THE SHAPING OF AMERICA

THE SHAPING OF AMERICA

Volume 1
Atlantic America, 1492–1800 (1986)

Volume 2
Continental America, 1800–1867 (1993)

Volume 3
Transcontinental America, 1850–1915 (1998)

Volume 4
Global America, 1915–1992 (in preparation)

THE
SHAPING
OF
AMERICA

A GEOGRAPHICAL
PERSPECTIVE
ON 500 YEARS
OF HISTORY

Volume 3
Transcontinental America
1850–1915

D. W. MEINIG

Yale University Press
New Haven and London

Set in Goudy Old Style type by The Composing Room of Michigan, Inc. Printed in the United States of America by Vail-Ballou Press, Binghamton, New York.

Library of Congress Cataloging-in-Publication Data
(Revised for vol. 3)

Meinig, D. W. (Donald William), 1924–
    The shaping of America
    Includes indexes
    Includes bibliographical references
    Contents: v. 1. Atlantic America, 1492–1800—v. 2. Continental America, 1800–1867.—v. 3. Transcontinental America, 1850–1915.
    1. United States—History.   2. United States—Historical geography.
E178.M57   1986   973   85-17962
ISBN 0-300-03882-8 (v. 1 : pbk.)
        0-300-05658-3 (v. 2 : cloth)
        0-300-06290-7 (v. 2 : pbk.)
        0-300-07592-8 (v. 3 : cloth)
        0-300-08290-8 (v. 3 : pbk.)

A catalogue record for this book is available from the British Library.

The paper in this book meets the guidelines for permanence and durability of the Committee on Production Guidelines for Book Longevity of the Council on Library Resources.

10 9 8 7 6 5 4 3 2

for
Lee

Think of the past as space expanding infinitely beyond our vision. . . . Then we choose a prospect. The higher it is, the wider and hazier our view. Now we map what we see, marking some features, ignoring others, altering an unknown territory . . . into a finite collection of landmarks made meaningful through their connections. History is not the past, but a map of the past drawn from a particular point of view to be useful to the modern traveler.

Henry Glassie

CONTENTS

ILLUSTRATIONS

PREFACE

Transcontinental America extends a special geographic perspective on American development into the twentieth century. It stands as a discrete, coherent work, self-contained in topic and treatment, but is best understood as a continuation of the kind of emphasis and interpretation set forth in *Atlantic America* and *Continental America.*

As mentioned in the Preface of *Continental America,* which dealt with the period 1800–1867, this third volume reaches back to 1850 to provide uninterrupted coverage of the development of the western half of the country from its midcentury status as a distant realm of empire, through the emergence of a set of distinct regions, followed by close articulation of these areas into the main body of the nation and full integration into the federation. And indeed, the dominant theme of this book is the shaping of the United States into an increasingly consolidated and relatively stabilized geographic structure—and its continued assertion of powerful pressures outward.

On similar grounds some topics that might seem to be pertinent to the span of this volume have been reserved for treatment in Volume IV. Automobiles were already of ever-greater interest in the early years of the twentieth century, but for the geographer the critical feature is not so much the existence of the vehicle as the creation of an effective network of roads for it to run on, and this enormous task was barely under way by 1915. The great impact of the automobile on the internal structure and outward spread of cities has invited deferral of those geographic topics as well, even though electric streetcars and interurbans were already having important effects. Whereas *Transcontinental America* is preeminently of the Railroad Age, *Global America* will feature the Automobile and Air Ages.

In the earlier volumes I have offered brief statements on the nature of geography and history, on relations between the two fields, and some basic geographic principles underlying this project. I have also commented on critical problems of terminology relating to various peoples, processes, and resulting formations. I shall not repeat these here, but I will again caution readers that *The Shaping of America* is but a limited form of historical geography, and it does not purport to deal with many important themes commonly found in more orthodox histories. It does, however, claim to offer a fresh perspective useful to a fuller comprehension of the character and course of American development, a new "map of the past drawn from a particular point of view to be useful to the modern traveler."

D. W. Meinig
Syracuse, New York

ACKNOWLEDGMENTS

My broadest debt is displayed in its usual place, the Bibliography, and much of this dependence is specified by author in the text or in the lengthy Sources of Quotations. Those lists include a considerable number of primary sources as well as studies by modern specialists, and this volume overlaps in time and place my own earlier historical geographies and regional interpretations of the American West, each of which has its own detailed list of references. Those books and years of fieldwork long ago now also undergird a good portion of *Transcontinental America* and call to mind my good fortune in having much university help in various forms and a Guggenheim Fellowship in support of regional reconnaissance and library research.

Each new volume of *The Shaping of America* deepens my debt and gratitude to Yale University Press, to its director, John Ryden, and to my editor, Judy Metro, for their patient and generous support; to Nancy Ovedovitz for her continuing fine work of design, to Laura Jones Dooley for her gentle, helpful touch as manuscript editor of yet another volume, and to the many others whose expertise and care have produced these handsome books.

Similarly, my debt and gratitude to Syracuse University grows with the years. Dean John L. Palmer and Associate Dean Robert D. McClure of the Maxwell School, and Professors John Mercer and Daniel A. Griffith, as chairmen of the Department of Geography, have given every needed support—best of all in the form of a special research professorship that allows me to devote full time to this project. All the costs of manuscript preparation and most of the cartographic work have been covered by the university. Kay Steinmetz transformed my handwriting into type for this "monster" as she did for its predecessor, and her keen editorial eye and sensitivity to language has had its usual corrective effect on my prose; she also prepared the index. Michael Kirchoff, manager of the Syracuse University Cartographic Laboratory, not only translated my crude sketches into clear, accurate maps but applied his varied skills to preparing all the other illustrations for publication.

I thank the following persons for their help—in some cases quite extensive—in the search for illustrations: Bruce Bigelow, Butler University; John C. Hudson, Northwestern University; Ralph Ehrenberg and Ronald E. Grim, Geography and Map Division, Library of Congress; Richard H. Smith, Cartographic and Architectural Branch, National Archives; Fred Pernell, Still Picture Division, National Archives; Michelle Anne Delaney, National Museum of American History, Smithsonian Institution; Jovanka R. Ristić, The American Geographical Society Collection at the University of Wisconsin–Milwaukee Library; Douglas R. McManis, former editor, *The Geographical Review*; Lowell C. Bennion, Humboldt State University; Mark J. Cedeck, John W. Barriger III National Railroad Library, St. Louis Mercantile Library Association; Dydia Y. DeLyser, Syracuse University; Gary Dunbar, Cooperstown, New York; Nelson Morgan, Hargrett Rare Book Library, University of Georgia; H. Vincent Moses, Riverside Municipal Museum, Riverside, California; Edward K. Muller, University of Pittsburgh; Miles Richardson, Louisiana State University; Susan Seyl, Oregon Historical Society; David H. Stratton, Washington State University; Norman Thrower, University of California–Los Angeles; Dina Vargo, Steel Industry Heritage Corporation, Pittsburgh. I again thank Boomer Kennedy-Raisz for permission to use portions of Erwin Raisz's landform maps in this multivolume project.

As an admirer of Roger G. Kennedy's fresh, insightful, and graceful depictions and interpretations of the American landscape and American history, I was delighted to receive his generous endorsements of *Atlantic America* and *Continental America*. Such support from beyond the confines of self-centered academic fields is a welcome specific for the laborer trudging through 500 years of geography and history.

Like its predecessors, this book is dedicated with deepest thanks to the one who has lived it with me day by day.

PART ONE
ARTICULATION: BINDING THE COASTS TOGETHER

Every city and State in the Union has an interest in the location of this road; for it is destined by its more or less favorable point of connection with their respective railroads and other channels of communication, to affect all their commercial and social interests.

Senator John Bell (Tennessee), February 5, 1853

Prologue

The mid-nineteenth century was a time of enormous geographical change in the extent, shape, and prospects of the United States of America. Part of this alteration was overt and abrupt: the firm, formal acquisition of a long Pacific frontage upon the division of Oregon and acquisition of California. Other changes were more of a transition, less obvious and more incremental but no less decisive: the emergence of the railroad as a space-conquering instrument of revolutionary possibilities.

It did not take much imagination to discern a strategic interdependence in these two developments; only a radically efficient system of communication and transportation could ensure the integrity of a truly transcontinental republic, and the construction of such a system would demonstrate the remarkable power of the railroad and display to all the world the entrepreneurial energy and genius of the American nation and people. Yet the basic issue of where to build this essential facility was so momentous, so geographically contentious, that it defied resolution for many years. We therefore take a closer look than is usually accorded this topic to consider what was at stake, what alternatives were considered, and what was finally accomplished in this protracted and provocative struggle to fix the first firm transcontinental axis of the United States. Having completed this essential bond, we shall be ready to delineate the formation and character of the several American Wests of the time.

1. Forging the Iron Bond

CONCEPT

Quite suddenly, at midcentury, the United States assumed a new position and prominence on the world map. In less than the three years between 1846 and 1849 the bounds of the country had been so enlarged and reshaped that it now spanned the continent from sea to sea as "a magnificent parallelogram" three thousand miles across and half that in breadth, "equal to the whole temperate zone" of North America. With such a transformation "the great idea" so long dreamed of, "an inland communication" from the Atlantic to the Pacific, was "now ripe to be realized." It was worth pondering "what a wonderful circumstance in the history of the world" had made it so: "that there should be a nation whose domain is so extensive that she is able to lay down as she chooses, by law, a road across a continent, the whole distance under one flag, and one law."

As might be expected, Thomas Hart Benton, the redoubtable Missouri states-man who propounded these views, was quite ready to lay down by law just where and what sort of road this should be. It must be a "great national central highway," he said, linking San Francisco with St. Louis, from where it would connect with routes already opened or in process to form a direct line to the Atlantic and provide ready access to "all the States and cities of this Union." And it should be "a great public highway," open to the people and adapted to the different means of convey-ance. "I propose," he said, to reserve a one-mile breadth of land "from the frontier of Missouri to the Pacific Ocean . . . for all sorts of roads—railway, plank, mac-adamized," as many tracks, independent of one another, as shall be necessary and practical, including a margin given over to "a plain old English road, such as we have been accustomed to all our lives—a road in which the farmer in his wagon or carriage, on horse or on foot, may travel without fear, and without tax—with none to run over him, or make him jump out of the way."

Senator Benton emphasized the "wonderful contingency" of the moment: the time was "ripe for action" because the whole country west from Missouri was "territorial" (and Congress need only "to conciliate the Indians—to get their consent"); the means "are ample" (indeed, the road "makes itself"—for it runs the entire way through public land and we simply take a per centum from the stimu-lated sales of that vast resource); "we have all the information that is necessary" (thanks to the "varied," "minute," and "accurate" investigations by John Frémont—Benton's son-in-law); and it is required and demanded of us, for obvious military, political, and commercial reasons—which he expounded in a grand rhetorical flourish.

Yet for all his vision and sense of urgency Benton was a voice more of the past than of the future. His emphasis on a set of parallel roads and of movement by wagons and horseback (and sleighs in winter) and his openly expressed doubts about the feasibility of a railroad through the mountains exposed him as only partially attuned to the transformations of the times. For thirty years he had presumed to speak for the West and dilate upon its vast potentials (though he had never himself ventured there beyond Missouri), and he self-consciously carried an assumed commission from the revered Thomas Jefferson (whom he had met in Jefferson's last months) to further the idea of a transcontinental trafficway. He therefore readily grasped the general significance of the acquisition of California, the inrush of people to the goldfields, and the imperative need to bind this Pacific Slope to the main body of the nation. Had he looked as intently eastward he might have discerned more clearly that the means for effecting those vital connections were becoming available at this same moment in history. For it had taken just twenty years to demonstrate what a radical, transforming instrument the steam-powered railway was. The building of several lines across the corrugated Appalachians, linking the Atlantic seaboard with the Ohio Valley or Lake Erie, confirmed the practicalities of such mountain engineering, the operation of these as single-company linear systems displayed a new dimension of geographic management, and the scheduled daily services set new standards of speed and efficiency in the conquering of distance. Henceforth there need be no doubt that the continents, however broad, lay open to penetration; that all places, however isolated, might be connected; that all resources, however difficult of access, might be tapped by the spreading tentacles of the modern world system.

This intersection of profound changes in the shape and position of America and in transport technology was recognized, in some degree, by many different persons. Whereas in 1846 a House committee had dismissed Asa Whitney's intensely promoted scheme for a railway from Lake Michigan to Puget Sound as "a project too gigantic, and, at least from the present, entirely impracticable" (although some congressmen and many interested state legislatures expressed support for it), by 1852 relatively few questioned either the necessity or the practicality of such a national project, a railroad to the Pacific was the main theme of commercial conventions, orations, pamphlets, newspapers, and national periodicals, and Pacific railroad bills became a staple of every session of Congress. From this time on the basic questions were not *could* and *should* we build a transcontinental band of iron but *how* and *where* to do so. Historians have examined at length the tangle of political and financial interests involved and exposed some of the reasons why it took twenty years from general recognition of the need to the actual completion of the task. We shall focus attention on the deeply divisive issue of *where* such a connection or connections should be built, and why it took thirteen years and a drastic alteration of geopolitical circumstances to come to a decision.

We may begin by noting the objectives, the declared purposes and benefits, of such a line. As a national project requiring broad public support, a varied mixture of these, ranging from the directly practical to soaring visions of national destiny, were expounded in every forum. Because the decision lay with the central government, we may conveniently confine our review mostly to those expressed in Congress (whose members certainly varied from the practical to the extravagant visionary).

The most obvious and simple objective was to create a *national trunk line.* Such a link was the essential "chain of union" ensuring "the integrity" of the whole. Inevitably, the famous imperial precedent was called into support: "we know that the Romans—from whom we borrow so many of our ideas, useful or grand—never considered a conquered territory added to the republic or empire until it was perforated by a road." To defend the Pacific Coast was an obvious primary task of empire (concern over British attack was commonly cited), and a railway would also greatly enhance the efficiency and reduce the costs of supplying the many intermediate posts already established along the way to protect emigrants and "keep in check the dangerous Indians." But the purpose here, as in the Roman case, was not only military but (in Edward Gibbon's cited words) to unite "the subjects of the most distant provinces by an easy and familiar intercourse." An American nation grounded upon popular government had an even more compelling need of such interaction. Not only was such a trunk line "necessary to the unity and promptitude of government, representation, administration, and defense," as the web of railways spread outward from this "great base line of connection. . . . the laws of contact and association . . . will bind society together in all its parts" until it becomes "coextensive with the boundaries which embrace the American family."

At least as much rhetoric was devoted to the role of the Pacific railroad as a *developmental line.* All advocates stressed its transforming power: "the western wilderness . . . will start into life under its touch." Whereas the "law of nature" kept population and the commercial economy bound to the riverbanks, "the railroad operates as the river did in olden time. . . . The railroad is the river produced by modern science. We can carry these streams over mountains and across valleys, and they will be followed by towns and cities along the plains. From this great stream rivulets will flow, so that . . . American civilization will spring up, and the land teem with life." "The geographical center of the Republic is almost unoccupied and uncultivated for want of the road we now seek," said Senator William M. Gwin, presenting a Pacific railroad bill for debate in 1854. Up to that time some saw a need first to establish a series of soldier-colonies along the main route (Senator Stephen A. Douglas's bill would provide special land grants for such) so as to secure the means of forming an eventual "continuous line of settlements," but most speakers simply pointed to the experience of the Eastern states and referred to "the teeming millions who will follow the track of the railroad," confident that, as one put it, "what the Erie Canal has been to the State of New York, a Pacific railroad is destined to be to the whole country." In the final debate of 1862, a California senator offered the full developmental rationale:

> The line of this great thoroughfare between two oceans, would offer the highest inducements, with every prospect of success in agricultural and mineral regions, now imperfectly developed. Soon, in fact, this almost blank in our geographical limits would be filled up by industrious producing classes, requiring all the appliances of civilized life. The effect in value upon such public land would be amazing, and the opening up of the arable surface and development of the precious and useful metals; the working of coal mines, establishment of machinery and workshops, would revolutionize the existing condition of "the plains," filling the waste places with occupation, and preparing the social and political condition of the country for a transition from Territories into sovereign States of the Union, linking by a great federative bond the whole political fabric from ocean to ocean.

And a *Pacific* railroad would be more than a national line. It was a decisive part of something far greater that was taking shape: the "last grand revolution in the commercial intercourse of the world"—"the consummation of the great idea which filled the mind of Columbus"—"the American road to India." Such a route was "destined to bear on its long lines that majestic procession of the commerce of the continents of Europe, America, and Asia." The rhetoric was extravagant, but dazzling visions of an *intercontinental trafficway* were connected, however tenuously, to some major discernible developments:

1. Communication, at a hitherto unimaginable speed, by telegraph, which was already transforming the means and expectations of commercial intelligence; most proposals for a rail included a telegraph line to the Pacific; the laying of a transatlantic cable, undertaken in 1857, was unsuccessful, but the attempt was quickly renewed and plans for a world-girdling network were under avid discussion;
2. More substantial was the emergence of the "Atlantic ferry": regular scheduled crossings by fast iron-hulled, screw-propelled steamships, a system that seemed readily adaptable to the Pacific to capture and expand the Asian trade; and
3. The rapid push toward consummation of another age-old commercial dream: a canal through the isthmus of Suez. In 1854 Ferdinand de Lesseps obtained a concession and formed his company, the next year he assembled an international commission of engineers and naval experts, and in April 1859 he turned the first spadeful of sand to begin excavation of this great ditch.

The Suez route was of course a direct rival of the American prospect, and there was fear that it would be augmented by a British "Asiatic railway from the Mediterranean, by the Persian Gulf and India, to the ports of China." Furthermore, warned Senator Gwin, British statesmen and engineers were "warmly advocating" a "scheme of a great continental railway from Halifax through British territory to the Pacific"; therefore, it was a contest "between London and New York, between Calcutta and San Francisco, between England and America, by land and by sea . . . [for] undisputed command of the commerce of the world." A keen sense of such rivalry (from the French as well as the British) was apparent through all these years of debate. A practical senator from Vermont might dismiss all this talk of overland Asian commerce as illusory, for "nothing but opium or silks" could pay the freight, but a sense of urgent need to secure for the United States a central position within a system that was "to produce a *radical* and *permanent* change" in the routes of world commerce remained a driving force.

Finally, a transcontinental railroad would be a *national symbol of American character*. Such a vast and challenging undertaking was "necessary to the highest destiny of the nation," it would "elevate our national pride, stimulate our national energies and consolidate our national character," and it would put the nation's virtues on munificent display to all the world. As an early senatorial endorsement phrased it, this "short route to the riches and marvels of the Indies" would soon be thronged with travelers, and

> this crowd must pass through the heart of our country, witness its improvements, the increase of our population, the activity, the genius, and the happiness of our people, and contemplate the wisdom and the advantage of those free institutions which have produced such glorious effects. It would certainly not be unreasonable to suppose that this intercourse would have an extensive influence upon the opinion and feelings of the civilized world in favor of free institutions.

The rehearsal year after year of this compelling set of incentives underscored the great paradox: a project of such national importance widely endorsed by public sentiment was repeatedly thwarted by the inability of the Congress to act. Although members were eager to respond to such public interest, support was dispersed among a host of competing routes, and Congress was paralyzed by that lack of focus and the enormity of such a fundamental geographic decision.

THE PROBLEM OF ROUTE SELECTION

In the restless search for a formula that would break the deadlock, four desired qualities permeate the discussions: the route must be *practicable, economical, national,* and *equitable*. A major early effort to find a way toward a decision focused on the first two. The act of 1853 authorizing explorations and surveys directed the secretary of War "to ascertain the most practicable and economical route . . . from the Mississippi River to the Pacific Ocean." The professed hope was that scientists and engineers could assess several alternative routes for their feasibility (grade and curvature, availability of water and timber, winter snows, and so on), calculate the costs of each route (distance, excavation and grading, bridging and tunneling, well-drilling), and present the Congress with a route of decisive attractiveness. As William Goetzmann has observed, "It was . . . characteristic of federal policy in the trans-Mississippi West when issues of public importance arose to seek recourse in the disinterested judgment of science. In a sense, this was a way of letting nature itself decide, not only because it placed the decision beyond the control of mere mortals but also because the decision seemed to depend on the overarching justice of the natural law. Upon such a premise was based the whole idea of the Pacific railroad surveys."

But that premise was inevitably compromised from the outset. Someone had to nominate the general routes to be investigated, select the leaders and members of the survey parties, and assess the results for presentation to Congress. There was no way of ignoring already vigorously competing interests or of erasing the experiences and biases of those assigned to the task. The Army Topographical Corps and the more than one hundred scientists who participated were for the most part a conscientious force, and they produced an immense amount of information in a short time—"an encyclopedia of western experience"—but they were not devoid of special interests and rivalries; and, indeed, the set of thirteen massive volumes includes some surveys sponsored by private promoters (such as some of Frémont's work), and several of the officers had invested in potential terminal sites.

In simple terms five "transcontinental" routes (the term is not literal in American railway usage but refers to companies and trunk lines extending from the dense web in the eastern half of the nation to the Pacific Coast) were examined, each designated by a particular parallel or parallels of latitude, and each implicitly related to interests focused on a particular city or cities or harbors at either end. On the Pacific Slope several longitudinal routes connecting the major terminals were also examined (fig. 1). We need not review in detail each route. Suffice it to note that four of the five were declared to be entirely practicable by their investigators (and each of these routes would eventually have one or more trunk-line railroads). Each had difficulties to surmount, chiefly the double mountain barrier of the Rockies and the Sierra Nevada–Cascades (or lesser extensions from these) and climatic conditions: the scarcity of water and timber on portions of the southern routes and (more controversial) the probability of deep snows on the northern routes. Only the Thirty-eighth parallel prospect (which had been included largely because of Senator Benton's intense lobbying) was dismissed as impracticable, no suitable pass being found through the complicated mass of the Southern Rockies.

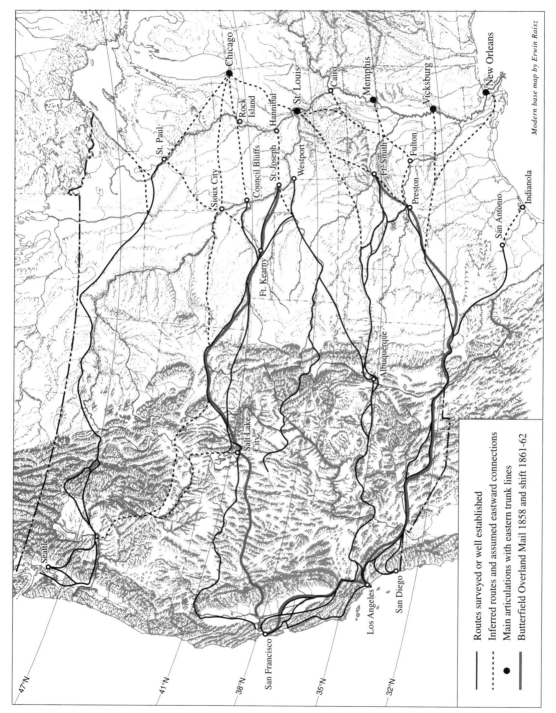

1. Pacific Railroad Surveys.

Based on "a hurried compilation of all the authentic surveys" to accompany the Report of the

Modern base map by Erwin Raisz

Routes surveyed or well established

Inferred routes and assumed eastward connections

Main articulations with eastern trunk lines

Butterfield Overland Mail 1858 and shift 1861-62

The effort expended on study of these several routes varied greatly, with the least devoted to the most central—the Forty-first parallel—in part because long portions of it were already familiar from previous surveys of the emigrant trails to Oregon, Utah, and California, though in fact the best prospective route for a railroad across the Continental Divide in this sector was not closely examined.

As for "most economical," the figures produced by the leaders of the several surveys were highly uneven in totals and reliability, based as they were on hasty and sporadic engineering investigations, surmises derived from earlier reconnaissances, estimates about little-known conditions (such as geology, weather, and prospects for water), and the predilections of the investigators. Those ultimately in charge, Captain A. A. Humphreys and Jefferson Davis, secretary of War, grossly adjusted some of these figures (most notably increasing the estimate for the northernmost route from $117 million to $141 million and decreasing the Thirty-fifth parallel route from $169 million to $95 million), thereby leaving the whole topic open to severe challenge. Furthermore, cost tended to recede in significance. The nation was not in debt (indeed, said Senator Gwin, the annual accumulations of "an overflowing Treasury . . . are a source of embarrassment, reversing the experience of all other nations"), nor, it soon became clear, was it going to finance directly the building of such a road but only underwrite bonds and offer land grants from the public domain of the territories. And, after all, for such a facility most would agree that it was important to select the best route, not necessarily the cheapest one.

Such a combination of special and inherent difficulties and complications doomed this strenuous sprawling search for "nature's decision" to failure. As Goetzmann concluded:

> In the end, the effect of the Pacific railroad surveys proved to be almost exactly opposite of their intended purpose as expressed by Congress. They did not furnish a conclusive report on "the most practicable and economical route . . . ." Instead, confusion was deepened and competition intensified by the most obvious results of the reconnaissance, which indicated first not one but several extremely practicable routes existed, and second that because of this the far-western country was possibly more valuable than anyone had previously imagined.

Thus when Jefferson Davis declared to Congress in early 1855 that a comparison "conclusively shows that the route of the 32d parallel is, of those surveyed, 'the most practicable and economical route'" because it was not only the shortest and cheapest (by a third) but could be completed much more quickly and would enjoy much less interruption of service once built, he was immediately accused of overweening sectional bias, and he succeeded only in turning the issue back to a contest completely focused on its *national* and *equitable* features.

In an early comprehensive report on transcontinental railroad proposals, *De Bow's Review* asserted that "a work so stupendous must be the common work of America, and for this it ought, as nearly as possible, to be *central.*" Senator Benton had already propounded that axiom in support of his own St. Louis–San Francisco design: "a central road is the most national in its character, because it accommodates the greatest number, and because it admits of branches to the right and the left with the greatest ease and convenience." Throughout these debates this simplest of designs—"one grand trunk central railroad" (as an 1855 amendment referred to it)—was repeatedly put forth as a logical and powerful proposition for such a national project.

Once California was acquired there was never great argument about the best Pacific terminus (although Southerners kept a fond eye on San Diego, and Puget Sound had its advocates) because "the bay of San Francisco, the finest in the world, is . . . central, and without a rival," and San Francisco would be "the Pacific seat of trade," a great "entrepôt" and the "equipoise" to New York, the great Atlantic emporium. At the outset St. Louis might call on the same kind of geographic logic. Since the days of Lewis and Clark it had been the unrivaled gateway to the West, and well-worn trails now led to Santa Fe, Utah, California, and Oregon. Pivotal to all the great waterways of Transappalachia, it would naturally become a prime objective of railroads in this rapidly developing interior. But any such claim was immediately challenged on other grounds. A resolution adopted by a Memphis convention, meeting just a week after a big one in St. Louis, pointed to the "special advantages" for "a national railroad" of "the route commencing at San Diego," thence via the Gila River, Paso del Norte, and "terminating at some point on the Mississippi between the mouth of the Ohio river and the mouth of the Red river" (the vagueness about an eastern terminus represented a compromise between Upper South and Lower South–Memphis versus Vicksburg–interests). By 1852 the claim for *sectional equity* had become overt: a Senate committee (chaired by Solon Borland of Arkansas) called for a national trunk line with two branches, one to St. Louis and one to Memphis, so as to "equalize the commercial interests of the States on the [Atlantic] seaboard, and, by these branches intersecting the Mississippi, upper and lower, those of all the western States by means of this noble river."

From this time on there was an intense contention between Northern and Southern interests; amendments to specify Memphis, or "not north of Memphis," were countered by those specifying St. Louis, or not south of St. Louis. A Kentuckian's proposal to designate the mouth of the Ohio (Cairo) as the eastern terminus got nowhere, but it openly declared the kind of centrality at issue: "[that point] may be said to be the mouth of all the rivers between the Alleghany and Rocky mountains, . . . [it] is half way from the head to the mouth of the Mississippi, and it is the point on that mighty river where the non-slaveholding and the slaveholding States come together. Thus, sir, it is not only geographically, but *politically, central."*

By this time, however, developments in the North had further complicated the issue. By 1855 several railroads fanning out of Chicago had reached the Mississippi and extensions across Iowa were under way. Northern interests favoring a trans-Iowa–Platte Valley route thereby emerged as vigorous challengers of St. Louis. Because of a general assumption that Congress could offer land grants only within federal territories (not within states), this issue was often defined in terms of a line commencing from the western boundary of Iowa versus one from the western boundary of Missouri. That differentiation, in turn, was quickly translated into the sectional rivalry between nonslaveholding states (Iowa) and slaveholding ones (Missouri). Because the designation of any point as an eastern terminus was so inflammatory, recourse was also taken in specifying a band of territory defined by latitudes. However, since "every town on the Mississippi, from St. Paul to the Gulf, is contending for the terminus," any such designation inevitably produced amendments to broaden the eligible band. Thus an attempt in 1855 to fix a terminus between 39°N and 40°N (Kansas City to just above St. Joseph) was quickly amended to 37°N–43°N (Cairo–Sioux City) and redefined the next day into two branches diverging from the trunk toward Lake Superior on the north and Memphis on the south. An 1859 bill underwent similar successive attempts at mutation until it reached the (obviously intended) reductio ad absurdum of 49° to the mouth of the Mississippi.

This broadening of the eastern terminus issue demonstrated that the selection of a route or routes was not just a national and a sectional issue but one of *regional equity* as well. The first major Pacific railroad bill was obviously designed to meet all these requirements. Presented by California's William Gwin, chairman of the Select Committee, it proposed a route from San Francisco southeastward in the Central Valley to Tejon Pass to pick up the general line of the Thirty-fifth parallel route eastward to Albuquerque, from whence the trunk line began to fan into half a dozen branches: to Matagorda Bay in Texas; to Fulton, Arkansas, with branches to Memphis, Vicksburg, and New Orleans; to St. Louis; to St. Joseph and Hannibal; to Dubuque via Council Bluffs. A long branch from the San Joaquin north to Oregon City and Puget Sound completed a vast "horseshoe" or "oxbow" system totaling 5,000 miles (fig. 2). Gwin was a Democrat well attuned to Southerners' interests and their insistence on a southern trunk line (he would later serve as a Confederate agent in Europe), but the design was obviously the creation of a committee seeking to cater to every regional interest. A flurry of opposition sent it back to committee.

Impasse over the horseshoe design led to a different means to satisfy the same variety of interests (fig. 3). A new committee began with the idea of proposing two

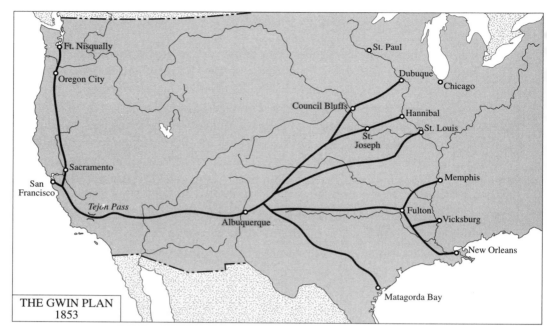

THE GWIN PLAN
1853

2. The Gwin Plan.

trunk lines, a northern and a southern, but "concluded that unless we proposed
. . . three routes, and gave the chances to the different sections, no bill could
pass." The result was a bill authorizing land grants and other aids to facilitate the
construction of three transcontinental railroads:

1. A Northern Pacific, from some point on the western boundary of Wisconsin to a
   port in Oregon or Washington Territory;
2. A Central Pacific, from the western boundary of Missouri or Iowa to San
   Francisco Bay; and
3. A Southern Pacific, from the western boundary of Texas to a California port.

Although such a major change in geopolitical strategy generated its own brand of
resistance—"Why, sir, as if the difficulty were not enough in the execution of one
railroad, . . . we are startled with the enormous proposition to make three"—the
Senate actually passed such a bill in 1855 and twice thereafter (1859, 1861), but
none were endorsed by the other house.

   In the House of Representatives the focus was on either one central trunk line
with eastern branches or, at most, two trunk lines. Toward the latter 1850s the
increasing power of the North in Congress and in the nation led to greater insistence on a single central route. As a senator defending such a proposal argued: "it is
more central as to the territory of the country; more central to population; more

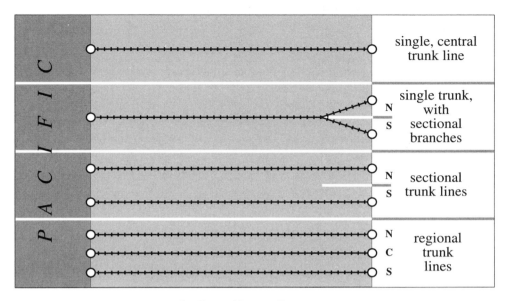

3. Some Abstract Concepts.

central to the line of emigration; more central to the great business interests of the country." Even so, chronic geopolitical realities were also taken into account: "it is proposed that the line shall have two short branches: one from a slave State, and the other from a free State—one from a northern State, and the other from a southern State—Iowa and Missouri." However, by this time (1859–60) such a limited gesture only infuriated militant Southerners. Just as a similar bill in the Senate the year before had caused Alfred Iverson of Georgia to demand that "the South shall have an equal chance to secure a road within her borders, to insure her benefit whilst the Union lasts, to belong to her when, if ever, the Union is dissolved," so now a Texas congressman bitterly accused the House committee of designing a bill "for the sole purpose of giving supremacy to one section of the country to the detriment and injury of the other" and threatened secession. Re-committed, the bill reemerged as a proposal for two routes, northern and southern, each with eastern branches to serve contending regional interests; passed by the House (95–74) in December 1860, differences with the Senate's three-route bill remained unresolved before being overwhelmed by the secession crisis.

In the wake of secession and the onset of war geopolitical pressures for a Pacific railroad took on new urgency. The need to defend the national territory became more compelling (fears of British intervention in California were now heightened), and the need to "cement the two coasts of our country, and make the East and the West parts of a well-united nation, easily governed" was now starkly apparent. Even as we proceed to "crush out this rebellion . . . [and] have an entire restoration," said Thomas Edwards of New Hampshire, a year into the war, we must

> look carefully into the future, and . . . guard in advance against all possible considera-
> tions which may threaten the dismemberment of the country thereafter. From the
> geographical face of the country, when the great region of the distant West shall have
> grown to the size of which it is rapidly tending, when it shall begin to feel its sense of
> independence, unless the relations between the East and West shall be the most
> perfect and the most intimate which can be established, . . . the empire will be in
> danger of breaking on the crest of the Rocky mountains, and of separating by the
> weight of its two sea-girt nations.

A central route across the Far West was now the obvious choice because of fresh developments therein as well as the removal of Southern votes in opposition. The new city of Denver was arising near the base of the Rockies to serve the sudden influx of people to nearby mining camps; at the same time, Virginia City emerged atop fabulously rich silver discoveries in the Washoe Mountains of Nevada, directly across the Sierras from the goldfields of California. Meanwhile, the cost and difficulties of dispatching an army to quell the Mormons had underscored the need to improve the arteries of empire. The overland mail service had been shifted from the Southern Plains to a St. Joseph–Denver–South Pass–Salt Lake City–Placerville–Sacramento route and an overland telegraph line completed along the same in late 1861. In spite of general agreement on a western extension it took weeks of debate to resolve where it should be attached to the existing eastern network.

The primary controversy was between interests centering at St. Louis and those at Chicago, translated into a terminus at or near the mouth of the Kansas River or the mouth of the Platte. The simplest response was to authorize two branches to serve those alignments. The attempt to do so, however, opened up two more issues: at what point the branches should be joined to the trunk, and exactly which places on the Missouri River should become the terminals. These were interdependent matters in that the point of attachment affected the angle of the branch, the distance to the trunk, and the amount of the land grant and other government aid given to the corporate builders. The original bill in each house set this point at 102°W longitude somewhere in the narrow band between the waters of the Republican River and the Platte in central Nebraska. A Minnesotan proposed a branch from his state to connect as far west as 106°W (beyond Laramie), but there were many more attempts to shift this junction eastward to Fort Kearney (99°W), or to 100°W (which was done), to shorten the branches and reduce the largess. The initial concept of two branches serving the Kansas and Platte river routes was quickly challenged and eventually amended to include several others. As the first and as yet only town on the middle Missouri River to be reached by a railroad, St. Joseph saw itself as having already won the race to be the new gateway to the Far West. The Pikes Peak gold rush had greatly increased its wagon and stagecoach traffic across the Plains. In the end, the designers of the bill gave in not only to St. Joseph but to Leavenworth and Sioux City as well (the latter to appease Dubuque and Minnesota interests). As a result, as one critic of the time observed, "What might have been a great artery . . . became nothing but a sprinkler." With such a lavish sprinkling of the chances for eager capitalists to make a lot of money without putting up much of their own, a Pacific railroad bill was passed by wide margins in both houses and signed into law by President Abraham Lincoln on July 1, 1862.

In summary, the following routes were authorized (fig. 4):

1. A Union Pacific trunk line from a point on the One-hundredth meridian between the Republican and Platte rivers, "thence running westerly upon the most direct, central, and practicable route" to the western boundary of the Territory of Nevada," there to meet and connect with the line that the Central Pacific Railroad Company was to construct from a point "at or near San Francisco, or the navigable waters of the Sacramento River, to the eastern boundary of California";

2. A Union Pacific line from a point on the western boundary of Iowa— designated by the president as Omaha, opposite Council Bluffs—by the most direct and practicable route to 100°W;

3. A line "from the Missouri River, at the mouth of the Kansas River" (Kansas City) to connect with the Union Pacific at 100°W (originally granted to the Leavenworth, Pawnee, & Western Railroad; soon renamed Union Pacific, Eastern Division);

4. An extension of the Hannibal & St. Joseph Railroad (and associated companies) to connect with the Union Pacific at any point east of 100°W;

5. A line by the Hannibal & St. Joseph via Atchison to connect with the line westerly from the mouth of the Kansas River (later named Union Pacific, Central Branch);

6. A line from Leavenworth to connect with the Kansas River line; and

7. Whenever a railroad across Minnesota or Iowa reached Sioux City, a branch from that city to connect with the Union Pacific east of 100°W (Sioux City & Pacific).

Various incentives and limitations relating to construction progress were built into the program and adjusted from time to time. Two are of particular note. A provision allowed either the Central Pacific or the Union Pacific to build beyond the California-Nevada line should the other road not have reached that point to "meet and connect" to form "the whole [trunk] line." Should the line from the

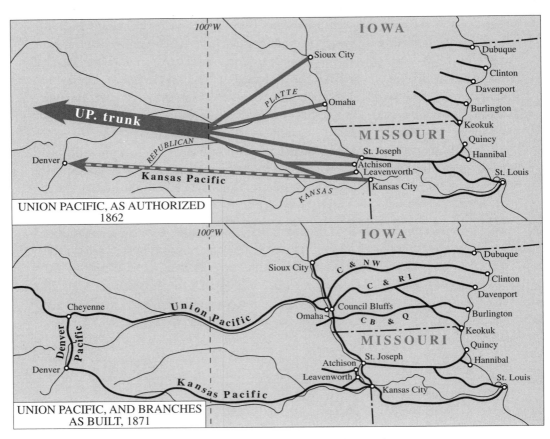

4. Union Pacific: Authorization and Actuality.

mouth of the Kansas River be completed to 100°W ahead of the Union Pacific from
Omaha, it could continue along the trunk route to meet the Central Pacific. In
1866 a further modification allowed this line (renamed the Kansas Pacific in 1869)
to build on past Fort Riley directly west to Denver and fifty miles beyond that city,
rather than join the UP at 100°W. These provisions relating to the Kansas route
were expressions of continuing intensive lobbying by St. Louis gateway interests to
offset the ever-more apparent advantages of Chicago. This competition was also
affected by the choice of gauge. The original act decreed a uniform width for the
entire line but left the choice up to the president. Lincoln selected five feet (the
width of most of the railroads in the South and of a short line in California);
whereupon Congress passed a new bill prescribing four feet eight and one-half
inches, so as to conform with all the western lines north of St. Louis. The whole
system was, by law, to operate "as one connected, continuous line" so that "cars

can be run from the Missouri River to the Pacific Coast," with grades and curves not exceeding the maximum of the Baltimore & Ohio Railroad (America's first Trans-appalachian trunk line).

Thus after a decade of impassioned, often bitter debate, and only after the federation had partially disintegrated was the central government able to determine where this essential national facility should be built. The difficulties were inherent in both the character of the government and the significance of the choice. The fixing of the nation's communications axis was such a momentous geographical decision as to produce "a trembling anxiety" in the leadership of every state and city; it was an issue that "so exasperates human passion and so enlists [selfish] human interest" as to paralyze a republican federation. Only by offering a spray of branches to every competing interest could an agreement be reached.

CONSTRUCTION AND OPERATIONS

The vast difference between authorization and realization of such an immense project was well understood, and the original legislation allowed fourteen years for completion. Leland Stanford, president of the Central Pacific, turned the first shovelful on the levee at Sacramento on January 8, 1863, to begin grading east-ward, but it was October before the first rails arrived by ship in San Francisco. The ground-breaking at Omaha did not take place until December 2, 1863, and little was accomplished for several months, in part because all materials had to be brought upriver during high-water season from St. Joseph, the only railhead on the Missouri, or hauled by wagons across Iowa from the several lines creeping overland from the Mississippi. Wartime shortages of labor and material as well as chronic problems of financing and adjudication ensured that progress would be discour-agingly slow for some years.

The two companies were faced with starkly different physical conditions in the early stages of construction: the Central Pacific with the formidable, heavily ra-vined wall of the Sierra Nevada a short distance east of Sacramento; the Union Pacific with the plains rising almost imperceptibly for nearly 500 miles to the west with no more than a few shallow streams to cross (fig. 5). Five routes across the Sierra Nevada were closely examined before the shortest route, Emigrant Gap, was decided upon in late 1865, and it took more than two years of heavy work, including many deep cuts (soon covered with forty miles of snowsheds) and several tunnels, to cross the mountains. Not until the spring of 1868 did the track reach Truckee Meadows (Reno) where the rapid push across Nevada could begin. By that time the Union Pacific had surmounted its first physical challenge at the Laramie Range, a spur of the Rockies, and was building across the Wyoming Basin; scarcity of water now posed the main difficulty for both parties. As track laying picked up

PROFILE

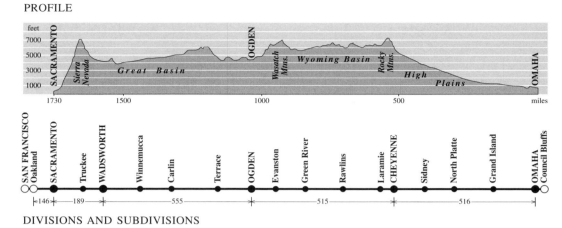

DIVISIONS AND SUBDIVISIONS

5. Profile and Operational Segments.

speed, two major decisions faced the converging forces: whether to skirt the Great Salt Lake on the north or the south and where to meet and to establish the official working junction between the two companies. In spite of the strong urgings of Brigham Young for a route through Salt Lake City and across the broad level salt flats on the south side, the more rugged northern route was chosen, in part because of grave uncertainty about the fluctuating levels of the famous inland sea. Just where the tracks would join was an issue of major financial importance (relating to land grants and per-mile subsidies). Although the heroic labors of the competing construction crews racing across the deserts would receive great public attention, the decisive contest was being fought in Washington, where the rival lobbyists filed hastily compiled survey and optimistic progress reports to induce government decisions in their favor. Rival survey parties ranged hundreds of miles ahead, those of the Union Pacific to Humboldt Wells (Wells, Nevada), those of the Central Pacific through Echo Canyon to the Wyoming border, and the accelerating construction crews graded parallel roadbeds more than a hundred miles past one another. The actual meeting point was negotiated privately in Washington in April 1869, between Collis Huntington of the CP and Grenville Dodge of the UP, who agreed to join tracks at Promontory Summit, to transfer 47.5 miles east of that point from the UP to the CP (for a price), and to create a new city adjacent to Ogden as their joint operating terminal. A month later, on May 10, 1869, "the most significant single act of the historical geography of American transportation was accomplished."

The telegraph that transmitted (or, rather, simulated) the sound of the hammer striking the golden spike set off celebrations all across the land and a gushing torrent of words proclaiming the immense, transforming importance of this long anticipated moment. On closer examination, however, "the importance of this accomplishment for many years was mainly psychological"; it was "a symbol that far transcended the event." When the well-traveled journalist Samuel Bowles, upon completion of his inspection trip, declared, "The Pacific Railroad—open, is a great fact to America, to the world. . . . It is the unrolling of a new map, a revelation of a new empire, the creation of a new civilization," he was confirming, along with many others, that the symbolic objective had been achieved. Other, more practical objectives were rather more elusive. In a new national icon, the engines at Promontory stood (in Bret Harte's famous phrasing), "Pilots touching,—head to head / Facing on a single track, / Half a world behind each back"—but it would take more than a spiking together of these two flimsy, hastily constructed tracks to wrench world commerce out of its accustomed paths. The Pacific Mail Steamship Company, principal American concern operating in that ocean, continued to focus on Panama and provide serious competition for transcontinental shipments, including much government business (for it, too, was a subsidized service). An 1870 agreement to apportion traffic with the railroads soon broke down, and the competition was considered so debilitating to the fragile railroads as to induce their leaders to invest heavily in the steamship company and try to enforce cooperation. Thereafter a slow trickle of teas and silk gave a tantalizing hint of the "colossal" commerce so long anticipated, but "the last grand revolution" in world intercourse was slow to develop.

Viewed as a developmental line, the results were sporadic but more substantial and assured. By 1870 the frontier of colonization was about a hundred miles west of Omaha, and the huge land grant (every other section in a twenty-mile belt) gave the Union Pacific a major means and incentive to extend this salient along its route as far as farming proved feasible. The three main settlement districts farther west along this central route, Denver and the Colorado mines, the Mormon oasis, and the Washoe mines around Virginia City, were quickly connected by local railroad branches and in every case greatly aided by the new trunk line service. As for the vast stretches in between, there was only a thin scattering of ranches and incipient mines and little local freight, and the towns created by the railroads to serve their own operations were the most substantial settlements (fig. 6). Thus Cheyenne, midway along the Union Pacific, became the main division point, with subdivisions breaking at Grand Island, North Platte, Sidney, Laramie, Rawlins, and Evanston between the Omaha and Ogden terminals. Each of these points of crew change, locomotive servicing, and car inspection, with their roundhouses and repair shops, employed scores or hundreds of men, with smaller numbers spaced along the line at various water, coaling, and helper stations. All across western Nebraska, Wyoming, and Nevada the railroads initiated and in large degree set the

6. Union Pacific at Laramie.
Such massive windmills and water tanks boldly attested that building across the high plains and desert was not as cheap as might be inferred from the terrain. In the background are a twenty-stall sandstone roundhouse and shops. (Andrew J. Russell, photographer; Union Pacific Museum Collection)

settlement pattern. Thus the main line was readied to serve as a "great stream" from which "rivulets" would flow and "American civilization . . . spring up," although much of this rugged and arid land would never exactly "teem with life."

Paradoxically, the most obvious feature, the physical creation of a railroad to the Pacific, did not in fact result in the primary objective: a national trunk line. When Thomas C. Durant, the erratic promoter and manager of the Union Pacific, cried out exuberantly after the commemorative spikes were driven, "there is henceforth but one Pacific Railroad of the United States," he might seem to be voicing a common assumption that the "one connected, continuous line" Congress had decreed was now ready for operation. But such was far from the case then (as he well knew) and would never really be the case in any full sense (as he helped ensure). What the public and orators had long envisioned—"unbroken communication by rail across the continent"—made its appearance only in such extravagant displays as the Pullman Hotel Express, a special train created to carry a group of affluent Bostonians (several of whom had helped finance the Union Pacific) on a weeklong journey to San Francisco, whereas the routine service was a daily passenger train each way between Omaha and Ogden and another between Ogden and Sacramento, with the option (after December 1869) of continuing by rail on a subsidiary line to Oakland, or by steamboat to San Francisco. The 1,800-mile journey was scheduled as five and a half days of travel and normally took at least another day because the two trains were not scheduled so as to connect and provide through service (many travelers welcomed the break and the chance to inspect the Mormons).

The fundamental fact was the existence of not "one Pacific Railroad" but two railroads, two separate corporations, authorized by Congress to provide service between Omaha and San Francisco, and any assumption that there would be ready cooperation to obvious mutual advantage was quickly negated. Created and shaped to the interests of powerful leaders, the CP and UP were competitive from the start and remained so long after their tracks were joined. They abandoned the idea of jointly building a new town near Ogden (partly because of Mormon opposition), and they engendered endless problems at the junction they did set up; schedules, transfer time, methods of operating, types of equipment, and, especially, division of rates required constant negotiation. It was soon apparent that the leaders of the Central Pacific saw a much better future in a rapidly developing California than in a debt-ridden elongated line across Nevada, and they created a new instrument, the Southern Pacific, and set out to dominate California and the Southwest. By 1881, through construction and acquisition, they had formed their own "transcontinental" from San Francisco to New Orleans (via the Thirty-second parallel route) as well as a connection at Deming, New Mexico, with the new Atchison, Topeka & Santa Fe to Kansas City and thereafter treated their Central Pacific subsidiary as a secondary line.

The Union Pacific, so emblematic in name and fame, was in fact no more than a segment of a trunk line within the emerging continental system, and a very vulnerable one. For years its Omaha-Ogden route generated relatively little local traffic. Much the most important area tapped was Colorado, but within a year of the golden spike that lucrative region was reached by the Kansas Pacific, offering an alternative route to the east. Moreover, the KP linked with the Denver Pacific comprised a competitive trunk line from Cheyenne eastward via Kansas City and St. Louis and claimed legal equality of access to transcontinental traffic. This Kansas Pacific was the extended redirected version of the original UP, Eastern Division, authorized by Congress to build west from the mouth of the Kansas River, part of the derided "sprinkler" attached to the eastern end of the transcontinental artery. None of the branches defined in the Pacific railroad legislation was built as originally programmed. For years the Central Branch from Atchison and the extension from St. Joseph were mere tap lines into the prairie, stopping well short of the UP; the Sioux City & Pacific elected to build more south than west (so as to qualify for grants of richer land in Iowa) and only belatedly effected a junction at Fremont, forty miles west of Omaha. As a result, the strategic focus remained on Council Bluffs–Omaha, and it was a point of chronic contention.

The first problem was the Missouri River. An ambiguity allowed the Union Pacific to regard Omaha as its legal terminus. This resulted in an awkward and exasperating connection by ferries, omnibus, and wagons with the several railroads that had reached westward to Council Bluffs. Only after extended litigation was the UP forced to construct a long bridge to comply with the congressional directive to build "west from the Iowa boundary." Even after this rail link was completed in 1872 a shuttle system (in which several railroad officials had an interest) was imposed on all passengers and freight between the two towns for several years. Much the most volatile problem was that of sharing rates on through traffic with the trans-Iowa companies offering competitive service to Chicago and points east. By 1870 there were three such roads and more would appear. Furthermore, the most vigorous of these, the Chicago, Burlington & Quincy, soon became a direct danger to the UP by invading Nebraska with a line from Plattsmouth to Fort Kearney and threatening to intercept trunk-line traffic (at the very point that had so often been cited in congressional debates as the ideal branching point). Before long the CB&Q would build clear to Denver and give the UP really severe competition. Desperate to find profits somewhere, the Union Pacific sent a long branch from Ogden north to the Montana mines and built the Oregon Short Line to connect with another building east from Portland. In this way it belatedly turned itself into a "transcontinental"—and soon into bankruptcy.

Anyone who traveled across America by rail in the 1870s or was familiar with the actual handling of freight had a clear—and severe—understanding of just how far the world-famed transcontinental was from being the "one grand trunk central railroad" so long envisioned. At best this band of iron was, quite literally, an articulation, "divided into joints," into four distinct legal and operational segments—Atlantic ports to Chicago, Chicago to the Missouri River, the Missouri to the Wasatch Oasis, the Wasatch to San Francisco Bay—linked at three congested, exasperatingly inefficient junctions: Chicago, Council Bluffs–Omaha, Ogden (and there were often more segments, depending upon which lines one took between the Atlantic and Cheyenne) (fig. 7). It took that form because that was the way the United States had decided to create its railroad system: by as many different sets of capitalist entrepreneurs as could survive the vicious competition to build and operate such facilities. Even so, there had still been the option of

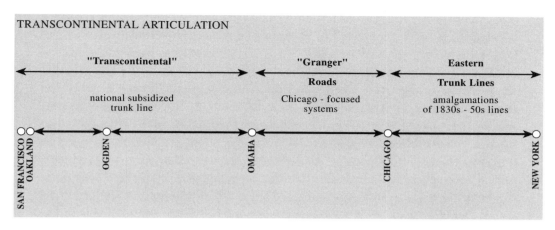

TRANSCONTINENTAL ARTICULATION

"Transcontinental" **"Granger"** **Eastern**

Roads **Trunk Lines**

national subsidized   Chicago - focused   amalgamations
trunk line   systems   of 1830s - 50s lines

SAN FRANCISCO OAKLAND   OGDEN   OMAHA   CHICAGO   NEW YORK

7. Transcontinental Articulation.

imposing upon private corporations a requirement that in the national interest this one great trunk railroad be operated (as a keen and sympathetic British observer had admonished) "as a united whole from the Atlantic direct to San Francisco" and not "be permitted to be worked in a disjointed manner." After all, it was widely agreed that building this first Pacific railway was a national task and could be accomplished only by lavish government subsidy. But although such aid was be-stowed upon these and many other railroad corporations in great amounts, such intervention was never guided by a rational design for a national transportation infrastructure.

The closest thing to such a design was the Gallatin plan of 1808, which was debated and chewed over in revisions and pieces for twenty years, leaving one partially built National Road (authorized earlier and incorporated into the plan) as its only direct legacy (see *Continental America*, 334–52). No similar plan for a national network of railroads was ever presented. Yet by fixing a first framework for the western half of the country and thereby profoundly affecting the network already in place in the eastern half, the Pacific railroad issue took on something of the character and significance of such a plan. Obviously the central government intervened here more directly in geographically decisive ways than it had anywhere in the East.

Such intervention was always under challenge. There were recurrent sugges-tions that the decision on the route of the transcontinental be left to the capitalists who would build the line, on the assumption that entrepreneurial risk takers would select the most economical, practicable, and traffic-generating route—that thereby no particular locality would have any advantage "except that given by nature herself"—but the idea was bitterly denounced in the inflamed political atmosphere of the 1850s. Southerners well understood the almost certain regional consequences of that policy: "Sir, this unequal flow of Government money and Government benefits into the great northern maelstrom has been going on long enough." Even more vehement was the condemnation of an early proposal to let the president of the United States do what Congress seemed unable to do. After the original Gwin plan was rejected, a new committee, despairing of getting any specific designation of an eastern terminal approved, proposed to leave the selection (as well as of the corporations to build the line) to the president as the decision maker most likely to respond to what was best for the nation as a whole. Such a radical deference was immediately denounced by senators from the older South: the granting of such "immense influence . . . in building up one section of the country where it goes, and in injuring that where it does not go" would be a giant step in transforming "a free confederacy of Republican States" into "a consolidated empire." Such "a rape of the Constitution" stood no chance of enactment. The most obvious alternative for such a government was to offer something to every interest. In this bicameral structure it is understandable that a Senate, in which each state had the same number of votes, would be pressured toward *three* Pacific railroads—despite the enormity of such a commitment at the time—as a way of breaking the stalemate, whereas the House, with proportional representation increasingly favoring the North, would tend to hold out for a *single* central trunk line. Had the federal crisis not become so nearly mortal on other grounds, it seems likely that a sectional compromise on a *two*-road program would have been approved, providing for a southern route and a central route (with branches). As it turned out, the Central Pacific–Union Pacific trunk stands as a distinctly *national* creation achieved on the collapse of the original federation and adapted to provide nominal equity to relentlessly assertive residual *regional* and *local* interests.

"Regional interests" refers not only to the rivalries over the eastern terminus but to the very existence of a Central Pacific and a Union Pacific. To the modern eye, in light of the chronic difficulties it engendered, the government's allocation of the proprietorship of this crucial national line to two distinct companies may seem a serious mistake. It was not, however, simply a reflection of congressional bungling or weary compromise. There was of course the practical need to build from both ends, the obvious difficulty that any one company might have in coordinating such a huge and disparate operation, and the value placed on competition as an incentive to hasten progress toward completion. But there was more to it than that. There was the fact of a thriving California, a vigorous diversifying nucleus of 400,000 people. This American colony was not an isolated outpost hanging precariously on the far fringe of the nation, desperate for subsidy and nurture from a distant government; it was a seat of productive wealth and entrepreneurship, a famous city and region already giving stimulus and shape to a larger Pacific world.

The Big Four of the Central Pacific—Huntington, Stanford, Hopkins, Crocker—were Sacramento merchants (all gold rush emigrants from New York State) who were organizing to build a wagon road and a railroad across the Sierra Nevada before any Pacific railroad bill was passed. When Congress finally did come to a decision, the provisions of the act and the efforts it set in motion represented California reaching out to the nation as much as the nation reaching out toward Pacific shores—indeed, considering the physical obstacles overcome and where the junction was effected, the Californians may be said to have made the more impressive response. Why this should be so, how California had acquired such qualities, calls for a much closer look at it and at other regions of this "distant West."

However hastily constructed and selfishly operated this famous band of iron across the continent might be, the daily trains trundling along to and from Ogden at a scheduled average of nearly twenty miles per hour wrought a revolution in Western travel. It fixed in place the first full axis and quickened the pulse of the

8. For the Extension of Western Travel.
A trainload of thirty coaches shipped by Abbot, Downing & Co., Concord, N.H., to Wells, Fargo & Co., Terminus, U.P.R.R., April 15, 1868. (Courtesy American Antiquarian Society)

nation in all its Western extremities. Stage lines now radiated from its stations to mining camps and to distant regions such as western Montana, Walla Walla, and Oregon, and branch railroads would soon follow as they already had to Denver, Salt Lake City, and Virginia City (fig. 8). The hazards of weather did prove greater than expected. In December 1871 blizzards blocked the Union Pacific for twenty-eight days—more than confirming the warnings so relentlessly sounded by proponents of southern routes years before. But by this time other transcontinental projects had been authorized by Congress: the Texas & Pacific, along the Thirty-second parallel route; the Atlantic & Pacific, along the Thirty-fifth parallel route; and the Northern Pacific, along the Forty-seventh and Forty-ninth parallels route. Although the progress of these was as yet barely discernible there could be little doubt but what all the Wests—the whole "magnificent parallelogram" of the United States—would become bound into one vast network by steam and steel. As a writer in *Leslie's Weekly* declared in 1870: "The railway has so abridged time and space, that the continent is rapidly losing its romance and becoming prosaic. . . . We have almost ceased to speak of the frontier."

PART TWO
DOMINION: THE EMERGENCE OF AMERICAN WESTS

Western America is one of the most interesting subjects of study the modern world has seen. There has been nothing in the past resembling its growth, and probably there will be nothing in the future. A vast territory, wonderfully rich in natural resources of many kinds; a temperate and healthy climate fit for European labor; a soil generally, and in many places marvellously, fertile; in some regions mountains full of minerals, in others trackless forests where every tree is over two hundred feet high; and the whole of this virtually unoccupied territory thrown open to a vigorous race, with all the appliances and contrivances of modern science at its command, —these are phenomena absolutely without precedent in history, and which cannot recur elsewhere, because our planet contains no such other favoured tract of country.

James Bryce, 1887

Prologue

Contrary to some expectations upon the completion of the first transcontinental railroad, Americans never ceased to speak of the frontier and the American West never lost its romance. Far from "becoming prosaic," it became enshrouded in myth and symbol and was accorded a special importance in the development of the American nation and of the character of the American people. But whereas myths and symbols may be important in shaping a nation, at this point we need to become quite prosaic and concerned with more mundane matters. And any shift of focus from symbol to substance, from the West as a place and a past in the imagination to actual places and events—insofar as we can discern such things—abruptly confronts us with great differences within the bounds of any generalized famous "West."

Our theme, therefore, is the fundamental reality and importance of American *Wests,* of deep and enduring features that distinguish various parts of this half of the country. Our method is that of the regional geographer concerned with identifying areas of similar peoples and sets of places bound by focused networks that form areal complexes of a common character recognizably separate and distinct from neighboring societies. Our half century or so of coverage embraces the transformation of a vast, newly acquired extension of the American empire into an integral, complex domain of the American nation.

1. Delineating the New West

Samuel Bowles assured the user of his little guidebook for the journey by rail across "the New West" that whatever one's intention and experience might be, the traveler was certain to gain "a new conception of the magnitude, the variety and the wealth, in nature and resource, in realization and in promise, of the American Republic,—a new idea of what it is to be an American citizen." And there were assurances in other works that such extended travel, however desirable, was not essential to an enlarged appreciation of "what a remarkable people we were and what a remarkable country we lived in." As J. B. Jackson goes on to note, many large volumes generous in format and illustration appeared at just this time:

> After a ruinous civil war the Republic was reunited, more prosperous, more vigorous than ever. The completion in 1869 of the Union Pacific had revealed to us some of the promise of the West, and as the public well knew, within a few years' time the hundredth anniversary of our independence was to be celebrated by an immense international fair. What could have been more natural than for us to remind our-selves of our accomplishments as a nation, and to seek to learn more about the vast new regions extending to the Pacific?

A large amount of material pertinent to such learning about those new regions had been accumulating all through the twenty-year struggle to forge that iron band, as the Pacific Railroad Surveys displayed. But beyond such compendiums of detail and mapping of routes there remained the challenge of synthesis and gener-alization. There was the need, for scientist and citizen alike, to have a relatively simple, ordered overall view of the entire country, a common reference for the American people of the basic geographical patterns of their transcontinental re-public. Hence the significance of the *Statistical Atlas of the United States, Based on the Results of the Ninth Census 1870.* Prepared under Francis A. Walker, director of the Census Bureau (and professor of political economy and history at Yale), this geographical reference contained fifty-four plates of maps and graphs, together with commentaries on selected physical, social, and demographic topics. If curi-ously incomplete and imbalanced by modern standards, it was an unprecedented and impressive work designed to serve as the foundation for a new emphasis in American education. The project proposal of 1871 called for 5,000 copies to be distributed "to public libraries, learned societies, colleges and academies" so as to help promote a "higher kind of political education" based on "the exact knowledge of our country" through "the study of political and social statistics" in an atlas format.

Much the most striking map in this landmark work was a double-page display of the distribution of population in the United States, as recorded in the 1870 census (fig. 9). And much the most striking feature of that map was the sharp contrast between the eastern and western halves of the country. The "line of population," that is, the inland edge of the contiguously settled part of the nation, approximated the Ninety-eighth meridian, almost exactly bisecting the Republic. West of that

9. Population Distribution, 1870, *Walker Atlas.*

The bland shadings on the original map preclude careful differentiations in density in this reproduction and can mislead about patterns in the Far West, where many of the large shaded areas merely denote Indian reserves.

margin only a wide scattering of settled districts, together with many Indian reservations, appeared amidst large expanses of apparently empty country.

This map was the final plate in a time series showing the patterns of such population densities for each decennial census. Designed to show "the Progress of the Nation—1790–1870," these maps stand as one of the most vivid depictions ever made of the shaping of America, and they established a mode for such historical geographic summations thereafter. Emphasis was on the dynamic population surface—the ever-changing patterns of extent and volume—and these areas were drawn with careful attention to inherent problems of translating numerical data into spatial form. Six degrees of density were depicted, with two inhabitants per square mile as the minimum qualification for "settlement"; below that was the "petty population": "the solitary ranchman, the trapper and the fisherman, the small mining party, and the lumbering camp." Special attention was directed to the "frontier line," the term now being appropriated to refer to the advancing edge of White settlement, and to the migrating national "centre of population," a new geomathematical calculation.

The general impression left by that series and its culminating map was that half of the country awaited settlement, and the continuing "progress of the nation" would presumably spread a population over that remainder. Yet it was also pretty generally understood by now that the western half of the United States was a very different kind of country and must thereby differ in its opportunities for development. Most any guidebook, such as that of Bowles, offered some sense of those regional differences. "There are four great natural divisions" between the Missouri and the Pacific, he wrote. The first was "the Plains," 500 miles wide, "the great natural pasture-ground of the nation"; next, "the Mountains," 500 miles of these "broken into a dozen sub-ranges, with vast elevated plains lying among and between"; third, another 500 miles of "the vast interior basin, which more properly than any other region . . . merits the name of the American desert"; and finally, that wonderfully varied section from the eastern foothills of the Sierra Nevada to "the muddy Sacramento and its broad alluvials" and on to San Francisco Bay: California. Such a simple segmentation was readily grasped, but a single central traverse could not provide a full picture of the western half of the country, and here, too, the new national atlas offered unprecedented help.

The opening section contained a set of maps and commentary on the position and character of the great physical provinces of the country. A new name, "Cordilleras," was proposed "as a comprehensive term for the vast complex of ranges west of the 104th meridian." This connected system, including the Rocky Mountains and their flanking plains on the east and the Sierra Nevada, Cascade Range, and Coast Ranges on the west, formed the "skeleton or framework" of the Far West, creating a "lozenge-shaped figure" containing within it a set of high plateaus, each strikingly different in character: the "stupendous volcanic" Columbia plateau; the series of elevated "parks" within the Rocky Mountains; the Great Basin, with its "very remarkable [interior] drainage"; and the horizontally stratified Colorado plateau, cut "in the most surprising manner" by "tremendous cañons." Identification of numerous lesser areas, an emphasis on such peculiarly Western features as desert "sinks," "salt valleys," "sage plains," and the "want of navigability" of Western rivers (a sixty-mile stretch of the Sacramento, and the Columbia—requiring two railway portages through the Cascade Range—being the only notable exceptions) rounded out the picture of a very distinctive half of the nation.

The atlas plates presenting these demographic and physical features routinely displayed another major framework covering this West (as well as the rest of the country): the geopolitical pattern of states and federal territories. Despite the presence of great mountain ranges and rivers, few boundaries followed such bold lines of nature: only the lower Columbia, a portion of the Snake, the lower Colorado River, and the Bitterroot Range were made to serve. Elsewhere the long-standing preference for straight-line geometric boundaries ordered this wonderfully variegated land into a simple set of political boxes. And for all the efforts of the cartographers and geographers of the time, it was the names affixed to these huge, more or less rectangular units that would provide the most influential guide for ready assimilation of this Far West into American minds. Several were already famous—California, Oregon, New Mexico, Mormon Utah—and each of these was in some degree understood as an area distinct in people and place. Others were newer or less well known—Nevada, Arizona, Colorado, Wyoming, Montana, Dakota, Idaho, Washington—and as federal territories (except for Nevada) their current bounds (and names and number) remained subject to change in response to subsequent Western developments—and congressional whim.

This gross grid of political territories was still a set of mostly empty frames. Fewer than a million of the more than 38 million persons counted in the 1870 census lived west of the "frontier line" of population, and more than half of these were in California. For the rest, the three oldest areas of colonization—New Mexico, Oregon, Utah—were each nearing 100,000; a decade or so of mining rushes had left about 40,000 each in Nevada and Colorado, and there were only the barest beginnings of American settlement in all the remainder. Such a disparate distribution placed the newly calculated "centre of population" in southwestern Ohio, barely midway between the Atlantic and the Mississippi. All of these population figures and maps referred to the "constitutional population" of the United States; that is, excluding "Indians not taxed." Had these indigenous peoples been included, the density patterns would not have been greatly altered, and their presence was at least partially indicated by the formal block of Indian Territory west of Arkansas and the numerous reservations and hunting areas shown on the map. However, such peoples were much more widely and variously present than was thereby suggested, and nearly half of this western half of the country was still Indian lands. Without quite saying so, in this one map of population the Walker Atlas sets before us a succinct cartographic portrait of the United States as at once a nation and an empire, an East and a West sharply separated and markedly different in character and in stage of and prospects for development.

Few readers of the time would have doubted that the whole of this New West would be conquered and domesticated by Americans as had a succession of older Wests. Yet there was also ample evidence to infer that the process of such incorporation into the body of the nation would take on a rather different pattern. Although folk colonization is always selective and uneven in area, in the older Wests of Transappalachia local clusters and salients in the vanguard were soon engulfed and integrated into a generally contiguous pattern of advance—as was now displayed in the historical sequence of maps on the "Progress of the Nation." Even though it might seem likely that the current "frontier line of population" would advance farther onto the Plains, it would surely not simply sweep forward on a continental front to the Pacific. Rather, this Far West would become settled chiefly by expansion and extension outward from the several primary nuclei already implanted. Because it was already clear that each of these—California, Oregon, Utah, Colorado, New Mexico—was isolated in location and distinct in kind, it should also have been apparent that in any program for a "higher kind of political education" based on "the exact knowledge of our country"—as provided by this new atlas format, or any other—generalizations and understandings about this American West as a whole must be firmly grounded on knowledge of its diverse regional parts.

Such an admonition and caution have been far more ignored than heeded, then and thereafter. Americans have never taken much to atlas study and have been far more attracted to sweeping generalizations about the nation as a whole than to knowledge of its regional realities. Hence the special need and value of a geographical perspective on the history of this West—as well as of the nation—to which we now turn.

2. California

THE GOLD RUSH TRANSFORMATION

"California has not grown or evolved so much as it has been hurtled forward, rocket-fashion, by a series of chain-reaction explosions," said Carey McWilliams in his penetrating interpretation of *California: The Great Exception.* "It was, of course, the discovery of gold that got California off to a flying start, . . . the lights went on all at once, in a blaze, and they have never dimmed."

We may well begin our sketch of the remarkable geographical transformation wrought by that famous event by noting that, in fact, a Golden California was forming in American minds and becoming fixed on American maps even before the sensational discovery of gold in Sierran streams. Fully six months earlier, in July 1847, a New York editor referred to California as "that remote conquest, the present Dorado of the American imagination" and directed his readers' attention to the character and position of San Francisco Bay as an obvious contender for the site of "the destined metropolis"—"that mighty city of the imagination, the Tyre or Carthage of the uttermost West, which is to wield the future sceptre of the Pacific . . . a world of empire, embracing all Oceanica, and the Asiatic and American shores of the South Seas." And shortly thereafter the restless American geopolitical explorer John Charles Frémont furthered such visions by bestowing the name "*Chrysopylae* (Golden Gate)" on the portal to that destined seat of commerce and empire, "on the same principle," he explained, that the great "entrepot of eastern commerce," "the harbor of Byzantium . . . was called *Chrysoceras* (golden horn)."

From their first acquaintance with this edge of the continent Americans had fixed their attention on this singular break in "an iron-bound and surf-beaten coast." Routinely praised as "one of the finest harbors in the world," it was much more than a mere harbor, more like a "miniature Mediterranean": a nest of bays connected to the ocean by a narrow defensible gate, deep enough for the largest ships, with bold and fertile shores suitable for towns and settlements, and serving as the single outlet by navigable river of the vast interior valley of the Sacramento and San Joaquin. With a climate like "that of southern Italy," "vast resources for shiptimber, grain and cattle," and a "geographical position on the line of communication with Asia," it was clearly the essential controlling piece of California, and it was the one part given highest priority in the treaty negotiations with Mexico.

Mexico gave up San Francisco Bay in the first round of those negotiations not just because, given American power and insistence, it had little choice but also because that part of California had never had the same meaning to Mexicans or their Spanish predecessors. Mexico, like New Spain, was a land-based society, grounded on local resources and the exploitation of local populations. Commerce tended to be controlled and limited, geared to periodic supply of essentials and staple exports. Thus Alta California was a linear system of sites in the coastal valleys, a tenuous string of missions (secularized in the 1830s), a few presidios and pueblos (towns), and, near the end of the Mexican era, a loose, more or less continuous patchwork of ranchos. The main areas of the thinly scattered population were in the Los Angeles Basin, Santa Barbara, Monterey, and San Jose. San Francisco Bay was a marginal district and treated as such. It is telling of Spanish perspectives and motivations that this astounding harbor was discovered in 1769 by a land party blundering northward, even though it lay on a seacoast that had been reconnoitered and claimed by Spain for more than 200 years. Once known, the principal concern of Spanish, and later Mexican, governments was to keep it out of the hands of rival powers. The last and northernmost of the missions, San Rafael and Solano (Sonoma), were founded in part to secure the area against the Russians.

Thus in all those years few Spanish or Mexican ships ever sailed through the Golden Gate. Monterey served as the capital and main seat of activities in the north, and the ranchos around the bay were served by annual visits of Yankee and British vessels in the hide and tallow trade. A sprinkling of foreigners drifted in, some marrying into *californio* families. For some years the Hudson's Bay Company had an outpost at Yerba Buena. In 1840 a new inland center began to emerge in the Sacramento Valley where John Sutter, who had gone to German Missouri fleeing family and debts in German Switzerland and spent some years floundering about various Far Western frontiers before inveigling a large land grant from the governor in Monterey, was building his baronial estate of New Helvetia into an eventually thriving combination of fort, farm, ranch, workshop, and trading center. The American farmer-emigrant families that began to filter in from 1841 on also settled in the Sacramento Valley more or less apart from the few californios. There was no great surge of such pioneers. Until 1849 emigration was running perhaps ten to one in favor of Oregon over California. Farmers were deterred not just by the serious complications of land grants and titles but by serious uncertainties over the agricultural potentials of California. Although there were numerous glowing reports, so knowledgeable an American as the Rev. Walter Colten, while ready to nominate a number of "insular spots" that "may be made perfect gardens," had to admit that "California as a whole . . . is not the country agriculturalists would select." And many an overland migrant arriving in the ovenlike heat of the Sacramento Valley in late summer must have felt like the forty-niner who exclaimed: "I say without hesitation, let no man come here for agricultural speculation while there is a corner left between the Alleghanies and the Platte."

When the United States assumed formal control there were probably no more than 15,000 Euro-American residents in all Alta California, and not a tenth of these were north of San Jose. Thus when the news of the discovery of gold in Sutter's new millrace in the Sierra foothills got out and the great rush gathered momentum, the force of the impact was directed at the farthest, feeblest reach of the Hispanic system and it created a pattern of settlement and circulation utterly disparate with the old linear coastal one. The outline of this new human geography emerged almost instantaneously: San Francisco (a renamed and transformed Yerba Buena), the instant city and international entrepôt—the waterway through the northern bays, Carquinez Strait, and up the rivers to the inland supply centers of Sacramento and Stockton—the pack trails and wagon roads fanning into the mountain camps in the broadening pattern of the gold region.

Although this indelible imprint may seem essentially inevitable in retrospect, there were serious rivalries and uncertainties in the first few years. It may seem surprising that the principal question was just where the premier city would be. In spite of San Francisco's sudden astonishing growth (to perhaps 30,000 in two years), there were complaints and doubts about its site and situation. These were succinctly put by the general in command of the new Department of the Pacific: San Francisco is "in no way fitted for military or commercial purposes," he informed his Washington superior in 1849; "there is no harbor, a bad landing place, bad water, no supply of provisions, and inclement climate, and it is cut off from the rest of the country except by a long circuit around the southern extremity of the bay." He therefore selected the new town of Benicia on Carquinez Strait for his military headquarters. A few years later the navy followed suit, establishing its naval yard on Mare Island at nearby Vallejo. Deep water, a mixture of fresh and salt, and the absence of the chilly dense fogs so common to San Francisco were important civilian attractions as well, and the Pacific Mail Steamship Company set up its main depot and shops in Benicia. Furthermore, strong majorities in the legislature twice voted to fix the state capital along this strategic trafficway, choosing Vallejo in 1851 and Benicia in 1853, but after one session in each of these raw new towns, whose promoters had far outpromised what they could deliver, they gave up and settled in Sacramento, which by then provided good facilities and seemed to be central to expanding agricultural and mining interests. San Francisco was considered too tumultuously urban and eccentric in location to be a serious contender for this geopolitical prize, but its leaders worked rapidly to improve its commercial facilities, especially by the extension of long wharves and infilling of the tidal mudflat of Yerba Buena Cove, and it was not long before its urban supremacy was secure.

There was much extension and infilling of this overall new geographical framework as well (fig. 10). The sudden influx of so many people created enormous demands for provisions, shelter, and fuel, stimulating a thriving sea trade with Hawaii, Oregon, and other Pacific sources, and giving rise to a whole set of specialty districts within California. The lateral thrust of this American invasion had cut across a rich sequence of local environments: the foggy redwood coast, the oak groves and prairies of the sheltered leeward valleys, the salt marshes of the bay and tule marshes of the lower Sacramento, the open grasslands of the great central valley, the prairie and riparian woods of the foothills, and the pine- and fir-clad slopes of the higher Sierras. And so lumbermen were soon felling the great trees back of Santa Cruz and Bodega Bay; farmers were marketing a remarkable variety of field, garden, and orchard produce from the valleys tributary to the bay; dairymen (mostly New Englanders) were shipping in butter and cheese from Monterey and the Marin peninsula; wheat, a staple of Hispanic California, was rapidly expanding in the Sacramento Valley, while barley was grown there and in the foothills to feed the tens of thousands of horses and mules used in the freighting business. All the while the number of productive gold placers was rapidly expanding. Within three years' time the main gold region extended as a more or less continuous belt from LaPorte and Downieville on the north to Mariposa on the south, with a dozen major camps in between.

There was much instability. The 1860 census recorded nearly 150,000 in these Sierran counties; ten years later there were considerably fewer, as large hydraulic or hard-rock mining operations took over from surficial placers, but there had also been a sudden extension eastward into Nevada, where sensationally rich silver ores had given rise to the big works at Virginia City. By 1870 San Francisco was a city of 150,000, there were another 50,000 in the bay area, 560,000 in the state as a whole, and the economy was much further developed and diversified. The Mediterranean-like climate of California, so unlike anything migrants from the

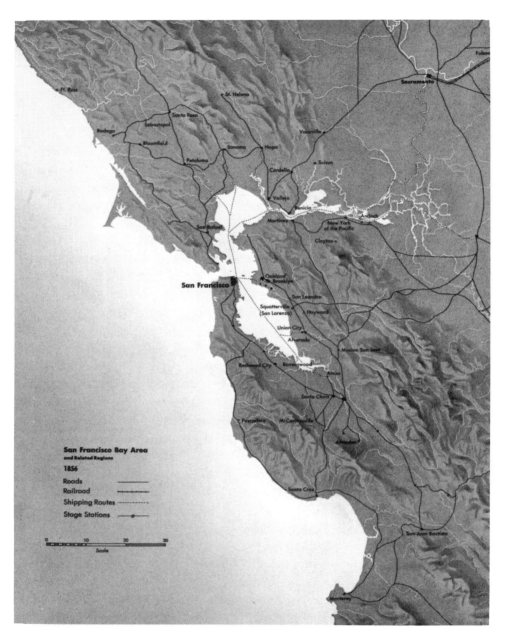

10. San Francisco Bay Area, 1856.
(Reprinted from Mel Scott, *San Francisco Bay Area: A Metropolis in Perspective.* 2d ed. Copyright © 1985, The Regents of the University of California)

Eastern states had experienced, was now better understood and its virtues made manifest:

> In the Atlantic States the storms of approaching winter put a stop to the labor of the farm and force both man and beast into winter quarters. In California it is just the reverse. The husbandman watches the skies with impatient hope, and as soon as the rain of November or December has softened the soil, every plough is put in requisition. . . . The planting season continues late, extending from November to April. . . . Owing to the absence of rain, harvesting is conducted in a plan which would confuse the ideas of an Atlantic farmer. There are no showers or thunder gusts to throw down the grain, or wet the hay, or impede the reaper. . . . In September and October the great grain-growing valleys may often be seen dotted over with cords of grain in sacks, as secure from damage by weather as if closely housed.

The quick maturing of orchard plantings, the succession of fruits and vegetables coming on the market through the year, and the bountiful productions of the many tributary valleys made San Francisco an enviable place: "it is probable that no market in the world is equal to it" in the "extraordinary variety of fruit" available at the same time. Whether true or not—what of Seville, Constantinople, or Suzhou?—Americans were much impressed. By any Eastern standard the sheer scale and mode of operations—the size of farms, orchards, and vineyards as well as the implements and organization of work—were also impressive. A single company in Marin County operated fifteen dairies with a total of 3,500 cows. Many wheat farms were not only huge in size, they were being worked by new kinds of machines: gang plows turning a broad swath of these lighter soils instead of the familiar deep furrows of the two-bottom sulky plow of the East, the header or even the combine in place of the binder. Primitive combined harvesters had been tried out in Michigan in the 1840s but provoked little interest. One was shipped to San Jose in 1853, and its revolutionary time- and labor-saving possibilities prompted further experimentation so that by the 1860s a successful machine was being locally manufactured and marketed to a rapidly expanding industry. By that time wheat farming dominated the Santa Clara and Sacramento valleys and was edging southward into the drier San Joaquin, aided by the decimation of herds and breakup of many ranchos after the great droughts of the mid-1860s and by the rapid expansion of its export market. The size and capitalization of California farming, the high cost of labor, and the assuredly dry harvest season had put this new region in the forefront of agricultural innovation, and these together with its geographical extent and position had made it one of the leading grain-export regions of the world.

The San Joaquin Valley and the southern Coast Ranges and valleys continued to be strongholds of cattlemen and sheepmen, the original Californian stock now much augmented and altered by herds driven in from Sonora, Texas, and the older American West. It was a volatile business, expanding over all the possible ranges but under heavy pressure from nature and speculations. These summer-dry pastures were far more fragile than the prairies of the Great Plains and were soon overgrazed, the native bunchgrass giving way to wild oats. Droughts took a heavy toll, ranchers were usually in debt, and speculators were eager to subdivide these lands into farms. The passage of a "no fence law" in 1873, by which the pastoralist was responsible for any damage done by his livestock to the farmer's crop, marked the essential end of a half century of the "rancho era" in California. The usual shift was from livestock to grain, but it was commonly expected that the ultimate shift, especially in all the drier southern half of the Great Valley and of the state, would be to irrigation and much more varied and intensive agriculture. No large-scale irrigation projects were undertaken before the 1880s, but there was much local experimentation, land companies were formed and large tracts purchased, colonies were designed, and as the railroad began to extend southeast from Stockton, founding a town at every river crossing, the prospects from this remarkable land seemed exhilarating and almost endless. In 1873 the California State Agricultural Society urged the cultivation of the following crops, all of which "have been produced in abundance by individual experimenters in different localities of the state": flax, sugar beets, hops, tobacco, olives, figs, sugarcane, pepper, cotton, dates, coconuts, mangoes, bananas, pineapples, rice, opium (poppies), tea, coffee, ramie, New Zealand flax, jute, and silk (under a state subsidy, with a silk mill at San Jose). Many of these crops, of course, would prove inappropriate to these summer-dry subtropics, but they attest the fervent speculations of the time and point toward the actual cornucopia to come.

All of these districts were brought into focus on San Francisco by an evolving network of riverboats, railroads, stagecoaches, and freighting teams (fig. 11). Services were continually being improved and extended. The launching in San Francisco in 1860 of the 1,050-ton sidewheeler *Chrysopolis,* which could carry a thousand passengers to and from Sacramento with all the speed and elegance of the best on the Hudson or Ohio, demonstrated the local entrepreneurial and industrial response to regional opportunities. The chief deficiency for industry and shipping was the inadequacy of local coal supplies. The small seams at Mt. Diablo, just south of the Sacramento Delta, had to be supplemented by large tonnages, much of it brought in as ballast, from overseas sources.

In addition to this main continuous body of Californian development, there were outlying areas, north and south, bound into this San Francisco focus. In the immediate aftermath of the first gold discoveries prospectors began to range through the tangle of rugged mountains toward the California-Oregon border— and Shasta, Weaverville, Yreka, and Jacksonville soon emerged as producing dis-

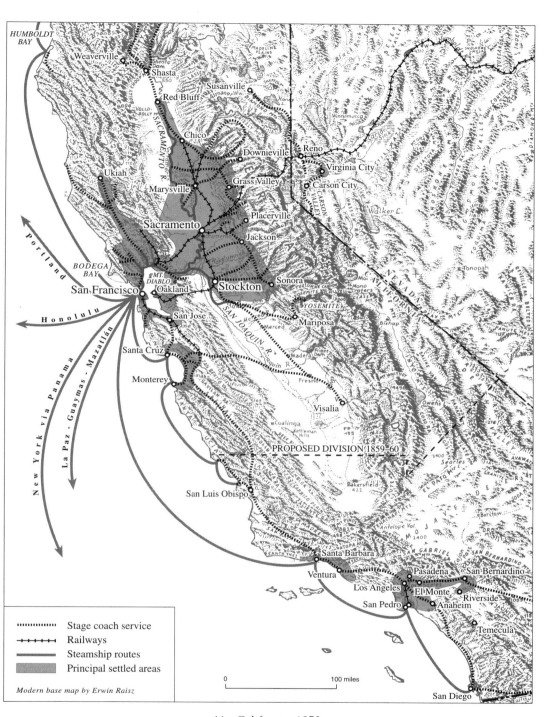

HUMBOLDT
BAY

Weaverville
Shasta
550
Red Bluff
Susanville
Chico
Downieville
Reno
Ukiah
Grass Valley
Virginia City
Marysville
Carson City
Sacramento
Placerville
Jackson
BODEGA
BAY
MT.
DIABLO
Stockton
Sonora
San Francisco
Oakland
San Jose
YOSEMITE
Santa Cruz
Mariposa
Monterey
Visalia

Portland

Honolulu

New York via Panama

La Paz – Guaymas – Mazatlán

PROPOSED DIVISION 1859–60

San Luis Obispo

Santa Barbara
Ventura
Pasadena
San Bernardino
Los Angeles
El Monte
Riverside
San Pedro
Anaheim
Temecula

••••••••••• Stage coach service
+++++++ Railways
———— Steamship routes
　　　 Principal settled areas

0   100 miles

Modern base map by Erwin Raisz

San Diego

11. California, 1870.

tricts. In 1850 a Klamath Exploring Expedition set out from San Francisco to probe the Klamath, Rogue, and Umpqua river basins for gold, townsites, and other lands worthy of investment. The company soon failed, but in its wake were a scattering of mining camps and coastal shipping points, such as Trinidad, Crescent City, Gold Beach, and Scottsburg. Humboldt Bay, much the most capacious harbor (but with a difficult entrance), was rediscovered at this time. Initially valued as a port for inland gold districts, it was soon colonized by fishermen and lumbermen from New England and Nova Scotia and became an important source of redwood. The meadows of the cool, humid valleys were well suited to dairying, and in the 1870s Danish and Italian Swiss immigrants joined these Yankee pioneers in expanding the production of butter and cheese. Here, therefore—and including the many sawmill hamlets along the rugged Mendocino coast—was a very different California: one of a limited range of resources in a quite different kind of country colonized by a small and limited variety of people, the whole quite detached from the characterizing swirl and growth of the main.

Southern California was also a markedly different scene, but one of greater significance to the whole. The Gold Rush had a relatively minor and selective impact on this 300-mile stretch of Hispanic California. There was some exodus to the mines, pastoralists enjoyed a brief prosperity from the sudden new market, and a stream of migrants came through following the southern transcontinental trails to the goldfields. Even before this influx American troops and companies of Mormons had arrived via this southern portal. Inevitably some of these migrants stayed on, sensing some sort of opportunity in this sunny subtropical land wedged between the mountains and the sea. One of the problems confronting commercially minded Americans was that the only decent harbor had no hinterland, whereas much the most attractive area had no harbor. The virtues of San Diego as a sheltered anchorage had been well appreciated by treaty negotiators and soon thereafter by railroad promoters, but the limitations of its larger position were starkly apparent to anyone who probed its rugged arid backcountry. Anglo speculators found only a few ranchos and a few hundred residents in the entire district, and although they quickly laid out new townsites around the bay and touted the health-giving powers of the desert climate, they were able to lure relatively few settlers or investors.

In contrast, the Los Angeles area was the largest coastal lowland along this entire Pacific frontage, with many good sites but no decent harbor. Ships had to lay well off from the Palos Verdes headland in the exposed bay and be served by lighters from San Pedro. The main districts of interest lay twenty to thirty miles inland, where the oldest pueblo, two former missions, and numerous well-watered ranchos were strung out along the base of the mountains. This became the main staging ground for American officials, merchants, colonists, and promoters and thereby much the most important focus of Anglo-Hispanic tensions in Southern California. The intersection of two sharply contrasting societies was soon apparent in various forms: in the set of American rectangular grids attached to the empirical Hispanic patterns in the pueblo of Los Angeles; in a townscape of new brick and milled-wood buildings amidst those of adobe, tile, and tar (roofs); in the rapid transformation of selected ranchos into American communities. A few of these new settlements were more or less informal agglomerations, such as El Monte at the end of the trail from Texas, but most were formal projects of one kind or another. One of the first was San Bernardino, a typical Mormon farm-village laid out at the base of Cajon Pass primarily to serve as a waystation for Utah-bound emigrants coming by sea. This soon-thriving settlement was abruptly abandoned in 1857 when such outlying populations were summoned home to Utah. In that same year another distinctive settlement was initiated by a group of German emigrants who after indifferent success in the goldfields formed the Los Angeles Vineyard Society, purchased a ranch on the Santa Ana River, and established Anaheim as a cooperative venture. Within a few years the community was shipping wine to San Francisco, and its success stimulated a number of other horticultural projects, but costs, agronomic problems, and isolation impeded progress. Anticipation of railroad connections to San Francisco and to the East caused a brief flurry of real estate promotions, such as Riverside, Pasadena, and Ventura, but growth remained slow. The first railroad was a short line connecting Los Angeles to Wilmington, a slightly improved harbor adjacent to San Pedro.

By 1870 probably a majority of the 15,000 people in Los Angeles County were newcomers, but few were to be found beyond the Los Angeles lowland. All along the coast to Santa Barbara and San Luis Obispo the rancho society was still intact even if under severe economic pressures, and scattered about the region were loose villages of Indians and mestizos living on small rancherias (as at San Juan Capistrano and Temecula) as yet little disturbed by the American takeover. Even farther away, on the margins of the Mojave, were many little Indian bands never caught up in or at least long free of any imperial system.

Southern California, therefore, was a distant, detached sector of the vigorous regional system anchored on San Francisco. It had been made distinct by the Gold Rush in a negative sense: by being so removed and lightly affected by that powerful event. Its Anglo residents of course envisioned and worked to change it into a fully "Americanized" region but could not do so quickly or comprehensively, and the contrast with the main body of the state remained stark: in 1870 the counties south of Monterey, containing a third of the state's area, had only 5.5 percent of its population. Such imbalance in growth and character had fostered political tensions from the first. At the 1849 Constitutional Convention a californio delegate from Santa Barbara had proposed a division of the state, and although brushed aside by the dominant northerners, the idea kept reappearing in legislative debates and bills all through the 1850s until a separation bill setting aside the six southernmost counties as the Territory of Colorado was actually approved by both houses, signed by the governor, and sent to Congress (underscored by a letter explaining that "the union of southern and northern California is unnatural") in 1860—where it died, lost in the turmoil of secession. Thus the political bounds of California remained discordant with the human geographic patterns of the time, and continued to be, under rapidly, radically changing circumstances, thereafter. The proposed division made good geopolitical sense then, and similar proposals, grounded on geographic arguments plausible to each era, have recurred quite regularly ever since. So near a thing in 1860, and so persistent a cause, prompt reflection on what effect such a division might have had on the shaping of the American West—and of the national federation.

Setting the eastern boundary of the state was also controversial but much less consequential. The initial question was whether to draw a "natural" or a geometrical line. For some "the snowy range of the Sierra Nevada . . . , a line traced by the Omnipotent," was the obvious choice because they felt there could be no effective connection or community of interest between the eastern and western sides of that formidable barrier. But others regarded the mountain range (and its gold-bearing innards) as an entity, its eastern valleys as useful oases, and some pressed for a longitudinal line much farther to the east (to fend off Mormon Utah). After long debate a simple geometric angle enclosing the Sierra Nevada and approximately parallel with the coastline was drawn. Subsequent attempts by California and by local residents to shift that boundary eastward so as to annex Carson Valley got nowhere, nor did Nevada's counterpetition (set forth in the first message of its governor and supported by a congressional committee) for California to cede all lands east of the Sierra summit.

In a broader view San Francisco was the focus of a realm that far transcended even the extensive bounds of California and adjacent Nevada. As the *Daily Alta Californian* noted in 1872, all through these years California had been engaged in "the building up and peopling of half of a great continent," and as a consequence (as a later student of western mining emphasized) "there was everywhere present, everywhere respected, everywhere vital—the Californian . . . carrying with [him] the methods, the customs, and the ideas of the mother region." By this time scheduled steamship services radiating to the north, west, and south offered some indication of how Oregon, Puget Sound, British Columbia, Hawaii, and northwest Mexico depended on San Francisco as a commercial and financial center. Passengers, mail, imports, and exports of this North Pacific Slope, including inland mining camps as far away as Idaho and Montana, were very largely funneled through this premier city by way of its powerful agencies, the Pacific Mail Steamship Company, the Wells, Fargo and Company, and, eventually, the Central Pacific railway. In 1849 speculators had surveyed the plat for "the City of New-York of the Pacific" at the mouth of the San Joaquin. Their brief energetic promotion came to nothing, but the concept was real enough, and by the 1870s there was no doubt that San Francisco was that "equipoise," the destined metropolis of the American Pacific World as New York was of the Atlantic World. It not only performed that role commercially, it did so culturally as well. It was the one great immigrant focus of the West, its cosmopolitan vitality was quite unequaled, and it was world famous. As Roger W. Lotchin summarized: "instant and urban and detached from other metropolitan areas by thousands of miles. . . . Anarchic, mis-sited, miserably planned, full of chaos, conflict, hope and greed, oft burnt and oft rebuilt, alternately a source of despair and extravagant expectations, San Francisco succeeded in a very short time in becoming the wonder of almost all who encountered it. And it has never stopped being just that."

RESULTANT REGIONAL CHARACTER

It is important to get a clear sense of the social and cultural shaping of this premier Pacific city and its region. And we begin with the fact that like its Atlantic analogue it would be difficult to discern within San Francisco any residual imprint whatever of the pre-European inhabitants and only minor vestiges—Mission Dolores, the Presidio—of the Europeans who preceded the Anglo-American era. These negatives are an essential dimension of the Californian scene.

The devastation of California's Indians by the Gold Rush is one of the worst in the long sequence of cultural collision horror stories in North America. In the preceding eighty years of contact with Euro-Americans, disease, disruption, and direct abuse by Whites had taken the kind of toll more or less common to such encounter, reducing a population of perhaps 300,000 by about a half. In the next decade or so most of the remainder was not merely shattered and shoved aside, it was in many places ruthlessly, intentionally destroyed. The peculiar power of this assault was the result of special features on either side.

In comparative terms the Indians of California were remarkable not only for the high densities of population in a nonagricultural economy but for the enormous number and variety of their basic sociopolitical units. As David Hornbeck notes: "each stretch of beach, each valley and each hillside had its own contingent of Indians, often very different from those living only a short distance away. In effect the California Indians exhibited a bewildering mosaic of regional differences in human occupance." All told these "tribelets" (as anthropologists have labeled such autonomous groups of rarely more than a few hundred persons occupying a territory "traversable in a day's walk") represented about 14 language families, perhaps "80 mutually unintelligible tongues, all divided into more than 300 dialects." Such intensive differentiation precluded either concerted resistance against sudden incursions or negotiation for cession and withdrawal from extensive areas. Such societies were not well organized for mortal combat; with no warrior tradition, no ready adaptation of horses and guns, they could survive only by flight, stealth, and isolation, retaliate only by sporadic murder and theft.

On the other side was, in effect, a vast mob running amok: tens of thousands of armed males swarming over the countryside, under no general leadership or discipline, restrained by no laws or police, driven by greed, imbued with contempt for all "lower" forms of humanity—and especially these "digger Indians" who grubbed a meager subsistence out of roots and nuts, insects and small game. Unlike many a land rush in the Transappalachian territories, the most eagerly sought areas were not the arable plains, valleys, and commercial sites (though these were quickly taken) but every stream and valley in the mountains, no matter how rugged or inaccessible. Thus the Indians had virtually no refuge; they were driven off, hunted down (there are actual cases of communities hiring hunters to be paid per scalp to extirpate these "vermin"), enslaved (the selling of children and holding them as indentured servants for many years was common and sanctioned by state law), or left to starve.

Technically, of course, Indians in California as elsewhere were dependents under the imperial care of the federal government. In addition, a special article of the annexation treaty ostensibly protected them from displacement—from "the necessity of seeking new homes." In response to the chaos of the first year or so of the Gold Rush three Indian commissioners were sent from Washington to attempt some amelioration. Working from south to north they negotiated eighteen treaties setting aside as many reserves and the cession of all remaining Indian lands west of the Sierra summit. These treaties followed the standard pattern of offering protection and recompense in the form of livestock, clothing, equipment, teachers, and gifts. In retrospect, these California treaties were more extravagantly flawed than others in pressuring legitimization of huge cessions of lands from tribelets or in some cases individuals who actually had not the slightest claim of authority over most of the territory defined. This entire set of treaties was denounced in California for the extensive reservations proposed and the intended removal of non-Indians already residing therein. To require, said a legislative committee appointed to assess the matter, that "large, permanent, and populous settlements of enterprising citizens who had located upon and acquired rights and interests" in such lands be forcibly removed "to make room for the introduction and settlement of a few tribes of ignorant barbarians" would not only be unjust and "have a most deleterious effect upon the general prosperity of the whole State," it would be counter to all American precedent and expectation: "These rights and interests have been acquired by the pioneer miner and agriculturist in good faith upon the implied assurance that the same privileges and immunities would be extended to the toil-worn emigrant in California that has been extended to the first settlers in other new countries with the limits of our Government."

Although a few voices were raised in defense of the Indians—"has the love of gold blotted from our minds all feelings of compassion or justice?"—the legislature petitioned Congress not only to reject all these treaties but to remove *all* Indians from the State of California "with all practicable dispatch." Congress rejected both the treaties and the idea of expulsion and subsequently made various feeble efforts to cope with the anarchy, primarily by setting up temporary reserves that were in effect "concentration camps into which as many Indians were herded as could be caught and transported"—and from which most fled as soon as possible. By 1870 only four small formal reservations existed, Indians had been expelled or extirpated over large areas of the state, and their number had been reduced to about 30,000, a considerable proportion of whom were in the least disturbed districts of Southern California. "Seldom has a native race been subjected to such a catastrophic decimation."

The first great wave of the Gold Rush surged across everything in its path and left a residue of destruction. The hospitable John Sutter, who had accommodated and assisted many a visitor and immigrant, was suddenly swamped and ultimately ruined. Squatters camped on his land, trampled his crops, slaughtered his live-stock, used his fences for fuel, and stole his goods. Already heavily in debt through his own extravagance Sutter transferred all his property to his son (newly arrived from Europe), who proceeded to have the plat for Sacramento surveyed and did reap some return. This impact on New Helvetia was symptomatic of what would befall many a rancho, and it quickly emerged as a regionwide clash of cultures. Two factors were fundamental in this antagonism: the contrast in land tenure systems and associated attitudes, and the pervasive American assumption of "Anglo-Saxon" superiority.

In its later stages the Mexican system of land grants tended to be loose and lavish even by Hispanic-American standards. Officially intended to encourage settlement in thinly occupied frontier zones, colonization laws allowed up to eleven square leagues (about 47,000 acres) per grant, to be made up of a combination of irrigable, arable, and pastoral lands. In remote Alta California governors were often lax with regulations relating to surveys and registration and inclined to reward favorites extravagantly. Thus even though the Treaty of Guadalupe Hidalgo guaranteed Mexican property rights, the validity of many holdings was readily challengeable. Furthermore, Anglo-Americans seeing miles of unfenced, unde-veloped, apparently unused countryside were ready to assume that it was public domain open to claim according to long-standing American practices—or, if not, that it ought to be, for no one, and certainly not indolent Mexicans, should be allowed to lock up such acreages. Further fueled by the near absence of police and judicial authority, squatting became an endemic and often riotous problem, cursed by many persons, then and later, as "a universal abomination of the California of the 1850s."

Under the special circumstances of California the clash between the two peoples and their contrasting systems was unavoidable and exceedingly difficult to mediate. The United States solution was to depend upon the courts and a special California Land Act of 1851 designed to ascertain the validity of land titles. But that act was shaped by an assumption that many of the Mexican titles were defective, and it placed the burden of proof upon the landowner, who had to defend his property within an unfamiliar, and certainly in some degree, unfriendly system. Typically, such adjudication proved to be far more complex, time consuming, and expensive than anticipated, and it beclouded land titles in many important districts (including the pueblo lands of Los Angeles and presidio lands of San Francisco) for many years. As Robert Glass Cleland concluded, "whatever may have been the intention of the sponsors" of this land act, "Its enforcement brought to fruition all of the evils which its [opponents] warned, it penalized legitimate land owners, often to the point of ruin; played into the hands of speculators; discouraged settlement and immigrations; . . . and by creating a resentful and disaffected landless element, served to produce a large measure of instability."

Any map of basic land surveys of California will display the state divided between two radically different systems: a fragmented mosaic of large individualized parcels marked out by metes and bounds covering the Hispanic coastal strip, with a scattering of fragments in the Central Valley, and all the remainder—including every interstice within the Hispanic pattern—parceled rigidly into the uniform mile-square sections of the American township-and-range system. However, this overall pattern of the two land systems must not be mistaken for, in effect, a social geography of the encounter and accommodation of the two peoples, for the older pattern had been heavily penetrated by the new people. By the time 514 Mexican grants (out of 813 claims) had been finally recognized, a third of them were held by Anglo-Americans. Few of these new owners were aspiring ranchers; they were land speculators eager to subdivide these large parcels into farms and towns. The prospects for such promotions varied greatly with land quality and location, but old Hispanic strongholds were soon punctuated by Anglo-American settlements (such as Watsonville, Gilroy, Ventura, Santa Cruz, and, in 1874, Lompoc), and Anglo merchants and professionals, agents of an aggressive encompassing system, were present in every district. Although some californio families persevered on at least a portion of their properties and even enjoyed some degree of social prestige, the Hispanic society as a whole, captive within an alien social, political, legal, and

linguistic imperium, was ever-more constrained, penetrated, weakened, and impoverished, its lower levels reduced to peonage, vagabondage, or, in some notorious cases, banditry.

It should be noted that the Hispanic population was momentarily greatly increased during the opening phase of the Gold Rush. Mexicans, after all, were much
the best positioned to seek this new wealth in their recently lost province. Some
estimates put the influx of Sonorans as high as 10,000 (but there was a tendency to
lump all Mexicans under that term), and they were joined by thousands of Chil-
eans and other Latin Americans. These people opened up much of the Southern
Mines (south of the Mokelumne) but soon faced heavy opposition. Resented as
interlopers—even "invaders"—gleaning American wealth from American soil,
they were driven out of many camps with a brutality and hatred well honed in the
just-completed Mexican War. Like most gold seekers, most of these Latinos had
come with the intention of eventually returning home—as many did seasonally. A
minority hung on, finding a niche as laborers, drovers, freighters, and as the placers
gave out, Sonoran experience with hard-rock gold mining and milling became
valued. Just how much the total Hispanic population was thereby augmented and
the extent to which these earliest immigrants made connection with older californio families is not clear, but they came to make up about a third of the Los Angeles
barrio (which Anglos usually referred to as "Sonora Town").

That there was in fact a significant human continuity and cultural imprint from
the Hispanic era is of course an important feature of this distinctive region.
Once the people were reduced to a feeble minority within a powerful Anglo
California the lore and landscape of mission and rancho would be romanticized and
celebrated. The more fundamental legacy came from the mundane activities of
those colonizing instruments: the routine introduction of Mediterranean forms of
agriculture and pastoralism that gave American settlers and entrepreneurs a head-
start on their development of what was to them an exotic environment. Thus the
tens of thousands of cattle, sheep, horses, mules, and burros were quickly put to
use; the established cultivation of well-adapted varieties of wheat and barley allowed ready expansion of those basic staples; the enticing remnants of "mission"
oranges, lemons, figs, olives, and vineyards—with or without irrigation—demonstrated the exciting potential of these summer-dry subtropics.

Unlike other areas annexed from Mexico, the stark Anglo-Hispanic confrontation in California was almost immediately complicated, subordinated, and diffused
by the mass influx of a great variety of peoples, for the news of gold lying in Sierran
streams reverberated around the world with unprecedented impact. Sonorans along
with Oregonians and Hawaiians were the first to respond, followed by Chinese and
Australians. Word of the discovery reached New York in August 1848, seven
months after the event, and spread rapidly thereafter with mounting credible

evidence, culminating in President James K. Polk's formal statement to Congress in December that "the accounts of the abundance of gold in that territory are of such an extraordinary character as would scarcely command belief were they not corroborated by authentic reports of officers in the public service."

Thus the great surge from Eastern America and Western Europe came in 1849. Facilitated by burgeoning new information and transportation systems and coinciding with widespread social and political upheavals in Europe, tens of thousands of young males representing, in total, dozens of countries and five continents set out to glean the fabled wealth. The convergence of these peoples upon the Golden Gate and Sierran slopes had a major impact on world traffic patterns, bringing into focus the several overland trails from the Eastern states, the shorter connections from Oregon and Mexico, the suddenly magnified isthmian routes, the long voyages around Cape Horn and across the Pacific.

Carey McWilliams saw this vast insurge epitomized in a momentary scene and a set of names on the land:

> Every state, nation, and race was represented in the gold rush migration. The flags which could be seen flying in the harbor of San Francisco in the late fall of 1849 told the story: England, France, Spain, Portugal, Italy, Hamburg, Bremen, Belgium, New Granada, Holland, Sweden, Oldenburg, Chile, Peru, Russia, Mexico, Ecuador, Hanover, Norway, Hawaii, and Tahiti. The names of the gold camps also indicate the diversity of the migration: Washington, Boston, Baltimore, Concord, Bunker Hill, Irish Creek, Italian Bar, French Corral, German Bar, Dutch Flat, Kanaka Bar, Malay Camp, Chinese Camp, Nigger Hill, Missouri Bar, Iowa Hill, Wisconsin Hill, Illinoistown, Michigan Bluffs, Tennessee Creek, Kentucky Flat, Minnesota Flat, Cap Cod Bar, Vermont Bar, Georgia Slide, Alabama Bar, Dixie Valley, and Mississippi Bar [and he might have added Portuguese Flat, Chilean Camp, Spanish Diggings, Peru, Cherokee, Texas Hill, and Mormon Gulch].

Such names suggest the tendency for people of common origins to settle together in "islands" or "pockets" and even amidst the great instability of the times to resettle in some degree as a group in some other district or town or city neighborhood. Thus this newly American California became instantaneously a cosmopolitan California, its settlement geography a mosaic of racial and ethnic areas. That about half of the population of San Francisco, and approaching 40 percent of the state as a whole, were foreign-born (1870) did not in itself markedly differentiate this frontier society from, say, Milwaukee, Chicago, or Wisconsin, but the sources and proportions of these new Californians were significantly, indelibly different. Furthermore, because all flocked in at once and the Americans were as new to this part of the continent as the rest, "foreigners became more co-colonists than alien immigrants," creating together a California self-consciously distinct from the common routines of American life.

To Anglo-Californians much the most visible and notorious of these groups was the Chinese. Established trans-Pacific links with Canton had given them early entry and the lure of gold and the unrest at home (the Taiping Rebellion following upon the British assault and forced opening of ports) brought 25,000 within the first three years. These frugal and industrious people, so alien in appearance and customs, were soon marginalized and harassed by all the other peoples, but they continued to arrive and were increasingly recruited as contract labor (more than 10,000 were employed in building the Central Pacific). By 1870 they numbered at least 50,000, a "Chinatown" was a visible part of most California towns, they had found numerous service niches (such as cooking and laundering), and they constituted half of the factory workers in San Francisco (especially in shoes, clothing, and cigars). During the economic depression of the 1870s assaults upon the Chinese as an unassimilable race whose "coolie-labor" undercut American living standards were intensified, and laws to prohibit further immigration and to limit their participation in the society and economy were strongly supported.

Among the Europeans the Irish and the Germans were much the largest groups, as elsewhere in the United States, with the several British peoples (from many parts of the empire as well as directly from the British Isles) forming another substantial body (Cornish were especially important in quartz-mining districts). The proportions of French (mainly lured by speculative French companies), Italians (mostly from northern Italy), and Portuguese (chiefly by way of Yankee whaling and shipping contacts with the Atlantic islands) were greater than elsewhere and unusual at all in newly settled North American regions.

People flocked in from all parts of the United States but not quite in proportion to regional populations. New York and New England were the largest contributors and dominated the business and professional ranks. Missouri and the Border South was an important source region, but the Lower South was not, partly because slavery could not be sustained legally or effectually in California. Vigorous attempts to enact a constitutional prohibition on the entry of any Blacks were defeated, but relatively few came (4,272 recorded as resident in 1870), although they were visible in nearly every county and suffered all the discriminations and abuse common to their lot elsewhere in the country. White Southerners, coming by way of the southern overland routes, were rather more prominent in the Los Angeles area, the southerly goldfields, and the San Joaquin (where Visalia was an early stronghold). They tended to join in local feelings of antagonism to San Francisco and Sacramento, in the desire for territorial separations, and, later, in support for the Confederate States (a training camp for soldier recruits was opened at El Monte).

From whatever source and by whatever route the journey to California was an unforgettable and life-changing experience. Few came with intention to settle, and some left after a few seasons (after the first gleanings gold mining became increasingly heavy and tedious work), but many prospered in some degree—or continued to hope to do so. Most stayed on (and a good number of those who left returned with their families), and by the very nature of their experience in the swirl of life in this new land they began to create a California that was cosmopolitan not only in being "composed of elements gathered from all parts of the world" but in the deeper sense of a society that was open to new ideas and ways of doing things: experimental, innovative—the opposite of provincial. Such things showed forth even in the most basic and mundane activities, as E. W. Hilgard, California's distinguished commissioner of agriculture, emphasized in his report of 1878:

> unlike the great agricultural States of the Mississippi Valley, California has not undergone the slow and regular process of settlement by pioneer farmers. . . . The great tide-wave of the rush for gold cast a far different material on the shores of the Pacific; and when the placer mines ceased to yield fortunes to the men of small means, and agriculture began to attract their attention as a surer mode of acquiring the coveted metal, very many of the hands that grasped the plow had never felt its touch before, while their owners would have been at a loss to distinguish a grain-field from a meadow; but among these, as well as among those who at that time returned to the plow after a few years' digression, there was an unusual proportion of progressive, thinking, and reading men, whose ambition and energy had carried them forward when others fainted by the wayside. Both classes of men soon discovered that in a great many respects the rule-of-thumb experience and practice of the older countries would not avail them here; and casting loose from precedent, they tried a "new deal" in constructing for themselves a practice adapted to the new conditions.

Their innovations involved more than tillage practices, machinery, and new crops; they developed a new kind of agriculture quite "outside the American [family] farm tradition": agriculture primarily as a business, and, to a more than ordinary American extent, a speculation based on an ever-expanding array of products and involvement in processing and marketing.

California, therefore, emerged as something new in the American scene. Formed out of a different combination of peoples, with amazing rapidity, under unprecedented social, economic, and political conditions, in a markedly different physical environment far removed from the advancing edge of settlement in the older West, it was neither an extension nor a transplant nor a replica of an established America or of any of its regions. Here there had been hardly a touch of the usual imperial and pioneering preludes, no constraining colonial phase as a federal territory (instant statehood in 1850), no inhibiting scarcity of capital: rather, money came flooding in seeking investment in a California generating its own wealth. Although emerging almost instantly in situ, it was not of course created utterly de novo. It was shaped under United States sovereignty, mainly by White American males who were conscious carriers of "American" values and concepts (the state constitution was modeled on those of New York and Iowa). But there were various versions of such things, necessitating a selection of specific ideas and designs, adaptations to new circumstances, and, in the absence of any dominant group, intense and at times violent struggles in the shaping of the regional society (as evidenced in the populist pressures resulting in a new constitution in 1879). Even as powerful interests emerged, the dynamics of California required "a constant reconciliation of things, a continuous renegotiation of the social contract." Californian political culture, therefore, was an important regional variant; "individualistic," certainly, but in a narrower, shallower sense than that characteristic of the great midland zone of American national politics (à la Elazar); not so deeply enmeshed in the variety of rural and urban interests common to a more slowly evolved society, it was an extreme "Lockean liberalism," focused on the "release of private energy and the increase of private options." Such openness to social change was undergirded and reinforced by a physical environment that was so different in character as to require experiment and so rich in its variety and rewards as to fuel speculation and recurrent surges of development.

Everyone who came to California knew that it was an extraordinary place, and their letters, newspapers, and all manner of reports and essays reinforced that view to an attentive world. Californians had taken the lead in formal scientific study of their lands and resources, and a good many thoughtful people asserted that it was not only new and different, it was important as the nucleus of—or at least a glimpse of the possibilities for—a new society, something closer to what America might—ought—to become. Seeing in this supercharged emergent California the equivalent work of a century accomplished in a few years, they set out to record its history, define its character, and interpret its meaning. From the 1860s on these self-conscious image makers, as varied in style and substance as Bret Harte, Mark Twain, Henry George, and Hubert Howe Bancroft, portrayed a cosmopolitan, creative, open, democratic, progressive way of life in a wonderfully attractive climate and countryside that made California a powerful symbol, the focus of a mythology that, continually reinforced, would help shape the human geography of America through a century ahead. As Kevin Starr summarized: "Whatever else California was, good or bad, it was charged with human hope. It was linked imaginatively with the most compelling of American myths, the pursuit of happiness. . . . [The] symbolic value of California endured—a legacy of the Gold Rush."

3. Southern California

A little less than forty years after the convulsion that initiated a new American California, a mutation in a marginal area suddenly created another major American region. It may be called a mutation because it was clearly Californian in important ways—in its general climate and countryside, its distant, detached location and exotic environment, the massive influx of long-distant migrants and quick emergence as a famous place—and yet its particular attractions and modes of development, the kind of people who came and the society they created, made it a distinct variant. In short, Southern California was at once a recapitulation and a redefinition of "California." Although bound within the same geopolitical frame and sharing in a general world-famous image, from the late 1880s onward it was clear to any thoughtful observer that the United States contained not just one California but two.

As already noted, important groundwork for this development was under way twenty years earlier. The initiation of horticultural colonies and experiments with crops and irrigation gradually produced a "citrus belt"—actually a rather sporadic pattern of groves rooted in the alluvial fans along the base of the environing mountains. Riverside, at the inland edge of the lowlands, was an important early nucleus. Here the first plantings of the Washington navel orange, a superior, winter-ripening variety obtained from Brazil, were made in 1873. When seedlings of the Valencia orange, a summer-ripening type suitable to more exposed coastal areas, were planted near Anaheim three years later, the botanical basis for the modern industry was established, although many years of experimental adjustment to soils, groundwater, and microclimates lay ahead.

Emerging more or less coextensive with the citrus belt was a "sanitarium belt." The long, dry summers and short, mild winters, and the fresh air of the mountains and the sea had been highly touted from the first American visitations, but few could be lured until the means of getting there were radically improved. Only after 1869, when one could arrive in northern California by train and take the stage or coastal steamer on south, did the numbers begin to swell and the facilities expand. Many of these newcomers were sojourners seeking seasonal respite from continental winters, but the developers of colonies always stressed the far greater benefits of permanent residence in this subtropical wonderland, and as these promotions were aimed primarily at Middle Westerners they found a receptive clientele among those afflicted with "consumption" (tuberculosis), malaria, asthma, rheumatism, and other ailments commonly blamed on the harshness and dampness of the Mississippi–Ohio Valley climate. The completion of the first Pacific railroad coincided with a postwar prosperity that allowed the idea of selling the family farm or business and seeking a better—and longer—life in a warmer climate to be assessed as a feasible alternative.

It must be emphasized that Southern California's location, position, and physical structure gave it a climate sufficiently different from the rest of the state as to enhance its attractions for many people. This small compartment was not only lower—warmer—in latitude, it was shielded by the mountains, moderated by the ocean, with the trend of the coast helping to ensure considerably warmer waters (the occasional blistering dust-laden desert winds—California's sirocco—were rarely mentioned in the literature of the day, or later).

Every new settlement and the area as a whole were featured in a mushrooming volume of propaganda from visitors and local publicists, but there was also a small cadre of men who sought to manage the development of the region in much more specific and calculated ways. They were not a cohesive body (there were at times bitter rivalries among them) but a loose association of capitalists (mostly from San Francisco) who shared some common civic interests. They were regional strategists who were determined to shape developments so as to ensure the success of their programs. Of critical concern was the creation of a regional infrastructure and vital connections with the larger world. Most of these men had invested heavily in Los Angeles as the primary focus of Southern California. Their first accomplishment was to connect Los Angeles by rail with an improved port, at Wilmington (and, not untypically, a rival scheme resulted in a line to a long wharf at Santa Monica a few years later). During these years productions from the local region were so limited that much effort was expended in competing for the modest mining trade of the desert interior, especially that of Cerro Gordo in the Owens Valley, but this traffic was soon diverted to the railroad advancing southward through the San Joaquin Valley. Much the greatest concern, however, was to ensure that this main line of the Southern Pacific came through Los Angeles as it was extended eastward to form a southern transcontinental link.

There were good reasons for this concern, arising from the rather complicated physical structure of this Southern California region (fig. 12). In the popular usage of the time Southern California was all that lay "south of Tehachapi"—beyond the curving ridge linking the Sierra Nevada and the Coast Ranges, closing off the southern end of the Central Valley. But there were distinct compartments within this southern sector. Crossing southward over the Tehachapi Mountains brought one directly into the Mojave Desert, a broad riverless wasteland studded with barren mountains and dry lake beds. All the productive districts of Southern California lay south of another wall of mountains trending parallel with and at varying distances from the coastline. Thus to reach Los Angeles the railroad would have to cross the formidable San Gabriel Mountains. Locally the great fear was that the Southern Pacific would regard such a route as a costly deviation and would elect to build more directly along the northern base of the San Gabriels to Cajon Pass, thence cutting across only the eastern extremity of the Los Angeles lowland via San Bernardino and exiting by way of San Gorgonio Pass on a direct line southeast-ward to the Colorado River crossing at Fort Yuma. Such a route would leave Los Angeles more than fifty miles off the main line and threaten to shift the primary focus to some junction in the San Bernardino area. Los Angeles leaders

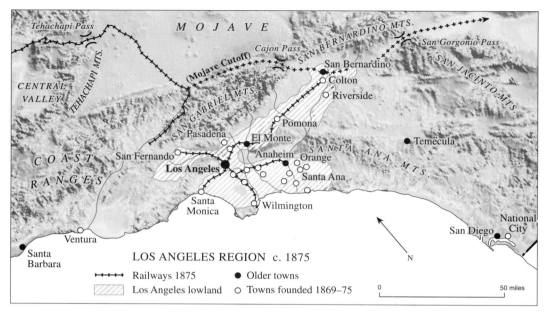

LOS ANGELES REGION c. 1875

Railways 1875 ┊┊┊┊┊   ● Older towns

▨ Los Angeles lowland   ○ Towns founded 1869–75

0 _____ 50 miles

Tehachapi Pass

M O J A V E

SAN BERNARDINO MTS.

San Gorgonio Pass

Cajon Pass

(Mojave Cutoff)

SAN JACINTO MTS.

CENTRAL VALLEY

TEHACHAPI MTS.

SAN GABRIEL MTS.

San Bernardino

Colton

Riverside

COAST RANGES

Pomona

Pasadena

El Monte

SANTA

Temecula

San Fernando

Anaheim

Orange

ANA

Los Angeles

Santa Ana

MTS.

Santa Monica

Wilmington

N

Ventura

San Diego

National City

Santa Barbara

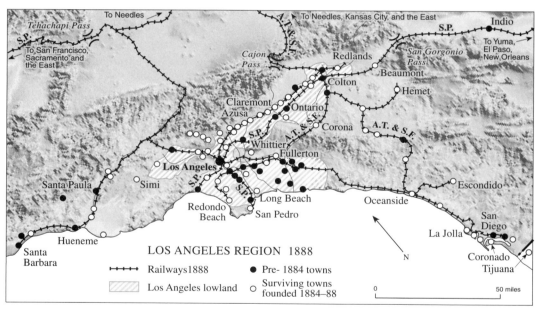

LOS ANGELES REGION 1888

Railways 1888 ┊┊┊┊┊   ● Pre-1884 towns

▨ Los Angeles lowland   ○ Surviving towns founded 1884–88

0 _____ 50 miles

To Needles

To Needles, Kansas City, and the East

A.T.&S.F.

S.P.

Indio

Tehachapi Pass

S.P.

To San Francisco, Sacramento and the East

Cajon Pass

San Gorgonio Pass

To Yuma, El Paso, New Orleans

Redlands

Beaumont

Colton

Hemet

Claremont

Azusa

Ontario

A.T. & S.F.

S.P.

Corona

A.T. & S.F.

Whittier

Fullerton

Los Angeles

S.P.

Santa Paula

Simi

S.P.

Long Beach

Escondido

Redondo Beach

San Pedro

Oceanside

N

La Jolla

San Diego

Hueneme

Coronado

Tijuana

Santa Barbara

12. Los Angeles Region.

were so alarmed that they tried to get Congress to prohibit this "Mojave cutoff" and force the Southern Pacific (in the words of their principal lobbyist) to "fix their *trunk* line definitely, permanently, and at once, through the City of Los Angeles." The railroad's charter already contained a less specific provision of this sort, and after intense bargaining, resulting in a sizable subsidy and control of the local line to the port, the SP agreed to follow this route. While the heavy work of grading and tunneling through the mountain barrier proceeded, track was laid north and east from Los Angeles as segments of the eventual main line.

By the mid-1870s the regional structure of an emergent Southern California was discernible. Rail lines radiating from Los Angeles to Colton (a new town between Riverside and San Bernardino), Anaheim, Wilmington, Santa Monica, and San Fernando approximated the main arena of development; a few localized centers of activity, such as San Diego, Ventura, and Santa Barbara, lay somewhat detached and further afield. But in spite of intensive efforts there had been no great surge, and by 1875 the national depression had not only halted growth, it had precipitated a decline: several thousand people left the region.

In September 1876 Angelenos celebrated the arrival of the first train through the San Fernando tunnel, giving their city and region an all-rail link with San Francisco, Sacramento, and the East. A few months later the first carload of oranges was shipped to St. Louis, but neither of the superior types was yet in production, the freight rates were high, and no great surge in exports followed. In fact, the Southern Pacific soon purchased the bankrupt Santa Monica line and Angelenos were cursing the "terrible power" that now closed them out from a cheap ocean alternative. In spite of these "shackles of monopoly," important developments did ensue. As would long be the case, incoming passenger trains were more important than outgoing freights. That a person of means could now cross the country in comparative luxury, step off the train directly into a comfortable hotel, and begin assessing prospects for investment in a wonderfully inviting land would have profound effect on the region. Before long a number of places—old towns, such as Santa Barbara, and new ones, such as Pasadena—emerged into prominence as "wealthy colonies" dominated by people of education and culture, leaders who had the vision and the means to establish libraries and colleges as well as paved streets, tree-lined boulevards, and other civic amenities. In such "millionaire towns" handsome mansions and luxury hotels were part of the formative (one can hardly call it "pioneer") phase of settlement.

A greater number alighting from these trains were tourists and winter sojourners, and these, too, were mostly persons who could well afford such travel and leisure. With the completion of this longitudinal line through California Americans were offered a new possibility: a Grand Tour within the bounds of their own nation, a chance to enjoy an exotic land without having to cope with foreigners.

As Carey McWilliams put it, referring to the main source of such travelers: "Unlike their colleagues on the eastern seaboard, the mid-America sections of this new middle class were intimidated by the thought of the Atlantic crossing. Italy, France, and Spain seemed forbiddingly remote. They wanted an Italy nearer home—an Italy without the Italians, an Italy in which, perhaps, they might settle and live out their days in the sun." These "tourists" (as they now came to be called) were well served by books and reports extolling the special lure of California, such as *The New Italy* (a monthly newspaper), *Semi-Tropical America* (1874), and *California: For Health, Pleasure, and Residence* (1873). This last, by a veteran popular writer, Charles Nordhoff, gave special attention to Southern California—"a region almost unknown"—and historians have stated that it deserves "more credit for sending people to California than anything else ever written about the section." Nordhoff opened his work with this emphasis on the peculiar attractiveness of this southwest corner of the nation:

> When a Northern American visits a tropical country, be it Cuba, Mexico, Brazil, or Central America, he is delighted with the bright skies, the mild climate, the wonderful productiveness of the soil, and the novel customs of the inhabitants; but he is repelled by an enervating atmosphere, by the dread of malarious diseases, by the semi-barbarous habits of the people, and often by a lawless state of society. Moreover, he must leave his own country, and is without the comfort and security he enjoys at home. California is our own; and it is the first tropical land which our race has thoroughly mastered and made itself at home in. There, and there only, on this planet, the traveller and resident may enjoy the delights of the tropics without their penalties; a mild climate, not enervating, but healthful and health-restoring; a wonderfully and variously productive soil, without tropical malaria; the grandest scenery, with perfect security and comfort in travelling arrangements; strange customs, but neither lawlessness nor semi-barbarism.

The "grandest scenery" referred to Yosemite, the redwood forests, Lake Tahoe, and other wonders; "strange customs" referred to the Chinese in San Francisco and, especially, the "Spanish Californians" in the south. These californios were real people to Nordhoff (he devoted a final chapter to the genuine rancho hospitality and rodeos he and his family had enjoyed), but it would be a short step soon taken to move from his low-keyed descriptions into a romanticized mission and rancho heritage assiduously cultivated by developers and publicists to enhance the exotic attractions of this sunset land.

Nordhoff devoted the bulk of his book to the virtues of California for health and residence, with much attention to agriculture. By the time a second edition appeared, in 1882, he could describe the obvious success of various colonies and offer enticing illustrations of the wealth to be obtained from a few choice acres of California land. Although his descriptions were favorable, they were not wildly fanciful nor devoid of sound advice and warnings ("California is subject to droughts"; "Be more careful to buy water than land"). And just at this time a new colony, Ontario (not mentioned by Nordhoff), was setting "a new standard in rural planning." This creation of the Chaffey brothers (from Brockville and Kingston) was perhaps the best example of the "developer's frontier" adapted to the Californian situation: the purchase of carefully selected rancho lands along the foothill belt, the construction of a complete water supply system (using, for the first time, concrete pipes—and, a few years later, the first hydroelectric pumping plant), the formation of a mutual water company to ensure allocation of water rights with each parcel of land sold, the building of streets, a broad central avenue, community center, and other facilities, and then—only when all these were in place—the chartering of excursion trains from Los Angeles and opening the sale of lots. (Like many others, Ontario was only loosely a "colony," although the largest group of initial investors was from Canada, but the term hung on in California because of such clustering and the need for a degree of cooperation in irrigation and horticultural operations).

By this time, this special combination of climate and countryside, of economy and society unique within the bounds of America was a powerful lure—"an orange grove is the perfect setting for a handsome suburban estate" (fig. 13). The only thing needed to unleash the flood was a sharp reduction in the cost of getting there, and the groundwork for that was being pushed forward strongly as well. The Southern Pacific built its new main line eastward across southern Arizona and New Mexico into Texas, where in 1881 it met the Texas & Pacific coming westward from Dallas and, by acquisition and construction, also extended its own system through San Antonio and Houston all the way to New Orleans. The first passenger train along this new Thirty-second parallel route arrived in Los Angeles in February 1883, but this second transcontinental had little immediate impact: the cost remained high, and most Texans and Louisianans remained too impoverished in their own sweltering subtropics to even think about moving to California (although the prize-winning oranges and lemons shipped via the SP to the New Orleans "World's Fair"—the Cotton Centennial Exposition—in 1884–85 may have prompted some dreams). The decisive event was the completion of a rival transcontinental line from mid-America ready to compete intensely for California traffic. The Atchison, Topeka & Santa Fe laid tracks along the general route of the Santa Fe Trail, sending a short branch to that famous destination and continuing along the Rio Grande to Albuquerque and El Paso. Purchase of the land grant of the Atlantic & Pacific gave the Santa Fe the right to build directly west from Albuquerque along the Thirty-fifth parallel route to the Colorado River. This advance impelled responsive actions within California: a line from Tehachapi across the Mojave to Needles, near the crossing point on the Colorado, as a defensive thrust by the Southern

13. The Middle West amidst the Orange Groves.
In 1887 C. T. Collier, local "photographic artist," lugged his camera up Mt. Rubidoux to get this shot of nearly the whole of the original Mile Square of Riverside. Laid out seventeen years earlier by the Southern California Colony Association, the simple plan now contained several substantial business blocks and an array of sizable houses surrounded by orange groves in various stages of development. On the back of this particular print the owner had noted that "the part inclosed by the red lines [the rectangle in the upper right] is our young orange orchard in the new part of Riverside." (Courtesy Riverside Municipal Museum)

Pacific; and a line (financed by local businessmen, with help from the Santa Fe) from San Diego to San Bernardino and Cajon Pass as the eventual western segment of this new transcontinental. After complicated negotiations and court battles the Southern Pacific (under financial distress) gave way, selling the Mojave line to its rival and allowing it trackage rights to San Francisco. The Santa Fe then built to Cajon Pass, and having purchased the line to San Diego and another short line to Los Angeles, it was finally in a position to compete for California traffic on its own tracks from Kansas City, where it had ready connections to the main body of the national network (and would soon have its own line to Chicago).

After a few months of sparring had brought modest reductions in the normal $95–$100 fare from Midwest points, the battle was suddenly intensified in early 1887. The price plunged to $25, to $10, momentarily to $1, then hovered between $10 and $20 for the rest of the year, accompanied by a massive publicity campaign by the railroads, California newspapers, and a host of special interests extolling especially the wonders of the Los Angeles area, the most direct focus of the railroad rivalry (an emphasis so heavy as to cause a San Jose newspaper to complain that "the average Eastern mind conceives of California as a small tract of country situated in and about Los Angeles"). The result of such a precipitous reduction was "an avalanche rushing madly to Southern California," requiring extra trains every day, putting a frantic pressure on accommodations, bringing an influx of townsite sharks, auctioneers, and promoters of every stripe from all across America, and unleashing the most flamboyant real estate boom the nation had yet seen. During this brief mania more than a hundred new towns were platted (in addition to the scores of tract extensions within the bounds of existing towns) on every conceivable kind of site, including riverbeds, cliffsides, and desert wastes—wherever a promoter could get hold of a block of land. One historian's research in the county recorder's office yielded the oft-cited conclusion that in Los Angeles County alone about sixty new towns, embracing in total 79,350 acres and subdivided into about 500,000 lots (sufficient, he suggests, for 2 million people), were platted in 1887–88—and in July 1889 had an actual population of 2,351. Although the frantic speculation in the sale and resale of lots soon collapsed and many of these paper towns evaporated, the impact was far from ephemeral. In the region as a whole about sixty new towns survived, and although thousands of people had departed by 1890, the census showed a decennial gain of 136,000 for the region, with nearly 40,000 of these newcomers in the epicenter, Los Angeles. More important than these sheer numbers were the influx of talent and capital and the impetus given to further promotion and development. Indeed, "Los Angeles as a modern American metropolis may be said to date from the end of the boom and the founding of the Chamber of Commerce" in the autumn of 1888: "In the next two years, more than a million pieces of persuasive 'literature' were broadcast in the corn and wheat belts. Exhibits of prize agricultural produce from southern California were established in Chicago and at fairs and expositions, and later a special train, 'California on Wheels,' made a two-year tour with prize fruits and vegetables, a brass band, tons of pamphlets, and a squad of high-powered Los Angeles salesmen."

Such efforts were essential to the continued development of the region because, despite the constantly expanding and improving citrus and related horticultural industries, the local resource base was very limited. A feverish scramble following an oil strike in 1892 jammed 2,500 wells in a small area just west of downtown Los Angeles, but although the region began to take a lead in new applications of this volatile wealth (such as the first oil-fired locomotives), it represented only a modest diversification of the regional economy (unlike later larger discoveries). Southern California remained essentially a real estate promotion, dependent upon the continual influx of new people and capital. "The major business of the region" was "expansion": "With a steadily increasing population, the construction industry expanded and payrolls mounted, new [related] industries were established, more shops and stores were opened, and opportunities in the professions and service trades multiplied. New capital imported to the region provided the energy for expansion and improvement. . . . Had the flow of population ceased or materially diminished, the consequences would have been as disastrous as a drought."

Thus a great deal of the development was focused on infrastructure: on water systems for cities and towns as well as for agriculture (with Los Angeles averting a crisis by gaining control of—historians say "stealing"—the water of Owens Valley, east of the Sierra Nevada, and conveying it by aqueduct 233 miles to the city); on electric lighting ("Los Angeles was the first city in America, perhaps in the world, to be completely illuminated by electric lights"); on railroads (formed in 1901, in ten years' time the Pacific Electric exceeded 1,000 miles—the largest such system in the country—linking all the towns of the Los Angeles Basin and—essential to the style of life—all these towns with the beaches); on port improvements (a new outer harbor, the first large shipyard, at Long Beach, and political annexation of San Pedro–Wilmington and a narrow connecting corridor to the City of Los Angeles).

It was also a time of intense civic development and emergence of a distinct Southern California townscape: urban and suburban life amidst the orange groves; streets lined with eucalyptus, acacia, and palms; city halls, banks, hotels, and mansions reflecting various interpretations of a Mediterranean style—Mission, Spanish Colonial, Italian Renaissance; ordinary house styles shifting from be-towered and gabled Victorian to the horizontal lines, wide eaves, and veranda fronts of the "bungalow" embowered in an array of exotic trees, shrubs, and flowers. Civic festivals were becoming expansive annual affairs (led by Pasadena's Tournament of Roses, founded in 1889). A dozen colleges were emerging from shaky boom-time beginnings into substantial institutions.

Climate was now routinely regarded as "a commodity that can be labeled, priced, and marketed." By 1900 the longing for a winter sojourn, retirement, or migration to our "own foreign land" had swept over the heart of the country. Although health seekers continued to arrive, promoters now veered away from such emphasis, not wanting to suggest that the place was filling up with invalids (the infectiousness of tuberculosis was more widely understood); instead, promoters in Southern California embarked on a program to send health to all the nation. In 1907, in one of the most remarkable advertising programs ever mounted, the California Fruit Growers Exchange ("perhaps the most efficient marketing cooperative in the world") sent gaudily bannered trainloads of oranges and blanketed the State of Iowa with the slogan "Oranges for Health—California for Wealth." Sales jumped by 50 percent (despite a higher price), and the migrations to Long Beach and vicinity swelled (where thousands gathered every January for the "Iowa Picnic"). Orange crate labels became a highly developed art form, placing in "the mundane grocery stores" of the nation vivid images of the exotic reality of America's own Eden.

In the first decade after the collapse of the Great Boom, Los Angeles doubled in size to 102,000 and then surged to 319,000 ten years later (in part by annexation). The regional population had surpassed 750,000. Growth was heavily concentrated in the Los Angeles lowland, but San Diego was now beginning to enjoy a long-awaited boom, filling in its extensive speculative tracts and laying plans for civic redesign in conjunction with a celebration of the opening of the Panama Canal. The population had reached 40,000, but it was still primarily a winter resort. After years of lobbying the U.S. Navy had finally been induced to make use of this superior harbor—establishing a coaling station in 1907. More important, the formation of the San Diego & Arizona Railway (with the backing of the Southern Pacific) seemed likely not only to provide the long-sought direct route east but to tap a promising hinterland in a heretofore sterile region. The Imperial Valley was the main sector of the Salton Sink, a below–sea level compartment formed when the silt-laden Colorado River had extended its delta across the Gulf of California, cutting off the ocean and leaving, eventually, only a small remnant Salton Sea. Bringing fresh water from the Colorado by a trunk canal to this level, fertile, arid tropical lowland had been envisioned for many years and was finally begun in 1892. In 1907 an unusually early and high seasonal flood diverted much of the river into the main canal, and before this alarming inflow could be checked, at great cost, it had greatly enlarged the Salton Sea. However, the main body of developmental lands was not seriously affected and the formation of this nearly tropical agricultural oasis was being carried forward. Railroad lines were being extended, a new county was formed (with El Centro as its seat), and towns and farms laid out. In conjunction with this major program, a subsidiary company established the town of Mexicali (opposite Calexico, the American headquarters) as the focus for a small Mexican sector of this irrigation colonization.

The development of the Imperial Valley and the Coachella Valley (the smaller northerly portion of the Salton Sink) would be an important addition to the productive base of, and the tapping of the Colorado River an important precedent for, a Southern California so narrowly confined by mountains and desert. Of course such barren wastelands may hold untold riches, and there were always visionaries and developers eager to add more such areas to their field of operations. With every surge of activity in Southern California there were those who looked southward and saw Baja California as an attractive and inevitable addition. Such common imperial and assimilationist assumptions were abetted during these years by the attitudes and actions of a Mexican government eager for dollars and development. In the 1880s an American company obtained a concession for colonization and municipal development in the northern third of the peninsula. Little was accomplished before the collapse of the boom, but the first act of the new Los Angeles Chamber of Commerce in 1888 proposed "that the United States should purchase the peninsula of Lower California from Mexico, annex it to Southern California, and create a new state." From 1900 on much of this Mexican borderland was under the control of California developers. After the Mexican Revolution broke out in 1910 a filibuster movement, originally led by Mexican exiles in Los Angeles but recruiting a motley band of mostly American adventurers and "socialist" idealists, seized Mexicali and within a few months controlled all the small borderland settlements. A Californian faction sought to proclaim a new "republic," locally annexation seemed likely, and a number of Americans sought to obtain lands and concessions for speculation. However, this insurgency soon disintegrated, and an augmented Mexican force from the capital at Ensenada drove them back across the border, where they were arrested (and eventually tried and acquitted) by American authorities. Mexico had good reason to be fearful and angry over this brief episode. Baja California was remote and lightly held, and American pronouncements and behavior were blatant and offensive. After the surrender of Tijuana to the mainly American force in May 1911, "hundreds of American tourists, charged fifty cents apiece for admission, crossed the border and aided the filibusters in looting stores and homes. This shameful procedure continued for several days, and perhaps caused greater resentment on the part of the Lower Californians than any other incident." Even though the Mexican government soon reasserted control, the tension between a rapidly developing, prospering region and a thinly populated, stagnant border province could not readily be lessened. Many Southern Californians saw a southward extension of their region as the logical counter to the power of the Alta California north of Tehachapi. Meanwhile, before and after the momentary disruption of 1911, the increasing popularity of tourist trips to the racetrack and bullring, shops, brothels, and bars of Tijuana (platted in 1889) served to remind that there were three Californias, not just the American two.

In the new century Southern California gained important new interregional links: the Los Angeles & Salt Lake provided a direct line northeastward across the desert to its parent railroad, the Union Pacific, and the East; the Southern Pacific completed its Coast Line between Santa Barbara and San Luis Obispo, providing an alternate route to San Francisco; and the Santa Fe purchased a new San Joaquin Valley railroad and by extending it to Richmond provided the first actual competitive railroad line between Los Angeles and San Francisco Bay (but the two companies soon came to terms and shared keeping the rates high).

This elaboration of the links between the two Californias was important to many intrastate activities—governmental and social, as well as economic—and it reflected the marked change in the demographic and developmental balance of the state as a whole. In 1870 Los Angeles had been a bicultural settlement of fewer than 6,000 people, its hinterland a distant minor sector of a San Francisco–centered system; by 1910 California south of Tehachapi contained nearly a third of the state's population and Los Angeles (319,000) was rapidly gaining on a San Francisco (417,000) badly shattered and still recovering from the 1906 earthquake. Still, such figures can mislead as to real balances of power and relative importance. San Francisco was the focus of a close network of bay cities (adding another 250,000 to the metropolitan total) and remained quite unrivaled as a commercial and financial center (its new Federal Reserve Bank of 1914 served most of the Far West). In spite of a considerable decline in many Sierran mining districts, San Francisco's California hinterland had been vigorously developing and diversifying. There had been a strong shift to horticultural production. California remained an important wheat exporter, although the great warehouses lining Carquinez Strait (Port Costa, Wheatport, Benicia, Vallejo) drew upon a diminishing acreage. Droughts, declining yields, and rising land prices spurred the breakup of huge grain farms, while legal provision for irrigation districts, adaptation of pumps and systems originally developed for hydraulic mining, improved agronomy, and expanding marketing facilities encouraged investment in far more intensive forms of farming. The San Joaquin was the main arena of action. The first rail line had bisected the long belt of coalescing alluvial fans along the eastern side of the valley; later parallel lines broadened this ideal irrigation belt. Most of the land was marketed by large companies, some of it in tracts to group purchasers. In keeping with cosmopolitan California a considerable variety of people responded, some of them forming ethnoreligious colonies, such as the Swedes at Turlock and Kingsburg, the Danes at Selma, the German Mennonites at Reedley, and the Japanese at Livingston; others maintained such identities amid variegated settlements, such as the Portuguese dairymen at Atwater and Oakdale and the Armenian grape growers around Fresno; at least a few Chinese were to be found in most every town. Most of these colonists were not new immigrants but had relocated from some other American, mainly Californian, area. By 1910 an already impressive volume and variety of fruits, nuts, vegetables, poultry, and dairy products, some of it from highly specialized districts, was being shipped to California cities and the nation. The existence of a "thermal belt," of slightly but critically warmer winters on the Keweah Delta around Visalia, had become apparent through experimental plantings of oranges. (Although this would eventually become a major producing district, it did not alter the image of oranges as distinctly Southern Californian.)

Important innovations continued to characterize Californian agriculture and industry. Stockton, the river port and northern gateway, was shifting from flour milling and grain farming implements to canneries, packinghouses, and specialized graders and cultivators for irrigation agriculture. In 1904 the Holt Company, which had pioneered the combined harvester, invented a track-laying tractor (later known as a "caterpillar"); designed to work in the mucklands of the Delta, it was quickly seen to be ideal for hilly farmlands and heavy construction work, and by 1910 branch plants had been authorized for Spokane and Peoria. At the southern end of the valley Bakersfield was booming from major oil discoveries at Taft.

In 1910 the State of California recorded a population of 2,378,000, far more than any other western state. Just over two-thirds of that total lived north of Tehachapi, within the primary hinterland of San Francisco. But almost exactly half of the nearly 900,000 added to the state's population during the previous ten years had appeared in Southern California, and it was now receiving the largest share of newcomers. Thus, only 27 percent of Angelenos were California-born, as compared with 66 percent of San Franciscans; furthermore, few of these new Southern Californians were foreign immigrants, whereas San Francisco continued to attract a wide variety of such people (including Japanese, mostly from newly acquired Hawaii, amid rising protests of White Californians). Thus the "state society," celebrating pleasant memories of former homes, was a folk movement (soon highly orchestrated) peculiar to Southern California, whereas the "Native Son" movement earlier emerged in the north as a politically powerful assertion of those long involved in Californian development who were determined to keep it a "White Man's paradise" ("native," typically, was very selectively defined). Such things of course point to the obvious existence, by this date, of two very different Californias within the bounds of a single state: two regional societies quite sharply set apart, each with its dominant city and networks of places, each with its particular patterns of economy and society. As noted at the outset, the one was a mutation from the other, mirroring some basic features but diverging sharply into distinction. The "Boom of the 80s" may be called Southern California's Gold Rush, but it was utterly different in character. Whereas the original was a rough, raucous adventure, drawing in a great formless heterogeneous mass of males from around the world, the later one was quite the opposite: "the least heroic migration in history," said Charles Fletcher Lummis, one of its most influential celebrators, "but the most judicious; the least impulsive but the most reasonable." He was referring of course to the movement of those prosperous families who arrived in comfortable trains from mid-America and invested in homes and businesses. San Francisco had little appeal for such people; it was too urban and urbane, too congested and cosmopolitan—too ethnic and Catholic; why move to and adapt to that when they could have a California on their own terms, shaped to their own image. And so they formed churches and clubs and state societies and impressed their strong Protestant, middle-class, Middle Western mores on every new community and the region as a whole. By 1910 the measure of their local success and the reality of two Californias within the one geopolitical frame was evident in the complete polarization of north and south on state legislation relating to such social issues as prostitution, liquor, racetrack gambling, and Bible reading in public schools. In such matters Southern California was even more of a minority region than its population indicated, for there was the usual lag in the shift of political power. Virtually no government aid or state institutions were allocated south of Tehachapi before 1900 (Los Angeles got a small teachers' college). At the national level Southern California did not gain a full congressional district until 1903. Such incongruities helped fuel recurrent movements for state division—and ensure their defeat. During the lively agitations in 1909 derision of Los Angeles by complacent northerners as "being composed of Easterners and not true Californians" might well bring the response: "We are different in pursuits, in tastes, manner of thought and manner of life. We call ourselves, not Californians but Southern Californians."

The emergence of Southern California resulted in a rapid, radical alteration of the regional character and structure of the United States. It was a remarkable phenomenon, by any measure, and in a simple but fundamental sense it was the result of the inclusion of a particular set of climatic and landscape contrasts within the spacious framework of a transcontinental nation: the contrasts between the midsection of the country and its far southwestern corner, between harshness and mildness of climates, between hot, sultry summers, cold, freezing winters, sudden temperature changes, and violent weather in the one region and the golden mean of soft light and air and gentle seasonal changes in the other; and the contrast between landscapes of broad uniformity—monotony—with little variation in the land or its human patterns for miles on end in any direction, and an inviting, comforting landscape of sunshine and orange groves and new towns nestled between the mountains and the sea. Once an easy, inexpensive passageway between these two was made available a mighty torrent of migrants followed; of course the timing had to be just right to impel it in 1887—but it has never ceased to flow thereafter. Such continued growth ensured that the internal contention would be not just for political dominance of the state but for the meaning, the image, of "California."

4. Oregon and the Pacific Northwest

Oregon was famous before California. The focus of America's first reach to the Pacific, contested ground resolved by bellicose diplomacy, occupied by families whose covered wagons on the overland trail became a powerful symbol of American intrepidity and purpose, Oregon was a substantial foothold before it was suddenly overtaken as a destination and overshadowed in national interest by

California. However, even if relatively obscured and marginalized by the Gold Rush, Oregon continued to develop, in part by its very contrast with this new rival region. Far greater numbers now trekked the Western trails, and even though the ratios in choice were now reversed, those who headed for the Willamette rather than for the Sacramento did so with a strong sense of the differences in regional character. Furthermore, this kind of "filtering effect" was at work directly in Oregon itself: thousands left there for the Gold Rush, some stayed in California, but many soon returned, having decided that the Willamette Valley offered a more attractive future.

As these two Pacific Slope regions took shape the contrasts between them became standard fare in travelers' accounts. "Oregonians have builded what they have got more slowly and more wisely than California," observed Samuel Bowles; but such comments were not always so flattering—"certainly they are not an enterprising people," said a Cincinnati reporter a few years later. As might be expected, Oregonians countered with their own versions of the matter, as Dorothy O. Johansen noted, relating the theme of an 1850s anecdote: "At Pacific Springs, one of the crossroads of the western trail, a pile of gold-bearing quartz marked the road to California; the other road had a sign bearing the words 'To Oregon.' Those who could read took the trail to Oregon." Such a canard was calculated to evoke a whole set of characterizations that Oregonians would self-consciously cultivate—and historians tend to confirm:

California	*Oregon*
young males	young families
impulsive adventuring	reasoned migration
in search of quick wealth	to build family competence
loose, unstable camps	kith- and kin-based communities
turbulence and conflict	order and tranquility
industrial and urban	agrarian and small town
heterogeneous and cosmopolitan	homogeneous and provincial
explosive growth	incremental growth
speculative	conservative
exuberant laissez-faire	"classical republicanism"
new kind of country	familiar kind of country
experiment and innovation	transfer and easy adaptation
discontinuity	continuity

When set forth in this summary form such contrasts (like those concurrently proclaimed between North and South in the beleaguered federation) verge into caricature, but—like good caricature—they were grounded in the realities of the historical geography of these new Pacific Coast societies.

The 1840s American foothold in the Willamette Valley was quickly expanded to the limits of its natural compartment, aided by the increased inflow of land seekers in the 1850s and by the continued allocation of land in generous amounts. Congress not only confirmed earlier claims made under the local Donation Land Law, which had allowed 640 acres to a married couple, but authorized half that amount (double the national norm) to be routinely available for some years thereafter. The scale of such holdings scattered the population thinly over the countryside and soon covered the valley (and much more limited areas along the upper Umpqua and Rogue rivers) with claims, but no family could put so much land to ready use and there was a continuing thickening of settlement as properties were subdivided. Speculation was muted not only by the wide availability of land for sale but by the fact that so large a share of those seeking it had come at the direct invitation or example of those already there. For rural Oregon grew mainly by the continuing inflow from its original primary source region: kith and kin from old neighborhoods in the Upland South borderlands of Missouri, Iowa, and the Ohio Valley lured by the chance to obtain a substantial family property in a healthy country wherein one could carry on a familiar way of life with one's own kind of people.

Those old spurs to migration—debts and personal problems and the ravages of diseases endemic in the Mississippi Valley—continued to operate, but the pull of Oregon was magnified by the ever-greater volume of reports on farming success and settler satisfaction. The well-wooded, river-laced Willamette Valley (fig. 14), with its many prairies and oak openings, sheltered by forest-clad mountains from the excessive rains of the coast on one side and from the cold and drought of the interior plateaus on the other, was the only country of its kind in the Far West, the only one at all akin to the farmlands of Eastern America. "*Indian Corn* and *Tobacco* do not succeed here as in the southwestern States [Kentucky and Tennessee]," reported an early pioneer, "owing I think to the coolness of the nights. Both are cultivated—tobacco for domestic use, and Indian corn more from attachment to the plant than its value." He thereby pointed to the only really significant agronomic difference facing these new colonists. Corn needed a hot, humid season, but wheat, oats, and barley, peas, beans, and potatoes, apples, peaches, and pears generally thrived in this more moderate land; there was luxuriant natural forage for horses, cattle, and swine, and fish and game and berries aplenty in these waters and woods. An occasional dry summer or harsh winter or seasonal floodings of the river lands gave no cause for doubt about the attractiveness of this fine valley for the farm family. Furthermore, it was a safe country, essentially cleared of Indians years ago by disease and attrition (although there could still be danger in getting there, as troubles in the Rogue River country, adjoining on the south, warned).

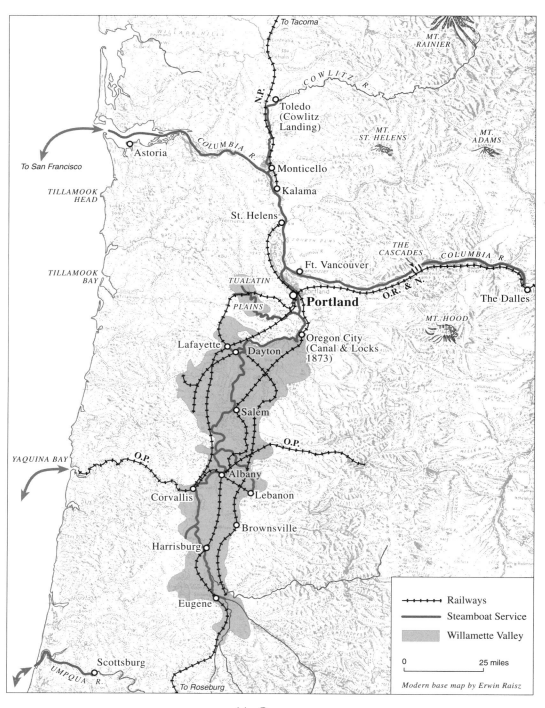

14. Oregon.

While this pioneering proceeded, another, complementary, dimension of Oregon development was under way, stimulated by the California Gold Rush, led by a very different set of people. For most of the promoters of towns, commerce, and industry were from New England or Upstate New York—as such names on the early maps as Salem, Albany, Syracuse, Oswego, and Portland (by a flip of a coin, not Boston) attest. In direct continuity with early American missionaries, sea captains, and traders, these Yankees avidly scouted for investment opportunities. Oregon City, at the great falls of the Willamette, already a milling center (initiated by the Hudson's Bay Company) and the first territorial capital (1849), was an obvious focus, but the fleets of ships coming up the Columbia to load cargo for California soon directed attention to more convenient anchorages on the lower Willamette. Portland, a good site on the west bank, promoted by astute leaders who invested in steamships for service to San Francisco and a wagon road to the Tualatin Plains, the nearest agricultural district, soon emerged as the primary center and worked assiduously on developing the commercial resources of its hinterlands (see fig. 14).

The Willamette Valley became the scene of intermittent competition between shipping companies, resulting in extensive service and the creation of stern-wheel steamboats of such minimal draft that they could, on occasion, chug all the way up to Eugene and up shallow, meandering tributaries. The state subsidized a canal around the falls at Oregon City, but by the time it was completed, in 1873, new railroads extending up the east and west sides of the valley had captured much of the traffic. Although competitive in conception, these railroads soon came under monopoly control, challenged only by local narrow-gauge farmers' lines fanning out from landings at or near Dayton. A California promoter extracted a heavy subsidy from Portland to ensure railroad extension, but there was no significant challenge to that city's commanding position. An attempt to provide the upper valley with an alternative route to the coast by the Oregon Pacific Railroad, connecting Albany and Corvallis directly west with Yaquina Bay, was an undercapitalized promotion of minor impact, although a line of passenger steamships operated out of that port for some years.

Thirty years of domestication and these extending tentacles of commerce produced a distinct regional landscape: an attractive patchwork of farms and forest spread across the broad mountain-girded valley, interrupted by raggedly timbered buttes, with embowered rivers and roads and railroads weaving through a nearly—but not rigidly—rectilinear pattern of fields and wooden fences of a prospering mixed agriculture of cereals, potatoes, orchards, and livestock (fig. 15). In architecture and layout farmsteads displayed all the variety of their Eastern antecedents and here and there the influence of newer national styles. While there was some grubbing away at the brushlands of the foothills (which had thickened

15. Willamette Valley Scene, 1885.
The dense spires of the evergreen horizon, oaks and other hardwoods of the middle ground, and young orchards enclosed in lavish wooden fences in the foreground exhibit a characteristic Oregon scene on the edge of Salem. (Oregon Historical Society, W. P. Johnson, 170 G 050)

rapidly in the absence of Indian burnings), the more important expansion was inward upon the valley floor by simple ditching and draining of sloughs and meadows. A moderate density of villages and small towns, many with gristmills, sawmills, sash-and-door factories, and an occasional woolen mill, were aligned on the rivers and roads. The number of denominational colleges rivaled that of an older West under Yankee influence, but the density of churches and schools was considerably less. All in all, it was a distinctly Oregon version of a common mid-American scene.

The developing alliance between the business leaders and politicians of Portland and Salem represented a commensurate political link between regional capital and hinterland. Central within the valley, on the site of a brief but famous American mission—with Willamette University claiming continuity with that venerated Yankee initiative—Salem had wrested the territorial seat from Oregon City in 1853, later fought off several rivals for the state capital (1859), and had risen above a dozen aspiring towns to become the principal inland center. The commercialization of agriculture, the extension of mercantile and industrial activities, and the unending pursuit of governmental favor brought the leaders of the two charter peoples of American Oregon—Yankees and Upland Southerners, town and country, Republican and Democrat—ever closer, allied in business, politics, society, and marriage. Since its founding in 1853, the annual banquet of the Sons of New England had exalted the heritage of leading Portland families. Over the years a selection of others were accorded courtesy membership and joined in inflating "professed pioneering New England virtues to the point where myth became reality" in common interpretations of Oregon. The basic truth was the existence of an establishment of prudent merchant capitalists that "between 1843 and 1913 . . . exhibited great stability and continuity" while shaping the character and structure of a major Western region.

Although Portland first emerged on the basis of its command of Willamette Valley commerce, a good deal of its subsequent wealth and leadership was derived from similar control over the Columbia Interior. Broadly speaking, that vast area was divided into three environmental regions: the Great Columbia Plain, an open country in the lee of the Cascade Range, more varied in terrain than this early common name might imply, with local areas of ridges, coulees, canyons, or steeply rolling hills and varied in cover from desert sage in the center to luxuriant bunchgrass prairies along its eastern margins; an almost encircling belt of forested mountains around that Plain, divided into many different ranges and coursed in numerous places by large rivers and lakes in old glacial valleys; and far to the southeast, the broad, arid Snake River Plain and adjacent High Desert. Emigrants on the Oregon Trail traversing this sequence in reverse order during the dry summer season found little to interest any prospective settler. A glimpse of large herds of Indian horses in the Grande Ronde or along the Umatilla might suggest good grazing, but it was all isolated and insecure country.

This emigrant trail was just one of a set of former fur trade routes that had converged on the Columbia River Gorge for the passage through the Cascade Mountains to Fort Vancouver. The Hudson's Bay Company had disbanded operations here following the imposition of the international boundary. For some years thereafter the Great Columbia Plain was the scene of intermittent warfare arising from Indian grievances against trespassing Whites. Initiated by the Whitman massacre and concluded by the army victory over a force of Spokane, Coeur d'Alene, and Palouse Indians in 1858, this decade saw the extension of Portland's reach into the Interior. Navigation on the great waterway through the mountains was normally interrupted in two places: a thirteen-mile stretch from Celilo Falls through the constricted rock-braided channel at The Dalles, where the Columbia made a thunderous entrance into the gorge; and a four-mile reach of rocky rapids, known as The Cascades, at the exit from this mountain passage. Military needs soon overtaxed the usual bateaux and portage trails and induced the building of steamboats and wagon roads or tramways so that by the end of these campaigns a three-segment river service was in operation, commonly referred to as the Lower River (Portland to the Cascades), Middle River (Upper Cascades to The Dalles), and Upper River (Celilo to Wallula, and seasonally up the Snake to Lewiston). By 1860 this entire system was under the control of the Oregon Steam Navigation Company (OSN) and was coining money for its Portland owners.

Following the defeat of the Indians and redefinition of a set of reservations, spaced around the margins of the Great Columbia Plain—Warm Springs, Umatilla, Nez Perce, Yakima (and a little later, Coeur d'Alene and Colville)—the Interior was opened to White settlement. At first only a trickle of Oregonians came to take up attractive ranching sites, but prospectors ranging over the region soon initiated a mining rush that shifted year by year from one set of districts to another, each relatively limited in yield but together sustaining an influx of thousands of people to instant camps scattered around the entire ring of mountains: Fraser River, Colville, Kootenay, Clearwater, Salmon River, Boise Basin, Owyhee, John Day, and many lesser places, as well as across the Continental Divide to Alder Gulch (Virginia City) and Last Chance Gulch (Helena) on the upper reaches of the Missouri. Portland was in the best position to respond to the sudden demands for supplies and services, making use, for the most part, of the pathways of the former fur trade system that had fanned out from The Dalles and Wallula (old Fort Nez Perces). An important addition was the Mullan Road, a military wagon road connecting Fort Walla Walla with Fort Benton on the upper Missouri, by way of Coeur d'Alene.

Although the stampede into these northern districts was not comparable in scale or fame with the California Gold Rush, it was an extension of that experience. The prospectors were applying what they had learned in the Sierran slopes, and most of the early influx was from California. Many of the merchants, teamsters, packers, and inland ranchers supplying beef to the camps were Oregonians, and the position of Portland and associated towns and areas was broadly analogous to the Californian case: Portland, like San Francisco, the single great entrepôt; the Willamette Valley, like the several productive districts around San Francisco Bay, the primary source of food and feed; the Columbia trunk line through the mountains like Carquinez Strait; Walla Walla, imitating Sacramento and Stockton, the principal inland supply center for a wide scattering of districts; the Columbia Plain, like the Sacramento Valley, a supplier of beef and horses and, eventually, flour and feed. Portland itself was of course dependent on San Francisco for most of its manufactures, and it could not dominate this entire northwestern region to quite the degree that San Francisco commanded its western hinterland. It faced competition in all the outer ring of districts: from Victoria in the Fraser River mines, from Sacramento in the Owyhee and Boise basins, from St. Louis and from later railheads on the Missouri in the Montana trade, and once the Union Pacific was completed, from Salt Lake City in Montana and southern Idaho. But Portlanders continually improved their service, building railway portages around the interruptions on the Columbia, rapidly enlarging their fleets of riverboats, and even putting vessels on upper reaches of the Columbia during the peak of traffic to distant camps.

Such mining traffic could be immensely profitable but was inherently unstable, and the more important development was the expansion of ranching and farming in the Columbia Interior. Herds and flocks were brought in from western Oregon and surpluses driven seasonally to the mining markets. In time cattle became a glut only relieved by long drives to stock newly opened ranges in Wyoming and Dakota. By the 1870s a considerable tonnage of wool was being shipped downriver, enlarging an Oregon industry as well as an important export. Over much of the Columbia Plain stockmen gave way to farmers, but only gradually at first for there was much hesitation about these open, summer-dry lands. Once it was demonstrated that wheat succeeded well in the hills around the Walla Walla oasis, settlers began to spread into the higher lands along the base of the Blue Mountains and in the 1870s across the Snake River into the Palouse country. Only after extensive trials on these moisture-retentive loessal soils did it become commonly understood that "wheat will grow and mature wherever the 'bunch grass' grows." It was a discovery of immense importance to regional development, but the potential of this highly productive grain country could not be realized without ready access to world markets. Trial shipments of flour downriver for sale in San Francisco were made as the mining market waned. In the late 1860s British ships began to come to Portland to load "Oregon" wheat and flour for direct shipment to Europe. The success of this new market orientation and expansion of production in the Interior initiated railroad construction: first a line from Wallula to Walla Walla, then extensions farther into the expanding wheat country, and, as the riverboats and portages became overtaxed with the mounting harvests (which coincided with the onset of low water), the OSN reorganized itself as the Oregon Railway & Navigation Company (OR&N) and built a line parallel with the Columbia all the way from Portland to Wallula. With this new system colonization of the Great Columbia Plain accelerated, "Walla Walla" wheat became a staple on the Liverpool market, Portland thrived on the tribute collected from a greatly expanded hinterland, and the merchant elite replaced their early self-consciously New England houses with opulent mansard mansions and villas styled by San Francisco architects.

Portland was benefiting from developments downriver as well, even if it could never bring that trafficway under such firm control. Indeed there was always some apprehension about rival ports along this oceanic entranceway (in the early 1850s the Pacific Mail Steamship Company had tried to make St. Helens its Columbia terminus—just as it had at first preferred Benicia to San Francisco). Lumbering and fishing were the main activities, with fish wheels pumping salmon out of the river for Chinese laborers to cut up for the canneries (first established by a California company in Astoria). Much of this product went directly overseas, but all these towns and camps were mainly supplied from Portland. Viewed from this regional capital the Cowlitz route to Puget Sound was a branch of its downriver realm. For years the most reliable mail to and from Olympia moved this way, and much of the business, government and private, of the Puget Sound region was transacted by way of Portland because of more extensive and regular services to the rest of the nation. This connection was greatly strengthened with the completion in 1873 of the Northern Pacific Railroad line between Tacoma and Kalama on the Columbia, with steamboat service between that port and Portland.

This Tacoma-Kalama line represented a brief Portland victory in a crucial contest over larger railroad strategies. The Northern Pacific was originally authorized by Congress in 1864 to build from Lake Superior to some point on Puget Sound. Although allotted an unprecedentedly generous land grant (alternate sections within an eighty-mile strip along the main line), it was long mired in difficulty (Albro Martin, an expert, declared it to be "one of the most poorly led railroads in American history"—a notable ranking in a crowded field). Actual construction did not get under way west from Duluth until 1870, and in that same year NP interests gained control of the OSN and got their charter amended to allow them to build their main line down the Columbia to Portland, with a connection from there via the Cowlitz to Puget Sound, relegating the original projected trunk line directly across the Cascades to Puget Sound to a lesser—and optional—branch. It was a change responding to Portland interests and resulted in the early construction of this isolated Kalama-Tacoma segment.

Oregonians were more concerned about their ties with the nation than with this improved link with Puget Sound. When the NP's financial backing collapsed in 1873 it had reached west only to the Missouri River at Bismarck, Dakota Territory, and during the ensuing severe depression the Portland Board of Trade, fearing that this northern transcontinental might never be completed, appealed to Collis Huntington to construct a link from the southern end of the Willamette Valley line at Roseburg southeastward across the desert to Winnemucca on the Central Pacific, the only operating transcontinental system. The California magnate declined to do so, and Portland's main overland link with the nation continued to be by way of California. A daily mail stage between Sacramento and Portland was initiated in 1860 (and a telegraph line completed in 1864), but it was years before the road was sufficiently improved to make service at all reliable. Railroad extensions in the Sacramento and Willamette valleys were a big help, but the 375-mile

gap through the tangle of mountains between Redding and Roseburg stood uncom-
pleted until 1887. Thus the ocean connection, by steam or sail, to San Francisco
remained the trunk line to the nation, a service continually improved in capacity
and quality, but never without latent peril; work on the dreaded Columbia entrance was only begun by army engineers in 1884.

Portland, like San Francisco, was the undisputed commercial capital of a very
extensive region, even though all was on a much smaller population scale: Portland
(including East Portland across the river) with only 20,000, serving a region of
little more than 250,000 in 1880 (by which date California and adjacent Nevada
were nearing a million). And Portland's relationship with Puget Sound at this time
had something in common with that of San Francisco with Southern California.
Both of these thinly populated outlying areas were rather detached and distinct,
and both had been sheltered from the direct impact of gold rushes and consequent
urban and economic developments. Connected to their regional capital by sea
more readily than by land, there was the possibility of them establishing direct
links to the East. Commercial interests on Puget Sound, like those in Los Angeles,
were obsessed with more direct overland connections across mountains and deserts, and their eventual success in obtaining competing transcontinental railroads
(and their propaganda machines) transformed the prospects and character of these
hitherto marginal areas. However, there were also important differences. Whereas
the lack of a good harbor to serve the main productive districts was the great
physical deficiency of Southern California, Puget Sound was a maritime wonderland of sheltered deep-water anchorages. And whereas Los Angeles never had a
serious challenger, Puget Sound was the scene of intense rivalries among at least
half a dozen promotions of apparent strong potential to become the premier port
and regional focus. Geopolitically the Los Angeles area was almost immediately
locked into the State of California and, failing to secede, was long under the
dominance of San Francisco and Sacramento; in contrast, a separate Washington
Territory was formed at the behest of Puget Sound interests in 1853. As a federal
territory, Washington was long under remote federal control, but eventual statehood was all the while being shaped in the Puget Sound region (fig. 16).

At the time of its creation there were fewer than 4,000 Whites and barely a
semblance of a town in all of Washington Territory. A small army outpost, Fort
Steilacoom, near old Fort Nisqually in the southern reaches of Puget Sound, with
its local village and mills, became the focal point for proposed military roads.
Olympia, near the industrial village of Tumwater, on the southernmost harbor (but
a mudflat at low tide) and therefore head of the shortest road between Puget Sound
and the Columbia River, became the territorial capital. On Elliott Bay, midway
along the eastern shore, local leaders of the small settlement of Seattle had

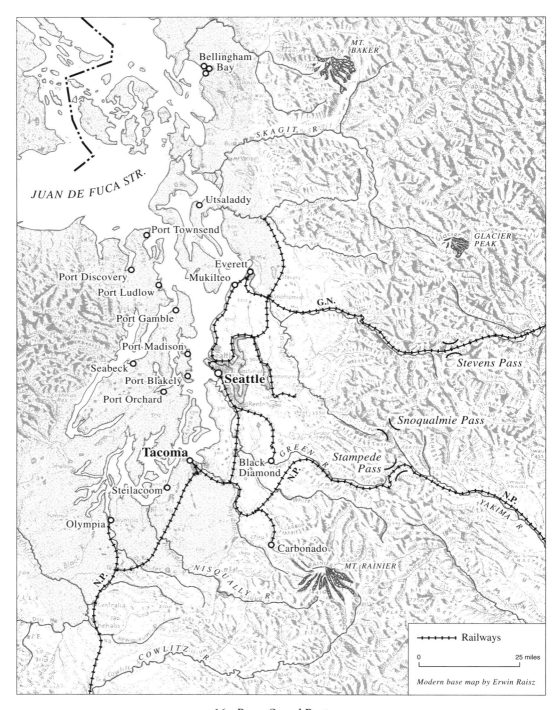

16. Puget Sound Region.

garnered the territorial university. To the northwest, Port Townsend, overlooking the oceanic entranceway to Puget Sound, soon obtained the customs station (initially at Olympia) and as the only official port of entry attracted businesses and, eventually, several consulates. For the rest, most of the American population lived in sawmill towns, which were mostly company-owned camps full of bachelor workers. The California Gold Rush had sent a fleet of vessels hurrying to the Northwest for lumber, causing a brief boom along the lower Columbia. But navigation on the river was hazardous and tedious, and in the early 1850s Californians turned to the marvelous tidewater forests of Puget Sound and soon had large steam-powered mills at work in such places as Port Discovery, Port Gamble, Port Ludlow, Port Madison, Port Blakeley, and Seabeck. Almost all of the big mills were financed and operated by San Franciscan Yankees who marketed this "Oregon pine" (mostly Douglas fir) in their company vessels throughout the Pacific World.

The population remained low—by 1870 there were barely 10,000 around Puget Sound—because there was so little to attract American settlers. These fragmented glaciated lowlands were densely forested, and the scattering of wetlands and small bracken-covered prairies could not compare with the Willamette Valley. The Coastal Salish Indians had been drastically reduced, for with the arrival of new infectious diseases their "huge cedar houses, once admirable adaptations to the environment, became deathtraps," but they remained sufficiently present and mobile to pose a threat to trespassing Whites. Numerous selections were made under the Donation Land law, but pioneering was heavy, discouraging work. Wheat did poorly in this cool, damp country, and settlers had to rely on gardens, livestock, fish, and game, with meager prospects for commercial marketing. Most attention therefore was focused on speculation, based on the conviction that cities, industries, and commerce must eventually arise and thrive in this strategic northwest corner. As an early governor extolled:

> It would be difficult to overestimate our commercial advantages . . . We have in Puget Sound the finest inland sea in the world. . . . With sufficient depth of water, in all of its parts, to float the largest ships of the line, it is yet so locked in and protected that it may be regarded as one immense harbor.
>
> . . . Nature has made this body of water the key to more than fifteen hundred miles of the north Pacific ocean, and it will, in obedience to nature's laws, sooner or later gather within its grasp not only the coast trade for this distance, but also a large portion of whatever commerce is carried on between the two hemispheres upon this ocean.

Coal and evidences of iron discovered in several localities awaited capitalists, and the whole region longed for the quickening touch of the northern transcontinental

railroad, surveyed and so vigorously advocated throughout the 1850s by Isaac
Stevens, the first territorial governor.

From the beginning, governors and legislators annually pleaded for federal
assistance to build a road across the Cascade Mountains to connect the two great
physically distinct parts of the Territory. It was considered essential for security,
hence the agitations for a Fort Steilacoom–Fort Walla Walla military road, for
which congressional appropriations were never sufficient for more than a reconnaissance. It was considered essential "for preserving the integrity and unity of
Washington Territory," especially in view of Oregon's attempt "to rob us of . . . so
valuable a portion of our territory" as the Walla Walla country. (Oregon was
happily responding to a petition of leading Walla Walla citizens to have the state
boundary shifted north to the lower Snake River, because "the Western part of the
Territory [Puget Sound] appears to the people of this valley like some foreign land,
and it is about as little talked of or thought of by them as is the Chinese empire.")
And it was considered essential for populating the country, for only by demonstrating the ease of passage across the mountains could Washingtonians intercept
emigrant trains in the Walla Walla Valley and divert some of these land seekers to
Puget Sound rather than have them continue on to the Willamette. Inability to
lure many along the Cowlitz corridor north from Portland was demonstrated year
after year—which Puget Sound propagandists blamed on the near impassable
condition of the roads rather than on the paucity of attractive farmlands.

More than all else, this agitation by government and business leaders alike for a
road across the Cascades was based on the need to demonstrate the feasibility of
such a route for the eventual northern transcontinental railroad. From the initial
explorations and debates over the Pacific Railroad, those favoring competing
routes always pointed to the heavy snows in these northern mountains as a formidable obstacle to any such line. But experience year after year showed that the snows
were no greater and the passes less difficult than those on the Central Pacific route
across the Sierra Nevada. As far as Puget Sound interests were concerned the
problem was not the difficulty of the mountain passage but the ease of the alternative: the Columbia River Gorge. The success of the Northern Pacific in getting its
charter altered to reach Puget Sound by way of Portland was bitterly denounced,
and the power of that company to select its own terminus on the sound compounded anxieties. The NP soon narrowed its choice to three harbors: Tacoma, on
Commencement Bay; Seattle, on Elliott Bay; and Mukilteo, in the lee of Whidbey
Island. Tacoma was selected, probably because it was the nearest to the track being
extended north from Kalama (the company was out of money and afraid of losing
its land grant if it failed to complete this segment), and because the NP could
obtain control of most of the land for a city and port. (The urgent need to sell lots

to raise money doomed Frederick Law Olmsted's overelaborate parklike plan for Tacoma, as the NP's land company opted to drape the slopes of this bold promontory with a quickly surveyed grid, resulting in some of the steepest streets in any American city.) Seattle responded by initiating the Seattle & Walla Walla Railroad. Although this line got no farther than the foothills, it tapped coal mines that provided a valuable export.

It would be fourteen years after it reached Tacoma from the south before the Northern Pacific did finally complete the long-awaited line across the Cascades, building up the Yakima and by way of Stampede Pass, the Green River, and on to Tacoma. Seattle responded by building a new railroad toward its preferred Snoqualmie Pass but, again, did not have the resources to extend it across the mountains and for the time being had to settle for a short branch connection with, and poor service from, the NP. It did not have to wait long for something better, however, for in 1893 it celebrated the arrival of James J. Hill's Great Northern Railway, a formidable rival built west without subsidy from Hill's prosperous St. Paul and Manitoba system along the northernmost—and shortest—route to Puget Sound. Reaching the sea by way of the Snohomish River, it momentarily thrilled speculators in the new town of Everett, then built on south, past Mukilteo, to Seattle. The Northern Pacific had undertaken its trans-Cascade line only after losing control of the OR&N down the Columbia to Portland, and shortly thereafter, this strategic Oregon company came under the control of the Union Pacific, which soon completed its full Oregon Trail route and became at last a truly "Pacific" railroad.

"Railroads," said an early territorial governor trying to reassure his longing constituents, are "not a mere convenience to local populations, but a vast machinery for the building up of empires. They are the true alchemy of the age, which transmutes the otherwise worthless resources of a country into gold." A generation later the machinery was in place and the alchemy at work. With three large railroad systems traversing the region, competing for its commerce, connecting it with the nation, the whole area underwent vigorous, transforming development. Between 1880 and 1900 the population of Oregon, Washington, and northern Idaho grew by about three-quarters of a million, entirely new areas were opened for settlement, new resources tapped, new towns created; but in addition to these commonplaces of American expansion there was a major reshaping of this far corner of the country, a realignment of its trafficways, with decisive, indelible effect upon competing centers. Three geographic alterations deserve particular notice: the development of the Columbia Interior and the meteoric rise of Spokane, the competition between Puget Sound and Portland for the commerce of that Interior, and the emergence of Seattle as the unrivaled city on the sound and leading port of the region.

The two northern transcontinentals followed glaciated valleys winding devi-
ously through the tangle of the northern Rockies to enter the Great Columbia
Plain at its northeastern corner. With the Union Pacific reaching northward from
its earlier (OR&N) entry up the Columbia from Portland, these giant systems now
built rival lines into the Walla Walla, Palouse, and Big Bend wheatlands and to the
newly discovered mineral wealth in the Coeur d'Alenes. Special trains brought in
land seekers, investors, and speculators, dozens of towns quickened into life, and
one mushroomed into a city. Spokane Falls, astride its powerful plunging river,
became the focus of its self-proclaimed "Inland Empire," embracing all the expanding wheatlands of eastern Washington, the immense white pine forests of northern
Idaho, and half a dozen mining districts in the adjoining mountains (fig. 17). The
reality of this new commercial region was geopolitically confirmed by the annexation of northern Idaho (the absurd "panhandle" that was inaccessible directly from
southern Idaho) to the incipient State of Washington. Strongly endorsed by most
local interests, this redrawing of the map was approved by Congress only to die
unsigned on the desk of President Grover Cleveland (made wary of political ramifications in remnant Idaho Territory, Nevada, and Utah). Largely burned in that
first year of statehood (1889), Spokane (it soon dropped "Falls" from its name) was
rapidly rebuilt with a substance and style befitting its pride in being the largest
inland city west of Minneapolis and north of Salt Lake City. A Dutch banker,
assessing its prospects, declared that he "had never seen a small town which offers
such an overwhelming impression of monumental buildings." With more than
20,000 people at the time it was already much more than a small town to Americans and—with significant help from Dutch investors—it quickly grew to a metropolis of more than 100,000, a phenomenal change from a village of 350 in thirty
years' time, even by American standards. Spokane had completely usurped Walla
Walla as the primary center of the Interior; bypassed by all the trunk lines, the
older town was reduced to serving only its own rich but local district.

A Columbia Interior so magnified in population and resources was an ever-
greater prize for Pacific ports. With two main line railroads across the Cascade
Range, Puget Sound challenged Portland's monopoly over its "natural" hinterland.
The greater costs of carriage over the mountains were offset by the greater costs of
navigation on the lower Columbia. Competition for the grain trade was intense.
Each of the railroad companies had affiliated systems of warehouses and mills. The
big grain companies in Portland opened branches in Tacoma and Seattle, and with
the rapid growth of flour shipments to Asia, Puget Sound ports took the lead in
milling and exports. These interregional rivalries were further complicated by
extravagant new railroad constructions that brought a third northern transcontinental, the Chicago, Milwaukee, & St. Paul, to Puget Sound, and a joint GN-NP
line between Spokane and Portland, following the north bank of the Columbia.

17. Spokane and the "Inland Empire," c. 1894.

A dozen years after the arrival of the first train, Spokane was the focus of a remarkable set of radiating lines, making it the unrivaled capital of a large diversified region. (Reproduced from a booster pamphlet; courtesy Eastern Washington Historical Society, L 85-122)

The cities on the Sound grew from vigorous development of more immediate hinterlands as well. Their new transcontinental connections to St. Paul and Duluth were soon followed by the arrival of large lumber companies eager to shift from depleted Great Lakes holdings to this newer Northwest. The Weyerhauser purchase of an enormous block of timberlands from the Northern Pacific was only the largest of many such relocations (there was a similar movement into northern Idaho). The erection of the "world's largest lumbermill" in Tacoma was soon followed by an even larger one in Everett, and these were simply the most conspicuous representatives of the new scale of capital and technology. The fishing industry, drawing upon another prodigious regional resource, was also greatly expanded in volume, range, and product. By the 1890s Puget Sound–based fleets and canneries were harvesting the seasonal salmon riches of the Alaskan coast. (In marked contrast to these expansions, several attempts to create an iron industry from local coals and ores failed.)

By 1890 these Washington ports were beginning to rival Portland in size as well as function:

Portland (including East Portland)	57,000
Seattle	43,000
Tacoma	36,000

In the ensuing economic depression Seattle began to forge rapidly ahead of industrial, company-dominated Tacoma. Already the seat of an array of small industries and Puget Sound services, Seattle was well poised to become the premier port, and James J. Hill helped to make it so. Gaining control of the NP as well as the GN, he ended the discrimination in rates and service favoring Tacoma, invested heavily in docks and shipping facilities, and worked out an agreement with Nippon Yusen Kaisha, the largest steamship line in the Pacific; in time Great Northern trainloads of silk leaving Seattle for the rush across the continent seemed a vivid fulfillment of the global axis of commerce so long dreamed of by Pacific railroad enthusiasts. The Alaska gold rush, beginning in 1897, compounded Seattle's surge. The city had already ousted San Francisco as the base for most Alaskan trade and mail, and its vessels took excursionists to Sitka and back to marvel at the new "American Switzerland"; now the chamber of commerce mounted a continentwide publicity campaign extolling Seattle as "the gateway to Alaska." Its superior position and leadership ensured its continuation as the commercial capital of Alaska, the principal seat of its industries, seasonal labor, finance, and commerce, for half a century after the stampedes to the subarctic wildernesses of the Klondike and Nome were over. Tacoma remained an important industrial and export center, but Seattle was clearly the superior service center. It was not clearly superior to Portland, however, because it was not easy to compete in banking, wholesaling, and related activities with well-established Oregon companies. In general terms, Seattle grew more from an influx of wealth invested in new areas and activities, whereas Portland continued to grow on the basis of older wealth invested in activities long fostered in its large hinterland.

By the time Washington had become a state (1889) it had surpassed Oregon in population, and it continued to grow at a much faster rate. By 1900 the three main subregions of western Oregon (including the lower Columbia counties of Washington), western Washington, and the interior country tributary to these Pacific ports were about equal in population (each about 300,000–350,000), their dominant cities were among the fastest growing in the nation, and they would continue to be for at least another ten years. If not quite equal in growth rate or size to Los Angeles, the results (1910) were nonetheless impressive:

Portland (East Portland now annexed)	207,000
Seattle	237,000
Spokane	104,000

Such a pattern of subregions and cities suggests how extensively the shape and character of the overall region had been altered. In simplest terms, it was a transformation of "Oregon" into the "Pacific Northwest": the change from a rather simple regional system patterned on the obvious lineaments of nature, with Portland as its focus, into a much more complicated and comprehensively developed region of three obvious main parts, with Seattle and Puget Sound quite the equal of Portland and the Willamette Valley in population and importance, and with keen competition between these urban rivals for the trade of the Interior and for transcontinental and oceanic commerce. The bounds of this newer system were reasonably clear and, except for the addition of Alaska, not much different from the old, with freight rates as well as distance limiting effective penetration of southern Idaho and western Montana.

As a regional concept this "Great Pacific North West Empire"—to use the term of an 1881 territorial governor envisioning the eventual emergence of such a thing—was rather vague and imprecise as to content and character. The sharp physical contrasts between coast and interior, the obvious lack of a single focus, the self-conscious rivalry of its leading cities, and the awkward parceling among three states all precluded any single, simple image. There were also differences among the peoples and societies of its parts that if far less obvious than those in many American regions were nonetheless apparent to careful observers (and cultivated by local chauvinists). It was common to contrast, with pride or derision depending upon one's stance—an old, stable, conservative Portland-Willamette establishment cultivating its strong sense of pioneer stock and the virtues of community and continuity with an aggressive, progressive "Seattle Spirit" powered by enterprising individuals. Such characterizations were grounded in differences in timing and impetus of development: between an Oregon founded on family-farm colonization and shaped through nearly forty years of modest growth as a rather isolated provincial economy and system centered on a single city and indirectly linked to the nation by way of San Francisco and a Washington that had boomed much later under the impact of direct railroad connections by which Eastern capital and corporations flowed in to take command of resources and exercise strong influence upon cities and politics. In Washington seasonal labor in lumbering, mining, fishing, and shipping played a larger role in a more volatile economy and fostered a more confrontational political culture. Whereas Oregon grew primarily from its own well-rooted population derived mainly from the older Middle West–Border South and from California, Washington's growth in population came strongly from the upper Middle West, with Scandinavians and Finns a conspicuous (but not the largest) element. Seattle's business leadership, like that of Portland, drew from the Northeast, but even more heavily from the upper Midwest. Consistent with these characterizations, Portland's new-century extravaganza, the Lewis and Clark Exposition (1905), called attention to a distinguished past, whereas Seattle's Alaska-Yukon-Pacific Exposition (1909) looked forward and outward.

Though it was rarely specified, such generalizations were almost entirely based on *western* Washington and Oregon—essentially comparing Puget Sound and the Willamette Valley. Spokane and the Inland Empire, subordinate backcountry obscured by the contrast with the "evergreen" image of the Raincoast, had their own distinct character (and early in the new century tried to create a new state— Whitman or Lincoln—conforming closely to these bounds, but it would have involved major concessions by three states, and however geographically appropriate, it was too late for such drastic geopolitical alteration). Although the railroads brought in many people from the Middle West and farms and towns in the Columbia wheatlands superficially resembled contemporaries in Minnesota, Dakota, and Kansas, they were actually initiated and influenced more from the Willamette Valley and California and few displayed anything like the bold ethnic mosaic of the Great Plains. And while Spokane sprang into life at the point in place and time where the Middle West was brought to bear on the older Oregon system, its character cannot be deduced simply from such an encounter for it was shaped as well by more local circumstances, and especially by the wealth derived from its mining hinterland that more than anything else created its remarkable commercial and residential townscape (shaped notably by an Eastern-trained architect bold enough to build occasionally with the local basalt) and its large complex of Roman Catholic institutions, including a Jesuit university.

Puget Sound was like Southern California in being a rather minor, marginal area transformed under the impact of competing transcontinental railroads, but the geographic context and results were significantly different. Seattle and Tacoma became direct rivals of Portland in a way that Los Angeles could not (as yet) rival San Francisco; and Puget Sound's divergence from Oregon in cultural character was nothing so bold as Southern California's emergence as a coherent culture region. Rather, this Pacific Northwest emerged as a more complicated, loosely associated realm of three distinct geographic parts, whose people were bound by common commercial networks (though divided in formal political focus) and understood themselves as set apart from other areas, sharing unique physical environments of bold Western beauty and immense local resources in a far corner that seemed destined to serve as the nation's nearest threshold to the Pacific and Oriental worlds.

5. Zion, Deseret, and Utah

The founding, within the space of three years, of a large and flourishing community, upon a spot so remote from the abodes of men, so completely shut out by natural barriers from the rest of the world, so entirely unconnected by watercourses with either of the oceans that wash the shores of this continent—a country offering no advantages of inland navigation or of foreign commerce, but, on the contrary, isolated by vast uninhabitable deserts, and only to be reached by long, painful, and often hazardous journeys by land—presents an anomaly so very peculiar, that it deserves more than a passing notice. . . . the success of an enterprise under circumstances so at variance with all our preconceived ideas of its probability, may well be considered as one of the most remarkable incidents of the present age.

So reported Captain Howard Stansbury, leader of an official exploring party engaged in making a survey of that natural curiosity, the Great Salt Lake, in 1849–50.

Americans, of course, had been giving the Mormons more than a passing notice for some years. Their presence in this Far Western refuge was the result of animosities that had been deepening for more than a decade: early rumblings in Ohio, suddenly severe in Missouri, disastrous in Illinois. Their apparent success in removing themselves as a body and colonizing a remote and unwanted wasteland only magnified their national notoriety. We need to review these antecedents and get some sense of what they attempted and failed to achieve in the East if we are to account for their remarkable presence in the Far West.

The Mormons were a *peculiar* people: they called themselves such, as the Lord's own, a chosen people covenanted to carry out the divine purpose; others called them that because they found them to be different, strange, even subversive and dangerous. Mormonism was distinctive in being deeply, assertively "American" and yet strongly divergent from the mainstream of American society; in purely religious terms it was, as Leland Jamison put it, "at once an irreconcilable Christian heresy and the most typically American theology yet formulated on this continent."

THE SEARCH FOR ZION

That the Mormons have a special place on this continent is central to their doctrines as well as to their history. The Book of Mormon sets forth an epic story of ancient peoples in America as descendants of dispersed tribes of Israel who once built great civilizations, fell from grace, and left behind only the remnant "Lamanites" (American Indians). Yet North America remained "a land choice above all lands" wherein there would be a restoration of the true church and the building up of the Kingdom of God on earth. It was in their struggle to carry out this divine plan that the new "Latter-day Saints" would have an important role in shaping the cultural geography of America.

Geographically Mormonism can be seen as an emanation from New England Extended that became competitively involved in American frontier colonization. Both Joseph Smith and Brigham Young were born in Vermont and moved to Upstate New York early in life. Smith had his transforming visions, produced his sacred text, and in 1830 formally organized what would become the Church of Jesus Christ of Latter-day Saints while resident in western New York. Early converts (such as Brigham Young) were gathered through preaching missions across this turbulent region that was being swept by such a succession of fervent religious movements as to become famous as "the burned-over district." The conversion of a Protestant congregation in the village of Kirtland in the Western Reserve provided an opportunity to build a full Mormon community. Within a few years nearly 2,000 converts had settled in that Ohio locality where, in 1836, they consecrated their first temple. By that time, however, a new focus had been selected, for Joseph Smith had gone west to help initiate a mission to the Indians and had proclaimed Independence, Missouri, as the true Zion. Indeed, not only was this heart of the continent to be the New Jerusalem, "it had in fact been the site of the Garden of Eden itself; not Mesopotamia, but the great valley of the Mississippi had been the cradle of mankind."

As Mormons began to arrive in Missouri, in what was at the time the farthest salient of Anglo-American settlement, troubles with the "Gentiles" (the Mormon term for all non-Mormons), already bubbling up in Ohio, quickly followed. Within two years of Joseph Smith's visit local Missourians were meeting to adopt measures "to rid themselves of the set of families called Mormons," who were under orders from their leader "to come up to Zion, [the] name they have thought proper to confer on our little village." Although disparaging them as a "singular set of pretended Christians," this local response was not simply an expression of endemic religious bigotry. The root of the matter lay in the very concept of "Zion." If to the Mormons it resonated with the heady prospect of building the Kingdom of God on earth, for other people in the area it seemed to sound the death knell of American society as they knew it. Mormonism was more than a set of beliefs, it was work to be done—*together*. The key concept was the "gathering"—in Smith's words, the Lord's call to bring together "mine elect" "unto one place upon the face of this land." The fundamental issue, therefore, was geopolitical: the control of territory and of the character of society therein. As the Mormons arrived in rapidly enlarging numbers and not only bought all the land they could but proclaimed themselves a chosen people who were destined to "possess the country" for their New Jerusalem, the Missourians countered with a declaration that "every consideration of self-preservation, good society, public morals, and the fair prospects . . . that await this young and beautiful country" required their expulsion. Add to this vital contest over turf some of the well-known social tendencies of these particular contestants—the moralistic, self-righteous Yankee fervent in his uncompromising views and the fiercely independent Upland Southern frontiersman ready to run roughshod over anyone who stood in his way and to take the law into his own hands to protect family and property; add, further, the larger state, regional, and national contexts of this collision—the politics of slavery and of party and sectional interests—and it becomes clear that these troubles in the West were a particularly ugly prelude to "Bleeding Kansas." (The assertion of a divine right to all Palestine by militant Zionists is more than just an obvious analogy; it is the modern expression of the original concept that the Mormons adopted.)

Driven out of Independence, the Mormons moved a short distance to the north, laid out new towns, and proceeded to build on an extension of hallowed ground: Adam-ondi-Ahman, their settlement along the Grand River, being, so Joseph Smith declared, the very place where Christ appeared to Adam after his expulsion from the Garden of Eden. But there were other colonists already in these districts as well and the results were the same. Failing to induce them to "become as other citizens," to "scatter" and liberate themselves from the "fetters of fanaticism" (and to vote as individuals and not en bloc as a means of group power), the governor of Missouri issued an "Extermination Order" to drive all Mormons from the state for the public good. Retreating eastward across the Mississippi, Mormon refugees purchased lands some miles upriver from Quincy where, augmented by the first inflow of converts from Britain, their new city of Nauvoo soon emerged as one of the showplaces of the West (and, momentarily, the largest in Illinois). All Mormons were now called to gather to "this corner-stone of Zion" to help raise a new temple and build the Kingdom. The ensuing influx and expansion, rhetoric and rumors, soon reproduced the same clashes with other citizens and officials. In an attempt to insulate the Mormons from harassments (and curry their favor in state politics) the Illinois legislature granted an extraordinary charter to Nauvoo, making it virtually a Mormon city-state, with its own officials and uniformed militia. As this did not resolve the problems, and despairing of effective state protection, Joseph Smith boldly took the concept to a higher level, formally requesting that this enclave be made a federal territory within the State of Illinois, a proposal that, as one historian put it, "approached the extreme limits of possibility . . . within the general framework of the American federal union."

Local tensions became incendiary. With Joseph Smith, the charismatic prophet of a theocratic imperium (now rumored to be fostering bizarre and offensive religious practices), boldly displaying himself as general of his own army and declaring his candidacy for president of the United States, "fear that monolithic Mormonism might insidiously engulf broad areas of the nation" became widespread. The explosion came following the arrest of Smith and his brother on civil charges and their incarceration in Carthage, the county seat, whereupon, on June 27, 1844, a mob stormed the jail and murdered both men.

In the bitter aftermath of this martyrdom Brigham Young, as the senior Apostle, struggled to hold the flock together while studying how and where to extricate them from their besieged situation. The harsh truth that the Mormons would not be tolerated as a cohesive, gathered, expansive, religious society in the midst of Gentile America had been bloodily confirmed; removal to some distant, insulated refuge was now imperative. Mounting troubles had spurred talk of such a thing for some years. Smith had spoken of establishing colonies in the Far West, apparently as outposts to be used in emergency, and had recently authorized exploring parties to California and to Texas. All of this was congruent with more general American interests, activities, and visions of the time. Smith, himself, was an outspoken proponent of national expansion, publicly stating that Americans "should grasp all the territory we can," and with characteristic audacity had proposed that the federal government use the Mormons as an armed instrument to conquer and secure a vast western realm. Manifest uncertainties about the future geopolitical pattern of North America impinged on any assessment of possibilities for a Mormon colony in 1844–45. Oregon, the most firm American foothold, could be dismissed because it was filling up with Missourians. An emissary sent to the Republic of Texas was a man of imperial visions who sought cession of the whole of west Texas and the Nueces Strip, which the Mormons would colonize and thereby provide a protective buffer between Texas and Mexico. It is unclear whether this negotiation had gotten anywhere before Young firmly rejected the idea of implanting his people in that volatile borderland. The governor of Illinois urged Young to remove to feebly held Alta California and build up his kingdom there; that, too, was rejected, though California would continue to tantalize and lure some Mormons and persist as a factor in the shaping of the Mormon region.

Seeking first of all an empty and isolated refuge, Brigham Young looked to the Rocky Mountains and soon focused on their western margins in the vicinity of the Great Salt Lake. It was a country well known to trappers, traders, and explorers. Since the first expeditions of Peter Skene Ogden in the 1820s it had been a contested borderland between British and American fur traders. The curious lake itself had quickly become a famous landmark amidst a vast new Western world, and it was set in a very striking kind of country, with sterile deserts to the west (the residue of its former greater extent), but on the east a narrow lowland crossed by many streams flowing from the steep wall of snow-capped mountains. Osborne Russell's *Journal of a Trapper* was not published until some years later, but his comments, recorded in February 1841, were not an uncommon assessment of the time: "This is a beautiful and fertile valley intersected by large numbers of fine springs which flow from the mountain to the Lake and could with little labor and expense [be] made to irrigate the whole Valley." Frémont's explorations a few years later confirmed that "a region of great pastoral promise, abounding in fine streams, the rich bunchgrass, soil that would produce wheat" extended south along the mountain front for 150 miles. After careful study of Frémont's published report and all other available information, a decision to remove to the Valley of the Great Salt Lake was made sometime in the summer of 1845. At the general church conference in October, Young announced the impending "exodus of the only true Israel from these United States to a far distant region of the west." Doctrinally, the way for such a drastic relocation had been opened by Joseph Smith a year before. Faced with the disconcerting problem of having abandoned Zion in Missouri, he announced to the elders in Nauvoo a new revelation: "I will make a proclamation that will cover a broader ground. The whole of America is Zion itself from north to south, and is described by the Prophets, who declare that it is the Zion where the mountains of the Lord should be, and that it should be in the center of the land."

In the following year, while his people were encamped on the Missouri River building up resources for their great trek, Young specified their impending exodus and destination in a letter to President James K. Polk:

> The cause of our exile we need not repeat; it is already with you, suffice it to say that a combination of fortuitous, illegal and unconstitutional circumstances have placed us in our present situation, on a journey which we design shall end in a location west of the Rocky Mountains, and within the basin of the Great Salt Lake, or Bear River valley, as soon as circumstances shall permit, believing that to be a point where a good living will require hard labor, and consequently will be coveted by no other people, while it is surrounded by so unpopulous but fertile country.

The American president had already instigated a war with Mexico that would soon determine that after their thousand-mile journey into this wilderness isolation the

Mormons would find themselves still within the sovereign bounds of the United States.

The three years between Smith's vast geographical broadening of the concept of Zion and Young's first implantation of the Kingdom in a remote region thereof was a tumultuous, defining period, a "glorious emergency" that tested, winnowed, hardened, and bonded the nucleus of a new nation in North America. In the aftermath of the death of the Prophet only one substantial group rejected Young's leadership. Eventually formalized as the Reorganized Church of Jesus Christ of L.D.S., they disallowed the concept of the political kingdom (as well as the practice of polygamy) and remained scattered about in the older West. The Exodus was the real test of Mormon cohesion and leadership, and it was carried out with greater efficiency and less hazard than any similar movement of its era. By that time they could follow a well-traveled route across the Plains (several thousand Americans had already gone to Oregon and a few wagon trains had veered off to California by way of the Salt Lake Valley), but it was the character and power of their American Moses that was critical. A man of dogged practicality wielding firm and complete authority, Young was soon put to a severe test by the need to get 15,000 followers out of Illinois and across Iowa in midwinter (he had already gained valuable experience in overseeing the move from Missouri to Nauvoo a few years before). After a year of preparations in encampments near Council Bluffs, Brigham Young led a vanguard across the Plains, and on July 24, 1847, he sat in his carriage on a high terrace overlooking the Valley of the Great Salt Lake and said, "This is the place." It became the most famous phrase in Mormon history (that is, in the common version of that history—there seems to be no actual record of his words), sufficient in itself to consecrate the new Zion and set in motion the creation of a genuinely expansive Mormon nation.

THE MORMON SYSTEM OF COLONIZATION

The Mormon accomplishment is so remarkable—as Captain Stansbury and every other observer of this formative time emphasized—that we must get a clear picture not only of the extent and character of this new Western region but of the peculiar conditions, principles, and processes involved in its creation. In general, we may summarize that the Mormons gained access to a huge area without competition from other American settlers and with little hindrance from local Indians, and were able to apply an orderly system of colonization under centralized church authority essentially unrestrained by U.S. laws.

The Great Basin lay open to Mormon colonists because it was "coveted by no other people." Thousands of land seekers had seen it, or passed along its margins knowing something of it, but hurried on to Oregon or California. The combined isolation and desolation were overpowering in comparison with those coastal regions. Even though recent reports, such as that of Frémont, spoke of attractive potentials, not only was the area far removed from any commercial network of the times, it was also apparent that any substantial settlement would have to be sustained by irrigation, a form of agricultural colonization foreign to the experience of American pioneers. Typically, the whole country was regarded as essentially empty, the lands lying open for the taking, reinforced in the Mormon case by the conviction that this was "the land of Promise, held in reserve by the hand of God as a resting place for the Saints." It *was* thinly populated: the Wasatch by Shoshones and Utes, closely related hunting and gathering peoples living in seasonal camps, whose life had been somewhat expanded by acquisition of the horse from the Spanish a few decades earlier, and the desert mountain and bolson country by widely scattered, small bands of Gosiutes and Paiutes, who gleaned a meager subsistence in a fashion most Americans considered degrading. Although Mormon theology defined all these "Lamanites" as a degenerate but redeemable people and Mormon policy called for amicable relations, friendly assistance, and missionary tutelage in farming life, church leaders brooked no interference with Mormon colonization. There were the usual harassments and small clashes, and within a few years Brigham Young was seeking to have all Indians officially removed from the region; in time almost all would be, overwhelmed by relentless, systematic Mormon expansion.

In 1847 the Mormons had actually moved beyond U.S. jurisdiction. The Treaty of Guadalupe Hidalgo changed that technicality, but Brigham Young became governor of the Territory as well as president of the church and for years carried out his program essentially unrestricted. Federal land laws were not applied in Utah for more than twenty years, during which time the Mormon system of settlement was extended without hindrance or adaptation, resulting, as Charles S. Peterson put it, in "the most widely applied and formally practiced system of squatter's rights ever devised in America."

The Mormon church is a highly structured centralized theocracy, operating under a president (officially "President, Prophet, Seer, and Revelator"), a set of high counselors (in effect a kind of cabinet), with a larger council as a quasi-legislative-endorsing-body (this ecclesiastical structure, titles, numbers, and duties were evolving during these years). Under this kind of authority the church proceeded to create the Kingdom in physical form: selecting the areas and often the specific sites to be occupied; "calling" a cadre of settlers to initiate a new colony at a particular time; decreeing the mode of settlement and continuing to supervise and assist in the management and welfare of each settlement as part of an expanding coherent whole.

The application of this system of colonization to create a Mormon nation in Western North America may be conveniently summarized under a set of major features.

1. *Nucleus: Valley of the Great Salt Lake.* The first task was to create a substantial base from which further extensions could be made. The Salt Lake Valley was the best of the lands and locations in the hundred-mile stretch of valley and bench-lands lying at about 4,400 feet above sea level along the base of the highest mountains and parallel with a New World version of Galilee-Jordan-Dead Sea. Within three years there were more than 11,000 Mormons living in thirty-five settlements "within the protective walls of the 'everlasting mountains,'" forming the Wasatch Oasis and the Mormon Core.

2. *Frame: Deseret.* Brigham Young not only envisioned a New Jerusalem, he placed it within a vast American Israel. He marked out that area on the map, gave it a name, Deseret (from the Book of Mormon, meaning honeybee, symbolizing productive industriousness), and hurried to establish a hold upon it. In 1849 Congress was petitioned to admit "the free independent State of Deseret," encompassing the whole of the Great Basin, the watershed of the Colorado River (as far south as the Gila, then the United States boundary), and a frontage on the Pacific in Southern California—an area of some 400,000 square miles (fig. 18). Failing in this, Young (at the suggestion of President Zachary Taylor) sent an emissary to California to explore the possibility of seeking admission together as one "consolidated state," with agreement to split into two states thereafter. Such a ploy was prompted by the fact that Deseret had far fewer than the 60,000 "free inhabitants" generally required for admission to statehood but might be expected to qualify within a few years. California rejected any such partnership with the Mormons and was admitted as a state in 1850. At the same time Congress created the Territory of Utah, a narrower band between the Forty-second and Thirty-seventh parallels but reaching from the summit of the Rockies to the California line.

But Young never really gave up on the larger concept. In 1851 he selected the site for a new capital 150 miles south of Salt Lake City as being far more central to the envisioned development of Mormonland. Named Fillmore, in Millard County (in honor of the new American president who was considered to be more friendly than his predecessors), it was technically the capital for seven years, although only one session of the legislature was actually convened there in the partially completed statehouse. Failure of Congress to provide the funds anticipated for such territorial buildings and changing relations with the outer world kept the seat of government in its original place. In 1862 a petition for statehood was again rebuffed, and seeing the United States mired in its own mortal crisis, Young began a practice of convening what became known as "the ghost legislature of Deseret" for one day following the close of each session of the Utah territorial legislature, a symbolic act in preparation for the day when Deseret might indeed become a "free and independent state," the embryo for the political Kingdom of God on earth.

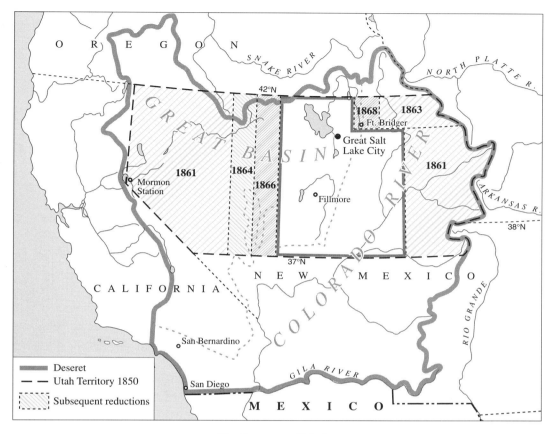

18. Deseret and Utah.

3. *Trafficways and Portals.* Building the Kingdom was predicated on a continued rapid growth in the number of Saints and their gathering together in Zion. Missionary programs in the United States, Canada, and Europe were producing a considerable number of converts every year, and there was need to establish an efficient system for getting them to Deseret. In 1849 the Perpetual Emigration Fund was created, and year by year the system of conveying people across the Plains was improved.

Young was determined to get control over the eastern approaches to the Wasatch so as to fend off Gentile traders and to provide a provision base. Accordingly Fort Supply was established in 1853, two years later Fort Bridger was taken over, and these would serve as operational depots for the annual "church trains" sent east to bring in the emigrants. Because most European converts had few possessions, the Mormons devised a handcart scheme, greatly reducing the number of oxen and wagons needed as well as the time of passage, and several thousand pulled their goods across the plains and mountains in this manner. From the first, however, Young hoped to redirect the path of such migrations so as to reduce expense and avoid the potential hazards of passage across hostile ground. In the early years almost all European converts came by way of New Orleans (making use of the cotton boats returning from Liverpool) and up the Mississippi to Missouri, Illinois, and Iowa. Young wanted a Pacific route, thinking first of the Colorado River as an entryway, and when explorations revealed how awesomely entrenched and difficult that would be, he sent a party "to select a site for a city or station as a nucleus for a settlement near Cajon Pass." Thus San Bernardino at the western base of that pass in the Los Angeles lowland was initiated in 1851 as a southwest portal to Zion, a subtropical colony, and (as the plat reserving a central block for a temple inferred) an intended focus of Mormon California. The head of the British mission was now instructed to find a way to send converts to Zion by way of San Diego. However, no such facilities were found and no such shipments were ever made. In the 1860s Young again looked to the Colorado River. He directed the Utah territorial delegate to ask Congress to "grant us about two degrees on one side or the other of the river to the Gulf of California . . . [to] give us an outlet on the western ocean as we need." He had a warehouse built at a river landing in Boulder Canyon, but nothing came of these efforts either, and once the Union Pacific project got under way interest in such alternatives ended.

A third portal and passageway became of concern just as Deseret was being defined. Even before Brigham Young could lead the vanguard across the Plains, two other Mormon parties were heading for a western Zion by way of California. One was the Mormon Battalion, recruited by the U.S. Army to serve in the war against Mexico (and approved by the Mormon leadership as a means of currying favor with American officials and getting several hundred men west at government expense). This troop marched to Santa Fe and on to San Diego. Upon discharge most of them went on to northern California en route to eventual reunion with their fellow Saints. The other party was a group of eastern Mormons who had departed New York by ship and arrived in San Francisco Bay in the summer of 1846 to await determination of just where the new Zion would be. In the following year their leader, Samuel Brannan, went overland to meet Brigham Young in Wyoming and try to convince him of the superiority of the San Joaquin (wherein a small settlement had been started) over the Salt Lake Valley for the main Mormon base. Failing to do so, Brannan returned in disgust to California (and in 1848 achieved his chief fame as the man who first shouted in the streets of San Francisco news of the gold discovery). The men working with John Marshall, who first found flecks of gold in Sutter's millrace, were Mormons awaiting travel weather across the mountains. The lure of Zion proved more powerful than that of gold for most of these sojourners, but the great overland surge to the goldfields suddenly magnified the importance of Carson Valley at the eastern base of the Sierra Nevada. A few Mormon traders set up in business there at what became known as Mormon Station, and in 1854 the Utah legislature organized Carson County, in part to fend off petitions from rival traders and settlers for annexation to California. In the following year Young sent sixty or so families to try to fix a firmer hold on this strategic margin of Deseret.

4. *Contiguous Expansion.* Even more compelling than staking out a capacious perimeter was the need to create a continually expanding, thoroughly Mormon region. The general strategy was to work outward from the Salt Lake Valley nucleus, successively occupying every habitable area, that is to say, wherever there was an appropriate combination of arable land, adequate water, long-enough growing season, and adjacent natural grazing lands. Beyond the almost continuous strip along the base of the Wasatch Mountains, such land was found in many smaller areas separated from one another by ridges, canyons, or stretches of barren country. In general the sequence of colonization was one of extension southward beyond Utah Valley along the front of the high plateaus; thence into a tier of valleys a thousand feet higher within the Wasatch Mountains and Plateau; then to a wider scattering of even higher backvalleys, and beyond the eastern margins of this highland mass into a thin scattering of isolated patches of habitable ground within the deeply sculptured canyonlands, as well as westward across wide expanses of desert to a few meagerly watered ranch sites along the base of the meridional ranges of the Great Basin.

5. *Extension into Outlying Areas.* By the early 1870s the Mormons were running out of land in their mountain stronghold. Brigham Young became much concerned about reaching beyond the girdling wastelands and establishing a line of Mormon footholds in areas that were still thinly populated by Indians, ranchers, and traders. He sent scouting parties across the canyonlands and beyond the Hopi villages and Navaho country deep into Arizona Territory, called colonists to take root in the Little Colorado area along the rim of the highlands, sent others on to the Salt River and the San Pedro far below that rugged edge, and talked of extensions deep into Mexico. All these colonies and a number of offshoots from them were very limited footholds in difficult country. Such lands usually had to be purchased rather than merely taken, because they were in the midst of Gentile ranching and mining country, and as railroads and land syndicates began to accelerate developments the dwindling number of Mormon colonists and available resources left them unable to compete for dominance of major districts. In the late 1880s, seeking a refuge for its leaders beyond the reach of federal marshals, the church purchased lands just across

the border in Chihuahua and Sonora—the last feeble extension of this long southward thrust.

Much of the strong southward bias of this outreach seems to have been the result of Young's prejudice against lands to the north. He made only one extended trip in that direction and was not favorably impressed. Mountain-girded Cache Valley (Logan area) had proved to be rather frosty, and he assumed (erroneously) that winters would be colder and the growing season shorter farther north. Furthermore, troubles with traders, ranchers, and emigrants along the Oregon Trail would be likely. Thus the Utah boundary approximated the limit of his colonizing interests, and only after his death in 1877 did Mormon land seekers spread quite rapidly up the Bear and Malad river valleys into the upper Snake River country, at first informally, then, as these lands proved to be better than the leadership had expected, with increasing church sponsorship and assistance. Although ranchers and traders had preceded them, Mormon farmers became the principal population, converting this outreach into a further extension of contiguous expansion from the Wasatch Oasis—and causing territorial politics in Idaho to take on a strong anti-Mormon stance. In 1886 the church sent a man from Cache Valley to reconnoiter western Canada for a suitable refuge for the hunted leaders of the northern settlements. After examining several valleys in British Columbia he chose an area along the St. Mary's River in southern Alberta, and a colony was initiated there the next spring, the northern counterpart of the Mexican colonies as refuge and terminus of cordilleran expansion.

6. *Specialized Colonizations.* An early reconnaissance found evidences of iron and coal near the southwestern edge of the high plateaus, and in 1851 the Iron County mission was formed to begin a works at Cedar City. British missionaries were instructed to search out converts familiar with mining and iron making and to send them along with essential equipment as soon as practicable. Some years later similar missions initiated coal or lead mining and smelting in several districts. In most cases these undertakings proved more difficult than anticipated, equipment was inadequate, and the product fell short of the quantity and quality hoped for, but they were important exhibits of the centralized program for the development of essential resources.

A more celebrated and successful colonization was the "Cotton Mission" in the Virgin River Valley 3,000 feet below the settlement at Cedar City. Initiated after the withdrawal from San Bernardino, it was expected to become a subtropical oasis. Young spoke of olives, almonds, figs, grapes, sorghum, tobacco, and cotton as appropriate products and sought colonists skilled in such work. The American Civil War made cotton a major emphasis, and within two years Southern growers and English textile workers were producing bales and cloth and the whole area became known as "Utah's Dixie." Although never fulfilling the hope of clothing all Mormondom in its own product, the venture was a considerable success (a bit was even shipped East and to California to take advantage of high wartime prices) and continued in production for several decades. Sorghum and fruit did well, and the mild winter climate lured Brigham Young into winter residence, making St. George in effect the seasonal capital of the Mormon commonwealth.

7. *Settlement Design.* From very early Joseph Smith directed Mormons to live as a "compact society," and he set forth a "Plat of the City of Zion" that would be influential in the eventual emergence of a regularized settlement pattern featuring populations gathered in farm villages similar in form and spaced out over the habitable area in orderly fashion.

Smith's plat, drawn up as a model for the new Zion in Missouri, was an approximately mile-square grid, with wide streets, a range of larger blocks for church use in the center, and a special orientation of lots block by block; all barns and stables were to be in the outlying agricultural lands. Although unique in some details, the general concept of nucleated residence amidst surrounding farmlands was common in New England and in utopian schemes, while the rectangular plan was of course typical in America. Nor was the City of Zion a rigid model for Mormon settlement, as the plats of Missouri towns and Nauvoo (supervised by Smith) attest. What was important was the adherence to a distinct pattern in the colonization of all Mormondom, a design—best exhibited in Salt Lake City—consisting of a gridiron aligned with the cardinal directions, of unusually large blocks (ten acres) and wide streets, subdivided into large lots (one and a quarter acres each) of alternating orientation and uniform setback of houses, with every street bordered by open ditches of flowing water. Applied to the smallest villages as well as the larger towns, these repetitive plats, soon filled with houses, stables, barns, orchards, gardens, trees, and shrubs, sitting in the midst of open fields and pastures and spaced out along the valley floor of some mountain-girded setting, stamped a characterizing imprint on the landscape of an extensive region of the American West (fig. 19).

Again, as a host of meticulous scholars have made clear, the design and the process were not invariable. Not every settlement was initiated and carried out under the direction of church authorities, but the great majority were, the general pattern was apparent in every valley, and the reasons for it were well understood and appreciated. In the very last stages of Mormon expansion, John Taylor, Young's successor as president of the church, responding to an inquiry from some families in Cache Valley who sought approval to move out of their village and build homes on their farmlands two miles or so away, set forth the authoritative rationale for the policy:

19. A Mormon Temple and Village.

Within a mile or two of the town the irrigated suburbs of Manti break in upon the sage-brush, and the Temple, which has been visible in the distance half the day, grows out from the hills into definite details," reported the English traveler-journalist Phil Robinson in 1882. Although he thought the style of Mormon architecture "heavy and unadorned," when "looked at from the plain, with the stern hills behind it, the edifice is seen to be in thoroughly artistic harmony with the scene, while the enormous expenditure of labor upon its erection is a matter for astonishment." And he found the town to be "pretty, well-ordered and prosperous." "The abundance of trees, the width of the streets, the perpetual presence of running water, the frequency and size of the orchards, and the general appearance of simple, rustic, comfort impart to Manti all the characteristic charm of the Mormon settlements"—all of which this photograph, taken about twenty years later, fully confirms. (Courtesy Utah State Historical Society)

In all cases in making new settlements the Saints should be advised to gather together in villages as has been our custom from the time of our earliest settlement in these mountain valleys. The advantages of this plan, instead of carelessly scattering out over a wide extent of country, are many and obvious to all those who have a desire to serve the Lord.

By this means the people can retain their ecclesiastical organizations, have regular meetings of the quorums of the priesthood, and establish and maintain day and Sunday schools, Improvement Associations, and Relief Societies. They can also cooperate for the good of all in financial and secular matters, in making ditches, fencing fields, building bridges, and other necessary improvements.

Further than this they are a mutual protection and a source of strength against horse and cattle thieves, land jumpers, etc., and against hostile Indians, should there be any; while their compact organization gives them many advantages of a social and civic character which might be lost, misapplied or frittered away by spreading out so thinly that inter-communication is difficult, dangerous, inconvenient and expensive.

That it allowed the local bishop and supervising elders to keep all under surveillance and for shepherd and flock together to pressure individual members into conformity went without saying.

8. *Allocation of Land.* On the second day in Salt Lake Valley, Brigham Young declared: "No man can buy land here, for no one has any land to sell. But every man shall have his land measured out to him, which he must cultivate in order to keep it. Besides, there shall be no private ownership of the streams that come out of the canyons, nor the timber that grows on the hills. These belong to the people: all the people." Such principles of community and stewardship were prominent throughout the colonization period. There was an intent to allocate land equitably, if not equally; church leaders usually received larger amounts (but they usually had larger families because polygamy was virtually an obligation for them), specific town and farm lots were distributed by lottery, mill sites were granted to those who would put them to community use. Family-sized holdings, productive use, and cooperative labor for the general good were esteemed, speculation and profiteering strongly discouraged. Nevertheless, although a fuller village communism remained a professed ideal and the object of several experiments (especially the United Order—a kind of Mormon kibbutzim), there was an easing of such pressures and increasing differentiation. Private "canyon grants" allowed tolls to be charged for the use of roads, bridges, timber, and Young and other leaders acquired extensive estates, although it was not always clear what was privately held and what was in some degree church property.

9. *Church Support of Facilities and Services.* In addition to those colonizations undertaken to provide supplies of basic goods, such as coal, iron, lead, and cotton, the church fostered the construction of woolen mills, a silk mill, a sugar mill (a famous first American attempt—a failure—to extract sugar from beets); established the *Deseret News*, the Bank of Deseret, and ZCMI, a mercantile chain store; and built roads, telegraph lines, and railroads. Some of these facilities became corporations, but their initiation was made possible by a strongly promoted policy of tithing by the church membership. Such monies also sustained the building of

temples, tabernacles, and other edifices, which were often initiated as public-works projects in times of labor surplus from large immigrations.

THE MORMON NATION

"While other millennialists set a time, the Mormons appointed a place," and in the process of finding that place they "became a genuine people, a covenant folk like ancient Israel with a shared history and at last a homeland. In so doing they had moved," William Mulder went on to say, "from near-sect to near-nation." Whereas most Americans tended to sit lightly upon the land, ready to sell out and move on at the slightest opportunity—as the many streams of migrants filling up all the other regions of the West well displayed—the Mormons took firm root; for them it was the end of a search, a culmination, and July 24, Pioneer Day, commemorating their entry into the Promised Land became the principal Mormon holiday and the annual occasion for celebrating—and elaborating—their official mythology of Exodus and Triumph. Thus the region they created took on a human geographic quality quite unlike anything in surrounding areas. It was a homeland in a more profound sense, with a unity, homogeneity, order, and self-consciousness not to be found in any other region in the United States (rivaled, if at all, only by that other peculiar nation of North America along the lower St. Lawrence).

The geographic creation of that homeland was in a profound sense a process of withdrawal. For nearly forty years not only had "Saints from across the world traveled through the wilderness to the valleys of the intermountain region," that process "was renewed and perpetuated . . . in the village system of colonizing. The exodus from the world as well as the arrival in the new Zion were ritualized by sending colonies . . . to establish upwards of five hundred villages by 1890." Their very choice of the kind of country in which to settle further differentiated them from other pioneers. The Mormons became America's main exhibit of an irrigation society, a system and a success entirely of their own making. If not admired as a society, they were nonetheless widely respected for having domesticated such an unpromising land and creating a commonwealth subsistence for an ever-growing flock. To proclaim Zion and to press for the Gathering of the Saints to such a land was surely a bold move, full of risk—an act of faith. It meant an intensive search for every acre of habitable ground and eventually pressure upon and penetration of borderlands to try to enlarge the perimeter—the capacity—of Zion.

Forty years of such search and pressure had carved out an elongated mountain and valley homeland for some 170,000 Mormons, stretching more than 600 miles from the upper Snake River to the lower Virgin (fig. 20). Much of that growth in numbers had come from European converts, for the British and Scandinavian missions had reaped a harvest unrivaled in America. When the vanguard of Saints

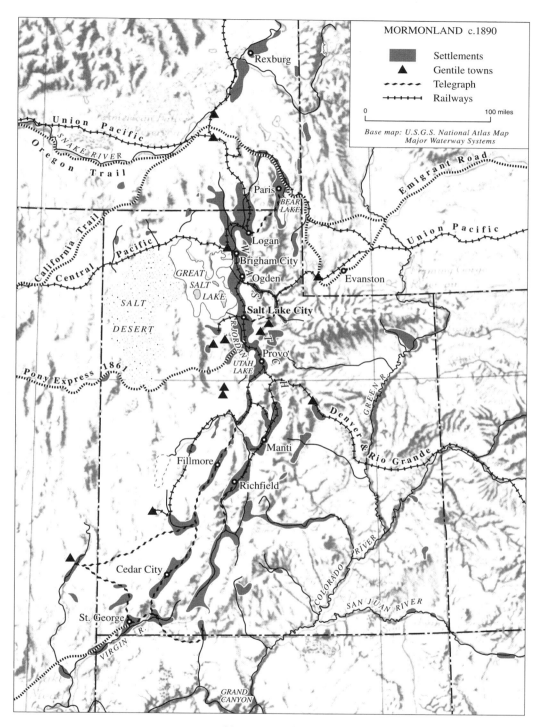

MORMONLAND c.1890

	Settlements
▲	Gentile towns
∿∿∿	Telegraph
┼┼┼	Railways

0   100 miles

Base map: U.S.G.S. National Atlas Map
Major Waterway Systems

Rexburg

Union Pacific

Oregon Trail

SNAKE RIVER

Union Pacific

Emigrant Road

California Trail

Central Pacific

Paris

BEAR LAKE

Logan

Brigham City

GREAT SALT LAKE

Ogden

Evanston

SALT DESERT

Salt Lake City

R. JORDAN

UTAH LAKE

Provo

Pony Express 1861

GREEN R.

Denver & Rio Grande

Fillmore

Manti

Richfield

COLORADO RIVER

Cedar City

San Juan River

St. George

VIRGIN R.

GRAND CANYON

20. Mormonland.

was taking root in the Great Basin there were actually more Mormons in England than in America, and over the next forty years more than 50,000, along with another 30,000 from Scandinavia, emigrated to Utah. The Mormon birth rate has always been high, with the emphasis on large families augmented by half a century of sanctioned polygamy. If the initiation of that "most famous of all Mormon peculiarities" might be understood as a logical part of Joseph Smith's "recapitulation" of ancient Israel precedents, Nels Anderson's assertion about Smith's successor's views has geographic pertinence: "there was no mistaking the reason for polygamy under Brigham Young. It was for the purpose of producing children"; it "was essentially a political expedient for speeding the rapid growth of Zion." The proportion of the population living in such families remains uncertain, but it was certainly high in some places. Because it was practiced largely by the leadership (who were under pressure to do so and could better afford it) the whole Mormon hierarchy was in large degree "a huge extended family, closely connected by blood and marriage."

That huge family was nurtured and disciplined by a highly organized patriarchy operating through a geographical hierarchy of central places. Such a system of places, evolving with the early church, was regularized by Brigham Young in his last years. The basic unit was the *ward* (equivalent of a Catholic parish); a group of wards formed a *stake* (from Smith's metaphor of "the church as a gigantic tent supported by stakes"); beyond this was an informal regional level created by the assignment of leaders to oversee church affairs from a set of larger places: Provo, Fillmore, Cedar City, St. George, Manti, and Richfield to the south, and Ogden, Brigham City, Logan, Paris, and (soon thereafter) Rexburg to the north. Incipient was a more specialized regional scale of temple districts: St. George (dedicated 1877), Manti (1888), Salt Lake City (1893), and Logan (1884). The whole system was anchored on Temple Square, the focal point and seat of power for all Mormondom. The life of the church pulsated through this hierarchy to the farthest reaches of Zion. Brigham Young not only sat as the great patriarch and kept a close eye on all activities, he "regarded it as part of his responsibility to visit each Mormon settlement in Utah at least once a year." Such tours, in spring to the northern settlements, in the fall to the southern, sometimes became large processions, the benevolent king inspecting, counseling, exhorting, and selecting new leaders, sites, and activities. Throughout the year messages and persons assigned to particular tasks moved through the system, and twice a year, just before planting and just after harvest, delegates and members from every ward and stake gathered in the great tabernacle in Salt Lake City for a week-long conference to hear the words of their leaders and to endorse the programs of the church.

Immigrants flowing into Salt Lake City were redistributed to the hinterland and bound into the community. Foreign converts were assimilated rapidly, for, as

Mulder noted, "the break with the Old World was a compound fracture: a break with the old church and with the old country . . . [and] the kingdom was interested in unifying the brotherhood, not in perpetuating backward-glancing cultural differences." Every ward had its school, literacy was high, and the church poured out an increasing volume of literature, all geared to what Brigham Young stated was the main purpose and his greatest satisfaction: welding a great variety of people "into one harmonious whole, one in faith and in practice." One of the more extreme examples of Young's projects—and a rare failure—was the Deseret Alphabet, a completely new orthography of thirty-eight symbols for English phonetics to be used for children's books so as to shield them in their formative years from bad literature. It failed to generate much interest and little was accomplished (two primers and the Book of Mormon were published), but it was a telling illustration of the separateness and defensiveness that permeated Mormon society.

In the early 1880s, Phil Robinson, an English journalist sojourning among the Mormons, was struck by many "points of resemblance" with another withdrawn, self-conscious, and defensive people: the Boers of South Africa. It was at the time (after Kimberley but just before the gold rush to the Rand) an analogy obvious to such a widely traveled reporter, and useful—within limits—to the modern student of the shaping of nations. Following the British takeover of Cape Province from the Dutch (formalized in 1814), the Boers had felt their way of life increasingly threatened and in 1837 began their Great Trek into the thinly occupied interior. Their ponderous ox-wagon trains toiled up the Great Escarpment and spread ever deeper into the continent, one branch curving off that rugged edge southeastward down into Natal (like the Mormons into Arizona); their spacious, rectangular little villages—focused on a church, parsonage, and few trading stores, embowered in orchards and gardens—soon studded the vast dry expanses of the High Veld (far more widely spaced than those of the Mormons for they were pastoralists rather than peasants). Having outrun effective alien control, they formed their own republics (eventually consolidated into two, Orange Free State and Transvaal), memorialized their sufferings and accomplishments, and emerged into Afrikaner nationhood. The great difference, of course, was the absence of a single authority to lead and control the shaping of the nation; there was also the absence of any system of bringing new members to the fold (and the Mormons rapidly surpassed them in number), but the large Boer family and interlocking networks of families were closely akin to their American counterpart.

In the last decades of the century this analogy was to be extended in the renewed intrusions of outside peoples, a reencounter with overpowering authority, and an enforced conformity. For, as Jan Shipps has put it, in their "re-capitulation of the Hebrew-Christian story," the Mormons "built what was in effect, a nation-state that was internally powerful and externally respected as strong enough to be dangerous, even dangerous to the government itself."

INTRUSION AND INCORPORATION

Robinson had also found what had become apparent to every traveler: the City of the Saints was in fact "a City of Two Peoples between whom there is a bitterness of animosity." It was the great irony of Mormon history that within two years of settling into their remote refuge they suddenly found themselves astride the main transcontinental trafficway of the nation.

The thousands of travelers hastening to the California goldfields were an opportunity as well as an intrusion. They needed supplies and services and they had money and goods—especially livestock—to pay for them, and the wealth derived from such exchanges may have been critical to Mormon survival and certainly gave a surge to development during these formative years. But of course some people came and stayed, and the old tensions reappeared in the very heart of the secluded society. Salt Lake City became the principal supply and service center between the Missouri and California. Missouri traders brought in wagon loads of goods to peddle; merchants, traders, craftsmen, Mormon as well as Gentile, set up in business; in the 1860s the Pony Express, then the overland telegraph, came through, and Brigham Young tried his best to get the transcontinental railroad to do likewise. Although he failed to lure them to his capital, he took construction contracts for much of the line through Utah, accepting part payment in supplies and equipment so that he could quickly complete a railroad connection with Ogden. Young worked with the railroads because he knew there was no way of avoiding such a radical intrusion, but he sought ways of blunting its impact, not only by providing good Mormon construction crews but by forming Zion's Cooperative Mercantile Institution as a means of serving all Mormon communities and shielding them from the corrupting—and enticing—influence of Gentile merchants.

Inevitably the presence and power of the Gentiles continued to grow. Ogden was the first city in Utah to elect a Gentile mayor, and its dual character was notorious: "The railroad traveller gets a very wrong impression of Ogden. He sees nothing but the Gentile part of town, the stations of the U.P. and C.P. Railroads, their offices and engine houses, and a dozen or two shanties occupied as restaurants, grog shops and gambling houses." The facilities listed were actually of minor significance, to be found in other railroad towns that sprang up along the routes across Mormon country, such as Corinne, Pocatello, Helper, and Winslow. More important were the large mercantile establishments, industrial plants, freighting companies, and much more in Ogden and Salt Lake City. The continued expansion of this pair of commercial centers was more the result of developments in their hinterlands than in transcontinental traffic. Mining rushes, first in Nevada and Montana and eventually in dozens of districts throughout this Far West interior, provided the main stimulus. Mining camps, towns of a kind utterly alien to the bucolic Mormon scene, began appearing in Utah itself in the 1860s, first at Stockton where the officer in charge of a military encampment encouraged his troops to comb the hills for gold and silver and, after the arrival of the railroad, in districts around the fringes of the Wasatch Oasis, such as Mercur-Eureka-Tintic, Bingham Canyon, Alta, and Park City. Heavy freighting, mills and smelters, and repair shops were routine accompaniments in the mountains; industrial supply houses, banks, and a stock exchange in the local metropolis. It was primarily these smoking, volatile, ramshackle camps that injected into the Mormon region an unprecedented, unassimilable variety: Roman Catholics, Orthodox, Protestants, Anglicans, Jews; Irish and Italians, Greeks and Slavs, Portuguese, Mexicans, Chinese. Insofar as these were separate settlements in the mountains, conflicts with local Mormons were minimized and a mutually profitable trade might ensue, but in the larger service centers Mormon-Gentile antagonisms were magnified, sustained by rival newspapers, political parties, and social institutions—and by small but vociferous groups of Mormon apostates.

Ever since the formation of Utah Territory the federal government had been the principal instrument of opposition to Mormon power and pretension. Federal appointees sent to Utah, finding themselves helpless to assert their authority in opposition to monolithic Mormonism, generated a stream of accusations about this dictatorial and seditious society. Inflamed by polygamy (openly declared as a church doctrine only in 1852) and entangled at the national level with slavery and partisan politics, such incriminations led—without any investigation or notification—in 1857 to the dispatch of a federal army to suppress a supposed rebellion in Utah. Upon hearing of this, Brigham Young issued a broadside to his people—"We are invaded by a hostile force who are evidently assailing us to accomplish our overthrow and destruction"—and prepared to resist in their mountain fastness. He called in all missionaries and outposts (he had already ordered a withdrawal from San Bernardino, considering it a beleaguered and troubled colony—though some members refused and stayed in California), and he oversaw the orderly evacuation of all northern settlements—some 35,000 people—to Utah Valley and southward. Mormon militia were sent to harass the approaching enemy (but "take no life"), and Young was prepared to put the torch to vacated Salt Lake City if necessary. However, as the army neared Utah (and after the Mormons had burned some of its supply trains) mediators worked out an agreement that Young would give up the governorship and the army would not occupy the capital but take up residence on the edge of the desert fifty miles to the southwest. Although this new accommodation momentarily stabilized practical relationships (as Young later remarked about his successor: "I believe that Governor Cummings came to the conclusion that he was Governor of the Territory as domain; but Brigham Young was Governor of the people"), it was deeply resented by the Mormons as an army of occupation.

These federal troops were withdrawn after the outbreak of war in 1861, but a year later a company of California infantry under Colonel Patrick E. Connor was sent in to guard the overland route. Connor reacted to what he regarded as Young's despotic rule by establishing Fort Douglas on a high terrace overlooking the capital city, its guns trained on Temple Square. He also supported an opposition news-paper, encouraged prospectors, and generally sought to subordinate this stubborn people. Like Thomas Jefferson in response to newly acquired French Louisiana, Colonel Connor had a favored solution for the problem: "My policy in this Terri-tory has been to invite a large Gentile and loyal population, sufficient by peaceful means and through the ballot-box to overwhelm the Mormons by mere force of numbers, and thus wrest from the church—disloyal and traitorous to the core—the absolute and tyrannical control of temporal and civic affairs, or at least a population numerous enough to put a check on Mormon affairs." However, whereas Jefferson thereby created a large Louisiana Territory to accommodate the anticipated influx, Congress, responding to the pleas of non-Mormon residents beyond the actual Mormon region, repeatedly reduced the broad bounds of Utah Territory, first carving out Colorado and Nevada on either side (Nevada in response to the surge of Californians to the Comstock Lode and Carson Valley), and, as the mining population spread eastward with new discoveries, enlarging Nevada with successive bands taken from Utah Territory (see fig. 18).

None of these reductions actually impinged upon the body of contiguous Mor-mon settlement, but there were attempts to do so. An 1861 bill in Congress proposed an extinction of Utah, dividing it along 113°W between Nevada and a proposed Jeffersonia (Colorado); in 1869 the chairman of the Committee on the Territories stated his wish "to blot out the Territory" as a step toward disposing of "the Mormon question," and his committee brought out a bill drastically reducing Utah so "that they shall not have territorial area enough left to make a State." Such proposals were attempts to accomplish by a gigantic gerrymandering what Congress could not muster the votes to do directly: an effective prohibition of polygamy. The extinction of Utah was avoided, but anti-Mormon agitation became intensified nationally into a moral crusade culminating in the Edmunds-Tucker Act of 1887. "One of the most far-reaching pieces of federal legislation ever passed in peacetime history," it gave unprecedented power to federal marshals to hunt down and arrest polygamists, vested complete control over voter qualifications in an appointed commission, and "dissolved the Church of Jesus Christ of Latter Day Saints as an incorporated body, placing its assets in the hands of a receiver."

In the face of such crippling measures, the aged president of the church, Wilford Woodruff, "undertook a psychic and physical journey which marked the end of one phase of Mormon history and ushered in the transition to a second." He traveled 2,400 miles throughout Mormonland and to California to assess the situation and hear from his people. Upon his return, concluding that "I am in the necessity of acting for the Temporal Salvation of the Church," in September 1890 he issued a "Manifesto" (subsequently unanimously endorsed by the church in conference) to give up the practice of plural marriage and to adhere to the laws of the United States. In spite of a good deal of skepticism and uncertainty, once that inflammatory issue had been resolved, the way to statehood was relatively easy. Former polygamists were granted amnesty and church property was restored; Utahans created a tax-supported secular school system, drew up an acceptable constitution, and in 1896 Utah at last became a full and equal member of the federal union.

Polygamy was far from being the whole—perhaps not even the central—problem in this long, rancorous relationship. Many Americans, near or far, didn't much care how the Mormons formed and ran their families, but influential people in Utah and elsewhere did care how they ran their sociopolitical system. For them, the real enemy was theocracy, the refusal to separate church and state and to establish the common American secular political pattern, with two parties, civil courts, public schools, and the like. "It was easy for prominent politicians in both national political parties to picture the territory as some kind of alien intrusion on the national polity and the majority of its people as *sub*-American if not actually *un*-American." In their enforcing of cultural and political conformity anti-Mormon legislators readily called upon the motives and means they had applied to Reconstruction in the South (not surprisingly, Southern congressmen strongly opposed the Edmunds-Tucker Act). In its capitulation the church was forced not only to give up polygamy but to "take on the political status of a client state." Thus the great creative questing phase of Mormonism, its recapitulation of the ancient sacred task of building the Kingdom of God on earth, was brought to a close: "With Zion and Babylon come to terms, that past was filled up. Complete." The challenge of coexistence now had to be squarely faced (just as the Afrikaners of Transvaal were about to find, with a suddenly emergent Johannesburg in their midst and an encompassing British authority forced upon them).

"We have come here to stay," a prominent apostle of the church assured his audience in 1891, "I do not see how we are going to be ousted. We are going to take root on the tops of these mountains and spread out." And indeed they had already taken root and spread out and would surely not be ousted. But the conditions and prospects had surely changed as well. A period of great growth and expansion was over. Mormon families might continue to be large and missionary efforts continue unabated, but the number of converts was much reduced. Moreover, the summons to Zion, heretofore virtually a command, was much subdued: "Respecting the gathering, the elders should explain the principle when occasion requires; but acting upon it should be left entirely to the individual." As Mulder notes, this 1891 statement marked "a startling transition from the days when the clarion call was to redeem the faithful and bring them singing to Zion. It was a day of pruning—the Saints were welcome, but at their own risk." The risks were primarily economic, for there was little land left to allocate in Zion and many parts of rural Mormondom were sliding into ever-deeper poverty from local population pressures, land deterioration, and lack of capital. (As the federal government began to undertake major irrigation projects, the serious relative deficiencies of the necessarily small-scale, incremental, Mormon pioneer development of water resources as compared with more comprehensive basinwide schemes became ever more apparent.) Yet the Utah economy was expanding in other ways under the initiatives of both its peoples. In the early 1880s the church abandoned its formal boycott of Gentile merchants, and the formation in 1887 of a Chamber of Commerce and Board of Trade that included both Mormons and Gentiles marked an "important indication of change in the character of the leadership in Salt Lake City" (and similarly in Ogden). Mormon entrepreneurs and workers began to range out over the West to compete for jobs in construction, mining, forestry, and transport, and the church itself fostered new commercial businesses.

In 1900 Salt Lake City was a commercial center of 54,000 and together with Ogden (16,000) accounted for a quarter of the population of the new state. Both of these centers were dual cities wherein the Gentiles competed in numbers, organization, and institutions as well as in business. By the time the massive, many-pinnacled temple—forty years abuilding—was finally dedicated in April 1893, the spires of many rival churches punctuated the landscape of the embowered capital. Temple Square, with its adjacent clusters of church offices and businesses, remained the great focus of the Mormon region, but a recognizable Gentile cluster of shops, banks, offices, and institutions filled out the downtown, while Gentile residences, together with their churches, schools, clubs, and hospitals, spread south and east to the nearest benchlands. Beyond, on the higher terrace, stood Fort Douglas, symbol now not just of the federal presence but of federal dominance, confirming Salt Lake City as the nexus of nation and subnation, of American culture and a subordinated regional culture.

Mormon nationalism had passed through several phases. From 1847 onward it was at first overtly separatist, seeking isolation and cultural integrity with the least possible affiliation with the United States, and welcoming independence should that fragile federal union fail. When that possibility ended in 1865 Mormon petitions for statehood were, as before, a means of maximizing local autonomy, "to join the United States in order to be free from it," as Leonard Arrington notes, referring to Brigham Young's forthright statement shortly before his death: "All we care about is for them to let us alone, to keep away their trash and officers so far as possible, to give us our admission into the Union just as we are, just as we have applied for it as near as may be to let us take care of ourselves, and they can keep their money, their lands and in fact everything which they can."

In standard imperial terms, the Mormons sought to be an *indigenous state,* and with Brigham Young as governor they were essentially that, a "native state" left largely undisturbed in its ways of life so long as it did not interfere with the larger interests of the empire. But the imperial agents sent to monitor the situation warned that it was indeed a threat to those larger interests—with respect to political systems and the moral basis of society—and so the United States insisted on Utah becoming a territory under *direct rule,* conforming with the laws and courts, the political and social practices of the ruling power. The disavowal of polygamy and admission to statehood marked the end of that process of enforced conformity but did not efface all vestiges of an imperial relationship. Fort Douglas remained in its commanding position, and the Mormons undertook new measures to reinforce their cultural integrity and separation, especially in the founding of many church academies to counter the secular school system. More important and far-reaching, however, was the remarkable change in attitude and image. It was a deliberate move—without further altering any basic theology, doctrine, or practice—to change themselves from "a peculiar people" into "model Americans," that is, into the kind of people Americans were thought once to be and ought to be: God-fearing, family-centered, sober, thrifty, industrious, *patriotic* people. They could undertake such a shift in stance without strain or falsity because they deeply believed that America was the chosen land, Columbus's voyage a divine mission, the American Revolution a divine preparation, the American Constitution an inspired document of freedom. Mormon separation from and resistance to the United States were not against the Constitution, only against those who had perverted it. Thus, on hearing of South Carolina's secession, Brigham Young had commented to his Utah delegate: "While the waves of commotion are overwhelming nearly the whole country, Utah in her rocky fortresses is biding her time to step in and rescue the constitution and aid all lovers of freedom in sustaining such laws as will secure justice and right to all regardless of creed or party." Whether in mountain exile, imperial territory, or statehood, Zion aspired to be the model for America.

6. New Mexico: Hispano, Indian, Anglo

In 1850 New Mexico was a newly captive territory. Real authority rested with an army commander seated in the old Governor's Palace in Santa Fe, symbolically backed by an impressive earthwork fortress hastily built on an adjacent hill and physically asserted by companies of troops stationed in all the main towns. A few local civilians had been appointed to carry out various public duties under an imposed legal code. The status and prospects of all these newly acquired New Mexicans within the suddenly much-enlarged United States remained quite uncertain, as did the actual bounds and extent of this vast territory and just how it was to be fitted into the overall geopolitical framework.

New Mexico had a long history as an imperial province, first of Spain and then of Mexico, but always as an outermost unprofitable and vaguely defined territory. Its general form was obvious enough: a narrow region of agricultural settlements along the Rio Grande, broadening out in the north along the several mountain slopes, with the whole of this well-populated area surrounded by vast reaches of open, dry lands dominated by wide-ranging nomadic tribes and bands that had never succumbed to imperial authority. How to subdue, integrate, and eventually assimilate this distant and different kind of place into the American federation and nation posed new problems for the American empire.

American officers found themselves faced with three very distinct groups of people. The most important were the "Mexicans," from whose officials they had accepted the local surrender of this land and who constituted its main settled population, numbering about 60,000, spread more or less contiguously in small towns, villages, and ranches from just below Socorro on the south to above Taos on the north, with minor extensions fanning up various tributaries and around the southerly margins of the Sangre de Cristo mountains to Villanueva and Las Vegas on the upper waters of the Pecos. Tracing its origins from the early Spanish conquerors, it was more properly seen as a largely indigenous mestizo population derived from generations of mixture of soldiers and colonists with a wide variety of Indian captives, servants, and neighbors; immigration into the region had been negligible for many years. It was a peasant and pastoral society, each locality a network of extended families cultivating their staples of corn, wheat, and beans on their irrigated long lots and running their sheep on the open ranges and mountain pastures, the whole served by a few priests, dominated by a small set of *patróns*, and splintered into various sociopolitical factions.

Embedded within this "Spanish-American" or "Hispano" settlement region (as these people would come to identify themselves or be generally categorized to differentiate them from later Mexican immigrants in this broadened borderland) were the Pueblo Indians, whose compact towns and farmlands had prompted the Spanish to fix their hold upon this distant north two and a half centuries earlier. The sixty-some pueblos of 1600 had been reduced to fewer than twenty, spaced along the Rio Grande Valley from Isleta to Taos, with Laguna and Acoma lying fifty miles west of the river (and not including Zuni and the Hopi villages much farther west and beyond sustained imperial reach). Nearly all of these pueblos had been in place for centuries and had been formally recognized and ostensibly protected by imperial laws. Such insulation had been much eroded over the years with considerable shift of lands to Hispanos, but despite shared problems of defense and mutual advantages of trade, the two societies remained clearly separate. Even the presence of a Catholic church within most of the Indian towns did little to unite them for such an imposition had never succeeded in replacing the kiva and the ancient rituals for most of the Pueblo people. Thus although their numbers had been drastically reduced to no more than six or seven thousand, their cultural integrity remained intact. They cultivated their maize, beans, and squash on communal lands, spoke their native tongues (remarkably diverse among the several clusters of towns), and lived their sharply compartmentalized, autonomous, local lives without major alteration of their customary ways.

In the broader imperial view these Rio Grande settlements seemed a kind of elongated island amidst a restless sea of "wild Indians." These wide-ranging nomads were composed of a somewhat uncertain number of distinct peoples: the Utes of the Southern Rockies; the Kiowas and Comanches, aggressive horse-mounted buffalo hunters dominating the Great Plains from the Arkansas deep into Texas; several bands of Apaches ranging out from desert mountain fastnesses between the Pecos and the Gila; and the Navahos, who had emerged into distinction and prominence as sheepherders of the Western plateaus. Each of these peoples had responded in particular ways to the intrusive Europeans: adopting horses, knives, and guns; participating in trade and extracting government gifts; plundering herds, flocks, and caravans. Relations with the Pueblo Indians and Hispano river settlements were unstable, varying with each group and characterized by periods of routine trade punctuated by raids on livestock and the capture of women and children. Lacking sufficient forces to forestall or punish many of these transgressions, New Mexican governors had recurrently sent emissaries and gifts to these *Indios bárbaros* to negotiate a fragile protection for their vulnerable province.

American officials inherited that challenging task, further compounded by the treaty that committed the United States to protect Mexico from Indian raids across the new boundary. They soon concluded that they must apply an aggressive new strategy, shifting troops from the Hispano towns (where they had been placed to guard against any resistance to American annexation) to the Indian periphery. Accordingly Fort Union was laid out where the Santa Fe Trail approached the mountains near the outer edge of Hispano settlements. This new portal to New Mexico would serve as the main supply base for an increasing number and shifting array of posts, of which Fort Stanton amidst the Mescalero Apaches, Fort Craig on the Rio Grande, Fort Defiance in Navaho country, and Fort Massachusetts (later Fort Garland) guarding the passes in Ute country were among the most important.

But it was also quickly apparent how ill equipped they were and how costly the task would be. As usual, the bitter rivalry between the Bureau of Indian Affairs and the army complicated the matter, with Indian agents deriding the military ("our troops are of no earthly account. They cannot catch a single Indian") and the military disgusted with the whole assignment. In 1852 the colonel in charge declared New Mexico to be a worthless country imposing "a very heavy burden" without "the slightest return" and argued for the withdrawal of all troops and civil officers. "As a conquered people," he went on to say, the Hispanos "feel a natural dislike towards us" and "with regard to their protection from the Indians, they would have the same that was extended to them by the Mexican government—that is to say, permission to defend themselves." Secretary of War Charles Conrad was sufficiently impressed that he recommended the United States pay the 61,000 New Mexican settlers to "abandon" their homeland and relocate in some more favorable region. But New Mexico was already a formal part of the American system, and even if, as the colonel had emphasized, "the only resource of this country is the government money" pumped in through the military and other agencies, it was now crossed by southern routes to California and the United States would soon spend $10 million to enlarge it by means of the Gadsden Purchase. Furthermore, no American government was likely to admit defeat in the securing of its national territory. And so expeditions mounted against the Apaches would prove to be but an early phase of a forty-year struggle to get firm imperial control over their new Southwest.

The Treaty of Guadalupe Hidalgo provided that New Mexico should be admitted to the Union "at the proper time (to be judged by the Congress of the United States)." It was generally agreed that the settled population should be accorded some sort of normal American government, but there was deep disagreement as to the form, content, and area to be included. Coming as they did, in the later 1840s, such geopolitical considerations were inevitably enmeshed in the bitter controversies over the extension of slavery and the sectional balance of power in Congress. The New Mexican case was further complicated by the attempted seizure of half its territory and people by an aggressive Texas. The Republic of Texas had claimed the entire course of the Rio Grande as its western boundary and had sent several expeditions toward Santa Fe to enforce its authority. Although these forays were all ignominious failures, Texas leaders never dropped the claim, and in the fluid aftermath of the Mexican War the new State of Texas sent officials to organize counties and judicial districts in all the areas east of the Rio Grande. New Mexicans had long regarded the Texans as enemies and they were soon supported by American officials, who considered New Mexico as a separate area under federal military authority. After being warned by a new president, Millard Fillmore, that any Texan attempt to enforce its claims would be countered by the U.S. Army,

Texas reluctantly agreed (as part of the momentous sectional Compromise of 1850) to be bought out by a congressional indemnity of $10 million for allowing a boundary to be drawn through the empty Llano Estacado along 103°W (fig. 21).

Before this resolution, one group of New Mexicans, encouraged by statements of the then President Zachary Taylor, had called a constitutional convention, submitted the results for public endorsement, and prepared a petition for immediate statehood. Although backed by some influential supporters in Congress, it was vehemently opposed by Texans and most Southerners and was eventually rejected in favor of recognizing New Mexico as a territory (as part of the great compromise). The boundaries proposed in these versions of a new American New Mexico are of geographical interest. The statehood convention confirmed Santa Fe as the capital centered not only within the Hispano area of the upper Rio Grande but within a broad, encircling belt approximating the lands of all those peripheral nomadic Indians who had at least occasional commercial relations with these New Mexican settlements. Given the new scale of territory considered suitable to these thinly

21. Boundaries: Some Proposals and Changes.

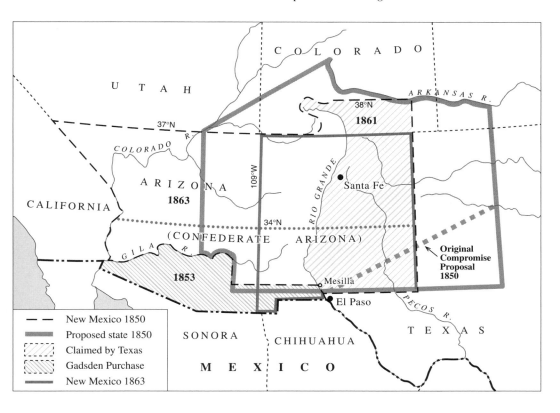

populated mountain and desert lands of the Far West—to say nothing of the gigantic concurrent designs of Deseret or Texas—it was not a grossly inappropriate claim. The original proposal in the congressional compromise for the New Mexico–Texas boundary was not drastically different with respect to that sector; both would have allotted what became the Texas Panhandle to Santa Fe jurisdiction. Of greater significance, however, was the acknowledgment in statehood, territorial, and other proposals of a long, westward-extending promontory giving Texas control over El Paso. The early presence here of Texas militia and successful organization of county government had put them in command of this portion of the new southern route to California already well trodden by Texas emigrants, and their hold was never seriously challenged. The Territory of New Mexico ultimately created by Congress was anchored on Santa Fe and contained all the land south of Utah (created at the same time) between Texas and California. The one anomaly in this simple geometry was a jog in the northern boundary to follow the crest of "the Sierra Madre" (interpreted, with some uncertainty, as the Continental Divide) northward to 38° so as to include the uppermost Rio Grande basin within a New Mexico vitally dependent on its waters.

With the annexation of New Mexico, the Hispanos had been abruptly altered in status from local rulers to distant subjects. Nevertheless they remained, for the time being at least, essential partners in the running of the territory, for the Americans, aside from the military, numbered no more than a few hundred and there seemed to be little immediate prospect of attracting a great many more. As in many an imperial case, the change of flag was not quite as abrupt or radical as it might seem. New Mexico had been penetrated and softened up all through the Mexican era. The occupying army had marched from Missouri over a well-rutted trafficway and negotiated its entry and taken control with the help of Anglo intermediaries long resident and influential in the local society. An Anglo-Hispano merchant partnership was already well established and would thrive on the large infusion of government expenditures and the growing traffic to California, and the great reinforcement of commercial ties with Missouri and the Eastern states would far offset any severance from Chihuahua and Mexico. Political movements reflected the same kind of practical ethnic combinations. Only a few northern New Mexicans fled the transfer of authority (although a considerable proportion in the El Paso district did so), and the various factions supporting statehood or territorial status contained many Hispano *ricos* whose families had dominated local and provincial politics for generations. Much of the business of the territorial legislature was conducted in Spanish (and in 1853 New Mexico elected a delegate to Congress who spoke no English). Party politics was not aligned with ethnicity because all Anglo leaders needed Hispano votes, yet it was far from an equal partnership, for Anglos controlled the key appointments and critical relations with federal authorities and of course were skilled in American law and political practice.

This imbalance in actual power was blatantly apparent in day-to-day imperial relations. Army officers and troops displayed the usual arrogance and roughness of occupying forces, and almost all American officials and observers expressed a deep-rooted prejudice against these provincial Mexicans. Anglos saw themselves charged with bringing civilization and enlightenment to a primitive and indolent people. It was generally agreed, as William Davis, a Massachusetts Yankee who served several years as U.S. attorney (and later acting governor), put it, that there was need to work for "the regeneration of the people of New Mexico, morally, socially, religiously."

Unlike some others, Davis was heartened by changes he had observed after only a few years of American rule. In the penultimate paragraph of *El Gringo*, his well-known book on New Mexico published in 1857, Davis responded to his own question about "whether the native Mexicans have been benefited by . . . having our institutions extended over them":

> I believe they have been improved in both a social and political point of view. They live under certain and written laws, and are protected in the enjoyment of all their rights instead of trusting to the caprice of an irresponsible individual as before. There is a decided improvement in the style of dress and mode of living; they wear a greater quantity of American goods, and tea, coffee, and sugar are becoming more common in use among the peasantry. Many are dispensing with the *serape* (blanket) as an every-day garment, and are wearing coats instead; and buckskin is giving way to woolen and cotton goods, and moccasins to leather shoes. There is also an improvement in the mode of building, and their houses are made more comfortable than before.

This last point referred to the use of adobe. Few things in this strange landscape seemed so foreign and contemptible to Americans; as General William Tecumseh Sherman said in a parting shot to New Mexicans in 1880: "I hope ten years hence there won't be an adobe house in the Territory. I want to see you learn to make them of brick, with slanting roofs. Yankees don't like flat roofs, nor roofs of dirt." Such were the relentless, pitiless pressures of American imperialism. Captive peoples could not be allowed to remain as they were; they must be made over into proper, progressive Americans, not just in allegiance, laws, and language but in dress and diet, in tools and trades ("you must get rid of your burros and goats," said Sherman), in habits and habitations, if they were ever to become "respectable citizens."

Moreover, American officials and their Anglo cohort were not the only agents working directly for cultural change. Upon the cession of the Mexican territories the Roman Catholic leadership in the United States petitioned the Holy See to transfer these areas to their jurisdiction. Accordingly New Mexico was taken from the bishop of Durango and placed in charge of a new vicar apostolic sent out from Baltimore. Jean Baptiste Lamy, a French priest recruited some years earlier to work in the Ohio Valley, arrived in Santa Fe in 1851 and was appalled by what he saw. The secularization accompanying the Mexican Revolution, together with the isolation and poverty of this frontier province, had taken a heavy toll. There were a mere ten priests to serve more than seventy places of worship, and the whole system seemed enfeebled and corrupted. Thus Lamy, who was soon made bishop of a newly created Diocese of Santa Fe, began a program of comprehensive and drastic reform, bringing in priests from his native land to replace local Hispanic incumbents and expanding facilities and services. Fifteen years later there were about fifty priests (nearly all Frenchmen), 135 churches and missions, and the usual complement of convents, schools, academies, a hospital, and an orphanage (and shortly thereafter a college and new cathedral). Although the Hispanic priests regarded him as a foreign usurper (he excommunicated several of them) and a tyrant (he attempted to suppress the Penitentes, a local New Mexican cult derived from older Spanish mystic brotherhoods), their local support was eroded by the obvious reinvigoration and expansion of valued services (all these new priests were required to learn Spanish and English). Thus by 1875, when he was made archbishop of the metropolitan see of Santa Fe (with suffragan bishops serving in Tucson and Denver), John B. Lamy had gained the high respect of Anglo and Hispano alike, and, with a kind of double irony, his Roman Catholic church (so deeply distrusted as a foreign presence by many in the Eastern states) had, through its own kind of modernization (so deeply opposed to the secular modernization sweeping the Western world), become a major instrument of Americanization throughout this Southwest.

The Hispano population may have been captive but they were not confined. Indeed, this early American era is a time of major geographic expansion, continuing an outward movement that had been gathering momentum during the Mexican era. It was powered by a search for pastures, water, and patches of arable ground, made possible by the gradual curbing and confining of the nomadic Indians, and eventually halted by running head-on into other settlers seeking the same resources. It was a centrifugal movement from the historic settlement core along the Rio Grande: broadly eastward across the mesas and shallow cutlands of the upper Pecos and Canadian rivers; northward along the flanks of the Sangre de Cristo and far into the San Luis Valley; northwestward up the Chama and across the divide into the upper San Juan; more narrowly westward from Albuquerque and Socorro, skirting the lava fields and dry plains to the rimland sources of the Little Colorado and the Gila; and very selectively southward across the deserts to a scattering of footholds in the Rio Mimbres and the Rio Ruidoso countries (fig. 22). As a result of this spontaneous unspectacular folk movement an indelible cultural stamp was imprinted upon the life and landscape of a broad area of the Southwest reaching from Tascosa in the Texas Panhandle westward into Arizona, and from outposts toward the southern margins of New Mexico (the Mesilla Valley was a Mexican era colonization from the El Paso oasis) northward well into Colorado (thus approximating the political bounds of the proposed State of New Mexico of 1850). This newer imprint was a thin scattering of *placitas,* little family clusters of simple adobe or stone houses amidst a rough nest of brush or pole corrals anchored on a patch of irrigable ground and winter shelter in some little valley, *rincón,* or shallow canyon, from where they ranged their flocks seasonally over the wide plains, mesas, or foothill and mountain pastures. No real commercial towns had been founded; links were maintained with older settlements through itinerant traders and family travel. Their hold on the land was discontinuous and unsubstantial, leaving them vulnerable to title challenges and competitive colonists. By the 1870s these were in strong force on all fronts: land grant speculators, Texas cattlemen, Colorado ranchers, Mormon farmers, California stockmen. The vanguard of Hispano shepherds was often repelled or pushed onto the poorer lands and their settlements soon enclaved within Anglo cattle country. With the arrival of the railroads this pattern of encirclement was followed by heavier selective penetrations of this much-enlarged but thinly spread Hispano homeland.

Although the shepherd and the cowboy were usually moving in upon apparently empty country, they were occupying the former hunting-and-gathering grounds, villages, and campsites of the nomadic peoples. The defeat and displacement of these several Indian groups was sporadic and episodic, carried out by federal troops, local militia, irregular forces, and the attrition of innumerable local clashes—an ugly, painful process for both sides and anyone caught in between. Having never been conquered by Mexico these people saw no reason to submit to American rule. They were often quite ready to allow Americans passage through their country and even to set up stations and depots along such routes, but not ready to change their way of life. To halt all raids upon the flocks and herds of traditional enemies would require an unprecedented change in their whole economy (they were particularly puzzled by the American attempt to restrain them from raiding into Mexico, the state that the United States had warred against and displaced). The Americans, having never fathomed the nature of Indian political life, were equally baffled by the maddening inability of the Indians to work together to uphold the treaties they had signed and by their irrational resistance to a settled agricultural life.

The most focused and decisive campaign was that carried out by the U.S. Army (with the help of key Indian allies) against the Navahos. After years of punitive expeditions had failed to halt raiding and defiance (including a massed assault upon

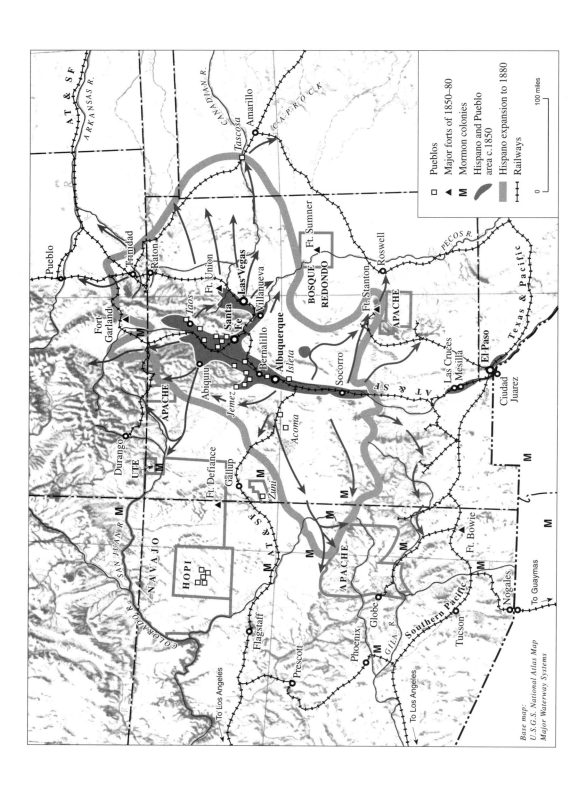

Legend:
- □ Pueblos
- □ Major forts of 1850–80
- ▲ Mormon colonies
- M Hispano and Pueblo area c.1850
- ⬭ Hispano expansion to 1880
- ┼┼┼ Railways

0   100 miles

Base map:
U.S.G.S. National Atlas Map
Major Waterway Systems

Fort Defiance set up in their midst), in 1863 an army force began a systematic campaign to destroy the basis of Navaho subsistence, methodically cutting down their canyon peach orchards (a staple of diet and trade that had been introduced by Pueblo refugees), burning fields, and slaughtering thousands of sheep. At the same time they tried to avoid human bloodshed and offered food rations and other aids to those who would surrender and agree to live under imperial supervision. As a result about 8,000 Navahos were eventually forced and lured into submission and herded to a reservation on the Pecos River 250 miles east of their homeland. There, at Bosque Redondo, the soldiers of Fort Stanton were assigned to assist them with setting up farms and building rectangular adobe houses, while officials devised new "tribal" divisions with designated leaders and tried to teach them the ways of American polity. The Navahos naturally resisted as best they could this forced remaking of themselves. After a year of confinement smallpox had killed a quarter of them, rations were meager (much of it stolen by corrupt officials), and in desperation a designated Navaho spokesman traveled to Washington to plead for permission to return to their homeland. After a special investigation exposed the heavy cost and failure of the policy, the Navahos were allowed to do so in 1868, walking back and receiving small starter flocks and continuing rations as they reestablished themselves within the confines of a newly delimited reservation (which with subsequent additions became much the largest in the United States). However, although the Navahos had resisted this programmed acculturation they were not unchanged; it had been an unprecedented, defining experience: "The memory of the 'Long Walk' to and from Bosque Redondo and of the suffering there stood as a historical incident with as much significance for Navajos as the Civil War, for example, for Americans. Events came to be dated from it, the sense of Navajo identity was heightened by it, and attitudes toward all Anglo-Americans were influenced by it."

A quite different but ultimately even more decisive sequence cleared the Comanches and Kiowas from the High Plains. Long-standing, if somewhat intermittent, trade relations between these people and the Hispanos flourished to new heights during the American Civil War as the Comanches raided almost undeterred deep into Texas, bringing back thousands of head of cattle and horses for exchange with Hispano "Comanchero" traders who came out from Puerto de Luna, Anton Chico, and Las Vegas to the Palo Duro and other camps under the edge of the Caprock. Such raids continued after the war. But the buffalo hunters were rapidly wiping out their basic subsistence, and after many minor clashes, in 1874 a set of converging army forces defeated and forced the remnants of these Comanches and Kiowas onto a reserve in Indian Territory guarded by Fort Sill.

The first Apaches to be challenged and forcibly confined were the Jicarillas, a quite distinct group long in close contact with the Pueblos and Hispanos, who roamed the northern approaches, often in alliance with neighboring Utes. A retaliatory attack on American wagon trains prompted a series of bloody campaigns that finally depleted them to the point of accepting peace, with rations, and eventually a reservation along the Continental Divide just beyond the northwestern margins of Hispano settlement at the time; a band of Utes were given a small reserve just beyond. The Mescalero Apaches of the Sacramento Mountains generally tried to stay clear of American entanglements but became implicated in various clashes and were reduced to submission by a winter campaign that destroyed their subsistence and shelter. Removed to Bosque Redondo, they had chronic quarrels with their fellow captives, the Navahos, and soon fled. Eventually they were confirmed in a Ruidoso reservation under the eye of Fort Stanton.

It was the Southern Apaches who proved the most difficult challenge to imperial management. The term as used by Americans referred to a variable set of related bands—Mimbreños, Chiricahuas, San Carlos, Tontos, and others, to use names conferred by the Spanish—based in the broad belt of rugged country between the Rio Grande and the middle Gila. These peoples had traditionally ranged far to the south (and occasionally to the north and east to the Pueblos) to plunder settlements. For them it was more a symbiotic relationship than warfare: they sought livestock and avoided wanton killings for they had no wish to destroy those who nurtured these vital supplies. For them the Spanish colonization of northern Sonora had simply provided greater and more accessible resources, which they exploited so extensively that by the end of the Mexican period there had been a marked shrinkage in such settlements in this "Apacheria." The Americans became quickly embroiled with these highly flexible, wide-ranging foragers. By drawing an international boundary straight across their homelands and attempting to constrain them from following their traditional patterns of movement they challenged their basic way of life. By creating a new trafficway through their territories, thronged with the overland mail, stagecoaches, freighting caravans, emigrants, and herds of cattle and sheep bound for California, as well as implanting stations, forts, depots, and ranches along the way, the Americans had lavishly augmented the prospects for plunder. The inevitable petty clashes quickly negated treaty agreements and unleashed protracted intermittent warfare that became increasingly brutal as frustrations mounted. By the 1860s a dozen army posts attempted to protect the trafficway and its settlers, and the Bureau of Indian Affairs sought to lure the Apaches with offers of protection, rations, and farms; in the 1870s, declaring this "peace policy" a failure, the army began a series of campaigns to enforce submission, declaring an intention to kill all who refused to settle down on reservations. Fifteen years later about 5,000 had been placed on the San Carlos and Fort Apache reserves in the rugged upper Gila watershed in central Arizona.

As a result of these forty years of "pacification" and enforced settlement these nomadic Indians had been confined to a set of precisely delimited territories in remote and rugged lands least coveted by their conquerors, forming a set of isolated outposts on the perimeter of a greatly expanded Hispano homeland. Meanwhile, the first New Mexico legislature had reconfirmed the Pueblo Indians in their immediate lands and local autonomy, and this was endorsed by later territorial action and courts. Technically they were treated as communities of citizens holding private lands rather than as Indians on reservations, although the Indian Bureau eventually placed agents in each village and provided various services (and Congress refused to recognize their votes in territorial elections). The western pueblos of Zuni and the Hopis remained beyond the reach of any program until the 1880s.

Thus the human geography of the new American Southwest had been extensively reshaped and the status of and relationships among its several peoples considerably redefined. The geopolitical pattern had also been altered, and that, too, involved a good deal of contention, including open warfare, and controversial results. The huge Territory of New Mexico created in 1850 was obviously an expedient certain to be subdivided in some way. Following the Gadsden Purchase, attempts to detach a latitudinal band enclosing the southern corridor between Texas and California got underway in earnest. Local leaders in the Mesilla Valley had never been part of the northern Hispano cliques, and the rest of this southern strip was dominated by Texans interested in land, cattle, and the traffic to California and deeply antagonistic to Santa Fe. There was always some congressional support for such a division, and by 1860 it appeared that a bisection along 33°40′N would be likely. Foundering in the national crisis, that concept was revived by Confederate interests, slightly enlarged northward to 34°N, and, backed by Texas cavalry, a Territory of Arizona was formally recognized as part of the Confederate States of America (see fig. 21). Leaving aside the larger national issues involved, such a boundary made good geographical sense at the time: it cut across the Rio Grande Valley near the southern tip of the main Hispano settlement region, through the rugged, as yet barely explored Mogollon rimlands, and on across empty desert to the Colorado, thereby enclosing the entire southern corridor and Gila River drainage. However, after bold thrusts northward to Albuquerque and Santa Fe, Confederate forces soon withdrew in the face of superior Union armies converging from Colorado and California. The U.S. Congress now reconsidered the matter, and in response to Santa Fe interests as well as Eastern capitalists eager to explore the mineral potential of various western districts, New Mexico was divided along the 109°W meridian, in direct contradiction of the earlier east-west design.

Although this bisection confirmed New Mexico's control down the Rio Grande to the border with Texas, it had, in a separate action, lost control of the uppermost waters: it had retained the Mesilla Valley but lost the San Luis. For in 1861

Congress had carved out a Territory of Colorado, and, with its usual predilection for geometric symmetry ("the lines exhibit more beauty and grace") and interest in enlarging the population of this "Pikes Peak" region (and, perhaps, favoring certain land grant speculators), had fixed the southern boundary along 37°N to form a simple block. This arbitrary bit of tidying severed several thousand Hispano settlers on either side of the Sangre de Cristo from their New Mexican kin. Santa Fe and the local Hispanos repeatedly protested this "unnatural union" and sought return of this "New Mexican notch," to no avail. The New Mexico defined by these 1860s boundaries was vulnerable to further changes during a long territorial phase, and there would be various attempts to detach southern districts as well as a later congressional move to reunite it with Arizona. But it would survive intact, and however awkward its large, boxy frame might be, it had the merit of enclosing all but the outer fringes of the enlarged Hispano region and all but the westernmost pueblos. Just how its remaining largely empty spaces might be filled awaited further settler movements.

Any strong Anglo influx into New Mexico was long delayed by the apparent lack of available lands or commercial resources as well as by the well-publicized dangers and the rooted Hispano presence. For twenty-five years Americans were there mainly as imperial agents—as soldiers or federal and territorial officials— and many of these were Western carpetbaggers "whose sole aim was to fleece a region and return East with the proceeds." There was only a small sprinkling in business in the few towns; there was no bank in the territory until 1871. And indeed many of those engaged in business were "Anglos" only in the broadest sense, for they were German Jews. Although themselves recent immigrants to America, they were part of the vanguard in New Mexico, arriving ahead of General Stephen Kearny, and they kept coming and stayed and spread out so that before long there was "the Jewish pueblo trading post; the Jewish sutler; the Jewish storekeeper in almost every settlement; the Jewish sedentary merchant of the cities who sat at the peak of the business hierarchy; the Jewish drummer peddling his way through every village and town as often as not to every ranchhold." Backed by superior sources of credit and supplies through their Eastern and European connections (the first in Santa Fe, in 1844, was an agent of a Westphalian firm), cosmopolitan and acute, ready to deal with anyone for any marketable goods, willing to assume local cultural and social leadership (some of them married into Hispano families), yet so few and so scattered in a land and society so foreign in kind to most Americans that they escaped much of the traditional ethnic animosity, these petty merchant capitalists have been recognized as "catalytic agents" in helping to link Anglo, Hispano, and Indian, to adapt old ways to new, to tie desert outposts to the industrial metropolis, helping, in short, to build a modern regional society out of disparate parts.

In the 1870s anticipation of railroad connections to the East began to alter the prospects for profits and position. Slowly forming over the years, the "Santa Fe Ring" now emerged into full notoriety: "it was essentially a set of lawyers, politicians, and businessmen who united to run the territory and to make money out of this particular region. Although located on the frontier, the ring reflected the corporative, monopolistic, and multiple enterprise tendencies of all American business after the Civil War. Its uniqueness lay in the fact that, rather than dealing with some manufactured item, they regarded land as their first medium of currency." "Land" meant litigation, and "down the trail from the states came . . . an amazing number of lawyers" who, "still stumbling over their Spanish, would build their own political and economic empire out of the tangled heritage of land grants." And so, somewhat belatedly, a general repetition of the Californian situation got under way, and with the same general results: "eventually over 80 per cent of the Spanish grants went to American lawyers and settlers." Important differences were the presence in New Mexico of a much greater number of Hispanic peasants and communities well rooted on the land, the considerable resistance and violence generated by this American assault, and the sullen resentment created in an increasingly constricted and impoverished people who felt they had been cheated out of much of their lands. In contrast to common representations it was not a case of a vigorous, expanding society moving in upon "a static culture," for "the Hispanos were still settling and conquering New Mexico, ever-extending their control" when the Anglos arrived. Here even more starkly than in California the conflict arose not just out of simple imperial imposition and crass chicanery but out of the clash of two fundamentally different sets of values, perceptions, and motivations. For ordinary Hispanos land was simply basic to a comfortable existence: "enough land to farm, enough pasture for stock, enough game to hunt, enough wood to burn, and enough material to build," all "to help one live as one ought to live"—including the continuity of such a life generation after generation. Although operating to a great extent on tradition and custom, this was not the simple, "primitive" society most Anglos took it to be; it had its own laws relating to land and water, its own complexities of status, politics, and factions. To the Anglos land was a commodity to buy and sell, to exploit as quickly as possible, a means of profit and a propellant of one's personal progress. Furthermore, "American land policy featured precise measurement and documentation, assumed individual ownership, and came out of a tradition that expected western land to be open for settlement." And it came out of eastern lands—out of the humid woodlands of Europe and America—and its assumptions about settlement and family farms, its rigid uniform rectangular survey system, its laws relating to water, cultivation, and seasonal use were incongruous with the needs and practices of Hispano farming and stock raising in the arid Southwest. Thus the most vulnerable parts of the Hispano system were the common lands, essential to the grazing economy, but often used without title, or held by a patrón who ultimately sold or lost his title, or by a community grant that was readily challenged under American law and likely to be declared by the courts to be public land subject to routine survey and sale. This process of Anglo encroachment went through several phases over several decades but reached an important victory in an early court approval of the Maxwell Grant, an infamous case wherein the original 97,000 acres was inflated to nearly 2 million covering a huge county-sized area of prime piedmont lands. Well before the owner had certain title to this baronial tract he had sold it to London speculators, and once the country that had "seemed worthless to Kearny's soldiers" became "an item in the stock exchange and a topic of interest in a dozen investment houses in Europe" the invasion of New Mexico had taken on a new momentum.

During this same time the railroad began its transforming work. The Atchison, Topeka & Santa Fe started out as a projected link between those two Kansas cities, but once aimed along that southwesterly route it was almost inevitable that its promoters would enlarge their visions and (spurred by the prospect of large land grants) seek to lay tracks along that first famous trafficway across the Great Plains. Backed by New England money the line reached Las Vegas in 1879 and Santa Fe a year later. However, that historic terminus tucked in a difficult mountain-girded setting seemed likely to generate little traffic, and the main line was extended along a more direct route to the Rio Grande and Albuquerque. And by that time new goals had transcended the name and the AT&SF sought to become a "transcontinental" line. Although first reaching the Pacific at Guaymas, the Sonoran port long coveted by American expansionists, the main objective was California, by a line west from Albuquerque across the high plateau along the old Thirty-fifth parallel route to the Colorado River, where, as we have noted, negotiations with its rival, the Southern Pacific, eventually provided entry (at the cost of the Guaymas line) into—and an enormous impact upon—the Golden State.

The "Santa Fe" (as the AT&SF was usually called) and the SP (building eastward to Tucson, El Paso, and New Orleans) certainly accelerated the Anglo invasion but in no way comparable in volume or extent with what happened in California. The population of New Mexico doubled in the twenty years thereafter but had not quite reached 200,000 in 1900—and only a quarter of these were Anglos. Rather, it was much more like the Gentile invasion of Mormonland: a selective intrusion that gave Anglos an ever-greater role in business and professions (much more so than in Utah, for there was no Hispano equivalent of the Mormon socioeconomic hierarchy), created a number of Anglo railroad and industrial towns (such as Raton and Gallup), and, most notably, transformed old centers into a set of dual towns displaying in their life and landscape the new bicultural realities. When the Santa Fe approached Las Vegas it did not attempt to enter that old trade center but laid out a new town across the river a mile away, and the same pattern was followed at Bernalillo, Albuquerque, and Socorro. These Old Town–New Town pairs, sharing a name but sheltering separate societies, were vividly distinct in age and architecture, the cluster of flat-roofed adobe shops and houses along the narrow streets radiating from the old plaza now paired with the formal blocks of Victorian facades of brick or wooden buildings lining the wide, straight streets and sidewalks leading to the depot (fig. 23); the single Roman Catholic church and parochial school on one side balanced by several Protestant churches and (eventually, after a long political struggle) public school on the other. The two centers were bound together physically by a busy traffic and socially by a set of bilingual intermediaries, with a few Anglos in business in Old Town and a growing number

23. Albuquerque, 1880s.
"The engineer and locomotive marked out the first straight line . . . and right angles, and fronts to the houses [were] adapted to the railroad, the regenerator," remarked William Burrows observing, as he put it, the impact of the nineteenth century on the sixteenth century in Hispanic New Mexico. In Albuquerque the traveler was greeted by this line of buildings on First Street of the New Town grid and could take the horsecar to Old Town plaza a mile and half away. (Center for Southwest Research, Gen. Library, University of New Mexico. Neg. No. 000-119-0569)

of Hispano workmen and servants resident in New Town; yet they remained a set of strongly, self-consciously separate communities, the one feeling beleaguered by alien forces, the other expansive and self-confident: in short, "natives" and "conquerors," the "colonial city," a classic imperial creation.

Yet it was not all quite that simple and obvious, as a visit to Santa Fe would confirm. For here old and new were closely intermingled, in the presence not only of adobe alongside modern brick and stone buildings but of hybrid forms—adobe with milled wood porches, windows, and trim, adobe faced in wood, ornamental brick coping on adobe walls—in what became known as the graceful New Mexican "territorial style," a physical expression of the more intimate and practical social and political relationships of two peoples interdependent in the governing and development of the territory they shared. That Anglos were only a quarter of the population of this old capital, whereas they were the majority in Las Vegas and Albuquerque (71 percent in this latter, the largest city) was of course a reflection of the failure of Santa Fe to compete as a commercial center with those main-line towns (and, indeed, it had to fight hard to keep from losing the territorial capital to Albuquerque, the new crossroads). Santa Fe remained the primary anchor of the majority people, it was the largest community of Hispanos, their religious as well as political focus, "the exact demographic center" of an Hispano homeland that despite selective penetrations, losses of lands, and blunted expansions remained solid and resistant to ready change, a *patria* embodying an "aggregate of hundreds of *patrias chicas* [native villages and localities] which," as Nostrand described it a century later, "ordinary Hispanos know intimately and for which they have sentimental and enduring feelings of attachment." (And, as Lamar noted, embedded within this region "those grand masters of cultural isolation, the Pueblo Indians, exercised their own arts of living as if the white man did not exist at all.")

The Anglos were a minority in 1900, but a steadily more dominant minority, in control of all the main instruments of development and change. They created new production and settlement areas, such as the coal-mining districts along the Colorado border, copper mining at Santa Rita, lumber camps in the higher mountains, dry farming on the mesas of the Canadian country, large irrigation projects in the Pecos Valley, as well as a strong expansion of tourism to this land of natural beauty, picturesque villages, and colorful Indians, and of health seekers to the high, dry climate. These activities brought in new peoples in considerable numbers: Slavs, Magyars, Welsh, and others to the coal mines, Mexicans to the copper mines and smelters, Middle Westerners to new farmlands and towns, Texans all across the southern half of the territory, and a small sprinkling of anthropologists, artists, writers, and others who began to undertake serious study of, and establish rapport with, the peoples native to the region. Such camps and colonizations further hemmed in the Hispano land seeker, but they also lured the Hispano laborer outward: to the section gangs along the railroad tracks all the way to Kansas City, to the mines and beet fields and orchards of Colorado, and all across and beyond their old rangelands where Anglo stockmen made ready use of Hispano skills as herders and drovers. Such things continually modified the social geography of the Southwest, creating new complexities and interdependencies among its peoples and a diffuse, uneven but ever-greater integration of this frontier territory, and the larger nation.

There were concurrent moves to formalize integration at a higher level. Statehood was a controversial issue in New Mexico, and the divisions were not clearly along ethnic lines. Most Anglos regarded it as an inevitable eventuality, and many felt that the sooner the better because an expanded public school system, pressures for the use of English, the practice of democratic politics, and other routines would advance integration and assimilation. Capitalists anticipated a rise in property values, politicians an expansion of offices. But powerful railroad and mining interests feared increased taxes and regulations (though based in the East they controlled influential local newspapers and politicians), and many Anglos were concerned that a Hispano electorate would be controlled by a few patróns. As for the Hispanos, many feared that statehood would indeed intensify pressures for cultural as well as political change, and the Roman Catholic hierarchy was determined to protect its role in education and morals, yet some Hispano leaders regarded statehood as an important badge of equality and respect as well as opening opportunities for themselves and their people.

As always, statehood was of course much more a national than a local decision, and the New Mexico case was unusually prolonged and embattled. Aside from Republican and Democrat assessments as to whether the new state would enhance their power (probably the most critical factor in any particular session of Congress), two major issues were recurrently cited against admission:

1. *Too few people.* Although New Mexico had always qualified by the old standard of at least 60,000 free inhabitants, Congress was not bound by such precedent, and there were now strong pressures to insist on something closer to the level of the smaller states, especially as the prospects for growth seemed very limited in these desert and mountain territories. The powerful chairman of the Senate Committee on Territories asserted that 1.5 million ought to be minimum standard in the new twentieth century, whereas New Mexico (195,000) had only caught up with tiny Delaware (185,000), and as the issue of its admission became coupled with that of Arizona (123,000), the idea of four senators from such a small population—and *Western* senators, at that—drew strong opposition (which often pointed to Nevada, the notorious, hastily admitted, "rotten borough" that now had only 42,000 and was *declining* in population).

2. *The wrong kind of people.* Probably more widespread but less overt was the feeling that the majority of New Mexicans were a "foreign people," "a race speaking an alien language." Newspapers put it more pungently: they were a "mongrel population," "not Americans, but 'Greaser,' persons ignorant of our laws, manners, customs, language, and institutions," and therefore "unfit for statehood." New Mexico therefore had to be "Americanized," and there seemed to be two ways of doing it: by a greater influx of Anglos and by changing the customs and language of the Hispanos. Opponents of statehood sought more such changes before admission, proponents argued for admission as a means of accelerating these.

After statehood for New Mexico had been blocked in Congress in 1889 and again in 1902, the idea of "jointure"—recombining the two Southwestern territories into a single State of Arizona, with its capital at Santa Fe—was put forward as a means of answering the one objection (too few people) and diluting the second (the Hispano proportion). The stoutest congressional leader of the opposition to two states now sang the praises of this one new "Arizona, standing midway between California and Texas, three great Commonwealths guarding the Republic's southwestern border." The proposal passed both houses and was signed by the president in 1906. However, the act required separate approval by the voters in each territory, and although New Mexicans voted in favor (although most of the main Hispano counties did not), Arizonans soundly rejected any such "miscegenation" and prospect of rule from a remote and corrupt Santa Fe.

Once this ploy was dead Congress seemed weary of the long struggle, and the movement for statehood for both of these last of the contiguous territories was revived. There was greater confidence among Anglos that the influx they had long sought was gaining momentum. In all the literature poured out by the Bureau of Immigration and other propagandists the presence of the Hispanos was rarely mentioned, and never emphasized. By 1906 Max Frost, one of the most active publicists, asserted in his popular book, *The Land of Sunshine,* that "a few more decades will witness the complete amalgamation of the native people, both as to language and as to customs, with the newcomers of Anglo-Saxon origin." However, political leaders were necessarily more attuned to realities and now worked assiduously on a constitution that would protect the interests of both peoples (this 1910 convention was a telling reflection of relative power: sixty-eight Anglos, thirty-two Hispanos, even though the Hispanos were still the majority population). It was agreed that Spanish be accorded equality with English in legal documents, that interpreters be made available in courts, that every citizen enjoy the right to vote, hold office, or sit upon juries regardless of "religion, race, language or color, or inability to speak, read or write" English or Spanish, that education be provided in both languages, that "children of Spanish descent . . . shall never be denied . . . admission and attendance in, . . . and never be classed in separate schools but shall forever enjoy perfect equality with other children in all public schools"; yet, as well, that the teaching of English be required in all public schools and that all state officials be able to read, write, and understand English. Here, then, was conformity and compromise; Americanization, certainly, but without suppression and dismemberment of the captive culture. Given the power and predilections of the American nation, which had always operated on assumptions of integration and assimilation and rejected the concept of ethnic territorial units as appropriate members of the federation, it must be judged, for the moment, a victory for the Hispanos. New Mexico therefore proved to be a difficult case, a resilient subnation that could be subordinated but not readily assimilated. It had of course been penetrated, its Hispano population geographically contained, and its most valued resources were firmly in Anglo control, and thus Congress did finally agree that after sixty-four years of territorial rule (under despotic officials like "an East Indian State under Hastings" as one statehood proponent had fumed) "the proper time"—in the words of the Treaty of Guadalupe Hidalgo—had arrived to accept this imperial province into the federal union. And it was formally done on January 6, 1912.

7. The Colorado Complex

Although nearest to the main body of the nation, Colorado was the last of the major Far Western regions to be initiated. The general locale had been known for forty years, but apart from the brief era of the fur trappers and traders the massive wall of mountains looming ever higher before the traveler crossing the Plains was not a lure but an obstacle. The great overland trails skirted its northern and southern flanks by way of the Wyoming Basin or the Southwest Plateaus. Intensive explorations failed to find a feasible way directly through the Southern Rockies; surveys for the Thirty-eighth parallel Pacific Railroad route, so avidly desired by influential interests, found passages through the Front Range but none across the broader mass beyond.

In the opening phase of Anglo-American settlement, Pikes Peak, the famous landmark for a generation of travelers moving up the Arkansas Valley, gave its name to the whole region even though the initial discoveries were seventy miles to the north. By the time of this "Pikes Peak Rush" in 1858 the main national settlement frontier was well into Kansas and Nebraska, crossing the Plains had become routine, and half a dozen Missouri River towns competed for this sudden new traffic. Thus mercantile houses and outfitters, freighting, stage, and mail services, newspapers, guidebooks, and maps extolled the special facilities and position of Kansas City, Leavenworth, Atchison, St. Joseph, Nebraska City, or

Omaha as the most advantageous for those rushing to the new goldfields. The intensity of such urban competition and the velocity and volume of this surge to the Rockies were an expression not only of the heady precedence of California and extensive experience with Western travel but of the business doldrums and general restlessness and uncertainties on the eve of a national convulsion. The initial insurge found only meager placer deposits, but in June 1859 bold headlines in the *Leavenworth Times* announcing "Immense Gold Discoveries" in the mountains and declaring "Pikes Peak a Glorious Reality!" were telegraphed to the nation, and such news revived the faltering boom.

The several competing routes across the High Plains came into focus on a small area near the base of and extending a short distance into the mountains along the upper waters of the South Platte. Here Denver, at the site of the first placers on Cherry Creek, and Central City, near the hard-rock discoveries in the mountains forty miles to the west, quickly emerged as the principal centers. Prospectors swarmed over the region and mining camps sprouted up across the tangle of canyons and high ranges in this "crest of the continent." But it was all a rather floundering beginning. Most placers were quickly exhausted and although many hard-rock deposits seemed rich, they proved to be difficult to process. In the fever of speculation eager companies hauled in a great array of stamp mills and machinery before the suitability of these to the local ores had been demonstrated. There followed a tantalizing, difficult period of experiment and instability. The census of 1860 recorded a population of 34,277 and ten years later only 39,864 (and this latter figure included the several thousand Hispanos annexed by the 1861 boundary change), but it has been estimated that as many as 100,000 people lived in Colorado for a season or a year or two during that period. The ease of travel to and from "the States" no doubt intensified such coming and going during a tumultuous decade in the nation as a whole.

In spite of these continuing uncertainties about just how substantial Colorado's resources and prospects might be, important groundwork was being laid. The scale and regularity of stagecoach, mail, and freighting connections with the older West of the prairie Plains were improved (despite severe disruptions from weather and Indian attacks), and from 1864 onward the westward progress of the Union Pacific and the Kansas Pacific was intently followed. Ties with New Mexico, an early source of flour and meat for the mining camps, were also maintained. Most of the land along the Piedmont, the narrow belt of valleys and benchlands along the base of the mountains, watered by streams and a somewhat higher rainfall than the adjacent High Plains, was taken up, and ranches and a few farms and orchards were begun. Much of that acreage was held on speculation, of course, as was that in the numerous townsites. In addition to Denver (clearly in the lead with 4,600 people), the most promising of these appeared to be Golden, Colorado City, Cañon City, and Pueblo, each positioned in an entryway to mining districts in the mountains. Such places, as well as the many mining camps, had an oversupply of merchants and services awaiting some new surge in development.

And a territorial government had been formed (1861), providing the usual American political arena for the unusually heavy influx of office seekers, lawyers, and associated professionals. Counties had been organized, courts established (modeled on Illinois), mining and water laws defined (following earlier Far Western precedents), a territorial survey authorized, and the first official map completed. A United States mint had been requested, granted, and completed in Denver, and that city, having survived successive challenges from Colorado City and Golden, seemed to have a pretty firm hold as the territorial capital. Overall the population was developing toward a more normal pattern: only 62 percent male in 1870 as compared with 95 percent ten years earlier.

All through this time Colorado was an exhibit of the magnitude of American speculation, of the amazing amount of money and energy and talent that could be attracted to a new mining region, even when the amount of actual wealth generated was as yet very modest. Frank Hall, editor of the *Central City Register* and territorial secretary, tried to reassure his mother back in Upstate New York that this was simply the normal pattern: "All new states are born in an outburst, a sort of tempest of speculative passion, which burns and surges until the material it feeds upon is exhausted and then the substantial foundations of the state are laid." Hall's generalization of 1869 was rather too broad, but it fitted Colorado very well, and those more substantial foundations were just then beginning to appear.

Of prime importance was the completion of railroad connections to the East. The Union Pacific reached Cheyenne in late 1867 and headed on west across Wyoming, but by 1870 Denver had its link to Cheyenne and later that year the Kansas Pacific arrived, providing direct service to Kansas City and St. Louis (fig. 24). The potential impact upon mining was immense, for these Colorado operations required much freighting of ores, concentrates, fuels, underground timbering, and machinery. And just at this time the first important resolution of the peculiar difficulties of Colorado ores was taking place. The rich sulfide gold deposits of the Central City district had not yielded well to American empirical methods, and it took a combination of European metallurgical science, specifically that of the ancient Saxony academy at Freiburg and the famous Welsh smelting works at Swansea, together with imported Cornish engineers and workers steeped in the problems and methods of deep underground mining, all backed by ample Eastern capital (well exhibited in the new Boston & Colorado smelter on the outskirts of Denver), to achieve a breakthrough.

A much more sensational event was the belated discovery that the annoying "blue stuff" that had clogged the gold sluices in the declining California Gulch

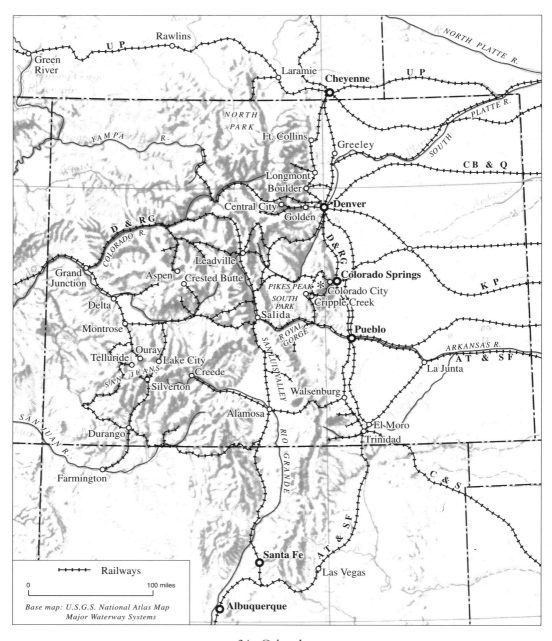

24. Colorado.

district on the headwaters of the Arkansas beyond South Park was actually very rich and easy-to-smelt silver carbonate, resulting in a wild rush in 1877–78 and the emergence of Leadville as one of America's greatest mining camps. By 1880 there were 15,000 residents in this town just below timberline at 10,200 feet and thousands more in the vicinity working the thick congestion of mines and smelters. Railroads raced to the scene, arriving in 1880 to help the rapid transformation from a wilderness jumble of tents and cabins into a formal grid-pattern city with multi-storied brick business blocks, an opera house and theaters, churches, social halls, and hospitals, all served by a municipal water system and gas lights. And basic to this new scene—to the hoisting, pumping, and smelting, and the gas lights—was the abundance of Colorado coal. It was found in many outcroppings along the mountain front, from near Boulder south into New Mexico, and eventually in a number of places well within the ranges, such as at Crested Butte. The high-grade bituminous coals at Trinidad and coke ovens at nearby El Moro were especially important to Leadville. Furthermore, the availability of good coking coal as well as local iron ore (chiefly from the Orient mine in the San Luis Valley) led to the building of an iron and steel works at Pueblo in 1881. For sixty years thereafter this Colorado Fuel and Iron plant was much the largest—and at times the only—such integrated facility (that is, working from iron ore rather than just scrap) in the Far West, turning out railroad iron, bars, pipe, wire, and nails for an extensive market in spite of severe competition from larger railroad-favored plants in the East.

Agriculture also attained a new level of development, aided by the arrival of the railroads. The Union Colony at Greeley became the most famous exhibit of the change. Conceived by Nathan C. Meeker and Horace Greeley and given national publicity in Greeley's *New York Tribune,* it was a mutation from the Fourierism of the 1840s (in which both men had been involved), now espousing colonization by the "doctrine of association," that is, by formal cooperation rather than by full communism. Clearly influenced by the example of Mormon success (both men had visited Utah as well as Colorado), the design called for membership by fee, village settlement of families, individual ownership of house lots and farms, with the community as a whole purchasing and subdividing the initial large block of land, constructing the vital irrigation system, and providing essential social facilities (schools, churches, library, town hall). The well-publicized initial success of these Eastern colonists with this well-managed program on a large acreage of good Piedmont land fifty-four miles north of Denver spurred others, of which the Chicago-Colorado Colony at Longmont and the development at Fort Collins (on lands of a vacated army post) were among the more prominent. There were, of course, failures as well (most notably the Chicago German Colony in the Wet Mountains west of Pueblo); even the more successful programs struggled with difficult problems of water management, and most agricultural settlements were more like ordinary American real estate promotions than formal cooperatives (and all these latter evolved toward ordinary towns). However, the need for major investment in irrigation systems and careful attention to local agronomic conditions was generally recognized, and the manifest results with grain, hay, potatoes, fruits, vegetables, and livestock were sufficient to attract Eastern and European capital and to sustain the spread of settlement across all the feasible lands of the Piedmont, in narrow strips down the South Platte and the Arkansas, and into a thin scattering of favorable valleys within the mountains. Meanwhile, the state, struggling with a morass of water litigation, eventually divided Colorado into water divisions and districts, set up agencies for local administration and adjudication, and evolved a "Colorado System" for public control of water "that proved to be one of the most successful innovations" of its kind. In 1905 the federal government added its powerful touch when the newly formed Reclamation Service began work on a tunnel nearly six miles long to divert water from the Gunnison River to irrigate 100,000 acres in the Uncompahgre Valley.

As elsewhere in the West, this expansion of agriculture was at the expense of open-range stock raising. Cattlemen had driven in herds from Texas to serve the mining camps, making use of a wide expanse of public lands from homesteads secured in some well-watered location. Railroad connections and codification of range laws led to a spate of speculation, overstocking, and collapse of the boom with the onset of unusually heavy winters and droughts in the latter 1880s. A more permanent form of ranching, with investment in land, fencing, water, and winter feed, emerged from this debacle and given the narrow environmental limits on agriculture endured as a substantial part of the regional landscape and economy.

Movements for statehood waxed and waned with all the instability of the mining industry. As Albert D. Richardson had facetiously observed while visiting Denver in 1859: "Making governments and building towns are the natural employments of the migratory Yankee. . . . Congregate a hundred Americans any where beyond the settlements, and they immediately lay out a city, frame a State Constitution, and apply for admission to the Union, while twenty-five of them become candidates for the United States Senate." Here, again, Colorado was a prime exhibit, for it attracted an unusual number of political promoters with extensive experience in territorial and state formation. But it took time to develop effective parties and to elicit the necessary support in Washington (President Andrew Johnson vetoed Colorado statehood in 1865), and proposed constitutions generated considerable opposition, especially among the Catholic Hispanic population of the southern counties. Only after signs of substantial permanent development and the favorable impressions made upon President Ulysses S. Grant during a visit in 1873 was success attained. Admitted to the Union in August 1876—the only new state for many years—Colorado proudly proclaimed itself the "Centennial State."

At the time of statehood only the central third of this huge rectangle had even the beginnings of American settlement, and there seems to have been no serious attempt to expand its geopolitical bounds (although one leader in the 1860s had proposed a northward extension so as to include the route of the Union Pacific). The High Plains on the east were crossed by two railroads and several old wagon trails but were still essentially buffalo and Indian country. Even though both bison and Indian seemed doomed, it would be a few years before the possibility of general agricultural settlement of these high, dry plains would even be considered. West of the Continental Divide there had been a minor mining rush into the San Juans, but the remainder was empty of settlements and mostly still Indian lands. Men of vision, of course, were not limited by the current geography of settlement, and the eventual shape and character of a distinct Colorado region—"empire" was the common term—were generally shared among an interlocking set of "entrepreneur politicians" who saw themselves in charge of its development. Heavily involved in land, mines, railroading, and government positions and contracts, these men were nearly all from New York, Pennsylvania, or the urban older West and had fruitful connections with Eastern, and in some cases European, financiers.

William Gilpin, who served briefly as the first territorial governor and then became heavily involved in land grant speculations, expounded upon the topic in his usual pseudo-scientific geographical manner. He (who a few years earlier had denominated the Independence–Kansas City locale as the destined site of the eventual great Centropolis of America) set forth his "1,000-mile" theory that assured the emergence of his newly adopted city as one of the four great metropolitan centers—New York, Chicago, Denver, San Francisco—spaced along the continental pathway of progress. The most obvious problem with that concept was the bypassing of Denver by the great transcontinental instrument of progress, the Union Pacific. More practical-minded leaders worked avidly to build a connection to Cheyenne and to ensure the arrival of the Kansas Pacific. Once those vital national links were in place (1870) they could begin to exploit Denver's potential as the focus of a great mountain and piedmont "island" set apart from the East by hundreds of miles of dry plains and from other Western regions by broad stretches of wastelands or sharp differences in peoples.

The most visionary and effective of these men was William Jackson Palmer, an experienced, well-connected Pennsylvania engineer who had been associated with the Kansas Pacific. In 1871 Palmer incorporated the Denver & Rio Grande, the name declaring his concept of a "Mountain-Base Railroad," to build south from Denver crossing into the San Luis Valley to the upper Rio Grande, and on to Santa Fe and El Paso to connect with a north-south Mexican line. Such a railroad would command the entryways into the mountains and allow branches to be extended to coal and mineral districts; he regarded northern New Mexico as a southerly portion of this mountain region, and links to Mexico important as sources of labor, trade, and seaports. The entire system was to be narrow gauge, not only to reduce construction costs but to create an insulated regional network. Within a few years his mountain-base line had reached El Moro, near the New Mexican border, with branches up the Arkansas and across La Veta Pass into the San Luis Valley to Alamosa on the upper Rio Grande. At this point he encountered new challenges and opportunities. The AT&SF ("Santa Fe") had reached west to Pueblo and sought to block Palmer from building into New Mexico. At the same time, the sudden emergence of Leadville made the Royal Gorge, a narrow passageway up the Arkansas, an alluring corridor to railroad riches. After a brief "war" for control of these critical routes, a complicated compromise left New Mexico to the Santa Fe and redirected the D&RG's main line westward from Pueblo up the Arkansas. The mountain-base line now became the premier mountain line; aided by the profits from Leadville, Palmer began what Robert Athearn termed his policy of "railroad prospecting," following "each new [gold or silver] strike with the avidity of a hard-rock miner," sending spindly narrow-gauge branches high up into the deepest recesses of the Rockies: to Gunnison, Crested Butte, Lake City, Aspen, Silverton, Ouray, Creede, and many others. As some of those names indicate, the entire Western Slope of Colorado had been forced open to settlement in 1880 (the Utes being sent off to a reservation in eastern Utah), and the railroad and associated townsite companies were immediately on the ground: Durango, Montrose, Delta, and Grand Junction were all founded in the next year. By 1890, the D&RG, along with a few lesser companies, had built an amazingly extensive and intricate net-work of lines in the most difficult terrain of North America (figs. 25 and 26).

Denver remained the great focus of this mountain network, though its leaders recurrently worried about rival junctions created by Eastern trunk lines at Colorado Springs and Pueblo. They remained obsessed with the desire to have a major railroad built directly westward through the towering Rockies so as to put Denver on a trunk line to the Pacific. (It was an old theme: the lowest crossing, at 11,300-foot Berthoud Pass, had been discovered in 1861 by a survey party seeking a route for the Central Overland California and Pike's Peak Express Company.) William Palmer did his best to make his winding developmental road into a trunk line as well. Once he had redirected his strategies westward, he envisioned a profitable exchange of Colorado coal and iron goods for Utah farm produce for the mining camps, as well as connections on to California. A line between Grand Junction and Salt Lake City was completed in 1883, but the commercial reciprocities were less than anticipated (excellent coal was being opened up in Utah) and the Union Pacific remained far better positioned, geographically and corporately, for trunk-line traffic. By 1890 the D&RG had standard gauged its main line between Denver and Salt Lake City along a rerouted mountain division over Tennessee Pass beyond

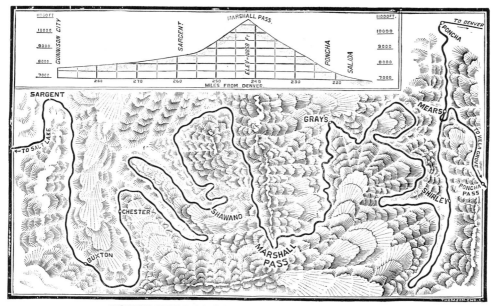

ALIGNMENT OF THE D. & R. G. RAILROAD OVER MARSHALL PASS, COLORADO.

25. "The marvellous railroading over Marshall Pass."
"The tortuous method by which the daring engineers of the Denver and Rio Grande Railroad have achieved this summit" of nearly 11,000 feet "can best be understood by studying this . . . alignment of the track," wrote William M. Thayer, who happily included it among his *Marvels of the New West* (1888). This crossing of the Continental Divide just west of Salida was on the original main line to Salt Lake City.

Leadville. This upgrading of facilities made the D&RG potentially more competitive, but the addition of this new route, linking the upper Arkansas with the Grand (upper Colorado) River Valley, was more immediately important in extending the regional system through another part of the state. By this time that system was essentially coextensive with the Piedmont, the High Rockies, and the Western Slope, defining a coherent functional region anchored on Denver. Only the very thinly populated far northwest—Middle Park and the Yampa country—remained untapped, awaiting the actuality of various proposals for a direct Denver–Salt Lake line.

If these Colorado lines could never match the efficiencies of the great transcontinentals to the north and the south they were themselves unmatched in the grandeur of the region they traversed. The arrival of the railroads initiated a vast campaign extolling this "Switzerland of America," and once its network was in place even Baedeker had to admit that "the somewhat ambitious title of 'Scenic Line of the World,'" adopted by the D&RG, "is, perhaps more justified by the facts

26. Salida Roundhouse, c. 1890.
This busy scene, with hotel and depot in the left background, well displays the railroad as an
important regional industry. It took two, three, or four of these narrow-gauge 2-8-0 engines to
haul and shove a train over Marshall Pass or into the remote recesses of the Rockies. (Courtesy
Denver Public Library, Western History Department)

than is usually the case with such assumptions," as could be confirmed by taking the
famous 1,000-mile "Around the Circle" excursion, featuring several mountain
crossings of up to 11,000 feet on a journey from Denver to Durango, Grand
Junction, or Gunnison, and back to Denver through "some of the grandest scenery
in the United States." It was early appreciated that tourists, recreationists, seasonal sojourners, health seekers, and those who could afford to live well in the
mountains would become an important part of the regional economy, and developers set out to cater to every kind and class of such clients. Much the most
elaborate project was William Palmer's Colorado Springs, handsomely laid out in
the afternoon shadow of Pikes Peak near Manitou Springs and the wind-sculptured
Garden of the Gods. Designed to implant an Eastern elegance in a spectacular
Western setting, the town was an immediate success, in part because Palmer set up
his estate there and had influential Eastern and English connections. Twenty years
after its founding Colorado Springs received a major injection of wealth and
leadership with the discovery of gold at Cripple Creek, just south of Pikes Peak.

The city's firm codes relegated the accompanying industries and saloons to nearby Colorado City, and newly rich investors soon further adorned the area with the Broadmoor and other resorts and attractions. All the while there were dozens of lesser spas and camps being developed throughout these American Alps, as well as all manner of hotels and services in all the gateway cities catering to this heavy seasonal traffic.

In the 1880s the Colorado region doubled in population, and Denver tripled; after the nationwide depression and crisis of silver in the early nineties a resurgence brought the region past half a million in 1900, of which Denver (134,000) together with the adjacent South Platte portion of the Piedmont accounted for about 40 percent. By that date the shape and character of this region was clear and essentially stabilized (Cripple Creek was the last great gold and silver rush). Unlike neighboring New Mexico and Utah, Colorado's distinction did not derive so much from its particular peoples. The great majority of these were from the northern states; the immigrant clusters in the mining and smelter districts, the northward spread of Hispano shepherds and laborers, and (after 1900) the Volga Germans and others recruited by the sugar beet companies were altogether a small part of the total. Rather, it was set apart by its particular combination of activities in a very striking physical setting. In spite of its inherent instabilities, mining remained a mainstay of dozens of local districts and of the regional economy as a whole, and, as Rodman Paul has made clear, Colorado was a major seat of American mining science and expertise. The Colorado Scientific Society (1882) and the Colorado School of Mines (1874) were only the more obvious formal exhibits of a special industrial culture that drew directly upon Old World skills and New World experience. Furthermore, coal was unusually abundant in Colorado. It was of course basic to the mining industry and to Colorado's special advantage in having its own iron and steel industry, and it fueled the locomotives and provided the largest tonnage of freight and the most reliable source of profits for the railroads that bound this rugged region together. Colorado agriculture was shaped not by the stereotypical pioneer farmer but by generally well-capitalized colony and other land development schemes; well served by railroads, it shifted rather quickly from diverse productions for the regional market to narrower specializations, so that, for example, by 1900 trainloads of Greeley potatoes and Rocky Ford melons were being sent to the East, and shortly thereafter it would take the lead in sugar beet production. So, too, stock raising was dominated by large companies and was an important part of the economy in nearly all parts of the region. All these features, together with the unrivaled role of resorts and tourism in this remarkable Rocky Mountain environment, made up what may well be termed a distinctive "Colorado Complex."

The bounds of that complex were clearly discernible. The easternmost tier of Colorado counties on the High Plains was the western edge of the Middle West, a hazardous grain-farming frontier that had advanced out of Kansas and Nebraska during a cycle of wet years in the 1880s only to shrivel in the droughts that followed, with up to half the population leaving and half the land left unplowed, and then undergoing a modest redevelopment based on widely hailed but still experimental dry-farming techniques. Such areas were tied more to Kansas City and Omaha than to Denver. But elsewhere the region corresponded more or less with the bounds of the state. On the north, aside from a minor railroad branch from Laramie aimed at the coalfields of North Park, the political boundary approximated the functional division between a Wyoming aligned with its Union Pacific axis and a Colorado awaiting the slow progress of "the Moffat Road," the pet railroad project of a Denver financier that had tunneled and tortuously wound up to and across Rollins Pass (11,600 feet) and made its way through Middle Park, ostensibly en route to Salt Lake City. On the west only a few Mormon outliers amidst the empty canyonlands punctuated the broad separation from Utah. Raton Pass, dividing the trade areas of Colorado and New Mexico, along the main north-south axis, was almost exactly on the state line; farther west the narrow-gauge Colorado system weaved along the boundary toward Durango and sent a branch to Farmington on the San Juan, thus tapping a few thinly populated districts of northernmost New Mexico. (The Farmington branch was designed to fend off any northward reach of the AT&SF from Gallup; the D&RG's belated narrow-gauge extension south to the city of Santa Fe proved to be an inconsequential completion of an original Palmer objective.)

This Colorado system had very limited links with neighboring western regions and half a dozen connections eastward across the Plains to the national system, a pattern reflecting the nearness, ease of access, and avid Eastern interest that so heavily shaped the region from the beginning. Complaints about freight-rate discriminations and the power that those Eastern-financed corporations held over the desired development of Colorado had prompted an early effort to find a geographical alternative, resulting in a railroad link between Denver and Texas (completed in 1888; later reorganized as the Colorado & Southern) and the formation of a Deep Harbor Committee of the Denver Chamber of Commerce to lobby for federal funds to improve the conditions at Galveston. Such a line might be seen as a variation on Palmer's original mountain-base concept, but it had little immediate impact on the main traffic patterns.

Denver, the proudly proclaimed "Queen City of the Plains," might therefore more accurately be called the "Queen City of the Mountains and Piedmont." It was an unusually strong regional focus. Its Union Depot stood as a great symbol of that fact, for it was a genuine hub: all trains began or terminated here, none passed *through* Denver (an ironic gain from the failure to get itself on a transcontinental trunk line). Its smelters, foundries, and mining equipment firms, its flour mills,

Union Stock Yards, and packinghouses, its big wholesaling and retailing houses, its banks, newly built mint, and mining exchange, its sanitariums and tuberculosis hospitals, its hotels, new convention center, and gigantic Welcome Arch erected opposite the depot were all tangible representations of the diverse regional economy; its big business blocks, opera house, ornate mansions, and country clubs were emblems of the men who found much wealth in the region and continued to exert much influence over it (some of whom, in their support of a new "city beautiful" movement, might be said to be reacting to the criticism of a British visitor of 1897, who found Denver "more plain than queenly").

Colorado was a new and famous region of America, a land of snow-capped peaks, rushing waters, narrow gorges, and high open country so strikingly different from all to the east that it became a compelling symbol of the West in the public mind. A euphonious name for a spectacular land, Colorado was a place a great many people longed to see, and every year thousands headed for the Mile-High City to begin their explorations of the sublime country beyond. And Colorado had an unusually clear definition on the American map. In both physical and functional terms—as a landscape and as a complex of activities—it had a coherence, a geographical integrity that was readily recognizable and set it apart from neighboring regions. Yet for all this distinctiveness, Colorado was also the least independent of Western regions, the most closely tied into the national system, the most dependent from its beginnings on surges of investment from the East, not only in mining but in land, townsites, and irrigation systems, in ranching, resorts, railroads, and most everything else. Late in its emergence, Colorado was—aside from the special case of 1880s Southern California—from its beginnings the least isolated, least provincial, the least resistant to rapid integration with the nation.

8. The Rest of the West

FILLING IN THE FAR WEST

These half-dozen major regions accounted for only about half of the area of the Far West. In between or on their margins were an equal number of others, some of them great in extent, but all distinctly smaller in population, simpler in economies, without major cities, and more dependent upon external services; in sum, they were markedly less important during this formative period in the shaping of this half of the nation. These six secondary regions were identified with, but not quite identical to, a set of names fixed in the framework of the federation: Nevada, Idaho, Montana, Wyoming, Dakota, and Arizona. In several cases these large geopolitical units had come into being more as nearly empty areas left over after the formation of territories and states around major developing nuclei than in response to the demands and designs of local settlers. We need to look briefly at the emergence of these several regions to see their relation to these geopolitical compartments and how these sets fit together to make up the Far West (fig. 27).

Nevada Nevada was an early and representative case. In origin and orientations it was simply an outlier of California, initiated by the rush to the silver riches of the Washoe Mountains. But these lay beyond the boundary of the Golden State, the mining population was eager to be freed from any possible allegiance to or interference from Salt Lake City, and so a large block of the western Great Basin was detached from Utah Territory. Only three years later, manipulations in national party politics elevated this still largely vacant expanse of mountain and desert land into a state, which was further enlarged eastward by the addition of bands of territory in response to a succession of rushes to new mineral discoveries. These locales, such as Aurora, Reese River (Austin), Belmont, Eureka, White Pine (Hamilton), and Pioche, all initiated within ten years after the formation of Nevada, sprinkled splotches of settlement and unstable networks of activity across the center of the state, while the completion of the Central Pacific fixed a firm axis and a sparse pattern of towns arched along the old Humboldt route across the northern sector. In the early twentieth century rich gold discoveries implanted 10,000 people in the new towns of Tonopah and Goldfield in the desolate country north of Death Valley. Stockmen from California drove in their herds and spread across the area in the wake of these mining extensions, securing their operations on the thin scattering of creeks, meadows, and mountain pastures. Basque sheepmen became a fixture along the Humboldt and its meager tributaries.

This great blunt wedge of territory (110,000 square miles) was more than 300 miles wide, yet it remained firmly anchored on its original Carson-Truckee-Washoe nucleus. The state was so sparsely populated that as late as 1900 the barely 20,000 in this small corner were nearly half the total, with Reno, on the main-line railroad, now surpassing Virginia City, astride the depleted Comstock Lode, as the largest town. Carson City retained the capital, and the state university had been shifted to Reno from Elko because so few students could be lured to that remote place (which had originally obtained it as the highest bidder).

The Boise Basin and Idaho Just to the north the overall pattern was not dissimilar. Prospectors struck gold in the Boise Basin in 1862, and within a year similar finds in the Owyhee district had attracted 20,000 people to the general area. A huge Idaho Territory was created in 1863, including the Clearwater mining district far to the north, then drastically pared down in the next year by the formation of Montana. These geopolitical actions arose primarily from the wishes of Washington and Dakota territorial politicians to excise such unstable mining populations from their

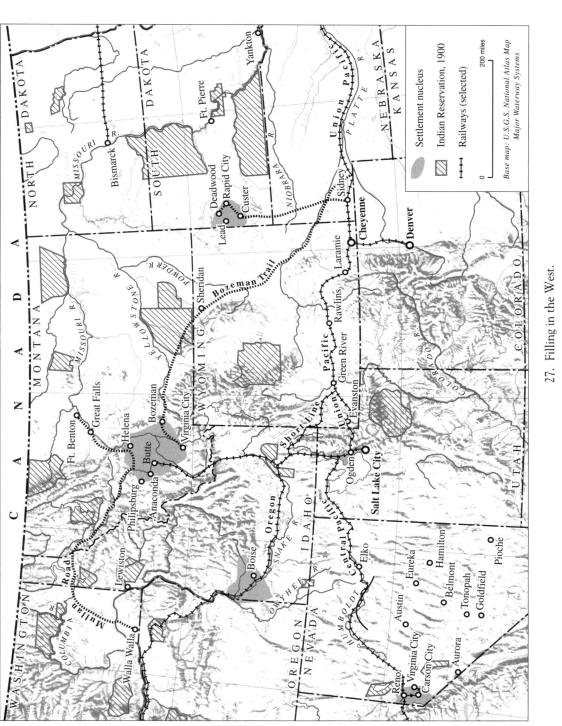

27. Filling in the West.

constituencies. The southern Idaho placers could not long sustain large camps, but a traveler of 1864 "found ranches and farms everywhere thickening up" and the attractions of these well-watered valleys along the Oregon Trail were enough to support a slow expansion of this Boise oasis. For stockmen the open range and ranching lands of this high, dry country were simply a northern portion of a larger intermountain region of similar general character. Boise City became a principal base and rendezvous for Basque sheepmen.

In 1865 Boise had wrested the territorial capital away from Lewiston and began to emerge as the undisputed focus of a broad region that included southeastern Oregon, the western Snake River Plains, and the mountain mass to the north. Earliest stage and freighting connections were with Walla Walla and down the Columbia to Portland, soon challenged by routes across the high desert to the upper Sacramento Valley and San Francisco, later reoriented southward to shipping points on the Central Pacific, and finally fixed when the Union Pacific built its Oregon Short Line directly through the Boise Valley. Various attempts were made to bring the boundaries of Idaho into greater concordance with this tributary region. Southern Idaho initially agreed that the absurd panhandle reaching to the British Columbia border, with which it had no connection whatever by road or river service, should become part of some redefined northern entity; the desired corollary and compensation would be the annexation of southeastern Oregon to Idaho. However, the transfer of northern Idaho to Washington that was actually approved by Congress in 1887 (but vetoed by Cleveland) was strongly opposed by Boise and related interests because they feared Nevada's designs upon themselves. Years earlier Nevada had petitioned Congress to annex the Owyhee district, and now with southeastern Idaho being rapidly colonized by Mormons and ever-more closely tied to Salt Lake City, southwestern Idaho looked like a tempting crippled remnant. Having staved off these reshapings Boise entered the twentieth century as the capital of a state incredibly awkward in design (in relation to north and south) and deeply divided in religiopolitical culture (as between east and west), and the primary commercial focus of an interstate region with only 50,000 inhabitants.

Montana Montana developed contemporary with Idaho, initiated by the miners from the first gold diggings of 1862 swarming out from the headwaters of the Missouri across a broad valley and mountain region overlapping the Continental Divide. Alder Gulch was the first big discovery, resulting in Montana's own Virginia City, quickly followed by Helena in Last Chance Gulch a hundred miles to the north. Many lesser ones added to the region's allure, but the 1870 census recorded only 20,595 inhabitants (of whom, typical of Far Western placer camps, 10 percent were Chinese). The next surge came in response to rich silver discoveries at Butte in 1876, soon compounded by the opening up of large, immensely rich copper deposits there whose development (concurrent with the rapidly emerging electrical age) would serve as the primary base of Montana's economic and political life for long after.

Montana was remote. Just before this influx the first steamboats had made the long, tedious ascent of the Missouri to the head of navigation at Fort Benton, from where a military wagon track, the Mullan Road, led on up that valley and westward across to Pacific drainage, thence by way of a steep pass over the Bitterroot Range to Lake Coeur d'Alene and down through the scablands to Fort Walla Walla— putting in place the portage connection that Meriwether Lewis had reconnoitered and suggested to Thomas Jefferson fifty-four years earlier. The sudden flurry of traffic on these two access routes represented the competition of Portland with St. Joseph and St. Louis for this new region. Attempts to open a more direct wagon road from Missouri River cities by way of the North Platte or Niobrara and the Bozeman Trail across the Powder River Basin were defeated by strong opposition of the Sioux, despite army escorts. By the end of the 1860s completion of the Union Pacific made Ogden and Salt Lake City the principal inland supply centers, and the riches of Butte lured the first railroad, a narrow-gauge line north from Ogden completed in 1881. Two years later the golden spike of the long-awaited northern transcontinental was driven west of Butte, completing the Northern Pacific trunk line between St. Paul and Portland, crossing the entire breadth of Montana, and further stimulating settlement expansion.

Montana was a huge block of land (147,000 square miles), and its population tripled in the 1880s, but when it was admitted as a state near the end of that decade most of its people were still in its early nuclear area. This Montana core was a roughly circular region extending from the fine ranching country of the Gallatin Valley around Bozeman to Philipsburg and adjacent silver camps on the west, and from Virginia City to Helena on the north. Near the center, almost astride the Continental Divide, Butte, already famous as "the Richest Hill on Earth," was the focus of one of America's largest mining complexes. It sent its ores to a huge smelter in the new satellite town of Anaconda, from where the copper was then shipped to Great Falls for final refining. Great Falls was also a new and integral part of the system but lay further afield and was much more than a satellite. It was founded in 1883 by a Minneapolis investor who saw in its waterpower potential and local coal the basis for a thriving industrial center. He had the backing of James J. Hill, and once Hill's Great Northern Railway reached there in 1887 and soon thereafter completed a connection with Butte, Great Falls boomed into the second largest city and new northern gateway, undercutting Helena's commercial position. To the west of the main region timber companies began to move in upon the fine forests around Missoula and the northwest, and much of this product was destined for the mines and smelters. Meanwhile ranching was spreading over the entire state, far outgrowing the local mining market and soon suffering the woes of overexpansion and unusually severe winters or drought common to most all such Western operations.

By 1900 Montana had a quarter of a million people, with a quarter of these in Butte-Anaconda. They had come in mainly from other western areas, from Nevada, California, Oregon, western Canada, and, later on, from Colorado. Half of the Butte population was foreign-born, with the Irish and Cornish especially prominent (the Chinese had been held down to their early numbers); Slavs and Italians were beginning to show up in the smelting and coal towns, Finns and Swedes from Minnesota and the upper Great Lakes in the timber camps. Similarly, capital and early leadership came especially from San Francisco (with a few important additions from Salt Lake City), and then as the railroad arrived and the successful companies expanded, became ever-more heavily controlled by Boston and New York. By the turn of the century Montana was already infamous as a "company state," its politics and development dominated by the copper barons and closely associated industrial and railroad interests, its workers responding with militant unions (the Western Federation of Miners was organized in Butte in 1893). Whether viewed as a whole or just in its historic core area Montana was distinctive; it was considerably more substantial than Nevada or Idaho, but even though similar to Colorado in important respects—in its great mining industry and mountain setting—it was not at all comparable in scale or diversity of development: its largest city was just another Leadville; it had neither a Denver nor a Colorado Springs.

Wyoming Wyoming was the great exhibit of a spatial remnant, a large, virtually vacant block of country left over after the formations of Nebraska, Dakota, and Idaho. Territorial status was conferred in 1868 in response to the building of the Union Pacific and the need for some minimal government for its incipient service centers. By that date the track had reached Rawlings Springs (Rawlins), halfway across the 370-mile expanse. Cheyenne, in the far southeastern corner—barely within the territory—was the only real town and therefore the capital. The townsite had been selected the year before as a railroad division point at the base of the mountains, and it seemed the likely junction for a branch to Denver. The first census, taken about a year after the completion of the railroad, reported 9,118 inhabitants in the entire territory; the first counties were five longitudinal subdivisions of the territorial rectangle, each anchored on a Union Pacific town: Cheyenne, Laramie, Rawlins, Green River, Evanston. Thirty years later these five towns plus Sheridan, a ranching supply center in the far north, were the only ones with as many as 1,000 people; Cheyenne, still the capital, had 14,000. During that time thousands of head of Texas and Oregon Country cattle had been driven in, and untold thousands of dollars—much of it from British investors—had fueled the speculative expansion of ranching over the whole state as fast as the Sioux and Crow Indians could be removed. Railroads had begun to penetrate the center and cross the northeast, but exploitable resources were limited and no new centers of development had emerged. Wyoming remained a vast, thinly populated expanse anchored upon its Union Pacific axis and still focused on its southeastern corner.

The Black Hills Cheyenne's eccentric position allowed it to compete for the trade of a major western mining boom typical of the West but strikingly absent from Wyoming (where an 1867 rush to South Pass proved to be an ephemeral affair). Rumors of gold in the Black Hills, an isolated compact mountainous dome forming a dark forested wall beyond the barren badlands 150 miles west of the Missouri and 100 miles east of the general Rocky Mountain front, had been building for some years, magnified by the fact that little was known about an area revered and closely guarded by the formidable Sioux (and locked in a "permanent" reservation by treaty in 1868). The Depression of 1873 and lack of other new diggings intensified agitations and probings. The army tried to halt or expel trespassing prospectors, and in an effort to replace rumors with facts and to locate a site for a protective post, the government authorized an extensive exploratory expedition in 1874 under General George A. Custer. However, gold was discovered by members of the party, given nationwide publicity, and generated uncontrollable pressures. Negotiations with the Sioux to cede and withdraw were unsuccessful, and the army gave up trying to protect the area. The ensuing invasion brought retaliations, an army campaign that resulted in the annihilation of the impetuous Custer's entire company before the subsequent defeat of the Indians, and the forced treaty of cession in 1876. The towns of Custer and Deadwood were early major camps, and Rapid City, midway between, was promoted as the main commercial center. The general application of methods learned in Nevada and Colorado, and, more specifically, the early development of the fabulously rich Homestake Mine at Lead by San Francisco capitalists, provided a sustaining base for the Black Hills to emerge as a coherent settlement region. Its early connections were south and east, with Sidney, Nebraska, and Cheyenne on the Union Pacific, Bismarck, a railhead on the Missouri, and Yankton and Sioux City (sending steamboats to Fort Pierre) competing for the coveted traffic. In spite of treaty provisions for wagon roads, the great belt of Indian reserves west of the Missouri impeded any direct railroad link between the two settled parts of southern Dakota for many years. Thus the first railroad to reach the Black Hills came in 1886 by way of the Niobrara route across northern Nebraska, providing connections with Sioux City and Omaha. Cheyenne continued to be an important gateway for traffic from other western mining regions.

This unusual "island" so clearly set apart and so different in every way from agricultural Dakota on the prairie plains east of the Missouri was inevitably restive under territorial rule from Yankton or Bismarck (the successive capitals). A petition for a separate Territory of the Black Hills was sent to Congress in 1876. When the idea of taking parts of adjacent Wyoming and Montana ran into opposition, a proposal simply to divide Dakota along 100°W received the enthusiastic support of Bismarck (which saw itself as the logical capital) but got nowhere in Congress. None of these ideas generated much interest outside the regions affected because the population was so small (the 1880 census found fewer than 15,000 in the Black Hills), and the prospects for general settlement (even if the Indian reserves were much reduced) appeared so limited that there seemed little point in wrangling over the redrawing of lines around empty country. When "the Hills" became a western outlier of a new South Dakota in 1889 it contained barely 10 percent of a population that had more than tripled with the great agricultural boom of the eighties, and thus in the larger map of America it appeared as a minor Far Western region captive within the bounds of a distinctly Middle Western state.

Arizona and the Copper Borderlands The early Territory of New Mexico, reaching from Texas to California, was a temporary geopolitical unit spread across two quite distinct physical and human regions: one anchored on the Rio Grande, with vital commercial connections eastward to Missouri, the other a thinly settled expanse of mountains and tropical desert of the Gila basin now oriented by a sudden new compelling commerce westward to California. As we have seen, it was not long before attempts got under way to subdivide this extensive territory so as to conform more closely to its human geography. Early efforts aimed at a latitudinal division to detach and encompass the southern corridor of trails to California (as briefly realized in Confederate Arizona), followed by the actual longitudinal division setting apart the western half as the new Territory of Arizona, and some years later some rather feeble attempts to detach southern or southwestern New Mexico and bind these to Arizona to form a more logical geopolitical entity of common interests and character. During these same years and recurrently thereafter various politicians and promoters, feeling that the Gadsden Purchase of 1853 was far short of American needs and opportunities, were urging the United States to purchase, occupy, or gain extensive formal concessions in adjacent Sonora.

For thirty years this southern corridor was a dangerous area of limited attractions and remained sparsely populated. Prospectors worked over the gravels of the Colorado River and the dry placers of the western desert, and in the 1870s Tombstone, Clifton, and Silver City became mining towns of considerable substance, drawing wheat and flour from Sonora and making use of Guaymas as a port with steamship connections to San Francisco. Only with the building of the railroads across the region and the defeat and confinement of the Apaches in the 1880s did stockmen from Texas and California begin to occupy fully these sparse rangelands and farmers take up all the lands along the thin scattering of perennial streams. By 1900 there were about 20,000 settlers in the Salt River Valley, an essentially new agricultural district. Phoenix, the first of its towns, named in recognition that Anglos were reoccupying the lands of an ancient agricultural people whose canals and village sites were still plainly discernible, was the territorial capital and largest center in this tropical oasis, where the landscape of palm trees and citrus groves, alfalfa, cotton, and winter vegetables, and the string of young towns with their largely Middle Western populations lured by shrill land promoters made the whole scene more akin to Southern California than to the older Southwest.

Tucson, the oldest and largest (7,500) of Arizona towns, was representative of the more common character of the region: largely Hispanic in population, with Papagos, Christian Indians, and Apaches nearby, dominated by an Anglo leadership thriving on a hinterland of mines and smelters, ranches, army posts, and Indian agencies, and with both Anglo and Hispanic businesses serving a busy transregional and international traffic. Anglo penetration of northern Mexico had been rapid after the rise of Porfirio Díaz, and especially in the 1880s with the completion of major railroad projects. The title of a book published in San Francisco in 1881 (the first of several editions) well expressed a common American view: *The Border States of Mexico: Sonora, Sinaloa, Chihuahua, and Durango . . . A Complete Description of the Best Regions for the Settler, Miner and the Advance Guard of American Civilization.* Sonora was unusually open to such "peaceful conquest of the country." It was very remote from the core of Mexico, walled off by almost impassable barrancas from adjacent Chihuahua, and for years its only railroad links with the rest of the country were by way of the United States. Furthermore, it had been devastated during the Apache raids and civil wars and was desperately short of capital to rebuild and exploit its well-recognized resources. Thus American and other foreign investors flooded in, buying up mines, ranches, and potential irrigation areas, building railroads, telegraphs, and telephone systems, and cooperating with a willing set of Mexican politicians, merchants, and hacendados. The human geography of the state was considerably remade (fig. 28). The new border city of Nogales became the main gateway, undercutting in some degree Guaymas's role; Hermosillo, midway on the railroad near new agricultural colonies on the Rio Sonora, replaced and surpassed the old capital at Ures and the old elite center of Alamos. But much the most radical change was the creation of great copper camps at Nacozari and Cananea. By 1905 the latter was the largest settlement in Sonora, and there were many lesser ones (fig. 29). These borderland mining developments were wholly American initiatives, extensions from a set of big American complexes, such as Santa Rita, Morenci, Globe, and, especially, Bisbee a few miles

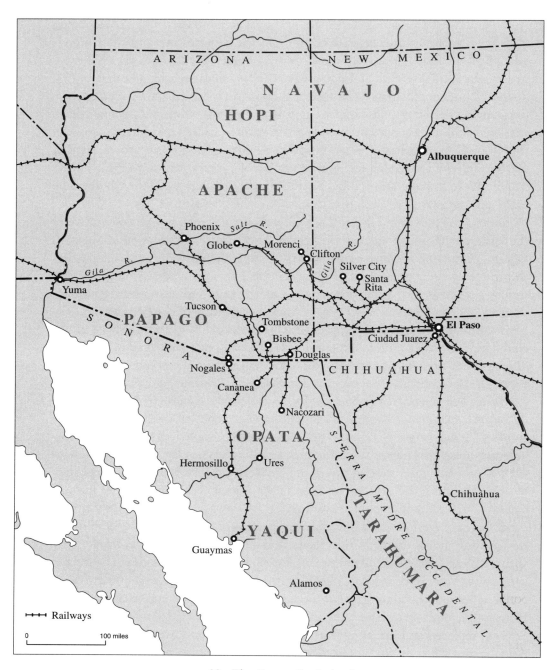

28. The Copper Borderlands.

29. Cananea, Sonora.

After William C. Greene built this large smelter in 1904 to serve a rich body of copper ore, Cananea Vieja, now lying within the curve of the railroad, became a village remnant within a settlement of 22,000. A formal company town, with neat cottages along straight broad streets, was laid out nearby for American engineers and managers. (Courtesy Arizona Historical Society, Tucson, AHS #52, 478)

north of the border. Bisbee's Copper Queen mine became the main base of the Phelps Dodge Company, which controlled Morenci and Nacozari as well, and in 1904 built a large smelter at the new border town of Douglas to handle all these ores. The company also built a railroad to connect with El Paso and to bring in coking coal from northern New Mexico.

El Paso was the eastern anchor of this borderland region. Located at a famous strategic site, the American city was almost entirely a modern creation of the railroads. Within a few years it had direct connections with Houston, Kansas City, California, and Mexico City. Its railroad yards, huge smelter, stockyards, and wholesale houses served a large area, reaching deep into Mexico and drawing workers north to this new border creation. By 1900 about half of El Paso's 16,000 people were Hispanics and another 8,000 lived in Ciudad Juárez (the former Paso del Norte, renamed in 1888), its largely residential and entertainment twin (bull-

ring, racetrack, gambling halls, brothels). Many of these Mexicans were daily
workers in El Paso, and thousands of others had moved on through to jobs in
smelters, mines, packinghouses, and railroad gangs. This burgeoning binational
complex was a prime generator of an important "border culture" featuring intricate
relationships between two peoples who retained their ethnic identities while inevitably altering one another. Here Mexicans on either side of the border were
sustained by a complete and lively Hispanic community, and those who moved
further into the United States usually maintained close links with kith and kin,
with much visiting on family and festive occasions. And so they routinely carried
on much of their folkways, while at the same time they were being shaped by the
practices and pressures of a modern commercial and industrial world, their children going to school and learning at least rudimentary English. Although generally
strongly class-structured and ethnically segregated, modern portals such as El
Paso–Juarez, Ambos Nogales, and Tucson supported a substantial Hispanic business and professional society working closely with its bilingual Anglo counterpart.

South of the border the penetrations and power of the Americans had given rise
to a common recognition within Mexico of a distinct *norteño* regional culture.
Broadly applied to all the border states, it was most apparent in Sonora (Chihuahua was ruled through all these years by a powerful entrepreneurial extended
family that did much business with Americans but retained firm control over
politics and many resources). Not only was the American presence and control
greater than elsewhere, but Sonora's isolation from major Mexican centers and the
ease of contact with American ones magnified such influences. Wealthy Sonorans
could travel to Los Angeles and San Francisco, or even to St. Louis, Chicago, and
New York, more readily than they could get to Mexico City. Most of their business
relationships were with Americans, they admired American styles and methods,
many of them sent their children to schools in the United States, English became
the main language of commerce, and their habits of thrift and enterprise prompted
others to refer to them as "the Yankees of Mexico." More common folk were also
exposed to foreign influences, they "purchased low-priced American goods, drank
St. Louis beer, and developed an interest in . . . baseball," and picked up English
words for a variety of new ways and things.

However, even if "for many Sonoran social groups, the United States rather
than Mexico became their cultural point of reference," they did not cease to be
Mexicans nor cease to be concerned about the political and cultural dangers of
offering so liberal a welcome to this "advance guard of American civilization." The
state tried in various ways to curb and control this insidious invasion, such as
prohibiting the use of English in official documents and private contracts. Furthermore, even to those at the highest levels, who were profiting the most from
American activities, the imperial character of this relationship was ever apparent:

"foreign arrogance . . . pervaded every sphere the outlander touched." There were actually never more than a few thousand Americans resident in Sonora at any one time. A few of these were settlers in new irrigation districts (and Mormons in their refugee colonies—mostly in Chihuahua), but most were managers or engineers in American-owned industries, railroads, and other systems. The ethnic hierarchy was most starkly on display in the big copper camps, which were "imperial enclaves complete with *guardas blancas* (company police) and extraterritorial rights . . . 'fiefdoms' ruled by a . . . foreign master." When a pliant Mexican governor invited a volunteer Arizona militia to come and help the American owners suppress a great workers' strike at Cananea in 1906 there was a strong upsurge of resentment over such subservience. The tensions building up over such imperial behavior would soon explode and become one of the driving forces of the revolution. Led by norteños, that long, costly civil war would end by having driven most of the Americans out and by stoutly reasserting the reality of the geometric boundary line as the firm northern edge of a proud nation. Such actions, however, could not impede the continued vital engagement between these peoples in this part of one of the world's great cultural borderlands, a sector that had emerged so strongly and portentously in the thirty years just before the revolution.

ALTERING THE EDGE: WHERE THE WEST BEGINS

All of these Western regions, major and minor together, made up the new half of the nation that emerged so rapidly, variously, and famously from midcentury onward, distant and distinct from the older Eastern half. It took the whole course of this period for this Far West to begin to be routinely recognized as simply the *West* and the older Transappalachian West to become the *Middle West*—and a large degree of uncertainty and confusion about such regional references would persist. For the historical geographer, the question "Where does the West begin?" (in the modern usage of this term) had all this while a relatively clear and simple answer: it began immediately beyond the westward advancing "frontier line of population" depicted in the Walker Atlas showing "the Progress of the Nation." That line always marked a sharp discontinuity: it was drawn along the current inland limit of contiguous Euro-American settlement; beyond lay an open, unsettled—or at least very thinly settled—country: an abrupt change in land and economy. It was a feature unmistakable on the map, or on the ground, because to get from the older half of the country to settlements in the newer half required a long journey: either a tedious trek across the Plains (across the "prairie ocean" by "prairie schooner," as early pioneers sometimes described it) or a far longer voyage on the high seas to circumvent that midcontinent expanse.

That intervening area was a physical region of great distinction, a land that made a powerful impression on all who encountered it. Yet the Great Plains was not in itself a region in the same sense as all those Western regions we have been sketching, for it was not a coherent regional system of settlements and activities but a particular kind of country, a whole area being probed, traversed, and its indigenous human ecology destroyed without a well-proven alternative system of domestication ready to replace it.

For a short while this sharp break in human geography was a formal boundary: the "Permanent Indian Frontier" drawn along the western borders of Missouri and Arkansas to separate an Indian America from a White America. The lower Missouri served as the main avenue of Euro-American advance and towns such as Independence, at the elbow of the Missouri, became the portals from which caravans embarked for Santa Fe or Oregon. These trafficways, hanging close to the shallow Arkansas or the Platte to get across the high, dry plains, carried a rapid increase in volume in the latter 1840s—the Oregon migrations, the Mormon exodus, the sudden surge to California—and this "tremendous stream of westering humanity" generated an expanding swath of disturbance across this midsection. Intruding upon hunting grounds, depleting the buffalo, spreading smallpox and cholera, provoking countless clashes between invader and invaded, it produced such a train of troubles that in 1851 the United States government convened a huge gathering of Indians at Fort Laramie (and soon thereafter a lesser one at Fort Atkinson on the Arkansas) to work out treaties of accommodation. After long parlays the Indians agreed not to interfere with American traffic along these routes in return for gifts and annuities and formal recognition of various tribal territorial lands and hunting grounds.

Some of these horse-mounted buffalo-hunting tribes were still formidable adversaries, and the United States was not yet in a position to shove them around as it might have wished. An attempt, without first obtaining Indian permission, to add the Bozeman Trail as a major branch angling off from the central trafficway to the Montana mines across the hunting grounds of the Sioux and Crow resulted in the annihilation of a small U.S. cavalry force and a new Treaty of Fort Laramie (1868) that closed that route and defined large Indian reserves in the Northern Plains in return for a mere reaffirmation of the open corridor along the Platte, including the rapidly advancing Union Pacific. But, of course, the completion of the Pacific railroad was decisive to the momentum and force of this invasion and suppression. It "has totally changed the conditions under which the civilized population of the country come in contact with the wild tribes," wrote the secretary of the interior in his annual report of 1869: "Instead of a slowly advancing tide of migration, making its gradual inroads upon the circumference of the great interior wilderness, the very center of the desert has been pierced. Every station upon the railway has become a nucleus for a civilized settlement, and a base from which lines of exploration for both mineral and agricultural wealth are pushed in every direction." Furthermore, the railroad greatly increased the range and power of military forces to respond to the inevitable uprisings of Indians provoked by such radiating trespass. As General Sherman put it, in good imperial prose: "the *railroad* which used to follow in the rear now goes forward with the picket-line in the great battle of civilization with barbarism."

The advances of the Kansas Pacific and the Santa Fe railroads across the Kansas plains further split the once vast North American buffalo herd and rapidly accelerated the slaughter of the southern remnant, impoverishing the southern Cheyenne, Arapahoe, Kiowa, and Comanche and thereby increasing raids upon travelers and settlements by desperate Indians. In 1869 the army began a program to force all of the tribes to surrender and remove to reservations or face extermination. Carried on intermittently year after year, it focused on attacking Indian camps and systematically destroying all property—horses, tepees, robes, blankets, food, kettles, and other belongings. After many clashes and much killing the assault was brought to a conclusion in 1875 when five army columns converged on the last winter camps of the Kiowa and Comanche in the sheltering canyons of the Caprock escarpment in the Texas Panhandle and proceeded to kill, devastate, and carry off the remaining peoples to a reserve in Indian Territory. Two years later the hide hunters completed the extermination of the southern buffalo herd.

Meanwhile, as these southern operations were coming to a close, retaliation for the annihilation of Custer's troop and other humiliations was being carried forth in the north. Although after the Bozeman Trail defeat General Sherman had declared that "we must act with vindictive earnestness against the Sioux, even to their extermination, men, and women and children," the Sioux (who were not a single people but a loosely associated set of tribes) were not hunted down to destruction but harassed, threatened, and bribed into accepting major reductions in their reservations, giving up their beloved Black Hills yet retaining much of the remaining land just west of the Missouri in southern Dakota. Meanwhile, the northern Cheyenne and other Indians in this sector—Mandan, Atsina, Arikara, Assiniboin, Crow, Blackfoot—became confined to a scattering of reservations along upper Missouri waters. In October 1883, after the Northern Pacific had built westward up the Yellowstone Valley (on a right-of-way extracted from the Crow), William Tecumseh Sherman, in his final report as general of the army, declared: "I now regard the Indians as substantially eliminated from the problem of the Army. There may be spasmodic and temporary alarms, but such Indian wars as have hitherto disturbed the public peace and tranquillity are not probable. . . . The recent completion of the last of the four great transcontinental lines of railway has settled forever the Indian question." Insofar as "the Indian question" was a matter of warfare, that was essentially true—excepting only the dogged pursuit of a handful of Apache and the pathetic horror of the Ghost Dance finale at Wounded Knee.

By that date "the buffalo question" was also settled forever. The last 75,000 or so of the northern herd, hovering north of the Yellowstone, were wiped out in that year. A few that had scattered into the Dakota badlands were killed in 1884; a Smithsonian expedition of 1886 had trouble finding 25 good specimens for taxidermy and estimated that no more than 300–400 bison remained alive anywhere in the United States.

Historical assessment of this rapid massive extermination has been complicated by many uncertainties. Estimates of the total North American herd in historic time have varied enormously, from as many as 100 million (proposed by nineteenth-century observers staggered by the immense numbers sometimes seen and extrapolating for the immense extent of their possible range) to something closer to 30 million, based on diverse modern research estimates (taking into account bovine reproduction, grazing capacities, climate cycles, Indian numbers, annual losses, and so on). Whether the horse-mounted Plains Indians were depleting the herds before the onslaught of the Whites remains controversial—though there can be no doubt that the introduction of the horse initiated radical ecological and cultural changes. Nevertheless, several features and phases in the nineteenth-century assault stand out: the systematic annual killings by métis and Indian hunters in Assiniboia and Saskatchewan to provide pemmican for the British American fur trade; the rapid increase in the shipments of buffalo robes from the upper Missouri with the introduction of steamboats serving an expanding St. Louis market; the heavy toll taken by provision hunters and casual marksmen in the broadening trafficways across the Central Plains; increased inroads on the southern herd by eastern Indians relocated into Indian Territory; a sharper decline in the 1850s, now attributed to drought, introduction of cattle diseases, and competition with expanding herds of horses; marked increases in the volume and range of White intrusion with various Rocky Mountain mining rushes; the advance of railroad construction, supported by professional provision hunters; the development of new long-range rifles and new tanning processes, creating a market for hides rather than robes, leading to the final slaughter.

The extermination of the buffalo was powered by more than profits and profligacy. Many influential people in the nation and ordinary people in bordering regions regarded it as a simple and effective way of "solving the Indian question." Although never explicitly declared as official policy, there was a growing acceptance by army officers and high public officials of the idea that "every buffalo dead is an Indian gone," for to destroy "the Indians' commissary" would "hasten their sense of dependence upon the soil" (as farmers, on reservations). The army routinely assisted large hunting parties of visiting royalty and other dignitaries in this famous sport of the North American Plains, and by the 1870s they were furnishing free ammunition, "protection, supplies, equipment, markets, storage, and shipping facilities" to commercial hide hunters. Officers might occasionally voice a kind of moral rationale—"if we kill the buffalo we conquer the Indian. It seems a more humane thing to kill the buffalo than the Indian, so the buffalo must go"—and, rarely, even an outright protest at "this wicked and wanton waste," but the policy was driven by the great difficulty and cost of defeating the Plains Indians in direct warfare. General Sherman therefore applied in the West what he had so effectively demonstrated in the South: that the best way to destroy the will to resist was to devastate the countryside. It was a work quickly accomplished and highly effective. As Sitting Bull attested: "A cold wind blew across the prairie when the last buffalo fell—a death-wind for my people."

After the slaughter came the bone men, scouring the Plains, hauling their cargo to immense piles at the railroad stations, from where they were shipped east to be ground up for fertilizer. This gleaning was essentially finished in a few years (but the *mining* of buffalo bones, that is, excavating the deep deposits at buffalo "jumps"— attesting to Indian hunting practices over thousands of years—especially in the rougher Northern Plains was carried on in a small way for half a century).

In his *Memoirs* General Sherman took satisfaction in, and expressed a common American view of, this imperial transformation of the Plains, "in having in so short a time replaced the wild buffaloes by more numerous herds of tame cattle, and by substituting for the useless Indians the intelligent owners of productive farms and cattle ranches." However severe his characterizations, there was no doubt about the great rapidity and extent of change. Terry Jordan has provided a definitive account of the emergence of distinct cattle-ranching systems that were poised to move in upon this "great natural pasture-ground of the nation." Much the most famous response came from Texas, featuring the cattle drives to Kansas railheads that resulted in "the largest short-term shift of domestic herd animals in the history of the world." But this Texan component was much more complex than commonly supposed and much less effective in the longer run than less colorful competing systems. As Jordan demonstrates, rather than being an obvious product of the encounter between Anglos and Mexicans in south Texas, as long assumed, one must look farther eastward for the real antecedents: in the late eighteenth century "Anglo-Americans bearing a mixed Carolinian-Mexican herding culture crossed the Sabine River from Louisiana mounted on horned saddles and swinging their lassos above their heads, accompanied by black and mixed-blood slaves possessing the same skills. 'Anglo-Texan' ranching, for want of a better term, was born in the humid prairies of Louisiana." Somewhat later, another system, essentially British in origin, was carried by Upland Southerners to the Blackland Prairies and Cross Timbers of North Texas, where it picked up traits from the older coastal system (such as equestrian skills, roping, and lack of care of livestock), and after the Civil War this area served as "the principal staging ground from which the Texas ranching system launched its spectacular diffusion through the Great Plains." In the vanguard was a spread westward to the Pecos Valley and thence north to the Colorado Piedmont, bringing beef to army posts, Indian reservations, and mining camps, and setting up ranches in attractive sites along the way, from which there would also be an eastward movement onto the Plains as the army and hide hunters finished their clearances. But although Texas stockmen ranged widely over the Plains, piedmont, and Rocky Mountain parklands, they failed to dominate most of these areas because, generally speaking, they failed to adapt to these new environments (especially in the care of livestock through harsh winters) and their tough, half-wild cattle were less desired by the markets. Texas longhorns also carried a fever tick that could devastate non-immune domestic cattle, and they became increasingly barred by law and by force from many northern ranges and shipping points.

The Texans lost out to a system superior in its quality of stock, management, and strategic position. This basically "Anglo-Celtic" system, with American anteced-ents in Pennsylvania and southerly Appalachian valleys, was well established before midcentury in half a dozen major districts in the Transappalachian West, including the Boonslick Country of western Missouri. It was thereby positioned for ready extension westward in the form of "road ranches" along the great overland trafficways, and especially the Platte River route across Nebraska into Wyoming and Colorado. Deriving stock from and serving as supply points for the swelling stream of emigrants, such ranches were in effect a series of experiment stations in the management of cattle under the special environmental conditions of this vast region. The "Midwestern system" that had already emerged just to the east featured smaller-scale operations, much greater attention to the quality and care of stock (especially fencing and winter feeding), and shorter drives to fattening areas before slaughter, and it proved better able to survive the blizzards and droughts, over-stocking, speculations, and depressions that battered the whole American indus-try. Missouri, Iowa, and Illinois were the main sources, but the great demand for cattle upon the sudden opening of large areas of the Northern Plains following the defeat of the Indians also drew large herds and stockmen from the Oregon Country, where ranching of a generally Midwestern type had been established some years earlier. Thus, in the longer run, while incorporating selected practices and para-phernalia from—and appropriating the romantic image of—its Texan and Califor-nian rivals, this basically British-derived system came to dominate the cattle industry of the entire West.

Sheepmen also moved out upon the Plains in competition, at times in open conflict, with and eventually in succession to the cattlemen in some of the rougher, drier, or quickly depleted lands. German stockmen and their Hispanic shepherds brought flocks of sheep and mohair goats to the Edwards Plateau. Hispano shepherds spread eastward and northward from their northern New Mexican home-land; Scottish drovers, some from Canada, others from Oregon, moved in upon Wyoming and Montana. With an upgrading of stock, wool became an important export staple of the western margins of the Plains and adjacent mountains.

These stockmen and their herds were both a replacement of the Indians and the buffalo and a continuation of the Plains as a distinct human geographic area. Even though the ranching system was largely a diffusion from the Eastern states, the scale of operations, the physical environmental conditions, and the separation from the great farming regions made it unmistakably a *Western* operation. How-ever, the line of separation between these ranching and farming realms was always unstable and for most of this era was shifting westward as farmer colonization advanced at the expense of ranching.

This farming advance upon the Prairie Plains was well under way before the Civil War. The notorious Kansas-Nebraska Bill of 1854 was a belated response to the massive trespass of White settlers upon the large Western Indian Territory. The attractiveness of such lands had not been in doubt. The commissioners who reconnoitered them in preparation for Indian removal had declared them well suited to the farmer from the Eastern Woodlands, and emigrant Indian agricultur-ists as well as Whites in similar lands in adjacent Missouri and Iowa soon proved them right. Wartime anarchy slowed the process, but thousands poured in after the war, aided by the recently enacted Homestead Act (the national monument to the first such claims stands just west of Beatrice, Nebraska) and the visible advance of railroads. In spite of the depression of the mid-seventies this massive colonization movement continued deep into Kansas and Nebraska, with an important branch reaching northward up the Big Sioux and James river valleys into southern Dakota.

These pioneers were routinely employing a system of farming, featuring corn, small grains, hogs, and cattle, together with a variable array of garden, orchard, and specialty crops, that had been successfully implanted all across this midsection of the Transappalachian West. It was a system under continual improvement with a growing variety of machinery for most every task and served by rapidly extending transport networks. When this advancing frontier moved onto the higher, drier plains, however, a good many adaptations had to be made to the more severe environmental conditions. Fuel, lumber, and fencing had to be purchased and imported, and water lay at greater depths, necessitating new kinds of windmills and further experiments with crops, tillage systems, and tree plantings. Cultivation was at first confined to the bottomlands along the shallow stream valleys, but many local trials soon seemed to demonstrate that good crops of wheat might be obtained from the vast expanse of these drier plains, and in the 1880s, bolstered by a popular belief (endorsed by some scientists) that the very act of cultivation on such a comprehensive scale would produce a permanent increase in rainfall, the surge of land seekers was carried well into eastern Colorado. In the Republican and Platte river areas of southwestern Nebraska corn was also successful on the uplands, and the corn-grain-hog complex was thereby extended nearly to the Colorado line.

Such a generalized sketch can offer little sense of the actual processes and problems of this pioneering. It was always fraught with hardship and risk from weather, insect plagues, animal disease, insufficient machinery, undercapitalization, and fluctuating prices, and it displayed high turnovers in farm operators and owners and in the local businesses that served them. But the momentum of this movement was not halted until the late 1880s, when a sequence of dry years and lower grain prices created a broad band of crop failures and a good deal of abandonment and retreat, followed by a long era of experimental adjustment to the more generally appreciated hazards of this capricious land. Although unstable in its drier western margins, the enduring result was the Winter Wheat Belt, based upon drought-resistant varieties of hard wheat brought in by Mennonite colonists from Russia, and extending from central Kansas into Colorado and eventually southwesterly into the Texas Panhandle, as one of America's major agricultural regions (fig. 30).

Colonization of the Northern Plains proceeded slightly later and with some important differences. The salient of typical Midwestern agriculture spreading up the Missouri Valley into southeastern Dakota and the early wheat-specialty area of southwestern Minnesota provided the thresholds for this advance. Railroad lines across the broad, level Red River Valley were soon followed by the famous "bonanza farms," created by investment syndicates, featuring huge acreages, great echelons of steam-powered equipment, armies of seasonal laborers, and industrial-type management to convert the heavy black soils of this former glacial lake bed into a richly productive grainland. Smaller operations of a similar type were not uncommon in nearby districts, but the "Great Dakota Boom" of the 1880s was mostly the usual family farm colonization that quickly spread the Corn Belt over southeastern Dakota and extended the Spring Wheat Belt north and west across all the smoother glaciated lands east of the Missouri. In this northern sector the great river approximates the edge of glaciation and thereby marks an abrupt change in the land: all to the west is heavily dissected drier country, at its worst the infamous badlands, and most of it so poor in farming prospects that it was left in Indian reserves. Eventually a few thin and broken lines of settlement would spread along the railroad corridors toward—and in the far north, into—Montana to form the frayed, unstable outer margin of contiguous Midwestern colonization.

The southern sector also featured important variations. Immediately south of Kansas, White colonization was prohibited until Congress forced open, in piecemeal but rapid fashion, the lands of Indian Territory. After passage of the Dawes Act in 1887, which imposed upon each Indian household an individual allotment

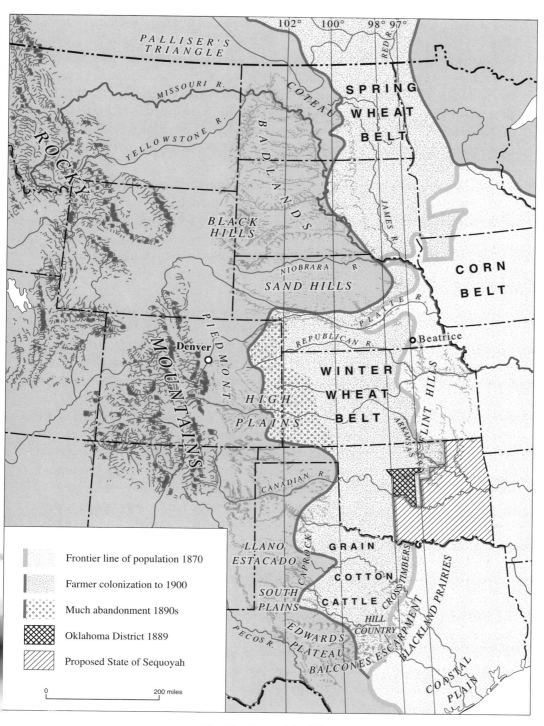

Legend:

- Frontier line of population 1870
- Farmer colonization to 1900
- Much abandonment 1890s
- Oklahoma District 1889
- Proposed State of Sequoyah

0   200 miles

Map labels:

PALLISER'S TRIANGLE
SPRING WHEAT BELT
MISSOURI R.
YELLOWSTONE R.
COTEAU
BADLANDS
ROCKY
BLACK HILLS
RED R.
JAMES R.
CORN BELT
NIOBRARA R.
SAND HILLS
PLATTE R.
REPUBLICAN R.
Beatrice
MOUNTAINS
Denver
PIEDMONT
HIGH PLAINS
WINTER WHEAT BELT
FLINT HILLS
ARKANSAS
CANADIAN R.
LLANO ESTACADO
CAPROCK
GRAIN
COTTON
CATTLE
CROSSTIMBERS
BLACKLAND PRAIRIES
SOUTH PLAINS
PECOS R.
EDWARDS PLATEAU
HILL COUNTRY
BALCONES ESCARPMENT
COASTAL PLAIN

30. The Edge of the West.

and relinquishment of claim to the leftover acreage, White pressures to occupy these "surplus" lands within the reservations mounted to near explosive proportions (the army was assigned to patrol the Kansas border to thwart trespass). The first release, on April 22, 1889, sent 50,000 people in a mad scramble to select lands in the Oklahoma District in the heart of the former territory and resulted in the instant creation of Guthrie and Oklahoma City as rival centers along the track of the traversing Santa Fe Railroad. A year later Oklahoma Territory was created, leaving a remnant Indian Territory to the east, and within a few years all of its lands had been opened to settlers.

This influx came most heavily from the north, but Texans also occupied a broad zone in what was in effect an extension of the pioneering that had gradually domesticated the rolling brushy lands west of the Cross Timbers, featuring grain, corn, cattle, and a bit of cotton. By 1900 this advancing frontier had spread thinly to the base of the Caprock, but it was all considered risky country, and despite a scattering of small colonies there was no general movement onto the vast, level surface of the High Plains.

Thus, by the outset of the twentieth century the westward-advancing frontier of contiguous settlement had moved deeply into this broad midcontinent expanse of open country. The familiar farmsteads and farming systems of adjacent regions were spread thickly across all the Prairie Plains and more thinly and selectively upon large parts of the higher, drier country, where parched dust-scoured grainfields, simple bleak forms of houses and barns, and scraggly bits of shrubbery and garden might suggest how far indeed had been the extension from the more congenial lands of Easterly origin. They also might reveal how ineptly Congresses (also largely of Eastern origin) had struggled from time to time to adjust national land policies to suit the changing needs of this westward advance. The Homestead Act of 1862 was more a culmination than a new departure, confirming a quarter-section (160 acres) as the appropriate basis for a family farm just as pioneers were reaching the drier plains. An attempt to legislate woodlots onto those plains by the Timber Culture Act of 1873 (just before the invention of barbed wire), which required 40 of the 160 acres to be planted in trees, was so misguided and misused as to be repealed soon after. By the time the Enlarged Homestead Act of 1904 offered 320-acre parcels in designated areas of the Western states there was little public land left fit for dry farming at any scale. Actually through most of this time more farmland was purchased than homesteaded, because the government allowed cash sales until 1891 and during a short period (1862–71) had granted an immense acreage, including broad swaths of alternate sections across North Dakota, Nebraska, and Kansas, to railroad companies that marketed and managed such holdings to suit their purposes.

We shall have more to say about the several settlement regions represented in this movement, but for now we simply focus on the fact that their unstable western margins continue to mark the western limits of "the East"—and thereby the eastern edges of "the West." Such a boundary does not closely approximate those simple surrogates that were so often employed to define this gross national division: it is not coincident with a meridian (the Ninety-seventh, Ninety-eighth, or One-hundredth) or with an isohyet (twenty inches of rainfall, or fifteen); rather it is a sinuous line reflecting terrain and soils and growing seasons as well as rainfall cycles and the systems of farming being applied. There will be further advances as well as retreats, and permanent farming derived from these systems will become established in a scattering of districts farther west, but these will be islands within vast reaches of largely open, unplowed lands (just as there were enclaves of ranching farther east, most notably the Bluestem Pastures of the Flint Hills in Kansas). Thus there remained a residual realm of ranching, a band of open country varying in width and in kind, reaching from the coteau, buttes, and badlands of Dakota, through the Sand Hills of Nebraska, the narrower contested High Plains of Colorado, the apparently level and almost waterless platform of the Llano Estacado, and on through the sandy scrub-covered South Plains to the mesquite-mottled grasslands of the Edwards Plateau rising abruptly out of the Coastal Plains of Texas: a visible, obvious, functional separation of the major settlement regions of the East from those of the West. (As we shall see, the contested border between steppe and sown extended on far to the north across the Canadian Prairies as well, but with very different meaning to larger national-regional perceptions and issues in that transcontinental confederation.)

Here indeed was "the real dividing line between the eastern and western portions of the continent," "a plain mark on the face of the earth," but one imprinted by human experiment rather than simply read from the appearances of nature. It coincided neither with the lines laid down upon the map by those who warned of the folly of trying to cultivate what nature had decreed to be uncultivable nor with those who assured that cultivation itself or new techniques thereof could extend the great "grain garden of the world" clear across the Plains. And the human experiment would continue—and continue to alter the edge.

9. Indians and Empire

To speak of "Filling in the Far West" is of course to view history and process from the standpoint of White American settlers and developers. After all, the whole area had been filled with Indians following their own patterns of life for many centuries. From this other side, filling in meant closing out, marking the end of Indian freedom and the completion of their conquest, confinement, and systematic subordination within the American empire.

Such a dual contradictory process was apparent at the time to anyone who thought seriously about the matter. As Francis A. Walker (of the Walker Atlas, who served a brief interim as commissioner of Indian Affairs) observed in 1872: "The freedom of expansion which is . . . to us of incalculable value [is] to the Indian . . . of incalculable cost. Every year's advance of our frontier takes in a territory as large as some of the kingdoms of Europe. We are richer by hundreds of millions; the Indian is poorer by a large part of the little he has. This growth is bringing imperial greatness to the nation; to the Indian it brings wretchedness, destitution, beggary." "Surely," Walker went on to say, "there is obligation found in considerations like these," and it was in fact a time of major reassessment of basic understandings and policies related to "the Indian problem."

A report prepared for the great Centennial Exposition in Philadelphia in 1876 concluded that "the usual theory" of decline and eventual disappearance of the Indian "must be greatly modified." The latest enumeration totaled about 300,000 (excluding newly acquired Alaska). That was surely a marked reduction from the early days of the Republic, but more recent trends were much less certain. Although a generation later the census reported only about 265,000, problems of definition beclouded all such enumerations, and by then there was even more reason to accept the 1870s proposition that "in all probability" the Indians were "destined to form a permanent factor, an enduring element of our population."

They were also, therefore, in all probability an enduring element on the map of the United States (fig. 31). By the opening of the new century the national pattern of Indian reservations appeared to be generally fixed, even though many local issues remained to be resolved by Congress or the courts and many details of the pattern would be modified in the years to come. That simple geopolitical pattern was a profound display of imperial history and policies. (We shall here confine our attention to the western half of the nation.)

The initial, compelling impression is one of brokenness, a shattering, a scattering of fragments and huge areas swept clean—a late stage in the relentless advance of a conquering population. Such a view gives appropriate stress to the pressures applied but can mislead as to the results obtained. For the wholeness that was shattered was a unit only in the general sense of "Indian Land"—a perception peculiar to the Whites—whereas that area was in fact composed of hundreds of tribal areas, greatly varying in size and shape, often imprecise in definition, unstable in location. Many of what may seem to be fragments were more precisely remnants, tribal territories still anchored on traditional ground, a persistence rather than a scattering, even though much reduced in scope. Indeed many such reductions were more drastic than any general map can convey for some peoples were left with only a few hundred acres; yet that attests that in some cases even bands of a few people tenaciously clung to some bit of ground and won formal

31. Indian Reservations, 1900.

Portion of Plate 36A, Paullin and Wright, *Atlas of the Historical Geography of the United States*, 1932 (Courtesy The Carnegie Institution of Washington)

recognition from the imperial power. Furthermore, such a map cannot show various other concessions, such as the right of taking fish or of hunting and gathering on designated waters and grounds.

And yet, there were indeed many fragments in this overall pattern, more than the simple outline of areas reveals, for a good many reservations now contained several different sets of Indians and many of these represented dislodgments and sometimes drastic relocations by imperial decree. The idea of creating a few large reserves to accommodate further mass removals remained alive long after the first great Indian Territory had been partially dissolved. The reduction of that entity to its original southern half (modern Oklahoma) led to the logic of creating a similar area north of the central transcontinental trafficway, where the Sioux still occupied a large area. Another one or two might be located somewhere in the Far West (the Yakima in the Northwest and somewhere in the Southwest were suggested). It is not clear that successive proponents of such a policy envisioned a complete removal of all Western Indians into a few collection areas. What is clear is their main concern with imperial efficiency and convenience. Such concentrations, they argued, would be far easier to protect and police ("the sale of liquors and arms could be more effectually prevented; bad white men could more easily be kept out of the Indian country"); shorter, well-defined boundaries would allow fewer possibilities for White contact and encroachment ("the danger of violence, bloodshed, and mutual wrong materially lessened"); many agencies "could be abolished"; and logistic costs would be greatly lessened ("many are so remote and difficult of access"). Most important, of course, was the fact that "large bodies of land would be thrown open to settlement"—entire states and territories could be freed of this nagging, miserable complication to their growth and prosperity.

But increasingly removal on such a scale had a bad reputation. The tragic history of the Cherokees on their Trail of Tears was becoming better known, the costly failure of the forced relocation of the Navahos to Bosque Redondo was fresh in the minds of pertinent administrators, and in the late 1870s new cases of similar tragedy and injustice (the Northern Cheyennes and the Poncas) received national publicity. Eastern sympathizers rallied to the cause of Indians in general; Westerners were alert to oppose any attempt to use their state or territory as a dumping ground for more Indians. A few prominent punitive removals were carried out, such as exiling recalcitrant Modocs, Chiricahua Apaches, and Chief Joseph and his band of Nez Perces to Oklahoma (these last were later released), but the concept of concentrating all Western Indians in a few large territories was never enacted. It would, of course, have been an immensely complicated, costly, and controversial program—but one backed by a powerful American precedent.

The ruling policy, more by default than by desire, remained one of many small reservations, ad hoc creations arising out of local circumstances. Ideally each reserve should be assigned as (in the words of an 1850s commissioner) "a permanent home, a country adapted to agriculture, of limited extent and well-defined boundaries; within which all, with occasional exceptions, should be compelled constantly to remain until such time as their general improvement and good conduct may supersede the necessity of such restrictions." In fact, such ethnic enclaves tended to be located on marginal lands least desired by Whites. Officials responsible for the management of such enclosures usually recognized the imperative corollary that these be made inviolable, free from the trespass of Whites, but Indian reservations in effect were protectorates without protection, for the imperial government never had the will to marshal the means and enforce its treaty obligations. As an investigative board concluded in 1869: "the arm which should have been raised to protect them has ever been ready to sustain the aggressor."

Policy makers always regarded Indian reservations as more than just holding pens for a marginalized people; each was to be a school for "civilization." Most Indian treaties included provisions for farmers, artisans, and teachers to reshape Indians into successful participants in American society. Proponents often envisioned large composite Indian territories as states in embryo, evolving into full (or perhaps special) members of the federal union. In such projections, tribalism would naturally have become subdued and tribal areas would become simply the constituent counties within the incipient state. Yet "tribalism"—the basic sociopolitical integrity of each traditional Indian group, whatever it might be called—was the one thing that virtually every Indian leader insisted on maintaining. That resolute stand proved anathema to a wide spectrum of Americans, including most of the self-defined "friends of the Indian." As one commissioner put it, to permit Indians to organize a local "government of their own" simply "to gratify this sentimentality about a separate nationality" would create a "political paradox"; it was an "un-American and absurd idea." And indeed by the time he was writing (1886), the practice of contracting treaties with Indian groups, no matter how large or small, as if each was "an independent nation, tribe, or power" had been abruptly ended by Congress fifteen years earlier. Such a change had been strongly advocated by many imperial agents, especially the military, which thought it absurd even to define each Indian society as a "domestic dependent nation" (long the official legal term) when they were in fact or in prospect simply helpless wards of the federal government.

As the work of conquest neared completion the next stage in the national program, to transform Indians into productive American citizens, received ever-greater attention. The reservation system, initiated long ago when much of "the Indian race was outside the limits of the organized States and Territories and beyond the immediate reach and operation of civilization," needed to be reassessed, for civilization now "surrounds these people at every point." Reservations, which had been initiated as a device for protecting Indians through separation, must now be adapted to foster integration.

There was by this time a broad consensus on what needed to be done. First of all, Indians had to be "de-tribalized." Their "excessive attachment to Indian tradition and nationality" had been "one of the most serious hindrances to the advancement of the Indian toward civilization," and thus "their tribal cohesion" must be dissolved so that they can "merge" into "the body politic as independent and self-relying men." Second, they must leave their old nomadic, shiftless ways and become anchored on the land as self-reliant farmers. Third, "the Indian will never be reclaimed until he ceases to be a communist": they must become individual owners of land and learn to manage private property. Fourth, Indians must forsake their traditional communal-consensual concepts and modes of law and authority ("a 'chief' in white terms was always a white invention") and embrace the American system of formal laws, rights, and procedures as well as hierarchical structures of power. Finally, Indians must become imbued with American patriotism. They must be compelled "to come out of isolation, into the civilized way . . . —into citizenship— . . . into the path of national duty." Native tongues must give way to English, native names translated into "decent and reasonable" names, native religious ceremonies replaced by standard Christian pieties; Indian youth should be instructed "in the elements of American history" and "the elementary principles of the Government," and schools should feature "the American flag," "patriotic songs," and "national holidays."

Individualism, self-reliance, private property, laws, courts, and leadership, patriotism, and Christian piety: in short, preparation for the fullest participation in "Anglo-Saxon civilization." There was little dissent among White leaders from the general intent of this program (their wards were not invited to contribute). Some members of the emerging field of scientific anthropology warned that whole societies could not be changed so readily, but even they—evolutionists all—accepted the concept that private ownership of property was the "principal instrument" of social advancement in the "natural order of progress . . . from a nomadic to an agricultural state." John Wesley Powell, famous expert on the American West and first director of the Bureau of Ethnology at the Smithsonian Institution, though warning of difficulties, strongly endorsed the necessity of some such initiative. It seemed at the time the only hope. As a commissioner bluntly put it in 1889: "This civilization may not be the best possible, but it is the best the Indian can get. They can not escape it, and must either conform to it or be crushed by it."

In the 1880s a rapidly expanding, ever-more centralized and standardized Bureau of Indian Affairs launched "what amounted to a wholesale assault on Indian culture and community organization," banning religious ceremonies and objects, altering marriage practices, sending children to off-reservation boarding schools (much the most famous, and far afield, was the Carlisle Indian School in Pennsylvania). But the really decisive move was the General Allotment, or Dawes, Act of 1887. Its central feature was *severalty:* the allocation of individual parcels of land to tribal members (160 acres to each household, half that to orphans and single adults). The title deed to such lands was to be held in trust by the secretary of the interior for twenty-five years, so as to preclude quick sale or lease to Whites and to await further progress toward civilization. The remaining "surplus" reservation lands were to be auctioned to White claimants and revenue from such sales applied to expansion of Indian schools and other aids. Upon finally receiving title to the land, each Indian was to become a citizen and subject to the laws of the state where he resided. As Frederick E. Hoxie concluded, the Dawes Act "stands as a pure product of the reformer mind of the age—hostile to every vestige of tribalism, coercive, well-meaning, certain that the Great Father knew what was best for his red children."

At the outset, officials emphasized the need to proceed gradually and carefully to carry out this radical transformation of Indian tenure and status. Each reservation was to be opened only at the discretion of the president and with the consent of the tribe. But local and national pressures quickly compromised every provision of this idealistic scheme. Empowered by new Supreme Court rulings, Congress proceeded to divest the Indians of their lands as quickly as possible. Necessity of Indian approval to begin the allotment process was abrogated, the right to lease lands approved, and shortly thereafter the right to sell; revenues were used to develop irrigation systems and other facilities to enhance development—virtually all for the benefit of Whites. Such a precipitous transfer of lands was often rationalized as the most effective means of "civilizing" Indians: by forcing them to labor on their own small plots and to follow the example of their White neighbors. (A Western senator had vigorously argued for including in the Dawes Act a provision allowing Indians to select only alternate quarter-sections, so as to create a checkerboard pattern of comprehensive contact with White settlers—the extreme opposite of years of support for the ideal of ethnic segregation.) The Indian school system was rapidly expanded but also increasingly altered in objective from education for citizenship to "industrial training" in manual skills. And the very concept of citizenship was modified in the Indian case to allow continued imperial management of unequal peoples.

The Five Civilized Tribes were excluded from the original Dawes Act (as were the Pueblo Indians, who were ostensibly secured in their lands and citizenship by the Treaty of Guadalupe Hidalgo). Because these peoples had "ignored their allegiance to the United States" during the Civil War parts of their original spacious reservations had been taken from them and used to accommodate the relocation of other tribes, but they lived relatively comfortably on the remainders, with herds of cattle on fine pastures, farms, orchards, and an array of modern institutions: tribal capitols and elected governments, courthouses, schools, churches, and seminaries, hospitals and asylums, newspapers, and much else. But they had been forced to allow railroads to cross their lands, the territory was studded with new towns, and there were already more Whites than Indians in residence. A national program for Indian allotments inevitably intensified agitations to break open tribal hold upon "this inviting tract of country, larger than all New England," and the creation of Oklahoma Territory in 1890 and sequence of large land openings therein generated explosive pressures from local "boomers" and government officials alike. The councils of the Five Civilized Tribes firmly resisted the concept of severalty, whereupon, in 1898, Congress forced it upon them, decreed the end of tribal courts, and set a deadline (1906) for the termination of tribal government.

In 1870 a bill to create a "Territory of Ok-la-ho-ma" had brought memorials from Indian leaders denouncing any such transformation as a violation of treaties and a White scheme to steal their lands, and had spurred the General Council of the Five Civilized Tribes to assess means of preserving local tribal control. Subsequent subdivision of their special territory, the actual creation of an Oklahoma, and insurge of White settlers propelled strong movements locally and in Congress for single statehood for "the Twin Territories." However, the wording of an 1899 agreement between a federal commission and the Cherokees seemed to recognize the real possibility of separate statehood for the residual Indian Territory, and within a few years Indians (and various interested Whites) had held a convention, drawn up a constitution, had their proposed State of Sequoyah (with the capital initially at Fort Gibson) endorsed by referendum by a huge margin (although the Creeks and Chickasaws were not supportive), and petitioned Congress for admission (cf. fig. 30). But the senator in charge of the Committee on Territories had already forthrightly declared that "no bill making Indian Territory a state has the slightest chance of passage," and such was the case. Nationally the issue of Oklahoma and Sequoyah became entangled with that of Arizona and New Mexico, with little congressional support for four new states and eight more senators from sparsely populated regions (and no administration support for a Sequoyah that it assumed would always vote Democratic). The alternative was "jointure" in both cases and was passed in 1907. However, whereas a combined Arizona–New Mexico required the approval of voters in each of those territories, no such dual endorsement was appended to the Oklahoma case and single statehood was ratified by 70 percent of the 255,000 voters. In the end most Whites and some Indians in Indian Territory gave their approval rather than continue as an increasingly undependable federal dependency. A few years later the superintendent of the Union Agency now administering the Five Civilized Tribes (Congress had relented on the schedule for terminating all tribal authority) reported that the work of allotment to the 101,216 enrolled members (including 23,381 "Freedmen"—former Black slaves or their descendants) was nearing completion.

Advocates of this national policy could point to reassuring signs in the new century that "the Indian problem" was heading toward a solution. The era of open warfare and bloody clashes seemed at last to be past; large numbers of Indians had been reduced to dependence on government rations for physical survival—for food, clothing, medicines; and an imperial management system was supervising a comprehensive program of culture change. In his first annual message to Congress, Theodore Roosevelt spoke with satisfaction of the allotment program as "a mighty pulverizing machine to break up the tribal mass." Anthropologists were avidly at their work of "salvage," to gather from the oldest living tribal members what Indian culture was like before it was distorted by the irresistible forces of contact and set on the path of disintegration and disappearance. Within a few years the first volumes of the ultimately twenty-volume work on *The North American Indian* by the famous photographer Edward S. Curtis ("a modern George Catlin") would appear, with its haunting opening shot of a band of Navaho fading into the desert haze, conveying, as the caption stated, that "the Indians, as a race, already shorn of their tribal strength and stripped of their primitive dress, are passing into the darkness of an unknown future." And indeed, the ultimate objective of the government's program was to make the Indian invisible: to vanish as a special category of people; to make American Indians into individual Indian Americans. It was inevitable, because one could not halt progress; it was appropriate because Indian societies were not worth saving—why preserve primitive "islands" in the midst of civilization?

Yet one did not have to look far to see that such assumptions and expectations were quite unreal. Severalty, the key instrument for change, was proving to be far more complicated and far less effective than expected. The process of defining those eligible, surveying the land, and assigning individual parcels was expensive and tedious and peaceably resisted by most Indians for as long as possible. Furthermore, the whole concept was simply inappropriate to many cases. Allotments were supposed to turn Indians into farmers or stock raisers, but large portions of reservation lands were desert, mountain, canyonlands, badlands, timberlands, or mere fishing stations. And so, although the program was put into effect in the fertile lands of the Great Plains and a few other arable areas (such as the Camas Prairie of the Nez Perces), after twenty years of effort less than half of all Indian lands had been allotted and less than 2 percent of that was actually cultivated by Indians. By then it was becoming clear that the "campaign for equality and total assimilation had become a campaign to integrate native resources into the American economy"—that is, to get these lands into the hands of Whites as soon as possible. In 1913 the commissioner of Indian Affairs admitted that, abetted by the Oklahoma legislature, the Indians there had been "subject to an orgy of looting." Furthermore, as Frederick

Hoxie summarized in his careful study of the topic, by that time "assimilation was no longer an optimistic enterprise born of idealism or faith in human progress; the term now referred to the process by which 'primitive' people were brought into regular contact with an 'advanced' society. When this process produced exploitation and suffering, it seemed logical to believe that it was teaching Native Americans the virtues of self-reliance and the evils of backwardness."

Most important, despite earlier expectations and still some wishful thinking, Indians were not vanishing. They were indeed "a permanent factor, an enduring element of our population." American policy makers had always considered "Indian Country" anomalous and temporary, yet there it was: nearly 200 "islands," forming several regional archipelagoes on the geopolitical map of twentieth-century America. However fragmented, reduced, marginalized, and compromised these scattered remains might appear, they represented the tenacious hold of Indian peoples on their own identities. However penetrated and subverted these territories might be, ostensible Indian reserves wherein White intruders, settlers, and leasees controlled most of the land and imperial agents asserted authoritarian rule over many dimensions of Indian life, these were more than hollow frameworks: they represented fundamental legal and psychological realities in basic geographic form. Furthermore, these were not just "Indian" lands but many kinds of lands containing distinct Indian societies greatly varied in numbers, character, and economy, in location, experience, and types of relationships with White America. Imperial agents in the field might be acutely aware of such deeply grounded variety, but national policies were always shaped by the general assumption that "Indians" constituted a single category of people who must all be changed in the same manner by similar processes. Such crude tools were bound to fail in a task so varied and difficult. On the other side, the failure to create an Indian state as a member of the federal union was less important than the success—despite a bitter, desolating history of assault—of hanging on to these many bits and pieces. For although the former might have become a powerful symbol of an "Indian" presence and participation in federal affairs, these dozens of enclaves scattered across half the national territory attested to a long roll call of captive peoples who continued as a real presence—as Pawnee, Papago, Paiute; as Apache, Comanche, Cheyenne, and Chinook; as Modoc, Makah, Mohave, and two hundred others. In the long run, these bits of territory—turf—matter.

10. American Wests—American Domain

The United States entered the twentieth century as a fully transcontinental republic and nation. Half a century of imperial conquest and management and the accompanying swirl of migrations, colonizations, and exploitations had spread an

American population over all this western half of the country. Even though it was, on the whole, still thinly settled compared to the rest, containing only a little more than 4 million of the 76 million enumerated in the 1900 census, there could be little doubt but that it would continue to grow in population and productions. Powerful business interests, lavishly aided by the federal government in some cases, had firmly bound all these distant centers and regions into the primary networks of the nation. Within a few years the transformation of the remaining territories into states would complete the formation of a transcontinental federation. In short, what had been no more than a vast imperial sphere of potential attraction and development in 1850 had become an integral domain of a vigorously developing nation in 1900.

Our review of this half century of developments has emphasized the distinct character of each major region and hence the necessity of thinking in terms of American *Wests* rather than a single great entity. Nevertheless it is also important to recognize what these areas have in common when viewed in this larger, national perspective. Obviously one thing they share is the very fact of this transformation, this eventual functional integration with the older half of the nation, and there were some common features of that process. Viewed broadly, a four-stage sequence can be readily recognized:

1. *Migration and Implantation.* Each of these areas was far removed from the main body of the nation and could be reached only by long journeys by land or by sea. Such movements require some special compelling attraction and tend to be highly selective of migrants. The initial nucleus must perforce begin in a high degree of isolation, with only seasonal or occasional connections to source and market areas. Formal government is likely to be capacious in frame but rudimentary in substance.

2. *Experimental Adaptation to New Environmental Conditions.* Physical conditions in the American West were sufficiently different from those in the East as to preclude the routine transfer of familiar agricultural and, in some cases, industrial practices, and in most regions major alterations were required. Furthermore, none of these areas was uninhabited, and in some cases deep-rooted populations were present in such numbers as to require sociopolitical adaptations by the invading Americans.

3. *Expansion and Regional Formation.* A continuing influx of migrants opens up new resources and leads to the occupation of all readily exploitable areas, creating a system of settlements connected by transport networks and focused on a regional capital. A distinct regional society emerges, attempts to shape a geopolitical frame-

work to fit its territorial aspirations, and retains a high potential for cultural divergence from the still-remote national society.

4. *Articulation and National Integration.* The extension of national trunk-line railroads revolutionizes time, mode, efficiency, and costs of contact with the main body of the nation. New inflows of people and capital begin to have major impacts on settlements, economic developments, and marketing; there are increasing pressures toward national control and cultural conformity, but regional distinctions based on marked physical and sociocultural differences persist.

Applying this general sequence to the six major regions reveals both the shared patterns and the anomalies to be expected among such a diverse set of areas (fig. 32). Among the greatest variations was the contrast in the opening stage between a Gold Rush California and a New Mexico annexed not for any resources of its own but because it provided access to that Pacific province. As for stage 2, Oregon required the least adaptation and Utah the most, for the Mormons had no direct experience with irrigation (but they at least understood the challenge they were facing, whereas the Mediterranean-type climate of California was unfamiliar to Americans and necessitated extensive experimentation). Colorado was anomalous in its late initiation and quick railroad connections so that its regional formation was simultaneous with heavy national investment. National integration was of course a powerful process for all these regions, but with marked variation in immediate geographic impact: bringing the least change to an already complexly developed California, the most to the physically complex Pacific Northwest with its divergent and competitive Columbia River and Puget Sound foci. The impact of new people and alterations in social geography during this stage were most apparent in Mormonland, New Mexico, and Southern California.

For all the importance of those iron bands connecting these Wests with the nation, there remained important distinctions of the *West* as a whole within the bounds of the United States. There was the sheer distance from the national core, the visible, experiential separation of East and West by those intervening open plains. Even the fastest trains took more than a day or a night to cross the narrowest band, between Omaha and Denver. Furthermore, there was the divergent pull of another ocean—hardly discernible perhaps in Colorado, minor in New Mexico, but palpable in Mormonland and powerful upon all within the real Pacific Slope. The attraction was not simply the existence of a great ocean and its invitation to the seacoasts of the world but the strong lure of vigorously developing American societies on that coast with their widely heralded resources and potentials.

Most obvious was the simple fact that this West was a different kind of country, a land and climate unlike anything in the East. Generalizations about that difference often foundered—then as now—on the great variety *within* the West, for it contained the wettest as well as the driest areas of the country, the hottest as well as some of the coldest, the highest as well as the lowest, scenes of rugged grandeur as well as some of the most monotonous of countrysides. No one could move here from the East without encountering those differences, look upon these landscapes without seeing the great contrasts with former homelands, experience Western seasons without feeling the change, till this ground for farm or garden without making adjustments in familiar practices. Those differences were what prompted the great series of government-sponsored surveys of Western lands (the most famous of which we now commonly identify by the names of their leaders: King, Hayden, Wheeler, Powell). Their massive, often beautifully illustrated reports and maps of geology, natural history, and physical geography were not merely contributions to science but tools to be put to use in developing the resources of these strange lands.

Furthermore, these great surveys were themselves a step toward what would become another general contrast between East and West: the continuing major role of the federal government in Western life. That unprecedented intervention arose in large part from those contrasts in geography, from the fact that American policies designed to transfer public lands into family farms simply could not work as intended in most Western areas. Thus "although Congress wanted to replicate existing landholding patterns, agricultural systems, and republican institutions in the West," not only did colonization processes, settlement patterns, and developmental sequences fail to follow Eastern precedents, a large proportion of the land (even after lavish distributions to railroads, states, and various special recipients) remained under federal control. How to find ways to bring these lands into beneficial use called forth extraordinary efforts and instruments, including not only those special surveys (and the famous rejection of John Wesley Powell's program for the Arid Region as too radical a departure from established land survey and allocation systems) but also the institutionalization of such study in the U.S. Geological Survey, the establishment of extensive government-administered reserves of lands (such as national forests and parks), and federal irrigation developments under the National Reclamation Act of 1902 (sixteen projects were authorized within the first three years). The administration of these activities produced an increasingly professional and centralized bureaucracy that was "often more powerful than local political interests in the West." Thus, just as the Bureau of Indian Affairs became a permanent fixture rather than an agency designed to terminate its own special business through the transformation of its wards into citizens, so, as Richard White noted,

	CALIFORNIA	**SOUTHERN CALIFORNIA**	**OREGON**
1 *MIGRATION AND IMPLANTATION*	gold rush sudden enormous influx from many sources sparse local populations overwhelmed worldwide shipping services to remote frontier	minor American influx incidental to gold rush Hispanic ranchos Indians few and marginal infrequent connections by sea or land	overland folk migration from Border South to Willamette Valley fur trade legacy Indians few and marginalized Yankee entrepreneurs irregular ocean connections
2 *EXPERIMENTAL ADAPTATION*	intensive experimentation with summer-dry subtropics Mexican land grant complications innovative mining techniques instant urban populations	Anglo borrowings from Hispanic prelude: grain, citrus, vineyards experimental irrigation colonies Mexican land grant complications	agricultural adaptation to Northwest Raincoast Donation Law allotments search for markets for flour, lumber, fish California as market and competitor for colonists
3 *REGIONAL FORMATION*	San Francisco as focus of California and Pacific Slope river, road, rail network early capacious state staple exports. local capital cosmopolitan population strong sense of regional identity	Anglo developers shape region with focus on Los Angeles new towns, improved port, local railroads citrus and sanitaria districts agitation for state subdivision	Portland as focus of Willamette and Columbia Interior river service and local railroads Columbia Plain as agricultural frontier Puget Sound as minor district Washington Territory
4 *NATIONAL INTEGRATION*	California railroads eastward to national network continued influx of heterogeneous population intensification of capitalist agriculture San Francisco as primary focus of Far West Hawaii as satellite	transcontinental railroads bring influx of middle-class Midwesterners instant towns, massive speculations, little industry, a new suburbia national fame as distinct and attractive region	competitive railroad connections transform regional structure: Seattle, Tacoma, Spokane, and Pacific Northwest national investment in staple exports Alaska as satellite

32. American Wests and the Stages of Integration.

MORMONLAND	NEW MEXICO	COLORADO
cohesive American theocratic society seeking refuge in isolated, unattractive area Indians few and marginalized	imperial conquest Anglo agents and opportunists intruding upon major Hispanic and Indian societies meager resource attractions	gold rush influx mainly from American North eager investors, modest rewards competitive connection with national network Indians defeated
experimental irrigation agriculture regional subsistence economy intrusion of Gentile merchants and federal officials attempt at Deseret	Anglo connivance for Mexican land grants Army suppression of nomadic Indians German Jewish merchants as intermediaries Anglo-Hispanic political negotiations	experiments with mining and milling problems. experimental irrigation colonies experimental ranching on high plains speculative investors and politicians
Salt Lake City as focus of Mormon nation centrally managed regional development theocratic society augmented by European converts extensions beyond Utah	Hispanic peasant and pastoral expansion Catholic reform of Hispanic church Anglo control of best lands and potential resources Anglo-Hispanic political tensions	Denver as focus of mining hinterland late initiation and ease of national railroad connections results in conflation of Stages 3 and 4
Gentile influx to Salt Lake City and Ogden and railroad and mining towns Federal coercion forcing Mormon conformity Mormon-Gentile business cooperation	Anglo influx development of lands, industries, resorts, bicultural towns Plural society under increasing Anglo dominance cultural compromise on statehood	major mineral discoveries regional railroad network rapid emergence of distinct complex of economic activities with strong focus on Denver Indians expelled early statehood

The federal bureaucracies of the land office and the territorial system were only to be a giant administrative scaffolding from which officials and citizens together would build models of older states. When they were finished the scaffolding would come down and the new states would stand as duplicates of the old.

Much of the scaffolding did eventually come down, but other sections of this administrative framework remained, and in fact the government began elaborating and adding to the framework until the scaffolding, in altered form, became a permanent fixture in the West.

Thus an unusual degree of "dependence on the federal government has been a central reality of western politics" and has helped shape a special political concern and character that is recognizable throughout the region even though varied in its particular state expression and rarely cohesive in any broader sense ("there has been no western equivalent of the solid South").

Although all the territorial scaffolding did eventually come down, it stood for much longer over much of the West than elsewhere because of those great differences in land and peoples. The thinness of populations over large areas for long periods of time retarded statehood in numerous cases (Washington was under federal territorial administration for thirty-six years), while the presence of captive, nonconforming peoples retarded the admissions of Utah, New Mexico, and Oklahoma even longer (sixty-two years for New Mexico). And the great spaciousness of the West, the wide separation of its several nuclear settlement areas, became built into the federal system. Aside from the State of Washington, with its great watery indentations, all the eleven westernmost states were larger than any state to the east (excepting of course the obvious anomaly of Texas, which was not a congressional design), averaging over 100,000 square miles, twice the average size of those in the older Transappalachian West. Even so, given their populations, almost all of these states enjoyed representation in the U.S. Senate far greater than comparable populations elsewhere—thus enhancing their voice in pertinent federal policies.

Finally, the West was distinguished by the presence of particular peoples, though each was unevenly distributed across the region. It was the home of most Indians (although the former Indian Territory, eastern Oklahoma, contained the largest concentration). It was home to the largest deep-rooted bloc of Hispanic peoples (in New Mexico) and to borderland Hispanic communities being augmented by immigrants from Mexico (as was the case in Texas). And it was home to most of the Chinese in the continental United States and to the more recent influx of Japanese. The great majority of these Asians were in the Pacific Coast states, but Chinese, especially, were to be found in industrial camps and railroad towns throughout the West. Although even taken together these peoples constituted but a small proportion of the regional population, each was regarded as a problem by the dominant Whites, and all were subject to special laws and treatment. Such discriminations and suppressions were specific to the West only in terms of these special groups. They were, of course, routine expressions of deep-seated and general American attitudes, with reference to which we should note that Blacks, the major pariah population of the United States, were present in all of these states but totaled only about 30,000 in 1900, two-thirds of whom were in California and Colorado.

Students of the West have often cited other features that help distinguish and define this half of the country, and closer examinations of society, economy, and politics might yield further evidence. But the geographer cannot but remain impressed with the limitations of many such generalizations, with how awkwardly or incompletely they fit upon the several regions within the West. Rather than strain to find what else California, Mormonland, New Mexico, and the others might have in common, it seems far more useful to conclude with a stress once again upon the bold reality and basic significance of American *Wests*. Having sketched something of the historical geographic character of these diverse parts it is time to turn once again to the East and trace the development of the other domains and core of the nation during this powerfully formative half century and thereby gain a clearer picture of what these several Wests and the West as a whole were being contrasted with and connected to in this continuous shaping of America.

PART THREE
CONSOLIDATION: STRUCTURING
AN AMERICAN NATION

The age we live in favours aggregation. The assimilative power of language, institutions, and ideas, as well as economic and industrial forces, is enormous, especially when this influence proceeds from so vast a body as that of the American people east of the Rocky Mountains.

James Bryce, 1915

Prologue

While the newer half of the United States was emerging into its distinct and diverse set of American Wests, the older Eastern half was becoming shaped into some decisive and long-enduring patterns. Simultaneous with the outward expansion and dispersal that created a fully transcontinental nation was an inward intensification and consolidation that concentrated formidable power of the national economy and society into a particular quarter of the country.

We begin with the need to put the United States back together and note how the South became bound more firmly into the national system even as it became an even more self-consciously separate region. Meanwhile the power of the dominant North was being greatly reinforced by industrialization and served by an elaborating transport infrastructure anchored on its great cities. So, too, the rapidly rising volume of immigration, altering the content and regional character of American society, had heaviest impact in this same region.

Overall, we are especially concerned with how the United States moved into the twentieth century as an increasingly integrated, unequal, stabilized—and contentious—set of regions and with the geographic networks sustaining its national systems.

1. A Re-United States

An unsuccessful civil war is likely to pose peculiar and painful problems. Such conflicts, when fought on a grand scale, create an internal wound that can be healed only by effort on the part of victor and vanquished alike. Being a "war between the states," the American case bore special peculiarities and ironies. A victorious North might assume that it would impose its will upon the defeated South, but its most basic, obvious goal was to restore the Union: to bring the Southern states back into full and equal membership in the federation. Yet to readmit these eleven states must inevitably alter the balance of political power in the nation, rewarding the part that had so gravely and grievously threatened the whole. Thus the aftermath of military conflict saw an intense, complicated political conflict: "a headlong collision of nationalism and federalism."

A further irony was soon apparent. All agreed that secession was a dead issue— that much, at least, had been resolved. However, the South, which had insisted that secession was a legal and practical solution to an intractable political problem, now sought to ignore or rescind secession and thereby automatically return in good standing to full membership, whereas the North, which had insisted that the Union was perpetual and secession illegal, now declared that these states had no standing (had "committed suicide," in one version of the matter) and could only be readmitted by becoming reconstituted on Northern terms. Whatever the ironies or illogics might be, the immediate problem was what those terms of readmission should be. No peace treaty defined such a thing, for—as usually the case in unsuccessful civil wars—no government had been recognized that could sign for the South. There had been simply an end to belligerence, an acknowledgment of Northern victory, but no agreement within the victorious party as to what they should do with the vanquished. "Mr. Lincoln gropes . . . like a traveller in an unknown country without a map," complained the *New York World* about (what would prove to be) the president's final speech on the matter, but it *was,* in effect, a new country for which only an incongruous set of crude sketch maps were being made available.

As noted in the treatment of the sundering of the federation (*Continental America,* 461ff.), the welter of proposals to deal with this problem may be simplified into three general categories. The simplest gave priority to *restoration,* to bring the Southern States back into the Union as quickly as possible. A second emphasized *integration,* the need to bind the South more effectively into the nation and help it partake of all the commercial, industrial, and modernizing trends of the time. The third insisted on the necessity for *regeneration* of the South, to enforce and nurture basic changes in society and polity to bring it into conformity with the North. These three formulations are of course gross simplifications of a highly complicated affair and they were not mutually exclusive. They could be combined selectively in various ways, and the struggle to define and sustain a national program to deal with "the Southern question" would preoccupy Congress and the administration for a dozen years after Appomattox.

At the end of the war, Andrew Johnson, the Tennessean who succeeded to the presidency, worked hard for minimal terms to restore the Southern States to the Union as quickly as possible. But Congress was in no mood for such a benign policy after such a bloody conflict, and competing presidential and congressional programs were stillborn until passage, over President Johnson's veto, of the Reconstruction Act of 1867. With this action "instead of a quick return to complete self-government, much of the South remained under federal domination for more than a decade." Our task is not to review all the complicated issues of this notoriously controversial era (which are treated at some length in every substantial American history text) but to focus on some important geopolitical features of that time and on some geographical changes in the South on through the end of that century and into the next.

THE SOUTH AS AN IMPERIAL PROVINCE

In 1865 the entire South became, in effect, a new imperial holding, and it displayed many features common to such conquered, captive territories.

1. *Military Occupation and Rule.* The area was initially divided into four territorial divisions (Atlantic, Gulf, Mississippi, Tennessee), each under the command of a major general, and these further subdivided into one or more military departments conforming to a state (fig. 33). Although "most generals preferred not to think of themselves as military governors," and none had been trained for the task, they and their subordinate officers faced immediate needs to provide for public order, protection of freedmen, disarming of local militias, relief of the destitute, for courts and schools, health and sanitation, repair of railroads, roads, bridges, and levees, and much else. Their problems were compounded by lack of manpower. Within two years the number of troops had been reduced to about 20,000 for the entire region, with further marked reductions in the 1870s. Although reconstituted civil governments (organized under the supervision of these military commandants) increasingly assumed their normal responsibilities, sporadic bloody disorders in the backcountry (and in some cities) were recurrent, and although the policing role of the army was at times officially reasserted, it was never given enough troops to cope with such problems.

2. *Imperial Agents Fostering Sociopolitical Changes.* Imperial management involved various other institutions and activities. Much the most notorious were the Northern men who dominated the early phases of governmental reorganization imposed upon the South. Working with newly enfranchised Blacks and a few Southern White allies, they manipulated elections in favor of the Republican party, which was regarded by most Southern Whites as the perpetrator of their miseries, a vindictive enemy instrument. In the new state governments of 1870 in the Lower South (the "Cotton States") four of the seven governors and ten of the fourteen senators were Northern men.

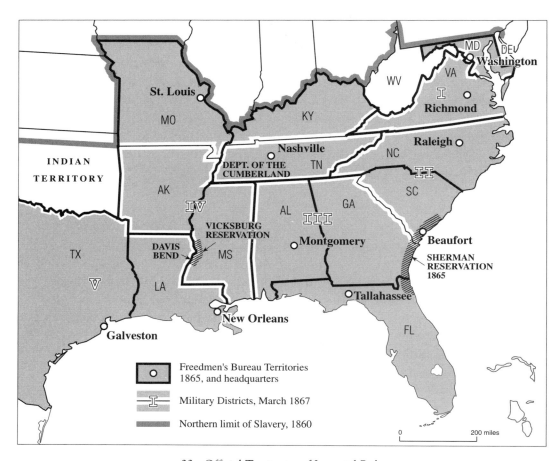

33. Official Territories of Imperial Rule.

The most notable new instrument of empire was the Bureau of Refugees, Freedmen, and Abandoned Lands, created within the War Department. Led by General O. O. Howard and a set of army officers ("the nation's most advanced experiment in social welfare . . . grafted onto the most conservative of American institutions"), this agency at its peak had 900 men in the field dealing with relief of the destitute (Whites as well as Blacks), confiscated and abandoned properties, and, especially and soon almost exclusively, the question of how to stabilize and sustain nearly 4 million freed slaves. Many more unofficial agents were also involved in such work, most especially schoolteachers, some supported by Northern philanthropy, others working in public schools created by Northern-dominated state governments (in defiance of widespread Southern White resistance to the very concept of tax-supported education). By 1869 about 5,000 Yankees were teaching in "Freedom schools," representing, in effect, that "light brigade of school mis-tresses" so earnestly advocated by New England interests as essential to Southern regeneration. Even more militant were the many Protestant ministers sent to reclaim and reform the region. Northern denominations sought to recover prop-erty from secessionist organizations of former nationwide bodies, rededicated themselves "to the task of building a Christian commonwealth in America," and regarded "the defunct Confederacy" as a missionary field.

3. *Seizure and Extraction of Wealth.* Much of the physical plant of the South was in ruins, its currency was worthless, leaving bales of cotton as its most obvious tangible form of wealth. Therefore "treasury agents scoured the South collecting cotton which had been the property of the Confederate government and hence was subject to seizure by the United States." Because of widespread disputes over ownership and accusations of fraud committed by these agents, such seizures were soon replaced by a federal tax on every bale—and by much fraud in the collection thereof. These revenues were intended to help pay for the costs of this temporary empire.

Far more extensive and onerous were the manifold means of plunder engaged in by a great variety of Northern and Southern opportunists through manipulation of state and local politics, laws, courts, taxation, and other means (for example, creating new counties in Arkansas as a way of creating new offices and the issuance of new bonds). Although government corruption became recognized as a nation-wide evil in this period, the imperial imposition of unpopular regimes greatly magnified that problem in the South.

4. *A Colony Opened for Settlement and Investment.* "Running through nearly all the plans of Reconstruction that filled the national agenda" in the years just after the war "was the assumption that northern colonization was a desirable and indispens-able agency in the process of remaking the South." The motives, and the re-sponses, were complex. Philanthropic leaders focused on helping the freedmen through demonstration farms and industrial schools, but the more general sense was that it would take "Northern capital and Northern energy," Northern leader-ship and example, to rebuild and remold the South. Underneath such rhetoric was many Northerners' sense of a chance to make money in a region that badly needed capital and new forms of management but had a proven valuable export staple—as Lawrence N. Powell put it: "seldom in our nation's history has so much energy gone into arguing the patriotic duty of making a quick killing." Momentarily, during this disruptive transition in society and economy, the South competed with the West as a frontier of opportunity.

Northerners (many of them former Union officers) flocked into the best cotton areas to buy or lease plantations. Leasing was much the more common because

Southerners were reluctant to sell except for the necessity of parting with some portion to save the remainder. To produce a crop the leasee had to obtain and manage workers, a highly uncertain, experimental matter in this new postslavery era. The common failure of local attempts to force and intimidate freedmen to do the usual gang labor suggested that Northerners might be more successful in recruiting and holding laborers through the crop season. And yet nearly all of these Yankee opportunists were young business or professional men who knew nothing about cotton growing and thus, as a Louisiana planter noted, an advantageous partnership was apparent: the planters could furnish the land and the knowledge of cotton cultivation, while "the Yankees furnish the niggers and the money."

Many leasees set up plantation stores to profit further from the presence of their wage-laborers, and within a few years an influx of petty merchants (Northerners, immigrants, and some Southerners) into the towns and countryside transformed the commercial system of the region. Whereas most of the business had been transacted through a few major port cities, much more comprehensive and competitive networks were forming in anticipation of the rehabilitation and elaboration of the railroads. A few months after the war Sidney Andrews found western and northern Georgia "full of 'runners' from Louisville and Cincinnati," and all over the South he found "a passion for keeping store, and hundreds of men are going into trade who should go into agriculture."

There was also much talk among Southerners of immigration as a "panacea for all present evils and troubles." Various Northern companies offered to supply workers to planters (Germans preferred, as hard workers who would not try to run society), land promotion companies undertook the establishment of colonies on cheap Southern lands, and the Southern states soon joined in with the establishment of immigration bureaus—all to little sustained effect.

The greatest focus of activity was Atlanta. Andrews found "a new city springing up with marvellous rapidity" from ruin and devastation, the "streets alive from morning till night . . . with a never-ending throng of pushing and crowding and scrambling and eager and excited and enterprising men, all bent on building and trading and swift fortune-making." From this time on visitors usually commented on the anomalous "Northern" character of the place. Great numbers of Northerners had "flocked to Atlanta," reported Edward King in 1873, creating an "eminently modern and unromantic" city "similar in character to the mammoth groupings of brick and stone in the North-west. There is but little that is distinctively Southern in Atlanta; it is the antithesis of Savannah." The imperial government had engineered the removal of the state capital from Milledgeville after the hotels of that "aristocratic and fossiliferous" place had refused to accommodate Black delegates to the constitutional convention. Northern railroad and commercial strategists regarded this high and healthy locale as "the great Exchange," the pivotal point along the broad arc of the Atlantic and Gulf South and between the Upper and Lower South, and they were welcomed by many leaders of this city at the edge of "Cherokee Georgia," an upland area of strong Unionist sentiment.

5. *An Exotic Province to Be Explored and Described.* The South was always understood to be different from the North, a land distinct in nature and history, society and economy, but the war and its aftermath had radically, roughly altered important features of that South and added to its distinctions and mysteries. A victorious North was avid for information about these changes, especially as regards Blacks and Whites, material conditions and prospects, and attitudes toward the North and reunion. Thus almost immediately after the war and for ten years thereafter reporters, business agents, politicians, and many curious individuals and visiting foreigners traveled through the region and filed lengthy descriptive and opinionated assessments of all manner of Southern conditions, attitudes, folkways, landscapes, and locales. As is often the case in newly acquired imperial provinces an element of danger added to the fascination. In 1865 Sidney Andrews reported from Georgia that "there are many counties in the State in which Northern labor and capital would not be safe but for the presence of the military," and ten years later Charles Nordhoff found that "Mississippi is still . . . a frontier State, with frontier habits. Men, and even boys of fourteen, go about with pistols in their pockets and murder is not a crime if the murderer . . . is not lynched, and his lawyer succeeds in delaying his trial." Northerners commonly referred to such people as "the natives," noted local usage of such terms as "crackers" and "hillbillies," and evolved "poor white" into "Poor White," as if a Southern species distinct from other Americans.

The most extensive and probably most widely read account was that by Edward King and the artist J. Wells Champney, who were sent by the editor of *Scribner's Monthly* to "exhibit, by pen and pencil, a vast region almost as little known to the Northern States of the Union as it is to England." King and Champney's "journey of observation through the Southern States" began in early 1873, covered more than 25,000 miles over the span of a year and a half, and yielded fifteen long, profusely illustrated essays for the magazine, which were then reworked into an 800-page book, *The Great South,* published in 1875.

No other part of the United States was subject to such intensive, searching inspection, and these reports must have had an important, if immeasurable, impact upon national political and social attitudes and thereby upon the fate of this postwar imperial experiment. For all their diversity in emphasis and quality, these many authors seem to have been in agreement with Edward King on at least one important conclusion: "The South can never be cast in the same mould as the North."

TRANSFORMATION OF THE SOUTH

The emancipation of slaves was clearly the most fundamental change imposed upon the South. Through a succession of decrees and completion of the conquest that much was accomplished and then firmly fixed in the national code with ratification of the Thirteenth Amendment in December 1865. But of course by its very nature that was only a beginning of a bitterly controversial, fearfully uncertain time. As a Tennessee planter recalled the situation, "all the traditions and habits of both races had been suddenly overthrown, and neither knew just what to do, or how to accommodate themselves to the new situation." Thus an intensely contentious, experimental redefinition of the relationships between Blacks and Whites got under way all across the South.

That experiment had actually begun during the war in several sectors. Two areas became especially prominent in this earliest stage of this fateful transition: the Sea Islands along the South Carolina–Georgia coast and the lower Mississippi Valley in the vicinity of Vicksburg, both major plantation areas with large Black populations.

Late in 1861 Union forces established a foothold at Port Royal Sound, lying between Charleston and Savannah in the heart of the rice and coastal cotton area. As the planters fled, this most African-American area in North America became even more so, and its residents readily adapted to their new circumstances. Having lived apart from Whites, often with their own garden plots, and worked more in small groups under a task system than in large gangs under a foreman, they now sacked the abandoned houses and storehouses, spread out upon the plantation lands, formed loose clusters of settlement, and diversified toward a sustaining peasant economy, including some truck for sale to Union troops. Officials in charge of this occupied territory struggled to define some sort of formal program. The prospect received great publicity in the North and lured schoolteachers, ministers, and others eager to help implement the radical Republican thesis that "the great plantations, which have been so many nurseries of rebellion, must be broken up, and the freedmen must have the pieces," but there also was much skepticism about the political, social, and economic feasibility of such changes. The arrival of General William Tecumseh Sherman's army, completing his famous March to the Sea, dramatically enlarged the scale of this development. Faced with the need to sustain thousands of Blacks who flocked to the shelter of his forces, Sherman issued a Special Field Order in January 1865 decreeing that "the islands from Charleston, south, the abandoned rice-fields along the rivers for thirty miles back from the sea, and the country bordering the St. John's River, Florida, are reserved and set apart for the settlement of the negroes now made free." An inspector of settlements and plantations was appointed to license and assist heads of families in the selection of plots of not more than forty acres of tillable ground and to furnish "a possessory title in writing." Whites were excluded from most of the area, and "the sole and exclusive management of affairs will be left to the freed people themselves," subject to U.S. military authority and laws. Within a short while about 40,000 Blacks were settled on about 400,000 acres. But the whole scheme was cut short by President Johnson's proclamation of amnesty to all but the topmost Confederate leaders. By the late summer of 1865 Sherman's program was officially abrogated and General O. O. Howard of the Freedman's Bureau undertook the painful task of dispossession (he stalled, trying to get approval at least for retention of small house and garden plots, but failed). Embittered Blacks generally had a choice of making some sort of arrangement with the restored planter-owners to stay on as laborers or to leave. Only about 2,000 of the 40,000 were able to get hold of some small plot of land. Many of the rest drifted off to towns and cities.

In 1863 Northern land and river forces captured much of the richest cotton lands of the lower Mississippi Valley. It was an area of considerable Unionist sentiment before the war, and some planters now declared their loyalty and hung onto their lands. But most of them had fled, and as more Blacks poured into these conquered areas the Treasury Department set aside a fifty-mile strip above and below Vicksburg to "line the banks of the Mississippi River with a loyal population and to give aid in securing the uninterrupted navigation of the river, at the same time to give employment to freed negroes whereby they may earn wages and become self-supporting." The contrast with the Sea Islands experiment was apparent: leases, not "possessory rights," and Blacks as the labor force, not a landed peasantry. Actually, 23 of 136 plantations were leased to Blacks, and many of these were subdivided into small plots, but the remainder were granted to Northern opportunists "whose highest thought is a greenback, whose God is a cotton bale" (or so it seemed to a White sympathizer with the freedmen at Natchez). Little worked out according to plan. Blacks refused to work under anything resembling the old plantation rules; leasees knew little about cotton production; weather and blight ruined much of the crop; Confederates from the unsecured backcountry raided, robbed, burned, and killed. By the end of the war a third of the land lay abandoned again, and as Union troops were withdrawn the formal program devolved into the chaotic experimentation common to the time.

One small locality persisted as an anomaly amidst this general failure. In 1863 General Ulysses S. Grant had ordered that Davis Bend, a 10,000-acre near-island lying within a great looping meander of the Mississippi, become a military reserve "exclusively devoted to the colonization, residence, and support of Freedmen." The reason for this selection was obvious: the home plantations of Jefferson Davis and his older brother, Joseph, occupied more than half the area. A free Black society already forming there in the absence of Whites was now brought under a good deal of supervision; land was leased to small "companies," mules and tools supplied, cottonseed distributed, the gin repaired, schools established. By 1866 about 4,000 Blacks were farming here, but as troops were withdrawn and planters pardoned (Jefferson Davis excepted), here, too, the experiment was soon absorbed into the common regional pattern—except for one small anomaly within: Joseph Davis sold his plantation to his trusted former Black manager, Benjamin Montgomery, who remained the leader of this colony for twenty years, and after his death his son moved a remnant group from the now flood-ravaged island and established the all-Black town of Mound Bayou on railroad lands in the Yazoo Basin.

These episodes are notable only as early formal attempts to deal with the sudden revolution imposed upon the Southern socioeconomic system. They were expedients driven by wartime exigencies, especially the need to provide sustenance to masses of newly free slaves. Such pressures grew with every advance of Union forces, gave rise to a variety of experiments, and caused local officials to see the problem more as what to do *with* the Blacks *now* rather than what to do *for* them in any longer-term constructive sense.

Freedmen were generally regarded as wards of the Whites—whether of the Whites in the localities they shared or of the nation that had rescued them from bondage was deeply in dispute. It soon became clear that the imperial government was not about to confiscate lands for redistribution to former slaves. Southerners, of course, cried out that a devastating confiscation of property had already taken place in the emancipation of slaves without compensation to the owners, and aside from that moral action few Northerners could support such a radical intrusion upon the laws of property. Both assumed that Blacks must remain in place as a laboring class; as the *New York Times* put it, the Emancipation Proclamation made slaves free, now comes "the further duty of making them work." Southerners insisted that if freedmen were given land they would never again work for the planters and the regional economy could never be revived. Northerners were eager to get Southern staples back into production for the health of the national economy (cotton had supported the largest Northern manufacturing industry and accounted for 60 percent of the value of the nation's exports), and they assumed that Blacks should become wage workers under supervision because they needed to be taught the virtues of industry, regularity, and thrift.

Other means of providing land for Blacks were feeble gestures. A Southern Homestead Act of 1866 offered 47 million acres of federal lands in five states (Florida, Alabama, Mississippi, Louisiana, Arkansas) in eighty-acre units to Blacks or loyal Whites, but most of it was piney woods or swamplands unfit for cultivation, local officials and citizens found many ways to inhibit Black applicants, and only a small number actually received patents. Various Northern philanthropic schemes to buy land for sale cheaply to Blacks resulted in no more than a few small patches of settlement scattered across the South. As for Blacks buying land on their own, not only did few have any means to purchase, they found little for sale, despite a region of impoverished planters. In localities all across the South landowners were agreeing never to sell to former slaves. For example, Andrews reported in 1865 that "in Beaufort District [S.C.] they not only refuse to sell land to negroes, but also refuse to rent it to them; and many black men have been told that they would be shot if they leased land and undertook to work for themselves." A year later Whitelaw Reid found that "in many portions of the Mississippi Valley the feeling against any ownership of the soil by negroes is so strong that the man who would sell small tracts to them would be in actual personal danger, . . . even the renting of small tracts to them is held to be unpatriotic and unworthy of a good citizen." And a year after that an agent of the Freedmen's Bureau in West Tennessee confirmed that "there is, in most localities, a determination that they shall not become free holders" and that the few Whites who actively sought to help them were "socially excommunicated from their churches." Several states attempted to prohibit by law Black ownership of farmland (as part of "Black Codes," soon abrogated under imperial pressure). Such deterrents were never absolute but everywhere apparent.

All across the region, therefore, "landowners without laborers confronted laborers without land" in a contentious search for some sort of survival accommodation. Southern planters simply assumed that Blacks must somehow be kept in place and made to work. They would probably have preferred some sort of federally decreed "apprentice system," as had been tried (with highly uneven results) in the West Indies, wherein former slaves would be required to remain under supervision as a workforce during a transition period of several years. Lacking that, they tried other methods to hold them on the land: by intimidation; by vagrancy laws making idle Blacks susceptible to arrest and forced labor; by yearlong contracts restricting workers to the plantation under customary rules in return for a meager wage. None of these was generally successful. Out of despair and disdain some planters were ready to expel all Blacks and replace them with Irish, German, or Chinese immigrants as contract labor. In the few cases where such workers were obtained they mostly fled after a season to some city or suburban refuge. A good many planters were willing to lease their land to Northerners in the hope that such ostensible friends of the Blacks would be more successful as labor recruiters. Some were, offering less restrictive conditions and new lures, such as schools and stores, but, as noted, most of these newcomers soon failed from poor crops and various financial and managerial problems; they had come to make a killing and found neither profit nor pleasure in their Southern adventure.

Through all this fractious, frustrating negotiation, the contrasting, conflicting objectives of Whites and Blacks were starkly apparent: the one wanted, above all, labor from a controlled, subordinate caste; the other wanted land, literacy, a secure family life, and basic social equity. As regards land and labor, the Sea Island experiment offered a telling basis for contrasting motivations and perceptions. Northern as well as Southern Whites commonly pointed to the failure of the Blacks to become efficient commercial farmers; they seemed to prefer to raise garden crops and keep a few chickens and pigs, to hunt and fish, rather than to produce as much cotton for the world market as possible; there was altogether too much "idleness," they needed to be "systematized" and taught the virtues of steady industry. For Blacks it was an obvious success; they had quickly created a productive peasant economy that not only provided essential support for their families but supplemental items from their crops and crafts and gatherings for sale on the local market; "most found bizarre the white folks' preoccupation with growing things that no one could eat"; they would ground their security in Mother Earth rather than in the capitalist system.

Because most Blacks were ousted from these occupied lands and only a few anywhere could obtain even so much as a freehold house and garden plot, they had to come to some kind of arrangement with White landowners. They were not helpless, their labor was needed, and they could bargain over terms. They stoutly resisted any semblance of gang labor under a foreman or any requirement that women and children do fieldwork; they often agreed to work in "squads," small groups managing themselves, and negotiated for supplies, tools, medicines, and housing. Planters generally found wage labor unsatisfactory: too much idleness, indifference to crop quality, disinterest in maintenance, resentment of any supervision. The most common compromise became some form of sharecropping in which the land was parceled out among tenant families for the production of a commercial crop (most often cotton). The owner usually supplied not only a house and garden plot but seed, fertilizer, fencing, and firewood, while the tenant supplied the tools and working livestock, but there was much variation in such details. Begun as an expedient in a cash-starved region it soon became apparent that landlord and tenant were locked into a market economy based on credit, and both became dependent upon bankers, merchants, and storekeepers—and indeed the "pall of debt" hung over all the land: "the merchants are in debt to the wholesalers, the planters are in debt to the merchants, the tenants owe the planters, and the laborers bow and bend beneath the burden of it all." Coupled with falling world prices for cotton, the crop-lien system soon reduced most tenants (in some areas more Whites than Blacks) to a form of "debt-peonage"—the common fate of landless farmers on many continents once enmeshed in the world commercial system.

Sharecropping was attractive to Blacks because it allowed them a larger degree of social freedom. Immediately after the war there was an intense, poignant effort to reunite families, sometimes across hundreds of miles of forced separations. White attempts to impose regulations on their marriages, residence, movements, and social gatherings were deeply resented and resisted. The most effective means of resistance was self-segregation, to live apart and form their own settlements and society. Sharecropping offered a degree of that, scattering families over the land away from the "big house" but still within ready contact with one another, allowing for easy gatherings for preachings and baptisms, weddings and funerals, harvest feasts, hog killings, and various country recreations. By the 1870s travelers often commented on the "little villages springing up here and there on the broad acres" of the plantations by a process "commonly known as 'segregation of quarters'" (fig. 34).

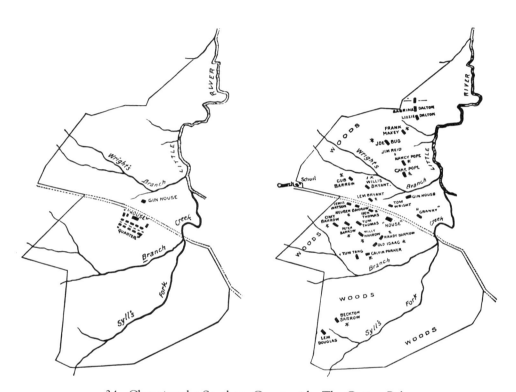

34. Changing the Southern Countryside: The Cotton Belt.
With these maps of Syll's Fork Plantation, his "Home Place" on an upper tributary of the Savannah River in the Georgia Piedmont, David Barrow, Jr., offered readers of the April 1881 issue of *Scribner's Monthly* a bold display of a radical change in settlement geography. On the left is the pattern of 1860, with the close row of slave quarters directly behind the Big House. On the right is that of 1881 showing the log cabins of Black tenants scattered over the entire arable area of the 2,365-acre holding (names marked by asterisk refer to families who were Barrow slaves in 1860). Barrow and two other Whites lived in the House; 162 Blacks lived in the twenty-six tenant houses (twenty feet square, with separate kitchen), each on a plot of about forty acres, most of which was devoted to cotton to pay the rent. Such families kept a garden, chickens, pigs, a cow, and a mule; the waters and woods were open to fishing, hunting, and pasture. Barrow donated an acre for a Baptist church (built by the freedmen, a Black preacher came twice a month to serve about 200 members) and for a school (kept open for three months a year by public funds, Black families paid to keep it open longer), and maintained a cotton gin. This print is from a copy provided by the *Geographical Review*.

Locally such loose clusters became commonly known as "settlements" (usually named after a leading family and often unrecorded on the map), and a group of such settlements was usually referred to as a "community" (often named after some natural feature, such as a creek, a cove, a hill). It was this latter aggregation that served more as a kind of dispersed village, with perhaps several churches, a school, social clubs, and meeting grounds, and, eventually, a post office, store, and black-smith shop, all laced together by paths linking farms and facilities (fig. 35). These settlement types arising out of sharecropping were common all across the Cotton Belt and in many tobacco districts. Where there was less possibility of a staple crop (and, therefore, of credit) and most Blacks were workers on White rural properties or were trying to scratch out a living on their own, the same desire for separation usually resulted in a scattering of ramshackle hamlets on some bit of least desirable ground: the Blacks "seem to form a little community in the woods," reported Sir George Campbell on his detailed inspection tour through northern Georgia, "the able-bodied men cultivate, the women raise chickens and take in washing; and one way or another they manage to get along." In the more prosperous areas White estate owners often created a short strip of formal allotments on some back road to ensure a local labor force (fig. 36). In most rural areas there was a responsive movement among White tenants and laborers (whom Campbell found living in the same kind of "miserable huts scattered about in an isolated way among the fields and the woods") who sorted themselves into their own settlements and commu-nities with their own churches and schools ("by general consent of both colors, there are no mixed schools," reported Nordhoff). As Milton Newton, Jr. noted in one of his penetrating studies of the rural South, "the separation of blacks and whites is fundamentally social and political; the separation is bridged, however, by a common cultural origin, a largely common history, much shared ancestry, many common values, and a broadly common inventory of material culture."

These folk communities were connected by roads to the county seat, the court-house town, the formal center of public life, the main focus of White society, with larger stores and shops, periodic open markets, churches, school, and newspaper,

---

35. Houses and Paths.

Rudolf Eickemeyer, Jr., has been called one of the three great developers of "pictorial photogra-phy" (along with Stieglitz and Hartmann), and he became famous for his fashionable portraits of New Yorkers. Early in his career, however, he visited a plantation near Mt. Meigs, Alabama, in the Black Belt a few miles east of Montgomery, and became fascinated with the Black tenants there. He returned several times in the 1890s, recording them at their work in fields of cotton, peanuts, sweet potatoes, and sugarcane and at other tasks. These two prints are from *Down South*, a catalogue of an exhibition in 1900. (Courtesy George Eastman House)

THE ANTEBELLUM BLUEGRASS ESTATE

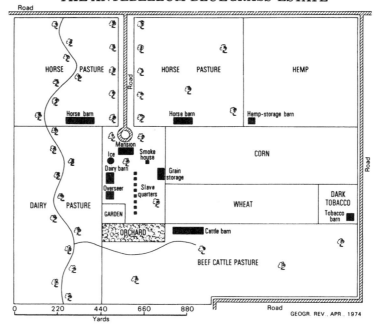

THE CONTEMPORARY BLUEGRASS ESTATE

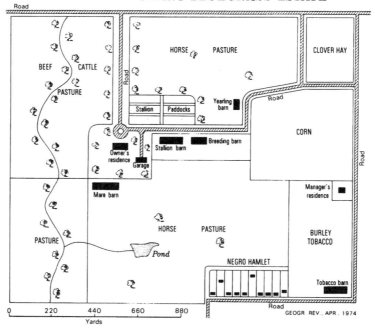

the home of lawyers, doctors, merchants, and some of the wealthier landowners (fig. 37). If they obtained a railroad, such rural centers also became a lively link with the commercial world, with perhaps a large public steam-powered gin, cotton warehouses, cotton-oil mill, fertilizer depot, and various workshops (fig. 38). In some of the smaller courthouse towns Blacks were confined to shacktown "quarters" on the outskirts, in the larger ones to definite districts within (in one Georgia county Whites even shifted the courthouse from a seat in the midst of a planter district—with the sudden prospect of many Black voters—to a village in an all-White small farm area). In the newer railroad towns the tracks created a simple separation and stark exhibit of an increasingly rigid segregation. "The negro quarter around the towns is as marked a feature of a Southern town as a Jew's ghetto anywhere in Europe," testified a White South Carolinian to Congress in 1901; for the ruling race such a pattern made it easy to recruit day labor and easier to police—control being ever a primary White concern.

These changes in the countryside were related to other regional transformations. For ten years or more reports from the South were studded with comments on a kind of general instability, of new systems on trial, and especially of people on the move: Blacks drifting out of the interior to the seaboard or to the big river towns, Blacks generally fleeing the plantations for the cities, Blacks and Whites alike heading west from the older cotton and rice lands to Louisiana, Arkansas, and, especially, Texas (in some cases recruited by agents from those states). It has been difficult to get a measure of such things—the 1870 census was considered so flawed that its total for the Southern states was later officially increased by 1,260,078. Some of it was the brief and impermanent, such as freedmen fleeing to the shelter of Union armies and federal agencies that soon faded from the scene. In many areas there were brutal attempts to keep Blacks from moving, yet there was a marked increase in the Black population of most Southern cities (fig. 39). In some old centers, such as Charleston, the pattern was not greatly changed, and "visitors in 1880 were struck by the 'proximity and confusion so to speak of white and negro houses' as they had been before the War," with Blacks living in lofts and alleys, in

---

36. Changing the Southern Countryside: Bluegrass Estates.
In parts of the Upper South slaves were more likely to have been stablehands, grooms, jockeys, cooks, and laundresses than cultivators of staple crops, and the need for such labor was even greater after the war. The change in settlement patterns thus tended to be merely a modest shift in location rather than in kind: from the slave quarters behind the Mansion to a concentrated "freetown" on a side road at the back of the estate, where small house and garden lots were given or sold cheaply to the new wage laborers. Peter Smith and Karl Raitz, who created these model diagrams, found twenty-nine such "negro hamlets" still extant in the Inner Bluegrass of Kentucky in 1972. (Courtesy the *Geographical Review*)

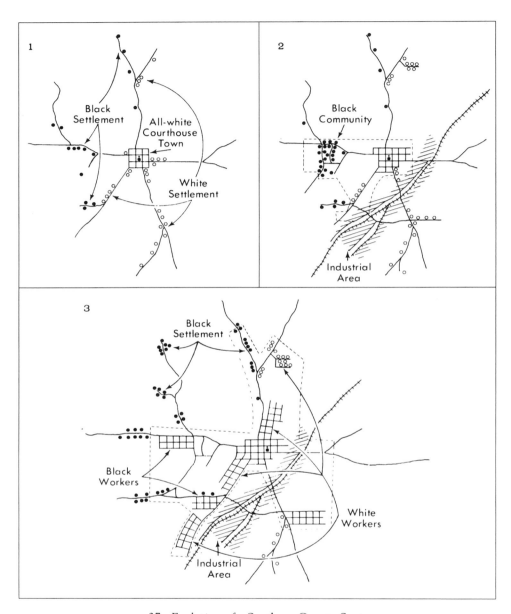

37. Evolution of a Southern County Seat.
This is the late Milton B. Newton, Jr.'s schematic summation, based especially on his intensive
studies in the Florida parishes of Louisiana, east of Baton Rouge. (Courtesy Louisiana State
University Press)

38. Cotton to the Country Gin.
Somewhere in Georgia in the 1890s. (Courtesy Hargrett Rare Book and Manuscript Library, University of Georgia Libraries)

and near stables, livery barns, and workshops, as well as in the rubbishy, swampy margins of the town. But elsewhere visitors were more commonly struck by the growth at the edges: in 1874 the German journalist-geographer Friedrich Ratzel found Richmond "surrounded by Negro villages, which far surpass in dirt, idleness, and demoralization as well as in picturesque disorder and lack of civilizatory amenities, the gypsy camps on the outskirts of Hungarian and Romanian cities." In the Black Belt of Alabama where in the generation after the war the Black population increased by 100,000 and the White by less than 5,000, most of the new Black majorities in such places as Montgomery, Selma, and Demopolis were to be found on the fringes and the pattern of segregation was more obvious (fig. 40), as was the case in such all new heavy industrial centers as Birmingham and Anniston, where large numbers of Blacks were employed as unskilled or semiskilled labor.

Although Blacks were excluded from many positions of skill, commerce, and profession, there were in all these larger centers Black mechanics and artisans of many kinds, Black-owned shops and businesses catering to their own people, including, eventually, banks and insurance companies, newspapers, doctors and

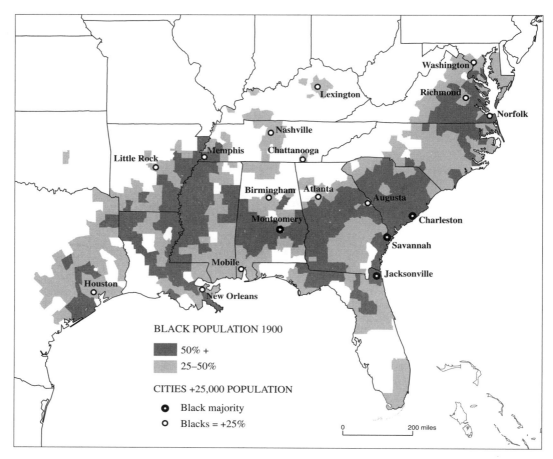

39. Black Population, 1900.
U.S. Census.

lawyers, and a considerable range of social services—and a social hierarchy at least
as self-conscious as in White society. Churches were vital institutions. In spite of
individual voices, White and Black, admonishing a Christian obligation to be
blind to color, leaders of both races had quickly sought separate local churches and
denominations. Black schools under Black principals and teachers provided educational grounding; advanced education was mostly limited to a scattering of meager
normal schools and church colleges, but a few institutions, initiated with the help
of Northern philanthropy, such as Fisk (Nashville), Morehouse (Atlanta), and
Spelman (Atlanta—the first for women) now stood as beacons for aspiring Blacks.
Under the pressure of law states were gradually establishing or assisting technical
colleges (Alcorn in Mississippi, Prairie View in Texas, and Huntsville in Alabama,

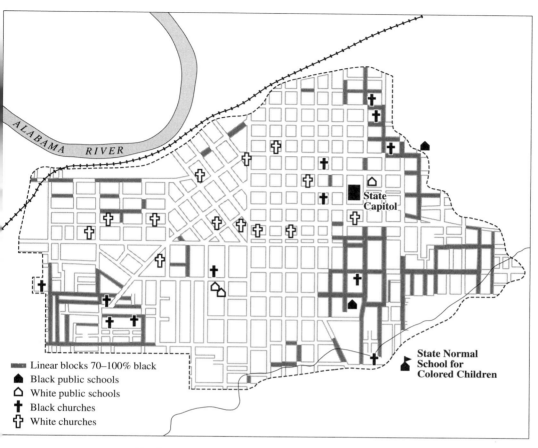

Legend:
▬ Linear blocks 70–100% black
◆ Black public schools
⬠ White public schools
✝ Black churches
♱ White churches

40. Racial Patterns in Montgomery, Alabama, 1895.
Adapted from Rabinowitz, *Race Relations.*

among the earliest), but none equaled in facilities or fame the Tuskegee Institute, which enjoyed Northern support and the leadership of Booker T. Washington. Washington was an inspiration to many Blacks, but his seemingly benign acceptance of segregation was bitterly criticized by others, such as W. E. B. DuBois, the prolific Harvard- and Berlin-trained Black scholar at Atlanta University, who noted that under such conditions, "despite much physical contact and daily intermingling, there is no community of intellectual life or point of transference where the thoughts and feelings of one race can come into direct contact and sympathy with the thoughts and feelings of the other."

In the early phase of this social revolution Southern Whites had tended to resist this trend toward racial segregation. Alarmed by the presence of companies of armed Black soldiers, fearful that Black preachers might foment "insurrection," suspicious of subversive messages from Northern missionaries and schoolteachers, and convinced of a natural Black inferiority, they felt a compelling need to assert their dominating power and presence in every community. But failing to subdue and discipline Blacks under customary rules, finding them "uppity" and "ungrateful," they came to regard segregation as an essential dimension of the caste system they were assiduously reworking in order to preserve a traditional social order. In his travels across the Cotton South in 1875 Charles Nordhoff found everywhere a "dread of social equality," an obsession with the necessity of "maintaining the color line," with the most virulent of such feelings asserted by the impoverished Whites in the backcountry—"in the more distant and obscure regions." Embittered by defeat and the social upheaval forced upon them by emancipation, such reactions had been greatly intensified by some of the highly visible results of the congressional Reconstruction program of 1867: Black voters (a majority in some districts), and Black legislators and other officials exercising power under imperial-sponsored state governments and legalizing unprecedented social equalities. The Southern response was a spontaneous, sporadic, largely uncoordinated upwelling of intimidation against Blacks that became nothing less than "guerrilla warfare" (the term often used by commentators of the time) that cost untold thousands of lives and inflicted countless beatings, burnings, tortures, and expulsions. The actions of the Ku Klux Klan (founded in Pulaski, Tennessee, in 1866) and the lynchings that became endemic across the South were only the most notorious exhibits of "what ought to be recognized as a true people's war on the part of the southern whites."

These relentless pressures toward White supremacy and enforced segregation reached their greatest intensity in the late 1870s and 1880s, following the formal end of imperial status with the Compromise of 1877 by which, in a tightly contested national election, the insecure Northern-based Republican party gained the presidency (in the person of Rutherford B. Hayes) in return for a complete withdrawal of its federal agents and programs from the former Confederate States. Henceforth, Blacks became effectively excluded from office and essentially from politics by systematic local intimidation and manipulation of voting procedures, and segregation in all public places was fixed in place by Jim Crow laws in every Southern state (and in many other localities touched by Southern migrations, as in Kansas and Arizona). These actions were subsequently sustained by Supreme Court rulings on voting laws (1898) and "separate but equal" facilities (1896). As Joel Williamson has summarized, during these years

the white elite acted vigorously to diminish substantially its previous heavy reliance upon black people as the mudsills of a higher cultural order and moved into the process of constructing instead a cultural system that put black people firmly to one side and tied the mass of white people tightly to the white elite. The final crusade of whiteness produced, among other things, all-white factories, all-white one-party politics, compulsory public education for every white child, public health campaigns that favored whites, segregation, a rage against miscegenation, and the relatively total divorce of white religion, language, and music from black. By 1915, the changeover . . . had been effectively completed.

Thus the defining pattern of Southern society was firmly fixed in place, a pattern imposed not by an imperial conqueror bent on "regeneration" but by fearful and vengeful White citizens determined to sustain their privileged position in a biracial society.

The "restoration" of the Southern states to formal equal membership in the federation had been completed earlier, beginning with Tennessee in 1866 and concluding with Virginia, Mississippi, Texas, and Georgia in 1870. Readmission depended upon ratification (by a majority of voters) of the Fourteenth and Fifteenth amendments and of a new state constitution conforming to approved federal standards. There followed in each case an internal struggle by Whites to "redeem" (their common euphemism) their state from radical Republican officials and replace them with conservative Southern Democrats, a process making use of armed militias as well as more normal electoral processes; accomplished first in Tennessee in 1869, it was not completed in South Carolina, Florida, and Louisiana until late 1876—after the Democrats had taken control of the federal House of Representatives and thereby ending any possibility of using federal troops to enforce electoral laws in the South.

With the readmittance of these eleven states, what had been a Union of thirty-three units on the eve of secession became a Union of thirty-seven (Kansas, West Virginia, Nevada, and Nebraska having been admitted in the interim); with the abandonment of the Reconstruction program what had been a Republican-controlled imperial government was once more a federal government with two strong parties in contention; and what had been a decade-long attempt to impose upon the former slave states nationally defined civil rights for American citizens was nullified by tacit and formal recognition of State's Rights and White Supremacy. "For better or worse, the American people made the decision to have the white South substantially control its own destinies." Such a response was not surprising; after all, as Carl N. Degler reminds us, "local control of government and negro inequality had long been values" not only of Southern life but "of American life nationally" (there were lynchings of Blacks, in lesser numbers, in most other states of the Union).

And so ended a reluctant imperialism, one that refused to respond as imperial powers have often done: execute or exile rebellious leaders, confiscate much of the best lands, fix its own ruling elite upon a suppressed people and province, grant special favors to allied minorities within the conquered province. There was talk of all these things, many proposals, several actual programs, but there was never the presidential determination or popular support to sustain any such geopolitical domination. The liberation of slaves was surely a great accomplishment, but it was more a wartime stratagem than an imperial policy. Emancipation could be hailed as an end of an embarrassing contradiction of American principles, but it became ever more obvious that the American leadership and the public at large had little grasp of the impact, magnitude, and ramifications of that change—not only on the South but on federal politics and the national society—and never defined an adequate response. Programs for Blacks relied on national democratic ideals rather than on local elemental realities, on the granting of citizenship and suffrage rather than on providing property and practical protections. But of course the latter would have required a far greater imperial establishment and a different sense of imperial purpose. For this was, after all, a temporary, intramural empire following upon a civil war; White Southerners were Americans, too, and the main objective was to get them back into the nation and the federation. And so sovereign separation had been defeated, but "the South had never been truly reconstructed or reformed, and in most respects it had not been fundamentally changed . . . . In the end the nation was reunited, but here had been no national settlement, merely a sectional and partisan stalemate." And thus, at the end of this brief imperial phase, as Vann Woodward commented, "the South might be said to have shared in the victory and the North to have shared in the defeat of the Civil War." But, it should be further emphasized that the North was far too absorbed in its own progress and problems—and far too little concerned with whatever might be going on in the South—to have any shared sense of "defeat."

RECONNECTIONS AND INTEGRATIONS

While politicians worked out ways to restore the former Confederate States to the Union, entrepreneurs and engineers were hard at work rehabilitating Southern railroads. It took about five years (and a massive increase in state indebtedness) to get these heavily ravaged facilities back into reasonable running order. Even when intact these roads bore only a bare resemblance of a regional system (as the Confederacy had found out under the pressures of war). Shaped by local interests and individual states, it was fragmented in pattern and gauge and much of it was flimsy in construction, designed primarily to carry seasonal produce to the nearest port. Initial postwar expansions were mainly continuations of such strategies, with the extension of tap lines from Norfolk, Wilmington, Savannah, Brunswick, Pensacola, and Galveston further into productive districts. Charleston, Mobile, and New Orleans undertook little new work, but all these ports were also soon reconnected by passenger and freight vessels with Baltimore, Philadelphia, and New York City.

In the 1870s these provincial lines became challenged by—and within a decade or so largely captive of—larger interregional strategies of Northern companies. "There is a grand scheme now on foot in the North to destroy the present commercial centers of the South," warned the Marietta (Georgia) *Journal,* "and to make the Southern railroads tributary to the commercial cities of the North." This cry of alarm was in response to an attempt by a powerful set of Northern and British capitalists to buy and to build a superior direct trunk line from Philadelphia via Baltimore, Washington, Richmond, Danville, and Charlotte to Atlanta, with further connections to Montgomery and Mobile. Although that particular initiative withered in the Panic of 1873, it completed important projects (such as a tunnel under Baltimore harbor, bridges over the Potomac and the Quantico estuary, and a new direct line to Atlanta) and established through Pullman passenger service to New Orleans ("sleeping-cars daily cross the Rappahannock, which a few years ago was red with the blood of Northern soldiers," mused Edward King), and its program was eventually completed by others (fig. 41).

West of the Appalachians the Louisville & Nashville Railroad, having prospered from heavy use by Union forces, acquired or built extensions south to Pensacola, Mobile, and New Orleans (and west to Paducah—to cut off Evansville's aspirations to be a rival gateway). Initiated by Louisville interests, this system came under New York and Philadelphia control in the 1880s. This early success in reaching deeply into the South was a cause of great envy in Louisville's great Ohio Valley rival. Only after extensive lobbying in three states did Cincinnati win approval to finance its own line to Chattanooga. Completed in 1879, this direct route needed twenty-seven tunnels to cut through the Appalachian Plateau; long derided by smoke-choked crews as "the Rathole Division," it became a busy link, with connections fanning into the Lower South. Farther west, Chicago and St. Louis competed for the Mississippi Valley trade. Chicago had an early lead, and its main instrument, the Illinois Central, eventually acquired its own line all the way to New Orleans, although the awkward steamboat transfer at Cairo was not wholly eliminated until 1889. Saint Louis gained access to this and other lower Mississippi routes but turned its main attentions toward an expanding Texas. By the early 1880s it had three trunk lines intersecting and cutting southwesterly across the elaborating Texan network. By then it had also radically improved its vital eastern connections with the completion of the splendid Eads Bridge across the Mississippi.

By 1890 Northern control of every major Southern railroad was virtually complete. A much-expanded regional network (doubled in mileage during the 1880s) had been standardized to the Northern gauge (largely accomplished in a single day,

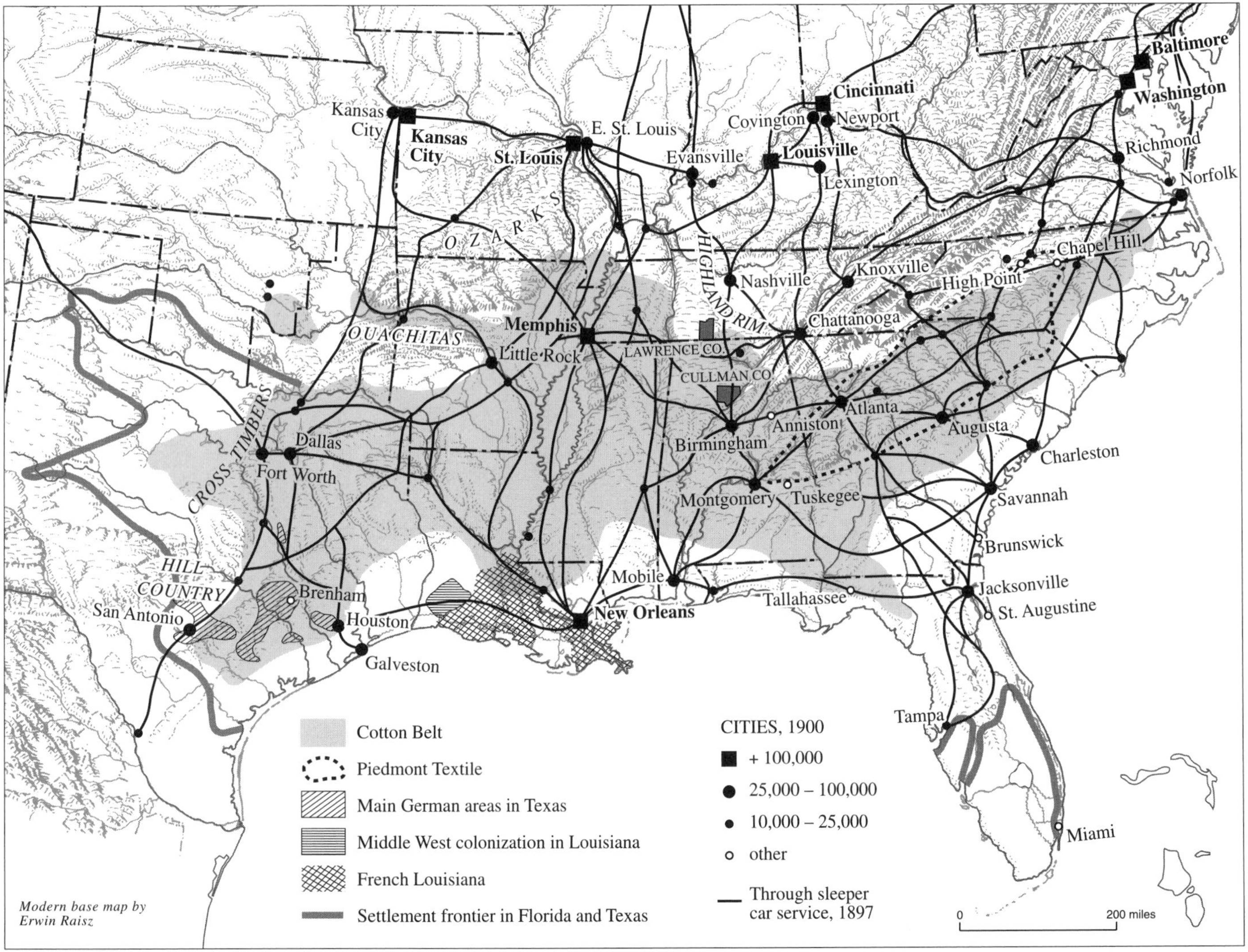

Baltimore
Washington
Richmond
Norfolk
Chapel Hill
Charleston
Savannah
Brunswick
Jacksonville
St. Augustine
Miami
200 miles
0
Cincinnati
Newport
Louisville
Covington
Lexington
Knoxville
High Point
Augusta
Atlanta
Anniston
Tuskegee
Tampa
Nashville
Chattanooga
HIGHLAND RIM
LAWRENCE CO.
CULLMAN CO.
Birmingham
Montgomery
Tallahassee
Evansville
E. St. Louis
St. Louis
Memphis
Little Rock
Mobile
New Orleans
Kansas City
A R K A N S A S
O Z A R K
Galveston
O U A C H I T A S
CROSS TIMBERS
Dallas
Fort Worth
Brenham
Houston
HILL COUNTRY
San Antonio

CITIES, 1900
■ +100,000
● 25,000 – 100,000
• 10,000 – 25,000
○ other

Through sleeper
car service, 1897

Cotton Belt
Piedmont Textile
Main German areas in Texas
Middle West colonization in Louisiana
French Louisiana
Settlement frontier in Florida and Texas

*Modern base map by
Erwin Raisz*

41. The South.

May 30, 1886, when traffic was halted on 13,000 miles of track while thousands of workers shifted one rail inward a few inches) and directly articulated with the main national system by way of four major centers: Washington, Cincinnati, Louisville, and St. Louis, with Chicago being served by lines crossing the Ohio at Cairo and Evansville. Through trunk-line service linked these cities with Atlanta, Jacksonville, Mobile, and New Orleans, with additional sleeper service along a dozen different routes to many much smaller Southern cities, such as Augusta, Macon, Tampa, Shreveport, and Austin. Service between Southern cities was incidental to these main trafficways.

Although Southern business and civic leaders generally welcomed these greater integrations of facilities and services, older aspiring commercial centers had good reason to fear these Northern strategies. Ports continued to serve local hinterlands, but often with volumes reduced despite major increases in production. For example, by 1890 half the cotton crop of Texas was moving northeast by rail through St. Louis rather than the far shorter shipment to gulf ports, a traffic diversion secured by the development in that city of cotton compress companies whose powerful steam presses changed 500-pound bales into nine-inch sheets for efficient rail shipment. On the Atlantic side Northern strategists pieced together systems from various local companies and then built cutoffs to provide direct routes for the booming Florida vacation and citrus traffic. Thus Wilmington, North Carolina, the early headquarters of the Atlantic Coast Line, became bypassed by New York–Florida "Solid Pullman Vestibule Trains" and by solid trains of refrigerated cars speeding subtropical produce to Northern markets. Meanwhile, wealthy Henry Flagler was indulging in his hobby of pushing his Florida East Coast Railway beyond his first great luxurious resort in St. Augustine, reaching Miami in 1896, and planning his audacious "overseas" extension to Key West (completed in 1912).

Maps also showed lines leading westward from those old contenders for a Pacific railroad: New Orleans, Vicksburg, and Memphis. The first of these (1880) linked New Orleans with Houston and was soon purchased by the Southern Pacific, completing at last the much vaunted Thirty-second parallel route; the other two converged on Dallas and the Texas & Pacific, which joined track with the SP near El Paso, thus forming eastern branches of the same "transcontinental." Although Southern ocean and river ports had long had "a lively ambition to get into direct communication with the Western States and the route to the Pacific," little interregional traffic was generated by or diverted to these routes.

Within this intensifying but captive regional network Chattanooga, nestled within the narrowing confines of the southern Great Valley, emerged as second only to Atlanta as a vital crossroads and was augmented by the development of new ironworks in the area in the 1870s. The ores of the southern Appalachians that had been tapped by a scattering of small furnaces before the war became the object of considerable speculation thereafter. But, as with cotton, much of this interest was from investors who knew little about the industry. New companies begun with great expectations (as expressed in the names of such new towns as South Pittsburgh, Sheffield, Leeds, and Birmingham) often floundered from hasty construction, poor equipment, inept management, and shortage of capital. However, the extraordinary proximity of rich ores, coking coal, and limestone remained a strong lure, and the expanding railroad network and new technologies eventually attracted stronger companies such as the Tennessee Coal, Iron & Railroad Company, backed by the L&N. In the 1880s this firm began investing in Birmingham, where others had been drawn to the best combination of resources, and that new city at the southern end of the Appalachians emerged as the principal focus of a heavy industrial district.

In spite of natural advantages in the cheap assembly of raw materials, productions were handicapped by the meager local market ("the whole state of Alabama cannot take the product of a single blast furnace for a month," said the English founder of Anniston in 1883). Superior quality railroad iron could be sent to the South cheaply by sea from large Northern mills. But as Southern firms began to market their products in the Ohio Valley and surplus productions occasionally precipitated "warfare between Southern and Northern furnaces," the big national companies became more interested. Although after an inspection tour in 1889 Andrew Carnegie declared the South to be "Pennsylvania's most formidable industrial enemy," he decided against purchase of its major producer (citing its poor management), but in 1907 the TCI&R came under the control of the new giant combination, United States Steel. Such a change represented recognition of Birmingham as an important iron and steel district—and as a regional industry firmly subordinated to Northern, national, control.

These works were among the more important "islands of industrialism scattered through the region," but more famous and significant was the denser archipelago of textile plants stretching along the Piedmont from southwest Virginia into Georgia. This, too, was not entirely new in kind, but it was certainly new in motivation, in the "public zeal" of its promotion, in the "extraordinary rate of growth," and in the extent and character of its impact. The Richmond-Atlanta "Air-Line Railway" provided the axis for this elongated cluster, the dozens of streams tumbling across the red hills onto the Coastal Plain provided the power (increasingly from electricity rather than the waterwheel), and the end of Reconstruction unleashed a surge of Southern determination to emulate rather than capitulate to Northern enterprise. As Vann Woodward noted, with this "civic crusade" for industrialism "old market villages . . . that had drowsed from one Saturday to the next since the eighteenth century, were suddenly aflame with the mill fever." Actually, many Piedmont villages and towns had never quite fit the stereotypes of the Cotton Belt, and a good deal of the business acumen came out of the Calvinist, Quaker, and Moravian ancestry of this most complex of Southern settlement regions. And many mills were set up in the countryside supported by a new company town, the orderly line of simple workers' houses, school, chapel, and company store bearing familiar marks of a paternalistic industrial plantation. Workers were drawn from the rural backcountry, with women and children forming a large portion of the force; Blacks were excluded. Such "mill people" were looked down upon by both "country people" and "town people," who tended to regard them as weak, shiftless, failures of some sort—"cotton mill trash"—but they came to constitute a lively proletariat, a distinct subset of Piedmont society.

The success of this industrialization was heavily dependent on cheap and docile labor as well as on ready access to raw materials and power, but, as David L. Carlton has demonstrated, it must also be seen in larger historical geographic context. Southern spokesmen eagerly cited the ever-increasing number of mills and spindles as proof that their region was becoming the successor to New England. However, textile machinery innovation and manufacture remained in the Northeast, and it was the sophistication of those machines in their tasks of carding, spinning, and weaving that allowed them to be tended by illiterate rural folk. And although some Southern mills served Southern markets with simple goods, most of their product was merely an intermediate stage and sent on to specialized firms in the North. Furthermore, the textile industry was extremely complicated, dependent upon a "vast store of accumulated and institutionalized expertise" among a great corps of specialists in Philadelphia, New York City, and New England. As capacities were expanded in the South, Northern capitalists moved in to bring this limited regional component of a complex national industry under ever-greater control.

This industrialization of the Piedmont was augmented by developments in the tobacco industry. Well established in Virginia and a few Carolina localities on the basis of the rather simple productions of chewing and pipe tobaccos, the industry boomed in the 1880s with the development of cigarette-making machines using the bright-leaf tobaccos that thrived in the sandy soils of southern Virginia and North Carolina. Aggressive firms fostered rapid increases in consumption through nationwide advertising and marketing, drove out weaker companies, and concentrated manufacturing in a few centers, such as Richmond, Winston, and Durham. Tobacco was a Southern-generated industry to an unusual degree, and the local reinvestment of tobacco fortunes in power systems, banks, and various philanthropies helped further differentiate the Piedmont from the more common regional pattern.

Other major industrial pursuits were more extractive and exploitative. Michael Williams has well described "the sudden massive transfer of capital, technology, and know-how" in the 1880s from the depleted Great Lakes pinery to begin the "assault on the southern forest." Lumbering and associated forest productions, such as potash, tanning bark, and turpentine, were centuries-old activities, but all was now suddenly on an utterly different scale. Railroad trunk lines to Northern markets had made the region newly attractive, Northern lumbermen and speculative syndicates purchased millions of acres of federal and state lands, and steam-powered locomotives, skidders, loaders, and sawmills had an "explosive" impact on the landscape. Sawmills sprouted up every few miles along existing railroad lines, and from these spurs were sent ever deeper into the forest and fanned out from company-owned sawmill towns. Special devices were developed to exploit the cypress swamplands along the coast. Whole counties could be stripped in a few years, the whole region heavily depleted within twenty or thirty, and much of the impact on settlements and employment (for many thousands of Blacks as well as Whites) was unstable and episodic. By the turn of the century the big companies were moving on to the Pacific Northwest. One small positive legacy of this forestry era was the emergence of a furniture manufacturing district in the North Carolina Piedmont. Drawing upon Appalachian hardwoods and an early history of craftsmanship, local entrepreneurs took advantage of their understanding of Southern tastes and pocketbooks and the new railroad system to develop a regional market for their products that competed well with national brands. High Point was emerging as "the Grand Rapids of the South"—but as yet on a scale similar to that of Birmingham compared to Pittsburgh.

Coal was analogous to forestry in that the railroads opened up remote areas to efficient exploitation, workers were drawn from the countryside into makeshift company towns, and the industry was completely dominated by Northern firms. Aside from the lesser Birmingham and Chattanooga districts its emergence was essentially a contiguous expansion southward from Pennsylvania and southeastern Ohio into West Virginia, westernmost Virginia, and eastern Kentucky. Much more volatile as an industrial activity (with a largely White labor force), it was less ephemeral in place than forestry. Mines were driven ever deeper into the earth, industrial and urban markets in the North kept expanding, and new heavy-capacity railroads carried solid trainloads across Virginia to huge export docks on Hampton Roads. For example, under the leadership of Collis P. Huntington of Central Pacific fame, the Chesapeake & Ohio, a consolidation of several Virginia lines, pushed on west to the Ohio River (at the new town of Huntington), tapped into the mountain coal region, and built east from Richmond to a new coal port at Newport News. The expansion of such specialized facilities made the combined ports of the Norfolk area the largest Southern urban complex on the Atlantic coast.

Travelers reporting on the South had rarely failed to speak of its great potentials for industrial development. Edward King, one of the more cautious, concluded that "the growth of manufactures in the Southern States, while insignificant as compared with the gigantic development in the North and West, is still highly encouraging." Within a few years, as the nationwide business depression faded, Southern spokesmen began propounding the theme of a "New South," a region to be made prosperous on the basis of its rich endowment of land, labor, waterpower, fuel, and other resources. Newspapers and new specialized periodicals with titles such as *Industrial South* and *Manufacturers' Record* proclaimed the cause and recorded its progress. More spectacular were the expositions sponsored by a succession of Southern cities, beginning with the International Cotton Exposition in Atlanta in 1881, followed by others in that same decade in Louisville, New Orleans, and Richmond. As Woodward notes: "The huge exposition structures of plaster and iron were temples erected to the alien gods of Mass and Speed. In their halls Southerners joined with millions of Yankee guests to invoke the spirit of Progress and worship the machine. . . . The expositions were modern engines of propaganda, advertising, and salesmanship geared primarily to the aims of attracting capital and immigration and selling the goods." There were continuities here with the long series of antebellum Southern commercial conventions, which had always expressed "a firm optimism about the potential for southern economic growth." In the 1880s it was becoming apparent that the South could attract capital but not immigration and, aside from tobacco products, was having little success in selling its industrial goods directly to a national market. As Carlton put it with reference to North Carolina developers (then and later), they "had in mind the creation of an industrial society modeled on the one they knew best, that of the North. That they created something different was due not so much to deliberate choice as to the business constraints under which they operated."

In large part, such constraints had long been in place. As noted in *Continental America* (388–91), the South had always been, at best, marginal to the rapidly developing geographic core of the American industrial system, and there was little hope of it becoming at all comparable to or—so long as it was part of the same sovereignty—autonomous from it. There could be no full imitation or "catching up"; there could only be participation, affiliation as an integral but limited, specialized, subordinate component of that powerful national complex. As Carlton stated: "southern industrialists thus faced a challenge common to 'backward' regions, of pursuing development in a context defined from the outside." They began with an extremely limited supply of relevant entrepreneurial experience and of skilled labor, and they undertook their task of regional transformation concurrent with powerful nationalizing trends in manufacturing and marketing. Thus the same railroad expansion that made efficient regionwide contacts possible also made the South wide open to national marketing that "brought a tide of mass-produced goods that eroded traditional small-scale enterprise" and placed any new development of local resources "in direct competition with one of the most dynamic and sophisticated industrial regions on earth." As Edward L. Ayers put it, access to that great array of eagerly welcomed goods "testified to the South's integration into the national economy, but the distant origins of those goods testified to the South's enduring provinciality."

Thus the South industrialized in the 1880s and 1890s, but with only a few kinds of industry, in limited specialized forms, and in only a few important subregions. It remained heavily dependent upon outside capital and especially upon Northern corporate and institutional seats of technology and innovation, commerce and marketing. And thus the relationship and result was not a case of the North consciously, imperiously imposing its control over a captive "colonial" South, but a South, once reintegrated into the federal political system, having no alternative to becoming subordinated within the national economic system. Such a result was inherent in the historical geographic regionalism of a re-United States.

REGIONALISM REINFORCED

Soon after the war the practice of annually decorating the graves of soldiers with flowers on a late spring day became ever-more common. Larger communities expanded the occasion with patriotic parades and orations, and by the 1870s many states had made Memorial Day a mandated holiday. In origin such things were of course distinctly separate between North and South, but as the past receded gestures of reconciliation increased. By the 1880s prominent men from both sections might be invited to address the occasion and soon veterans of the Blue and of the Gray were marching together; in the 1890s they stood together as battlefields were dedicated as national preserves, and near the end of the century a new generation of men (and proportionately more Southerners than Northerners, and Blacks as well as Whites) rallied to the call to arms to defend the honor of the Republic.

But there was another side to the matter. Although the federation had been reunited, a fully American nationalism reasserted, and practical integrations extended, a cultural divide had also been notably deepened. Regional distinctions between North and South had been redefined and magnified, in part by further diverging developmental trends, in part by feelings, perceptions, and attitudes expressed about the relationship of these parts to one another. Certainly the South entered the twentieth century in some ways more self-conscious of its separateness than ever before.

The obvious new and unique feature of the South was its searing experience of defeat, destruction, occupation, and assault upon some of its basic values and institutions (unique, that is, for an Anglo-American region; it was, after all, an experience common to, and continuing through all these years for, a growing multitude of American Indian nations). Such an experience generated among the surviving Southern Whites a defensiveness about their culture as well as a determination to recover control over local affairs. Suffering and endurance were translated into virtues, the necessary burdens of having valiantly supported an honorable cause. A Southern heritage was elaborated to present a society that had held fast to old and basic ideals in the face of an arrogant cultural imperialism from a modernizing North.

Thus the contest between starkly different versions of "Americanism" was reasserted. As Woodward noted, "the rupture between North and South had come earliest in the great Protestant sects, and there it was slowest to heal." Southern religious leaders became influential shapers and celebrators of the "Southern Way of Life" as "a distinctive culture and . . . the need for continued commitment to it." With an imperial North attempting to reshape its politics "the life of the South [was drawn] with increasing earnestness into the denominational organizations of the Church. These, at least, were loyally and securely Southern." Such security had come only with conscious resistance. At the end of the war many Northern church leaders assumed that the divorce of the 1840s would be annulled and reunification of the denominations would soon follow. But antagonisms had been intensified by the war and by the aggressive attempts of Northern denominations to reclaim properties and positions in conquered territories (in some cases they had even called for Southern "apostates" to confess to the error of their ways). Thus not only the big Southern denominations—Baptists, Methodists, and Presbyterians— but even the small body of Lutherans voted to maintain their organizational independence to serve "our beloved Zion in the South." Eventually, reluctantly, the Northern churches came to recognize these Southern denominations as "separate but equal." (The Episcopal church, prominent among Southern civil and military leaders but relatively minor in numbers, drew upon its historic formal structure and traditions and quickly and routinely reasserted its unity through the participation of bishops from both North and South in the consecration of new bishops, although a strongly Southern flavor permeated its congregations and new theological college at Sewanee.)

Some resistance to reunification arose from fear of Northern numerical domination in the conduct of church affairs, but, as in broader political realms, more fundamental were differences in emphasis and ideology. "Southern religion became entwined with the Lost Cause"—as it had with slavery—and had to defend the regional mythology. Whereas Northerners had talked loudly about the need "to impregnate the South with Northern ideas and civilization" (to quote an 1865 Pittsburgh Methodist paper), Southerners were warned to be militant against such an assault and conception, for (in the words of a leading Methodist evangelist) "the great defect of Northern civilization is its materiality." Even the widely promoted vision of a New South risked succumbing to "Mammon," to "money-mania," and becoming "like the conquerors." Southern evangelical Protestantism, together with the more extreme pentecostal sects proliferating across the region, focusing on suffering and salvation, prophetic preachings and emotional responses, was increasingly divergent from dominant national religious patterns and symptomatic of broader regional differences. As David Goldfield concluded: "by 1900 a distinctive civil religion was evident, distinguishing Southern culture from the optimistic, scientific, social gospel sweeping Northern ecclesiastics and society."

Much of this regional divergence in civil religion stemmed from the strongly rural character of Southern culture. The difference was not simply a matter of numbers and proportions, of the lack of large cities and industries, it was also, and more important, that most of the population in its cities, industrial districts, and mill towns were gatherings from the countryside, enmeshed in kinship ties and continuing their rural folkways. Furthermore, such people came out of an unusually narrow, limited, provincial society, as many an observer recorded: "Stopping for two or three days in some back county," said Sidney Andrews, "I was always seeming to have drifted away from the world which held Illinois and Ohio and Massachusetts. The difficulty in keeping connection with our civilization did not so much lie in the fact that the whole structure of daily life is unlike ours, . . . as in the greater fact that the people are utterly without knowledge. There is everywhere a lack of intellectual activity; while as for schools, books, newspapers, why one may almost say there are none outside the cities and towns." Schools, books, and newspapers would become much more numerous and widespread, but even in the towns and cities the relative lack of interest in and support for such services would persist as a regional trait, as many a subsequent commentator would attest, and recurrent measures and mappings of national patterns of various indicators (such as expenditures on education and libraries, years of schooling completed, and rates of illiteracy) would confirm. This persistent power of traditional attitudes, reinforced by the regional chauvinism of religious leaders, "helped make Southern cities bastions of conservatism, . . . rather than of change, as in cities elsewhere in the United States."

Maps of census data on the "foreign-born population" reveal one of the starkest of regional contrasts, and Southern spokesmen long claimed great virtue in the difference—in the absence of an "alien influx" (cf. fig. 57). "The South above any other section represents Anglo-Saxon, native-born America," said a Southern bishop at the end of the century, and sixty years later religious leaders in Lubbock were still expressing pride that their area had been settled by a "pure blooded, homogeneous, population . . . from the great Anglo-Saxon centers of the South." When a local historian added that Lubbock "still maintains much of the spirit of small town individualism, together with a rather strait-laced moral attitude . . . [and] a certain suspicion of such attributes of a modern industrial nation as government bureaucracy, labor unions, and commitments to foreign nations," he was confirming the persistence of those powerful rural influences on urban life. Such purported qualities and self-consciousness gave rise to the modern characterization of WASP Southerners as an ethnic group. Lubbock, at the farthest reach of an extended South, was in fact more Anglo-Saxon than any of its Southern sources because of sustained efforts to discourage Black migration into West Texas, but its sense of "racial pride" (as it was long called) was of course rooted in the Southern experience of a biracial society under disturbance and continuing challenge. The general antipathy to "foreigners" was not simply a response to their strange creeds and tongues but to the fear that they would not readily assimilate and become loyal supporters of the Southern Way of Life.

That much vaunted way of life was anchored on White Supremacy. The South was distinguished from the North not by discrimination against Blacks (which was endemic in the nation) but by the presence, almost everywhere, of large numbers of Blacks and Whites locked in a rigid caste system: two peoples equally native to the region, sharing a long history—indeed, co-creators of this South—interdependent but segregated, with Black subordination enforced by law and intimidation and operating through meticulous social custom. Rationalized as a "doctrine of race integrity," such segregation and subordination was (in the words of a Southern apologist in 1910) "the elementary working hypothesis of civilization in our Southern States." As an unchallengeable tenet of Southern society caste subordinated class, holding Whites together however much they might differ in position, wealth, and interest. Such unity undergirded the Solid South—one-party control under a self-sustaining political leadership. The old planter families had largely survived; augmented by newly wealthy merchants and professionals and supported by religious leaders, they governed. Paternalistic in many traditional ways, the political culture shifted strongly toward the *hegemonic* (see *Continental America*, 292) and increasingly under local demagogues who united town and country, rich and poor—however reluctantly—simply because White Supremacy could be maintained only by force. Blacks did not willingly accept such severe restrictions upon their rights as citizens and were subordinated only by a sustained campaign of threats and violence. Revolt was latent in such a social system, enhanced by those formal statements of civil rights declared in postwar amendments to the Constitution; although Radical Reconstruction had been defeated in the region, it had secured important provisions in the national charter, and fear of renewed "meddling" from external forces linked "Southern identity" with "a siege mentality."

These broad characteristics of religion, peoples, and politics were basic to any consideration of the South, but, as always, the incidence and intensity of such things was uneven and impinged upon any attempt at geographical definition of the region. Common references to a block of states were too crude and inconsistent. Just as there had been ambiguities and uncertainties as to what constituted the Confederacy (which claimed Missouri and Kentucky as formal members and reserved a place for Maryland), so there was no firm agreement on just what states constituted the South (Kentucky? usually; Missouri, Maryland? partly at most; Florida? becoming less Southern year by year). Such large geopolitical units might vote together on certain federal issues but were inappropriate for any refined sense of region. Clearly the most critical, controversial issue of all these years was the presence of large numbers of freedmen and the struggle to define new working relationships between Blacks and Whites. If we therefore direct our attention to the existence of a comprehensive biracial society—in countrysides, towns, and cities—a familiar pattern comes quickly into focus: the "Old South," the "Planter South," extending from southern Maryland and Virginia through the Cotton States, together with the estate country of the Nashville and Bluegrass basins.

That South had been extended in area and undergone some important shifts in population. Throughout these contentious years Texas had served as the great frontier. Impoverished but physically undamaged by the war, it had much land attractive to Southern modes of settlement. In his travels across the Lower South, Edward King repeatedly spoke of the thousands fleeing to Texas ("the flood of emigration from South Carolina, Alabama, and Georgia is formidable") and of local concern over the exodus ("something should be done to arrest the drainage toward Texas; it is dwarfing the development of the Alabamian towns"). Much of the blame was put on the troubles at home, especially with former slaves, but most such migrants moved into East and Central Texas to carry on their traditional ways, including the use of Black labor. North Texas had become a refuge for many Border Southerners (Marshall, Texas, had served as the capital-in-exile for Confederate Missouri) following the paths of earlier migrations to the Blackland Prairies. Toward the end of the century farmers were pressing westward well beyond the Cross Timbers, extending their grain-cattle-cotton complex thinly across the brushy plains to the base of the Caprock and northerly into southern Oklahoma, where they were soon halted by the insurge of Midwesterners. Such expansions were concurrent with the extensions of railroads, and behind that frontier there was a continuing intensification of settlement associated with clearing and draining and expansion of the commercial economy, and the emergence of Dallas, Fort Worth, and Waco as new regional centers. By 1900 Texas had more than 3 million people, a fivefold increase in forty years, and Arkansas, which also drew large numbers of migrants from the older South, had tripled in population.

The southern margins of that Planter South continued to be more diverse. New generations of Northern businessmen, foreign agents, and immigrants, including Irish and German Catholics and German Jews, came to the port cities. French Louisiana persisted as a strong cultural enclave, complex in its creole components, further penetrated by Anglo-American planters and businessmen and under insidious pressures from crude national racial categories and practices, but expanding in numbers, exercising local political power, and undaunted in its linguistic and cultural identity and pride. Annual official celebrations of Mardi Gras in Mobile (instituted in the early eighteenth century) proclaimed a persisting creole presence, but it was a diminishing minority in such lesser coastal footholds. On the west a small new ethnic outpost emerged on the margins of Cajun Country when American colonists from the Middle West with their grain-farming machinery transformed the cattle pastures of the Coastal Prairies into a productive rice area.

A resumption of German immigration enlarged the several districts in Central Texas initiated by their compatriots before the war, and it included, as before, a sprinkling of Poles and Czechs from imperial Germanic homelands. Distinctive in landscape and economy, clinging rather strongly to native dress and language (there were German newspapers in more than a dozen Texas towns and cities), their neighborhoods marked by their own churches and social halls, such people thickened the settlement and expanded the boundaries of older districts (buying land from eager Anglo sellers), and became prominent among the diverse populations of the larger towns (such as Brenham, Cuero, and Victoria) and important in the business and cultural life of San Antonio (perhaps a third of that city's population), Houston, and Galveston (where, said Edward King, "a steady current of sturdy Germans" was "the best of all imports"). German identities persisted in some of the old Piedmont settlements, but elsewhere there was little more than a thin scattering of tiny "cultural-agricultural islands" created by Europeans lured by promoters after the war to settle on what proved to be marginal lands, such as the German communities on the knobby Highland Rim in Lawrence County, Tennessee, and on the sandy soils of the Appalachians in Cullman County, Alabama. Such colonizations displayed their ethnic identity not only in their Catholic or Lutheran churches but in their tidy houses, big barns, profusion of gardens and shrubs, and productive mixed agriculture. Later on analogous little clusters from a new wave of immigration—Italians, Greeks, Hungarians, Poles—began to show up in the cutover forest lands along the Gulf Coast, struggling to survive usually on some form of market gardening.

Aside from the spread of the Cotton Belt onto the prairies around Tallahassee, Florida was more a subtropical colony of the North than an extension of the traditional South, but the need for labor in the citrus groves and vegetable fields, warehouses, docks, and fancy resorts attracted large numbers of Blacks, and Northern managers readily adapted to Southern social mores. Cuban refugees and businessmen, long a major presence in Key West, were moving north to Tampa. By 1900 the state had just over half a million people and the boom was still rather deflated from the national depression and a severe citrus freeze, but more and more Northern sojourners swelled the winter population.

When we shift our focus to the northern sectors of the South a major variation comes into view. We have not given it as much attention in this assessment of changes because it was marginal to the most critical of postwar features: the legacy of plantations and large numbers of freedmen. Here tobacco was in many areas an intensive and valuable crop but grown in small fields largely under the care of farm families. This was corn, grain, hog, and cattle country—the Upper South, Virginia Extended in all its forms: yeoman farmers in the better valleys and uplands, country elite on their livestock estates on the richest lands, poor Whites subsisting in coves and hollows of the Appalachians and in similar rough country farther west in the Highland Rim, the Ozarks, Ouachitas, and Texas Hill Country (including an anomalous outlier in what would become southeastern Oklahoma, where in 1865 there were 12,000 former Black slaves of the Indian nations that had been forcibly removed from the South a generation earlier. And this was the Border South, Southern in sympathies but divided over secession, sending sons to both sides, ravaged by local bands throughout the war, but less seared by postwar policies (Kentucky and Missouri did not have to undergo Reconstruction). It, too, was a rural, Anglo-Saxon, evangelical Protestant South, but with its own variations, such as Cumberland Presbyterianism and the rapidly growing Disciples of Christ (and continuing presence of a Roman Catholic enclave in rural Kentucky, implanted from Catholic Maryland). White Supremacy was routinely present but maintained with less fear and force (total lynchings a few dozen rather than the hundreds in nearly every state in the Lower South), and the political culture continued to be more of the older Virginian traditionalistic paternalism rather than driven toward the hegemonic.

These two Souths coexisted as major subregions in patterns determined by the paths of early migrations, qualities of country, and resulting agricultures. Postwar developments in the Piedmont with its mill towns and tobacco industries overlapping the margins of the Cotton Belt represented a kind of convergence between the two. The South as a whole was bound together by the railroads and served by a more extensive set of urban centers, but the number, scale, and character of its cities continued to differentiate it. New Orleans, world-famous entrepôt and by far the largest indisputably Southern city (287,000), had fallen far behind the great Northern commercial centers it had equaled or exceeded before the war—Cincinnati, St. Louis, and Chicago. The observations of the astute Friedrich Ratzel, made in 1874 while the South was still in the throes of recovery, were still generally valid a generation later:

The general character of Southern cities [is] . . . very different from their Northern and Western counterparts. Those that are located on the seacoast and possess good harbors have, as is well known, a considerable commercial importance based primarily on the export of the South's main products: cotton, wood, tobacco, and rice. This importance is, however, one-sided, since imports by sea run far behind exports, and because for many necessities these cities are dependent on the big Northern commercial centers. Although in the last decade many indications have shown that healthy, independent economic activity was beginning to develop, the commerce of this area is still not connected to any industrial activity to speak of. For that reason, besides the big merchants here there are not big industrialists, no skilled workers, nor a vigorous white working class of any size worth mentioning. The shopkeepers and handworkers cannot make up for the lack of these hearty classes that create civilization and wealth. Therefore, . . . this society has an incomplete, half-developed profile like that which one tends to associate with the industry-less large cities of predominantly agricultural countries. In this regard, New Orleans, Mobile, Savannah, and Charleston look more like Havana and Veracruz than, say, Boston or Portland.

He found most of the Southern interior cities similarly constituted, though smaller and less active, but he thought that many of them "now have a bright future" because of their waterpower and plentiful wood and the rapid extension of railroad lines. Much of that was realized over the next twenty-five years as a more comprehensive set and hierarchy of service centers emerged, but still the scale and character of the result was hardly comparable with the course of developments in the North and West. The biggest of the Southern textile towns had 10,000–20,000 people, whereas Lowell and Fall River had 100,0000; Birmingham and its satellites had fewer than 50,000. Memphis, largest of the river towns before the war, remained far in the lead with 100,000 (despite thousands of deaths from yellow fever in the 1870s), while Atlanta, so much a creation of Northern investment and the railroad age, had 90,000. Ratzel's further comment that "the intellectual life of the Southern cities cannot even be remotely compared with the breadth or depth of those in the North and West" was still valid as well, despite many expansions in local schools, libraries, and other activities.

There had been talk during the war that Atlanta might be the most advantageous site for the permanent capital of a postwar Confederacy. Railroads had further enhanced its position, it was a major wholesaling center, much the most vociferous voice of the New South, and always impressive to visitors ("a perennial stream of progress . . . in the heart of the South"), but it was far from being the capital of the entire region. That fact pointed toward the larger truth that the South had no obvious core or capital. Such geographic patterns are not essential to regions or regionalism but are telling clues to important matters. The South was a large area, 1,300 miles long and 600 miles broad, an approximate quarter of the nation, nearly equal in extent to the whole of the Far West. But whereas that West was a composite of discrete, sharply differentiated regions, each anchored on some nuclear area and dominant city, the South was characterized by a wide dispersal of essentially similar peoples, indeed widely interrelated peoples, across a variety of physical regions but with no marked separations among them, with several areas of above-average density but no single area of unusual concentration. Its extensive network of railroads was anchored on a widely spaced set of gateway cities on the north and an even more dispersed set of ports on the south and east, with no strong internal regional focus. There was a remarkable degree of political uniformity across the region, a South solid in much more than just federal actions, but there was no informal influential seat of leadership directing and nurturing such cohesion and resistance, which is to imply as well that there was no outstanding Southern cultural center: no voice of the South emanating from the seat of major publishing houses (regional literature was dominated by church publications); no distinguished academic institution training a regional elite; no cluster of creative artists exploring and expressing the Southern Way of Life. (Perhaps the most visible contrived assertion of Southern identity was the line of massive statues of Confederate heroes along Monument Boulevard in Richmond, a kind of mausoleum of the Lost Cause in the former capital of a defeated nation.)

Such patterns reveal the South to be more a folk culture than a nation—"a great family"—a regionally rooted, interrelated, dispersed population united into political action when its basic social system was challenged by external forces. Defeated in mortal combat, forced to accept the end of slavery, that same broad body of people dug in, resisted, and with even greater unanimity eventually overturned further programs of social reform and reestablished firm control over its own sociopolitical affairs. All of that was accomplished by an upwelling of action in every locality, without central direction, and the resultant redefined racial caste system continued to be enforced by the people as a whole—that is, by the *ruling* people as a whole: White Southerners in every city, town, and countryside. Such folk solidarity was an expression of insecurity as well as conviction, for this new mode of social control, based on a suppression of civil rights and protected by a political armistice at the highest national level, was ever vulnerable to some renewal of attack from external forces—and from an upwelling of revolt from those suppressed. Ironically, much of the cohesion and character of this militant regionalism was grounded in that other folk culture with which it was interlocked and interlaced, one as deeply rooted and thoroughly Southern as its oppressors. As James Bryce concluded: "someone has observed, with the exaggeration deemed needed to enforce a neglected truth, that the Negro, powerless as he is, still dominates the South, for his presence is never forgotten, and makes many things different from what they would otherwise be."

2. New Economic Regions

If North and South might be said to have ultimately shared in both victory and defeat with reference to social policies, there could be no mistaking which was the victor in economic terms. For whereas most of the South's industry and infrastructure lay in ruins and its labor system dismantled, the Northern economy, adapting to the diversion of hundreds of thousands of men and sudden insatiable demands for military supplies, had boomed along without major disruptions. Thereafter, while the South struggled to reorganize and recover, the North moved on to become the world's most prodigious industrial power.

"The growth of an industrial economy remains a mysterious process to those engaged in studying and describing it," said Peter Temin in the opening of his "inquiry" into the iron and steel industry. "It involves changes in thought patterns as well as changes in the means of production. It requires a transformation of agriculture as well as an expansion of industry." We cannot effectively engage here in such study, but we do need to sketch a few of the bolder regional changes affecting the basic geographical structure and balance of power in the nation. And we may well begin by noting that, broadly speaking, the Civil War was little more than a surficial disturbance in the economic development of the United States because the basic systems and conditions for continuing expansion—all those characterizing features of paleotechnic industrialism and capitalist enterprise—were already in place: the coal-iron-steam complex, the machine-driven factory, the new "American system" of mass production, the space-conquering railroad, established areas and centers of specialized production and distribution, and all the vigorous workings and potentials of an essentially "unfettered market economy" fueled by vast resources and a growing population.

In simplest geographic terms, expansion could be seen in two forms: the continued outward extension of settlement and resource exploitation into new areas, and the inward intensification of production and processing in selected older areas. Agriculture offered major displays of both. We have already traced the most important extensions in area in noting how the westward advancing edge of the East altered the eastern margins of the West (see fig. 30). That advance continued in fragmented form into the new century, but this later pioneering would result in only minor productive additions to the great agricultural specialty regions of the midcontinent whose basic character and outline were becoming discernible much earlier. As in other activities, a set of new industrial tools for a much-intensified agriculture was rapidly elaborated in scale and capability: new plows, drills, corn planters, cultivators, mowers, rakes, reapers, and threshers; new breeds of livestock and plants and more attention to crop rotations and fertilization. Such things were touted in a proliferation of farm journals, county fairs, and railroad promotions and by new state agricultural agencies, although adoption of the most advanced tools and methods tended to depend upon a few local leaders and spread rather slowly. Increasingly elaborate and efficient machinery might radically reduce the time and labor needed for many tasks, yet agriculture could not partake fully of paleotechnic industrialism not only because it remained inherently an organic activity but because steam power was generally unsuited for fieldwork on most farms. Giant steam tractors might pull great gang plows across the lacustrine levels of North Dakota and huge combine harvesters in the San Joaquin, but such heavy, costly, and cumbersome operations (huge intakes of fuel and water) could only be undertaken by the largest operators in a few special regions. For the rest, horses and mules continued to supply the motive power, supplemented only by the steam-powered stationary thresher. Hints of the fuller force of industrialization appeared in the new century with the development of gasoline-powered caterpillar tractors and combine engines (initially in California), but the horse remained supreme in all regions (sustained by large acreages of oats, the primary feed of working stock).

Much the greatest intensification came with the spread of a mixed agriculture of maize, small grains, and grasses devoted primarily to the fattening of livestock, all across the rich, deep-soil, well-watered prairie lands of ample growing season. Tile-drainage of extensive wetlands laced through this glaciated expanse kept adding more and more highly productive acreage, new varieties of corn allowed a slow expansion northward, and improved breeds enhanced the efficiency of meat production. By 1900 the concept of the "Corn Belt" as a distinct and centrally important American agricultural region was emergent, soon taking its place in the common vocabulary of American writers and fixed on the map by economic geographers (fig. 42).

On such maps the Corn Belt became the centerpiece of a set of great agricultural specialty regions. Each of these was in some degree derivative of the same broad midcontinent pioneering and had become differentiated through expansion into critically different physical conditions. As settlers pushed on westward they eventually found that wheat—always an important frontier crop in this new West—proved more reliable than corn, and in the 1870s and 1880s a Winter Wheat Belt began to emerge on the higher, drier plains of Kansas and Nebraska. Spreading on into Colorado during a short period of wet years, this advance was soon halted and partly repelled by drought and underwent a long period of further experiment and adjustment, drawing upon fervent promotions, such as "dry farming" (featuring special tillage of fallowed ground to conserve moisture) and expanding scientific investigations. Meanwhile, this wheat specialty region was extended southwestwardly across western Oklahoma and into the Texas Panhandle.

Northwest of the Corn Belt the shorter growing season, colder winters, and

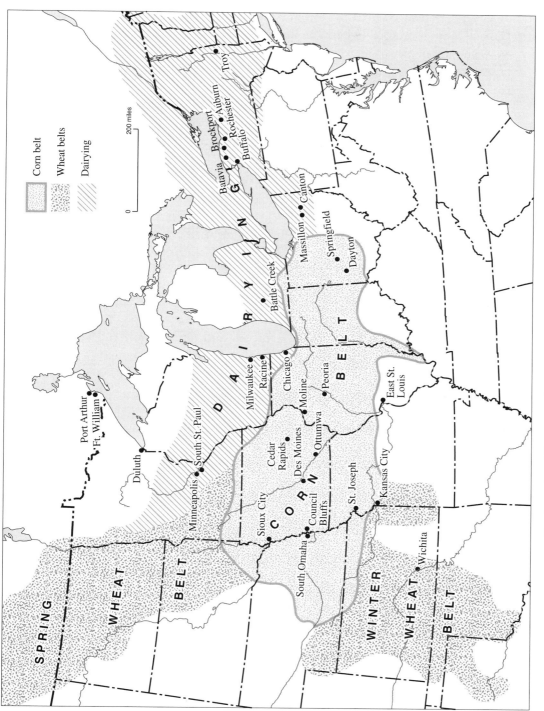

Corn belt

Wheat belts

Dairying

200 miles

0

Port Arthur
Ft. William

Duluth

Minneapolis
South St. Paul

SPRING

WHEAT

BELT

Sioux City

Cedar
Rapids

Des Moines

Council
Bluffs

South Omaha

CORN

St. Joseph

Kansas City

Wichita

WINTER

WHEAT

BELT

Milwaukee

Racine

Chicago

Moline

Peoria

Ottumwa

BELT

East St.
Louis

Battle Creek

DAIRYING

Massillon

Canton

Springfield

Dayton

BELT

Brockport
Batavia
Rochester
Auburn
Buffalo

Troy

42. Agricultural Regions and Some Associated Manufacturing Centers.

limited snow cover fostered an emphasis on spring-sown grain and the emergence of a Spring Wheat Belt reaching from southwestern Minnesota across the eastern Dakotas, into Manitoba (where the Red River Colony had also served as an early experimental nucleus), and, following a great flurry of railroad building and surge of settlers in the opening decade of the new century, broadly across the prairies and parklands of the new provinces of Saskatchewan and Alberta.

The emergence of these new wheat regions, producing huge harvests on large farms with the biggest machines and armies of seasonal laborers and served by specialized marketing systems, put wheat growers in older, less-favored areas under severe pressure. Well before the war, under competition from Ohio and Illinois, Upstate New York, once a major producer, had diversified into other lines, especially dairying, and in the 1870s the northerly portions of Ohio, southern Michigan, and the rougher, colder lands of Wisconsin and Minnesota were undergoing a similar shift. Implanted in all these areas primarily by Yankee settlers, dairying became the dominant commercial activity all across a northern belt from the upper Connecticut to the uppermost Mississippi Valley, aided by critical inventions (such as the centrifugal cream separator and the Babcock butterfat tester), greatly improved breeds of cows (especially holstein-friesian, guernsey, and jersey), and, toward the end of the century, research help from major agricultural colleges (especially Cornell and Wisconsin). Railroads and refrigeration and vigorously growing urban populations all along the southern edge were also important, especially to the marketing of fresh milk, and this entire Dairy Belt became parceled into an overlapping set of "milk sheds," each focused on a major metropolis (and the "milk train" stopping to pick up the farmers' cans in every town and village and at trackside platforms spaced through the countryside became a synonym for slowness in a society now attuned to express train speeds).

The simple labels of these belts can be misleading. They were not sharply set off but graded into one another (geographers would often disagree on just where to draw the boundaries), and even well beyond such border zones other crops and activities might be of considerable importance: cattle and other grains in the wheat belts (especially barley in the north), barley, oats, and hogs on the dairy farms, and all across this latter belt there was a sprinkling of districts devoted to orcharding, potatoes, vegetables, poultry, hops, or some other specialty. Furthermore, although these grand divisions were becoming fixed on the map of American agriculture, defining basic realms of major productions and their accompanying styles of farming life, such things are never really stable but respond recurrently to changes in markets, technology, and science—they are part of the continuous shaping of human geography.

These extensive regions were directly bound into the industrial geography of the nation—indeed, some economic historians would see their associated manufactures as central to the rapid changes in technology, scale, and pattern characteristic of the time. In general, local processing of farm products gave way to larger and larger factories in fewer and fewer places and controlled by a handful of powerful companies, but there were many variations. Dairying, with its daily perishable raw product and dense pattern of cooperative creameries and cheese factories, was a major exception. More representative was the changing geography of meat packing. The modern factory industry had emerged in the Ohio Valley and spread westward to river towns along the Wabash, Illinois, and middle Mississippi. In the 1850s railroads made possible new orientations and the rapid raise of productions in Chicago and Milwaukee (and in Indianapolis in the older sector). After the war, as the industry spanned the breadth of the Corn Belt, Cedar Rapids, Ottumwa, Des Moines, Council Bluffs, St. Joseph, and Kansas City joined in, and Chicago became much the largest pork-packing center in the nation. As this was taking place a further dimension was being added. The slaughter of local cattle had always been part of the industry, but as the Great Plains became occupied by ranchers and crossed by railroads, cattle could be shipped in from these western ranges, fattened for several months on Corn Belt farms, and then sent to the packinghouses. Actually for some years large numbers were sent east to be slaughtered near Atlantic Coast markets, a system challenged only with the development of refrigerated railroad cars and intensive campaigns by the big companies to undermine the resistance of Eastern packers and butchers and to enlist them as agents in a national system for the marketing of "Chicago dressed beef."

In 1871 the Armour Company opened a plant in Kansas City to receive the "torrent of Texas cattle pouring" in. That particular influx soon diminished with tightening restrictions against Texas fever and the availability of better beef cattle from ranches on the High Plains, Sand Hills, and other ranges. This new interregional relationship favored a set of cities serving as Western gateways to the Corn Belt, each with converging railroad lines, huge union stockyards, and big packing plants of the four or five largest companies that had developed fleets of refrigerator cars, icing facilities, and cold-storage warehouses spaced through much of the national market. Thus "Chicago was the industry prototype, Kansas City its first copy," and these soon joined by East St. Louis, South Omaha, and South St. Paul, then filling in with St. Joseph and Sioux City, with Wichita as an outlying gateway near the Flint Hills.

Flour milling displayed a further variation of such emergent national patterns. The local waterpowered gristmill long dominated the industry. Larger mills and clusters of mills arose at major receiving and shipping points, especially Baltimore and Richmond, and, as wheat began to arrive in large amounts from the West, at numerous sites in Upstate New York, especially Rochester and Buffalo (where in 1842 the first large steam-powered grain elevator was erected). In the West, St.

Louis was the leader in grain receipts until the mid-1850s (when it was overtaken by Chicago) and in flour milling for another fifteen years. A major shift occurred in the 1870s after Minneapolis millers developed a "new process milling" featuring steel rollers (adapted from Hungarian models) for the milling of hard wheat and repeated siftings to "purify" the flour (a French design to remove bran and produce an unprecedented whiteness). Minneapolis soon became much the largest flour-milling center in the world, followed by Buffalo (which was now receiving spring wheat from big new shipping facilities at Duluth and Fort William-Port Arthur) and Kansas City. A few giant firms invested heavily in these primary centers, but many lesser companies maintained mills in smaller cities throughout this agricultural midland. By the turn of the century firms specializing in newly developed and widely advertised breakfast cereals, such as rolled oats and cornflakes, had given new industrial prominence to such places as Cedar Rapids and Battle Creek.

Foundrymen, blacksmiths, artisans, inventors, and entrepreneurs followed the spread of agriculture westward, and we can readily discern the sequential emergence of important implement-manufacturing districts. It was not simply a case of local response to routine needs but of creating demands for new, ever-more complex machinery. As a special report in the 1880 census put it, the industry became "mainly dependent upon an agriculture revolutionized by agricultural machinery itself—a manufacture . . . which has created its own demand." The industry was complicated by the variety of seasonal tasks (plowing, harrowing, seeding, cultivating, harvesting, threshing), the needs of different crops (small grains, corn, potatoes, hay, and others), the large number of firms, and the role of patents. American law allowed a patent holder to issue exclusive rights to a specified territory, and this diffusion of designs rather than the shipment of implements tended to create a cellular pattern of production areas, each dominated by an independent local firm. Such licensing was more effective with complicated machines (such as reapers and binders, as best exemplified by the McCormick Company) than with simpler ones (such as plows and cultivators); most firms produced a limited variety of implements and the number of manufacturers remained large. After the war there was a notable increase in scale and character, from local workshops to much larger factories, and wider marketing by means of the ever-improving railroad system. Several loose geographical clusters of major machinery manufacturers emerged from a widely diffused and unstable industry: Upstate New York, especially Auburn, but also Troy, Brockport, Batavia, and Buffalo; Ohio, especially Canton-Massillon and Springfield-Dayton; and Illinois—southern Wisconsin, especially Chicago, Peoria, Moline, Racine, and Milwaukee. The formation of the International Harvester Corporation through the merger of major Chicago firms and quick acquisition of an array of specialized producers marked the

beginning of a new stage of diversified corporate dominance, yet important companies continued in a number of smaller cities.

Viewed more broadly all these agriculturally related industries were specialized
components within or on the margins of a vigorously developing American Manufacturing Belt. The backbone of that complex geographic structure was the iron
and steel industry, wherein, as with agriculture, major developments were related
both to extensions into new areas and intensifications in selected older ones. Such
changes were shaped by uneven distributions of essential resources and major
breakthroughs in technology. These latter were especially important in fuels and
furnaces. The early American iron industry was based on charcoal, lavishly available from Appalachian forests. By the 1850s the rich anthracite resources of
eastern Pennsylvania were replacing charcoal in the larger furnaces throughout the
East. At the same time, experiments with producing coke from the enormous
bituminous coalfields of western Pennsylvania were under way, and with the heavy
demand for high-quality railroad iron, larger coke-fueled furnaces were beginning
to replace charcoal ones in the West. But much the greatest change came with the
introduction of the Bessemer hot-blast furnace. Experimental plants of this British
invention were built in the United States in the mid-1860s, and within a few years
this "unorthodox leap" in technology had transformed steel from a small, expensive specialty into a cheap, mass-produced item (U.S. output increased fortyfold
between 1869 and 1880). Toward the end of the century production by a new open-
hearth process (which could make use of a wider variety of ores and also scrap iron)
began to compete with Bessemer in the growing demand for high-quality structural
steel (for new high-rise fireproof buildings and bridges).

Much the biggest geographic change was the shift to ever-heavier dependence
on Lake Superior ores. These came from a set of rich and enormous beds of iron
(the Marquette, Menominee, Gogebic, Vermillion, Mesabi "ranges"—to list them
in order of their development) all within a short haul to lake ports (Marquette,
Escanaba, Ashland, Duluth, and Two Harbors—the major ones of 1900). Early
shipments from Marquette made use of small wooden sailing vessels and the new
(1855) Soo Canal bypassing the rapids on the St. Marys River outlet of Lake
Superior (undertaken by the U.S. government to get the wonderfully rich Ke-
weenaw copper to Eastern consumers). It took years of experiment with these iron
ores (testing them in various kinds of furnaces) and later enormous investments in
shipping facilities (high-capacity railroads, special steam-powered iron-hull ore
vessels, huge mechanized docks) as well as successive enlargements of the Soo
Canal (1876 and 1896) and a parallel one on the Canadian side (1895) before
these bountiful resources could be put to maximum use. Annual shipments did not
reach a million tons until 1872, but with a great surge of investment in the 1880s
"the transport of Lake ores had become an intricate ballet of large and complex

machines," and the movement of more than 20 million tons during the eight-month, ice-free season of 1900 represented three-quarters of the nation's total iron ore production.

Concurrently, experiments demonstrated the superiority of Connellsville coke for blast furnaces, explorations broadened the known extent of the "Pittsburgh seam" of such coal, and the valleys of southwestern Pennsylvania became lined with tens of thousands of ovens producing this concentrated fuel for shipment downriver. By the 1880s the heartland of American heavy industry had shifted from southeastern Pennsylvania and the anthracite region to the meeting ground of Connellsville coke and Lake Superior ore, a short broad belt extending from Pittsburgh and the valleys to Cleveland and nearby lake ports. Pittsburgh itself became the greatest center of this land of fire and smoke, mass movement and mass production, gigantic riverside and railroad-enmeshed factories (fig. 43), but there were clusters of similar facilities: Steubenville and Wheeling on the Ohio, Newcastle and Sharon in the Shenango Valley, Youngstown and Niles in the Mahoning, Lorain on the lake, and the banks of the Cuyahoga in Cleveland. At the opening of the twentieth century more than two-thirds of America's steel was being produced

43. Mass Movement and Mass Production in a Land of Fire and Smoke.
Coal barges and steel mills on the Monongahela at Pittsburgh, c. 1901. (Courtesy Steel Industry Heritage Corporation)

here, and much of it was supplying a dense array of rolling mills, wire and rod mills, tube plants, tinplate companies, and a host of other specialized manufacturers within this belt and such nearby industrial centers as Canton, Massillon, Columbus, and those in the oil district of northwestern Pennsylvania.

Viewed broadly, such a development represented a relatively moderate northwestward extension and gross magnification of a well-established upper Ohio, Pittsburgh-centered industry, a response to new sources of materials, and the rapidly improving advantage of a position central, pivotal, within the main industrial markets of the nation. A much greater alteration of earlier patterns was the rise of the Chicago area as a major focus of the iron and steel industry. In the 1860s St. Louis was the leading center in this western region, with iron ore nearby and coal available by river shipment (and some Missouri ore was being sent east to upper Ohio furnaces), whereas Chicago had only a few foundries and a rolling mill. But in the next decade new Bessemer furnaces at Chicago and vicinity were making use of Lake Superior ores and Connellsville coke (eventually mixed with upgraded Illinois-Indiana coals), and a plant at Joliet, in the short industrial corridor developing along the Illinois & Michigan Canal, became the largest producer of steel rails. Missouri ore lost its wider market, St. Louis's prospects as a heavy industrial center faded, and the triumph of Chicago was firmly fixed when the new capitalist colossus, the United States Steel Corporation (fig. 44), selected a nearby strip of Indiana shore for the erection of the largest steelworks in the world at the new town of Gary (completed in 1908).

At the same time, the closure of a large works in Scranton and shift of operations to a new mill in a new town (Lackawanna) on the Erie shore adjacent to Buffalo represented the lure of Lake ores and the relative inefficiency of anthracite in the blast furnace. Nevertheless, even though eclipsed in production by these lakeward and westward shifts the older Eastern iron and steel district in Pennsylvania (Lehigh Valley, Harrisburg, and the Philadelphia area), New Jersey (Trenton), and New York (Troy) continued to play an important role. New mills were built, new methods (such as mixing coke with anthracite) adopted, and a new center added with the construction of a large plant at Sparrow's Point at the entrance to Baltimore harbor to make use of inexpensive imported ore (chiefly from Cuba).

Although the market had spread westward with heavy demands for rails, structural steel, agricultural implements, and shipbuilding (much of this last market generated by the industry itself, with more tonnage launched on the Great Lakes than in all the rest of the United States during many of these years), the more elaborate engineering industries were still primarily in the older industrial districts of the East. The major locomotive works, for example, were in Philadelphia (Baldwin, dating from 1831 and now much the largest), Schenectady, Paterson, Providence, and Pittsburgh. Furthermore, Eastern mills were well situated to re-

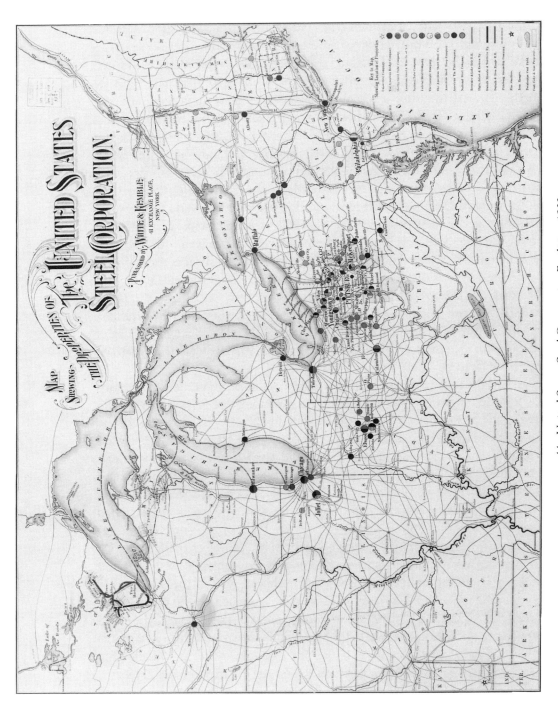

44. United States Steel Corporation Facilities, 1903.

The original is in color, differentiating among the various associated companies. (Courtesy the Library of Congress)

spond to increasing demands for high-grade steels for an expanding array of specialized manufactures, such as hardware, cutlery, small arms, and textile machinery, which were still strongly anchored in various districts of New England, New York, New Jersey, and the Philadelphia area. New inventions tended to enhance the same areas, as displayed in the huge Singer sewing machine factory at Elizabethport and the Remington typewriter factory at Ilion in the Mohawk Valley (but cash registers were coming from Dayton, Ohio). Similarly, Philadelphia, Providence, Worcester, and Hartford continued as leaders in the machine-tool industry, although Cincinnati was now actually the largest center and Rockford, Illinois, a rising one.

Associated heavy industries tended to conform to a similar pattern. Smelting and, especially, refining of copper, lead, and zinc continued to be important in East Coast ports despite the strong emergence of the tristate lead-zinc region centered on Joplin, Missouri (with some smelting and refining locally and at Kansas City and St. Louis), and new massive copper operations in the Far West (as at Anaconda and Great Falls). Two-thirds of the nation's Portland cement, a major new construction material, was produced in the Lehigh Valley; pottery and porcelain remained primarily in East Liverpool (local clays) and Trenton (imported clays). The heavy concentration of the new mass production of machine-blown glass in Pittsburgh and vicinity was loosened when cheap natural gas (soon wastefully depleted) lured major companies to Toledo and Muncie.

Petroleum and natural gas were new fuels and resources, increasingly important but as yet without radical impact on the geography of manufacturing. "Colonel" Drake's famous first well of 1859, drilled near Titusville, Pennsylvania, in an area of oil seepages long known to the Seneca Indians, set off the kind of wild, speculative scramble that would characterize the American industry for the next hundred years. An industrial historian of 1878 offered a bold sketch of the lurid scene and its ramifications:

From the year 1860 the development of the petroleum-industry was so rapid and vast as to be without parallel in American history, all things considered. Though the oil-lands proper were contained within a small geographical area, the influence of the excitement and greed of gain thereby aroused extended all over the country, and even to foreign lands. Companies were formed to bore for oil in thousands of places where traces of petroleum had been noticed for years previous. Land that was heretofore, and even then, worthless brought fabulous prices. In the oil-region itself it was next to impossible to buy land. The business of getting out and refining oil grew like Jonah's gourd. Derricks, tall, strange, but useful sprang up by the thousands. Cities, even, came into being almost in a day. Huge fortunes were made in weeks. There was a new class of shoddy aristocracy created by the wealth produced by petroleum. The ignorant but lucky, the low but shrewd, suddenly became immensely rich. New branches of industry essential for the operations of the oil-interest—improved mining apparatus and processes, railroad extensions, new kinds of cars, pipe-lines, oil-boats, tanks, refineries, barrel-factories, lamp-factories, ship-building, co-operative organizations of producers, transporters, refiners, and exporters—were required to meet the exorbitant and pressing demands of the petroleum-traffic. Banking, insurance, and other interests, were required to enlarge their facilities. The arteries of domestic trade and transportation were made to pulsate with unnatural life and vigor, and our whole business-system was quickened into abnormal activity. Our foreign commerce was rapidly extended, petroleum leaping to the third rank among our exports inside of fifteen years.

Drake's New England sponsors were seeking a source of kerosene, a new illuminant that with the invention of appropriate lamps was much in demand. Initially distilled in small quantities from shale or coal (hence "coal-oil"), this lavish new source had an immense potential market awaiting. Kerosene not only remained the principal petroleum product for forty years, more than half of that production was exported: "indeed, few products associated with America have had so extensive an influence . . . on the daily living habits of so large a proportion of the world's population." Not until the end of the century did refinery by-products (such as fuel oil, naptha, paraffin, vaseline, lubricants, and gasoline) become its equal in value.

Avid drilling extended the producing area up and down the Allegheny River valley and into lesser districts along a set of narrow belts reaching into southwestern Ohio, West Virginia, and Kentucky (giving rise to a theory of "oil belts" as an early stage of geological reasoning). The first pipelines led from wells to river port or railhead. Legal rights to extend and operate such systems were uncertain, and railroads fought them in courts, legislatures, and on the ground. Furthermore, intense rivalries between railroads for this new lucrative traffic influenced oil company strategies regarding pipelines, refineries, and marketing. A pipeline to Pittsburgh ignited an intense contest between Philadelphia and Baltimore railroad and commercial interests, but a few years later the first long-distance pipelines were laid to the Delaware (at Marcus Hook, downriver from Philadelphia) and to New York Harbor (Bayonne), and Baltimore faded as a contender. Small refineries had been quickly erected within the oil region, and barrels rafted downriver helped make Pittsburgh an early center, but a Cleveland refinery of 1865 became the nucleus of John D. Rockefeller's Standard Oil Company, which soon dominated the industry.

In 1882 Rockefeller led the transformation of an extensive alliance of oil refiners into the Standard Oil Trust, which undertook a drastic rationalization, reducing the number of members' refineries from fifty-three to twenty-two, focusing many of this remainder on specialized markets, and directing most crude oil production to three new gigantic refinery centers at Cleveland, near Philadelphia, and on New York Harbor. As this was taking shape the first major new American field emerged at Lima and was soon broadened across the Maumee Plain of northwestern Ohio

and Indiana. The heavy sulfurous oil of this field required special treatment and led
to the first extensive marketing of fuel oil as a power source competing with coal.
To protect its dominance Standard Oil began to buy producing properties in this
field and in 1890 built a huge new refinery near Chicago, at Whiting, Indiana. By
that time it controlled more than 80 percent of U.S. refining capacity, and its
"headquarters at 26 Broadway in New York City housed what was then the world's
largest managerial hierarchy which coordinated, monitored, and planned the
activities of . . . [an] integrated global enterprise." With the development of the
Baku field on the Caspian, Russia, the first foreign producer to rival the United
States, gained momentary parity in 1898 only to fall quickly far behind with the
opening of immense new sources in Texas (especially Spindletop, near Beaumont)
and Oklahoma (Bartlesville).

It was soon apparent that these new American discoveries would be bound by
pipeline or coastal shipment to the giant market-oriented refinery complexes on
the northeastern seaboard. Thus despite its volatile, sporadic character, the emergence of the petroleum industry, heavily shaped by the strategies of Standard Oil,
whose roots were anchored in the original Allegheny-Cuyahoga field of activity,
reinforced the basic geographic form of the American Manufacturing Belt (fig. 45).

45. Principal Oil Pipelines and Refineries, c. 1900.

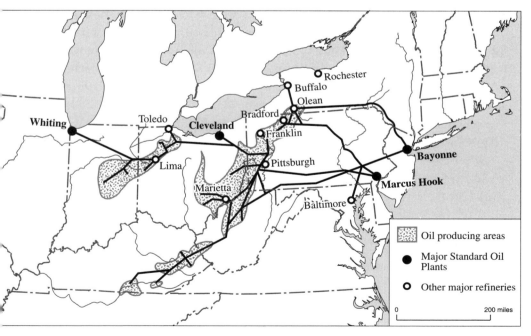

Cleveland became a major center in petroleum at the same time that it became one in iron and steel, and the huge Whiting refinery was a precursor by a few years of the enormous Gary steelworks a few miles away. Other wholly new industries also emerged within that industrial belt, such as the first great electrical-generating project at Niagara Falls (completed in 1895) and its associated industries (aluminum reduction, abrasives, electrochemicals); electrical manufactures at Schenectady (General Electric), Pittsburgh (Westinghouse), and Lynn (Thomson-Houston); the rubber industry at Akron (following an earlier emphasis on shoes and fabrics in New England and New Jersey); and photographic cameras and supplies at Rochester (Kodak).

The emergence of this American Manufacturing Belt was the geographic expression of an unrivaled industrial growth, scale, and diversity of operations. By 1900 the United States produced one-third of the world's industrial output—more than Great Britain, France, and Germany combined. Multiplying fivefold in forty years, these developments had shaped the geographic structure of the national economy into the form it would hold far into the next century. It was a bold and, for all its internal complexity, rather simple pattern on the map (fig. 46): an approximate parallelogram with corners at Milwaukee and St. Louis, Baltimore and Boston, modified in detail by an outward bending of the western boundary to pick up Dubuque and Davenport–Moline–Rock Island on the middle Mississippi and a stretching of the northern corners to catch the mill towns on the Fox and on the rivers of southern New Hampshire and Maine. By this date all the northern forests had been heavily cut, and the big lumber centers just beyond the edge of this belt—Bangor, Glens Falls, Bay City–Saginaw, Wausau, Eau Claire—were shifting to paper and other specialized products. To the west lay the great gateway agricultural processing centers; just to the south was Louisville, the only Southern city to exceed 20,000 workers, engaged mostly in the processing of its own region's specialties (as earlier noted, even the largest of the new mill towns in the South remained tiny "islands of industrialism" in that broad region). In the Far West only San Francisco (42,000) ranked as a large and diverse manufacturing center.

America's early industrial regions (described in *Continental America*, 374–99) remain readily visible within this pattern but further enlarged and diversified. New York City (including the New Jersey cities sharing its harbor) was now far in the lead in all common measures of industrialism: well over a billion dollars in capital investment, more than half a million workers, and a billion and a half in value of product—about twice that of Philadelphia in each category (and these two metropolises were unrivaled in their diversity of manufacturing, with virtually every skilled trade represented). The textile industry continued to dominate dozens of New England towns and various specialized centers in the Mohawk Valley, New Jersey, and Philadelphia environs and continued to develop new methods and articles

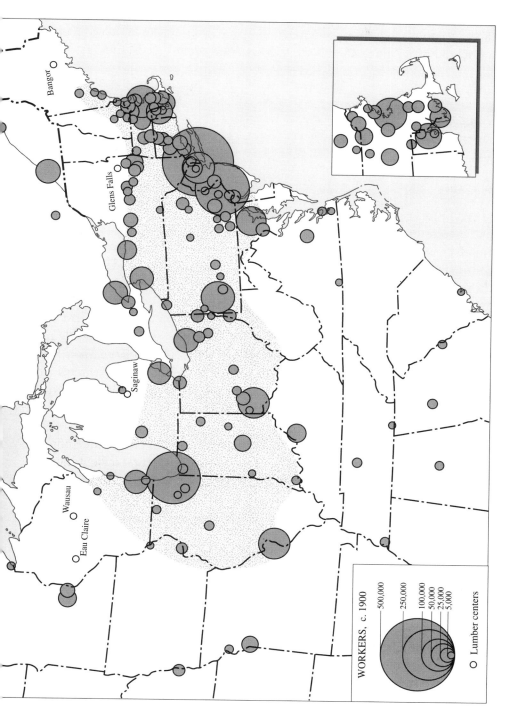

WORKERS, c. 1900

500,000
250,000
100,000
50,000
25,000
5,000

○ Lumber centers

46. The American Manufacturing Belt.

The scale refers to the average number of wage earners employed during the year and does not include "such salaried employees as general superintendents, clerks, and salesmen." Suburbs adjacent to major cities have been added to the city total. In a few cases towns close together (within walking distance) have been grouped to form a total sufficient for a particular level. In the great majority of places, manufacturing that employed 5,000 wage earners also represented at least $10 million in capital investment and $10 million in value of production. Data from the U.S. Census, 1900; Canadian cities, 1911 data from *Historical Atlas of Canada*, vol. III.

(especially to serve the ready-made clothing market), and it remained the largest manufacturing employer and a major industry by every measure, but iron and steel, combined with machinery and engineering, was now the leader in investment and value of product, marking an important shift toward capital goods. Even so, Walter Licht has cautioned against overstressing such a change because we should

> not lose sight of the impressive array of products that flowed from American manufactories. It is the *completeness* of the manufacturing system that deserves emphasis: Americans turned out steel rails and machines, but also clothing, ceramics, jewelry, and beer in great profusion. Visitors to the country in the late nineteenth century might be drawn to the imposing mass-production steel plants of Pittsburgh and the meat packinghouses of Chicago as they went to the textile mills of Lowell fifty years earlier, but missed again would be that large universe of firms in city and town that produced fine goods on a small-batch basis. Diversity and specialization persisted.

Similarly, our particular map of industrial centers can mislead as to the actual density of manufacturing, for there were more than three hundred additional towns within that belt that had more than a thousand wage earners engaged in manufacturing.

Thus the great majority of the nation's industrial capacity and diversity was concentrated in only a portion of its northeastern quadrant, occupying less than 10 percent of its continental expanse. Furthermore, despite the longings and fervent promotions for industrial growth in every other part of the country there were many indications that this fundamental economic pattern, this gross imbalance in regional development, was essentially complete and stabilized. Such persistence was based not just on the enormous investment in physical plant and systems of operation (for capital was ever seeking new areas of promise) but on the unprecedented efficiency of procurement and marketing on a continental scale. Once the railroad network neared completion, this specialized region, itself complexly laced together with the most modern trunk lines, could bind the rest of the nation into its orbit for "no transport technology in history has been more centralizing than the railroad." As noted, Southern industrial leaders found that they could not simply copy and create a diversified industrial South; they could participate only as a province constrained and subordinate to this powerful Northern complex. David R. Meyer has noted how the Middle West avoided similar subordination by undergoing rapid and diverse industrialization during a "window of opportunity" between 1850 and 1880 before Eastern-based railroad and marketing systems were capable of dominating the vigorously growing transappalachian market. Thus when those systems became able to conquer space more effectively, the result was a joining of two industrial regions, and this portion of the West (which had been populated by many of the same people and from the first had enjoyed advantageous familial and financial ties with the older commercial-industrial East) became, in effect, an equal partner, with Chicago the counterpart of New York City and St. Louis and Milwaukee matching Baltimore and Boston at the corners of a region extending a thousand miles from New England shores to the Mississippi. Here was the economic core of the nation; all the rest was peripheral and subordinate to it.

The railroad was not only vital to the creation of such a complex, it was, as Lewis Mumford wrote, "the most characteristic and the most efficient form" of the maturing paleotechnic age in which "size, speed, quantity, the multiplication of machines" became a mark of progress. Although railroads could be extended almost anywhere, a good one was costly to build, rigidly fixed in place, and efficient only for routine mass movement of standardized commodities (including passengers) in a limited variety of uniform vehicles. Railroads were not only "the first modern high-fixed-cost business," the complexities of their operation made them "the pioneers in modern management," providing the basic techniques essential to large industrial enterprises. Furthermore, just as competitive pressures led to extensive mergers of railroad companies to form large systems seeking control of major intercity connections and profitable territories, similar pressures and propensities came to characterize all industrial America. Economies of scale led to heavy investment in huge power plants and enormous factories full of massive machinery, and thus to mass production in place and the need for mass distribution therefrom. Manufacturers were driven by both opportunity and necessity, the prospect of serving a huge expanding domestic market and the dangers of ruinous competition in the unfettered American capitalist environment. Under the special conjunction of a severe economic depression following upon the rapid expansion of many capital-intensive industries, "a great wave of mergers swept through the manufacturing sector" between 1895 and 1904. International Harvester, U.S. Steel, and Standard Oil Trust were expressive of the kind of vast horizontal consolidations of formerly competitive firms that took place in most sectors of American industry. Many of these integrations were not very successful in the longer run, but this sudden surge toward concentration of control had marked geographic and political effects. Most of these powerful new companies soon moved into vertical integration (achieved to a large degree earlier by Swift and Armour), buying control of raw materials and of consumer firms and creating nationwide marketing systems managed by a bureaucratic hierarchy from a central headquarters. Among the devices used was "single basing point" pricing policies (such as "Pittsburgh plus" in the steel industry, whereby consumers paid the nominal price of shipment from Pittsburgh even if the item purchased had been produced and shipped from a nearby point) and special favorable freight rates negotiated with railroads of the region (an issue of such chronic complaint that as late as 1937 a congressional report stated that "for nearly three generations . . . the country has been accepting influences and conditions which have made a workshop region in one section," with the other sections condemned to be subordinate suppliers). Such moves were meant to stabilize prices, enhance profits, and in so doing sustain the heavy investments already committed to major facilities (and allow rational planning for new ones)—and, thus, in effect, to impose a high degree of stability on the geography of American manufacturing.

The United States entered the twentieth century, therefore, as an increasingly "administered market society" (to use Licht's terms). It had been far from a simple, seemingly inevitable, evolution in scale from small to large; it was in fact a highly uneven, tumultuous development marked by tensions not only among contending corporations but by bitter and at times bloody conflicts with labor (as in the case of the first massive strike, against the railroads in 1877), the upwelling of the Granger political protest movement in farm country, and nationwide community concern of local businesses and others over the economic and social ramifications of such concentrations of business power. Attempts by individual states to regulate railroads and grain companies marked a beginning of public political response, but the reaction of the federal government was hesitant and limited. It had of course long played a role in American industrial development through subsidies to railroads, banking and taxation policies, and, more directly, tariff legislation (especially important to the textile industry), but it was loath to intervene directly in the conduct of business. It took a generation of apparent, exploitative rate manipulations and scandals to bring about the creation of the Interstate Commerce Commission in 1887 to attack "unjust discrimination between persons, places, commodities, or particular descriptions of traffic" (to quote a Senate report recommending such a commission), and it was some years before further legislation gave it much actual power to do so. Similarly, the Sherman Anti-Trust Act of 1890, prohibiting any collusive or monopolistic "restraint of trade or commerce among the several States, or with foreign nations," had little effect until the "merger mania" at the turn of the century made "trust-busting" a lively political issue for the Roosevelt administration. By that time, critiques such as Thorstein Veblen's *Theory of the Leisure Class*, Ida Tarbell's exposé of Standard Oil, and many others were famous works, and the "muckrakers" were in full cry exposing the more vicious sides of this unprecedented industrial expansion.

"The growth of an industrial economy . . . involves changes in thought patterns as well as changes in the means of production"—to return to our opening quotation from Peter Temin—and it produced changes in the thought patterns of American workers and the public in general as well as in those in charge of the means of production. It was neither a case of deep conflict between old and new, nor of resistance to change, for (despite the brooding of Henry Adams and a few other prominent skeptics) most Americans seemed to have been fascinated with machines, celebrated technology, admired bigness, made heroes of many a business leader, and taken great pride in the progress and strength of their nation; yet they entered the new century with a good deal of unease about the social and political ramifications of this emergent managerial capitalism.

3. Railroads: The Contest for Territory

"To eyes unfamiliar with the nineteenth century it would appear as if society had found in railroads a substitute for war," said the historian Maury Klein:

> The correspondence of railroad men rang with the clang of arms. They fought wars, launched or repelled invasions, made treaties and broke them, forged alliances, claimed suzerainty over territories, disputed boundaries, and squandered their resources in hopes of gaining the spoils of victory. Other roads were referred to as foreign lines or simply the enemy, who must be "slaughtered," or "crushed" or "routed" if they would not agree to terms. Every road was a sovereign state whose officials ruled their domain with possessive zeal, providing services, granting favors, collecting taxes, punishing dissidents, and regarding outsiders with suspicion. Relations between companies were a form of diplomacy of which war was, as always, the last extension. . . . A railroad company occupied a large territory and was organized much like an army, which in fact provided the model for its administration.

The metaphor was apt and the analogy compelling because of the special context and conditions of the American case: the unrestrained opportunity for an unlimited number of capitalists to carve up a continent, parceling out large territories, creating intercity axes and interregional connections, defining the trade areas and therefore the commercial prospects of cities, towns, and villages, setting the basic network, and controlling the pulse of circulation for the internal body of the nation. We need, therefore, to look at some of the strategies and tactics employed in the intense and immense struggles that shaped and fixed in place this formidable geographic structure and system.

We are dealing with a half century of prodigious expansion leading to the essential completion of this national network. In the aftermath of the Civil War the total mileage was doubled (to 70,000) by the onset of the Depression of 1873, was doubled again in less than fifteen years, and reached 250,000 miles before 1915. (The first decline was registered in 1918, most notably effected by abandonment of the Colorado Midland's main line across the Rockies.)

Over the course of this vast and complicated expansion a succession of *general spatial strategies* can be discerned, a sequence driven by the dynamics of expansion itself. As noted earlier (*Continental America*, 323–31, 359–61), the first major railroads were initiated in the great Atlantic ports, each an instrument of urban mercantilism to extend and dominate the inland reach of a particular city, asserting the concept of a "natural territory" geographically, logically, bound exclusively to that entrepôt—a segmentation often initially defined (even legally) by state boundaries as well (as in the cases of New York and Pennsylvania). Once beyond the Appalachians there was a subsequent drive to connect with important mercantile centers on the great waterways (such as Buffalo, Pittsburgh, Cincinnati, and soon thereafter even such anticipated centers as Sandusky, Rock Island, and Keokuk). Thus in this inland arena monopoly could not be sustained, and the interlacing of lines seeking the same several terminals represented a regional strategy to compete for the traffic of this Old Northwest Territory. These strategies were still much apparent during the first surge of expansion after the war, as feeder lines were multiplied within natural territories and further connections made with interior cities (especially, now, Chicago and St. Louis).

The 1870s and 1880s brought a new emphasis on the creation of long-distance *trunk lines* in the form of high-capacity routes designed to compete effectively for profitable through traffic between major national centers and, intertwined with this, the reassertion of regional strategies by large, single-company systems seeking a competitive presence over a selected territory by means of links with its major centers and a dense pattern of feeder lines. In the 1880s and early 1890s a full set of "transcontinental" systems was completed, connecting the Middle West with the Pacific Coast, each anchored on a long main line across a separate segment of thinly inhabited country and thereby reviving the concept of "natural"— monopolistic—territories. There followed serious assessment of what seemed to be the logical next step: the creation of a fully integrated, truly transcontinental single system reaching from coast to coast. What was probably the most formidable prospect of the time failed to materialize when James J. Hill decided not to add the Baltimore & Ohio to his then-powerful Northwest system, concluding that he did not "believe it is possible to make a strong combination covering the country between the Atlantic and the Pacific." The one actual attempt to do so, George Gould's patchwork of existing companies (chiefly the Western Maryland, Wabash, Missouri Pacific, and Denver & Rio Grande) and new construction (in the Pittsburgh area and the Western Pacific from Salt Lake City to Oakland), soon collapsed from the costs of such new lines and lack of internal strength.

Concurrent with this great expansion of mileage and of corporate systems was a rapid improvement in physical facilities, management, and service. Heavier rail, double-tracking, more powerful locomotives, and better rolling stock greatly increased the capacity for moving goods and people. Automatic couplers, air brakes, and steam-heated passenger cars (banishing "the deadly car stove") made trains and travel far safer. Telegraph dispatching and large management systems brought manifold efficiencies. Fast-freight lines, specialized car fleets and luxurious passenger trains established new standards of service. Such improvements were more or less apparent within every major railroad company. However, intercompany relations, so critical to the functioning of a national network, were another matter. "One frequently hears the expression 'railway system of the United States,' but the truth is that no such thing as a railway system exists in the United States," said a railway specialist in an early Interstate Commerce Commission (ICC) report. He was referring especially to the bewildering varieties of management and accounting that affected business relations between companies, but his observation applied much more broadly, as every interested person knew.

Given the nature of the early stages of the railroad era, its sporadic, localized beginnings, the concept of exclusive territories, and incremental expansion, all by separate corporations, it is not surprising to find at the time little concern about the eventual creation of a national network. This was perhaps most obviously the case in the lack of uniformity of gauge. But, as noted, the choice of a particular width was sometimes a conscious device to dominate a territory and fend off potential intruders already committed to a different gauge, and such incongruities were often sustained for years as a defensive tactic despite mounting cries for more efficient interchange and through service. Various adaptive devices (such as a third rail, adjustable wheels, hoists to shift car beds to a different undercarriage) were put in use, but the pressures of competition caused most Northern companies to shift to standard gauge some years before the dramatic event of 1886, when the Southern lines were brought into conformity with the North.

A more common and difficult complication was the entire lack, or at least awkward form, of rail connections between companies within many cities. Here, too, the separate, limited early objectives account for some of the problems, but it was soon apparent that the perpetuation of such gaps could also be a form of defensive warfare. Such breaks in the network often fostered entrenched interests in local transfer services that extracted heavy fees from shippers and passengers. Even where the fee was hidden in the cost of the ticket ("free transfer between all depots for through passengers") the time and effort required could be a great annoyance. By the 1890s, Chicago, much the greatest node in the national system, had seven separate main-line passenger stations, Philadelphia and Cleveland five each, and most cities more than one. It is not surprising, therefore, that the creation of great *union stations* became a major dream of city leaders and planners in the great flush of urban improvements in the new century—and in virtually every case they had to overcome the strong reluctance of the railroads to participate (it was of course an expensive undertaking). Meanwhile, physical connections for the direct interchange of freight were eventually put in place, but the geographical dispersal and complexity of such local relationships endured as a legacy of the segmented and competitive character of network development. In many of the larger centers such interchange was often handled by special switching and belt-line companies (fig. 47).

In the 1870s competition on a major scale became the driving force in the formation of the American network. The concept of territorial integrity and cooperative alliances between connecting companies was rapidly eroded. "One new road after another appeared, slicing up domain, multiplying points of dispute, and tangling the calculus of diplomacy with Byzantine complexities. Every new competitor clamored for its share of traffic and posed the threat of becoming a link in some new through line, a beachhead for invasion." The strongest companies were not always the most aggressive, for whether by purchase or construction extensions were costly and risky, and they were often undertaken reluctantly, defensively, as the only means of continuing viability. The "peculiarly liberal" American environment, wherein "anyone could build a road anywhere, providing he could obtain means for the purpose," gave rise to mere adventurers who built roads for which there was no real need and whose purpose was to "make fortunes by

47. Belt Line.

The EJ&E connects with twenty-four railroad lines in its 130-mile circumvention of the Great Node. (Reproduced from *Official Guide*, September 1897)

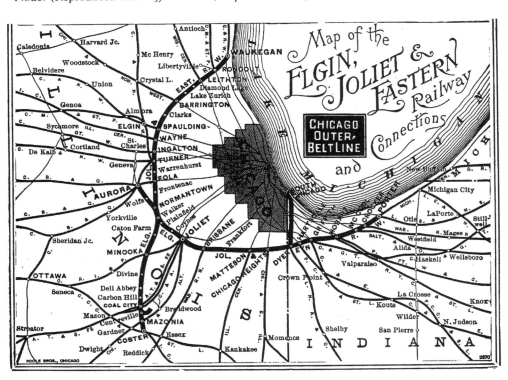

forcing them on others." The most blatant exhibit was surely fresh in the mind of the writer of that 1890 comment: the construction of the West Shore line parallel to Commodore Vanderbilt's prosperous New York Central all the way from New York Harbor to Buffalo and (by a separate company) of the NYC&St.L (the Nickel Plate Road) parallel to the NYC from Buffalo to Chicago. Within a year of the completion of this nearly 1,000 miles of main line it was purchased by Vanderbilt to keep it from falling into the hands of a powerful rival. More common was the competition among several companies for through traffic between major centers even though each main line followed a different route and could also draw traffic from its own swath of territory. Sooner or later one or more of these roads would cut their freight rates even below the cost of carriage between the two points. Such action was "almost invariably" regarded "as an act of open and avowed warfare, entered upon not to benefit the public, but to injure the rival line" (weak railroads might carry traffic at a loss to produce at least some income to apply against high fixed costs). Such warfare weakened all who engaged in it; defeated foes did not go out of business—they became insolvent, wiping out investments, and were ripe to be picked up by some other company as a possible weapon in wars to come.

A popular form of peace treaty between such combatants was a "pool," by which competing lines agreed to set firm rates and divide and share the traffic between specified points according to a carefully worked-out formula. One of the more successful—and notorious—was the Iowa Pool, formed in 1870 by the Chicago lines connecting with the new transcontinental axis at Omaha. Many others were tried, but few survived for any length of time; they were complicated to administer, easily violated, unenforceable by law—and they were the target of powerful public voices.

"When railroads began to be built the demand for participation in their benefits went up from every city and hamlet in the land," said the chairman of the newly formed Interstate Commerce Commission. "The public was impatient of any obstacles to their free construction and of any doubts as to the substantial benefit to flow from any possible line that might be built." Public money or credit was given "on the assumption that almost any road would prove reasonably remunerative." He went on, in this first annual report of 1887, to stress that "in time it came to be perceived that these sanguine expectations were delusive" and to describe some of the "serious evils" that had arisen from the "recklessness of corporate management," the speculations, discriminations, and "abuses of corporate authority" that made "interference by national legislation imperative." The crux of the problem was that "the railroads . . . have become altogether indispensable" for business and society, yet "those who have controlled the railroads have not only made the rules for the government of their own corporate affairs, but very largely also they have determined at pleasure what should be the terms of their contract with others." For many communities and producing districts the railroad was a monopoly; where it was not, the presence of a second company gave no assurance of competition as a guarantee of reasonable charges and an incentive to good service. Indeed, "towns and cities favored with a line . . . eagerly contributed to aid in the construction of a second" only to find that the one company took control of the other or the two formed a pool to fix rates and thus the people found that they had "imposed upon themselves grievous burdens of taxation . . . , doubled the power with which they have to contend, . . . and quartered upon themselves a new and expensive organization which must be supported from the products of their toil"—so declared a select committee of the Senate in 1874.

The report of that committee, chaired by Senator William Windom of Minnesota, was the first in a series of lengthy investigations of transportation issues. The Windom committee's focus on "Routes to the Seaboard" came in the wake of an annual sequence of conventions held by Western commercial interests (the first held in Detroit, followed by St. Paul, St. Louis, Dubuque, Louisville, Cincinnati) in their search for more adequate and equitable services for the rapidly expanding produce of the great "granary of the world." From 1867 on the rising voice of the Patrons of Husbandry—the Grange—joined in the clamor for political action on the "railroad problem." By the time of the Windom hearings, 83 percent of the Western grain surplus was shipped directly eastward, two-thirds of it by rail, the rest by a combination of water and rail or (a small amount) entirely by water (Great Lakes–Erie Canal–Hudson). A popular theme in the West was the need to break "the deadly grasp" of the East over all these systems. Some regulation of rates seemed essential, but direct federal control over such a vital feature of corporate operations seemed far too radical at the time so the focus was on selective government assistance to enhance competition, primarily through canal and river improvements. (A bold proposal, fostered by Granger interests, that the "General Government" should "own or control" a first-class freight-only railroad to be operated between the West and East at the lowest remunerative rate as a means of establishing a proper standard was dismissed in the next federal report on the problem as not economically feasible—nothing being said about the incredibly contentious geopolitical issue that would arise over what cities should be served.)

During these years an ever-stronger Granger political movement, fueled by persistent complaints of corporate exploitations and recurrent economic pressures from a volatile international grain market, had succeeded in obtaining various regulations of railroads and warehousing by individual states. When in 1886 such laws were disallowed by the Supreme Court as exceeding state authority, Congress passed the Interstate Commerce Act the following year. This first federal regulatory agency was created by large margins in both the House and the Senate, but its actual powers were limited. Nevertheless, it forthrightly declared that "railroads are a public agency. The authority to construct them with extraordinary privileges in management and operation is an expression of sovereign power, only given from a consideration of great public benefits which might be expected to result therefrom," and it proceeded to examine and hold hearings on issues relating to such expectations. It gave routine public exposure to both public complaints and railroad responses and thereby began to display ever-more clearly the enormous complexity of railroad operations and the powerful effects they could have on every place they touched. As the American network neared completion in the early years of the new century, the ICC would become increasingly empowered to sit in judgment on the strategies and tactics of its owners and operators.

Much the greatest issue between the public and the railroads was the matter of *rates*—the charges for the carriage of goods between two points. The topic as a whole was immensely, inherently complex, involving as it did thousands of kinds of goods, thousands of pairs of places, and hundreds of railroad companies. Practicalities required reductions of these multitudes to sets of generalized categories, a process undertaken by various railroad associations but inevitably involving arbitrariness and controversy. In the face of public outcry that railroads routinely charged whatever the traffic would bear, the ICC asserted that "rates can not be arbitrarily charged on the mere discretion of the carrier. They are to be equitably adjusted with regard to the public interests as well as the carriers." The notorious fact that railroads often charged more for a short haul than for a long haul on the same route seemed so obviously illogical and inequitable that several state legislatures had tried to forbid it. A similar prohibition was included in the Interstate Commerce Act but with a provision that rates may take into account "all the circumstances and conditions that affect the traffic to the respective points," such as "the length and character of the haul; the cost of the service; the volume of business; the conditions of competition; the storage capacity and the geographical situation at the different terminal points"—in other words, most all those factors that the railroads always insisted were appropriate to rate calculations. (Because of high fixed and terminal handling costs long hauls were in fact less expensive per mile; a Chicago, Burlington & Quincy manager, presumably weary of complaints, put the matter succinctly: "A railroad is a cheap means of transportation for long distances and relatively less cheap as the distance diminishes until, when it becomes very small a wheel-barrow is the cheapest—and for still smaller distances a shovel.")

However, as the deluge of complaints and subsequent court cases attests, existing rate differentials between places often revealed a disparity that could not be plausibly sustained by local "circumstances and conditions." The shippers and business representatives of aggrieved communities insisted that such "mischievous discrimination" was a vital matter, for it displayed how railroad managers had been given "the power to determine what localities shall pay and what shall receive tribute," and thereby "some towns have grown, others have withered away under their influence." An early typical case illustrated (in the words of the ICC) "the special iniquity of the system." Troy, Alabama, served by two railroads, was charged higher rates than shipments that went *through* Troy to Montgomery, fifty-two miles farther on the line, because the railways had established Montgomery as the basing point for that area (in response to the potential of waterborne competition). Accumulating evidence suggested that this kind of preferential treatment might be a power in shaping the economic geography of a whole region long after the network of tracks had been laid. A later detailed study of the South concluded that Atlanta emerged as the main regional traffic center in part because rates from Baltimore and all Ohio River gateways were equalized (a major commercial advantage that existed until 1914). The study further declared that "the status of Nashville" as a large distributing center "is due largely to the purposeful intent and efforts of the railroads." Rates were adjusted so as to assure Nashville and Memphis "an equitable proportion of trade," to the detriment of local centers (such as Bowling Green, Murfreesboro, and Columbia), and specifically to discourage Chattanooga (located at one of the great natural crossroads) "from invading the region allotted to Nashville." As in the Troy case, freight from South Atlantic ports moving through Chattanooga to Nashville or Memphis was charged a lower rate than that shipped only to Chattanooga.

Just how influential such discriminations were on city growth and services cannot be directly measured. The ICC began with the assumption that "the preeminence" of major commercial centers "has probably been increased by . . . such disparity of rates" and that such a "condition of affairs tends to perpetuate itself" and "to increase steadily the disparity in growth and prosperity" of the favored cities over others. Allan R. Pred, in his landmark study of "the spatial dynamics of U.S. urban-industrial growth," generally supported such a reading: "railroad developments probably had the most profound influence on the growth of some centers at the expense of others. . . . The *availability of lower freight tariffs in a relatively few cities on the major trunk lines,* the consequence of both rate competition and freight-volume economies, *acted as an urbanization* (agglomeration) *economy,* capable of attracting new manufacturing establishments and stimulating the expansion of existing production capacity, *and thereby diminished the importance of less favored points.*" In part, of course, an influential pattern already existed: most early railroads were projections of established cities and sought connections with early regional centers (such as Nashville and Memphis), but the unrestrained manipulation of rates allowed the compounding of such preeminence. Pred's reference to "freight-volume economies" points to cumulative and multiplier effects at major traffic nodes and the railroads' response of improved services and lower charges ("lessening the significance of distance") for major shippers, making it increasingly difficult for smaller companies at less-favored places to compete. Whatever may have been the power of railroad managers to shape such basic patterns by their arbitrary actions, it was a distinctly American phenomenon: "It is believed," said the ICC in 1897, "that in no other part of the civilized world is such a [practice] tolerated at the present day."

THE MATURE AMERICAN NETWORK

Browsing through most any atlas of about 1900 one can get a ready impression of the great density of the American network (fig. 48). But leafing through the maps of the states page by page one is confronted with a mind-numbing tangle of lines (fig. 49). No routes are featured, nothing is differentiated; it is as if one were given a modern state map with all the roads—interstates, state highways, county roads, country lanes—drawn in the same width, color, and symbol. Yet the railroad network of that day was about as varied as our roads are today. It had its great superhighways (four to as many as six parallel tracks in some cases), its lesser main lines, bypasses and beltways, meandering branch lines, and the rough rusting tracks of country short lines barely discernible amidst the grass and weeds. It is important, therefore, to make at least a simple geographical appraisal of that comprehensive national pattern, to identify major terminals, nodes, and links, regional systems, and structural breaks in its actual operation.

At the broadest level the railroads themselves routinely recognized four major "territories" in their multifarious relations with one another: Trunk Line, Western (or Granger), Transcontinental, and Southern. These four territories constituted the basic structure of the network, marked by major terminals that served as articulation points for the interchange of traffic between major systems. Each territory had its own characteristic lines, set of dominant companies, various subsystems, and anomalies.

Trunk Line Territory was an area bound together by those railroad systems projected inland from New York City, Philadelphia, and Baltimore to western waterways and ultimately to Chicago and St. Louis (fig. 50). Originally segmented axes, each with its own territory and terminals, these great companies (New York Central, Erie, Pennsylvania, Baltimore & Ohio) became competitive at both ends and many places in between. All had trunk lines between New York and Chicago, all except the Erie had routes to St. Louis, and selectively they offered rival service between those terminals and Pittsburgh, Cleveland, Columbus, Cincinnati, Indianapolis, and Louisville. A fifth competitor was created when the Grand Trunk, early axial line of the Canadas, built on westward across Michigan to Chicago and thereby provided a link on its own tracks to the Atlantic at Portland (as well as a

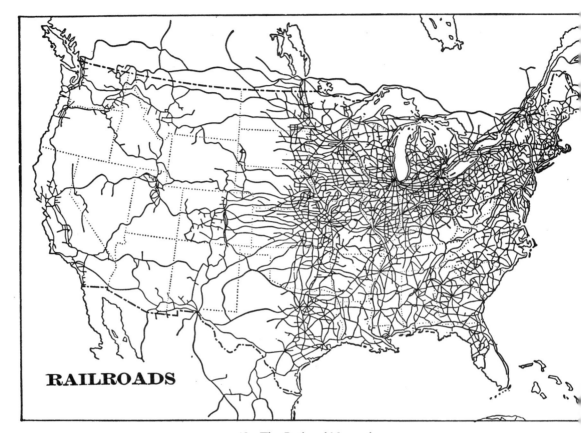

48. The Railroad Network.
(Reprinted from Jacques Q. Redway and Russell Hinman, *Natural Advanced Geography*, New York: American Book, 1901)

connection to Buffalo). The integrated international dimension in this network was further apparent in the New York Central control of the Canada Southern between Buffalo and Detroit, giving the NYC alternative trunk lines on either side of Lake Erie.

Portland was a distinctly minor port but useful as the nearest Canadian outlet to the open sea during the long Laurentian winter. More significant was the position of Boston, whose early attempt to reach westward by a "Great Northern Route" skirting the Adirondacks to Ogdensburg was a competitive failure. Subsequent links with Canadian systems provided devious and inefficient alternatives to the line directly west to Albany. Because that connection left Boston dependent on Vanderbilt's powerful New York Central, other possibilities were recurrently pursued, most notably by way of the long Hoosac Tunnel (built through the Berkshires by the State of Massachusetts) to a link with the Delaware & Hudson near Troy,

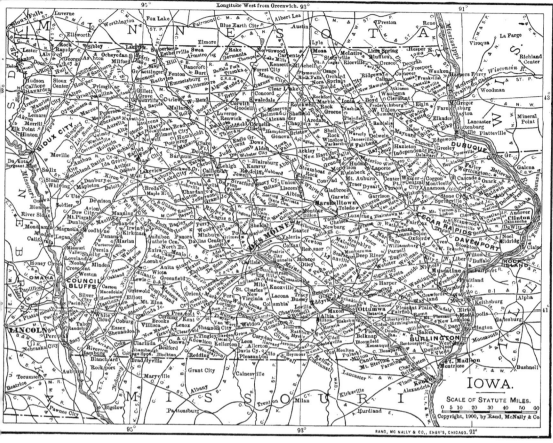

49. Railroads of Iowa.
(Reproduced from *Rand-McNally Dollar Atlas of the World*, Chicago, 1900)

and various patchworks of companies to the lower Hudson in search of connections with the Erie or other western lines. These routes became important in the coal traffic from Pennsylvania and, with the completion of a span at Poughkeepsie, as a "bridge line" bypassing the interruption and congestion of New York Harbor (a rail connection through New York City by way of underwater tunnels and bridges to connect with the New England system was not completed until 1910). Meanwhile, Boston became an ever-more efficient hub of the great density of local lines as these were consolidated under the New Haven system in southern New England and (rather less completely) under the Boston & Maine to the north. In general, New England functioned as a distinct subsystem of the national network, with high-capacity lines (by three routes) between Boston and New York and a through

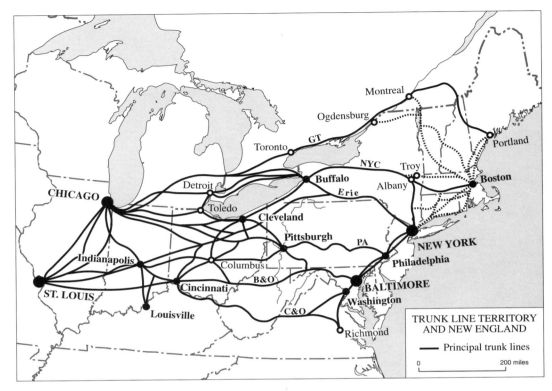

50. Trunk Line Territory and New England.

trunk-line route between Boston and Albany (which came under the complete control of the NYC in 1899).

Another internal feature of Trunk Line Territory was the dozen or so primarily coal-hauling companies radiating out of the anthracite and bituminous districts of Pennsylvania to New England, Upstate New York, and to Lake Ontario ports for export to Canada. Just to the west were several lines (mostly owned by the steel companies) serving the Pittsburgh and Lake Erie heavy industrial traffic. By the end of the century this official territory had been extended southward beyond the structural divide between north and south along the Potomac to include the Chesapeake & Ohio, which now provided trunk-line service from Washington and Richmond to Cincinnati and Louisville, in addition to its heavy coal business.

The western side of this territory was anchored on Chicago and St. Louis. Several lesser companies competed for the traffic between these great commercial centers, but no company offered passenger or freight service *through* them; they were the great "breaking points" between the Eastern and Western networks, binding together not only totally different sets of companies but two quite different types of systems. The Western Territory was dominated by five big companies, four with lines radiating out of Chicago (Northwestern, Milwaukee Road, Rock Island, and Burlington—to use the shorter versions of their names), one out of St. Louis (Missouri Pacific) (fig. 51). Each of these companies controlled dense patterns of branch lines in some large portion of the corn and wheat belts of this Granger realm. Formed out of early tap lines and extensions, expanded by constructions and consolidations, seeking to gain swaths through the richest districts, the lines of these big companies were complexly interlaced, with the regional pattern

51. Western Territory and Transcontinental Connections.

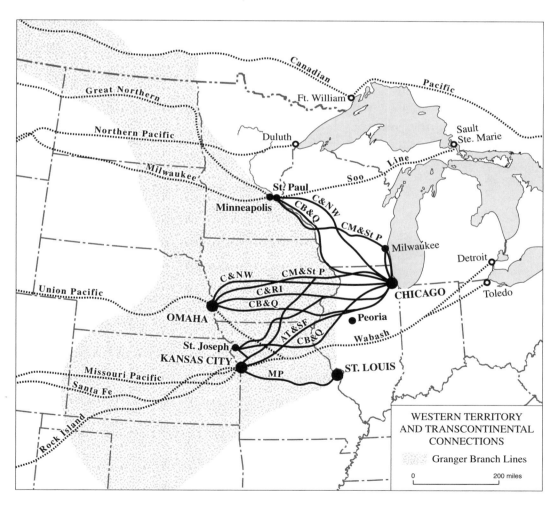

augmented by many local roads. Small cities, such as Cedar Rapids, Sioux Falls, Lincoln, Wichita, were served by four or five different railroads, many lesser towns by two or three, no farming area was untapped, and few farmers were more than four or five miles from a railroad siding with its elevators, warehouses, stockpens, and loading platforms (fig. 52). These Granger systems were feeders, the Eastern trunk lines were receivers: "the latter are saved the expense of picking up this [local] business by driblets. It comes to them in volumes."

Each of these Western companies had its own internal trunk lines connecting with most of the western gateways to this midcontinent area: Kansas City, St. Joseph, Omaha, Minneapolis–St. Paul. Each had also sent a long tentacle westward, partly lured by the potential traffic of the Black Hills or Colorado, but also to establish a position for a possible extension or more forward connection to gain access to a share of Pacific Coast traffic.

The principal anomaly in this regional pattern was the existence of several companies that sought to thrive on binding the Trunk Line and Western territories with routes across central Illinois, bypassing Chicago and St. Louis. The Wabash Railroad connecting Detroit and Toledo with Kansas City and Omaha was a prominent example; Peoria was an interchange point for several lesser companies. To the north Minneapolis millers sponsored the building of a line east to Sault Ste. Marie to avoid the power of Chicago interests. This Soo Line came under the control of the Canadian Pacific and was transformed into a Granger competitor as well, with aggressive branch-line extensions in Dakota and, eventually, a leased line to Chicago.

52. Railroad Extension and Farmer Access.

Trade area boundaries are drawn equidistant from grain elevators. This thickening of centers aided the farmers but reduced the trade area of each town, condemning most of them to hamlet size. (Adapted from John C. Hudson's detailed study of North Dakota in *Plains Country Towns*)

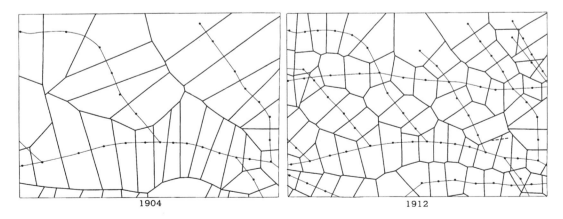

1904   1912

Having already noted the railroads in the several regions of American Wests we need only summarize a few characteristics of the Transcontinental Territory. The early design of a set of long axes, each monopolizing a broad swath of country between a midcontinent terminal and a Pacific port was approximated with the completion of the Union Pacific–Central Pacific, Northern Pacific, Southern Pacific, and Santa Fe. These soon became bound more directly and firmly to the great Chicago focus by way of St. Paul rather than Duluth (NP), Kansas City rather than Houston and New Orleans (SP via the Rock Island), and by the Santa Fe's extension of its own trunk line from Kansas City to Chicago. Large territories remained dominated by these first companies (notably much of California and western Oregon by the SP), but intensive competition (or threat thereof) soon developed for through traffic. This was especially true in the Pacific Northwest with the completion of the Canadian Pacific to Vancouver, Great Northern to Seattle, Union Pacific to Portland, and, in 1909, the Milwaukee's extension of what had been a Dakota branch line all the way to Puget Sound. These resulted in considerable duplication within the region as well (such as parallel high-capacity lines between Spokane and Portland, and a granger tangle of branch lines in the Columbia Basin wheat region). The attempt to create similar competition on the central trunk route by linking the Missouri Pacific, Denver & Rio Grande, and new Western Pacific to Oakland was much less successful. The D&RG's intricate Colorado network, Denver's position as a terminus (no trains through it), and the long reach to Galveston as an alternative to connections eastward stand out as important anomalies.

In 1901 James J. Hill formalized his control of the NP, GN, and CB&Q (Burlington), and Edward H. Harriman got firm control of both the UP and SP. The formation of these gigantic systems seemed in keeping with the merger mania affecting all big business at the time, and the companies involved had enjoyed close working relationships for some years (the Western Pacific was a response to control by the UP-SP over the "Ogden Gateway," and the Milwaukee's Puget Sound extension was a response to Hill's Northwest system), but the courts ruled that these particular combinations were too powerful and not in accord with national and regional interests. However, forced separation need not end cooperation and did little to resolve chronic complaints from all Western regions about the burden of high and arbitrary freight rates. Spokane, for example, was recurrently in court complaining that it "had been prevented from fully developing as a city" because the rate structure allowed Seattle and Portland firms to market Eastern rail-shipped goods to Spokane's own Inland Empire cheaper than Spokane wholesalers could obtain such goods themselves.

As noted earlier, the railroad pattern of the South became controlled by the North and generally anchored on a set of major gateways: Washington, Cincinnati, Louisville, and St. Louis. Several companies competed along the coastal plain for the traffic of the subtropical resorts and agricultural districts. The Southern Railway, an amalgam of several companies, had the main Washington-Atlanta trunk line and dominated the Piedmont. West of the Appalachians the principal companies competed for the traffic between the North and Gulf ports. The Louisville & Nashville was the major system and the Illinois Central an important contender and anomaly in having a main line that reached all the way from Chicago to New Orleans. The Mississippi River was a common company divide, those to the west binding Texas and its ports to St. Louis or Kansas City. One anomaly here was a line from Kansas City southeast across the Ozarks to Memphis and Birmingham.

These broad regional territories were historical creations shaped by the enlargement of railroad systems to a certain scale of management operating within perceived arenas of competition, as well as by a few natural features (such as the Ohio River and the western shores of the Great Lakes), and the general character of regional traffic. Putting them together to look again at the national network we can recognize an overall pattern obviously related to the distribution of population and the maturing economic geography of the nation, but it was not simply a reflection of such things, the logical spatial patterning of the unrivaled transport technology of its time. Rather, as we have seen, it was shaped by intense unregulated capitalistic competition not only for the control of territory and traffic but in the speculative pursuit of profit by other means. Such an environment was not peculiar to the United States (the British and some of the Canadian networks were developed under broadly similar conditions), but nowhere else was competition such a dynamic force—such a warfare—in the creation of a vital national system on such a scale. Some important geographical legacies of that environment were:

1. Extensive *duplication of main lines*—"a needless paralleling of existing systems," "unnecessary and uncalled for" by "public necessity" (to quote a railroad leader and a financial observer of the time).

2. A *surplus of major intercity trunk lines*, resulting in redundant service, excessive costs, and ruinous rate wars. For example, one high-capacity line between Omaha and Chicago could have handled the traffic that four lines struggled to share.

3. An *unusual density of branch lines*, resulting from the drive to control, if possible, or to invade and obtain a share of the traffic of a productive territory. (The spacing of Great Northern feeders in North Dakota and the Soo Line's calculated latitudinal bisection of them is an unusually clear example of these two strategies; fig. 53).

4. Large *railroad systems as incremental patchworks*, rather than networks designed to serve a region efficiently. Most were combinations of smaller companies (plus reactive expansions) held by lease or partial stock control, and some were quite unstable, coming apart under bankruptcies and financial manipulations with the pieces sometimes picked up by different systems.

5. Railroad companies *under the control of variable sets of financiers and speculators* whose strategies were tied more to Wall Street than to the interests of particular cities in securing hinterlands and critical links; "as perceived by those who ran it, a railroad was a pool of capital designed to make more capital."

6. *Traffic flows impeded by the articulations of so many different companies.* To the commonplace inefficiencies of such disjointed operations, freight might be with-

53. War Strategy on the Plains.
Map prepared by the Soo Line readying to build its famous Wheat Line directly across six Great Northern branch lines in North Dakota, together with their calculations of the grain acreage they would thereby command. (Adapted from copy supplied by John C. Hudson; original in Minnesota Historical Society Archives)

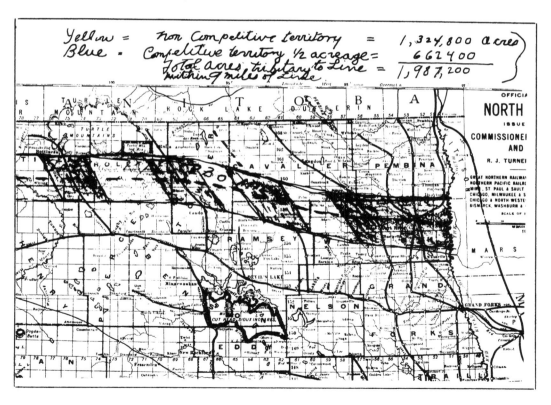

held from one connecting company and shifted to another because of changing patterns of amity and hostility; rate manipulations and desperate need of income could cause traffic to move along very indirect routes.

These features so characteristic of this half century of network creation became subject to an increasingly powerful role of the federal government in the new century, with the ICC and the courts asserting strong supervision over rates, traffic sharing, territorial competitions, constructions, consolidations, and intercompany relationships, and thereby imposing an unprecedented stability (some would say rigidity—"enterprise denied") upon the American railroad system.

In the broader geographic view there was of course a North American railway network. We have already noted several interpenetrations of United States and Canadian systems, and there were many more points of connection. To the south there were four links across the U.S.-Mexican border. The westernmost was the Southern Pacific's line from Nogales to Guaymas; the others, crossing at El Paso, Eagle Pass, and Laredo, were tied into the Mexican network, and the first two of these offered through freight and sleeper service to Mexico City (the Mexican link from Laredo was narrow gauge until 1903). Unlike the Canadian lines, all of these Mexican companies were American built and owned.

Furthermore, some waterways were an integral part of the railroad system, most obviously in the several ferries across Lake Michigan, owned and operated by the railroads by which freight cars could be forwarded between Michigan and Wisconsin ports, avoiding Chicago. Aside from ore boats, much of the shipping on the Great Lakes was owned by railroads, most notably the sets of modern passenger and freight vessels of the Great Northern Railway plying between Duluth and Buffalo (with passenger stops at Mackinac Island, Detroit, and Cleveland), bypassing Chicago and much of the Trunk Line Territory. In those early congressional investigations of transportation to the seaboard the Mississippi naturally received much attention. Many Westerners saw nature's great artery as the obvious route for the traffic that the railroads, through the disruptions of the war, had diverted to New York. But there were many problems with this alternative. The mouth of the river had so silted up that large vessels could not reach New Orleans. After much contention over a solution, James Eads (of St. Louis bridge fame) was awarded a contract to build jetties to narrow and induce the river to deepen itself, and in three years a thirty-foot channel was opened. Westerners looked to New Orleans not only to undermine Eastern dominance but to enhance American export competitiveness. Increasingly Russia and India, being served by expanding railroad networks, were regarded as impending threats on the world grain market. But despite further improvements upriver, investment in elevators and other facilities, relatively little traffic was diverted from the railroads or released from the grasp of the East. Railroads crossed the upper Mississippi at many points above Alton and drained virtually all the regional traffic to the vastly superior marts of Chicago. The coal shipments on the Ohio River and reaching west to St. Louis and Kansas City were much the heaviest traffic remaining on the Mississippi system.

In 1900 railroad companies still controlled the Pacific Mail Steamship Company, with its New York to San Francisco service by way of the railroad crossing of Panama, as a means of guarding against pressure on transcontinental rates; within a few years the ever-more assured prospect of a successful Panama Canal would pose ominous changes. Some major railroads also invested in, or made contracts with, major oceanic services as a means of ensuring or enlarging traffic through their preferred ports; notable examples were the Baltimore & Ohio with the North German Lloyd line and the Canadian Pacific and Great Northern with steamship services to the Orient.

Virtually every line of the American network offered passenger service to every village and town along its route, even if only by a coach attached to the tail of a freight—a "mixed train"—on some country short lines or branches. But of course the tedium of that kind of train had become the dread of every intercity traveler, and major companies competed for customers with "express trains"—"limiteds"—making few, if any, stops between major centers (water, fuel, and crew change stops were necessary on longer runs). Such trains could vary considerably in their number of cars and capacities (actual numbers of passengers carried was closely guarded information of each company), but the simple number of daily express trains offers a useful measure of the volume and intensity of movement between commercial centers— and brings us closer to the actual pulsations of the American system (fig. 54).

The great power of the railroads over the nation's pulse was starkly evident in their imposition of *standard time* upon every village, town, and city they touched. The complexities, confusions, and dangers of operating a multiplicity of trains on single tracks through hundreds of local (solar) times became ever-more apparent. Studies by a commission of railroad officials culminated on Sunday, November 18, 1883, at successive noons in four time zones when clocks were reset to the new standard (which in places was as much as forty-four minutes different from local time). Each of the four zones across the United States approximated fifteen degrees of latitude (1/24th of 360°) anchored on a designated meridian west of Greenwich (upon which Great Britain had adopted a uniform standard time in 1848): Eastern (75°W), Central (90°W), Mountain (105°W), Pacific (120°W); a fifth zone, the Intercolonial (now Atlantic), encompassed Atlantic Canada. Although there were flutters of resentment at the very idea of such artificial, "unnatural" time and the railroads' imposition of it, it was actually widely accepted almost immediately

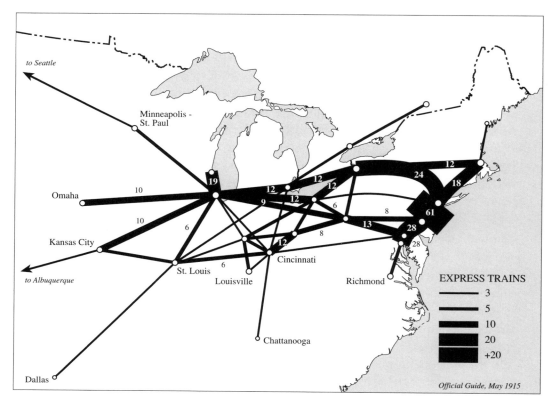

54. Express-Train Service, 1915.

This schematic map depicts service between major cities *in excess* of two express trains each way each day. Definition of "express," denoting very few intermediate stops, is necessarily somewhat arbitrary. (Based on *Official Guide,* May 1915)

as a practical necessity for a modern world (though uneasiness over its ramifications upon ways of thought and life lingered for a generation). The initial time zone boundaries would be adjusted in numerous places to suit local patterns of business, and the railroads selected points for time change to suit their own operations, often at division points of crew change (for a time the Southern Pacific changed clocks two hours at El Paso, ignoring Mountain Time altogether).

The movements throbbing through these railroad arteries touched the lives of every person who received mail. All railroad lines were post routes (by an 1838 act of Congress) and thereby served as an agent of the government in this comprehensive daily service to the social and business life of the nation. In the 1870s the Post Office Department organized a new Railway Mail Service featuring special cars for the sorting of mail en route and began to negotiate with railroad companies to carry mail cars on express trains and also to establish fast exclusive mail trains between the largest cities; by 1905 these mail trains had reduced the time between New York and Chicago to eighteen hours, and late-night trains fanning out from major centers brought the same newspapers and reports to a widening radius of towns and cities as were being read that day in the metropolis.

Such a quickening of the pulse of the nation had wide business ramifications. Major commercial centers were necessarily major railroad centers, and the sheer volumes and radiating patterns of traffic were important measures of the status of any particular city within the system. Although the telegraph, expanding as a companion system (and becoming essential to efficient railroad operations), had quickly worked its revolution in the commercial markets, the circulation of signed documents remained essential, and as the *Banker's Magazine* stated in 1905, "the bank that cannot profit by swift railroad service has a great handicap on it, and cannot perform the full functioning of the institution." Cities avidly competing for selection as a regional center in the new Federal Reserve system laid great stress on railroad connections and the frequency and rapidity of service. As George L. Anderson noted, Kansas City's advocates pointed to its already prominent banking clearinghouse system, its 260 daily passenger trains, and its 126 daily dispatches of mail into its hinterland and along interregional trunk lines. So, too, the astounding success of that revolutionary marketing device, the mail-order catalogue, by which Montgomery Ward and Sears, Roebuck of Chicago became by 1900 "the two greatest merchandising organizations in the world," was made possible by the regularity, rapidity, security, and national ubiquity of the railroad system. As Maury Klein concluded about this half century of railroad expansion:

> It bound together a huge, sprawling nation into a national market that in time would grow more homogeneous through the spread of standardized products, reading matter, cultural activities, and ease of travel. This fostering of economic and social homogeneity may be its single most important byproduct, for it helped nourish a sense of nationality that had surprisingly weak roots prior to the Civil War. In that sense the one supreme effect of the railroads may have been their role in literally making the United States a nation.

4. Populations and Peoples

The United States continued its prodigious population growth through the nineteenth century and into the twentieth. Its 31 million of 1860 was doubled in thirty years, reached 75 million by 1900, and rose to 100 million by 1915 (such rounded figures are to be taken as no more than general indications of totals and trends; demographic specialists conclude that official enumerations were often as much as 20 percent or more short of actual populations in many areas). Such growth of 21– 26 percent per decade was powered by strong natural increase and generally rising levels of immigration that maintained the foreign-born population at about 13–14 percent of the total in every decade.

As always there was much movement from place to place at every scale: local, regional, and interregional. The new industrialization fostered major increases in urbanization. In 1860 just under 20 percent of Americans lived in urban areas, whereas by 1915 nearly half of them did so (using in both cases the low census threshold of 2,500 as "urban"); a fifth of the population lived in large cities (100,000 or more), and that proportion was rapidly increasing (fig. 55). Such

55. Metropolitan Areas and Large Cities.

In 1910 the Census Bureau established a new category of "metropolitan districts" to deal with suburbanization that had spread beyond the political boundaries of cities of 200,000 or more and with clusters of urban centers closely bound together by efficient transport facilities. Thereby on this map several cities of 100,000 or more are amalgamated with a nearby larger center, such as Cambridge with Boston, and Jersey City, Newark, and Paterson with New York City. Cities of more than 100,000 in other parts of the country were San Francisco (with Oakland, 687,000), New Orleans (348,000), Denver (219,000), Portland (215,000), Seattle (239,000), and Spokane (104,000).

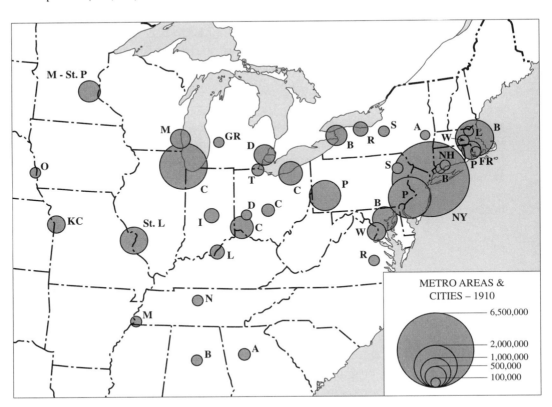

changes involved strong rural-to-urban migrations ("at least a third of the total urban population of 1910 were American natives of rural origin") as well as the accumulation of ever-greater proportions of the immigrant influx.

NORTH AMERICAN MIGRATIONS

Through much of this period, however, there also continued to be large expansions in space: a westward advance of the outer margins of contiguous settlement and a rapid filling in of the more attractive areas just behind. A broadening band of Eastern states contributed to this expansion. By 1870 northern New England, rural New York, and parts of Pennsylvania and Ohio were losing more people than they gained, and many of these were settling in Wisconsin, Iowa, Missouri, and Kansas. By 1890 Wisconsin, Illinois, and Iowa were contributing people to the Dakotas, Nebraska, and western Kansas, and as this contiguous westward expansion was drawing to a close in the new century, Kansas and Nebraska began to show a net loss of migrants (mostly to Oklahoma and the Far West).

There were important latitudinal continuities with earlier westward movements (fig. 56). New England Extended was stretched further to place a recognizable

56. Westward Extensions.
(Adapted from Hudson, "North American Origins")

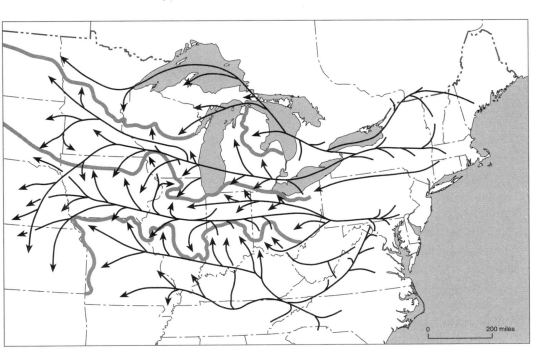

Yankee presence in much of Minnesota and the Dakotas, and the Midland belt reached across Iowa, Nebraska, and Kansas. But there was much overlap and interpenetration as these Easterners responded to the widely touted lures of western opportunities. Thus Yankees also showed up in southeastern Nebraska and along the Kansas Pacific line well beyond their early colonies in the Kaw Valley (implanted before the war in the geopolitical contest for Kansas), and several distinctly Midland peoples (such as Pennsylvania Germans and German Brethren from Indiana) formed a sprinkling of small clusters in North Dakota. The main Midland belt continued to be well supplied with its characteristic variety: American Methodists (and many Methodist and Wesleyan colleges), a number of Quaker settlements (most notably the early cluster around Oskaloosa, Iowa, with its William Penn College), and the full variety of German pietist sects. Yankees were much involved in land and town development and planted their emblematic Congregational churches and liberal arts colleges (among them Carleton, Yankton, and Washburn), but their hold upon many localities tended to be shallow and short. They were likely to sell out and move on after a few years of farming trial and as business prospects dimmed in these harsh and unfamiliar lands, and towns and townships with such unmistakable New York names as Niagara, Cayuga, Unadilla, Owego, Utica, and Syracuse eventually became filled with German, Swedish, Norwegian, or other immigrant families.

North of these regional culture extensions was a newer pattern formed by the movement out of the St. Lawrence Valley into the lumbering regions of the Upper Great Lakes. It was typically a commingling of Americans and Canadians. There was considerable instability, by the very nature of the main industry, but a good many stayed on in the cutover lands, and mining, railroads, and resorts provided a new basis for local economies. Canadians were especially prominent all across central and northern Michigan, and several thousand Ontarians settled on the rich farmlands of eastern North Dakota, most of whom had probably been intercepted by American land agents while en route to Manitoba by way of Duluth or St. Paul (there being no all-Canadian railroad connection until after 1885).

Such diversions were deplored by Canadian authorities, who were eager to fix a strong hold on distant Manitoba, and they stationed their own agents in key American cities to try to prevent such "loss in transit"—and to lure back some of the thousands of Canadians who year after year had been dispersing to what they perceived as far better opportunities in the United States. That southward flow was the least noticeable within the swelling tide of immigration to the United States— a drift across local borders by English-speaking North Americans who so readily integrated into the life of their new communities that they were commonly not even regarded as "immigrants." It involved loggers, fishermen, and others from Atlantic Canada and Newfoundland into Maine and Massachusetts, with ambitious youth especially attracted to Boston. Similarly, Ontarians left lumbering and limited farms for industrial centers in Upstate New York and southern Michigan (they were a large part of Detroit's immigrant population) or homesteads in the Middle West, while many seeking commercial or professional positions took their Grand Trunk to Chicago.

A distinct exception to this "invisible" immigration was the well-established movement of French Canadians to New England mill towns and the growing size of such clusters within most of that region's cities. Focused on a Roman Catholic church, served by convents, parochial schools, and French newspapers, bound by relatives and friends to villages in Quebec—and with much traffic between—such cohesive communities were in many respects essentially exclaves within the body of the Republic, and in their homeland the whole of them together were referred to as "le Québec d'En-bas," Lower Quebec. A scattering of French were also to be found along those Canadian paths of westward migration, but only occasionally were their numbers sufficient to form strong ethnic settlements (such as at an early outpost, Bourbonnais-Kankakee in Illinois, and its offspring in and around Concordia, Kansas).

Near the end of the century, when there were perhaps a million Canadian-born living within the United States, an important variation in these relationships got under way. The opening and avid marketing of the great prairie and parkland belts of what would soon become Saskatchewan and Alberta, coinciding with a major upswing in the world business cycle and grain prices, attracted large numbers of settlers from the United States. Canadian agents actively recruited in the United States and were especially successful in Minnesota and the Dakotas, where residents were familiar with this kind of country and farming. The total of this influx was not enough to offset the usual strong drift southward from Laurentian Canada (and some of these Prairie incomers were expatriate Canadians), but it was an important countermovement and a blurring of the boundary in a much altered borderland.

An important feature of immigration from Canada is that throughout the half century from 1851 to 1901 about half of all European emigrants arriving in Halifax and Quebec were declared to be in transit to the United States, and a large but uncertain portion of the remainder (hopefully classified by the Canadians as "intending settlers") eventually moved on to the United States. Such persons (estimated by American officials at 40,000–50,000 annually in the early 1890s) were almost entirely from Great Britain and Ireland and thus represented simply a northern strand of a long-established braided stream of transatlantic movement.

IMMIGRATION: GENERAL FEATURES

The topic of immigration is of course fundamental to any treatment of the shaping of America, indeed to the very concept—and changing and competing

concepts—of "American," but it is immensely complicated and fraught with problems of definition, measurement, and assessment. In *Atlantic America* we noted
how the mosaic of peoples in British North America represented all the regional
and religious diversity of Atlantic Europe from Göteborg to Gibraltar as well as
captives from a long stretch of the African coast and commented briefly on some of
the processes and sociogeographic patterns associated with such implantations and
acculturations. In *Continental America* we noted how new and larger streams of
immigrants from Europe further altered the content of American society, magnified major regional differences, and challenged its assumed powers of assimilation.
We must now extend this brief survey of selected themes to a period of far more
massive immigration and change. It can be no more than a simple sketch of an
extremely complex geographic topic that has yet to be systematically described
(there is no comprehensive atlas of immigration, although the retrospective commentary in James Allen and Eugene Turner's detailed mapping of 1980 ethnic data
is a valuable surrogate).

Our geographic perspective suggests a broadened view at the outset to remind us
that the United States (or North America) was not the only frontier of settlement
and land of opportunity of this time. Many thousands of Europeans from some of
these same sources were moving to other continents: to Brazil, Argentina, and
Uruguay, to South Africa, Australia, and New Zealand, and eastward to the
prairies and parklands of Siberia and the steppelands of Russia and Central Asia
(including many Germans continuing their centuries-old movement in this direction, now into Volhynia, Bessarabia, Crimea, and Azov). Nevertheless, the westward flow across the North Atlantic, which totaled about 25 million during the
period 1860–1914, was much the largest and does constitute one of the great
episodes in the history of human migration.

Annual volumes were much affected by conditions on either side. Crop failures,
chronic agricultural depressions, political and cultural restrictions, military con-
scriptions, ethnoreligious conflicts, and brutal pogroms provided strong reasons to
depart the Old Country, but far more people came in good times than in bad, and
the great surges and slackenings most clearly reflected periods of prosperity and
depression in the New World. Thus the Panics of 1873 and 1893 were followed by
deep declines in the number arriving on American shores. Such historical variations are prominent in the statistics, graphs, and literature on the topic. Less
apparent are the numbers of immigrants who left American shores and returned
home, to stay—or perhaps to come again. It is far less appreciated—indeed, it can
be something of a surprise or even shock to those nurtured on America as the
eagerly sought land of freedom and opportunity—that "the United States was not a
land where every immigrant came to stay; it was a country seen by many foreigners
as a means rather than an end"; a land of opportunity indeed, but offering the

chance to work for a few years to improve one's condition at home: "the striving for status . . . emerges as one of the main forces behind remigration as well as emigration." Thus the assumption that one could always return to Europe "must be added to the list of new encouragements" to cross the Atlantic, and it applied to men bound for the steel mills of Pittsburgh or women bound for the silk mills of Paterson as well as to the thousands of Italians—the famous *golondrinos*—who made the seasonal trip to Argentina for the harvest.

One of the main reasons why such countermovements remain so much less visible is the lack of reliable data for most of this era. The United States began to register such departures only in 1908 (when the number returning to Europe was well over half that of those entering—both figures being affected by the economic downturn of 1907). The proportion of sojourners to settlers varied greatly among ethnic groups but is estimated to have run as high as 20 percent on the part of English, Germans, and Scandinavians, long considered among the most welcome and readily assimilable of all. Such figures challenge common assumptions, make "the American immigration story . . . less unified, more diverse, when remigrants are considered within the broad picture of the peopling of a continent," and, as Mark Wyman concludes, place "the American experience . . . largely within the mainstream of the world's historic migrations."

The volume, character, and geography of all these movements were much affected by technology. The spread of the European railroad network eastward and southward, lacing loosely through the Austro-Hungarian Empire, the Balkans, and across the broader reaches of Russia and the Ukraine, began to open up the possibility of emigration from what had been very remote regions. At the same time, the rapid expansion of steamship service was transforming the oceanic voyage from a month or more of misery into a relatively quick, safe, and cheap passage, which together with the regularity of such sailing was attractive to sojourners as well as settlers. Seasonal or longer-term labor migration was an old feature of many places and peoples in Europe. Industrialization had lured workers to the Rhineland, to the Low Countries, and to the spreading number of inland mining and manufacturing centers, and in the later nineteenth century the steamship enlarged the geographic field of such movement. It was a big and competitive business. Steamship agents plastered towns and villages with alluring advertisements (local governments often tried to prohibit such propaganda), and early trickles turned into torrents flowing to Trieste, Fiume, Naples, Palermo, Patras, and Odessa, or by rail across to the more frequent shipping services of Rotterman, Antwerp, Le Havre, Bremen, and Hamburg. Similar flows to the Baltic were commonly shuttled to the big German emigration depots, just as many Scandinavians crossed the North Sea and sailed out of Liverpool or some other British port.

A broad view of general source regions shows that emigrants from the British

Isles made up at least 40 percent of the Europeans arriving on American shores up to the 1880s, and they continued to form an important stream even as their proportion declined with swellings from other sources. The number entering from Germany was about equal to that from Britain and Ireland, and when it lessened after 1895 (coincident with a strong upsurge in the German economy) the growing number from Scandinavia maintained the volume from Northwest Europe. In the 1880s the numbers from Southern, Central, and Eastern Europe—Italians, Greeks, Romanians, Magyars, Slovenes, Croats, Serbs, Bulgarians, Czechs, Slovaks, and Poles, Lithuanians, Latvians, Jews, Russians, and Ukrainians (and some of these "nations" further subdivided into lesser regional and ethnoreligious groups)— began to increase rapidly, surpassing those from Northwest Europe in the 1890s, and by 1906 (when the total annual influx from Europe first reached 1 million) constituted three-quarters of this transatlantic movement.

Migration flows are strongly shaped by a few basic factors. They tend to follow established channels because of the pull of kith and kin. The presence and persuasion of those who have gone on before are often the most powerful inducement, and they can provide initial shelter and assistance. Such "chain migration" leads to ethnic clustering, and the larger the cluster the more powerful the attraction because of the services and support provided: familiar churches, schools, clubs, newspapers, foods, shops, and many social and professional aids. Such clusters can become almost exclaves of the country left behind—a "community transplanted," as in the case presented by Robert C. Ostergren of a single Swedish parish that contributed over 100 families in a twenty-year period to a compact new settlement district in Minnesota. In the longer run all these clusters serve as halfway houses, decompression chambers, mediating the transition into American society, but overall they vary greatly in the rate of such change and may persist selectively in ways that alter the content and character of the encompassing receiving society.

Opportunities for work may be closely related to such ethnic clusters, but there were other means as well. Labor agents, including *padrones* from the Old Country, worked the American docks to recruit gangs of males for steel mills, mines, lumber camps, and railroads (where they were sometimes used as strikebreakers) and female workers for textile and other light industrial plants. Once any particular group became established in a town or industry, more would follow as long as any work was available. But such jobs were often only temporary, and more moves were made, sometimes of long distance, before a more secure niche was found. Only a few workers with special skills (such as Welsh foundrymen, Belgian glassblowers, and English textile experts) were recruited directly in Europe by American firms, but others of such kind as well as those with money to invest in a shop, business, or profession may have arrived with a broader view of possibilities; yet these, too, were likely to be guided in some degree by fellow nationals already on the ground.

Finally, there were those seeking land to farm. Many of these came in some sort of group, whether ethnoreligious, formal company, or informal association seeking to establish a colony or a neighborhood of their own people. They commonly had some area in mind, perhaps already contracted for, derived from the efforts of railroads, land companies, and state immigration bureaus, whose agents in America continued to compete for them with special fares and inducements. Those unable or unwilling to homestead or purchase immediately might work as laborers for a while or lease a farm for a few years, testing the country and the costs while searching for the most attractive district in which to put down roots.

PORTALS AND PATHS

New York City was always the principal portal to the United States, and it became much the greatest after the war and especially so in the steamship era, with thousands processed daily at Castle Garden until 1892, and at Ellis Island thereafter. Boston, Baltimore, and Philadelphia were other Atlantic receiving stations. A considerable proportion of this influx never got much beyond these thresholds, for there they found work, sheltering kin, social agencies catering to their own kind—or were too destitute to move on. New York and its Jersey satellites held on to some of every ethnic and religious group, ever compounding the great variety already present and sustaining and enlarging the vast array of industries and trades centered there. In 1910, 2 million of the city's 5 million were foreign-born, and it became a New York boast that it had twice as many Irish as Dublin, more Germans than Hamburg, more Italians than Naples, and more Jews than the whole of Western Europe. In marked contrast, Boston continued to be a major destination only for the Irish and for lesser numbers from Great Britain, with Italians and Portuguese showing up in later stages as they gained footholds in particular textile towns. Rather similarly, Germans were greatly dominant in the stream to Baltimore, as steamship connections with Bremen reinforced a migration pattern established years earlier in the tobacco trade. The busy port of Philadelphia had extensive shipping connections, but most of its immigrant population had entered via New York and made the short overland journey or had drifted back from the coal camps and steel mills of its hinterland (and its somewhat smaller proportion of foreign-born was a source of pride to local leaders who spoke of it as "the most American of our greater cities").

Beyond these entrances immigrants moved inland along the main trafficways. Large numbers of Irish and Germans had already done so before the war and thereby created strings of ethnic way stations deep into the continent. The Irish had helped build the canals and railroads and provided much of the heavy labor all across southern New England, New York, and the Lower Lakes to Chicago, branching off to various other cities and towns. Their paths were now clearly marked by Roman Catholic parishes, their more substantial presences by large churches, convents, schools, orphanages, colleges, and hospitals. They were to be found in every commercial and industrial center across the Manufacturing Belt; well experienced in dealing with English institutions, their rapidly growing numbers were soon translated into political power and municipal jobs. Thus incoming Irish found a ready welcome, help in finding a job, and a place to begin, and the increase in the number of American Irish took place largely within the geographic patterns early marked out.

Germans, who had begun to arrive in large numbers in the 1850s, had also spread widely across the North, but with important regional differences from the Irish. Entering by way of New York and Baltimore they moved westward, avoiding New England (there were relatively few in any of the big textile towns), and although they were quickly prominent in Upstate New York and Lower Lakes industrial centers, the largest stream had taken the Ohio Valley route, making Cincinnati and St. Louis big German centers and leaving important deposits in Louisville, Evansville, and the river cities above St. Louis, such as Quincy, Keokuk, Burlington, Davenport, and Dubuque. These two western paths converged at Chicago and extended thickly on to Milwaukee and smaller cities beyond.

Generally arriving with more skills and resources than the Irish, Germans found jobs in crafts and industries and soon created many of their own firms. They, too, were recognizable by characteristic facilities: churches and schools (Lutheran, Roman Catholic, Reformed), breweries, butcher shops, and bakeries, social clubs and musical societies, and, especially important, German newspapers, libraries, and literary groups, attesting to strong pressures by community leaders to hold onto ancestral language and culture. A small but important urban component of this influx from the German Confederation and Empire were the Jews, varied in economic status but soon emerging as shopkeepers, merchants, and professionals. As soon as numbers allowed, synagogues were formed, cemeteries set aside, and communities established that would have at least modest influence on the geography of the later massive influx of Jews fleeing the Russian Empire.

Large numbers of Germans came in quest of farmlands, heading west to join the vanguard of pioneers or, more often, with enough resources to buy or lease land already under cultivation. Here, too, a good many German settlements had been established before the war, and some of these became bases for further expansion. German Americans had sponsored several rural colonies (such as Guttenberg, Iowa, by Cincinnatians; Grand Island, Nebraska, from Davenport; New Ulm, Minnesota, by a German society in Chicago), and occasionally a German priest and a few associates set up an outpost and avidly recruited a settlement around it (as, notably, at St. Cloud, Minnesota, where a missionary to the Chippewa soon obtained, with diocesan help, a college, a convent, a large Benedictine abbey and initiated what would become one of the largest, most thoroughly Roman Catholic rural areas in the United States). Both Roman Catholic and Lutheran organizations had agents in New York City and Baltimore to direct immigrants to German rural districts in the West. By the 1880s Germans from the Russian Empire began to arrive, some of them as religious groups seeking land for colonies. Railroad land agents avidly sought such German farmers. James R. Shortridge, in his detailed ethnic mapping of Kansas, notes the remarkable role of Carl Schmidt of the Santa Fe, who made thirty-seven trips across the Atlantic and is credited with bringing in 60,000 Germans and doing "more than any other individual to influence the emerging cultural geography of the state." He was especially successful in recruiting Mennonites and various other Volga Germans to central Kansas (where Newton and Hillsboro became important ethnic centers). Less directed but similar in pattern and impact was the success of agents for the Chicago, Milwaukee & St. Paul who induced a flow of Germans from Bessarabia and the Ukraine to South Dakota. William C. Sherman details how these people fanned out from a railhead base at Eureka to spread northward over a huge area, eventually achieving an almost complete rural occupation of a solid block of a dozen counties in the two Dakotas. These large, focused inpourings stand out geographically but constitute only a small part of a vast dispersal of German settlers into Wisconsin, Minnesota, Iowa, and the Plains states. Much of the German population in the latter tier had moved there from German areas in the older West rather than directly from overseas, but many of these were foreign-born, having come first to an ethnic receiving area and later responded to opportunities in newly opened lands. Even the South tried to tap into and divert some portion of this German tide. In the 1880s Alabama sent a railroad display car to Ohio and on across the Midwest as far as Sioux City to proclaim its lures of land and industry. But the real motive, as Southern newspapers reported, was to build up the White population so as to "de-Africanize" the state, and little came of the campaign.

Scandinavians followed a somewhat similar if smaller and more northerly pattern in the Middle West. They, too, had established several clusters before the war, the Swedes notably in Rockford and Moline, Illinois (as well as Chicago), the Norwegians in northeastern Iowa (around Decorah) and southern Wisconsin. Much larger numbers began to arrive in the last quarter of the century, and they came primarily to Wisconsin and Minnesota. Finns first came to the Lake Superior copper and iron mines and were soon involved in lumbering, many taking root in the cutover lands. Scandinavians were heavily involved in all these activities (and as seamen on the Great Lakes) and became much the largest foreign-born population in the Iron Ranges, Duluth-Superior, and the Twin Cities. Although Swedish Americans sponsored a few colonies in various states (such as Lindsborg, Kansas, and in the Holdredge area in Nebraska), Swedish emigration became strongly focused on a few districts north and west of Minneapolis. Norwegians spread more widely, filling in much more land in western Wisconsin and southeastern Minnesota, and later in the Red River Valley and broadly across eastern and northern North Dakota. They were not always the first to settle in a particular area but came in groups, formed strong ethnic neighborhoods, and eventually became the dominant population of extensive districts, their locales marked by Lutheran churches in town and country and a strong emphasis on schools.

Communities of Danes, Dutch, Belgians, Luxembourgers, Swiss, and Icelanders were scattered about this West but were far fewer in number and did not dominate extensive districts. There were also settlements of Czechs (commonly known at the time as Bohemians) closely associated with German migrations, such as in northeastern Iowa (including the village of Spillville, later notable as the place Antonin Dvořák spent a summer and began his *Symphony from the New World*) and eastern and southern Nebraska (made famous by Willa Cather). However, by the 1890s raw land fit for farming was becoming scarce and scattered in the United States, and more land seekers from Eastern Europe headed for the Canadian prairies (where greater official accommodation of group settlement and closed villages was also available in some areas).

As a result of this immigrant influx contemporary with or following closely upon pioneer American settlement, the variety characteristic of the older Midland Belt was greatly extended in area and expanded in complexity (fig. 57). As an intensive field survey of many parts of this broadened Middle West in 1918 reported, "There are whole counties and even a number of neighboring counties . . . populated by immigrants of the same race and nationality. Such provinces have become self-sufficient; they have their own towns, their own schools, churches, industries, stores, select local public officials of their own nationality, speak their own tongue, and live according to the traditions and spirit of their home country." Those "traditions and spirit" were much emphasized in those local churches and schools but could not actually insulate such "provinces" from many practical changes. Initial imprints on the landscape in houses, farmyards, and fields, crops and animals, and ways of doing things would undergo rather rapid selective adaptations to American means and opportunities and thereby join in the shaping of broader regional patterns. Anchored by land holdings, these ethnoreligious mosaics tended to change shape slowly, with those groups most firmly committed to rural community life expanding at the expense of those (most commonly native-stock North Americans) more ready to seek fresh opportunities elsewhere. As Michael Conzen concluded from his study of German Americans in the Middle West, these "ethnic islands" also tended to become interconnected in varying degree to form an "ethnic archipelago," "a large, differentiated, evolving . . . macro-geography" of

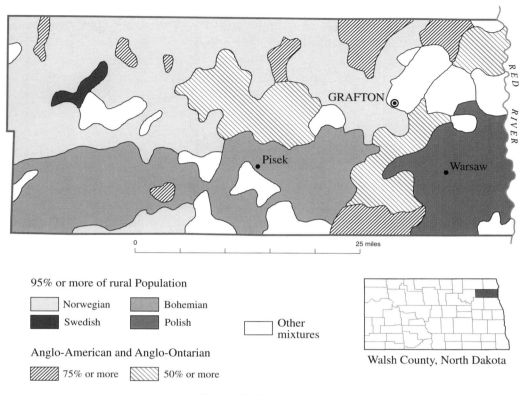

57. Rural Ethnic Mosaic.
(Adapted from Sherman, *Prairie Mosaic*)

continuing importance in the shaping of American society. In general these new-comers taking root in these broad open lands were also rapidly integrated into the American commercial system. As a geographer of 1915 concluded, this "great population has become naturalized to its new continental home with a success that recalls the spread of thistles in Argentina and rabbits in Australia; and although uncomplimentary, the comparison is based on sound biological principles."

But most of the rapidly increasing influx in the new century ended up in the Manufacturing Belt and its outlying industrial satellites (there were more Czechs in Cedar Rapids and in the packinghouses of Omaha than nearby on the land) (fig. 58). The great diversity thereby added to American cities also varied in content and proportions from place to place, shaped by established ethnic clusters, the needs of particular industries, and various opportunistic influences on migration flows. For example, the proportion of foreign-born in the 1910 populations of cities across Upstate New York were not very dissimilar (22–29 percent), but Italians were markedly the largest in Utica and Rochester (textiles and garments), Poles in

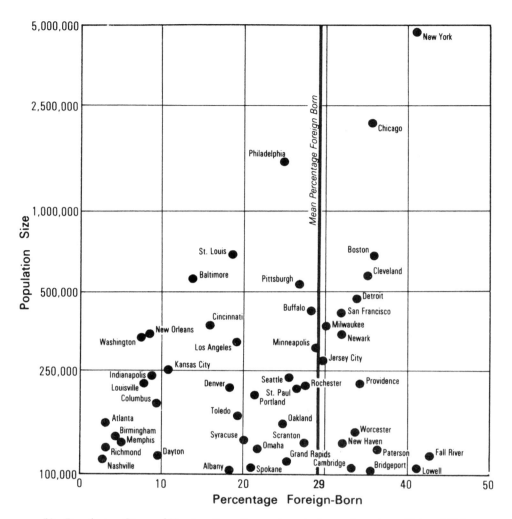

58. Population Size and Foreign-Born Proportions in Large American Cities, 1910.
Such a diagram displays the extreme difference between the South (lower left) and New England industrial cities (lower right), as well as interesting geographic variations within the Manufacturing Belt. (Reproduced from Ward, *Cities and Immigrants*; courtesy Oxford University Press)

Buffalo (steel mills), and Swedes in outlying Jamestown (furniture), whereas Irish, Germans, Italians, and Poles were about equal in Syracuse (no dominant industry). After the turn of the century Slavic immigrants were heavily recruited by the steel and coal companies. In the Pittsburgh-Cleveland belt they often constituted a third or more of the foreign-born population and as much as 70 percent of the labor force in the plants. Ethnic clustering and recruitment of fellow nationals ensured selective concentrations, as, for example, in Steelton, Pennsylvania, which had "large numbers of Croats, Slovenes, Serbs, and Bulgarians from specific regions but almost no Slovaks, Ukrainians, Russians, or Poles," whereas Youngstown had primarily Slovaks, Slovenes, and Poles. In thirty years time the working force in the Anthracite Region shifted from English, Welsh, Irish, and German to predominantly Slavic (plus Hungarians and Italians). The change began in the southern Schuylkill field and spread north to the Lackawanna, powered by coal company policies seeking to lower wages and break strikes. Small textile and shoe factories followed, employing wives and daughters. Italians dispersed much more widely, in part because of the padrone system of labor contracting, which sent construction gangs into every region (they became much involved in railroad track maintenance); they were recruited by textile mills, and they moved quickly into basic levels of many urban shops and services. Jews were heavily concentrated in major metropolitan areas but also spread widely in small numbers through the activities of peddlers and subsequent networks of suppliers and wholesale and retail merchandising.

There were numerous cases in which an initial immigrant connection with an expanding industry or company might impress a particular ethnic character on a whole community (such as Azoreans in New Bedford, where early whaling connections were readily turned to textile recruitment, Poles in the cotton mills of Chicopee, or Hungarians and a new big medical gauze plant in New Brunswick), but the great variety pouring into America commonly implanted a whole set of ethnic clusters in all the larger industrial centers, and most especially in New York City, where, as Jacob Riis reported, "a map of the city, colored to designate nationalities, would show more stripes than on the skin of a zebra, and more colors than any rainbow. The city on such a map would fall into two great halves, green for Irish prevailing in the West Side tenements, and blue for Germans on the East Side. But intermingled with these grand colors would be an odd variety of tints that would give the whole the appearance of an extraordinary crazy-quilt." Riis knew that variegated pattern well from his powerful photographic report on *How the Other Half Lives*—in vast, crowded, filthy tenements.

A mosaic of ethnic neighborhoods, each with its peculiar shops and services, was apparent in all these larger Northern cities, but they were not discrete, enclosed exclaves (fig. 59). Such *urban villages* (to use a later calculatedly benign term) were not sharply set off one from another, were not—could not be— replicas of Old World communities no matter how much they sought to create a familiar environment, and were not insulated but were nodes in extensive networks connecting with other clusters of their own kind in America and in Europe, as well as with neighboring ethnic groups and with the encompassing American society.

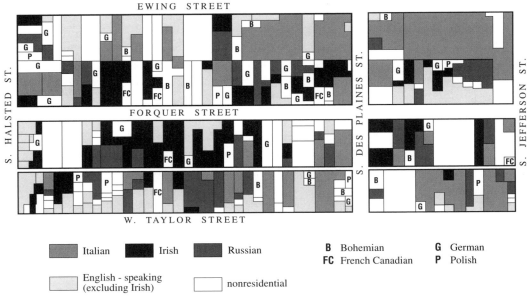

59. Urban Ethnic Mosaic.

A small portion, slightly simplified, of a "Nationalities Map" of twelve blocks of the immigrant district of Chicago produced by Hull House, in cooperation with the U.S. Department of Labor, in 1895. The full map displays fourteen categories (including "Colored"). (Adapted from a color reproduction in Duis, *Chicago: Creating New Traditions*)

THE IMMIGRATION "CRISIS"

A growing concern over the ever-greater massing of poor wage laborers into American cities took on a new intensity and perception toward the end of the century. *Slums* were turning into *ghettos,* calling into question not only America's capacity to absorb a continuing influx of foreign workers but its ability to assimilate such a great variety of alien peoples. Thus students of immigration have noted the irony that the October 1886 ceremonies dedicating the erection of the Statue of Liberty lifting her lamp by the golden door took place "at precisely the time when Americans were beginning seriously to doubt the wisdom of unrestricted immigration" (but of course the statue was not created to be such a symbol and Emma Lazarus's famous inscription about the "world-wide welcome" to "huddled masses" and "wretched refuse" was not inscribed on the pedestal until 1903). Such doubts were generated by many concerns and expressed by disparate factions, but they converged toward a general feeling that the current character and volume of this "immigrant invasion" posed "the most far-reaching problem of our national family."

The problem was viewed as being deeply rooted in the cultural geography of Europe. As John R. Commons, professor of political economy at the University of Wisconsin, explained in 1908:

A line drawn across the continent of Europe from northeast to southwest, separating the Scandinavian Peninsula, the British Isles, Germany, and France from Russia, Austria-Hungary, Italy, and Turkey, separates countries not only of distinct races but also of distinct civilizations. It separates Protestant Europe from Catholic Europe; it separates countries of representative institutions and popular government from absolute monarchies; it separates lands where education is universal from lands where illiteracy predominates; it separates manufacturing countries, progressive agriculture, and skilled labor from primitive hand industries, backward agriculture, and unskilled labor; it separates an educated thrifty peasantry from a peasantry scarcely a single generation from serfdom; it separates Teutonic races from Latin, Slav, Semitic, and Mongolian races. When the sources of American immigration are shifted from the Western countries so nearly allied to our own, to Eastern countries so remote in the main attributes of Western civilization, the change is one that should challenge the attention of every citizen.

Commons's book on *Races and Immigrants in America* was one among many on the general topic and like most others drew upon William Z. Ripley's *The Races of Europe*, a large synthetic compendium representative of an emerging field of anthropogeography struggling to formulate a scientific classification of the human variety around the globe. Strongly influenced by Social Darwinism and neo-Lamarckism, trying to sort out the relative influences of "blood" (heredity), "environment" (physical geography), and "tradition and custom" (culture), quite ready to impute social and psychological behaviors as inherent or especially characteristic of particular "races," "nations," or "ethnical divisions," the whole field was a muddle of contentious theories and assertions, with a strong tendency to pronounce upon superior and inferior peoples. At one extreme this pseudoscience led to a strident Anglo-Saxonism (often broadened into Germanic, Teutonic, or Nordic) that saw the strength and genius of the American people threatened with contamination and debasement by the influx of inferior peoples from Southern and Eastern Europe, a proposition most cogently presented in the title and content of Madison Grant's *The Passing of the Great Race* (1916). The Immigrant Restriction League, an influential pressure group formed in 1894 by a number of Harvard men (including the prominent geographer Nathaniel Shaler), generally espoused such racial theories, with Senator Henry Cabot Lodge, their fervent voice in Congress, warning of "the perils at the portals of our land" and the need "to check, to sift, and to restrict these [newer] immigrants."

But other voices insisted that any such "radical departure" from our traditional welcome to "all who came to us from other lands" would be "illiberal, narrow, and un-American." The United States had long been a mixture of many peoples, its absorptive powers were great, its century of "tremendous growth" was "largely due to the assimilation and thrift of millions of sturdy and patriotic adopted citizens," and worries about the quality of the latest wave had arisen time and again in the past only to be refuted by the success and contributions of those very people and their descendants. As for "race deterioration," it ought to be dismissed as a "Frankenstein . . . conjured up" in fearful imaginations; it had neither been demonstrated nor argued convincingly. As Emily Balch (who had done fieldwork all over Austria-Hungary and in many Slavic communities in the United States) stated forthrightly: "We are paralyzed by our comprehensive ignorance" about race mixing. "Those who should be expert give the most contrary opinions."

In 1907 Congress ordered an extensive inquiry into this vexing national issue. Four years and forty-one volumes later this Dillingham Commission offered an eclectic mass of testimony and statistics and a few tentative suggestions for new policies. The commissioners largely skirted the "racial problem," relegating it primarily to "Oriental immigration" (and supporting the rationale for exclusions already in practice), and focused on the need to correlate "demand for labor" with protection of the "standard of living" of our own "wage-earning classes"—but offered no formula for doing so. Their recommendation that every adult male be required to pass a literacy test (in any language) was enacted by Congress in 1913 and again in 1915 (as it had been in 1897) but was vetoed by successive presidents on the grounds that it constituted selection by opportunity rather than aptitude and would fail to screen out undesirables (such as anarchists; its sponsors clearly had in mind screening out large numbers of Southern and Eastern Europeans). Although no important changes were imposed at this time, as J. C. Furnas bluntly summarized, these recurrent debates, deliberations, and public discussions "helped to confirm among responsible persons the popular distaste for the generic Immigrant—a term become sweepingly pejorative, implying a slum-creating, soap-shy, illiterate, jargon-speaking, standoffish interloper, labeled variously dago, wop, hunky, bohunk, polack, yid"—and thereby prepared the way for the really radical changes that would follow hard upon the nation's direct participation in Europe's massive convulsion of 1914–18.

The distinctions between the New Immigration and the Old that seemed so obvious to so many at the time and would eventually have such a "decisive influence upon American immigration policy" were quite superficial in some ways. As Maldwyn Allen Jones has argued, this "traditional classification . . . has served to obscure the essential truth about immigration, namely, that as a social process it has shown little variation throughout American history." That is, in terms of motivations, traumas of uprooting and relocation, resources and skills brought, and ability to adapt to American conditions, such a distinction seems "both unhistorical and misleading." What did differ importantly were the specific eth-noreligious identities and the timing and geography of their attachment to the United States. The later waves did include a greater variety of people from less similar societies, and "their connection to America begins much later and is fused with the nation's Industrial Revolution." Thus they tended to be concentrated in cities and industrial camps; they could have no experience of America's great westward movement or its horrendous civil war and the impassioned patriotism generated by such vast dramas. They had their own histories that would have to be grafted on to the American celebratory sequence. As a North Dakota editor complained about students in rural ethnic neighborhoods: they "do not know anything about America, but know well the history of Hohenzollern and Hapsburg dynasties in Europe."

Problems of integration seemed magnified. Immigrants were routinely classified upon arrival according to political country of origin and further subdivided (chiefly by "mother-tongue") into "national" groups. In the decennial census they would be categorized as "foreign-born," their American-born children as of "foreign-parentage," and their next generation would be "unrecognized . . . and swallowed up in the category 'native.'" Acculturation was of course quite a different matter, and it little resembled the "Americanization" that most leaders of the receiving country wanted to happen as quickly as possible: the shedding of all foreign identi-ties and assimilation as individual conforming members of "American society." But there was no such monotype to conform to, there was no national program de-signed to shape such a process, and the rate and character of such change would vary greatly among these many peoples and places.

In many cases their "Americanization" involved alterations in their own sense of *European* identity. Most came with little or no experience of a modern nation-state, and even some who did might still define themselves primarily in terms of an ancestral province or district (such as the Dutch of Kalamazoo, who were subdi-vided into Friesians and Zeelanders and could barely cope with one another's dialect). Thus for many the concept of themselves as Italian, Czech, Slovene, Lithuanian, or whatever, grew out of their situation in America—"We Slovaks didn't know we were Slovaks until we came to America and they told us"—and such ethnic mobilization was shaped by the character and context of their New World settlements, the pressures they felt, the response of their local leaders, by broader movements within the United States (especially as fostered by the foreign language press), and, as well, by nationalist developments in Europe. As a group process this transformation of immigrant identities from local homelands (*Heimat*) to a larger sense of ancestral nationality (*Vaterland*) has been termed "the inven-tion of ethnicity." Such a process was not peculiar to the newer immigration. The deep animosity toward the first heavy influx of Irish Roman Catholic proletariat (especially in New England) generated a wider and more militant sense of nationality on the part of the Irish, with priest and parish taking on a more influential role in the Little Dublins of America than they had commonly enjoyed in Ireland.

Germans in America, who represented an unusually broad cross-section of their originating society, generally displayed a strong sense of pride in their cultural identity (and a keen interest in pan-Germanic political movements in Europe), and they reacted with such widespread strength against growing American pressures for conformity in such irritable matters as temperance, Sunday closing, and school language that they forced recognition of the actual "existence of ethnicity in the American public sphere" and its legitimacy "as a political factor." Thereafter the rapid increases in volume and variety of immigrants soon brought the concept of "hyphenated Americans"—Italian-American, Polish-American, Greek-American, and on down the lengthening list—to the fore and thereby confirmed the actuality of the United States as, for the time being at least, an unusually heterogeneous society. In the face of that tangible complexity, what "Americanization" should mean—*could* mean—became a vigorously debated question. *Anglo-Conformity*, the insistent goal of "nativists," seemed increasingly distant and difficult—hence their alarm; the *Melting Pot* so vividly proclaimed and widely popularized in Israel Zangwill's melodrama of 1908 envisioned a glorious fusion of all ethnicities into a new amalgam (recalling Crèvecoeur's famous remark of a century and a quarter earlier about "the American, this new man")—and thereby seemed a threat to both WASP nativists and new ethnic leaders; *Cultural Pluralism* (to continue with Milton Gordon's terms for these "ideologies of assimilation") was not only a reality for the moment but was implicit as a goal in the intensive efforts to hang onto ancestral languages and religions, and was made explicit by Horace Kellen in his 1915 attempt to counter the "almost hysterical fear of 'hyphenated Americans'" with his concept of a democratic federation of nationalities—the same year in which the president of the United States declared that "America does not consist of groups. A man who thinks of himself as belonging to a particular national group in America has not yet become an American."

IMMIGRANT RELIGIONS

An instructive and important display of "Americanism" as a contentious and complex issue became apparent within the Roman Catholic church during these same years. The emergence of that church from its colonial Maryland obscurity to become the largest religious body in the United States by midcentury and to claim 15 million by 1910 (membership numbers of this and every other church should be treated as a kind of rough guesswork) was of course closely linked to overall immigration patterns; indeed, it became clearly identified—and often derided—as "the immigrant church." Here, too, internal ethnic tensions arose before the war, when German Catholics found themselves "foreigners in an Irish-dominated church" and began their campaign to be served by German priests. Much more was involved than simply wanting "one of their own"; Irish bishops insisted that English was the appropriate lay language in the American church, and there were obvious differences in many aspects of parochial life. German resistance eventually resulted in the church's reluctant departure from the normal *territorial* parish (wherein all who live are expected to attend its church) and formal recognition of *national* parishes serving a particular ethnic group—"separate, but equal, churches" (just as there were separate Black and White churches within every denomination in the South and most everywhere else that Black members could sustain a separate church). Thus by 1865 there were eight German parishes among the thirty-two in New York City. This German-Irish ethnic rivalry became a major feature, involving conflict not only over language but over schools, religious orders, temperance, and much else. Subsequent growth from sequential influxes compounded such problems. By 1915 half of the 200 parishes in the Archdiocese of Chicago (coextensive with the State of Illinois) were national parishes, subdivided as follows:

33 Polish	5 Slovak	1 Belgian
30 German	4 Croatian	1 Chaldean (Assyrian)
10 Italian	4 French (Canadian)	1 Dutch
10 Lithuanian	2 Slovene	1 Hungarian
		1 Syrian

Many national parishes were "ethnic fortresses," jealously guarding their particular liturgical and devotional practices, pastoral styles, and social services, and as ethnic networks they had created an impressive array of schools, seminaries, colleges, hospitals, orphanages, asylums, recreational halls, and fraternal organizations (by 1900 it was claimed that every German national parish in the country had a parochial school). That "national" mosaic was so fundamental in the life—and problems—of the church then and for generations after that a modern sociologist felt it necessary to warn that "every generalization about . . . Catholic values and behavior is likely to be misleading, if not erroneous," unless it takes into account these "ethno-religious" subgroups. Contentions arose not only out of differences rooted in the distinctive European backgrounds of these groups but out of differences over what "Americanization" ought to mean with reference to all sorts of practical matters relating to schools, language, taxation, hierarchical authority, and much else. Indeed, certain trends within the American church (especially identified with a number of prominent Irish bishops) seemed to reflect so much tolerance of individualism, democracy, and accommodation to the sociopolitical

order that conservative European (and some American) Catholic leaders denounced "Americanization" as a heresy and obtained a formal papal statement
declaring certain features of "modernization" as especially dangerous.

Whatever the doctrinal issues might have been, there were overt displays of
extensive adaptations to American conditions built into the structure, context,
and local character of the church. Its geographic framework was fitted upon the
entire country, the strength of its regional presence reflecting the selective patterns
of annexation and immigration (with more than half of its seventy-six dioceses
subdividing the Manufacturing Belt) (fig. 60). Although New York had the largest
Catholic population, Baltimore, seat of the first bishop (1789), remained the
titular center of the American church. Whatever the language in the parish,
English was the norm at diocesan and higher levels. And for all its hierarchical
dependence on Rome (for whom the entire United States was technically a missionary realm until 1908), its alleged foreign character, its ancient ceremonies and
Latin mass, its awkward "fit . . . with established American Protestant patterns,"
no adequate definition of "America" nor description of its social geography could
exclude or marginalize this Roman Catholic population. In a basic sense this
Church and this State entered the new century struggling with the same intrinsic
problem: *E pluribus unum, In uno plures*.

The social geography of Lutheranism was also transformed by immigration, with
important impact on American regionalism. In 1865 it was essentially a Midland
religion, having spread from its Pennsylvania base across much of Ohio and Indiana, with firm footholds farther west (and several older outliers in New York, the
Carolina Piedmont, and Texas). Subsequent German and Scandinavian migrations made Lutheranism dominant over large portions of the upper Middle West
and, together with the very considerable number settling in older industrial centers, made it the third largest Protestant church in the United States. Divided
within itself primarily by ethnicity (German, Norwegian, Swedish, Danish, Finn-
ish, Slovak), secondarily by differing emphases in doctrine and piety arising in part
by different degrees of accommodation with the American context (an ethnic
splintering best exemplified by the rapid growth of the ultraconservative German
Missouri Synod), its many synods were nevertheless bound by a strong "underlying
unity in faith and practice" and consciousness of their bold Reformation origins (all
subscribing to the Augsburg Confession of 1530). In spite of an initial inward-
looking rural ethnic character in much of its presence, this immigrant Lutheranism
increasingly opened out and blended with a foundational Yankee imprint in the
upper Middle West to reinforce an enterprising, community-minded, moralistic
political culture that would be characteristic of the region thereafter.

A moralistic ingredient was also reinforced, in a different manner and in areas
where it had not been strong, by another immigrant religious group, whose signifi-

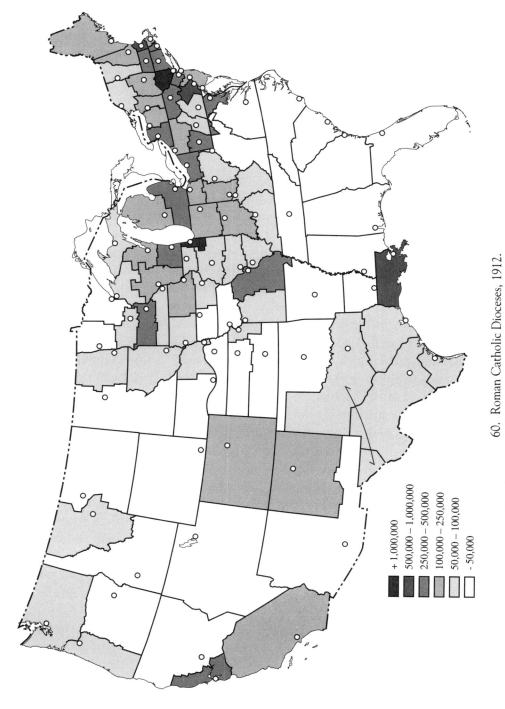

60. Roman Catholic Dioceses, 1912.

(Based on map and statistics in *Catholic Encyclopedia*, 1915, vol. 15)

+ 1,000,000

500,000 – 1,000,000

250,000 – 500,000

100,000 – 250,000

50,000 – 100,000

- 50,000

cance in American society and culture would far outreach its numbers and whose experience in America would also have profound effects upon its religious organization and practice. The marked threefold division in Jewish religion—Reform, Conservative, Orthodox—was very largely an outgrowth of the American scene. The Reform movement emerged in Germany but came into full flower as a formal body and radical departure from Talmudic Orthodoxy in America among midcentury German Jewish immigrants. Arriving as an integral part of a larger German population (and commonly regarded as such by Americans at the time), they shared in that larger pattern of dispersal and relatively rapid integration in American business and civic life. New York City was their largest seat, but Cincinnati became their most influential and symbolic center.

The massive influx of a Yiddish-speaking Ashkenazi Orthodoxy from the shtetls and ghettos of Eastern Europe into the Lower East Side of Manhattan and other northeastern cities transformed the overall social geography and the religious shape of Judaism in America. These newcomers were almost as much strangers to the German Jews as they were to other Americans, and they were a stark representation of what the Reformers had consciously moved away from. Their own strict, enclosed world came under powerful pressures of adaptation in their new American environment, and, rather expectedly, a new movement intermediate between the confining rigidities of Orthodoxy and the liberal secularism of Reform slowly emerged as an "historical Judaism," a distinct American Conservative tradition. These vigorous contentions and creative currents were further complicated by Zionism, anti-Semitism in the United States and abroad, and the intense emotional question of whether Jews would—should—become more of a religious or an ethnic minority in American life. Meanwhile they were moving into the turbulent marketplace of "individualistic" urban politics, civic leadership, and philanthropy to further the interests of their people and to seek broader protections, equities, and social services for Americans as a whole.

As the frontier of emigration moved ever deeper into Europe it not only opened the floodgates of the Jewish Pale but passed beyond the margins of Western Christendom into the land of the Orthodox and other Eastern churches and thereby initiated trickles of entirely new additions to the remarkable variety of faiths already in America. None became at all prominent before 1915. There were perhaps 100,000 Greek and a few thousand Serbian, Bulgarian, and Romanian Orthodox parishioners by that date but no resident bishops of these autocephalous churches. Ostensibly all were under the care of a Russian archbishop in America whose own flock had been doubled by accession of a body of Ruthenians who had broken away from the Roman Catholic church because American bishops refused to recognize its distinctive rites and practices (though such forms had long been recognized by the Vatican in its "Uniate" constituency). This priority of Russian

Orthodoxy stemmed from its early inclusion in the purchase of Alaska, where a cathedral had existed at New Archangel (Sitka) since 1848. In 1872 the Russian Orthodox headquarters for America was shifted to San Francisco and in 1905 to New York City, moves made in each case to better serve Orthodox of various nationalities. The growth of churches was slow because of the poverty of parishioners and because early emigrations were largely male, with high rates of return. Only after World War I did the onion dome begin to appear amidst the steeples and towers in the ecclesiastical landscape of anthracite valleys, New England mill towns, and other industrial districts (the surprising formation of a Greek Orthodox parish in Salt Lake City as early as 1905 resulted from labor contractors making the Mormon capital their base for serving the mines, mills, and railroads of the Intermountain West).

OTHER SOURCES

For most Americans "immigrants" and "Europeans" were all but interchangeable terms during this period and long after, but the case of Alaska and the Orthodox points toward other means and avenues of entry. The influx of Chinese to Gold Rush California and their later role in constructing the Central Pacific are well-known topics in American history, and, less appreciated, such actions were part of a long tradition of worker emigration from South China—Chinatowns were to be found throughout maritime Southeast Asia. San Francisco long remained much their greatest seat, but they spread in small numbers to many mining camps and construction projects in the Far West. Commonly identified with such lowly jobs as cooks, gardeners, and laundry workers, in California they were also successful fishermen, farmers, merchants, and small industrialists. Like many other groups, the initial influx was almost entirely males, who clustered with their own kind while in the United States and planned to return home within a few seasons or years. San Francisco Custom House records of such comings and goings for twenty years before 1876 show an average of about 8,000 arrivals and nearly 4,000 departures annually; by 1880 there were more than 100,000 in the Far West and a few thousand scattered elsewhere.

"What makes the Chinese experience unique in American ethnic history is not what they did but what was done to them," writes Roger Daniels as he reviews the peculiarly virulent public and scandalous political record of abuse and discrimination against these people. The intimidation and mob violence that they had suffered recurrently since early mining camp days reached a new level in the 1870s when the California economy underwent a brief depression and dislocation. Eagerly excused or actively exploited by politicians at all levels, such agitations resulted in a Chinese Exclusion Act, passed by Congress in 1882. It actually provided only for a ten-year suspension of immigration of laborers, but it was nevertheless "the first significant inhibition on free immigration in American history." Extended for another decade in 1892, it was made permanent in 1902. All the while, California laws had subjected the Chinese to special taxation, restrictions on employment, residence, and court protections, and denial of naturalization. This last, upheld and broadened by federal action, would remain in effect nationally until 1943. The Chinese were a "colored race" of alien dress and habits widely regarded as unassimilable; by and large they were also (as confirmed by careful studies of the time—they had at least a few stalwart American supporters) industrious and thrifty, skilled and reliable workers, shrewd in business, socially responsible among themselves—and widely characterized as "coolie labor" undercutting American workers (who in California were mainly Irish immigrants: "the shock troops of the anti-Chinese movement"). Certain categories of Chinese could still be admitted to the United States, but it had been made clear that they were not welcome.

These attitudes and discriminations were readily applied to the Japanese, who began to show up in Pacific ports after Japan legalized emigration in 1885. The 1900 census recorded only about 24,000 in the Western states, but 61,000 in newly acquired Hawaii, where they had been imported as laborers by sugar companies. As more came to San Francisco and began to take the lead in several lines of horticulture and intensive farming, pressures from California induced President Theodore Roosevelt to negotiate a delicate "Gentlemen's Agreement" in 1907 by which Japan (a victorious new Pacific power of great geopolitical significance to the Pacific interests of the United States) agreed to limit emigration to the United States severely. With this in place it would be an easy step ten years later to include in the first general immigration restriction act a specific "Asian Barred Zone," defined by longitude and latitude, to prohibit entry from Asia and the Pacific Islands— excepting, of course, from America's new Pacific possessions.

Whereas the United States decisively rejected Asians and was inclining ever more toward some sort of selection among the many kinds of ethnic Europeans, it remained essentially indifferent to peoples from the other Americas. There was movement from all the Hispanic- and Afro-American borderlands, but the impact was so local or the numbers were so few as to go virtually unnoticed in national discussions. The census of 1900 reported just over 100,000 Mexican-born residents, 70 percent of them in Texas, but it was generally regarded as a product of routine local traffic serving local needs, a coming and going to mutual advantage— and there was no official monitoring of it. Mexicans crossed the border to jobs on ranches, farms, and railroads, or in mines, mills, and smelters (just as Americans crossed into Mexico as owners, managers, and engineers of such facilities). If these Mexicans technically were immigrants, in a larger sense this whole borderland was their homeland, and such movements remained a regional matter of little national interest. As the U.S. consul general in Mexico City reassured his superiors in 1903: "the number of emigrants from Mexico to the United States is small and there is no probability of any considerable increase therein in the future."

The number of emigrants from the West Indies was so small as to be ignored (14,500 in residence in 1900), but a close look would have disclosed that with the multiplication of steamship connections, ease of travel, and American economic penetration, the idea of migration to the United States spread through the islands and the idea of West Indians as a labor force spread into North America. They came as field hands, factory workers, servants for hotels, resorts, and steamships, but they also came as artisans, shopkeepers, and professionals, and their impact on Black American society would be all out of proportion to their number (and that refers not just to those from the English-speaking islands, as the arrival of Arturo Schomburg from Puerto Rico in 1891 attests). Initial footholds in New York, Florida, and other ports became focal points for further migrations (just as the little communities of Cabo Verdeans in Fall River and New Bedford had been for the nearly century-old movement of Portuguese creoles from what might be considered a distant outlier of the Afro-American World). The geopolitical changes that followed upon the abrupt 1898 intervention and expansion into this American Mediterranean must surely alter potentials for emigration, but just how would not be at all clear for some years.

The maps accompanying the Thirteenth Census of 1910 offer the usual periodic summations of important geographic patterns at the national scale (continuing the depictions initiated by Francis A. Walker in his *Statistical Atlas* of 1870). One of these provides an interesting view of the local and regional impact of the two generations of immigration we have been considering. Entitled "Percentage of Foreign-born Whites and Native Whites of Foreign or Mixed Parentage combined in total population, by county," it displays not the simple distribution of the more than 32 million of such "foreign white stock" but their proportionate position relative to the population in each county (fig. 61). Nationally such persons represented 35.2 percent of the population, but the map offers three categories above that proportion and five categories below and displays a remarkably uneven surface. The boldest colorations (75 percent or more of such foreign stock) are found in the borderlands with Mexico and the Upper Great Lakes and in rural areas of Minnesota and the Dakotas. Relatively high proportions noted in our previous regional chapters are also discernible, such as in the mining and lumbering camps of the Far West, European Mormon converts settled in their New World Zion, the continuing modest influx into Central Texas, and Cubans in Key West and Tampa. But much the most striking pattern is the almost complete blankness of the South, confirming that a half century of massive immigration had hardly touched that

PER CENT OF FOREIGN-BORN WHITES AND NATIVE WHITES OF FOREIGN OR MIXED PARENTAGE COMBINED IN TOTAL POPULATION,
BY COUNTIES: 1910

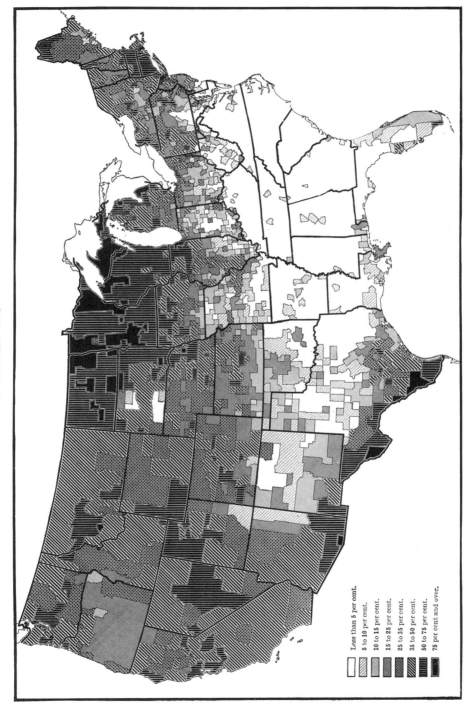

Less than 5 per cent.
5 to 10 per cent.
10 to 15 per cent.
15 to 25 per cent.
25 to 35 per cent.
35 to 50 per cent.
50 to 75 per cent.
75 per cent and over.

61. Foreign Stock Population, 1910.
(Reproduced from *Statistical Atlas of the United States*, Bureau of the
Census, 1914)

See text for explanation.

large region and thereby, as noted earlier, had strengthened Southern cohesion and separateness within the re–United States.

5. Systems and Symbols

A NATIONAL SYSTEM

As a result of the great geographical changes we have been describing it seemed to many Americans as if "a new United States, stretched from ocean to ocean, filled out, and bound together, had miraculously appeared." Toward the end of the century "publicists were savoring the word 'nation' in this sense of a continent conquered and tamed. It was a term that above all connoted growth and development and enterprise," lending itself to "sweeping, uniform description: nationalization, industrialization, mechanization, urbanization." All that would continue, of course, but there was also a special sense of accomplishment, a new status achieved. "We have come to full maturity with this new century," said Woodrow Wilson in 1902, "and to full self-consciousness as a nation." Like many others, the then-president of Princeton University was referring especially to a new American position in world affairs following upon its sudden expansion in the Pacific, but, as he well understood, that position rested upon the formidable material strength of the United States.

And the *national* quality of that material wealth was impressive to visitor and native alike. "Where else in the world will you find such a volume and expanse of free trade as in these . . . United States?" asked James F. Muirhead, the German-educated Scot whom Karl Baedeker had dispatched to America to prepare the first guidebook on the country for his famous series:

> We find here a huge section of the world's surface, 3,000 miles long and 1,500 miles wide, . . . containing seventy millions of inhabitants, producing a very large proportion of all the necessities and many of the luxuries of life, and all [its states] enjoying the freest of free trade with each other. . . . Collectively they contain nearly half of the railway mileage of the globe, besides an incomparable series of inland waterways. Over all these is continually passing an immense amount of goods. . . . The internal commerce of the United States makes it the most wonderful market on the globe.

The wonder of that national market had been further enhanced by common weights and measures, a national currency, the relatively easy flow of capital and credit, nationwide express shipment services, a comprehensive and inexpensive postal system (with free rural delivery recently initiated), and a common tongue proclaiming the language of business in a society devoted to enterprise and growth, progress and profits. (The telephone was still primarily an urban and local facility, but a national system was in the making: Boston and New York were linked in

1884, and long-distance trunk lines extended successively to Chicago [1892], Midwestern gateways, Louisville, Memphis, and Atlanta [1897], Dallas [1905], Denver [1910], and San Francisco [1915]; but long-distance tolls were very high and reliability uncertain.)

The language of business on such a scale required new forms and forces of advertising, thereby setting that industry on its way to becoming "the omnipresent, most characteristic, and most remunerative form of American literature." Company departments and independent agencies eagerly undertook the training of readers and consumers "in a new kind of symbolic shorthand. Compressed images, seals, and signs began to penetrate the American consciousness. . . . Ivory soap, Quaker Oats, Sapolio, and Hire's Root Beer were among the pioneers in this new sensory education." New mass-market magazines, low-priced because supported more by advertisements than by subscriptions, such as *Cosmopolitan, McClure's, Ladies Home Journal,* and the *Saturday Evening Post* (resurrected from near extinction to a million copies), together with the gigantic mail-order catalogues of *Montgomery Ward, Sears, Roebuck,* and *Spiegel,* became powerful agents in the surge of nationwide consumption of standardized goods and nationwide response to the caprices of fashion—and thereby in "the victory of market over market-place," that is, of the printed word and image defined by national companies over the face-to-face transaction with the local merchant or traveling salesman.

Concurrent with this "invention" of a "consumer culture" was the formation of nationwide trade associations (such as the National Association of Manufacturers and U.S. Chamber of Commerce), labor unions (American Federation of Labor, United Mine Workers), and professional guilds (American Bar Association, American Medical Association). In the universities there was a major shift in emphasis from the classical curriculum to more practical arts, from the past to the present, including training for business management (Wharton School of Commerce and Finance at the University of Pennsylvania, 1881; the first graduate business program, at Dartmouth, 1900), as well as engineering, agricultural science, and the emergence of the social sciences (such as sociology, at the new University of Chicago) to begin their analytical study of national characteristics and problems. These particular agencies are little more than hints of a large, varied, and interrelated set of movements that blossomed into what contemporaries and later historians (with some unease) called the Progressive Era. Initiated by business, professional, and voluntary associations, its most famous impact was upon government, and especially in the much-magnified role of the national government.

These governmental initiatives represented imitation of, assertion of power over, and a new kind of partnership with the business world. Big corporations provided the model of managerial efficiency for the drive to create an enlarged bureaucracy of career specialists. The Interstate Commerce Commission and anti-trust acts were strengthened and joined by commissions and legislation dealing with banking, commerce, labor, food and drugs, and other matters. The federal government assumed permanent protection of a few areas of remarkable natural beauty set aside as national parks (Yellowstone, Yosemite, Sequoia, Mt. Rainier, Crater Lake, and Glacier, by 1910) and, after 1907, the preservation of various smaller special sites as national monuments (such as Devils Tower, Mesa Verde, Petrified Forest—resistance to government preservation of historic sites remained strong for many years). More radical and controversial was the assumption of long-term control and management of large areas of the remaining public lands. The first forest reserve of 1892 was soon expanded into an immense acreage of national forests scattered across all the Western states. In 1908 President Theodore Roose-velt convened a large White House conference to preach the need for such "conser-vation of natural resources" and to try to assuage the outrage of Western leaders, over what they regarded as federal "imperialism," by offering a policy of scientific management and "multiple use" of public lands in conjunction with local and corporate interests. Meanwhile, the new Federal Reclamation Service was provid-ing subsidy and science to continue the expansion of settlement into lands whose conquest was beyond the capabilities of the farm family or the interest of corporate investors—a role vindicated in the courts as a promotion of the "general welfare" of the country. All of this unprecedented assumption of power by the central government was aptly characterized by its most vociferous exponent, Theodore Roosevelt, as a "New Nationalism" necessitated by "new problems" vividly appar-ent in this "new United States" that seemed to have suddenly appeared in the new century.

In her brief historical interpretation of the United States, Mary Platt Parmele concluded that "we are now passing through a period of centralizing forces"; however, observing the great urbanization taking place and reflecting upon "the ebb and flow from the centripetal to the centrifugal tendencies" of power, she wondered whether it might eventually become "diffused . . . in a Federation of Cities." Actually, in the American federal system cities were and would remain peculiarly powerless ("marginalized from the beginning in the . . . apparatus of national government"), but insofar as one might choose to view the United States as a vast market and unified world of business and commerce it already functioned as a great system of cities. The national government had played no direct role in that creation, but with the Federal Reserve Act of 1913 its current centralizing tendency intervened and reshaped one of the fundamental networks of that sys-tem. This initiative was not radically new in concept. A banking act of 1863 had designated a set of cities to assist New York City in the management of a new national currency, and subsequent acts allowed expansion of that network more or less commensurate with expansion of the market. The 1913 act formalized this system with new regulations, standards of participation, and a regional framework with designated primary centers—in effect completing the nationalization of this vigorous and volatile component of capitalist America.

The creation of the Federal Reserve system is of special geographical interest because of what it displayed about the existing networks of commercial banking. The act directed the organization committee to "'designate not less than 8 nor more than 12 cities to be known as Federal reserve cities'; to 'divide the continental United States . . . into districts'; . . . and to apportion the districts 'with due regard to the convenience and customary course of business.'" Regional hearings were held, representations from more than 200 cities were received, and 7,471 banks were queried by mail; 37 cities formally asked to be designated headquarters of a district (fig. 62). Given the great pressures to accommodate many regions and cities it is not surprising that the maximum of 12 districts was created (and the committee suggested that if continued growth in the Pacific Northwest allowed that area to meet minimum reserve requirements Seattle interests might petition Congress for an additional district). In the face of inevitable local disappointments and criticisms the committee felt it necessary to stress that "the Federal reserve banks are banker's banks" and that "the ordinary every day banking relations of the community, of business men, and of banks will not be greatly modified or altered."

62. Regional Reach of a Banking Center.
Map submitted by Minneapolis interests to show the extent and density of its banking field and the boundaries they proposed for a reserve district. (S. Doc. 485, 63d Cong., 2d sess.)

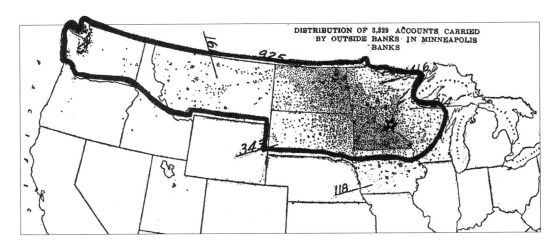

The initial map of this specialized system reflects the national commercial system only at a very general level, and it can mislead as to important features (fig. 63). A few of these boundaries would soon be modified to provide a better fit with the "convenience and customary course of business," and a set of branch districts, each with its reserve center, would be created within these primary districts. As Richard Bensel has carefully displayed, this latter configuration of subsidiary banking areas was thereby getting closer to the actual pattern of metropolitan trade areas (soon made explicit by studies of the Department of Commerce) (fig. 64). It was this

63. Federal Reserve Banks and Districts, 1914.

In their report the committee commented on a few especially difficult cases: New Orleans and its request for a district embracing all the Gulf states (rejected because it was a declining banking center, now far surpassed by Atlanta, overtaken by Dallas, and Texas bankers disdained any tributary connection with it); the choice of Richmond over Baltimore (justified on the basis of the scale of services already being rendered to Southern states—and, one suspects, the pressure to select a thoroughly Southern city); the selection of Kansas City over Omaha and rejection of a large mountain district centered on Denver (based on strong preferences expressed by banks within the bounds of proposed districts). Unremarked by the committee but noted recently by Richard Bensel was the selection of Cleveland, probably as a compromise between the contending claims of Pittsburgh and Cincinnati, both of which had greater assets and more votes from area banks. (S. Doc. 485, 63d Cong., 2d sess.)

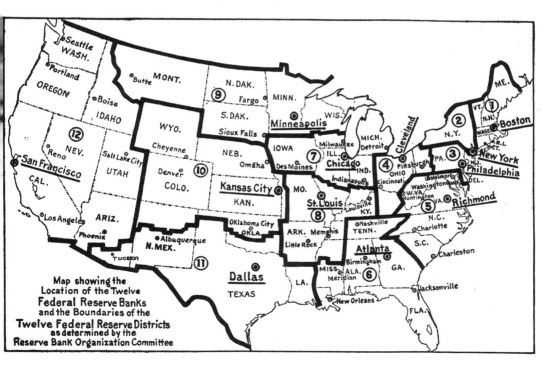

1. Chattanooga
2. Cincinnati   6. Nashville
3. Cleveland   7. Pittsburgh
4. Columbus   8. Sioux City
5. Indianapolis   9. Toledo

64. Trade Centers and Areas.
In the early 1920s the Domestic Commerce Division of the Department of Commerce began compiling maps and county data relating to retail and wholesale marketing. This pattern of fifty major areas was valid for fifteen years earlier, once the railroad network was essentially complete. The jagged edges follow county boundaries, approximating actual trade divides. (From Stewart, *Market Data Handbook*)

more detailed set of major wholesale centers and railroad nodes that defined the basic networks of the national market (wholesaling, like so much else, had been transformed into a much more efficient, regularized business, with big firms issuing standard contracts and credit in conjunction with big banks). However, it is also important to understand that this geographic pattern was functionally only the base level of a nested hierarchy; that is, just as Federal Reserve branch cities were subordinate to their district center, so most of these market area cities were subordinate to one or more still larger metropolitan centers (fig. 65). New York provided an array of financial and commercial services for the entire nation; Chicago was the principal financial and marketing center for a huge portion of the midsection of the country; St. Louis and Cincinnati had wider hinterlands in some activities than these standard banking and marketing maps indicated. It was through this network of fifty cities and hierarchy of several levels of geographic reach that the United States actually functioned as a single vast market.

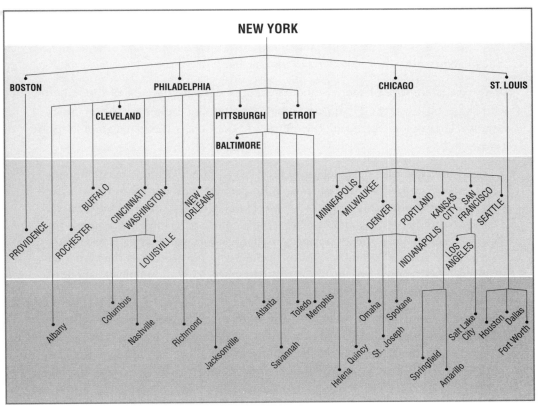

65. Urban Hierarchy, 1910.
Based on banking hinterlands. (Adapted from Conzen, "Maturing Urban System"; the shaded levels are derived from Borchert, "American Metropolitan Evolution")

The very look of these cities was powerful confirmation of that national market. European visitors seem to have been strongly struck by it, whether from a quick first impression, as in the case of Arnold Bennett ("Having regard to the healthy mutual jealousy of the great towns, I feel that I am carrying audacity to the point of foolishness when I state that the streets of every American city reminded me on the whole of the streets of all the others") or from extensive, reflective study, as in the case of James Bryce:

The uniformity is . . . remarkable. With [few] exceptions, . . . American cities differ from one another only herein, that some of them are built more with brick than with wood, and others more with wood than with brick. In all else they are alike, both great and small. In the same wide streets, crossing at right angles, ill-paved, but planted along the sidewalks with maple trees whose autumnal scarlet surpasses the brilliance of any European foliage. In all the same shops, arranged on the same plan

> . . . the same street cars passing to and fro . . . . I admit that in external aspect there is a sad monotony in the larger towns of England also, ... that American towns . . . are in some ways pleasanter; they are cleaner, there is less poverty, less squalor, less darkness. But their monotony haunts one like a nightmare.

Well, yes, there was a sameness and a generalized distinctiveness of the America scene (fig. 66); as a Scottish geographer thoroughly familiar with both sides of Atlantic later noted, "cities are the cultures of their countries made graphic in the landscape":

> American cities strike the European as being quite distinctive: they are rarely dominated by a castle or a cathedral, their street patterns have not crept out over the centuries testing and reflecting every shade of local relief, they do not often have the anomalies due to a long and complex history, they are less full of the echoes of singular personalities, they are much more changeful, more utilitarian, they attempt to be more businesslike and are more concerned with the masses and the needs and drives of their times. They are, in fact, American: reflecting an American attitude to life and the American way of using land.

The late Wreford Watson went on to refer to such characteristics as optimism, affluence, brashness, materialism, the sense of freedom and destiny, and especially the primacy of economic values—the common sort of list that Michael P. Conzen (another keen British-born student of the American urban pattern) has more analytically related to that special "American Victorian consensus" grounded in selected aspects of "republicanism, perfectionism, and domesticity" that seems to have coalesced just at this time.

American cities were distinctive because American values and the American context were distinctive; American cities looked alike because Americans placed a high value on being modern and up-to-date, on having the latest in facilities, facades, and furnishings; "keeping up with the times" meant keeping up with the examples on display in New York, Chicago, or whatever the biggest city was in one's region, and the American network kept such things on constant review and readily available to customers nationwide. Pressures to produce a modern national style and standard that had been apparent for half a century were now making use of new technologies in a new scale of urban life. Development was both upward and outward. "The symbolism of height with corporate power had become established in American society." Buildings of ten stories or more began to punctuate the townscape in many of the larger regional centers, emulating in smaller scale the soaring skyscrapers of New York or the big, boxy twenty-story office buildings in Chicago (all made possible by the electric elevator and steel-frame construction, and feasible by the telephone, which allowed concentrations of office work separate from the factories and enhanced the internal efficiency of such vertical massings). Such symbols of competitive urbanism stood alongside those great seats of marketing and mobility: huge department stores, big hotels, and capacious railroad stations. The kinetic level as well the areal expansion of urban life had been accelerated by electric trolley car systems radiating from downtowns to streetcar suburbs that were being rapidly extended by eager tract developers and sectorially sorted by class: "in places like Kansas City and Chicago one finds miles on miles of suburb filled with neat wooden houses, each with its tiny garden plot, owned by the shop assistants and handicraftsmen who return on the electric-cars in the evening from their work," observed an admiring Lord Bryce. A large share of the houses were mass-built by developers or mass-marketed as plans or sets of materials to smaller towns and rural areas by huge Chicago firms, offering variety within a limited range of styles.

The uniformity-regularity-monotony of the American urban scene was imitative, concurrent, and increasingly corporate-controlled. Big companies proclaimed themselves across the land by standardized emblems, colors, slogans, and even whole storefronts in the case of spreading chain stores, such as Woolworth's. But Frank Woolworth created another symbol as well: a fifty-seven-story headquarters building towering over Manhattan, by the insistence of its owner the tallest office building in the world (and it remained so until 1930) (fig. 67). Completed in 1913, this "Cathedral of Commerce" was not only "a huge sign advertising the [worldwide] business of the Woolworth company to the whole world," it also represented the "money, ambition, and drive for power" that proclaimed New York City as the great seat of corporations, of business and banking, insurance and investment houses—the undisputed "control point" of the national system.

A FEDERAL SYSTEM

Economically the nation might function increasingly as a vast network of cities, but it remained fundamentally a political federation of states and the geography of that essential framework was also reaching maturity. By 1912 the dozen units added since the Civil War had filled in the transcontinental pattern and stabilized the Union at forty-eight states for the next forty-seven years.

As the common map of America displays, most of these new states were huge areal boxes (Idaho a conspicuous exception), two of which appeared to be identical in shape (Colorado was slightly larger than Wyoming); all were bold exhibits of the republican principle and congressional preference that new constituent units of the federation be arbitrary compartments rather than organic societies, mere districts of population drawn to some general standard of size and shape rather than designed around a particular people rooted in time and place (hence no Sequoyah, boundaries of Utah and New Mexico that excluded important bodies of Mormons

Main Street, Richmond, c. 1900.

66. The Monotony of Main Street.

These three views of cities in three very distinct regions illustrate what Arnold Bennett and James Bryce were reacting to. The 110 additional views in Cynthia Read-Miller's *Main Street, USA in Early Photographs* amply confirm their impressions. All these prints were from a massive collection of the Detroit Publishing Company, a nationwide photographic and distribution center where much of the work was directed by the famed Western photographer William H. Jackson. (From the Collections of Henry Ford Museum and Greenfield Village)

Broadway, Los Angeles, 1911.

Market Street, Philadelphia, c. 1908.

and Hispanics, and attempts to combine New Mexico and Arizona). The scale of these units seems adjusted in some degree to lesser densities of Western settlement: from about 75,000 square miles in the tier of Plains states to about 100,000 in the Mountain states (with Montana nearly the size of anomalous California). In the railroad age such enlarged standards were still in keeping with the informal principle that states be "of suitable and convenient size for the purpose of government"— or so they were in the abstract, if not necessarily so on the ground (in 1900 a rail journey from northern Wyoming to the capital required a devious loop through two other states).

New states are officially created by Congress, but they are not mere creatures of Congress; they are systems within an encompassing system but not simply subordinate units within a national hierarchy. That they were more than that was of course basic to the idea of—and the need in the first place for—a federation and was carefully defined in the Constitution. States are sovereign over most of the political life of Americans. State law is the basic law of civil society, with the federal government restricted to establishing certain rules and playing an active role only in selective matters. Individual states set their own laws and programs relating to crime and public order, suffrage and elections, education, public welfare, licensing, chartering of corporations, regulation of industries, aids to economic development, and much else. Whatever the general trends of the times, American government remained in its basic structure a noncentralized government.

State legislatures created their own internal geopolitical framework of counties, townships, cities, districts, and the allocation of powers to such subunits. They selected their own primary seat of government and the location of an array of state institutions. In these new states the old principle that the capital ought to be at or near the center of the state was most apparent in the Dakotas (where in each case it was eccentric to the most populous districts), and shifts toward the center were made (before or after statehood) in Arizona and Oklahoma, and seriously attempted in Washington (where a majority voted against Olympia but split their support between Ellensburg and Yakima). In these as in earlier states there were strong pressures for "filling in the region with public facilities" and most distributed

---

67. Woolworth Building.
Towering over City Hall Park and the domed U.S. Post Office in the foreground and, by specific intent, over the forty-seven-story Singer Tower in the background, this soaring, attenuated Gothic-styled structure by the architect Cass Gilbert set a new aesthetic standard for New York skyscrapers. (Reprinted from a tinted photograph in Cochran, *Cathedral of Commerce*, a lavish descriptive brochure of 1917)

the major prizes (capital, penitentiary, university) and many lesser ones (agricultural college, reform schools, insane asylums, schools for the blind and for the
deaf and dumb, soldiers' home, soldiers' orphans' home, armories) widely among
competing cities and towns, with smaller places often preferred for schools and
asylums. (Nebraska, however, concentrated the penitentiary, university, agricultural college, and several asylums in the capital city, all helping as a makeweight
for Lincoln as opposed to Omaha.) During this era most states enacted compulsory
education laws for children and set up normal schools for teacher training, and
these were usually established in various regions for the convenience of local
clientele (in Nebraska at Peru, Kearney, and Chadron by 1912).

These member republics might serve as territorial building blocks for national
political change. Social movements such as compulsory education, prohibition of
liquor, and women's suffrage (to cite three characteristic of this "progressive era")
first gained adoption in a particular state and then spread incrementally state by
state until achieving nationwide endorsement (the last two of these by amendments to the Constitution in 1919 and 1920, such action requiring ratification by
three-quarters of the states). However, such movements did not diffuse from a state
of origin to bordering states and contiguously across the nation. Patterns of adoption were much affected by the internal character of each state with reference to
the values and interests of its people, and these were rooted in its historical human
geography: in sources of people, types and patterns of settlements and economies,
and political culture.

Superimposing the federal map of states upon these other national patterns
reveals great areal discordances and thereby something of the great variations in
internal geopolitical character of the states. Without attempting a full typology, it is
easy to recognize several kinds: rural states homogeneous in economy and political
culture (North Dakota, Mississippi); those with one large metropolitan area and a
generally compatible cultural hinterland (Minnesota, Georgia); large metropolitan
area with generally oppositional hinterland (Chicago and downstate Illinois, New
York and upstate); those strongly divided between two metropolitan areas (Missouri, Pennsylvania); those with strong regional socioeconomic contrasts (Washington, Florida). Many states were more complex (as were these when examined
more closely), and thus while states were complete coherent political structures,
many were not at all cohesive civil societies. The internal geopolitical framework of
counties and electoral districts in these bicameral republics commonly gave dispro-
portionate power to rural areas over rapidly growing urban centers.

The great national instrument of the states was of course the U.S. Senate,
where the primacy of territory over population was built into the federal system.
The admission of new states, each adding another pair of senators, was perforce a

major political issue. Although nothing as bitter and dangerous as the slave-free confrontations bedeviled postwar negotiations, important matters were at stake. We have noted special ethnic and religious issues affecting some Western cases and the smallness of populations in several others. Imbalances in the latter were ever more extreme (by 1900 the 42,000 residents of Nevada enjoyed the same power of vote as the more than 7 million of New York), but party not population was the critical factor. Nebraska and Colorado, considered to be safely Republican, were admitted while that party was fully in power during Reconstruction (just as Nevada had been admitted during the Civil War). But after 1876, as the Democratic party returned in full force and the Republicans were weakened by scandal and the accumulation of public grievances, "statehood politics"—the admission of new states—again became a major and protracted contest.

Nine territories remained on the map of the continental United States. These were dependent areas in thrall to the federal legislature as to when and in what geographic shape they would be considered for admission to the Union "on an equal footing with the original States in all respects whatever." During most of the 1880s the two parties were equal or nearly so in their number of seats in the Senate, and each party sought a strategy that would enhance its position. The old concept of paired admissions (so prominent in prewar North-South contentions) was revived in argument and tactics. Thus when the Republicans offered an "omnibus bill" to admit four new states, North Dakota, South Dakota, Montana, and Washington, the Democrats countered by offering to support Montana and Washington but substituted New Mexico and a single-state Dakota (they expected New Mexico to be Democratic and hoped to build a majority in Montana and Washington). Much of the debate on this and earlier related bills focused on the division of Dakota Territory, a partition avidly sought by southern Dakota leaders after they had lost the territorial capital to Bismarck and feared being closed out of a whole set of state offices. It was generally understood that Dakota was strongly Republican, and thus to admit two states from that area would, as a senator from South Carolina complained, "settle, perhaps, for some time to come, the question of political supremacy in this body." His fears were well founded. After complex maneuvering in the House as well as in the Senate, the Republican omnibus version was passed, and in the next Congress a Republican-dominated Senate admitted Wyoming and Idaho, further adding to their strength (a margin of fifty-one to thirty-seven in 1891). Democratic Utah was admitted in 1896, but the Republican leadership held off New Mexico and Arizona until 1912, meanwhile admitting Republican Oklahoma.

The effects of this timing and shaping of a suddenly enlarged federal union—the addition of six states in less than nine months—obviously ramified far beyond those large areas directly affected in the West, as our reference to party strategies implies. Just what those effects may have been cannot be exactly measured, but political scientists Charles Stewart and Barry Weingast cogently argue that the Republican party's success in "stacking the Senate"—that locus of fixed territorial power in the federal structure—"played a key role in the evolution of the New American State and the particular American form of industrial capitalism." Even though the Republicans had no strong, consistent electoral majority (for twenty years after 1876 the Democrats more often controlled the House), they were able to dominate court appointments and legislation relating to monetary politics, tariffs, railroad regulation, and other economic issues so as to support their desire for a nation of capitalist enterprise favoring big business with limited governmental regulation. In the aftermath of the severe depression of 1893 they successfully fended off powerful populist uprisings and in the new century defused some of the basis of those protests by carefully expanding the role of federal regulatory power under the "progressivism" of the New Nationalism.

In the other wing of Congress population prevails over territory (the 1900 census gave Nevada one representative, New York thirty-seven), members are elected every two years and patterns of party power are more unstable and tend to reflect more directly the interests—especially economic interests—of local congressional districts. Therefore to assess voting alignments in the House of Representatives, Bensel correlated congressional districts with urban trade areas to establish an appropriate geographical framework (and one that changes moderately in pattern era by era as political economies change). Even though he continues to use the terms "sectional" and "sectionalism," his geopolitical analysis offers a much more refined regional assessment than common simplicities of North-South-West and political mapping by blocs of states (which latter may be appropriate for the Senate). The result of his examination of a selection of key issues over a century of time (1880–1980) was a display of an "extraordinary stable" pattern of sectional alignments that pits the Northeast and Upper Midwest (with varying extensions in Mountain and Pacific states) against the South and Southwest: "the ebb and flow of political conflict across the American nation has almost always produced the same basic geographical pattern" and that constitutes "the most massive and complex fact in American politics and history," a geopolitical feature that defines the structural imperatives" of the American federal system.

Patterns of course do not by themselves explain things, and Bensel goes on to note that this "consistent spatial form of sectional stress in history belies the complexity of its influence on the evolution of American political institutions, the growth of the state, the development of party competition, and the emergence of national ideological-belief systems." These particular topics are largely beyond our purview, but the existence of that strikingly stable spatial form in this historical geographical view of important operations of the federal system points us toward the need to look further at American regions and regionalism as patterns that both underlie and transcend such political and economic topics.

A SET OF REGIONS

Division of the United States into groups of states sharing important characteristics was as old as the federation. New England, Middle States, and Southern States routinely appear in early geographies, census listings, and common reference. Expansion soon added a West to this standard set, then California and Oregon a distant Pacific pair, but as the full continental expanse began to be filled the need for revision became increasingly apparent. The Bureau of the Census was recurrently faced with this geographic problem. For several decades it featured a gross threefold Atlantic-Interior (or Central)-Western set, further broken down into North and South divisions of the first two. In 1910 it reordered this scheme into a North-South-West framework, subdivided into nine divisions, and this pattern has remained largely unchanged ever since (a united North Central or Middle West region was finally recognized in 1940) (fig. 68). As the primary source of geographic data for businessmen, scholars, journalists, and publicists this official practice must have had wide currency, and when we find that most school geographies of the time made use of generally similar groupings we may assume that some such set of sections-divisions-regions (the terms were used more or less interchangeably) was commonly understood as a convenient way of thinking about the internal structure of the United States.

Pondering such problems of division in response to an 1896 invitation to contribute to a set of essays on American sections for the *Atlantic Monthly*, Frederick Jackson Turner suggested to the editor: "Perhaps a more scientific method would be to ignore state lines. My work in American history is based on natural physiographic divisions as outlined by Powell . . . I find it revolutionizes the study." He was referring to John Wesley Powell's new *Physiography of the United States*, which included a large map covering sixteen regions. Powell's map was a landmark (published as the first monograph of the National Geographic Society of Washington, founded in 1888), but the more influential figure in the field was William Morris Davis, professor of physical geography at Harvard, famous for his theoretical work on landforms and a leader in promoting a broader view of a new scientific geography and fostering formal study of it at all levels (fig. 69).

As teachers and textbook authors, chairmen of new departments (the first graduate level program, in 1903, was one of many innovations at the University of

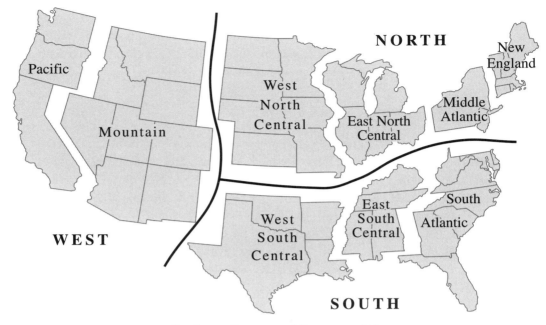

68. Census Sections and Divisions, 1910.

Chicago), and organizers of professional associations, Davis and his students shaped the new field. They made enduring contributions to physical geography, but in human geography the results tended to be simplistic in analysis and limited in topic. As a specialist on landforms and an evolutionist who viewed geography as a study of organic responses to inorganic controls, Davis logically regarded physical provinces and subregions as the essential template for understanding regional patterns of population, economic activities, and commercial cities ("the individual State is still a unit for the politician and the lawyer, but it is a fraction for the geographer and often a very improper fraction"); yet reasoning about human "responses" or "adjustments" to physical "controls" or "influences" was inherently vague and superficial, reflecting the failure of a geography emergent from geology to establish effective relations with the new social sciences and history.

A different approach was developing at the Wharton School, where the economist Emory R. Johnson began offering courses in geography in the 1890s and was soon joined by an energetic young J. Russell Smith. Smith was well versed in physical geography but focused on individual industries and commerce, on "the 'whys' and 'hows' of location, production, marketing, competition, and all other human and natural aspects which are necessary for an understanding of American industrial society" (he also taught and wrote books on industrial management). Smith was working toward a comprehensive view of North America as a set of

69. Physical Divisions.

As presented by William Morris Davis in his overview of the United States in Mill's *International Geography,* 1915.

"human use regions" (and, as an ardent conservationist, with increasing attention to human *misuse*), in which physical conditions were fundamental but use was also shaped by economic systems, technology, and cultural values. Smith's influence, however, awaited publication of his major books on industrial and commercial geography (1913) and regional geography (1925), and even though these were much more substantial studies than Davisian human geography, they remained limited in focus, even as economic geography.

The new geography, like the old, had the virtue of according the same formal attention to all parts of the country, and it provided ever-richer descriptions of selected features region by region, industry by industry, but offered little illumination of how the United States functioned as a complex of areal systems (no geography of the day helped the Federal Reserve define urban trade areas or banking hierarchies because most geographers would not have considered such topics as part of their field). Thus a new geography made its way into school and university curricula, but geographers had little influence in shaping a better public sense of regional structure and regional systems within the American nation.

Frederick Jackson Turner had a broader sense of geography than the geographers of his time. In 1892, before the appearance of Powell's map, he had declared "the need for a thorough study of the physiographic basis of our history . . . to see how these physical differences correspond to social and economic differences among the people who inhabit" these regions. The critical difference from Davis and other geographers (and especially Albert P. Brigham and Ellen Churchill Semple, who each wrote a popular book on the influences of geography on American history) was Turner's understanding of history as a "comparative and genetic study" of events and processes affecting all spheres of human activities with reference to specific peoples rather than some kind of inferred response to environment. A keen student of census maps and other distributional data (and creative in thinking of new kinds—"One might ascertain how business houses in the great centres divided up the 'territory' of their commercial agents"), Turner early saw, as he later phrased it, that "there is and always has been a sectional geography in America based fundamentally upon geographic regions. There is a geography of political habit, a geography of opinion, of material interests, of racial stocks, of physical fitness, of social traits, of literature, of the distribution of men of ability, even of religious denominations." (His mention of "men of ability" seems a direct reference to Henry Cabot Lodge's 1891 analysis of the more than 14,000 persons in the *Encyclopedia of American Biography*, which declared that while the South was strong in statesmen and soldiers, "almost all the literature, art, science, business, philanthropy, and music; almost all the physicians, educators, inventors, engineers, architects, and actors were produced by the Middle and New England States.") There, in effect, was a call for a kind of geography—cultural geography—that American geographers had yet to recognize.

In an early paper on the nature of his field, Turner emphasized that *each age writes the history of the past anew with reference to the conditions uppermost in its own time.* Viewing his country when the completion of conquest and of pioneer colonization were conditions uppermost in many thoughtful minds, he declared that it was time for a new "connected and unified account of the progress of civilization across this continent," and in 1893, in the address and essay that made him famous, Turner offered a prospectus of how American history must be written anew. We have already offered a brief assessment of his "frontier thesis" that "the existence of an area of free land, its continuous recession, and the advance of American settlement westward, explain American development" (*Continental America*, 258–64); our focus now is on his corollary that "the true point of view in the history of this nation is not the Atlantic Coast, it is the Great West."

Turner always emphasized that his West was more a matter of process than place, "a form of society, rather than an area," but his conflation of the West and the frontier, and thus of a succession of Wests as the frontier advanced across the continent, was not the full story. For the first Great West was the inland west, beyond the Appalachians, where pioneers of a new nation moved essentially unrestrained upon a vast, rich region of "free land," and thus it was the Old Northwest, drawing especially upon the Middle Atlantic states (the most "typically American" of colonial source regions) that produced the first full florescence of those "striking characteristics" that Turner's eloquence and influence were to make emblematic of the fully *American* character: "That coarseness and strength combined with acuteness and inquisitiveness; that practical, inventive turn of mind, quick to find expedients; that masterful grasp of material things, lacking in the artistic but powerful to effect great ends; that restless nervous energy; that dominant individualism, working for good and for evil, and withal that buoyancy and exuberance which comes with freedom—these are the traits of the frontier." The impact of Turner was, of course, the result of timing and context as well as content: during a formative time in his profession, he set forth a radically new way of looking at American history; at a major transitional period in American development ("and now, four centuries from the discovery of America, at the end of a hundred years of life under the Constitution, the frontier has gone, and with its going has closed the first period of American history") he was proposing a new way of understanding what had taken place; at a moment charged with a new American sense of achievement and stature among the nations, Turner, imbued with "Darwinian metaphors of evolution and organism," had "placed the American West at center stage in world history."

Thus as the United States entered the new century this young Wisconsin historian became the most influential spokesman about the shaping of America. He was applying a geographical perspective to one hundred years of American history, and now, one hundred years after his challenging thesis, we need to assess just how his West did at that time fit into the regional structure of the nation. Having provided our own geographical perspective on the shaping of the several distinct regions of the West and South—of American domains—we need to look closer at the special character of the North and East, and especially of the American Core at this critical stage of structural development.

PATTERNS OF POWER

A general outline of that generic core region may be readily inferred from several of the major patterns we have already treated, such as the manufacturing belt, trunkline territory and express-train service, large urban centers, and major immigrant destinations. All those imprints reveal that while still firmly anchored upon its original Atlantic seaboard nucleus this powerful complex had been extended beyond its midcentury western salients at Buffalo and Pittsburgh to form a great parallelogram now cornered on Milwaukee and St. Louis, with New York City–Chicago as its obvious main axis. Some of the defining characteristics of a core were well expressed in these patterns: *intensity*—a zone of concentration featuring the greatest density of population and industries, diversity of activities, and complexity of organizations; *focality*—the focus of circulation, magnet of selective migration drawing youth and talent from the provinces; *authority*—the greatest seats of power and influence. This last, however, includes a number of features less easily defined and depicted.

"Societies are constituted of multiple overlapping and intersecting sociospatial networks of power," asserts Michael Mann in the opening page of his extensive historical exploration of the topic. We may well take his four categories of power—ideological, economic, military, political—and put them to our own brief use (in different sequence). As noted in our treatment of the structure of the United States at midcentury, the *military* establishment was firmly seated in the core, not only in the obvious case of Washington as the command center and West Point and Annapolis as leadership training centers but in the array of arsenals and shipyards, factories and supply sources, and a heavy dependence on immigrants for annual intakes of new troops. With the century-long internal conquest completed and no bordering enemies there was now no frontier field of action (until the flare-up of the Spanish-American War and its distant and nonthreatening legacies), and thus the military was a realm of power peculiarly unimportant in this huge nation (labor strikes and other perceived threats to civic order were handled by local police or state militias—except in the great Pullman strike of 1894, when federal troops were sent, ostensibly to ensure movement of interstate mail trains).

Political power in the United States is of course both national and federal—central and dispersed—and, as we have noted, is further profoundly shaped by deep-rooted regional alignments. The core area contains the formal seat of the central power (Washington being included in the core only because of that role) and, equally important, "Wall Street," the seat of great influences upon the exercise of power by elected and appointed officials. Furthermore, the high density of population in the core gave it nearly half of the seats in the House of Representatives (169 of 357 in 1901, and during this period a huge majority of these members from core districts were Republicans).

As the home of virtually all the most powerful corporations, banks and other financial institutions, and stock and commodity markets and the base of all national communications networks, the *economic* and decision-making power of the core was so obvious—and in outlying domains so notorious—as to need no elaboration at this point.

Mann treats ideological power on two levels: "transcendent" and "immanent." The first refers to that which unites a large body of people in believing in their own special character and purpose as part of some larger cause and destiny. Nationalism has been the most obvious exhibit of such a thing in the modern world. American nationalism was grounded on a set of ideals rather than on ethnicity, a civic philosophy set forth in the Declaration of Independence and the Constitution rather than proclaiming a common ancestry and homeland. In the aftermath of secession and civil war (between rival nationalisms) there had been a gradual ameliorative shift in emphasis from "the Union," the ideal relentlessly asserted by the North, to "the Nation," and "as American society became simultaneously more integrated economically and more diverse culturally" there was a determined effort "to create a more abstract form of national unity that would appeal to various regions and groups." There was a great upwelling of emphasis at the end of the century on the flag, national anthem, routine recitation of the pledge of allegiance in schools, and the like (all powerfully reinforced by the Spanish-American War).

A parallel effort to proclaim the United States officially as a "Christian Nation" found outspoken support at all levels, though certainly not from all groups. No such legislation was enacted, but even so, as Bryce observed, "Christianity is in fact understood to be . . . the national religion," and its Protestant supporters achieved partial victories in temperance and other social legislation. "Christianity" in such terms was a vague nondoctrinal concept proclaimed by increasingly liberal Protestant leaders who fully aligned themselves with the optimistic, materialistic, expansive, "progressive" destiny of the nation. Such abstract and diffuse forms of power did not radiate from a single great center. It was spread and sustained from pulpits, lecterns, classrooms, patriotic organizations, historical societies, newspapers, magazines, books, and other media, but of course the most influential of these were in the big cities and institutions of the core. So, too, most of the major places becoming consecrated as national shrines, such as Plymouth Rock, Bunker Hill, Valley Forge, and Independence Hall, were within that frame (but Mt. Vernon and Monticello were not).

It was also apparent, however, that the formal capital had taken on more symbolic as well as practical power. The now world-famous capitol had been joined by other imposing structures, such as the Library of Congress, National Museum, State, Army, and Navy Building, and, most impressive of all, the purely symbolic Washington Monument, completed in 1884. And in a great flurry of construction in the new century, the federal government, after a long interlude of eclecticism, reestablished a national style. Bates Lowry credits the influence of the great White City, created as a stage for the Chicago World's Fair (officially the World's Columbian Exposition) of 1893, which was, in effect, "a full-scale, three-dimensional realization of the kind of city envisioned by L'Enfant for Washington. . . . The force of the idea and the emotional impact of the appearance of these [mostly impermanent] buildings was so strong that classical architecture [that is, a Beaux

Arts extension of that tradition] as the correct symbolic expression of the political values of the nation once again became dominant in the minds of its citizens and a particular group of its architects."

Such things were not simply inevitable accretions at this particular place in a growing nation. In 1869–70 various resolutions, petitions, and memorials to Congress from several Midwestern states had sought to halt further expenditures in the District of Columbia pending serious consideration of removing the capital to the Mississippi Valley, "from the circumference to the center, from the money chests of the East to the millions [of people] of the West," as a St. Louis newspaper put it when reporting on a convention in that city, the principal seat of such agitations. The movement never gathered much cohesion and strength and there was never any likelihood of such a radical shift, yet it was an expression of important regional tensions and the concept was not absurd but could be seen as a logical response in a democratic republic to the enormous shifts in the human geography of the country since the selection of that original compromise site.

"Immanent" refers to a different scale, to that which empowers a social group with a special sense of position and purpose: leadership groups with important national impact, "elites" of particular realms. A large national society requires a multitude of such elites to coordinate the activities of its many national systems. The most powerful group in America comprised the heads of its great corporations and associated capitalist institutions, but taken as a whole these decision makers were a factionalized, competitive, unstable set. Less decisive but rather more cohesive were those smaller bodies that asserted a diffuse social power by the prestige accorded them in "setting the standards" for the upper levels of "society." Such groups were found in every large community; they were the "establishment"—in claim, if not always in general recognition and effect. Furthermore, they were, viewed broadly, a generic type, similar from place to place because they were imitative, emulative of the forms and activities of the social leadership in what were regarded in such circles as the most prestigious places. As Beatrice Webb concluded from her meetings with civic leaders during her tour across the country in 1898 (recorded while resting in a mountain "villa" near Denver): "there was a restless admiration for Eastern America, an uneasy consciousness of their inferiority to New York, Boston, or Philadelphia, a dread of the ridicule of the Eastern newspapers, a desire that their children should have the advantage of an 'Eastern' education."

Those three cities had long been recognized as the most influential in this realm of national life. Although they varied significantly in particular character and status, their social leadership all exhibited that special defining combination of overt displays of wealth and taste, assertions of superiority and exclusiveness, and dedication to philanthropic causes, as exhibited in the grandeur and richness of their houses, furnishings, and fashions; in their dinners, balls, and expensive recreations; in their support of hospitals and asylums, libraries and museums, theaters, galleries and orchestras, schools and colleges, churches and benevolent agencies. Examined closely such groups were never really cohesive or exclusive (least of all in volatile, entrepreneurial New York), their "power" never really measurable, but their existence and importance had to be acknowledged, even by ardent republican critics. However, as Frederic Cople Jaher cautions in his monumental study of this phenomenon, "emulation is not absorption," and this "unification of elite life-styles that accompanied the development of a national economy" did not result in an integrated "national upper class" branching through the urban hierarchy. Local sovereignty prevailed in the selection of agencies and institutions to sponsor and in the kind of funding and direction conferred. And despite similarities across the nation, there were exceptions and variations in such emulation: as in Charleston, absorbed in its own past and patriarchy; New Orleans with its distinctive creole character; and San Francisco, where Beatrice Webb found "none of that extreme sensitiveness of Eastern opinion. . . . It seems isolated and unconcerned with any other part of America. It is out and away the most cosmopolitan city I have yet come across"—and, she concluded, the most anarchic.

And yet there was more than a semblance of hierarchy in the corollary of clusterings of talented professionals associated with all those institutions in some degree sustained by those urban establishments. As Peter Dobkin Hall put it:

> What the railroad and the telegraph did for the economies of American localities, the rise of national universities and professional associations did for its intellectual life, its occupational structure, and its world view. Just as the depot and the telegraph office had . . . become outposts of national economic coordination in nearly every American town and city, so the school, the doctor's office, the lawyers' chambers, the church, and the library became the recruiting stations and transmitters of national intellectual and professional life.

The most powerful and prestigious of those institutions were clustered in or near a few metropolitan centers. We do not as yet have maps of the networks and ranks of these various influential institutions, but there is a good deal of evidence and common inference about some. It seems clear, for example, that New England still reigned supreme in education. Jaher found that "beginning in the 1880s prominent citizens of Los Angeles, Philadelphia, New York, Cleveland, Pittsburgh, San Francisco [contrary to Beatrice Webb], Chicago, and other places markedly preferred to send their children to exclusive New England preparatory schools, . . . and to Yale, Harvard, and Princeton rather than to local academies and colleges."

Not only was "the role of the college as custodian of culture" and agent in the validation of social status becoming much stronger, by 1900 it was clear that the pull of New England was powered by professional prestige as well. Harvard had transformed itself from a club for the provincial elite into a great university in the modern sense, and Yale was not far behind. Many other colleges in the East, including several for women, were making analogous changes in character, as were some of the older universities, such as Columbia (New York City) and Pennsylvania (Philadelphia). There were also newer foundations, most notably Cornell at Ithaca (1868) and Johns Hopkins in Baltimore (1876), the latter quickly becoming "the southernmost university of wide resort" (in 1901 half of its advanced students were from Southern states). In general wealthy benefactors from the urban industrial world became more important than denominational and other traditional support.

The other major development in higher education was the rise of the great state universities in the Middle West, with Michigan and Wisconsin in the lead. The national government also played a role through the Morrill Act (initiated by the Republican Congress in the residual North of 1862), which allocated federal lands to each state (in proportion to their congressional representation) to provide funds in support of at least one college specializing in "such branches of learning as are related to agriculture and the mechanic arts . . . in order to promote the liberal and practical education of the industrial classes." Some states endowed a wholly new or separate college (such as Michigan State), others added one to an existing state university (as in Wisconsin) or, in the East, as a state affiliate of a private university (as at Cornell; and Massachusetts allocated one-third of its share to M.I.T.). Often popularly referred to as "cow colleges," the best of these Morrill-related institutions were becoming important scientific research centers. This older West, like the East, had long had a great number of denominational and other private colleges, a few of high quality, and the addition of the new University of Chicago (1892, munificently subsidized by John D. Rockefeller), surpassing all others in the resources and talent applied to its planning, building, and staffing, anchored this corner of the American core with an institution of instant national prominence. Washington University, founded "with Harvard firmly in mind" under Yankee leadership in St. Louis in 1853 and now on a handsome new campus, provided solid quality at the southwest corner.

In comparison with prestigious centers in the East these Midwestern universities were more regional than national in their lure, but taken together these seats of major institutions spaced across the core from the Atlantic to the Mississippi set the standards of higher education in America and, as George W. Pierson has detailed, would long exert an attraction and an influence upon American leadership in virtually all walks of life far out of proportion to their size (with Harvard far in the lead in many professions). The University of California at Berkeley and recently founded and richly endowed Stanford at nearby Palo Alto were the only ones at all comparable in quality or promise at the time—further exhibits of California's wealth and leadership in the Far West. (The idea of federal support for a great University of the United States in Washington as a national research and advanced teaching center was being proposed in Congress once again—it had been debated at the time of the Smithsonian bequest in the 1840s—but fear of centralization, government interference, and the resolute opposition of the president of Harvard ensured against any action.)

"The United States is the only great country in the world which has no capital," said James Bryce, who went on to assess and dismiss the five cities (Washington, New York, Chicago, Philadelphia, Boston) that might have some claim for consideration. But of course he was measuring by the European standard (and in line with the common definition of a primary center in our concept of geographical morphology):

> By a Capital I mean a city which is not only the seat of political government, but is also by the size, wealth, and character of its population the head and centre of the country, a leading seat of commerce and industry, a reservoir of financial resources, the favored residence of the great and powerful, the spot in which the chiefs of the learned professions are to be found, where the most potent and widely read journals are published, whither men of literary and scientific capacity are drawn.

Once we begin to think in terms of *sociospatial* power we could respond by saying that the United States had in fact several capitals—and be reminded of Mann's caution that "societies are much *messier* than our theories of them" (and we have made only the simplest use of his own scheme).

In the course of his review Bryce declared Chicago to be "perhaps the typically American place in America." Such an assessment directs attention to a further item in the generic concept of a core: that such an area is *representative* of the nation, best displaying the most characteristic features of the society in question. Bryce was not original in asserting such an emblematic status for Chicago; as early as 1874 a local literary periodical claimed that the city combined "the concentrated essence of Americanism," and similar comments by locals and visitors alike were common by the new century. But such a conclusion was far from obvious and was open to vigorous challenge—even derision. For again, the United States was not a typical example of these generic features. Its core area extended across a thousand miles, on an axis linking New York City and Chicago, binding two major, contrasting—and in important ways contending—cities and regions.

By 1900 Chicago was unrivaled as the Second City in almost every quantitative and functional measure of the national system. Its claim to priority in more symbolic terms was grounded upon its location, hinterland, and prospects as well as more specific internal features. It was the undisputed Central City of the American

Heartland, gathering point of half a continent, service center for 30 million people, growth pole of the new century. The city itself was a world wonder of phenomenal growth (and regrowth—after the Great Fire of 1871), and it was now in the midst of an era of cultural creativity. Its architects were designing new functional forms on a new scale, its huge department stores and mail-order houses were famous agents of American consumerism, its urban planners and reformers were leading theorists and practitioners in their attention to social problems, its journalists and writers were defining an American vernacular (and its big carto-graphic companies had popularized a new kind of "vernacular" map: relatively crude but simple, functional, versatile, cheap to produce and easy to revise—a handy tool instead of an artistic science). These and related features welling up during "a time of extraordinary civic confidence" had sufficient impact to allow later commentators to speak of "the Chicagoization of America."

But much of the acclaim for Chicago was not so much in terms of the city as in the region it represented: the Middle West, and especially the richest part, the Corn Belt, the heart of the Heartland. Here the transformation of "an immense wilderness into a fruited plain" (to use Timothy Dwight's phrase and the title of Gordon G. Whitney's fine account of it), thickly dotted with comfortable farm-steads, small towns, county seats, and regional trade centers, proclaimed "the sanctity of the agricultural way of life and the virtue of life in the towns." As Andrew Cayton and Peter Onuf note: "at the beginning of the twentieth century a great many people continued to insist that the typical American was the white, middle-class, Republican businessman in a small town in the Midwest" (fig. 70). Here, said Frederick Jackson Turner, was the true "Center of the Republic."

New York City was a famously great center but was surely not the typically American place. Its jagged skyline—"a cluster of mountains, with their bright peaks glistening in the sun far above the dark shadows of the valleys in which the streams of business flow"—was spectacular, and the whole scale and power and energy of the place bespoke of much that Americans took pride in and foreigners considered definitive of national characteristics. It was the quintessential urban place, and if not the most admired it was nevertheless "the most visited place in the country." It contained many tourist shrines, such as the Statue of Liberty, the Brooklyn Bridge, Wall Street, Central Park, and Grant's Tomb, but the great "crowd-center" was now Times Square (so named with the rise of the Times Building in 1904), as "Mid-Manhattan became a sort of permanent World's Fair, with particular streets reserved for the display and sale of clothing, housewares, jewelry, appliances, automobiles, books—as well as the music, arts, fashions, and theatrics of commercial culture."

But New York also represented a lot that Americans were uneasy about and certainly did not want to think of as typical—it had long been the most reviled

70. Main Street of Middle America.

Crawfordsville, Indiana, was centered in an early Corn Belt county forty-seven miles northwest of Indianapolis. On the northern margins of Upland Southern colonization, it was soon in the path of westward-moving Midlanders and attracted the common sprinkling of Yankee business, church, and civic leaders, who founded Wabash College as an enduring emblem. By 1915 this county seat of 10,000, with these solid business blocks facing the broad well-paved street and streetcar line leading from the Civil War monument at the courthouse corner to embowered residential areas, was a good display of the scale and character of community undergirding all those Middle Western virtues being extolled at the time. (Courtesy Indiana Historical Society, postcard col. C7608)

place in the United States. At one level it was too heterogeneous and squalid, full of "insoluble clots" of "aliens" in congested, filthy, crime-ridden slums, at another, too cosmopolitan and urbane. It could not be fully American because it was so richly international, a world city in many respects, a great conduit of European influences, whereas, in the eyes of inland critics, the Middle West, "by its geographical position, escapes the temptation to look constantly across the water and model itself on Old-World . . . patterns. Screened in a measure from the sapping seductiveness of foreign example, it seems destined to be the most 'American' part of our country." As Thomas Bender has emphasized, New York City displayed a commitment to a public culture that embraced diversity and conflict, a politics of difference rather than the consensus and conformity of preferred Middle America models. New York, too, had a rural hinterland, some portions of which, such as the best parts of Upstate, were highly productive and attractive, but that had nothing to do with its image (the idealized New England village loosely clustered around its church and green now seemed a world apart in time and space). If pressed to think about its regional hinterland, visions of stone-bound hill farms drained of youth and talent ("fished out communities") and narrow valleys crammed with mill towns, steel plants, mining camps, and dangerously volatile foreign workers would likely appear. But then Chicago, too, was a great industrial center full of immigrants and "a cauldron of class conflict."

The fact was, of course, that the American core area included both New York City and Chicago and everything in between (fig. 71). All of it was representative in some way, no one part of it was typical. Claims of what was most "typically American" in terms of specific cities, types of towns, or regions were actually assertions of what Americans—or, more accurately, particular sets of Americans—*wanted* to believe about themselves and their country. They were sketches of *model* communities, mythologies about the patterns of American development.

They were also politically charged programs, weapons in a national contest for transcendent ideological power. For in this as in so much else there was a sense of anxiety and urgency. That new sense of "maturity" and "self-consciousness as a nation" that Woodrow Wilson reported, that completion of "the first period of American history" defined by Frederick Jackson Turner, was accompanied by a new

71. Core and Contention.

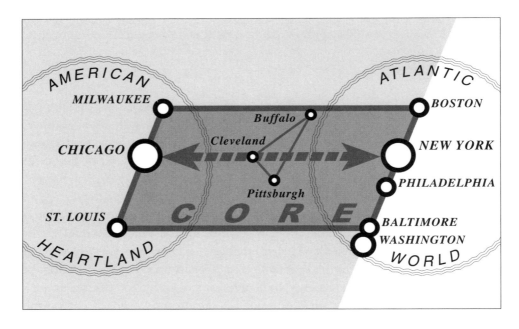

portentous stage in the geographical shaping of America. There would of course continue to be movement and development, but it now seemed likely to take place within a more fixed set of regions. "A new sectionalism began to show itself," said Wilson in 1902, and he clearly recognized the dominant section: "from the Atlantic seaboard to the Mississippi and the great lakes there stretched, north of Mason and Dixon's line, a region substantially homogeneous in all the larger interests of trade and industry, not unlike European countries in the development of its resources and the complex diversification of its life." But he gave it no name, and it wasn't easy to do so. The crude simplicities of the cardinal directions could not serve: if this was obviously a North distinct from the South, it was not simply an East distinct from the West, for the heart of the Midwest was firmly bound into it. However homogeneous it might be in important ways, this powerful section contained self-consciously discrete parts, a contentious regionalism within the frame of the national core, a struggle over what should be the model for America in the new century.

As was explicit in his essays and letters, Turner's frontier thesis was a revolt against the East, against a history establishment that viewed America as a youthful extension from European civilization—as more a continuation than an invention. More generally, Turner touched a chord of regional resentment of what was regarded as a cosmopolitan and condescending East that looked upon the West (that is to say, primarily the Midwest) as a country province open to its leadership and exploitation. Less consciously, Turner "provided the scholarly and theoretical basis for the growing celebration of the individualistic, democratic, enterprising middle class commercial society," assuring his fellow Midwesterners that not only had they created "a prosperous and orderly civilization" in their own region, "they had created the United States in their own image."

However, as Cayton and Onuf go on to say, Turner did this "at precisely the moment" when all this "was in fact rapidly fading in power." Fading in power, indeed, but not in all kinds of power equally. Wall Street and massive urban and industrial developments of a pluralistic, cosmopolitan, corporate capitalistic society emerging as a great power on the world stage were surely apparent—and the Middle West was heavily involved in it—yet Main Street of Middle America remained a powerful image and ideal, a touted model of domesticity and community, of family life and republican values, buttressing an American exceptionalism and isolationism well into the new century. This core area, this gross geographic imbalance in national patterns of power, together with this complicating contentious feature internal to that core, would prove to be an extraordinarily stable and important structural pattern in the continuous shaping of America.

PART FOUR
SPHERES: AMERICAN INFLUENCE
AND OUTREACH

*Twenty years ago the expression "world power" was unknown in
most languages; to-day it is a political commonplace, bandied about
in wide discussion. . . . The term is . . . not scientifically exact; for
each of the so-called world powers has spheres in which its interests
are vitally important, and others in which they are comparatively
small, if not inferior to those of less powerful states.*

Archibald Cary Coolidge, 1908

Prologue

During most of this time the United States must have seemed to most of its people a world in itself—a continental expanse set apart by broad oceans on either side, with ample room for the spread of settlement, accommodation of population growth, and development of resources. And in important ways it was always larger than its formal bounds, for by its mere presence—and often by design—it exerted a strong influence upon neighboring peoples and polities, generating critical problems of response in those adjacent lands. That it would intervene in foreign states to build and control a great canal to augment and ensure its transcontinental systems and security was entirely characteristic of its dominant and domineering role in North America.

At the opening of the twentieth century, partly by its own precipitous expansion and partly by geopolitical changes utterly beyond its control, the United States suddenly found itself in a much larger—and more dangerous—world. Although proud of its well-earned status as a World Power, its continental history had left the United States ill-prepared for and uncertain of the meaning of its new role in truly global affairs. It had boldly extended its sphere of imperial interests across the Pacific, while it had seemed indifferent to geopolitical developments across the Atlantic. It would soon be faced with assessing where the spheres of vital American interests lay.

1. Canada and Continentalism

While the United States, following its great internal convulsion, was engrossed in reconstructing and expanding the federation, binding its Atlantic and Pacific

coasts together, filling in its great Wests, consolidating its industrial and metropolitan power, and asserting a new sense of national accomplishment and maturity
on a transcontinental scale, its neighbor to the north was doing essentially the
same thing—albeit somewhat later in time, much lesser in content, and rather
more uncertain in result. Such parallelism was more than simply analogous in
general with developments in its powerful neighbor to the south, it was in important ways responsive, in part defensive, in part imitative—yet, so its leaders
insisted, it was also distinctly Canadian.

The Dominion of Canada was formed in 1867 to give some greater coherence
and degree of independence to British colonies in North America and to overcome
its chronic internal geopolitical confrontation between French and English in the
Laurentian Canadas (see *Continental America*, 533–46). The initial formation
joined only Nova Scotia and New Brunswick with the two Canadas (Quebec and
Ontario), but the architects of confederation were working on a much larger design
and immediately set out to lure other colonies and take over the vast Hudson's Bay
Company lands in the West. Because it was all British territory political negotiations allowed rapid progress, but not always quite as the Canadian leadership
desired. On the Atlantic side, Newfoundland preferred to continue as a great
fishing station under London rather than join a continental system. In spite of
widespread reluctance ("our individuality—our identity as a people—will be forever sunk and lost in the abysmal 'Dominion of Canada'") a debt-ridden Prince
Edward Island was pressured and induced to join in 1873 by promises of large
subsidies (especially to buy out absentee landlords, a long-standing local vexation)
and regular ferry service with the mainland. On the Pacific side, the existing
colony of British Columbia was obviously more important to any transcontinental
design than the Confederation was to it. Alternatives were widely discussed locally, with many of its considerable number of Americans preferring annexation
and political regularization of existing commercial relations with San Francisco
over impractical links with Ottawa. But British allegiance prevailed and the offer of
subsidies together with the promise of a transcontinental railway brought this
large, thinly populated province into the system in 1871.

Accession of the former territories of the Hudson's Bay Company made the
Canadians proprietors of half a continent, and it transformed Canada "from a
federation of equal provinces into a veritable empire, with a vast domain of subordinate colonial territory." In routine imperial manner the central government
appointed a lieutenant-governor and dispatched surveyors to Assiniboia to begin
parceling the public domain. But the métis of Red River, alarmed and resentful at
being "bought like the buffalo," refused the governor entry, seized Fort Garry, led
the formation of a provisional government, and pressured Ottawa into negotiation. The result was the creation in 1870 of a Province of Manitoba, initially a
small rectangle (half the size of New Brunswick) surrounding Red River Settle-

ment, with recognition of local land rights, of French as well as English in official use, and of dual Catholic and Protestant school systems. Thus this first new Canadian province "embodied the old rivalry and long co-existence of French and English in the Northwest"; at that time, the two peoples were about equal in number. Following this unexpected, reluctant recognition of a new province the remainder of this vast realm was organized as the North-West Territories under the direct supervision of Ottawa.

Thus in a span of four years the entire length of the borderland beyond the United States on the north became organized into a transcontinental federation. Yet so much of its extent was so remote and difficult of access, so thinly populated and little developed, and still considered to be so vulnerable to American expansion or attraction that the leaders of this young and fragile Dominion saw the need for extraordinary efforts to fill in and secure this enormous extension. "We must do, in one or two years, what had been done in the United States in fifty," said George Grant, accompanying Sanford Fleming on his "Ocean to Ocean" reconnaissance for a railroad route, and Sir John Alexander Macdonald, the first (and a subsequent) prime minister, sought tirelessly to do so by means of his National Policy of three interrelated parts: a transcontinental railroad, rapid settlement of the interior West, and tariffs to protect and nurture Canadian industry. Impelled by American example and pressure these persist as major themes in the shaping of Canada during this period, and we may well consider them in the form we have used for the United States: articulation, dominion, consolidation, and continentalism.

ARTICULATION

The vision of a "grand National Railway from the Atlantic to the Pacific" was about as old with reference to British North America as it was in the United States, but the Canadian context of 1870 was critically different. The length of new construction was a thousand miles greater (about 2,800 miles compared with the 1,800 of the Union Pacific–Central Pacific) because the existing railnet only reached a short distance above Ottawa, and, furthermore, the first thousand miles west from the Ottawa Valley was through an extremely difficult Precambrian granite and swamp-studded wilderness, a wasteland of little colonization potential. However, the Canadian project did not have to contend with geopolitical deadlock over routes and terminals. Montreal and Toronto interests could readily converge on this new westward axis, and it was commonly assumed that the Pacific terminus would be somewhere on the Strait of Georgia. The commitment to undertake such an enormous task was made only after the Americans had celebrated the completion of theirs.

The American example was analogous and influential in general objectives as well as practical accomplishments. This Pacific railway, too, was first of all to be a *national trunk line.* Not only was it initiated to lure and hold British Columbia, "until this great work is completed," said Macdonald, "our Dominion is little more than a 'geographical expression,'" and therefore it must be an all-Canadian route. The project in fact initially foundered politically on revelations that Macdonald's chosen Montreal financier had secretly collaborated with Americans to build the transcontinental south of Lake Superior from Sault Ste. Marie by way of St. Paul or Duluth en route to Winnipeg (and be subservient to the Northern Pacific). Recurrent entrepreneurial arguments that such a route was the only realistic way to avoid the fantastic expense of building across the sterile Canadian Shield were as recurrently declared to be politically unacceptable.

Second, it must be a *developmental line*, an essential agent in carrying settlers to the West, distributing them over the land, and hauling their produce to market. Third, it would become a great *intercontinental trafficway*, "the last link between Europe and Asia, it's the road that leads to the gold of Australia, the shawls of Cashmere, the diamonds of Golconda, the silks of China, the spices of Malabar and the Moluccas." (Pacific mail and steamship services were initiated shortly after completion, and one of the earliest eastbound transcontinental shipments was ten cars of tea.) And, finally, the completion of such a vast work would be a *national symbol* of character and accomplishment, giving Canada "an impetus that will make it a great and powerful country at no distant date," as the minister of Railways put it. The line itself would be a sinew for survival of a distinctly northern nation, a modern version of the Northwest Fur Company's great system reaching from the St. Lawrence to the Columbia, successfully fending off American encroachment.

Construction had barely gotten under way before being halted by political scandal and the 1873 depression and was not resumed until the formation of a new company in 1881, from which time it was carried forward with great vigor until the final spike was driven in the British Columbia mountains in November 1885 (regular service did not begin until some months later after much testing and rebuilding of the hastily constructed line). The original plan to arch northwestward from Manitoba through the parkland belt had been changed to a route directly west across the drier country, and the original Pacific terminus on Burrard Inlet was shifted westward a few miles from Port Moody to deeper water and a broader site, where a new plat "destined to be a great city" was therefore given a name "commensurate with its dignity and importance" (and indisputably British in its historic associations): Vancouver.

Sixteen years after the golden spike at Promontory Summit, the Canadians had emulated the Americans and achieved something their great southern neighbor never managed: a truly transcontinental railroad operated by a single company. A trip along the whole length of this iron band displayed four broad kinds of country (fig. 72): the first 300 miles from the docks of Montreal up the Ottawa Valley, then 1,000 miles across the Shield, 900 miles over the Plains to the base of the Rockies, and a final 600 winding miles through rugged British Columbia (no equivalent of a Sacramento Valley here) to mountain-girded Pacific shores. However (like an American journey starting west from Chicago), such a traverse scarcely touched the most important region: the Laurentian axis trending southwest from Montreal through Toronto and across the full length of the Ontario Peninsula. Here was the core of Canada, the seat of the power that had envisioned and created this trans-continental confederation and sought to manage its development.

72. Canada: Physical Regions and Political Units.

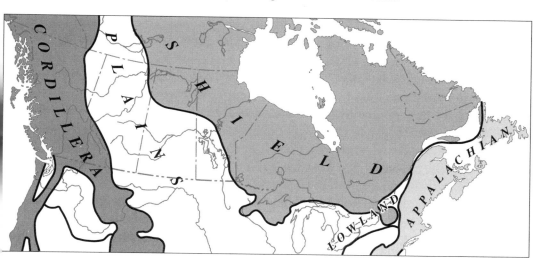

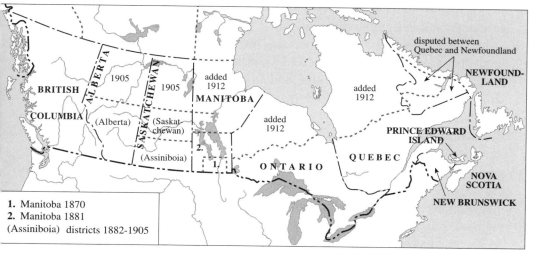

DOMINION

It was clearly the intention of these Montreal and Ontario interests to create an extension of "English Canada," that is, of an English-speaking British Protestant society—an Ontario West—and in important ways they did so, though on a scale and completeness short of their hopes.

A critical feature in this program (based on the example of the United States) was federal retention of public lands in the West "for the purposes of the Dominion," a policy sustained with respect to Manitoba (but not British Columbia, which—like Texas—was left in control of its own lands as part of the lure into confederation). A federal survey system of townships and sections (essentially identical with the American scheme) was applied, with half the sections available for homesteading and half for sale; some lands were retained by the Hudson's Bay Company (as part of the price paid for relinquishing Rupert's Land) and others would be allocated to the Canadian Pacific Railway and subsequent "colonization railroads." Concurrent was the need to extinguish Indian title to these lands (and a determination *not* to follow American examples). Treaties were to be concluded ahead of White settlement, Indian leaders were to choose the locations of their reserves, the size of which were to be commensurate with the number of families, and such lands were to be promptly surveyed and various farming or pastoral aids supplied. The Royal North West Mounted Police was created to suppress the notorious transboundary whiskey trade and ensure public order. Although Canadian policies were more equitable in intent and partly so in practice, the ultimate aim was similar—to prepare the Indians for cultural assimilation into the mainstream of Canadian society—and the immediate results less different than intended: little bloodshed, but scattered sets of marginalized, impoverished people, a status created more by the near extinction of the buffalo than directly by imperial confinement and settler expansion.

It was, of course, the initiation of this imperial program that had produced an immediate clash with the métis of Red River, and westward extension resulted in a recurrence fifteen years later on the Saskatchewan, whence many of these people and Indian associates had shifted in an attempt to prolong their way of life and establish a larger redoubt along the northern margins of the parklands. The first of these confrontations had brought about the creation of a dual-language Manitoba; the second resulted in a bloody defeat of the métis, the execution of their charismatic leader, and an end of any formal recognition of the West as a replication of the dual society of the St. Lawrence.

Ontarians had voiced strong opposition to "making Manitoba a New Quebec," but there was actually no attempt on the part of the Quebec leadership to do so in 1870 or thereafter. They were not interested in nation-building on a transcontinental scale. They had joined the Confederation to obtain autonomy and equality as a province, and they were concerned with consolidation of the one true nation of Canada, *La Patrie*, their deep-rooted homeland on the St. Lawrence. Their expansionism focused on colonizing every scrap of habitable land in their own North and building up their numbers in the English borderlands of the Eastern Townships and Ottawa Valley. Emigration to faraway Manitoba was opposed as a dispersal and diminution, worse than going to New England, which by now had many strong French communities. In time, they began to pay more attention to pleas for help from those French, mostly Catholic, officials who were trying to protect their position in Manitoba and extend the "civilizing mission" of French society on across the West (the métis, conscious of their special heritage and identity as the "New People" of the Northwest, had little reason to relate to Quebec). When the reality of these national dangers were confirmed in 1890 by Manitoba legislative moves to abrogate legal protections of the French language and schools, Quebec declared such actions to be "a declaration of war . . . against the French race" but chose to fight that battle at the highest political level in debates over the basic intention and true spirit of the Confederation, insisting that it must always confirm the "perfect equality of the two races before the law."

Thus in Canada as in the United States westward expansion had exacerbated the cultural differences and geopolitical tensions built into the original federation. As an Ontarian noted in 1874: "Manitoba has been to us on a small scale what Kansas was to the United States. It has been the battle-ground for our British and French elements with their respective religions, as Kansas was the battle-ground for Free Labour and Slavery." Whether the writer meant to imply that in each case one was right and the other wrong is not clear, but the French saw ample reason to receive such commentaries as such, with enduring meaning for the life and times of Confederation in Canada.

Given these disparate attitudes about migration, Ontarians were soon the largest element in the population of the West, augmented by a modest number of British immigrants, and "during the 1870s and 1880s the West was Canadianized." However, developments were much slower than expected. The long delay in completion of the Canadian Pacific, the competition of more accessible lands in Dakota, limitations in wheat varieties for these northern lands, the high costs of shipments, and the political crisis and military campaign against the métis all contributed to an embarrassing gap between expansionist rhetoric and Western reality. The province of Manitoba had been enlarged and three formal districts (Assiniboia, Saskatchewan, Alberta) marked off on the Prairies (see fig. 72), but after twenty years of promotion the 1891 census recorded only 250,000 in the region, mostly in Manitoba, with a thin line reaching west along the railroad to Regina, laid out as the new capital of North-West Territories. Furthermore, these new Westerners increasingly blamed Eastern indifference, incompetence, or imperialism for this retardation, and an emerging regional consciousness began to look for Western solutions, such as proposals for a railroad to Hudson Bay ("Churchill Harbour is only four hundred miles from the edge of the greatest wheat field in the world"), bypassing Ontario and the St. Lawrence in a reassertion of the Hudson's Bay Company's direct link with London (the wheat would go to Liverpool). On the Pacific Slope two-thirds of British Columbia's nearly 100,000 people were clustered in or near Victoria and Vancouver, and most of the remainder were Native Americans scattered widely over this huge province.

The great Depression of 1893 further dampened all development, and Canada neared the end of the century and thirty years of Confederation as a fragile structure, a vast outline of seven grossly unequal provinces and dependent territories tenuously stitched together along a railroad, with not quite 5 million people in total, meager in population and substance over most of its extent, and weakened in Dominion authority, for pressures from the provinces over a variety of social issues had led to new interpretations of constitutional allocations of power and undermined Macdonald's conception of a centralized federation engaged in nation-building on a transcontinental scale. Indeed, serious doubts about the future of this grand scheme were being voiced, and closer relationships with the United States—even some sort of union—were being discussed in some circles.

CONSOLIDATION

This bold but lean formative period was followed by a great surge of development, beginning with the general recovery of the world economy in the mid-1890s. The population of Canada increased by two-thirds in twenty years to 7.2 million in 1911. New resources were tapped in the once barren Shield, massive construction programs tripled the railway mileage and opened new areas, industrialization and urbanization proceeded apace. At the turn of the century the Anglo-Boer War gave a strong boost to the emotional ties of empire, and in 1914 a clearly more substantial and self-confident Canada stood ready to assert with pride its enhanced position in the worldwide Britannic family.

These years resulted in important new expansions and differentiations within the Confederation. The greatest transformation was the settlement of more than a million people on the Prairies and the creation therein of two large new provinces. The availability of quick-maturing, high-quality wheats, testing of more northerly lands, expansion of regional railroads, and drastic reductions in ocean export rates (and the filling in of attractive areas in the Dakotas) provided the basis for rapid development. Despite an inflow from rural Ontario and British immigrants, the overall result was no longer an Ontario West but a distinct region of varied content. The large American influx contained many Germans and Scandinavians from adjacent states, and these were joined by about as many Germans, Ukrainians, Poles, Hungarians, and others from Eastern Europe. Canada's willingness to adapt its land policies to accommodate group settlement was a strong attraction to various communal sects (the first of which were Mennonites to Manitoba in 1874). Thus Winnipeg, the great entryway and focus of this vast, broadening agricultural triangle, became an unusually diversified ethnic center, the countryside a mosaic of ethnoreligious districts, and in population and economy this great northern extension of the Spring Wheat Belt across Manitoba and the new provinces (1905) of Saskatchewan and Alberta became a region much more like adjacent Minnesota, Dakota, and Montana than like anything in the East.

Canada's Pacific province remained a strongly *British* Columbia. More than half of its newcomers were from Ontario or Britain, relatively few were from Eastern Europe; Victoria, left behind by the commercial emergence of Vancouver, continued to attract Empire retirees to its soft climate and English gardens. However, its fishing, lumbering, and mining industries—and its Chinese and Japanese minorities living under strong animosities and restrictive laws—resembled and were related in some degree to earlier and broader developments on the Pacific Coast.

If Ontario failed to impress its image firmly upon the Canadian West it nevertheless kept those distant areas pretty firmly under its economic and political power. While they were developing into new regions and provinces, the Laurentian base of Confederation was consolidating its position as the core of Canada. In spite of an extensive rural exodus, this area (including Montreal) received half a million immigrants and underwent strong urban and industrial growth. Coal (more readily available from Pennsylvania than Nova Scotia) and electricity (Niagara, Shawinigan, and many lesser points) fueled steel, engineering, machinery, textiles, food processing, and other industries. Railroad construction in the Shield had opened up riches in copper, nickel, gold, silver, iron, and cobalt, making Toronto's position as a corporate and financial center equal to Montreal, though still second in population (382,000 to Montreal's 491,000). Corporate consolidations similar to those in the United States (such as Massey-Harris in agricultural machinery and Dominion Steel) and the rise of big wholesale and retail houses (such as Eaton's and Simpson's) resulted in Canada-wide marketing networks.

Magnification of power at these centers had a depressing effect upon the lesser partners in Confederation. The Atlantic Provinces enjoyed only modest benefits from this general growth period. Tariff protections, new railroads, and cheaper freight rates, together with local coal and nearby iron ore (Newfoundland), fostered iron and steel and engineering expansions (Canada's largest integrated works was at Sydney, Nova Scotia), fishing and lumbering remained staples, and Halifax and Saint John were Canada's only ice-free Atlantic ports, but the generally small scale of most enterprises and eccentric regional location left the area highly vulnerable to external changes in political policies, market fluctuations, and corporate control. Heavy rural depopulation and little immigration resulted in low population growth, and the relative position of these small provinces in the economy and polity of confederation was weakening—as symbolized in the shift of the headquarters of the major Bank of Nova Scotia from Halifax to Toronto.

Consolidation at the center required ever-more efficient means of integration of the periphery, and the most spectacular and emblematic development was the construction of two new transcontinental railroad systems—vast and expensive undertakings reflecting the optimism and the assertive geopolitical designs of nation-builders (fig. 73). The first of these arose out of regional needs. By 1901 grain traffic from the Prairies had swelled so rapidly as to overwhelm the capacity of the CPR ("the hopper was too big for the spout"—September harvests had to be moved quickly to Lakehead before shipping was closed by winter). Manitoba, eager to support a competitor, assisted a local company to build a second line from Winnipeg to Lake Superior (and the CPR soon double-tracked the original "spout"); these entrepreneurs then organized the Canadian Northern to extend their prairie feeders

73. Transcontinental Canada.

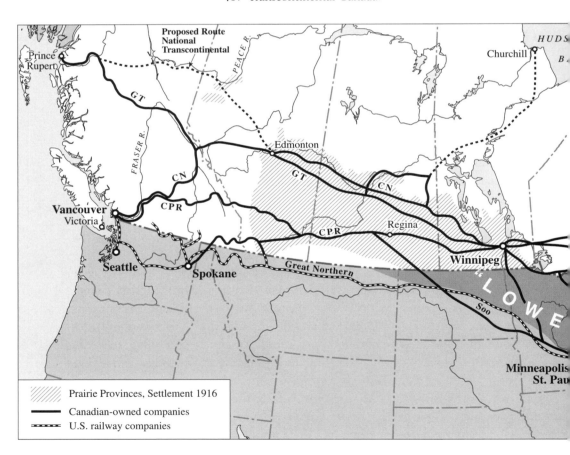

into a trunk line via Edmonton to Vancouver and also to build eastward from Port Arthur (Thunder Bay) across the Shield to connect with lines they had acquired or were constructing to provide direct access to Toronto and Montreal.

The second system was a more complicated and extravagant scheme, shaped by a peculiar combination of corporate competition, political compromise, and grandiose geopolitical visions. The Grand Trunk Railway, primary axis of Laurentian Canada, had chosen not to join in Macdonald's plans for Canadian expansion. Its economic interests were quite at variance with his all-Canadian vision, for its full line extended west to Chicago and east to Portland, Maine. However, seeing the Canadian Pacific profit from the swelling traffic of the Prairies, the Grand Trunk began to plan for invasion and extension in the West. Failing to get the Grand Trunk to cooperate with the Canadian Northern on sharing track across the Shield, the government (yielding as well to provincial pressures from the Maritimes and Quebec) agreed to build a new National Transcontinental line from

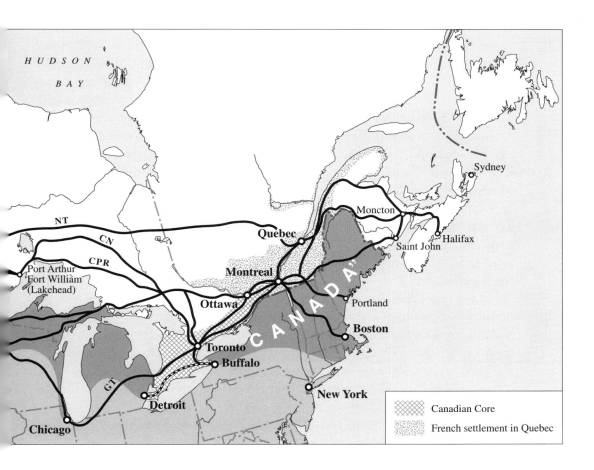

Moncton, New Brunswick (an eastern base selected to serve both Halifax and Saint John), to Quebec City, thence westward far north of existing settlements for 1,800 miles to Winnipeg. From there the Grand Trunk would build the "western division" of this 3,600-mile scheme, to Edmonton, across the Rockies, and down the Skeena River to the Pacific at or near Port Simpson, 500 miles north of Vancouver. With the help of enormous government subsidies and lavish loans from British and American investors, these two entirely new transcontinental systems were completed by 1915—and quickly faced bankruptcy.

The Canadian railroad network came to display some of the extravagances of the American, especially in some very expensive duplications (such as three long main lines across the empty Shield and parallel lines down the Fraser River Canyon), but the central government was much more involved and geopolitical concerns played a larger role. Whereas the Canadian Pacific was essential to hold the parts together, the National Transcontinental was designed to create a broader belt of Canadian-ness from sea to sea. Opponents stressed the practical folly of such an ostensible trunk line: it could never become a great conduit of Prairie traffic because wheat would move to Lake Superior, not travel 1,500 miles to the Canadian Atlantic; Prince Rupert, the new Pacific port, was 500 miles closer to Yokohama and China, but ocean transport was cheaper than rail and this raw, isolated little facility could never compete with Vancouver. But the concept of a northern axis for a northern nation carried the day (with the help of complicated political and economic interests). Railroad politics connected with a growing nationalist rhetoric that made a virtue of Canada's location: *We are the Northmen of the New World,* of a racial lineage and geographic environment that imparted a superior strength and hardiness, self-reliance and vigor to cope with these "Stern Latitudes." With the western borderlands filling up this mythology extolled the North as the next, indeed the genuine, *Canadian* frontier. Having the eastern division of the National Transcontinental connect with the St. Lawrence at Quebec City rather than Montreal was a way of responding to Quebec's insistent stress on northern develop-ment (and did in fact open up an unknown Clay Belt to limited colonization). In the West the Parklands had proved to be very fertile, and a vast area farther north seemed to await development by a hardy people. Original sketches of the western division had the main line arching to the upper Peace River (56° North—which would later be tapped and opened for settlement) en route to a Pacific terminus just south of the Alaska boundary. Interests in the North also resulted in extensions of the boundaries of Quebec, Ontario, and Manitoba to Hudson Bay, Canada's "Medi-terranean Sea," in 1912 (Saskatchewan's rival claim for a corridor to its natural outlet was rejected by Ottawa).

The first great rush to the North had actually thrust far beyond the margins of this settlement frontier directly to the Klondike, a tributary of the upper Yukon,

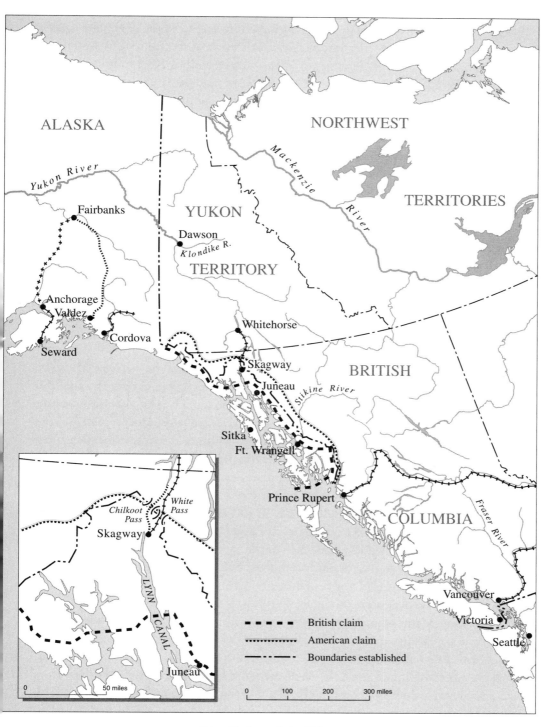

ALASKA

NORTHWEST

Yukon River

Mackenzie River

TERRITORIES

Fairbanks

YUKON

Dawson
Klondike R.

TERRITORY

Anchorage
Valdez
Cordova

Seward

Whitehorse

Skagway

Juneau

Stikine River

BRITISH

Sitka
Ft. Wrangell

Prince Rupert

COLUMBIA

Fraser River

Vancouver

Victoria

Seattle

British claim
American claim
Boundaries established

0   100   200   300 miles

Inset:

Chilkoot
Pass
White
Pass
Skagway

LYNN CANAL

Juneau

0   50 miles

74. Alaska and the Yukon.

and thereby generated new problems with the United States (fig. 74). The nearest portal to this remote corner was Skagway, and most of the influx was Americans sailing out of Seattle. A Territory of Yukon was created in 1898 to bring law and order to the mining camps. The sudden volume of trade made the exact location of the boundary a major issue. Serious friction over customs fees, licenses, bonding loomed; rival railway bills were introduced in Parliament and Congress. Canada reasserted claim to a line that would leave the heads of several long ocean inlets (including the site of Skagway) within Canadian bounds. The American claim, based on its Alaskan purchase and earlier arrangements between Russia and Great Britain, was drawn farther inland so as to enclose all these fjords. After a brief period of rival maneuvers the problem was submitted to a boundary tribunal consisting of three Americans, two Canadians, and one British representative. On the evidence of existing maps and tacit recognitions the Canadian claim was weak, but Theodore Roosevelt also waved his "Big Stick" behind the scene to induce British support for an award that satisfied all American interests. The two Canadians refused to sign and the whole episode generated bitter criticisms of both Britain and the United States. A treaty of 1871 had opened the Yukon and Stikine rivers to free Canadian navigation, but more ready access to the sea across the Alaskan Panhandle would be a recurrent issue in Canada.

By this time Americans were becoming more concerned about access to the main body of their own distant North. For thirty years they had paid only the slightest attention to Alaska. A San Francisco company had quickly moved into the richest sealing areas, but only a few traders, prospectors, and missionaries roamed into the vast interior. The entire area was declared to be a Military District, with half a dozen tiny posts under a general seated in Sitka, the old Russian capital; in 1877 it was turned over to the Treasury Department, its coasts patrolled by a few revenue cutters. The census of 1890 (conducted with the help of missionaries and a scattering of other informants) recorded only 4,300 Whites in a total population of 32,000. The Klondike and a quick series of lesser discoveries suddenly lured thousands into these boreal lands, made Seattle the great gateway and supply center, and drew the attention of investors and promoters. Salmon canneries and sawmills were set up, gold mines, copper, and coal staked out (this last was of particular interest for it was scarce and expensive on the Pacific Coast). Skagway, the instant town at the head of Lynn Canal, soon had a narrow-gauge railroad over the pass to Whitehorse, where it connected with steamboats on the upper Yukon, but the government sought to foster all-American land routes from the Gulf of Alaska to Fairbanks, which was emerging as the chief trade center of the interior. Rival schemes from Cordova and Valdez were proposed and a railroad was begun from Seward, but all were interrupted when the Theodore Roosevelt administration imposed new conservation controls over forestry, fishing, and coal mining. Alaskan interests howled in protest, insisting on the same "just and generous treatment" that had allowed their forebears a century of unhindered exploitation of resources across the American continent. Alaska was now touted as America's Last Frontier ("a territory equal to one-fifth of the continental United States, and capable of supporting a population larger than that of Norway, Sweden, and Denmark combined"), but it was not a vigorous one. The 1910 census recorded only 36,400 Whites—and their number was declining. Native Americans totaled 25,300, and although disease and disruptions had taken a toll, American activities were so sporadic and marginal that they had not suffered the massive destruction typical of American expansions. In 1912 Alaska was finally formalized into a Territory, with a local legislature at Juneau. Two years later the government itself decided to build a railroad from Seward to Fairbanks, and in 1915 the main construction camp was surveyed and lots auctioned for the new town of Anchorage.

These interrelated developments in the Yukon and Alaska extended and underscored the sharing of a continent by two enormous geopolitical systems, one a federation of nine provinces and a vast North, the other a federation of forty-eight states and its own huge detached North, with a boundary of 5,500 miles between them, equal in size (Canada, 3.8 million square miles, United States, 3.6 million) but grossly unequal in population (Canada, 7.2 million, the continental United States, 92 million). In general such a relationship was an obsessive reality for the one country, and a matter of no more than episodic interest to the other.

This obsession with sharing a continent with the United States dated from the early nineteenth century (the War of 1812) and was based on several corollary realities of the early twentieth. Politicians might speak grandly of a population "destined to be as numerous as that of the United States," but the current differences were enormous and grounded in fundamental geographical conditions, and it was clear that there could be "no balance of power in North America." Far more complex and controversial was the fact that Canadian nation-builders had not yet built a nation. Even the editors of the grand multivolume history and geography of *Canada and Its Provinces* (twenty-two volumes being prepared as an important component of the national project) felt compelled to state that "there remain differences of environment, of local interest, of language and race. Under such conditions the danger of sectionalism, in spite of material success, is greatly to be feared, unless this destructive tendency is met by the positive and constructive idea of the Nation."

But the common concept of a nation accepted by those who had undertaken the task embodied a people sharing a language, culture, and tradition, and such commonality emphatically did not exist in the Canada they were assiduously trying to construct. There was the implacable presence of a French Canada firmly embedded in the midst of this vast structure. Such a presence could not be ignored, of course, but since at least the famous Durham Report of 1839 (that had led to the first United Canada), English Canadian leaders had openly regarded the French as a conquered minority—"the remains of an ancient colonization . . . isolated in the midst of an Anglo-Saxon world," as Lord Durham had put it—that must eventually become assimilated into the larger polity and culture. Hence the quick attempts to undo the Manitoban duality forced upon Confederation in 1870 and to stamp out any expansion of official recognition of the French language, because, as the leader of that movement stated, it was "expedient in the interest of national unity of the Dominion that there should be community of language among the people of Canada." This and many related actions made it increasingly clear to the French that this new "Canada is not Canada for all Canadians," and thus while the English routinely—and to them, logically and necessarily—pressed for *national unity*, French leaders increasingly insisted—logically and justly, to them— on equality, on a *harmonious duality*. As their great spokesman Henri Bourassa insisted, the British North America Act (which created the Dominion in 1867) was intended to build a structure "that would be French and English in each of its parts as well as in its whole—not French and English in the sense of some bastard fusion of the two races, in which they would lose their distinctive qualities and characteristics, but a fruitful alliance of the two races, each one remaining distinctly itself, but finding within the Canadian confederation enough room and liberty to live together side by side."

In the larger context of these two federations and their problems such a stance seems an echo of Calhoun's anguished militant cry of sixty years earlier to "cease agitation of the slave [cf. language] question," give the South "equal right" to acquired territories in the West, and establish in Congress a "concurrent majority" system so as to restore the political "equilibrium" intended by "the hands of [the Republic's] framers" (*Continental America*, 459–60). The disintegration of the American federation was of course ever present in the minds of Canadian leaders; it was also obvious that the Union had been forcibly restored and was much stronger than ever before. But such restoration and strengthening was accomplished because from the time of its revolutionary inception the United States had expanded as a nation as well as a federation. The South may have been locked into a peculiar and divisive system, but it was not a distinct internal nation; historically, fundamentally, it was as American as the North. In contrast, the Canadian transcontinental polity had been organized (with the help of some pressure from London) by a small group of leaders who neither sought nor obtained popular support for their undertaking, and their vision of a unifying Canadian nationalism could not comprehend and subordinate the militant dualism of their Laurentian heartland— there was no "ideological Canadianism" sufficient for that task.

If not a nation, Canada was certainly a federation, an empire (on its own, as well as still part of the largest of empires), and, most obviously, a set of regional societies. Macdonald's National Policy was a success in its basic intention to create a transcontinental geopolitical structure within which disparate regions would be bound by practical systems of railways and tariffs. But how solid, how beneficial—how enduring—was this articulation? That had become *the* Canadian question, and the answer, important voices insisted, lay in geography. "Whoever wishes to know what Canada is, and to understand the Canadian question," said Goldwin Smith,

> should begin by turning from the political to the natural map. The political map displays a vast and unbroken area of territory, extending from the boundary of the United States up to the North Pole, and equalling or surpassing the United States in magnitude. The physical map displays four separate projections of the cultivable and habitable part of the Continent into arctic waste. . . . They are . . . the Maritime Provinces . . . ; Old Canada . . . ; the newly-opened region of the North-West . . . ; and British Columbia. The habitable and cultivable parts of these blocks of territory are not contiguous, but are divided from each other by great barriers of nature. . . . Each of the blocks, on the other hand, is closely connected by nature, physically and economically, with that portion of the habitable and cultivable continent to the south of it which it immediately adjoins, and in which are its natural markets. . . . Whether the four blocks of territory constituting the Dominion can for ever be kept by political agencies united among themselves and separate from their Continent, of which geographically, economically, and with the exception of Quebec ethnologically, they are a part, is the Canadian question.

An "artificial Canadianism" or a "natural Continentalism": the debate on that alternative lay "near the centre of Canadian politics" for the next twenty years.

CONTINENTALISM

Goldwin Smith's *Canada and the Canadian Question* (1891) and Samuel E. Moffett's *Americanization of Canada* (1907) were the most powerful statements of the time in support of continentalism, and they complement each other well in their geographic arguments.

A mere glance at the "natural map" confirmed the north-south alignment of the great physical divisions of North America—with the great exception of the Canadian Shield, which simply magnified the problem, the illogic, of a transcontinental Canada. The "habitable and cultivable" portions of the four great "blocks" within Canada were merely small northern compartments of vast continental regions. Furthermore (as we have confirmed in our several sections on these borderlands), these Canadian sectors were in part peopled by movements from the south, and each was bound by trafficways with its adjoining American region before becoming articulated by rail across the "great barriers of nature" with other Canadian blocks.

Moffett reviewed the historical sequence of the "intricately interlaced strands of communication" between the two countries, noting of the most recent form that, as with its predecessors, "the different sections of the Dominion are all in direct telephonic communication with the United States, but not with each other." By the time he was writing Canadian companies were making much use of ice-free U.S. Atlantic ports, the CPR—that nationalist lifeline—had obtained control of the Soo Line to St. Paul and Chicago, and the important new Kootenay mining region was primarily bound to Spokane.

Moffett emphasized the need to look at a "Greater Canada," spanning the full breadth of these borderlands. The real homeland of Canadians, he said "reaches down to Long Island Sound, westward south of the Great Lakes, and on to the Pacific Coast." Thus there was a "Lower Canada," not just a Lower Quebec, for "fully half the area actually settled by people of Canadian race" lay south of the international boundary (see fig. 73). New England held nearly a million persons of Canadian stock (more than all the Maritime Provinces), the Lower Lakes states about as many (equal to half the number in populous Ontario), and the Northern Plains and Pacific Coast states (including California) had more Canadians than the western half of Canada (he was using the latest census figures). Viewed in this perspective, Montreal, Toronto, Boston, Quebec City, Chicago, Ottawa, Detroit, and New York City were the top eight cities in the number of resident Canadians.

The high position of these American cities on that list displayed the power of modern metropolitanism and the inherent vulnerability of Canada, said Moffett, for

> there is no city in Canada which does not have to meet the competition of a more important American city within drawing distance of its own constituency. . . . The tariff does something to counteract the most powerful attraction of the larger places, but it cannot do everything. It cannot interfere with pleasure and education; it cannot compel people to take local newspapers in preference to metropolitan journals, nor can it stop the migration of ambitious youth to the points of greatest opportunity. A metropolis draws in currents of life from all directions and sends them back transformed. As London has unified England, as Paris has unified France, as Berlin is unifying Germany, so the great American border cities are unifying the regions over which their attraction extends.

Evidence of such transformation and unification seemed to be obvious and pervasive, covering everything from business practices, labor unions, and fraternal orders to decimal coinage, baseball, slang, and much else. The emphasis was on how much more American than English was Canada, and both Smith and Moffett wrote extensively about that bias in the style and tendencies of Canadian political life. There was more at work here, however, than just the power of propinquity and the gross imbalance in population and resources; there was the shared experience in North America that had molded a common society distinct in its fundamentals from Europe. Whatever their differences in details, Canadians and Americans were alike in the simplification and democratization, openness and expansiveness generated by having an entire rich continent an ocean apart all to themselves.

Goldwin Smith was a prominent English-born liberal, long resident and respected in Canada and well acquainted with the United States (he taught history at Cornell briefly before moving to Toronto); Samuel Moffett was an American journalist and social scientist of wide experience. Both men were "progressive expansionists" who saw a single great North American society taking shape. Neither gave much attention to the formidable geopolitical issues any real integration of the two federations would face. Smith referred to the Union of Scotland and England as a possible model; both men assumed an inexorable process at work, with formal commercial union as a probable first stage (the broader topic being greatly enlivened in Canada at this time by debates over "reciprocity" in trade relations with the United States). In general, these men were offering an updated and greatly elaborated version of the continentalism extolled half a century earlier by such geopolitical evolutionists as Arnold Guyot, who spoke confidently of the "geographical march of history" wherein the "law of progress" and the "law of nature" would culminate in a great Anglo-Saxon civilization across all North America.

Our current perspective offers a ready counter to these arguments and visions. Nations are not "logical" creations, and continentalism was not a "natural" geopolitical concept. If Canada was "united by no bond of geography," neither was the United States; the American Union was in fact a great exhibit of the articulation of unlike regions across the rugged grain of the continent, and it was not internally organized along great natural features of river basins and mountain barriers. Indeed, the waterborne system of the Northwest Fur Company connecting the St. Lawrence with the Columbia River pointed to a more powerful "geographic logic" for a transcontinental Canada than did any combination of natural systems for the United States. Canadian nationalists at the time tended to give more emphasis to "northernness" than to waterways, and they readily assumed that the concurrent work of natural scientists on the distribution of distinctive flora and fauna and physiographic conditions reinforced the notion that "the development of a transcontinental Canadian nation not only could be compatible with both its 'historical' British heritage and the influence of its North American environment but would also be natural and perhaps inevitable." (In such formulations the French were readily included, for intensive genealogical research was revealing that they were mostly of Norman and Breton stock, hardy races of the northern seas.)

That historical British heritage was far from being the fading and fragile thing described—even denigrated—by continentalists. It was, however, a complicated relationship. Some Canadians readily joined in with the Anglo-Saxonism of late Victorian England, taking pride in the Empire and its institutions as a great moral force for a better world. Furthermore, such a stance helped Canadians "look the Americans in the face on something better than equal terms. America was still adolescent but the British Empire was established and supreme." Indeed, Canada had a greater role to play in imperial affairs because its Atlantic and Pacific harbors were important naval bases and coaling stations and the Canadian Pacific was a vital logistical line in a worldwide system that was facing the rise of German and Japanese power. Most important, the imperatives of imperial participation allowed Canadians to increase their pressure for autonomy, for British recognition of Canada as a partner in a reformed system of dominions, a new stage in Canada's laudable history of "building up a nation without separation" from the motherland. Such issues were as central to the Canadian Question as were relations with the United States. Heritage, after all, is part of the human geography of nation-building, and a long Britannic presence in North America was deeply imprinted on this land. As a Conservative member put it during the reciprocity debates of 1911: "This land is ours, we have made it, we and our fathers. . . . We have not wrought so in order to bestow a great gift upon a rich nation, we have wrought to build ourselves a national home."

If Canadians routinely or even avidly accepted a wide spectrum of American influences, there remained important features of American society they did not admire: all that looseness, restlessness, lawlessness; the notorious political scandals, bombast, and jingoism—such things made the Canadian foundational triad of peace, order, and good government seem superior to such characteristic expressions of life, liberty, and the pursuit of happiness. That every year thousands of Canadians moved south and quickly blended into American society attested to attractions and similarities but did not negate the concept of a separate polity; after all millions did not emigrate and remained Canadians by choice. That much was shared between the two countries did not mean that the most important things were shared; most pertinently, they could not share their most difficult human problems: there were few Blacks in Canada (whereas those in the United States outnumbered the total population of Canada), and there was nothing in the United States to compare with the French-English dualism of Canada. Visions of a great Anglo-Saxon North America, whether British, Anglo-Canadian, or American, assumed an eventual assimilation of the French, but after a century and a half there was little evidence of such a thing. Indeed, in the midst of continentalist debates a prominent French Canadian editor evinced no fear of American expansionism, for "once the United States have engulfed the whole of North America, then their dismemberment will begin, and from that ephemeral confederation will be born a number of independent republics, of which not the least will be a New France." Such confidence was a reminder that the only solid nation as yet built in northern North America was to be found downriver from Montreal, and therefore the Canadian Confederation was a geopolitical experiment of distinct and profound importance for all North Americans.

Canadians were, unavoidably, North Americans. They were acutely conscious of being minority North Americans, of "the sustained pressure of ninety-three millions to eight millions," but (with the slight, momentary exception of the Montreal manifesto of 1849) "no political party, and no important political group, has ever advocated the union of Canada and the United States." Indeed, in the twentieth century as in the nineteenth they defined themselves by their determination not to be Americans. "Canadians feared and envied the United States. . . . No country . . . was as important to them as their immense, frequently turbulent neighbour. The task for Canadians was somehow to obtain the benefits of American society without its faults, while at the same time assuring that Canadian society remained distinct from the nation to the south."

2. Mexico and an American Mediterranean

America's long turbulent relationships in its southern borderlands were punctuated by two major explosions during this period that brought dramatic changes. On the mainland a Mexico that for thirty years had been wide open and welcoming to American penetration and exploitation was suddenly engulfed in a civil war initiated in its northern border states, implicating American influences and reverberating across the international boundary. In the island world to the east the eruption of yet another phase of the long-festering Cuban revolt and its sudden transformation into an American war with Spain allowed the United States to act upon its long-standing determination to make that strategic island an integral piece in its continental security system. That accomplished, the way was open for selective penetration almost at will of this tropical island world and the initiation of a long-awaited Isthmian canal, the critical segment of a new transcontinental trunk line.

The United States marches with Mexico for nearly 2,000 miles (about half the length of the boundary with Canada), but although this borderland includes Mexico at its broadest extent, it lies far from the Mexican heartland and consisted of a set of small, localized population districts distantly separated from one another. Thus whereas Canadian nation-builders gave highest priority to an all-Canadian transcontinental railroad to bind its borderland provinces together, the centralized Mexican government would give high priority to railroads that would bind its frontier states southward to the national capital and core.

This Mexican network would be built and operated by American companies, but such a program was initiated amidst a good deal of understandable fear and opposition. "Border nations are natural enemies," exclaimed a Mexican congressman in 1878, and current incursions and animosities along the Texas border could well be cited as but the latest phase of forty years of strife. On the other side, American conquest and subsequent pressures for purchase of large chunks of Mexican territory had been mostly replaced by a simple confidence in the power of America's republican ideals and capitalist instruments to work a peaceful conquest. "Fate has permanently placed two very dissimilar peoples in contiguity," said Secretary of State Thomas F. Bayard,

> and great good sense, constant forbearance, and careful self-control are indispensable requisites to keep matters in pacific train between them. The overflow of our population and capital into the bordering states of Mexico, must, sooner or later, saturate these regions with Americanism, and control their political action, but until they are prepared for our laws and institutions, we do not want them, and when they are fit they will find their own way to us.

Such views were being expressed while Porfirio Díaz, Oaxacan hero of the war expelling the French, was consolidating his power following an 1876 coup against a foundering liberal republican regime. His dictatorship attracted the support of a small professional elite who promulgated an ostensibly scientific program of "Order and Progress" to make Mexico a powerful and prosperous nation. While Díaz was establishing control over the Mexican frontier, the United States was doing essentially the same thing on its own side by its conquest of the Apaches, imposition of greater security and services (consulates, to reduce smuggling), and linking of a string of borderland towns by rail with the extension of the Southern Pacific from California to Texas.

Having established a large measure of order (and received formal diplomatic recognition from the United States) the Mexican government was ready to partake of modern material progress. During the 1880s new laws favoring foreign investment in land, mines, industries, and commerce "opened the floodgates of American capital" and initiated thirty years of vigorous development under the "Pax Porfiriana." We have already treated the impact of this new era on northwestern Mexico where Sonora was transformed by railroads, great copper camps and other developments, and the emergence of an increasingly distinct norteño society. In part this particular pattern reflected the failure to connect Sonora directly by rail with central Mexico, but heavy American investment and a northern regionalism were apparent all across the borderland. American companies built railways along the ancient trafficways from Mexico City to El Paso–Ciudad Juárez and to Laredo–Nuevo Laredo; another important line extended from the Southern Pacific at Eagle Pass–Piedras Negras (then called Ciudad Porfirio Díaz) across Coahuila to Durango (along a planned but never completed connection across the mountains to Mazatlán) and a later one tied Brownsville-Matamoros to Monterrey (fig. 75). By 1888 the value of imports and exports moving by land exceeded that moving through Mexico's Gulf ports. Furthermore, the integration of the American and Mexican networks involved far more than these geographic linkages and the traffic through them: "the vast system of railroads is operated generally, managed, and controlled by American citizens. The railway conductors, the division superintendents, the section foremen, the roadmasters, the clerks in the offices, the yardmasters at the terminals—indeed, a very large proportion of the persons who furnish the directing genius of the railroads of Mexico are citizens of the United States."

By the early twentieth century Mexico was served by a vastly improved infrastructure, an array of modern industries, and an expanding export economy. The first oil gusher was brought in by an American near Tampico in 1901, soon followed by major discoveries in the south (in Tabasco, by a British firm), and by 1910

75. Mexican Borderlands.

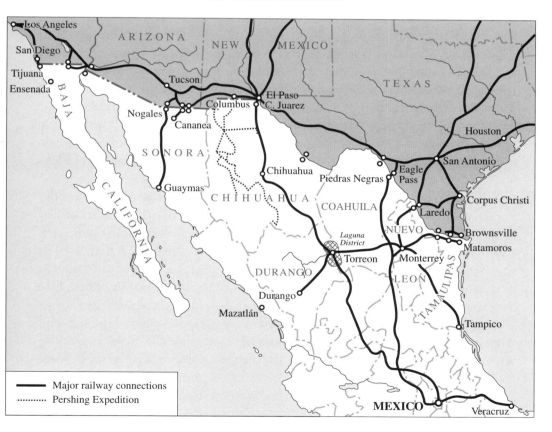

Mexico was the third largest producer in the world. The centers of the main cities had been modernized with paved streets, lighting, water and sewage systems, tramways, and telephones. The census of 1910 recorded an increase from just under 9 million to just over 15 million during the thirty-four years of the "Porfiriato." The borderland states contained only 1.7 million, but their population had been augmented by more than 300,000 migrants from central and southern states. If the total of only about 15,000 Americans in the North showed that contrary to confident expectations there had been no great "overflow of our population" (the census recorded only 25,000 foreign-born in the entire country), evidence of the overflow of American capital was everywhere to be seen. Foreigners (there were large British and German investments also) were reported to own a fifth of the land surface of Mexico as well as most of its large industrial and commercial firms.

Yet there were important geographical exceptions to this foreign domination, and especially in these borderlands. We have noted how Chihuahua, in contrast with Sonora, remained largely in the control of powerful local families. Much the most important exhibit was in the Northeast. Monterrey merchants had made a lot of money during the American Civil War when the Confederate cotton trade had been diverted through Matamoros, and the local elite responded energetically to opportunities during the Porfiriato. They invested in land, cattle, and cotton (this last in the Laguna District, Mexico's largest reclamation project); in local industries, such as breweries and flour mills, glass and cement, textiles and leather; and they created the largest metallurgical center, with smelters and iron and steel mills (based mostly on Coahuila ores and coal). As the commercial focus of an extensive region, the major financial center and largest city in the entire North, it was not uncommon—nor inappropriate—to refer to Monterrey as "the Chicago of Mexico."

There were important changes on the American side of this eastern sector of the borderland as well. All through these years San Antonio had persisted as an anchor of Hispanic presence, with about a third of its population concentrated on the west side of the river in a barrio locally known ("by way of distinction or derision") as "Mexico." The entire belt of country south of San Antonio–Corpus Christi was long little changed in people or pattern in spite of the relentless shift of land into Anglo ownership. *Patrón* and *peone* remained the norm, and the few larger towns such as Brownsville and Rio Grande City continued to have both Hispanic and Anglo merchants and some ethnic intermarriage between leading families. Anglos represented less than 10 percent of the population. In geocultural terms this was "occupied Mexico"—and it was treated as such by rustlers, raiders, smugglers, bandits, and local militias from both sides, who recurrently exploited this ambiguity. As the open range was turned into fenced ranches, cotton edged westward along the coastal plain, and railroads were built across the region to Laredo, greater security was imposed, and demands for labor lured more Mexicans across the Rio Grande. But a more drastic change was initiated in 1904 when a railroad was built from Corpus Christi to Brownsville, irrigation systems were begun, and land companies launched a campaign to lure American settlers and investors to the "Magic Valley." Thousands responded, mostly from the Middle West, and began to transform this long-secluded area into a dense pattern of new farms and towns and a dual society of Anglos and Hispanos, economically interdependent but socially segregated. The whole process would take twenty years, but from its inception the relentless subordination and marginalization of the local Hispanic population in their own homeland (100,000 by 1910) and the obvious contempt for "Mexicans" on the part of the invading Anglos compounded tensions in this long-contested area.

On the other side of the border, resentments against an increasingly rigid national dictatorship were mounting. Order seemed to have been purchased at the price of liberty, progress at the cost of making Mexico an economic colony of foreign capitalists; changes in laws had allowed rich hacendados to gobble up ancient communal lands, wealth was in the hands of a few. Political exiles in San Antonio, St. Louis, El Paso, Tucson, and Los Angeles began plotting and publishing; the great Cananea strike, suppressed only with the help of militia called in from Arizona, was a telling symptom and incitement. Regional revolts in the North and South exposed the hollowness of the long-ruling regime, and in May 1911 an aged Porfirio Díaz resigned under pressure and retired to France.

The Mexican Revolution was a decade of often bewilderingly complex civil war among many contending forces. It resulted in profound changes in the life of the nation, but its conclusion and significance for borderland relations lie beyond our coverage at this time. We should, however, note that by its very position and character the borderland was much involved in this upheaval. Most of the main leaders of rebellion (such as Madero, Villa, Carranza, Obregón) were norteños; they looked across the boundary for arms and supplies, for support from exiles and sympathizers, and they and lesser leaders might flee to the shelter of Hispanic communities in the United States in times of danger. Tens of thousands of ordinary Mexicans took refuge in nearby American cities, and nearly all of the thousands of Americans in Mexico eventually returned home (except for the 500 or so who lost their lives in the turmoil).

Moreover, this civil war welled up momentarily within South Texas in 1915, inspired by the revolution and fueled by similar grievances and Anglo dominance. Proclaimed under a "Plan de San Diego" (from the Texas village of that name), it was an irredentist movement calling for "Tierra y Libertad" (the slogan of Zapata's great rebellion on behalf of the Indians of southern Mexico), an end to "Yankee tyranny," and the creation of an independent republic out of all the territories stolen from Mexico (as well as establishing a separate Black nation out of several other U.S. states and returning tribal lands to Indians). Various political influences were involved in this program, especially the international anarchist movement, but its force was generated by the humiliations routinely imposed upon non-Anglo persons. As the preamble stated, "In Texas [Whites] have paid their workers with an unjustified race hatred that closes to the Mexican, the Negro, the Asian, the doors of schools, the hotels, the theaters, of every public place; that segregates them on railroad cars and keeps them out of the meeting places of the 'white-skinned' savages who constitute a superior caste." Anglo Texans did not at first take whatever they knew of this fantastic geopolitical agenda seriously, but an onset of sabotage and terrorism brought an equally savage response, with wanton killings by both sides. The area was turned into a war zone overlapping the political boundary and produced an extremely serious diplomatic crisis—an international problem complicated by American uncertainty over which of the contending rebel forces to recognize as the legitimate government of Mexico. De facto recognition of Venustiano Carranza's party in October 1915 allowed collaboration in reestablishing reasonable security in this sector. However, a reverberation occurred a few months later when Pancho Villa, incensed at American recognition of a rival, attacked and burned the border town of Columbus, New Mexico, killing several Americans. In response to the instant uproarious reaction in the United States (including retaliations against Mexicans in nearby El Paso), President Woodrow Wilson sent General John J. Pershing and 6,000 troops into Chihuahua in pursuit of these invaders. Pershing had chased Apaches through this same country years before and there was precedent for this kind of response to border insecurities in both official and informal relations between the two nations. In this case the humiliation of having a foreign army ranging deep into Mexican territory was matched by the embarrassment of Pershing's failure to catch any of the attackers, and an eventual diplomatic conciliation was achieved (despite a number of other incendiary clashes). By that time the United States had mobilized the entire National Guard and had 120,000 troops along the border. However, much greater concern over the immense war raging in Europe caused the American government to fend off public pressures for punishment of Mexico—and would soon set Pershing to a rather larger task.

By this time it was apparent that this borderland was being redefined quite at variance with earlier American expectations. For the time being at least, the "Advance Guard of Civilization" had been repelled out of Mexico; not only had Americans not "overflowed" and "saturated" the bordering states with Americans and Americanism, Mexicans had overflowed the boundaries and augmented their presence and importance in the bordering United States. Not only did American borderland cities prosper from this decade of disruption in Mexico, the war in Europe generated an economic boom throughout the nation and more Mexicans came seeking employment than merely political refuge—the total probably surpassing a million. John R. Chávez noted, with reference to various Mexican revolutionary leaders and their entourages, that "ironically, as these groups moved back and forth across the boundary they revealed the cultural unity existing along the border even as they transferred the deep divisions of Mexican society to the [American] Southwest." And in broader perspective we can see that having forcibly annexed half of Mexico's territory and several small districts of its population in the mid-nineteenth century, the United States had inadvertently created a set of reception areas, and by its own continuing assertive developments created a need for more and more people to sustain its economic transformation of those areas, ensuring, ironically, an ever-greater Hispanic "saturation" of its own borderland.

CUBA

To the east in the world of coastlands, islands, and waters, the relationships between the United States and its Hispanic neighbor had long had a special significance in both countries. From the time the United States obtained Louisiana and Florida, American leaders had fixed their own geopolitical design upon Cuba. The waters flowing through the Florida Straits were declared to be a natural extension of the Mississippi system, the island itself was called a "natural appendage" of North America, and American security made it an essential, eventual addition to its national territories. Cuban leaders of every kind—Spanish imperial officials, local nationalists, or whatever—well understood this American stance, factored it into their policies, and assumed the United States to be a major potential agent of change.

From the time of President James Madison's first overture the United States made repeated attempts to purchase Cuba, and although these were as repeatedly— and at times vehemently—rejected, Americans tended to assume that those "laws of political gravitation" that John Quincy Adams had cited with respect to such geographical situations would bring it into the fold whenever a weakening Spain loosened its hold. Meanwhile support of Spanish rule even if despotic seemed the best way to ensure stability in this strategic corner of the American sphere. That Havana, the Gibraltar of this New World Mediterranean, together with Cuba should never fall into the hands of an unfriendly power was the paramount consideration.

Cuba also became an expanding economic frontier for American capital and commerce. Whole districts, such as Matanzas and Cárdenas in the west and Gibara and Holguín in the east, were often referred to as "Americanized," and investments in sugar, coffee, and tobacco, iron ore and copper, railroads, telegraphs, telephones and public utilities were scattered throughout the island (fig. 76). The United States became much the largest market for Cuban exports and supplied the largest share of its imports. Frequent shipping services linked Havana with half a dozen American ports, and it became much easier to go to Spain via New York than

76. The American Mediterranean.
The Canal Zone was also protected by coast artillery fortifications.

THE AMERICAN MEDITERRANEAN

U.S. and possessions 1915

U.S. Protectorates
(formal and informal)

△ Proposed U.S. naval bases

▲ Active U.S. naval bases

0   500 miles

await the far more limited direct connection. As a U.S. consul reported in 1882: *"De facto,* Cuba is already inside the commercial union of the United States." Spain's attempts from time to time to stem this development with new taxes, tariffs, and regulations only led to severe economic distress in Cuba, followed by further American inroads on debt-ridden firms and estates.

Cuban interest in the United States was rather more complex than its counterpart. America was a symbol as well as a source of goods. "Cubans could not help but stand in awe at the prodigious accomplishments of North American material culture," but the United States was the seat of progress in many other walks of life as well: in politics (democratic institutions contrasted with centuries of Spanish rule); in religion (the attractions of Protestantism over the rigid Spanish hierarchy of the Roman Catholic church—the first president of Cuba was a Quaker convert who had spent many years in the United States); in education (the elite patronized American schools at all levels); in recreation (the Cuban League, formed in 1878, is the world's second oldest professional baseball association); "in habits, tastes, preferences . . . Cubans partook freely of North American culture."

Such influences were fostered not only by proximity and ease of contact but by the tens of thousands of Cuban émigrés who settled in Key West, Tampa, Jacksonville, New York, Baltimore, Philadelphia, Boston, and other communities along the Atlantic and Gulf coasts. They came for various reasons and they represented a considerable range of Cuban society: political refugees, businessmen and professionals seeking wider opportunities, agents of shipping and other American facilities in Cuba, workers badly in need of jobs (most notably thousands of cigar makers in Florida). Some maintained a residence in each country, some became naturalized citizens, some married Americans, but almost none severed connections with their native land and "their experiences guaranteed that North American influences would penetrate Cuban society deeply and indelibly" (and 50,000 returned to Cuba in 1898).

These connections and experiences complicated the Cuban liberation movement. *Annexationists* included some Cuban elite who were frightened of the rebellion and feared the rise of an underclass (recently emancipated and unemployed Blacks were a large presence as leaders as well as common soldiers in rebel forces); others were alarmed by the anarchy and military despotism that had followed upon independence in so many other Spanish American republics. Even before the U.S. invasion there were numerous *interventionists* who thought that a transitional period of American oversight would be the best insurance of republican stability and economic rehabilitation. *Nationalists* insisting upon full independence—*Cuba Libre*—included a good many whose experience had not made them admirers of all things American. They were repelled by the pervasive racism, labor suppression, and common American contempt for Hispanic societies; José Martí, foremost

Cuban leader and martyr, urged his compatriots to "block with our blood" annexation "to the turbulent and brutal North that despise them. . . . I lived in the monster [for fifteen years], and know its entrails."

The movement culminating in the end of Spanish rule passed through several phases. A revolt in 1868 initiated ten years of guerrilla warfare, largely in the eastern provinces, that devastated property and caused many Americans to regard these insurgents as little more than bandits. A greatly enlarged Spanish army and rebel factionalism eventually induced a negotiated peace. Thereafter a more comprehensive revolution was plotted, mainly by émigrés. At conclaves in New York and Key West in the 1890s the Cuban Revolutionary party was formed, José Martí elected head, and an invasion organized. The United States thwarted this 1895 attempt (as it had numerous filibustering efforts), but a small party of leaders landed and over the next several months Martí was killed in action, generals took charge, independence was proclaimed, and a constitution and provisional government for the Republic of Cuba was announced.

Through all of this turmoil the United States, despite loud support for Cuban independence from many citizens and congressmen, officially recognized Spanish sovereignty but worked behind the scenes to pressure Spain into granting Cuba genuine autonomy. Spain, however, reinforced its army and began a vicious policy of forced removal of populations out of the threatened rural areas. After three years of devastation and heavy loss of life, Spanish refusals of American offers of mediation or of purchase of Cuba, two months after the destruction of the U.S. battleship *Maine* in Havana harbor (a mystery never solved), and amidst a strident newspaper campaign and heavy congressional pressure for war, the president of the United States declared that "in the cause of humanity," "the very serious injury to the commerce, trade, and business of our people," and because "the present condition of affairs in Cuba is a constant menace to our peace and entails upon this Government an enormous expense," the United States had the right to intervene "to secure a full and final termination of hostilities." Congress quickly followed by empowering the president to use whatever force necessary to cause Spain to relinquish all its authority and withdraw from Cuba. By August 1898, following the destruction of the Spanish fleet at Santiago de Cuba (and of its Pacific fleet at Manila) and a short land battle, this was accomplished. Spain relinquished Cuba and ceded Puerto Rico (and the island of Guam in the Marianas and agreed to American occupation of Manila, bay and city, pending disposition by treaty).

As Louis A. Pérez, Jr., noted, with the U.S. intervention, "the Cuban war of national liberation became the 'Spanish-American War,' nomenclature that in more than symbolic terms ignored Cuban participation." The rebel government had been eager for American arms and supplies but not intervention, and it quickly found that the United States considered this its own war of conquest and pacification. It had not recognized the Cuban government, did not consider it to be "representative of the Cuban people as a whole," and regarded its army as little more than a rabble of "adventurers," peasants, and former slaves. As they began their occupation of the country American generals quickly complained about Cuban interference. While the United States tried to decide what to do with its new holding, the island was placed under an American military governor.

Historically, the United States had thought only of purchase or seizure, but Congress had inserted a clause in its war authorization (the Teller Amendment): "That the United States hereby disclaims any disposition or intention to exercise sovereignty, jurisdiction, or control over the said Island except for the pacification thereof, and asserts its determination, when that is accomplished, to leave the government and control of the Island to its people." If annexation was prohibited American domination had to be secured by other means. Cuban leaders had hoped that the relationship between the two countries would be defined by treaty negotiations between the two governments, but the United States insisted on dictating its own terms. After heated debate in Congress the result was the Platt Amendment of 1902, which included provisions that Cuba "consents that the United States may exercise the right to intervene for the preservation of Cuban independence, [and] the maintenance of a government adequate for the protection of life, property, and individual liberty"; to enable it to do so Cuba "will sell or lease to the United States lands necessary for coaling or naval stations." Furthermore, Cuba will never make a treaty with any (other) foreign power that might in any way "impair" its independence or gain any "lodgment in or control over any portion" of the island. News of this imposition provoked widespread popular protests in Cuba, and its reluctant acceptance by most Cubans came only because the choice was "limited sovereignty or no sovereignty" and "independence with restrictions was better than continued occupation."

Nearly four years of American military government brought vast changes. At the beginning, "Cuba lay in ruins. The population had been decimated; the economy was in a shambles; the backbone of the class structure had been shattered." A major program of reconstruction was undertaken to restore the infrastructure, get land back into cultivation, and vastly improve sanitation (for yellow fever and malaria were common and a danger to American coastal connections). The second governor, Major General Leonard Wood, was much concerned with courts, schools, and Protestant missions as well. A later American historian called him "one of the greatest colonial administrators in history, comparable to Britain's Curzon or France's Lyautey"; a more recent Hispanic-American historian described him as an autocrat "bent on 'Americanizing' the island as a preliminary step to annexation." Some support for annexation persisted in Cuba as well as the United States, but in Cuba, as an American visitor reported, such advocates would insist on "the status and rights of a state," not a mere territory, and he was no doubt correct in his skepticism that the American nation would ever confer statehood on a population that was Roman Catholic, Spanish speaking, and had so much "negro blood in their veins." The American-directed census of 1899 reported a third of the total population of 1,573,000 as "colored" (but as an American commented on a subsequent enumeration, census takers in Cuba "displayed an indifference regarding the location of the 'color line' which would not be tolerated in large parts of the United States").

That census listed 129,000 Spanish-born, reflecting rather large immigrations in the 1880s (mostly as laborers, although more than half the merchants in Cuba were Spanish), and that influx was renewed in the new century, numbering 270,000 by 1912. Much more visible were the many fewer thousands of Americans who "arrived as carpetbaggers and gamblers, brokers and vendors, homesteaders and settlers." Speculators and real estate agents bought up defunct or debt-ridden estates and touted Cuba as a "new California," a tropical frontier awaiting American energy and ingenuity. Small colonies were initiated in every province and a much larger number of Americans invested in land. The Isle of Pines, much the largest of outlying islands, received special geopolitical and speculative attention. Because of its position it was regarded as a potential American base, and the Platt Amendment excluded it from the territories of Cuba pending further treaty "adjustment." An ambiguity in the 1898 treaty encouraged speculators to assume that it was already and would remain American territory, a colony was quickly formed, and a local American Society was soon promoting its attractions and reasons for its retention (such as a location "midway between Hampton Roads and the Isthmus of Panama" and "a matchless opportunity of planting a distinctly American colony in the very heart of the West Indies, which would be an example and a lasting object lesson for the neighboring Latin Republics"). The very idea of such annexation had been extravagantly condemned by a minority in Congress ("the most apparent illustration of the Anglo-Saxon greed for land ever presented in a legislative body"), it was soon declared unsuitable for a naval station, and once the United States had decided to lease Bahia Hondo and Guantánamo for that purpose there was little official interest in Isle of Pines (but it was not formally returned to Cuban control until 1925).

Once the protectorate was formalized a Cuban government under President Tomás Estrada Palma took charge. In 1906 he asked for U.S. intervention to quell a rebellion over disputed elections. When a token American force landed the rebels asked it for aid in restoring fair elections. The American administration was deeply reluctant (for its own domestic political reasons) to get drawn into any such intramural dispute and sent Secretary of War William Howard Taft to assess the situation. Taft saw little merit in either party and when the Cuban president rejected his proposed compromise, he declared himself provisional governor of Cuba (backed by warships and 6,600 troops distributed among twenty-seven posts across the island). This Second Intervention for "Cuban Pacification" lasted two years, featured an extensive public works program, and another surge of American investment. By 1910 there were still only about 7,000 Americans resident, but their power and influence were great. The American colony in Havana was a major presence, and large enterprises such as sugar and mining dotted the landscape with American enclaves (each major sugar *central* was the focus of "a huge feudal territory," said a Cuban writer, "Everything there is private-ownership, industry, mill, houses, police, railroad, port"). Furthermore, the official American attitude underwent an important change. Whereas the powerful business interests behind President William McKinley were not at all eager for war and annexation (fearing it would be disruptive of the prosperity they were enjoying after the miseries of 1893), by the time William Howard Taft became president (following the lesser but worrisome depression of 1907) the role of foreign markets in support of "the vastly augmented power of [American] production" was being routinely emphasized and the era of "dollar diplomacy" was well under way. Expansion and protection of American property abroad took on new economic and strategic interest, and the emphasis of policy in Cuba "shifted away from armed intervention to restore political order to political intervention to prevent armed disorder"—a protectorate, after all, is designed to protect a great power's interests.

The United States and Cuba were indeed bound by those "ties of singular intimacy" that McKinley spoke of in an address to Congress. The American interest, said the secretary of State to his minister there in 1911, "arises out of and is dependent upon its economic and commercial relationship with Cuba, and upon the imperative necessities attendant upon and growing from the geographical propinquity of Cuba and the considerations inseparably inherent to the general problem of national defense." The primary Cuban interest was to survive as a nation under the thumb of the Colossus of the North. Various Cubans had good reasons for collaborating with American interests, but it seems likely that most would have agreed with General Maximo Gómez, leader and hero of liberation (who himself felt the need to cooperate with "those rich northerners, owners of a continent"), when he reflected, "None of us thought that [peace] would be followed by a military occupation of the country by our allies, who treat us as a people incapable of acting for ourselves, and who have reduced us to obedience, to submission, and to a tutelage imposed by force of circumstances." As Pérez, contemplating the history of this relationship ninety years later, put it: "North American resolve to control Cuba and Cuban determination to resist control have become part of the character of each and something of an obsession for both."

PUERTO RICO

For the United States as for Spain, Puerto Rico was a minor adjunct of Cuba. Whereas Cuba was Spain's most valuable colony, smaller mountainous Puerto Rico was of distinctly minor commercial importance, and whereas Cuba and the United States were interrelated and important to each other in so many ways, Puerto Rico was the most distant of the Greater Antilles, more than a thousand miles east of Miami, with little American investment or contact. And thus whereas the United States was determined to assert control over Cuba in some firm manner to further its own complex interests, it took over Puerto Rico for one simple reason: to get Spain out of the Western Hemisphere.

Once it took command of the island and its nearly 1 million inhabitants, however, the United States began to bring it into clearer focus and formulate a program for its retention and development. And once the Puerto Ricans (for the most part) had welcomed the Americans as liberators they also began to see their new situation more clearly. Puerto Rico was immediately placed under a military governor while the United States administration and Congress debated just what its status should—could—be. There were those who believed that permanent acquisition of such a foreign overseas territory violated both the letter and the spirit of the Constitution. Despite all the jingoism of the day, a sizable body of Americans had an "uncomfortable feeling that imperialism, the subjugation of alien peoples, was a betrayal of our heritage and the promise of our future" (the case of the American Indians was of course commonly considered fundamentally, geopolitically different—and over and done with). The issue was mainly argued with reference to the Philippines but was especially pertinent to the case of Puerto Rico because alternatives to its annexation were little considered. Proponents of expansion, needing an interpretation that would allow the holding of territories and peoples "differing from us in religion, customs, laws, methods of taxation and modes of thought, [where] the administration of government and justice, according to Anglo-Saxon principles, may for a time be impossible," came up with a distinction between "incorporated" and "unincorporated" territories, wherein the latter were not recognized "as an integral part of the United States" and need not be until "the wisdom of Congress" determined that they had "reached a state where it is proper that it should enter into and form a part of the American family." The cases of Louisiana and Florida were cited as precedents. Thus under the Foraker Act of 1900 Puerto Rico became an unincorporated "insular territory," its people "citizens of Puerto Rico" rather than of the United States, and Congress imposed a government on its new colony without consultation with its subjects. The Supreme Court upheld this imperial act by the narrowest of margins, with minority opinion dissenting strongly against such an "occult" concept of territories and the

substitution "for the present [American] system of republican government, a system of domination over distant provinces in the exercise of unrestricted power."
But such opinions quickly faded from the scene as the United States got under way
with its sudden new phase of empire.

The Puerto Rican leadership was bitterly disappointed in this substitution of
American colonial rule for that of Spain. As in Cuba there had been a long history of
agitations and sporadic revolts (though no sustained warfare) for independence or at
least home rule. They had expected to receive at least as much autonomy from their
new overlords as they had at last been granted by Spain in the months just before the
American takeover; what they got was a good deal less in local power and a set of
officials who spoke no Spanish and regarded them with a degree of disdain.

The Americanization program brought important physical changes with the
construction of roads and bridges, sanitation systems (and inoculations), and
agricultural experiment stations; American investors were soon modernizing and
expanding sugar and tobacco production; a university was founded, the public
school system was expanded, and "a peaceful invasion" of American schoolteachers
and Protestant missionaries ensued. Language was of course a critical matter.
Between 1905 and 1915 English became the official language in all public schools for
all subjects at all levels, as it was in most of the parochial schools now staffed by
priests and religious orders from the United States (the island was placed under the
Diocese of New York). Even the name of the island "was arbitrarily changed to 'Porto
Rico' to suit American pronunciation and usage" (a controversial matter that flared
up immediately in *National Geographic*: after an article on "Porto Rico" by Robert T.
Hill, the editors added a note "that in acceding to Mr. Hill's request in this trifling
matter that they are not establishing a precedent," which brought responses in a
later issue scorning this departure from proper Spanish usage and a report that the
U.S. Board of Geographic Names had decided on "Puerto Rico"—yet the changed
usage was common for some time even in government reports).

AN AMERICAN MEDITERRANEAN

The idea of the United States obtaining one or more naval bases in the Caribbean
was as old as the annexation of California and gold rush traffic across the Isthmus of
Panama. Puerto Rico had rarely been mentioned among numerous prospective
sites, but once under American military control it was immediately pushed to the
fore. Alfred Thayer Mahan, America's most famous and influential geopolitician of
the day, was quick to instruct the American public and its leaders on "the lessons of
the War with Spain": "Puerto Rico, considered militarily, is to Cuba, to the future
Isthmian Canal, and to our Pacific coast, what Malta is, or may be, to Egypt," Suez,
and the route to India. More attention, however, was directed to the islands

immediately to the east, which had been of interest to various American leaders—if not Congress—for many years. "There is no harbor in the West Indies better fitted than St. Thomas for a naval station," said an American admiral in 1865, and Secretary of State William Seward soon arranged to purchase it and its neighbor, St. John, from Denmark. However, a Congress immersed in the bitter politics of Reconstruction left the treaty unratified. The idea was revived in the early 1890s, and after the radical changes of 1898 the Senate in 1902 endorsed purchase of all the Danish West Indies. But this time the Danish Parliament, swayed by the sugar interests of St. Croix and the hope that an Isthmian canal would bring new traffic and profit, failed (by one vote) to ratify. However, the outbreak of the Great War in Europe soon altered the perspectives of both nations, and as relations between the United States and Germany deteriorated and fear of a German seizure mounted, a new American offer was made and accepted by Denmark. Thus for the price of $25 million (five times the 1902 price) the Danish Virgin Islands, with their 26,000 people, became another insular U.S. territory in 1917.

Before the war with Spain the United States had revived the prospect of leasing a naval base at Samaná Bay in the Dominican Republic and had sounded out Haiti on a similar position at Môle St. Nicholas, each site commanding a major passageway into the Caribbean. Neither proposal got very far, but they further illustrated American concern with obtaining a position commanding the approaches to an Isthmian canal. All through these years American leaders were also concerned over geopolitical instabilities in the region. The West Indies were divided among Britain, France, Spain, Denmark, and The Netherlands, and a latent fear that some of the possessions of the lesser powers might be sold to (or, later, that the home country might be seized by) a major imperial power became manifest with the rise of a blatantly expansionist Germany. Hispaniola, the exception amidst this complexity of colonies, was divided between two recurrently bankrupt and war-torn states: Haiti and the Dominican Republic. In 1869 the president of the latter actually sought annexation to the United States as the resolution of its problems; President Ulysses S. Grant was eager to attain it, but Congress refused approval. In 1904 the Dominican Republic was again bankrupt and Theodore Roosevelt, fearing that European powers (and especially Germany) might try to enforce repayment of debts (as Germany, Britain, and Italy had recently done in Venezuela), proclaimed his famous corollary to the Monroe Doctrine, by which "in flagrant cases of such wrongdoing or impotence" the United States would assume the "civilized" burden of intervention—in this case with a show of force, taking control of customs houses and allocating a portion of the receipts to repayment. Within a few years it would similarly intervene in Nicaragua and Haiti (and, on rather different grounds, seize and hold Mexico's chief port, Veracruz, for a few months in 1914).

This American assumption of "an international police power" (to use Roosevelt's words) marked the completion of a fundamental revision of imperial relations in the Caribbean. In 1850 a transcontinental United States and a maritime British Empire had agreed (in the Clayton-Bulwer Treaty) to cooperate on the construction of any Isthmian canal, to install no fortifications nor exercise exclusive control over such a canal, and to allow no further foreign occupation or dominion over any part of Central America (Britain had just imposed a protectorate over the Caribbean coast of Nicaragua). This agreement had been harshly criticized in the United States at the time as an impediment to America's expanding interests, and by 1900 pressures for drastic revision were irresistible. When a bill was introduced in Congress providing for the construction of a Nicaraguan Canal in defiance of the treaty, Great Britain, involved in the Boer War and faced with serious challenges on several imperial fronts, agreed to negotiate. The result was the Second Hay-Pauncefote Treaty, which gave the United States the right to build, control, and fortify an Isthmian canal (the first version had not included fortification and was rejected the U.S. Senate). This British recognition of American supremacy was followed by a reduction in its West Indian naval force and garrison at Kingston, Jamaica, and a few years later by the American decision to make Guantánamo Bay its principal Caribbean base.

Two months before the signing of that treaty in 1901 Theodore Roosevelt had become president (following McKinley's assassination), and building a canal became one of his foremost objectives. With Cuba and Puerto Rico in hand and Britain inviting the United States to create an all-American waterway, the principal question was where to build it: Panama or Nicaragua? Each had a considerable history of studies and supporters and a Panama Canal had actually been undertaken by a French company under Ferdinand de Lesseps, famous builder of Suez (completed in 1869). Excavation had begun in 1883 but ended in defeat six years later from lack of funds and the ravages of tropical diseases. The French company failed but its concession from the Republic of Colombia remained valid. In 1895 President Grover Cleveland had appointed a board to investigate the Nicaraguan route, and this was soon broadened into an Isthmian Canal Commission to evaluate various possibilities. In November 1901 this body recommended Nicaragua (primarily on the basis of cost, given the very high price of the French concession). When the House endorsed that proposal, the French company and its American and Panamanian associates hastily lowered their price and lobbied intensely for support in Washington. Their success became famous partly because of their ploy with the fortuitous coincidence of the issuance of a new Nicaraguan postage stamp featuring a volcano just as the horrendous explosion of Mt. Pelée on Martinique killed 29,000 people. The Isthmian Canal Commission and Congress quickly switched to Panama—if rights could be secured from Colombia in a reasonable time. A treaty was negotiated but it was rejected by the Colombian Senate (which

wanted more money, especially for such an unpopular and unprecedented concession of sovereignty as demanded the United States), whereupon Roosevelt determined to get it in a more direct way by supporting a carefully staged "revolt"
(planned in New York City and engineered primarily by the current holder of the
French concession) and granting official recognition to the new "Republic of
Panama" two days after it had proclaimed its independence. A few days later, for
the sum of $10 million and a quarter-million-dollar annuity, the United States was
granted a ten-mile Canal Zone (excluding the cities at either end) in which it
might exercise "all the rights, power and authority" as "if it were the sovereign of
the territory"—in perpetuity. Critics at home and abroad had ample grounds for
denouncing this kind of "piracy," "indecent haste," and "cooked-up republic," but
the furor soon died down. On the other side of the matter the Panamanians were
desperate to get the canal (though not necessarily at such a cost to their sovereignty) and had at various times before revolted against an unresponsive Bogotá.
Given the general context of the times most Americans—and Europeans—
probably agreed with Theodore Roosevelt's vigorous defense of his actions as
exercising "a mandate from civilization" to create an "interoceanic canal."

Thus in the opening years of the twentieth century, the United States had
transformed this Mediterranean into an American lake, its hegemony un-
challenged. It did so in response to what it believed to be geopolitical necessities; it
expanded upon these for economic advantages—and it generally considered its
moves and motivations to be in the best interests not only of Americans but of the
peoples of this region. Yet in this realm of empire as in others there was always
ample evidence of contradictions and resistances to such policies. The U.S. hold
upon Cuba, Puerto Rico, the Virgin Islands, and Panama assured its geopolitical
security, but this imperial imposition also extended and compounded its long
involvement in one of the world's most complex cultural borderlands. In this
fragmented realm, where the Anglo-American, Hispanic-American, and Afro-
American worlds intersect and overlap, the arrogance and racism ever apparent at
every level of American participation was bound to undermine and warp expected
results. An insular empire in a tropical world was a significant departure from a
century of continental imperial experience—as its concurrent expansions in the
Pacific would also attest.

3. Hawaii and an American Pacific

HAWAII

By 1850 Hawaii, the most remote corner of Polynesia, had become the central
crossroads of a Neo-European Pacific World. Traders, whalers, and missionaries

made it their primary base, navies of the leading powers kept an eye on this new strategic site, and in Honolulu, the bicultural capital town, Hawaiian royalty, foreign advisers, consuls, and various opportunists formed uneasy relationships during a time of impending change. King Kamehameha III's request in 1843 for legal recognition of Hawaii as an independent state had not been formally accepted, and an 1850s treaty of annexation and statehood was never acted upon by the U.S. Senate. The king had felt driven to these positions out of fear that irregular forces might seize power; the Americans locally involved in the matter regarded annexation as economically advantageous and geopolitically essential.

Expansionists of the time were not looking on across the Pacific; they regarded Hawaii as an outpost of North America, a natural adjunct of the continent because ships rounding Cape Horn bound for Oregon or California swung north and west to Hawaii following the currents and trade winds, thence north and east to the mainland. As the reality of an isthmian canal came nearer, the importance of Hawaii was compounded: "The annexation of Hawaii would make the canal a necessity as the construction of the canal will make annexation a necessity." Above all else, Hawaii must not be allowed to fall into the hands of a foreign power. In 1867 the American minister began to push for a commercial reciprocity treaty that would aid in the "quiet absorption" of the islands, and the treaty signed in 1875, allowing sugar duty-free entry to the American market, soon did make them virtually an economic colony. Sugar production soared, bringing great prosperity to a small *haole* elite of planters, merchants, bankers, agents, and shipping firms. (Originally a general term for all foreigners, *haole* was soon narrowed to light-skinned Europeans and Americans.) The one great continuing problem was labor. As Hawaiians generally refused to engage in such hard regimented work in their bountiful native land, Chinese, who had been drifting through since the California gold rush, were now recruited in large numbers. However, they usually left the plantation at the end of their contract, and in response to their complaints of abuse the Chinese government prohibited emigration to Hawaii in 1881. Concerned over the continued decline in the number of Hawaiians and the increase in Asians, the government and planters offered subsidies to Europeans, bringing in several thousand Portuguese from the Atlantic Islands and a sprinkling of Germans and Scandinavians, but these, too, left the hard tasks of the canefields as soon as possible (many Portuguese became plantation foremen and artisans). In 1885 they turned to Japan and it became the most reliable source for many years.

In 1887 the haole elite forced King Kalakaua to accept a new constitution giving principal power to themselves as property owners, and movements for closer ties with the United States gained new momentum. The United States had already been granted exclusive rights to Pearl Harbor, but a proposed comprehensive protectorate aroused strong opposition from the Hawaiians and was dropped. In

1892 a secret Annexation Club was formed in Honolulu, and the American minister to Hawaii worked avidly for the cause, insisting to his superiors in Washington that "Hawaii has reached the parting of the ways. She must now take the road that leads to Asia, or the other, . . . [that] gives her an American civilization and binds her to the care of American destiny." When in 1893 Queen Liliuokalani (who had succeeded her late brother) attempted to proclaim a new constitution restoring greater power to the Hawaiians, the Americans, backed by U.S. marines, staged a coup, formed a new provisional government (quickly recognized by their accomplice, the U.S. minister), declared Hawaii to be a protectorate of the United States, and sent commissioners to Washington to negotiate annexation. The Harrison administration readily agreed with its minister that "the Hawaiian pear is now fully ripe, and this is the golden hour for the United States to pluck it," and a treaty of annexation (providing annuities to the deposed queen and her heir) was signed on February 14, 1893.

Before the treaty was considered by Congress, however, a new administration took office and President Grover Cleveland, suspicious of this takeover (and generally against such overseas expansion), sent a special investigator to Hawaii. His report was a scathing critique of the affair, concluding that the queen had been overthrown by force with the complicity of American officials, and so after intense debate in Congress the United States decided not to accept this ripened pear. The haoles in power therefore proclaimed a Republic of Hawaii and began plotting anew how to achieve annexation so as to secure their access to the American market without undermining their local position (some sugar barons were hesitant, fearing that they would no longer be allowed to bring in Asian laborers).

In the debates and commentary of the time the pros and cons of the case for this particular expansion were expounded. Supporters insisted that Hawaii was one of "the necessary outworks" for the security of the nation, and some raised the specter of a British or German takeover (European powers were gobbling up the Pacific islands, as the United States had found out in Samoa). Influential voices took up Mahan's new theory that "without sea power no nation has been really great" and Hawaii was the key to the whole system of Pacific commerce and larger strategies. As for the constitutional legality of such expansion, clearly the time has come (said a senator from Oregon in 1893) when "we must abandon the doctrine that our national boundaries and jurisdiction should be confined to the shores of the continent," for (as a San Francisco paper later put it) "now that the continent is subdued, we are looking for fresh worlds to conquer," and "the colonizing instinct is now pushing us out and on to Alaska, to the isles of the sea—and beyond."

Opponents had plenty of answers. A powerful United States did not need bastions lying 2,500 miles across empty seas to defend its coastline; as for the canal, San Diego was 2,000 miles closer than Hawaii. Big navies and bases were a needless expense; with Pearl Harbor under lease we did not need to take over the whole island chain to participate in Pacific commerce. The Constitution clearly did not contemplate the acquisition of overseas territories that would not be routinely colonized and absorbed into the body of the Republic. As for our "colonizing instinct," after half a century of contact Americans made up less than 5 percent of the population, and, as Carl Schurz stated in a celebrated critique of "manifest destiny," "no candid American would ever think of making a State of this Union out of such a group of islands with such a population as it has and is likely to have" (about 60 percent Asian, 25 percent Hawaiian or part-Hawaiian—Americans of any experience in the islands generally liked Hawaiians as a people but did not consider them good prospects as citizens). At the very least, there should be no annexation without a plebiscite (an idea rejected by the haole government).

The Hawaiian Islands became a formal American possession by a destiny not at all manifest until the sudden astonishing victory of Commodore George Dewey 5,300 miles to the west in Manila Bay and its instant enlargement of American visions of the Pacific. Within a few weeks (before the war with Spain was over) a joint resolution of annexation was passed by Congress and on July 7, 1898, was signed by President McKinley.

What we got, said historian Lawrence H. Fuchs, was "a curious amalgam of a tropical European colony and a New England settlement." Honolulu, the polyglot, multicultural crossroads, displayed many of the marks of a colonial capital, more like a Colombo or a Singapore than any place in North America. The view from the comfortable mansions of the ruling elite was dominated by their architecture, businesses, and social and religious life, but the palaces and entourage of the native royalty were also readily apparent, as was an array of small shops and services, houses and shacks of a variety of immigrants (the Chinese were a quarter of the population). The lowlands of the countryside on all the major islands were studded with sugar plantations wherein the great house and the mill dominated the landscape, but the local society was most likely a Japanese enclave with its own language, games, gods, "attitudes toward family, property, and authority," and strong sense of cohesion and apartness. Scattered around the edges of these great estates and in remote villages was "the Hawaii of the Hawaiians . . . where some natives prayed fervently to Madam Pele, the Goddess of Fire, to shake loose molten lava from the mountains and wash foreign customs into the sea." Those customs were manifold and widespread because here the Western imprint was much more comprehensive and indelible than in the typical tropical colony; changes had appeared half a century earlier in such basic adaptations as monogamy and private property, Christianity and constitutions. It was in these things, together with the great emphasis upon schools and libraries, philanthropy and moral uplift, that displayed the mark of New England. By 1900 there were nearly 200 schools (public and private); there were many Hawaiian teachers and there was a generally high rate of literacy among Hawaiians and part-Hawaiians.

This new insular territory was treated very differently from Puerto Rico. Hawaii had already been strongly "Americanized," its inhabitants became American citizens, and its first territorial governor was a prominent haole. Hawaiians were actually a majority of the legislature, but they were coopted by members of the haole oligarchy, who worked assiduously and successfully to maintain their power and preserve a way of life that had made Hawaii—for them—"a veritable paradise on earth." Meanwhile the population continued to grow and diversify. Asian contract labor was no longer allowed, but Asians, including a brief influx of Koreans, continued to arrive. Plantation owners quickly turned to new American tropical possessions, bringing in several thousand Puerto Ricans and, beginning in 1906, Filipinos. At the same time a good many earlier immigrants moved on to mainland America. The 192,000 enumerated in the 1910 census offered some basic categories of the remarkable diversity in this new imperial holding (see table).

Asians 56%	Japanese	76,675
	Chinese	21,674
	Koreans	4,533
	Filipinos	2,361
Aboriginal 20%	Hawaiians	26,041
	Part-Hawaiians	12,506
White[a] 15%	Portuguese	22,301
	Spaniards	1,990
	Puerto Ricans	4,890
Other Caucasians[b] <8%		14,867
Blacks <1%		695

Notes: [a]Mostly imported as laborers.
[b]Includes American haoles as well as some imported laborers.

THE PHILIPPINES

Wars usually produce unintended results. Dewey's mission in Manila Bay was to destroy the Spanish fleet and thereby hasten an end to the war in the American Mediterranean and the expulsion of Spain from the Western Hemisphere. His sensational victory would prove a costly success, for it led to an American war of conquest and rule over 7 million Filipinos in a large archipelago half a world away. This "almost inadvertent takeover of the Philippines" posed serious geopolitical problems at the outset and would continue to do long after.

The Philippines were the extreme case in the bitter political battles over American imperial alternatives. There could be no pretense that these distant islands were essential to the security of the continental United States. To impose our rule upon an alien people in such a far-off foreign land would, opponents said, make the United States no better than predatory European colonial powers, compromising its highest ideals. Furthermore, such colonialism would burden the country with costly armies and navies because, as in Cuba, the Filipinos had revolted against Spanish rule and would surely resist simply being handed over to the Americans. Others of course extolled the opportunity so fairly won ("this island empire is the last land left in all the oceans") and the destiny so clearly revealed (the Pacific as the next stage in our westward advance and Manila as "the greatest commercial and strategic point in the East"). McKinley's cabinet debated a full range of alternatives: take nothing, take only a naval station at Manila, reserve only a coaling station and a free trade zone at Subic Bay, take Luzon only, take Luzon and establish a protectorate over the rest of the islands, take them all (fig. 77, inset). But they came to no conclusion, and the treaty ending the war left the matter hanging: "The United States will occupy and hold the city, bay and harbor of Manila, pending the conclusions of a treaty of peace which shall determine the control, disposition and government of the Philippines."

Resolution of the matter hinged on arguments that Spain (as had been so long apparent in Cuba) was an infamous and moribund imperial power and that the islands could not in good conscience be returned to its despotic rule, nor could they be left alone to be grabbed by some vigorous expansive power, such as Germany or Japan. Furthermore, as the Filipinos were not a nation but an aggregation of many tribes and tongues and quite unfit as yet for self-government, it was America's duty and mission to—in McKinley's later phrasing of it—"educate the Filipinos, and uplift and civilize and Christianize them." By a margin of one vote in the Senate the United States annexed the Philippines—and, as opponents had warned, it then had to undertake a military conquest of the islands. The Filipino revolutionary movement, under the leadership of Emilio Aguinaldo, had sought recognition from and alliance with the United States in liberating the country from Spanish rule. When the Americans had first arrived on the scene Aguinaldo claimed that he had received assurances from officials (including Dewey) that Filipinos would be allowed their independence under American protection. However, as in Cuba, the Americans shunned any partnership with these "insurgents." Both laid siege to Manila; the Spanish chose to surrender the city to the Americans, and the Americans refused to allow the Filipino forces entry. The Filipinos proceeded to defeat and oust the Spanish from much of central Luzon, set up their government in Malolos, thirty miles north of Manila, and sought to participate in the treaty negotiations between the United States and Spain being conducted in Paris (to no avail). Early in 1899 a minor incident flared into open conflict between the American and Filipino armies, which after a series of American victories changed

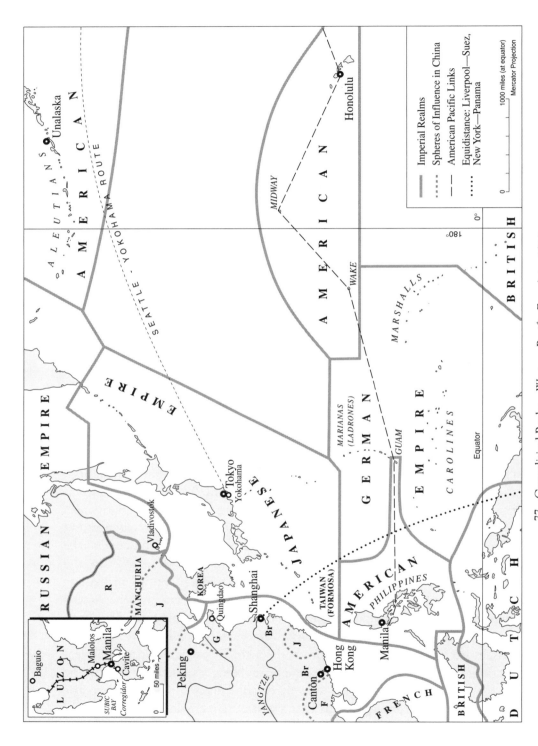

77. Geopolitical Realms: Western Pacific–East Asia, 1914.

The imperial sea boundaries shown merely outline generalized zones rather than formal

into a guerrilla warfare that became increasingly vicious on both sides as it was gradually compressed into the central islands and brought to a close in the spring of 1902. It had taken 125,000 troops to crush this "insurrection" at a cost of several thousand American and perhaps 200,000 Filipino lives. For the American army it was a continuation—"the long twilight"—of a century of imperial campaigns against indigenous peoples (nearly every high officer in this fray "had spent most of his career terrorizing Apaches, Comanches, Kiowas, and the Sioux").

Well before this military phase had ended the American government had sent commissions to assess the general situation and prepare a program for civilian rule, and on July 4, 1901, William Howard Taft took charge as governor. This long imperial reach across the Pacific was in itself nothing new to the Philippines, for through most of the more than 300 years of Spanish rule it was the westernmost outlier of New Spain, tethered to Acapulco by the annual voyage of the famous Manila Galleon carrying on the limited but profitable exchange of Chinese goods for Mexican silver. An old American influence was apparent in such crops as tobacco, pineapples, and especially maize, the food staple in many of the drier and poorer lands. The Spanish had needed little military force to extend their control over most of the islands because, with the important exception of the Moros (Muslims) of Sulu and Mindanao, the native peoples generally accepted and adapted to the Spanish presence. The gridiron town with its plaza, church, *convento* (priest's residence), government office, barracks, and houses of the principal families, together with the settlement and organizational hierarchy of *cabecera* (church village), *población* (district seat), *municipio, provincia,* and capital (Manila), imposed a rigid new skeletal frame upon the rather formless Philippine body. Because this distant land was not an attractive frontier of European colonization and exploitation, it escaped the common horrors of massive dislocations and forced labor in mines and plantations. Here Spanish rule focused on the spread of the faith; much of the country was run by Filipinos under the close tutelage and supervision of Spanish religious orders and was quite insulated—in the friars' view, protected—from the modern world. At the end of this empire few Filipinos were fluent in Spanish, but most were at least nominal Roman Catholics. Commercial life had long been dominated by Chinese traders and shopkeepers.

The nineteenth century had brought important changes. Foreign merchants were now allowed in Manila, and the Mexican Revolution ended the Acapulco connection and brought more direct links with Spain, later magnified by steamships and the Suez Canal. Roads, railroads, telegraphs, and interisland shipping services linked all substantial settlements and served an expanding commercial agriculture (tobacco, sugar, spices, and *abaca,* also known as Manila hemp). The population grew rapidly, older racial-ethnic categories (including complex concepts of "mestizo") became blurred, and an emerging elite of Filipino families (in which, like the country as a whole, "the Spanish element is less than often presumed, and the Chinese element greater than often admitted") prospered as landowners and businessmen, and they contributed to an intelligentsia (the *illustrados*) that worked at formulating a Filipino national identity (with José Rizal, "scientist, physician, linguist, poet, and novelist" as the "pre-eminent exemplar"). Caught in the pressures of "a modernizing convulsion" the Spanish hierarchy resisted demands for autonomy or independence with increasing severity. The Filipino revolt was against Spanish rule (in church as well as state) not Spanish culture.

The Americans soon developed an imperial program also and imposed their mark upon land and society, but there was a good deal of continuity as well. Their energetic expansion of roads, bridges, telegraphs, telephones, harbor facilities, and sanitation systems was an acceleration of developments already under way, yet the much greater facility of communications and easing of controls encouraged settlement dispersal, reversing a longstanding Spanish emphasis on stable concentrations. They continued to administer the country through the established geopolitical hierarchy, but they also brought in Daniel Burnham, famous chief architect of Chicago's great Columbian Exposition, to place an American stamp upon an expanding Manila, adding public buildings of classical Federal architecture, wide boulevards, and spacious parks. (Governor Taft, huge in bulk and suffering miserably in the tropical heat, also had Burnham create a summer capital 150 miles north at Baguio, a mile-high "health retreat" like Simla and Darjeeling in British India, a "City of Pines" that reminded Americans of the Adirondacks.) The Americans established modern currency and banking systems, purchased the huge holdings of the religious societies, and devised land policies to favor small operators (which, as in the United States, were far from wholly successful). They separated church and state and loosed a vigorous evangelical missionary effort upon the islands. The proselytizing had little direct effect upon an already Christian population, but the loosened hold of the official Roman Catholic church was quickly followed by the emergence of a schismatic Philippine Independent church and the beginnings of the indigenous charismatic Church of Christ. The biggest agents of cultural change were the American schoolteachers who came to staff or oversee mostly new schools at every level from primary to university as well as many specialized types: normal schools, trade schools, and nursing, nautical, and agricultural institutes. They taught in English, not only because they were imperial agents but because there was no obviously national language of instruction. Tagalog, the principal language of Luzon, was the leading aspirant and Spanish the tongue of the Filipino elite, but as an American education superintendent said, "English is the lingua franca of the Far East. It is spoken in the ports from Hakodate to Australia. It is the common language of business and social intercourse between the different nations from America westward to the Levant. It is without rival the most useful language which a man can know . . . and to the Filipino the possession of English is the gateway into that busy and fervid life of commerce, of modern science, of diplomacy and politics in which he aspires to shine." As indeed it proved to be.

As the historian H. W. Brands observed, such a program displayed that "to a considerable degree, American imperialism of the early twentieth century . . . was progressivism writ large." Throughout this imperial era "the United States refused to be labeled a colonial power and even expunged the world *colonial* from its official vocabulary" (its colonies were administered through a Bureau of Insular Affairs). In their own eyes Americans came not as masters but as missionaries of modern democratic life—"emissaries of good will," as one schoolteacher put it. They came, in fact, not only as masters but as military conquerors, but once that embarrassingly ugly phase was over their ambivalence about being there at all caused them to work assiduously at a policy of attraction and participation to gain Filipino support for their program of tutelage and modernization. They found powerful allies in a Filipino elite that was itself alarmed by revolutionary militarism and peasant uprisings. This "cosmopolitan upper class, composed mostly of Spanish or Chinese *mestizos* who were intellectual equals or even superiors of their U.S. masters" quickly "demonstrated their mastery of the imperial game, turning the American presence to their own ends." For the first twelve years under Republican administrations in Washington it was in effect an alliance between two elites, conservative men of property and position who regarded hierarchy and deference as a natural feature of society-limited agents of social reform. Despite much cooperation, attraction and consensus were undermined by racism and arrogance (in common imperial fashion, the "Manila Americans" did not allow Filipinos in their clubs and societies). American businessmen proved far less eager to invest in the Philippines than annexationists had assumed, partly because American officials were themselves divided as to whether the ultimate objective was to prepare the Filipinos for independence or to win them over to some sort of permanent affiliation ("benevolent assimilation" in McKinley's words) with the United States (hardly anyone envisioned eventual statehood). That difference was explicit in American party positions. Whereas Republicans sought to avoid the issue—and thus continue their program of tutelage—the Democrats in 1912 offered a bold denunciation of the entire affair:

> We condemn the experiment in imperialism as an inexcusable blunder which has involved us in enormous expense, brought us weakness instead of strength, and laid our nation open to the charge of the abandonment of the fundamental doctrine of self-government. We favor the immediate declaration of the Nation's purpose to recognize the independence of the Philippine Islands as soon as a stable government

can be established, such independence to be guaranteed by us until the neutralization
of the islands can be secured by treaty with other powers.

With the election of Woodrow Wilson major change was initiated. A new set of
American officials arrived to begin the "Filipinization" of the administration in
anticipation of the end of American rule a few years hence. Although no Filipino
party could be against independence, many of the elite were not as yet so secure in
their sociopolitical positions to be eager for it quickly. Under their astute leader,
Manuel Quezon, they sought greater home rule and a firm commitment by the
United States to eventual independence—without a specific date set. In the Jones
Act of 1916 they got exactly that.

The annexation of the Philippine Islands was the catalyst for the sudden creation of a new transpacific geopolitical axis and the emergence of the United States
as a major Pacific power (see fig. 77). The central line of bases was San Francisco–
Honolulu-Midway-Wake-Guam-Manila. Midway, a set of uninhabited atolls
claimed by the U.S. Navy in 1867, was now (as then foreseen) a useful outlier of
the Hawaiian chain. American forces en route to Manila in 1898 laid claim to
uninhabited Wake Island and took possession of Guam from an astonished Spanish
officer who in that remote bit of empire had not heard that the two nations were at
war. Guam was selected and retained from the longitudinal line of the Spanish
Ladrones (today's Mariana Islands) as a perfect complement to this itinerary. It had
a good harbor and enough land and people (about 10,000 Chamorros) to be a
valuable supply center (long ago it had been a routine stop for the westbound
Manila Galleon). Two other distant positions now took on new importance. Far to
the south near the margins of Polynesia and about halfway between Hawaii and
New Zealand and Australia the fine harbor at Pago Pago on Tutuila in the Samoan
Islands, long attractive to Western mariners and under some degree of American
claim since 1872, was brought under full possession in 1899. Far to the north the
spacious harbor of Unalaska in the Aleutians was midway near the shortest shipping routes across the North Pacific. Critics of Hawaiian annexation had stressed
that contrary to common impressions Unalaska was far more important than Pearl
Harbor for transpacific shipping because the shortest routes to Japan and China
followed the Great Circle 2,000 miles north of Hawaii. However, Hawaii itself was
a focus of American interest, and its strategic importance to shipping (inherent in
the days of sailing ships) would be greatly magnified with the completion of an
isthmian canal.

These widely spaced positions were well suited for the technical needs of the
day: coaling stations for steamships and points of safety for naval strategy ("coal
endurance," explained Captain Mahan to his coterie of influential imperialists, is
the distance, about 3,500 miles, that a battleship can steam without recoaling,

allowing a reasonable margin of safety); and relay stations for submarine cables (maximum also about 3,500 miles)—the new Pacific axis was quickly hailed as "a continuous line of great telegraph poles upon which we may string a wire or series of wires . . . across this great body of water . . . on our own territory and protected by the American flag"; and this was very soon done, with a further extension from Manila to Hong Kong. "Commerce follows the cables, and as we offer the most direct cable route, so should we offer the most direct steamship route . . . [and] the carrying trade will fall into our hands very largely when the Nicaraguan Canal is opened," wrote Senator Henry Cabot Lodge in an 1898 memo urging the need to hold Hawaii and the Philippines. Certainly trade was the great motive—the commercial possibilities of 400 million Chinese consumers fevered the minds of expansionists (fig. 78)—but contrary to common assertions an American hold upon Manila gave no guarantee of success; one must have a foothold in China itself and especially, as Captain Mahan instructed, in the Yangtze Valley, which by the laws of geography must become the commercial core (and, ideally, the political capital) of "a renewed China." The United States made a hesitant effort to obtain such a position but found itself in a competition for which it was not prepared.

The United States arrived in East Asia just as other imperial powers were voraciously carving up the feeble Chinese Empire. Japan had opened the way in 1895 when it decisively defeated China in a war over dominance in Korea and had taken the large Chinese island of Taiwan as a major territorial reward. The ease of Japan's victory had surprised the European powers and impelled them to grab their share. In 1897 a German naval force pressured the empire into granting a lease for a naval base and commercial privileges in the major port and hinterland of Qingdao (Tsingtao), and in the summer of 1898 (while the Americans were laying siege to Manila) Germany, Great Britain, Russia, France, and Japan formally parceled virtually the entire coast of China among themselves as exclusive "spheres of influence" (each involving commercial concessions and military bases). Actually, while Dewey was still at Hong Kong (the U.S. Asiatic squadron was dependent upon British coaling stations) before setting sail for Manila, his navy superiors had instructed him to ascertain "the best attainable port in China" should the United States decide to enter this competition, and during the next two years secret inquiries were made about Zhoushan (Chusan) Island lying south of the Yangtze entrance and Sansha (Samsah) Bay in Fujien Province; however, the first had already been allocated to Italy (which had belatedly entered the imperial race but would soon withdraw from participation in this East Asian event), and Japan firmly objected to Sansha Bay as an encroachment upon its own sphere opposite Taiwan. These geopolitical gestures never had the firm support of the American administration, which rather than directly compete in this dangerous game fell back upon getting all these other powers to support an equality of commercial opportunities in

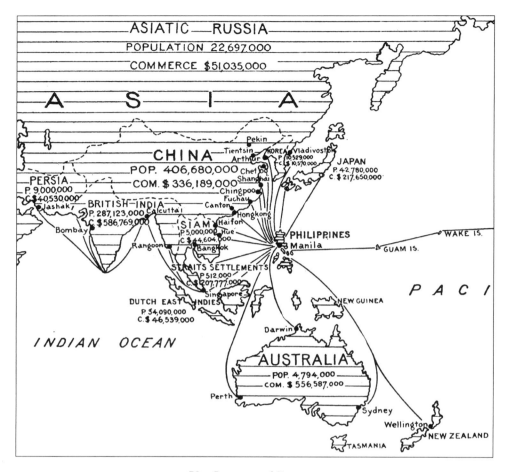

78. Commercial Fantasy.
O. P. Austin, Chief, Bureau of Statistics, U.S. Treasury Department, prepared this map to show his 1902 audience at the National Geographic Society "the position of Manila as a distributing point for the commerce of that great semicircle of countries stretching from Bering Strait to Australasia, containing half the population of the earth and importing a hundred million dollars worth of merchandise every month of the year."

China. Secretary of State John Hay's "Open Door Policy" was hailed by many Americans as a laudable altruistic response to an unseemly imperial struggle, but it was (as he well knew) a feeble instrument in East Asian affairs. It was implicitly a declaration to American business interests that their government was not going to use force or pressure on their behalf in China (which at the time accounted for only about 2 percent of American foreign trade).

By its sudden, unpremeditated expansion to the China seas the United States found itself in a new and difficult geopolitical situation. The Americans were there largely because of their own self-conceit, so long nourished. The public had been thrilled by the victory and heady with the prospects: it was the "final movement" in that great westward march of empire-progress-civilization "across the great ocean, step by step, and island by island" until today "American man" stands in the Philippine Islands "knocking at the door of China." As Harvard Professor Archibald Coolidge told his Sorbonne audience, one must take such rhetoric seriously: "Whatever pertains to the Pacific Ocean appeals strongly to Americans at the present day. There is something in the very immensity of the field which makes it seem appropriate for the display of their superabundant energy. They believe that they have an unequalled advantage, and are entitled to foremost place." Henry Gannett, government geographer who served as assistant director of the Philippine Census, supported the popular conviction that "because of our possession of the Philippines we shall become the dominant power of the Pacific both politically and commercially." Another prominent geographer put it a bit more specifically in a popular theory of the time: the war with Spain, wrote Ellen Churchill Semple in her *American History and Its Geographic Influences,* had only "accelerated the progress of history," for the United States was destined to find a forward base and enter "into the maelstrom of Asiatic affairs," which is an "international struggle for existence, . . . a struggle for space." But that surely defined something rather different. For once the United States had won its independence it had acquired its immense continental space with scarcely any struggle at all, and it was surely hard to discern any spatial pressure on its existence. This Ratzelian Lebensraum (Semple had studied under him in Germany), this competitive expansion for worldwide empire, had little precedence in American experience and the complications were soon apparent.

The United States had selected Guam as a practical stopover on the route to Asia, whereupon Spain sold the rest of its Pacific islands—the Marianas, Marshalls, and Carolines—and this new American base was suddenly a lone foreign enclave in the midst of the German Pacific empire (the German government had attempted to buy or lease some of these islands some years earlier). Furthermore, as Akira Iriye has emphasized, those shrill popular assumptions about America's expansive destiny "ill prepared the nation for coping with a totally different phenomenon: expansion undertaken by non-Western peoples." Much the greatest challenge came from an Asian power equally "self-conscious about civilization and race" and similarly supportive of colonization as an instrument of expansion. As a Japanese author wrote in 1890: "It would be to our great advantage if our countrymen moved outside the limits of the nation, scattering themselves in overseas settlements and colonies, engaged in their respective activities, provided food for themselves, but still maintained contact with the mother country so that while they were physically abroad they would internally be still part of Japan." (This sounds very like Jefferson's formula for taking over Louisiana and the common American assumptions about its pioneer settlers in Mexican Texas, California, or Oregon.)

The Pacific was the obvious realm for the establishment of these "new Japans." Hawaii was a prime target and seemed, for a time, a success: by 1895 it had become, said one author, "our branch house," and the Japanese government hoped for its continuance as an independent republic. With the acquisition of Taiwan the Philippines loomed as a logical extension, and even though Japan could not block American annexation the hope remained that "if we continue to send emigrants and create Japanese villages and towns, the result would be almost like extending the limits of our empire" (sounds like the confident expectations for "the advance guard of American civilization" in northern Mexico). It is not surprising, therefore, that Japanese leaders regarded the American takeover of Hawaii and the Philippines as a setback and the suppression of Filipino resistance as a flagrant case of Western aggression against an Asiatic people. However, the maintenance of good relations with the United States was too important to allow official protest of these events; deterioration of those relations would stem more directly from pressures exerted within the United States than from imperial competitions in the Pacific.

By 1905 there were more than 100,000 Japanese in Hawaii and on the American West Coast, and emigrants continued to prefer this wealthy land of opportunity over much closer areas now open to them, such as Korea and Taiwan. Fear of an impending flood of Japanese had made West Coast Americans adamant that Asian immigration must be halted. (If it was not easy to make the case that hard-working, thrifty Japanese were an inferior species, it was true that the first-generation immigrants were resistant to rapid assimilation into American life—which was of course true of some European ethnic groups as well.) The Japanese at home were well informed and deeply offended by the racial-cultural discrimination they encountered at all levels in the United States. Local correspondents kept them abreast of "the California Question," as they called it, and that question was deeply embarrassing to the government in Washington, for it had little legal power over state protests and practices. Only with great difficulty did Theodore Roosevelt get the State of California to cancel the establishment of separate schools for Asians and persuade the Japanese government to halt the issuance of emigration permits for Japanese laborers bound for the mainland United States (they were redirected to Korea and Manchuria). Roosevelt had special prestige as the mediator of a peace treaty to end the 1904–5 Russo-Japanese War (although the Japanese were disappointed in the results).

Japan's decisive defeat of Russia was another great surprise to Western leaders, a heady tonic to Japan's own expansionists, and an alarming portent for its competitors. Suddenly Americans felt vulnerable. The possibility of a war with Japan sometime in the future became widely discussed, Japanese immigrants were regarded as agents of conquest, reports of Japanese spying were common. Military authorities took such tales seriously and conducted extensive investigations; the war colleges began drawing up plans for future conflict (what to do with the Japanese on Oahu was a most "vexatious" question—"reconcentration" into guarded camps seemed the only practicable answer). The army and the navy had an acrimonious debate over the merits of Manila or Subic Bay for a major base, but in the end Pearl Harbor was chosen because the Philippines were considered too vulnerable (a secondary naval base at Subic Bay and fortification of Corregidor Island in the entrance to Manila Bay were approved). Theodore Roosevelt had said that "if we are not prepared to establish a strong and suitable base for our navy in the Philippines, then we had far better give up the Philippine Islands entirely." An increasing number of influential people began to agree, however reluctantly, that we should never have taken them in the first place. (Archibald Coolidge suggested in 1908 that had Japan been as strong a power in 1898 as it had become in ten years' time it might have saved the United States from having to decide about retaining the Philippines because Japan might have declared that it could not allow the Spanish *East* Indies and Western Pacific empire to be turned over to any external power—on the same grounds as the United States was determined that the Spanish *West* Indies must not be taken over by any European power.)

If the Philippines could not be defended militarily, one could try to protect them diplomatically. Because the United States could not consider fighting Japan to prevent its expansion on the Asian mainland, it tried to get something in return for officially recognizing the inevitable: specific Japanese disavowal of any aggressive designs on the Philippines in return for American recognition of Japanese dominion over Korea (1905), and (in 1908) the two powers agreed to maintain the status quo in the Pacific, respect each other's territorial possessions, and support the independence and integrity of China—the careful wording of this last tacitly approved Japanese dominance in Manchuria. The Anglo-Japanese Alliance of 1902 and the subsequent defeat of Russia had given Japan naval supremacy in the China seas. When Theodore Roosevelt sent the Great White Fleet of warships on their remarkable around-the-world cruise to display the new power of the United States, it was clear that their most important stop was to be in Japan (where, as elsewhere, they received a rousing welcome).

Thus the United States expanded precipitously, fortuitously across the Pacific without the slightest preparation or design. It annexed a large territory with millions of people that before 1898 most Americans had hardly, if ever, heard of, and few knew where it was (the president candidly admitted he hadn't known). There was vigorous debate in Congress and various forums about what to do with this surprising prospect, but in the end the issue was decided far more by domestic politics and national pride than by any real assessment of vital interests and potential dangers. Such geopolitical naïveté has its costs. That the United States would quickly be confronted with a formidable Pacific rival was not the destiny manifest to its turn-of-the-century expansionists. That Japanese expansion was powered by a rather analogous racial and cultural pride (but not self-confidence) and determination to dominate what it regarded as the geopolitical arena essential to its national interests was never appreciated by American policy makers or public. That American territorial security would become endangered by its own immigration policies and deep-seated racial and cultural prejudices was also a new and unanticipated complication.

That the United States moved into the twentieth century as a powerful nation was apparent to all. But its century of transcontinental imperialism had not been very pertinent preparation for transoceanic empire. If it was now generally acknowledged as a World Power, it found itself engaged in world politics in a place with dangers it had not foreseen.

4. Panama and Transcontinental Completion

THE PANAMA CANAL

Quite suddenly, in the new century, the United States assumed a new position and prominence on the world map. In less than six years between 1898 and 1904 the reach of the country had been extended over near and distant seas and included a strip of territory spanning the American Isthmus. With such a transformation the great idea so long dreamed of, a short waterway passage between the Atlantic and the Pacific, was now ripe to be realized.

Our adaptation of Senator Benton's rhetoric on the Pacific Railroad half a century earlier is fully appropriate to this new case. Now as then few questioned the necessity or practicality of such a vast national undertaking, and our review of the objectives, declared purposes, and benefits of such a waterway may well follow the framework used for that first transcontinental project.

The most obvious and simple objective was to create a *national trunk line.* This had been made clear—to the nation and to the world—in a famous pronouncement years earlier by President Rutherford B. Hayes: "The policy of this country is a canal under American control. . . . An interoceanic canal across the American Isthmus will essentially change the geographical relations between the Atlantic and Pacific coasts of the United States and between the United States and the world. It will be the great ocean thoroughfare between our Atlantic and Pacific shores, and virtually a part of the coast-line of the United States." The creation of this alternative trunk route was the primary motivation: "the United States Government built the Canal in order to join the two coasts of the country together and give it compactness." As in the case of the transcontinental railroad, the new ease of shipments was expected to have larger implications. As the president of the University of California put it: "The eastern and western coasts of the United States will be drawn closer together. They have been wide apart. Their interests are different. They do not understand each other. Closer relations will, however, show how admirably they supplement each other. . . . Interchange with the development of interdependence will make their very differences a source of union." Within a few months' time coast-to-coast shipments were double expectations. (It had been generally agreed that American intercoastal vessels should pay no tolls; however, when British protests made it embarrassingly clear that this would directly contradict the Hay-Pauncefote Treaty, the Senate hastily rescinded that exclusion. Even with the tolls the cost of shipments between the two seaboards was reduced by one-third in the first year of canal operation.)

It would also be a *developmental line*. If it would not, by its very nature, enliven quite every mile along the way as did the Pacific Railroad, it would stimulate all the main ports and hinterlands served. The impact was expected to be especially great on the Pacific Coast, where "ports which formerly were about as far from New York as from Liverpool now find themselves drawn within the circle of New York trade, and 2500 miles nearer the latter than the former." All Pacific Coast cities from San Diego to Seattle (as well as Vancouver and Prince Rupert) were in the midst of harbor improvements and expansion of shipping terminals in anticipation of being "quickened into new life when the stream of commerce begins to flow through the new channel." Gulf ports also expected an upsurge, portended by a first shipment of cotton from Galveston to Yokohama.

With this piercing of the last barrier Panama became the complement of Suez in a great *intercontinental trafficway* girdling the globe along the most direct routes. American shipping interests now saw the oceanic world divided between New York (via Panama) and Liverpool (via Suez) along a new equidistance line arching from Shanghai to Adelaide (see fig. 77). And—far more even than the Pacific Railroad—the prodigious work of creating this short forty-three-mile waterway was a *national symbol of American character*: the "greatest material achievement in the nation's history," "a service to the cause of universal progress and civilization," "America's gift to the world."

The military significance of the canal was an important addition to this list of objectives (defense of California had been cited in the Pacific Railroad debates but was not a major consideration). Public fascination with the long voyage around South America by the battleship *Oregon* in 1898 had generated acceptance that a canal was essential for American naval strategies. Military experts cautioned that it would also become an obvious major target and quarreled over the best modes of defense, but a modest program was begun. (Foreign warships had equal rights of passage in times of peace with the United States.)

Unlike the Pacific Railroad, the choice of route, though protracted and ulti-mately tumultuous, was not a paramount issue affecting the internal geographical patterns of the United States. A powerful Southern senator might emphasize the superiority of Nicaragua over Panama because it was closer to Gulf ports, but engineering feasibility and costs were commonly regarded as decisive. Tehuan-tepec, Nicaragua, and Panama were the only serious contenders for an isthmian canal, and from 1846 on the United States made numerous and varied efforts to secure transit rights across these narrows. Surveys essentially eliminated the Mexi-can route in 1876 (although a few years later James Eads, famed bridge builder, proposed a gigantic boat-carrying railway there), but Nicaragua and Panama re-mained in contention for more than half a century (fig. 79). Once Ferdinand de Lesseps got under way in Panama, American interests tended to focus on Nicara-gua. That route was much longer (about 187 miles), but its extensive use of a natural river and lake and a lower crossing of the Continental Divide made it attractive, whereas the Panama route became tarnished by the French failure and alarming losses from disease. The Isthmian Canal Commission appointed to assess "the most practicable and feasible route" (echoing the Pacific Railroad surveys initiated in 1853) endorsed the Nicaraguan scheme, but as we have earlier noted, Theodore Roosevelt was by then in charge and determined to build a canal quickly and in Panama by whatever means. That was not quite the end of the matter, however; in 1914 the United States pressured Nicaragua into a treaty granting rights to a canal zone and a naval base on the Gulf of Fonseca should the United States wish to undertake such a project—or to prevent any other state or company from doing so.

Construction of the canal took ten years (not counting the considerable usable work accomplished by the French). It was an engineering task unprecedented in scale if not in kind—no project had ever moved so much material or poured so much concrete—and it was a great drama presented to the public in a torrent of literature and photographs, lectures and orations, its magnitude often described in more imaginable form, such as the amount of material excavated being equal to that from a ditch ten feet deep and fifty-five wide across the United States from New York to San Francisco, or the amount removed from the Culebra Cut equal to a pyramid higher than the Woolworth Building, with a base covering eighteen city blocks. The initial authorization and early plans calling for a sea-level canal were abandoned only reluctantly in the face of formidable physical problems, chiefly the great fluctuations of the Chagres River (because of seasonal periods of torrential rains followed by several dry months) and excavation problems with unstable

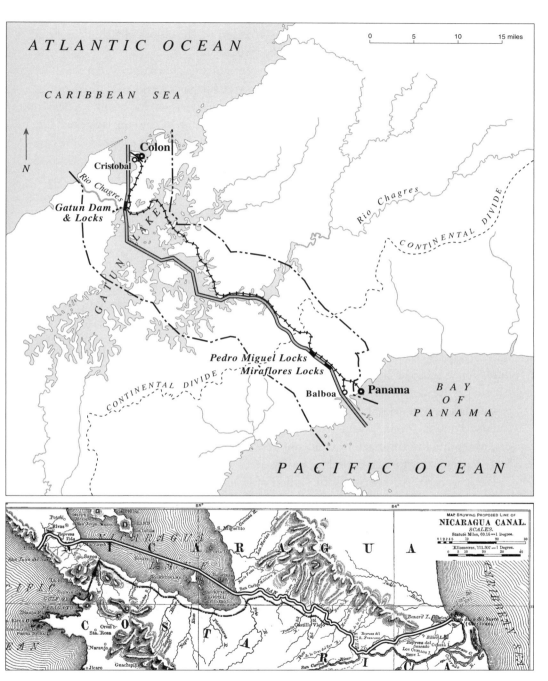

79. Panama and Nicaragua Canals.
Nicaragua map from Rand McNally, *New Imperial Atlas of the World*, 1900.

slopes in deep cuttings. The first was solved by a huge dam creating an artificial lake reached by a flight of locks; the second by broadening the slopes of a shallower cut necessitating a pair of locks on the Pacific side.

The human dimensions of the project were equally challenging. Foremost in time and importance was the need for a drastic reduction of endemic diseases (an estimated 20,000 having died during the French project). The American success in wiping out yellow fever and nearly eliminating malaria under the supervision of Dr. William Gorgas became world famous, although his critical experimental success of having already done the same in Havana in 1901 is less widely understood (deaths from disease were fewer than 5,000 from the far larger American work-force, and many of these were from a variety of other afflictions). The recruitment of labor for this "largest public work ever attempted anywhere" was a major task: nearly 50,000 were employed in the later phases. Environmental and racial theories of the day undergirded the routine assumption that heavy labor in the tropics must be done by "colored" people "naturally" suited to such tasks. The French had depended heavily upon Jamaicans, but the legacy of losses and costs from that venture caused that government to prohibit any renewed recruitment. Proposals to bring in Blacks from the United States "met with strenuous opposition from southern congressmen who foresaw their home states suddenly drained of their natural supply of cheap labor" (a few did come). Barbados proved to be the most ready source (about 20,000), and large numbers came from other depressed sugar islands of the Lesser Antilles. Dissatisfaction with the efficiency of such laborers resulted in a proposal to bring in Chinese, which was firmly opposed by the United States, Panama, and China—each hypersensitive in its own way to issues of exclusion and discrimination. Eventually thousands were also attracted from Spain and other Mediterranean countries (and paid twice the wages of the West Indians).

In sharp contrast, nearly all the skilled workers were White Americans. A rigid comprehensive "color line" was imposed, and it was primarily for this small minority (at most about 3,500 men, 6,000 including families) that entire new settlements were built. Much the largest were the terminal towns of Cristóbal and Balboa built alongside the old cities of Colón and Panama (which lay outside the Canal Zone). Laid out on spacious plans of the city-beautiful movement, they contained offices, houses, barracks, mess halls, hospitals, schools, churches, club houses, hotels, commissaries, and laundries, all standardized in design for healthful, efficient tropical living (fig. 80). Elsewhere many barracks, mess halls, and other facilities were constructed for the other workers, but the majority of the West Indians elected to live in their own ramshackle huts or city slums rather than conform to regimented housing. Officials eventually realized that allowing West Indians to bring in their wives and families resulted in a much more satisfied and stable workforce. Many chose to remain in Panama or the Canal Zone. As the

80. Balboa.
Administration Building in the background and the whole town set apart from Panama City by the hills beyond. (From Goethals, *Government of the Canal Zone*, 1915)

project neared completion, concentration of the entire Zonal population into a set of segregated towns within formal "sanitized zones" at either end of the canal was begun.

The overriding concern to get the job done led stage by stage to rule of the Zone and everything connected with the project by a single individual, Colonel George W. Goethals, a "benevolent dictator" responsible solely to the secretary of war and the president. When the canal was completed the Zone became an "unorganized overseas territory" under the jurisdiction of the secretary of the navy, with Colonel Goethals as governor. Unlike Guam or Samoa, however, it became in effect "a Government owned reservation dedicated to the operation, maintenance and protection of the Canal and its appurtenances"; there was no private land, and only licenses were available to companies or individuals. The Republic of Panama was a protectorate of the United States under a formal treaty that allowed the United States to intervene in Panamanian affairs on any matter that might affect the integrity of the canal. The most common kind of intervention had to do with sanitation and policing problems arising from the juxtaposition and interdependence of the Panamanian and Canal Zone cities at either end of the canal; those bicultural clusters were but local representations of the larger special geopolitical character of this unusual imperial position.

Such an immense achievement called for an immense celebration. More than a hundred warships from many nations were to gather off Hampton Roads on January 1, 1915, and follow the *Oregon*, under its 1898 commander and with President Woodrow Wilson as guest, in stately formation through the canal to San Francisco, where "the most modern city in the world" (because it had been so extensively rebuilt after the disaster of 1906) had prepared a resplendent Panama-Pacific Exposition to celebrate "the first cutting of . . . the long, broad dyke of the Americas . . . , the avenging of Columbus, the end of the four-century halt, the resumption of the [westward] advance to the Orient." But the actual opening of the canal had taken place on August 15, 1914, two weeks after the European powers had begun what was soon to become "the most Titanic war in world-history"; a humble freighter of the Panama Railroad Company made the first passage and no grand celebratory procession took place.

THE AMERICAN SPHERE

Nevertheless, Americans took great pride in their accomplishment and widely proclaimed its larger implications: "Beyond its significance as a great scientific achievement or commercial aid, the Canal stands as a triumph of man over nature, a new linking of the East and the West, a new step toward national unity, a new act of national expansion. Like the watershed that divides the streams in their courses, it marks off the old time from the new." Completed half a century after the Civil War, it was an important capstone of American geopolitical development, a vital instrument in the consolidation of a fully transcontinental nation and federation. It was also a critical addition to the greatly expanded American sphere of influence we have been describing. As our periodic (1800, 1850s) geographical morphologies have shown, the United States had always had a large space within its political bounds that awaited colonization and incorporation into the body of the nation. But that famous frontier West was now gone, and the only possible place for the continuation of that great American experience and process seemed to be Alaska, a detached "last frontier" where the American presence was still confined largely to a scattering of coastal footholds. For the rest, the American sphere in the new century was a very different and complex set of peripheral areas.

If we continue with another of our periodic summations of the United States in North America (fig. 81) (as we did for 1800 and 1867) and turn our attention to the American tropics, we find our simple classic definition of a sphere—"a peripheral area open to penetration and a measure of control by an imperial power"—in many guises. Americans were nowhere more than a small minority of the population, but American power ranged from complete control of an American-designed territorial entity in the Canal Zone, to full administration of Hispanic Puerto Rico

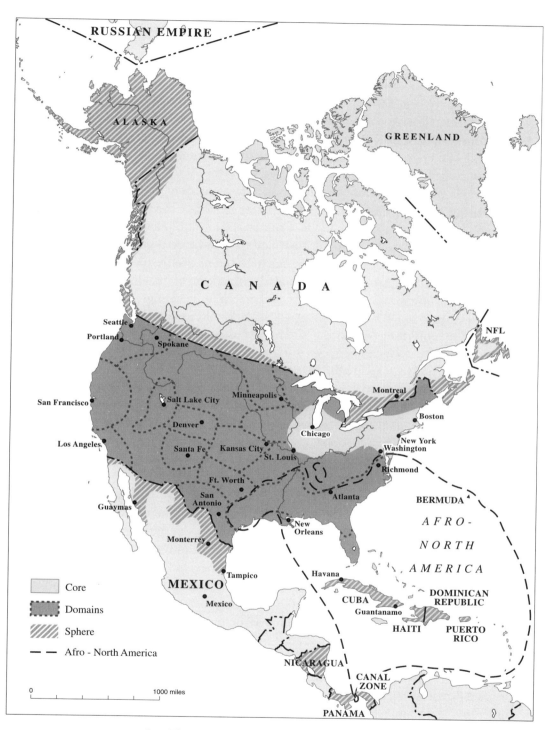

RUSSIAN EMPIRE

ALASKA

GREENLAND

C A N A D A

NFL

Seattle
Portland
Spokane
San Francisco
Salt Lake City
Minneapolis
Montreal
Boston
Denver
Chicago
New York
Los Angeles
Washington
Santa Fe
Kansas City
St. Louis
Richmond
Ft. Worth
Atlanta
San
Antonio
BERMUDA
Guaymas
AFRO -
New
Orleans
NORTH
Monterrey
AMERICA
Tampico
Havana
MEXICO
DOMINICAN
REPUBLIC
Mexico
CUBA
Guantanamo
HAITI
PUERTO
RICO

Core
Domains
Sphere
Afro - North America

NICARAGUA
CANAL
ZONE
PANAMA

0   1000 miles

81. The United States in North America, 1915.

as an "unincorporated insular territory," to rights of intervention and selective supervision in the formal protectorates of Cuba, Panama, and Nicaragua, to episodic military presence in the Dominican Republic and Haiti and recurrent diplomatic pressures on all the small independent states in this sector. None of these countries were generally regarded as attractive frontiers for American family-farm settlement. All were wide open to American investment in plantations, mines, railroads, public utilities, and other forms of capitalist penetration. Longer-term cultural influences were often less obvious or measurable but were profoundly important in some areas, as we have noted with respect to Cuba and Puerto Rico (especially the imposition of English as the language of instruction in an American-designed school system in the latter country—the spatial diffusion and geographic variations in these kinds of cultural penetrations await detailed study).

The two border states on the continent offer further variations. Until 1910 all of Mexico was a major field for American investment and business activity. The revolution was demonstrating how vulnerable that kind of foreign penetration was to internal disorder, fueled in part by anti-imperialist feelings. However, it also seemed certain in 1915 that the United States would be applying strong imperial pressure in one form or another to try to ensure the right of such American participation in Mexican economic affairs. Meanwhile American cultural influences upon the Mexican border states remained and were even being reinforced by routine and episodic transborder relations. Canada was still another special case: under the least political pressure (tariffs and trade being the only prominent issue of "penetration") but open to the most pervasive cultural influence. What Americans regarded as entirely benign, and Canadian nationalists might regard as insidiously imperial, clearly put most of populated Canada within the American sphere.

An American outreach in the Pacific was not a new feature. Hawaii had been within the sphere of strong American cultural and economic influence for half a century before annexation. It was now under formal control with Americans completely in charge of political and economic affairs, yet they remained a minority within its expanding immigrant population. Guam and Samoa and other lesser islands had been selected as simple strategic utilities and undergone little other development. The Philippines were a large conquered territory subjected to a calculated program of Americanization intended to produce indelible cultural change (with, as in Puerto Rico, the imposition of English through a comprehensive school system as the most powerful instrument).

This new American power and influence was a lively topic of the time outside the United States as well as within. For example, William Thomas Stead, well-known British editor and journalist, proclaimed a much broader American impact as already discernible and the most important "trend of the twentieth century." His book, *The Americanisation of the World*, published on both sides of the Atlantic in

1902, emphasized the influence of exemplary forms of republicanism, freedom of religion, various social movements, and the eager worldwide acceptance of ingenious American machines. Stead's main purpose was to press for the formation of a great "United States of the English-speaking World" as Britain's only hope for enduring participation as a world power, and his loose, eclectic commentary offers little guide for the kind of geographic assessment we shall need to make of an expanding American presence in the world in the twentieth century. For the moment, however, we must look a bit further at American impressions and the realities of their world position as they moved into that century.

"The most important geographical fact in the past history of the United States," wrote Ellen Churchill Semple in the opening sentence of her influential 1903 book, "has been their location on the Atlantic opposite Europe; and the most important geographical fact in lending a distinctive character to their future history will probably be location on the Pacific opposite Asia." That spoke to a new sense of position in the world: a fully transcontinental United States and a completed Isthmian Canal would give it *centrality* within a new set of global systems. Its destiny lay not so much in a continued "westward march of empire" (there had been a marked "dying down of the sudden imperialistic impulse of 1898–1910," noted James Bryce) but in that "new linking of the East and the West." Thus Semple reemphasized in her conclusion: "'Enthroned between her subject seas,' the United States has by reason of her large area and her geographical location the most perfect conditions for attaining preëminence in the commerce of the world ocean." Such a view called for a new standard map focused on the United States (and thereby splitting the Old World through Central Asia)—and Rand McNally was quick to issue a *New Imperial Atlas of the World*, opening with a map of "The Territorial Growth of the United States" and maps of its new overseas possessions, followed by a Mercator map of the world centered on the United States (rather than the usual double page featuring Western and Eastern Hemispheres).

But position is only a potential. The United States was enmeshed in globe-girdling systems but was not actually central to or in command of any. The world had been ordered into a common system of longitude and a fixed set of twenty-four time zones (first formalized at an International Meridian Conference in Washington in 1884 and adopted by most of the world by 1912), but the Prime Meridian was anchored on Greenwich. In Panama "the youthful American republic had triumphed where the old world had failed," but mere completion of the canal would not ensure preeminence in world commerce. Vaughan Cornish had reported that "in spite of geographical advantages, there is . . . some ground for the extreme opinion sometimes expressed . . . , that the canal is being built with American money for the use of Europe—and, one may add, of Japan." There was precedent for that: "To everyone's surprise the [Suez] Canal only reinforced Britain's domination of world shipping" (many had expected that nations of the Mediterranean would now enjoy a great advantage, reversing their 400-year-old eclipse). Britain's continuing advantage lay in "the ability to make merchant ships pay a profit," and that rested not only on its paleotechnic industrial leadership and supportive financial systems but also on its need for huge imports and its worldwide markets, more or less balancing inward and outward cargoes. Thus although American domestic shipments were flowing through the Panama Canal, the American merchant fleet was insignificant in the commerce of the world ocean. E. H. Harriman's grand scheme for an extension of his Union Pacific–Southern Pacific system into a world-spanning network of steamships and railroads incorporating Manchurian lines and the Trans-Siberian quickly foundered on resolute Japanese opposition.

As Peter J. Hugill emphasizes, Britain's dominance also included vital communications facilities: "Britain gained an early lead in building the first global information infrastructure, establishing itself securely as the information hegemon by the late 1880s at the geographic center of the global network of submarine cables" (fig. 82). American companies gained access to important segments of this system and even operated some of them under lease, but the fixed focus, the principal

82. World Submarine Cable Network.
(From Brigham, *Commercial Geography*, 1911)

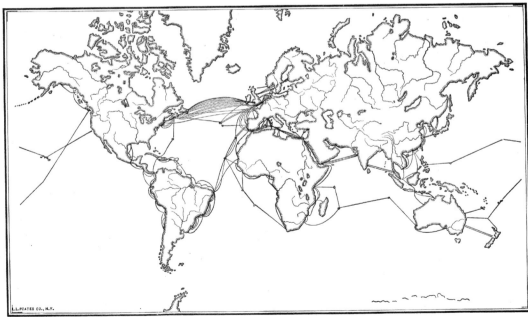

intelligence center, remained in London. As telegraph systems became critical for military strategy, Britain undertook to build several "all Red Routes" connecting British imperial territories (such as the longest cable in the world, connecting Vancouver with New Zealand and Australia, bypassing Hawaii, and providing an alternative to the American transpacific line to Manila and Hong Kong); American naval leaders became increasingly restive at their heavy dependence on British networks.

The new century did indeed require a new map of the world, but that depiction should feature more than the emergence of this great transcontinental republic; it needed to display a much more complex geopolitical transformation: *"the simultaneous appearance of three new world powers"*—a tremendous phenomenon in world history. That would call for more than common atlas reference maps and rather more than the immature and insecure academic field of geography was generally prepared to offer. Nevertheless special maps dealing with these broad geopolitical issues did occasionally appear. For example, Henry Cabot Lodge, powerful disciple of Alfred Thayer Mahan, lectured his fellow senators on the imperatives of sea power in 1895 (and, more specifically, on the strategic importance of the Hawaiian Islands) and displayed a world map on which "British naval stations and fortified places" were marked to show how Britain asserts "her control of the great pathways of commerce" and its desire "to put us in a position where we can not fight, if we wish, except at a great disadvantage" (fig. 83). We may be sure that leaders of the great powers were aware of that formidable pattern because Mahan's instantly famous book was translated into many languages and served as a text in military academies of Japan and Germany, among others.

The fervent embrace of sea power under the leadership of Theodore Roosevelt was a marked alteration of the American military stance. The United States had spent a century building itself into the great power of its own continent, and geopolitically that is all it had aspired to do. Its "exaggerated sense of right to expand" (its manifest destiny) was accompanied by confident expectations of "unlimited growth" on the basis of its own immense resources and, increasingly, by a sense of "total immunity" from any rival expansionist power—a century of "unearned security," to use Walter Lippmann's theme (referring to an Atlantic protected by the British fleet acting in its own interests). Those same continental resources and security allowed it to become a formidable sea power in the new century, but for all its riches and the wonderful harnessing thereof, North America was one of the lesser continents. The United States might be a great exhibit of the transmuting power of transcontinental railways, but "nowhere can they have such effect" on "the conditions of land-power . . . as in the closed heart-land of Euro-Asia," said Halford J. Mackinder in what would become in time a famous lecture to the Royal Geographical Society in London in 1904. It was true, he went on to say,

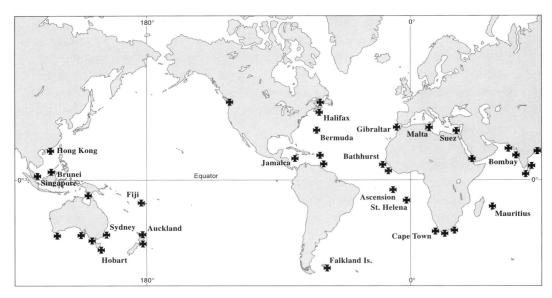

83. Sea Power.
Simplified from map of "British naval stations and fortified places" accompanying speech of Senator Lodge, March 2, 1895, in the *Congressional Record*.

"that the Trans-Siberian railway is still a single and precarious line of communication, but the century will not be old before all Asia is covered with railways. The spaces within the Russian Empire and Mongolia are so vast, and their potentialities in population, wheat, cotton, fuel, and metals so incalculably great, that it is inevitable that a vast economic world, more or less apart, will there develop inaccessible to world commerce." Should such an inland power expand over the marginal lands of Euro-Asia and apply its vast continental resources to fleet-building, "the empire of the world would then be in sight. This might happen if Germany were to ally herself with Russia" (fig. 84).

Such was the view of a British geographer who had recently completed an eloquent book on *Britain and the British Seas* (in which he mentioned Mahan in a brief chapter on "Strategic Geography") and was deeply concerned about the security and future of the British imperial system. In his scheme the United States and North America were relegated, with little comment, to an "Outer Crescent," a distant oceanic realm essentially the creation of the 400-year Columbian epoch. But that period of history was over and no longer provided to such outlying areas the security they once enjoyed. "From the present time forth," said Mackinder, "in the post-Columbian age, we shall . . . have to deal with a closed political system . . . of world-wide scope . . . [wherein] every explosion of social forces . . .

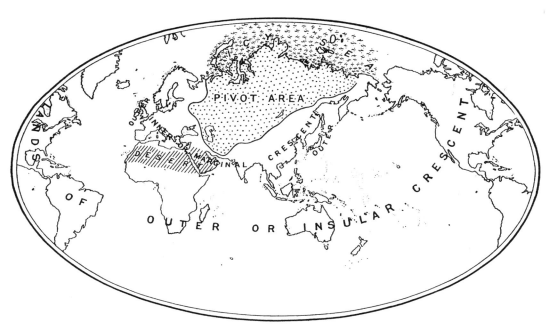

84. Land Power-Potential.
As depicted by Halford J. Mackinder in his presentation to the Royal Geographical Society. He referred in his text to this "Pivot Area" as "heart-land of Euro-Asia" closed to the reach of sea power; in his 1919 revision it became the "Heartland" of his famous geopolitical formula:
"Who rules East Europe commands the Heartland:
Who rules the Heartland commands the World-Island:
Who rules the World-Island commands the World."

will be sharply re-echoed from the far side of the globe, and weak elements in the political and economic organism of the world will be shattered in consequence." Whatever the merits of his particular geographic formulation (he would elaborate extensively upon it in 1919), his recognition of this kind of reverberation latent in a world transformed by vast colonizations, encompassing imperialisms, and radical technological changes was surely apt.

Americans were not well attuned to such perspectives. Typically, they understood the end of the Columbian Age in continental, not global, terms. It marked the end of the frontier and the onset of having to contain and cope with explosive social forces within their own closed national space. Having long asserted their hegemony over the Americas they generally regarded the mounting geopolitical crises in Europe and Asia with some concern but a comfortable degree of detachment behind their oceanic moats.

But the outbreak of war among all the other great powers quickly brought discomfiting changes. In the Pacific an opportunistic Japan seized all the German

Asian and Pacific possessions north of the equator—thereby leaving Guam a single American position within, and the Philippines a large American territory beyond, a sudden new Japanese imperial screen projected across the Western Pacific (see fig. 77). In 1915 Japan promulgated its Twenty-One Demands upon China, which, if successful, would make all of China a Japanese protectorate and much of it open to Japanese exploitation. The United States sent a protest.

As for Europe, America's own geopolitician had warned in 1900 that the United States would have to readjust its views because "we can never see with indifference, and with the sense of security which characterized our past, a substantial, and still less a radical, change in the balance of power there; . . . the declension of a European state might immediately and directly endanger our own interests." But Mahan was a militarist and expansionist and not representative of the common view of the nation or its leaders in 1914. As Samuel Flagg Bemis noted, "Neither the people of the United States nor the persons whom they had placed in governance knew very well what [the war] was all about" and "all leaders of American life were in favor of neutrality, when the President promptly proclaimed it." On May 7, 1915, a German submarine torpedoed the unarmed British liner *Lusitania* off the coast of Ireland with a loss of 1,198 lives—including 128 Americans. The president sent a note of protest but also began preparing for the possibility of American intervention.

The United States aspired to lead the world, not to conquer it by arms. It saw itself as having become a world power through the "Law of Progress," not through the "laws of spatial growth" in an international struggle for existence. As William Appleman Williams has emphasized, the United States had accepted "empire as a way of life" through several mutations, always proclaiming its expansionism as a benevolent necessity. Its series of unrelenting successes in that kind of geographic growth through the whole span of the nineteenth century had brought it abruptly into a very different world in the twentieth. "Powerful and persuasive minds" were now "focused on the explicit or implicit need to transform the idea and the tradition and the reality of continental empire into global empire"—but they faced an ambivalent, hesitant, and uneasy nation, federation, and set of regional societies. The "old time" was indeed marked off from the "new" by great events—by much more than just the completion of a long-awaited passageway between the seas.

Sources of Quotations

PART ONE

p. 4 "a magnificent parallelogram," etc.: Benton, *Cong. Globe*, 30th Cong., 2d sess., February 7, 1849, 472–73

p. 5 "a project too gigantic": H. Report 773, 29th Cong., 1st sess., July 13, 1846, 2

p. 6 "we know that the Romans": Benton, *Cong. Globe*, 30th Cong., 2d sess., February 7, 1849, 473

p. 6 "keep in check the dangerous Indians": Gwin, *Cong. Globe*, 32d Cong., 2d sess., April 10, 1854, 879

p. 6 "necessary to the unity and promptitude of government": Yates (Illinois), *Cong. Globe*, 33d Cong., 1st sess., December 13, 1853, 42

p. 6 "great base line of connection": Gwin, *Cong. Globe*, 33d Cong., 1st sess., April 10, 1854, 880

p. 6 "the western wilderness . . . will start into life": Benton, *Cong. Globe*, 30th Cong., 2d sess., February 7, 1849, 473

p. 6 "the railroad operates as the river did": Kelley (Pennsylvania), *Cong. Globe*, 37th Cong., 2d sess., April 9, 1862, 1594

p. 6 "the geographical center of the Republic": Gwin, *Cong. Globe*, 33d Cong., 1st sess., April 10, 1854, 881

p. 7 "the teeming millions who will follow": French (Maine), *Cong. Globe*, 36th Cong., 1st sess., May 29, 1860, 2444

p. 7 "what the Erie Canal has been": Phelps (California), *Cong. Globe*, 37th Cong., 2d sess., April 9, 1862, 1592

p. 7 "The line of this great thoroughfare": Latham, *Cong. Globe*, 37th Cong., 2d sess., June 12, 1862, 2677

p. 7 "last grand revolution": Loughborough, *Pacific Telegraph and Railway*, 11
"consummation of the great idea": Dunn (Indiana), *Cong. Globe*, 37th Cong., 2d sess., April 17, 1862, 1701
"the American road to India": Benton, *Cong. Globe*, 30th Cong., 2d sess., February 7, 1862, 473

p. 7 "destined to bear on its long lines": Yates, *Appendix, Cong. Globe*, 32d Cong., 1st sess., April 23, 1852, 476

p. 8 "Asiatic railway" and "scheme of a great continental railway": Gwin, *Cong. Globe*, 33d Cong., 1st sess., April 10, 1854, 881

p. 8 "nothing but opium or silks": Morrill (Vermont), *Cong. Globe*, 37th Cong., 2d sess., April 17, 1862, 1708

p. 8 "to produce a *radical* and *permanent* change": Loughborough, *Pacific Telegraph and Railway*, 11

p. 8 "necessary to the highest destiny": Yates, *Cong. Globe*, 33d Cong., 1st sess., December 13, 1853
"elevate our national pride": Loughborough, *Pacific Telegraph and Railway*, 11
"short route to the riches and marvels of the Indies": Breese (Illinois), *Senate Report on Public Lands*, No. 466, 29th Cong., 1st sess., July 31, 1846, 12–13

p. 9 Goetzmann, *Army Exploration*, 262–63

p. 9 "an encyclopedia of western experience": Goetzmann, *Army Exploration*, 336

p. 11 Goetzmann, *Army Exploration*, 295

p. 11 Jefferson Davis: Ex. Doc. 78, 33d Cong., 2d sess., Feb. 27, 1855, 29

p. 12 "a work so stupendous must be . . . *central*": DeBow, "Intercommunication," 20

p. 12 "the bay of San Francisco": Benton, *Cong. Globe*, 30th Cong., 2d sess., February 7, 1849, 472
"the Pacific seat of trade," "entrepôt," "equipoise": Gwin, *Cong. Globe*, 33d Cong., 1st sess., April 10, 1854, 882

p. 12 Memphis convention on "special advantages": Wender, "Southern Commercial Conventions," 72

p. 12 Borland committee report: S. Report, No. 344, 32d Cong., 1st sess., August 18, 1852, 3

p. 12 the mouth of the Ohio "may be said to be the mouth of all the rivers": Grey (Kentucky), *Cong. Globe,* 33d Cong., 2d sess., January 17, 1855, 288

p. 13 "every town on the Mississippi . . . is contending": Geyer (Missouri), *Appendix Cong. Globe,* 32d Cong., 2d sess., February 18, 1853, 186

p. 14 "concluded that unless we proposed . . . three routes": Bell (Tennessee), *Cong. Globe,* 33d Cong., 2d sess., February 19, 1855, 811

p. 14 "Why, sir, as if the difficulty were not enough": Pearce (Maryland), *Cong. Globe,* 33d Cong., 2d sess., February 19, 1855, 806

p. 14 "it is more central as to the territory": French (Maine), *Cong. Globe,* 36th Cong., 1st sess., May 29, 1860, 2444

p. 15 "it is proposed that the line shall have two short branches": Curtis (Iowa), *Cong. Globe,* 36th Cong., 1st sess., May 29, 1860, 2330

p. 15 Iverson, "the South shall have an equal chance": *Cong. Globe,* 35th Cong., 2d sess., January 6, 1859, 244

p. 15 "for the sole purpose of giving supremacy": Hamilton (Texas), *Cong. Globe,* 36th Cong., 1st sess., May 29, 1860, 2445

p. 16 Edwards, we must "look carefully into the future": *Cong. Globe,* 37th Cong., 2d sess., April 7, 1862, 1703

p. 17 "What might have been a great artery": quoted in Boorstin, *Americans: National Experience,* 256

p. 17 on routes authorized: *Statutes at Large,* vol. 12, July 1, 1862, 489–98

p. 19 an issue that "so exasperates human passion": Bayard (Delaware), *Cong. Globe,* 32d Cong., 2d sess., January 13, 1853, 707

p. 20 "the most significant single act of the historical geography of American transportation": Vance, *Capturing the Horizon,* 312

p. 21 "the importance of this accomplishment . . . mainly psychological": Martin, *Railroads Triumphant,* 29

p. 21 "a symbol that far transcended the event": Klein, *Union Pacific,* 222

p. 21 Bowles, *Pacific Railroad,* 5

p. 22 Durant, "there is henceforth but one Pacific Railroad": quoted in Klein, *Union Pacific,* 226

p. 22 "unbroken communication by rail across the continent": Cronise, *Natural Wealth of California,* 669

p. 25 be operated "as a united whole": Petro, *Resources and Prospects,* 306

p. 25 "except that given by nature herself": Gwin, *Cong. Globe,* 33d Cong., 1st sess., April 10, 1854, 876

p. 26 "Sir, this unequal flow of Government money": Iverson (Georgia), *Cong. Globe,* 35th Cong., 2d sess., January 6, 1859, 242

p. 26 "immense influence . . . in building up one section of the country": Mason (Virginia), *Cong. Globe,* 32d Cong., 2d sess., January 13, 1853, 676

p. 26 "a free confederacy of Republican states": Butler (South Carolina), *Appendix, Cong. Globe,* 32d Cong., 2d sess., February 5, 1853, 178

p. 28 *Leslie's Weekly,* "The railway has so abridged time and space": quoted in Davidson, *Life in America,* vol. 2, 259

PART TWO

p. 31 Bowles, *Pacific Railroad,* 116

p. 32 Jackson, *American Space,* 13

p. 32 Walker, *Statistical Atlas,* 1

p. 33 on the "petty population": Walker, *Statistical Atlas*, "Progress of the Nation," 1

p. 34 Bowles on regional differences: *Pacific Railroad*, 8–14

p. 34 on "Cordilleras" and other features: Whitney, "Physical Features . . . ," 1–4, and Brewer, "Woodland and Forest Systems," in Walker, *Statistical Atlas*

p. 36 McWilliams, *California: Great Exception*, 25

p. 36 "that remote conquest, the present Dorado": *North American*, 2–27–47, quoted in Garner, *Letters*, 190–92, n. 1

p. 36 Frémont, "Geographical Memoir," 532–35

p. 38 Colton, *Three Years*, 371

p. 38 "I say without hesitation, let no man come here": *Alonzo Delano's California*, 54

p. 38 General's report on San Francisco: quoted in Scott, *San Francisco Bay Area*, 28

p. 41 "In the Atlantic States": Cronise, *Natural Wealth of California*, 347–48

p. 41 "it is probable that no market . . . equal to it": Cronise, *Natural Wealth of California*, 348

p. 42 "have been produced in abundance": California State Report, in *Report of the Commissioner of Agriculture, 1873*, 375–82

p. 46 "union of southern and northern California is unnatural": cited in Hunt, "California State Division Controversy"

p. 46 "snowy range of the Sierra Nevada": McDougal in debate October 8, 1849, cited in Davis, "California East of the Sierra," 103

p. 46 *Daily Alta Californian* quotation: in Paul, *California Gold*, 196

p. 46 "there was everywhere present . . . the Californian": Trimble, *Mining Advance*, quoted in Paul, *California Gold*, 194

p. 47 Lotchin, *San Francisco*, 342

p. 47 Hornbeck, "California Indian," 24

p. 47 "traversable in a day's walk": Kroeber, "Nature of Land-Holding Groups," 96

p. 47 on languages: Hornbeck, "California Indian," 24

p. 48 protect Indians from "the necessity of seeking new homes": Heizer and Almquist, *Other Californians*, 79

p. 48 legislative committee report against removal of "large, permanent, and populous settlements," etc.: Heizer and Almquist, *Other Californians*, 70–72, 74

p. 49 "concentration camps" and "Seldom has a native race": Cook, *Population of California Indians*, 45, 44

p. 50 "a universal abomination": Roske, *Everyman's Eden*, 326

p. 50 Cleland on land act: *Cattle on a Thousand Hills*, 49

p. 52 Polk on discovery of gold: *Appendix, Cong. Globe*, 30th Cong., 2d sess., December 5, 1848, 2

p. 52 McWilliams: *California: Great Exception*, 67

p. 52 "foreigners became more co-colonists": Starr, *Americans and the California Dream*, 66

p. 54 Hilgard, "Agriculture and Soils," 476

p. 54 "outside the American [family] farm tradition": Paul S. Taylor, quoted in McWilliams, *California: Great Exception*, 100

p. 55 "a constant reconciliation of things": Lotchin, *San Francisco*, 342

p. 55 "Lockean liberalism": Johnson, *Founding the Far West*, 7
"release of private energy": J. Willard Hurst, quoted by Johnson, *Founding the Far West*, 7

p. 55 Starr, *Americans and the California Dream*, 68

p. 59 "fix their *trunk* line . . . through . . . Los Angeles": Judge Robert M. Widney, quoted in Nadeau, *City-Makers*, 119

p. 60 McWilliams: "Unlike their colleagues on the eastern seaboard": *Southern California Country*, 96

p. 60 historians giving Nordhoff "more credit for sending people to California": Morrow Mayo, quoted in Dumke, *Boom of the Eighties*, 30

p. 60 Nordhoff, "When a North American visits a tropical country": *California*, preface, 12

p. 61 "California is subject to droughts": Nordhoff, *California*, 132

p. 61 Ontario as "a new standard in rural planning": McWilliams, *Southern California Country*, 155

p. 61 "an orange grove is the perfect setting": McWilliams, *Southern California Country*, 214

p. 63 San Jose complaint, "The average Eastern mind conceives of California": quoted in Dumke, *Boom of the Eighties*, 40

p. 63 "an avalanche rushing madly": Dumke, *Boom of the Eighties*, 25–26

p. 63 "Los Angeles as a modern American metropolis may be said to date": *Los Angeles: A Guide*, 45, 44

p. 63 "The major business of the region" was "expansion": McWilliams, *Southern California Country*, 134

p. 64 "Los Angeles was the first city . . . to be completely illuminated": McWilliams, *Southern California Country*, 129

p. 64 climate "a commodity that can be labeled": McWilliams, *Southern California Country*, 6

p. 64 "perhaps the most efficient marketing co-operative": McWilliams, *Southern California Country*, 211

p. 64 "Oranges for Health—California for Wealth": *Los Angeles: A Guide*, 50

p. 64 placing in "the mundane grocery stores": Starrs, "Navel of California," 30

p. 66 L.A. Chamber of Commerce proposal "that the United States should purchase . . . Lower California": McWilliams, *Southern California Country*, 129

p. 66 "hundreds of American tourists . . . aided the filibusters in looting": Gerhard, "Socialist Invasion," 302

p. 68 to keep California a "White Man's paradise": McWilliams, *Southern California Country*, 178

p. 68 Lummis on "the least heroic migration in history": quoted in McWilliams, *Southern California Country*, 150

p. 69 Los Angeles "being composed of Easterners": Hunt, "California State Division Controversy"

p. 69 "We are different. . . . We call ourselves, not Californians but Southern Californians": quotation of that era, exact source unspecified, in Hutchinson, *California*, 311

p. 70 "filtering effect": Johnson, *Founding the Far West*, 45

p. 70 Bowles, "Oregonians have builded": quoted in Johansen and Gates, *Empire*, 297

p. 70 "certainly they are not an enterprising people": quoted in Johnson, *Founding the Far West*, 269

p. 70 "At Pacific Springs": Johansen, in Edwards and Schwantes, *Experiences*, 46

p. 70 "classical republicanism": Johnson, *Founding the Far West*, 9, 55

p. 71 "*Indian Corn and Tobacco*": Applegate, "Report," 473

p. 75 "professed pioneering New England virtues": MacColl, *Merchants*, 108

p. 75 "between 1843 and 1913": MacColl, *Merchants*, xvi

p. 77 "wheat will grow . . . wherever the 'bunch grass' grows": *The Pacific Northwest* (1882), quoted in Meinig, *Great Columbia Plain*, 264

p. 78 "one of the most poorly led railroads": Martin: *Railroads Triumphant*, 29

p. 81 "huge cedar houses . . . became deathtraps": White, *Land Use*, 28

p. 81 "It would be difficult to overestimate": Governor Moore, December 9, 1867, in Gates, *Messages*, 139

p. 82 "for preserving the integrity": Governor Pickering, December 12, 1863, in Gates, *Messages*, 51

p. 82 "Western part of the Territory [Puget Sound] appears": *Walla Walla Statesman*, December 9, 1864,, quoted in Kingston, "Walla Walla Separation," 94

p. 83 "Railroads . . . not a mere convenience": Governor Moore, December 9, 1867, in Gates, *Messages*, 142

p. 84 "had never seen a small town which offers such": Isaac C. Jolles, quoted by Fahey, in Stratton, *Spokane*, 181

p. 87 "Great Pacific North West Empire": Governor Newell, October 5, 1861, in Gates, *Messages*, 229

p. 89 Stansbury, *Exploration*, 123

p. 90 Jamison, "irreconcilable Christian heresy and the most typically American theology": quoted in Hansen, *Quest for Empire*, 26–27

p. 90 "it had . . . been the site of the Garden of Eden": Mulder, "Mormons in American History," 21

p. 90 "to rid themselves of . . . Mormons": Missouri newspapers, October 8, 1833, reprinted in Mulder and Mortensen, *Among the Mormons*, 77–78

p. 91 the Lord's call to gather "mine elect": quoted in Hansen, *Quest for Empire*, 47

p. 91 destined to "possess the country"; "every consideration of self-preservation": 1833 accounts reprinted in Mulder and Mortensen, *Among the Mormons*, 82, 79

p. 91 to "become as other citizens" . . . to "scatter": Arrington, *Brigham Young*, 69

p. 91 Nauvoo as "this corner-stone of Zion": Flanders, *Nauvoo*, 49

p. 92 "approached the extreme limits of possibility": Flanders, *Nauvoo*, 286

p. 92 "fear that monolithic Mormonism might . . . engulf": Arrington and Bitton, *Mormon Experience*, 65

p. 92 J. Smith, Americans "should grasp all the territory we can": Flanders, *Nauvoo*, 289

p. 93 Russell, *Journal of a Trapper*, 120

p. 93 J. Smith, "I will make a proclamation": quoted in Flanders, *Nauvoo*, 298

p. 93 B. Young letter to President Polk: Arrington, *Brigham Young*, 128

p. 95 "the land of Promise, held in reserve . . . for the Saints": Wilford Woodruff Journal ms, quoted in Wright, *Rocky Mountain Divide*, 163

p. 95 "the most widely applied . . . system of squatter's rights": Peterson, "Mormon Village," 11

p. 96 thirty-five settlements "within the protective walls": Hansen, *Quest for Empire*, 122

p. 96 "the ghost legislature of Deseret": Hansen, *Quest for Empire*, 167

p. 98 "to select a site for a city . . . near Cajon Pass": Campbell, *Establishing Zion*, 82

p. 98 ask Congress to "grant us about two degrees": Jackson, *Mormon Role*, 39

p. 101 "compact society" and Plat of the City of Zion: Jackson, "Mormon Village," 232

p. 102 Taylor, "In all cases in making new settlements": quoted in Anderson, *Desert Saints*, 427–28

p. 103 "No man can buy land here": quoted in Anderson, *Desert Saints*, 68

p. 104 "While other millennialists set a time": Mulder, "Mormons in American History," 19, 14

p. 104 "Saints from across the world traveled through the wilderness": Shipps, *Mormonism*, 60

p. 104 "was renewed and perpetuated . . . in the village system": Peterson, "Mormon Village," 10

p. 106 "most famous of all Mormon peculiarities": Shepherd and Shepherd, *Kingdom Transformed*, 81

p. 106 Anderson on polygamy: *Desert Saints*, 391, 390

p. 106 Mormon hierarchy "a huge extended family": Bennion, "Mormon Country," 6

p. 106 *stake*, "the church as a gigantic tent": Hansen, *Quest for Empire*, 9

p. 106 "regarded it as part of his responsibility to visit each Mormon settlement": Arrington, *Brigham Young*, 306

p. 107 "the break with the Old World was a compound fracture": Mulder, "Mormon Angles of Historical Vision," 20

p. 107 welding a variety of people "into one harmonious whole": Arrington, *Brigham Young*, 286

p. 107 Robinson on Mormons and Boers: *Sinners and Saints*, 117–18

p. 107 "re-capitulation of the Hebrew-Christian story" and "built . . . a nation-state": Shipps, *Mormonism*, 63, 124

p. 108 Robinson, "a City of Two Peoples": *Sinners and Saints*, 69

p. 108 "The railroad traveller gets a very wrong impression of Ogden": 1874 traveler quoted in Roberts, "Railroad Depots," 76

p. 109 "We are invaded by a hostile force": Arrington, *Brigham Young*, 254

p. 110 "I believe that Governor Cummings came to the conclusion": Arrington, *Brigham Young*, 268

p. 110 Connor, "My policy in this Territory": Lamar, *Far Southwest*, 361

p. 110 Committee on Territories, "to blot out the Territory": *Cong. Globe,* 40th Cong., 3d sess., January 14, 1869, 364

p. 110 "One of the most far-reaching pieces of federal legislation": Lamar, *Far Southwest,* 398

p. 111 "undertook a psychic and physical journey": Alexander, *Mormonism in Transition,* 3

p. 111 "I am in the necessity of acting for the Temporal Salvation of the Church": reprinted in Mulder and Mortensen, *Among the Mormons,* 416–17

p. 111 "It was easy for prominent politicians": White, "Prelude to Statehood," 304

p. 111 "take on the political status of a client state" and "With Zion and Babylon come to terms": Shipps, *Mormonism,* 63

p. 111 "We have come here to stay": quoted in Bennion, "Mormon Country," 17–18

p. 112 "a startling transition from the days when the clarion call": Mulder, *Homeward to Zion,* 30

p. 112 "important indication of change . . . of the leadership in Salt Lake City": Alexander and Allen, *Mormons and Gentiles,* 105

p. 112 "to join the United States in order to be free from it" and "All we care about is for them to let us alone": Arrington, *Brigham Young,* 238

p. 113 "While the waves of commotion are overwhelming nearly the whole country": Arrington, *Brigham Young,* 294

p. 116 "our troops are of no earthly account": John Greiner, Indian agent, 1852, quoted in McCall, *New Mexico in 1850,* 188

p. 116 New Mexico "a very heavy burden": Sumner, "Reports from . . . New Mexico," 24, 23

p. 116 Treaty, New Mexico admitted "at the proper time": Larson, *New Mexico's Quest,* 13

p. 119 "regeneration of the people" and "whether the native Mexicans have been benefited": Davis, *El Gringo,* 255, 431–32

p. 119 "I hope . . . there won't be an adobe house" and "you must get rid of your burros": General Sherman, October 28, 1880, quoted in Chavez, *Illustrated History,* 125, 92

p. 119 "respectable citizens": Sumner, "Reports from . . . New Mexico," 24

p. 123 "The memory of the 'Long Walk'": Spicer, *Cycles of Conquest,* 219

p. 126 "the lines exhibit more beauty and grace": Mr. Bocock of Virginia, *Cong. Globe,* 36th Cong., 2d sess., February 18, 1861, 1003

p. 126 carpetbaggers "whose sole aim was to fleece a region": Lamar, *Far Southwest,* 14

p. 126 "The Jewish pueblo trading post": Parish, "The German Jew," 326

p. 127 Santa Fe Ring, "it was essentially a set of lawyers, politicians, and businessmen": Lamar, *Far Southwest,* 146

p. 127 "down the trail from the states came" and "eventually over 80 per cent of the Spanish grants": Lamar, *Far Southwest,* 135, 149

p. 127 "the Hispanos were still settling and conquering" and "enough land to farm": Rosenbaum, *Mexicano Resistance,* 117

p. 127 "American land policy featured": Rosenbaum, *Mexicano Resistance,* 23

p. 128 "seemed worthless to Kearny's soldiers": Lamar, *Far Southwest,* 150

p. 130 "the exact demographic center" and an "aggregate of hundreds of *patrias chicas*": Nostrand, *Hispano Homeland,* 230, 225–26

p. 130 "those grand masters of cultural isolation": Lamar, *Far Southwest,* 201

p. 132 a "foreign people," "a race speaking an alien language," a "mongrel population," "not Americans, but 'Greaser'": Larson, *New Mexico's Quest,* 350, n. 60, 218, 148

p. 132 "Arizona, standing midway between": Larson, *New Mexico's Quest,* 239

p. 132 Frost, "a few more decades will witness the complete amalgamation": Lang, "New Mexico Bureau of Immigration," 210

p. 132 State Constitution, Art. 7, sec. 3; Art. 12, sec. 8, 10

p. 133 "an East Indian State under Hastings": Governor Prince, 1902, quoted in Lamar, *Far Southwest,* 499

p. 134 *Leavenworth Times,* June 10, 1859: quoted in Ubbelohde, *Colorado Reader,* 95

p. 135 Frank Hall, "All new states are born in an outburst": Abbott, *Colorado*, 269

p. 138 "Colorado System . . . that proved . . . one of most innovations": Abbott, *Colorado*, 151

p. 138 Richardson, "Making governments and building towns": quoted in Reps, *Cities of the American West*, 732, n. 27

p. 139 "entrepreneur politicians": Lamar, *Far Southwest*, 298

p. 140 Athearn on "railroad prospecting": *Rebel of the Rockies*, 98, 90

p. 141 Baedeker, *United States*, 488, 475

p. 145 Denver "more plain than queenly": quoted in Leonard and Noel, *Denver*, 141–42

p. 148 "found ranches and farms everywhere thickening up": quoted in Winther, *Old Oregon Country*, 283

p. 153 "peaceful conquest of the country": Pletcher, *Rails, Mines, and Progress*, 39

p. 156 they "purchased low-priced American goods": Salas, "Sonora," 435

p. 156 "for many Sonoran social groups": Salas, "Sonora," 448

p. 157 "foreign arrogance . . . pervaded every sphere": Ruíz, *People of Sonora*, 70

p. 157 "imperial enclaves complete with *guardas blancas*": Ruíz, *People of Sonora*, 82–83

p. 158 Secretary of the Interior, It "has totally changed the conditions": Prucha, *Documents*, 129

p. 159 General Sherman, "the *railroad* which used to follow in the rear": Prucha, *Documents*, 159

p. 159 General Sherman, "we must act with vindictive earnestness": Andrist, *Long Death*, 124

p. 159 General Sherman, "I now regard the Indians as substantially eliminated": Prucha, *Documents*, 159

p. 160 "every buffalo dead is an Indian gone" etc. through Sitting Bull: Smits, "Frontier Army and Destruction of Buffalo," 325, 328–35, 338

p. 161 General Sherman, "in having in so short a time replaced the wild buffaloes": quoted in Smits, "Frontier Army and Destruction of Buffalo," 337

p. 161 "the largest short-term shift": Jordan, *North American Cattle-Ranching*, 222

p. 161 "Anglo-Americans bearing a mixed Carolinian-Mexican herding culture": Jordan, *North American Cattle-Ranching*, 188

p. 161 "the principal staging ground from which the Texas ranching system launched its spectacular diffusion": Jordan, *North American Cattle-Ranching*, 220

p. 167 "the real dividing line between the eastern and western portions": Cyrus Thomas, 1872, quoted in Malin, "Agricultural Regionalism," 210

p. 167 "a plain mark on the face of the earth": Smythe, *Conquest of Arid America*, 21

p. 167 "grain garden of the world," Hardy Webster Campbell of the Campbell System of dry farming: quoted in Malone and Roeder, *Montana*, 181

p. 168 Walker, "The freedom of expansion": Prucha, *Documents*, 141

p. 168 "the usual theory" . . . "must be greatly modified": Selden N. Clark, quoted in Dippie, *Vanishing American*, 127

p. 170 "the sale of liquors and arms could be . . . prevented" and subsequent quotations: John Q. Smith, commissioner, 1876, quoted in Prucha, *Documents*, 149

p. 171 reservations assigned for "a permanent home": Luke Lea, quoted in Kvasnicka and Viola, *Commissioners*, 51

p. 171 "the arm which should have been raised to protect them": Report of the Board of Indian Commissioners, in Prucha, *Documents*, 131

p. 171 a "government of their own" simply "to gratify this sentimentality": J. D. C. Atkins, 1886, in Prucha, *Documents*, 170–71

p. 171 "the Indian race was outside the limits of the organized States and Territories": President Cleveland, 1886, quoted in Dippie, *Vanishing American*, 141

p. 172 Their "excessive attachment to Indian tradition and nationality": J. D. C. Atkins, commissioner, 1886, in Prucha, *Documents*, 170

p. 172 "their tribal cohesion" must be dissolved: Mohawk conference report, 1884, in Prucha, *Documents*, 163

p. 172 "merge" into "the body politic as independent and self-relying men": Carl Schurz, commissioner, 1880, in Prucha, *Documents,* 154

p. 172 "the Indian will never be reclaimed until he ceases to be a communist": George E. Ellis, 1884, quoted in Dippie, *Vanishing American,* 109

p. 172 "a 'chief' in white terms was always a white invention": Berkhofer, "North American Frontier," 62

p. 172 "to come out of isolation, into the civilized way": John H. Oberly, Commissioner, 1888, in Kvasnicka and Viola, *Commissioners,* 190

p. 172 "decent and reasonable names": Dippie, *Vanishing American,* 180

p. 172 instructed "in the elements of American history," etc.: Thomas J. Morgan, commissioner, 1889, in Prucha, *Documents,* 181

p. 172 fullest participation in "Anglo-Saxon civilization": John Wesley Powell, quoted in Hoxie, *Final Promise,* 24

p. 172 private ownership . . . the "principal instrument" of social advancement in the "natural order of progress": Hoxie, *Final Promise,* 19, and Dippie, *Vanishing American,* 108

p. 172 "This civilization may not be the best possible": Thomas Jefferson Morgan, quoted in Kvasnicka and Viola, *Commissioners,* 194

p. 172 "what amounted to a wholesale assault on Indian culture": White, *"It's Your Misfortune,"* 112

p. 173 "stands as a pure product of the reformer mind of the age": Hoxie, *Final Promise,* 175

p. 173 "ignored their allegiance to the United States": Treaty with the Creeks, 1866, Prucha, *Documents,* 99

p. 174 "this inviting tract of country, larger than all New England": King, "Indian Country," 603

p. 174 "no bill making Indian Territory a state has the slightest chance": Maxwell, "Sequoyah Convention," 318

p. 175 "a mighty pulverizing machine": quoted in Dippie, *Vanishing American,* 244

p. 175 "the Indians, as a race, already shorn of their tribal strength": quoted in Dippie, *Vanishing American,* 209

p. 175 "campaign for equality and total assimilation had become a campaign to integrate": Hoxie, *Final Promise,* 187

p. 175 "subject to an orgy of looting": Cato Sells, quoted in Kvasnicka and Viola, *Commissioners,* 244

p. 176 "assimilation was no longer an optimistic enterprise": Hoxie, *Final Promise,* 187

p. 179 "although Congress wanted to replicate": White, *"It's Your Misfortune,"* 137

p. 179 "often more powerful than local political interests": White, *"It's Your Misfortune,"* 58

p. 182 White on "the federal bureaucracies of the land office," "dependence on the federal government has become a central reality," and "there has been no western equivalent of the solid South": *"It's Your Misfortune,"* 137, 353

PART THREE

p. 188 "a headlong collision of nationalism and federalism": Gillette, *Retreat,* 364

p. 188 "Mr. Lincoln gropes . . . like a traveller": quoted in Foner, *Reconstruction,* 74

p. 189 "most generals preferred not to think of themselves as . . . ": Sefton, *United States Army,* 38

p. 191 "light brigade of school mistresses": Power, *Planting,* 22

p. 191 "to the task of building a Christian commonwealth": McFeely, *Yankee Stepfather,* 72, quoting T. Smith

p. 191 "defunct Confederacy": Buck, *Road to Reunion,* 62

p. 191 "treasury agents scoured the South": Sefton, *United States Army,* 38

p. 191 "Running through nearly all the plans": Powell, *New Masters,* 6

p. 192 "Yankees furnish the niggers and the money": quoted in Powell, *New Masters,* 48

p. 192 "full of 'runners'" and "a passion for keeping store": Andrews, *South,* 365–66

p. 192 "panacea for all present evils": Andrews, *South,* 207

p. 192 "a new city springing up": Andrews, *South*, 340

p. 192 King on Atlanta: *Great South*, 351, 350

p. 193 "there are many counties . . . in which Northern labor and capital": Andrews, *South*, 378

p. 193 "Mississippi is still . . . a frontier state": Nordhoff, *Cotton States*, 74

p. 193 "the natives" . . . "poor white" . . . "Poor White": Woodward, *Origins*, 109–10

p. 193 "exhibit, by pen and pencil, a vast region": quoted in Buck, *Road to Reunion*, 131

p. 193 "The South can never be cast in the same mould": King, *Great South*, 793

p. 194 "all the traditions and habits of both races": quoted in Roark, "Lords to Landlords," 128

p. 194 Sherman's Special Field Order: Andrews, *South*, 209, 211

p. 194 "the great plantations, which have been . . . nurseries of rebellion": Senator Charles Sumner, quoted in Garraty, *American Nation*, 439

p. 195 "line the banks of the Mississippi River with a loyal population": Treasury Department Circular, October 27, 1863, quoted in Currie, *Enclave*, 57

p. 195 "whose highest thought is a greenback": Currie, *Enclave*, 57

p. 195 "exclusively devoted to . . . Freedmen": quoted in Currie, *Enclave*, 101

p. 196 *New York Times*, "the further duty of making them work," January 3, 1863: quoted in Foner, *Reconstruction*, 50

p. 197 "in Beaufort District [S.C.] they . . . refuse to sell": Andrews, *South*, 206

p. 197 "in many portions of the Mississippi Valley the feeling against": Reid, *After the War*, 564–65

p. 197 "there is . . . a determination that they shall not become free holders": McFeely, *Yankee Stepfather*, 297

p. 197 "landowners without laborers confronted": Roark, "Lords to Landlords," 128

p. 198 "most found bizarre the white folks' preoccupation": Fields, "Ideology and Race," 166

p. 198 "the merchants are in debt to the wholesalers": DuBois, *Souls*, 126

p. 199 "little villages springing up": King, *Great South*, 652

p. 201 "able-bodied men cultivate, the women raise chickens": Campbell, *White and Black*, 375–76

p. 201 "miserable huts scattered about": Campbell, *White and Black*, 292

p. 201 "by general consent . . . there are no mixed schools": Nordhoff, *Cotton States*, 22

p. 201 "the separation of blacks and whites is fundamentally social and political": Newton, "Settlement Patterns as Artifacts," 351

p. 203 "The negro quarter around the towns is as marked a feature": quoted in Burton, "Rise and Fall," 183

p. 203 on Charleston, "visitors in 1880 . . . struck by the 'proximity and confusion'": Radford, "Race, Residence, and Ideology," 344–45

p. 205 Ratzel on Richmond: *Sketches*, 147

p. 207 "despite much physical contact . . . no community of intellectual life": DuBois, *Souls*, 183

p. 208 "dread of social equality" and "maintaining the color line": Nordhoff, *Cotton States*, 111–12, 16

p. 208 "what ought to be recognized as a true people's war": Degler, *Place Over Time*, 108

p. 208 Joel Williamson on "the white elite": *Crucible of Race*, 513

p. 209 "For better or worse, the American people made the decision": Wharton, "Reconstruction," quoting Donald Sheehan, 314

p. 209 "local control of government and Negro inequality": Degler, *Place Over Time*, 108

p. 210 "the South had never been truly reconstructed": Gillette, *Retreat*, 379

p. 210 "the South might be said to have shared in the victory": Woodward, "Gone with the Wind," 5

p. 211 "There is a grand scheme . . . to destroy the present commercial centers": quoted in Coulter, *South During Reconstruction*, 244

p. 211 "sleeping-cars daily cross the Rappahannock": King, *Great South*, 795

p. 213 "a lively ambition to get into direct communication": Somers, *Southern States*, 34

p. 214 "the whole state of Alabama cannot take the product": Warren, *American Steel Industry*, 72

p. 214 "warfare between Southern and Northern furnaces": Rothwell, *Mineral Industry*, 301

p. 214 "Pennyslvania's most formidable industrial enemy": Woodward, *Origins,* 127

p. 214 "islands of industrialism," "public zeal," "old market villages": Woodward, *Origins,* 150, 132, 133

p. 215 "vast store of accumulated and institutionalized expertise": Carlton, "Revolution from Above," 468

p. 215 "sudden massive transfer of capital": Williams, *Americans and Their Forests,* 238

p. 217 "the growth of manufacturers in the Southern States": King, *Great South,* 792

p. 217 "The huge exposition of structures": Woodward, *Origins,* 124–25

p. 217 "a firm optimism about the potential": Vicki L. Vaughn, quoted in Alexander, "Dimensions of Continuity," 88

p. 217 "had in mind the creation of an industrial society modeled on": Carlton, "Revolution from Above," 474

p. 217 "southern industrialists thus faced a challenge," etc.: Carlton, "Revolution from Above," 449, 457, 458

p. 218 "testified to the South's integration": Ayers, *Promise,* 81

p. 219 "Southern Way of Life" . . . "a distinctive culture": Wilson, *Baptized in Blood,* 119

p. 219 "the life of the South [was drawn] with increasing earnestness": Murphy, *Problems,* 32

p. 219 "our beloved Zion in the South": Anderson, *Lutheranism,* 208

p. 219 "Southern religion became entwined with the Lost Cause": Goldfield, "Urban South," 1021

p. 219 "to impregnate the South with Northern ideas": Morrow, *Northern Methodism,* 22

p. 219 "the great defect of Northern civilization is its materiality": Wilson, *Baptized in Blood,* 84, 85, 86

p. 220 "by 1900 a distinctive civil religion was evident": Goldfield, "Urban South," 1021

p. 220 "Stopping for two or three days in some back county": Andrews, *South,* 387

p. 220 "helped make Southern cities bastions of conservatism": Goldfield, "Urban South," 1023

p. 220 "pure blooded, homogeneous, population . . . from the great Anglo-Saxon centers": Graves, *History,* 473, viii

p. 221 "the elementary working hypothesis of civilization": Murphy, *Problems,* 34

p. 221 "Southern identity" . . . "a siege mentality": Reed, *Enduring South,* quoting Sheldon Hackney, 88

p. 222 "the flood of emigration," "something should be done to arrest the drainage": King, *Great South,* 99, 519

p. 225 "the general character of Southern cities [is] . . . very different": Ratzel, *Sketches,* 147, 148

p. 225 "a perennial stream of progress": Russell, *Atlanta,* quoting a Philadelphia reporter of 1885, 261

p. 226 "a great family": Wilson, *Baptized in Blood,* quoting a Georgia Methodist bishop, 167

p. 226 "someone has observed . . . that the Negro . . . still dominates": Bryce, *American Commonwealth,* vol. 2, 548

p. 227 "The growth of an industrial economy": Temin, *Iron and Steel,* 1

p. 227 "unfettered market economy": Licht, *Industrializing America,* xvi

p. 231 "torrent of Texas cattle": Hudson, *Making the Corn Belt,* 144

p. 231 "Chicago was the industry prototype": Hudson, *Making the Corn Belt,* 174

p. 232 "mainly dependent upon an agriculture revolutionized by agricultural machinery": quoted in Pudup, "From Farm to Factory," 211

p. 233 "unorthodox leap" in technology: Temin, *Iron and Steel,* 4

p. 233 "the transport of Lake ores had become an intricate ballet": Temin, *Iron and Steel,* 197

p. 237 "From the year 1860 the development of the petroleum-industry": Bolles, *Industrial History,* 773–74

p. 238 "indeed, few products associated with America": Williamson and Daum, *American Petroleum Industry,* 725

p. 239 "headquarters at 26 Broadway . . . housed world's largest managerial hierarchy": Chandler, *Scale and Scope,* 74

p. 242 "not lose sight of the impressive array of products": Licht, *Industrializing America,* 129

p. 242 "no transport technology in history has been more centralizing than the railroad": Cronon, *Nature's Metropolis,* 374

p. 242 "window of opportunity": Meyer, "Midwestern Industrialization," 933

p. 243 "the most characteristic and the most efficient form" and "size, speed, quantity, the multi-plication of machines": Mumford, *Technics and Civilization,* 199, 196

p. 243 "the first modern high-fixed-cost business" and "pioneers in modern management": Chandler, *Scale and Scope,* 54

p. 243 "a great wave of mergers swept through": Lamoreaux, *Great Merger Movement,* 1

p. 243 "for nearly three generations . . . the country has been accepting influences": H. Doc. 264, 75th Cong., 1st sess., 51, quoted in Perloff et al., *Regions, Resources and Economic Growth,* 219

p. 244 "unjust discrimination between persons, places, commodities": S. Report 46, 49th Cong., 1st sess., vol. 3, quoted in Faulkner, *American Economic History,* 499

p. 245 "To eyes unfamiliar with the nineteenth century": Klein, *Union Pacific,* 385

p. 246 James J. Hill did not "believe it is possible to make a strong combination": Martin, *James J. Hill,* 486

p. 247 "One frequently hears the expression 'railway system of the United States'": Henry C. Adams, Statistician, Interstate Commerce Commission (I.C.C.), *Second Annual Report* (1888), 245

p. 248 "One new road after another appeared": Klein, *Union Pacific,* 387

p. 248 "peculiarly liberal" American environment, wherein "anyone could build a road anywhere": I.C.C., *Fourth Annual Report* (1890), 291

p. 249 "almost invariably" . . . "an act of open and avowed warfare": I.C.C., *Fifth Annual Report* (1891), 332

p. 249 "When railroads began to be built," through subsequent quotations, ending with "those who have controlled the railroads have not only made the rules": I.C.C., *First Annual Report* (1887), 2–9

p. 250 "towns and cities favored with a line . . . eagerly contributed to aid": U.S. Cong., *Report of Select Committee, Transportation,* 118

p. 250 "General Government" should "own or control": U.S. Cong., *Report of Select Committee, Transportation,* 140

p. 250 "railroads are a public agency": I.C.C., *First Annual Report* (1887), 9

p. 251 "rates can not be arbitrarily charged on the mere discretion": I.C.C., *Fourth Annual Report* (1890), 173

p. 251 "all the circumstances and conditions that affect the traffic": I.C.C., *Second Annual Report* (1888), 108

p. 251 "A railroad is a cheap means of transportation for long distances": quoted in Cronon, *Nature's Metropolis,* 84

p. 252 "the power to determine what localities shall pay": I.C.C., *Eleventh Annual Report* (1897), 45

p. 252 "some towns have grown, others have withered": I.C.C., *First Annual Report* (1887), 7

p. 252 "the special iniquity of the system": I.C.C., *Eleventh Annual Report* (1897), 45

p. 252 "the status of Nashville" . . . "is due largely to the purposeful intent": Joubert, *Southern Freight Rates,* 177, 186

p. 252 "the pre-eminence" of major commercial centers: I.C.C., *First Annual Report* (1887), 82

p. 252 "railroad developments probably had the most profound influence": Pred, *Spatial Dynamics,* 49, 52, 78

p. 253 "It is believed that in no other part of the civilized world": I.C.C., *Eleventh Annual Report* (1897), 45

p. 258 "the latter are saved the expense of picking up this [local] business": Nimmo, *First Annual Report, Internal Commerce,* 24

p. 259 Spokane "had been prevented from fully developing": Smart, "Spokane's Battle," 24

p. 260 "a needless paralleling of existing systems" and "unnecessary and uncalled for": quoted in Grodinsky, *Transcontinental Railway Strategy*, 271, 277

p. 261 "as perceived by those who ran it, a railroad was a pool of capital": Cronon, *Nature's Metropolis*, 81

p. 265 "the bank that cannot profit by swift railroad service": quoted in Anderson, "Banks, Mails, and Rails," 281

p. 265 "It bound together a huge, sprawling nation": Klein, *Unfinished Business*, 17

p. 267 "at least a third of the total urban population": Glaab and Brown, *History of Urban America*, 136

p. 270 "United States was not a land where every immigrant came to stay," and subsequent quotations: Wyman, *Round-Trip*, 207, 205, 27, 204, 208

p. 273 "the most American of our greater cities": Golab, *Immigrant Destinations*, 11

p. 275 Shortridge on Germans in Kansas: *Peopling the Plains*, 99

p. 276 "There are whole counties": Speek, *Stake in the Land*, 130–31

p. 276 Conzen on German Americans: "German-Speaking Ethnic Archipelago," 89

p. 277 1915 geographers on "great population has become naturalized": Davis, "United States," 713

p. 279 "large numbers of Croats, Slovenes": Bodnar, *Immigration and Industrialization*, 25

p. 279 "a map of the city, colored to designate nationalities": Riis, *How the Other Half Lives*, 25

p. 280 "at precisely the time when Americans were beginning seriously to doubt": Jones, *American Immigration*, 247; also Thistlethwaite, *Great Experiment*, 226

p. 280 "immigrant invasion": *King's Portfolio*, 33

p. 281 "A line drawn across . . . Europe": Commons, *Races and Immigrants*, 69–70

p. 281 Senator Lodge, "the perils at the portals": *Cong. Record*, 54th Cong., 1st sess., March 15, 1896, 2820

p. 281 "radical departure" from welcome to "all who came": President Cleveland, *Cong. Record*, 54th Cong., 2d sess., March 2, 1897, 2667

p. 282 "race deterioration" a "Frankenstein": Senator Gibson, *Cong. Record*, 54th Cong., 2d sess., February 17, 1897, 1935

p. 282 "We are paralyzed by our comprehensive ignorance": Balch, *Our Slavic Fellow Citizens*, 404

p. 282 on Dillingham Commission report: Jenks and Lauk, *Immigration Problem*, 371–72

p. 282 Furnas on "the popular distaste for the generic Immigrant": *The Americans*, vol. 2, 840

p. 282 "decisive influence upon American immigration policy": Jones, *American Immigration*, 178, 4

p. 283 "their connection to America begins much later": Golab, *Immigrant Destinations*, 163

p. 283 "do not know anything about America": Speek, *Stake in the Land*, 164

p. 283 "unrecognized . . . and swallowed up": Taylor, *Distant Magnet*, 258

p. 283 "We Slovaks didn't know we were Slovaks": Daniels, *Coming to America*, 218

p. 284 "existence of ethnicity in the American public sphere": Conzen, et al.: "Invention of Ethnicity," 11

p. 284 "almost hysterical fear of 'hyphenated Americans'": Higham, *Send These to Me*, 206

p. 284 "America does not consist of groups": Gordon, *Assimilation*, 101

p. 285 "foreigners in an Irish-dominated church": Dolan, *Immigrant Church*, 6

p. 285 "separate, but equal, churches": Liptak, *Immigrants and Their Church*, 65

p. 285 list of national parishes, Archdiocese of Chicago: Liptak, *Immigrants and Their Church*, 194

p. 285 "ethnic fortresses": Liptak, *Immigrants and Their Church*, 98

p. 285 "every generalization . . . about Catholic values": Greeley, *American Catholic*, 252

p. 286 awkward "fit . . . with established American Protestant patterns": Hennesey, *American Catholics*, 175

p. 286 "underlying unity in faith and practice": Ahlstrom, *Religious History*, 761

p. 288 "historical Judaism": Herberg, *Protestant-Catholic-Jew*, 177

p. 289 "What makes the Chinese experience unique": Daniels, *Coming to America*, 245

p. 289 "the first significant inhibition": Daniels, *Coming to America*, 246

p. 290 "the shock troops of the anti-Chinese movement": Higham, *Send These to Me*, 108

p. 291 "the number of emigrants from Mexico . . . is small": U.S. Department of Commerce . . . , *Emigration to the United States*, 175

p. 293 "a new United States, stretched from ocean to ocean": Wiebe, *Search for Order*, 11–12

p. 293 "We have come to full maturity": Wilson, "Ideals of America," 734

p. 293 "We find here a huge section of the world's surface": Muirhead, *Land of Contrasts* (1898), excerpted in Harris, *Land of Contrasts*, 35

p. 293 "the omnipresent, most characteristic, and most remunerative form of American literature": Boorstin, *Americans: Democratic Experience*, 137

p. 293 "in a new kind of symbolic shorthand": Harris, *Land of Contrasts*, 8

p. 293 "the victory of the market over market-place": Boorstin, *Americans: Democratic Experience*, 135

p. 295 T. Roosevelt on "New Nationalism": speech of August 31, 1910, in Hart and Ferleger, *Theodore Roosevelt Encyclopedia*, 385

p. 295 "we are now passing through a period of centralizing forces": Parmele, *Evolution of an Empire*, 290, 292

p. 295 "marginalized from the beginning": Conzen, "Moral Tenets," 281

p. 296 "designate not less than 8 or more than 12 cities": S. Doc. 485, 63d Cong., 2d sess., 1914, 361, 367

p. 299 "Having regard to the healthy mutual jealousy of the great towns": Bennett, *Your United States*, 41–42

p. 300 "The uniformity is . . . remarkable": Bryce, *American Commonwealth*, vol. 2, 880–81

p. 300 "cities are the cultures of their countries made graphic": Watson and O'Riordan, *American Environment*, 79

p. 300 "American Victorian consensus": Conzen, "Moral Tenets," 281

p. 300 "The symbolism of height with corporate power": Domash, *Invented Cities*, 95

p. 301 "in places like Kansas City and Chicago": Bryce, *American Commonwealth*, vol. 2, 871

p. 301 the Woolworth building as "a huge sign advertising": Landau and Condit, *Rise of New York Skyscraper*, 382, xiii

p. 306 "filling in the region with public facilities": Brunn, *Geography and Politics*, 107

p. 307 "settle, perhaps, for some time to come, the question of political supremacy": Matthew Butler, *Cong. Record*, 50th Cong., 1st sess., 4–10–88, 2836

p. 308 "stacking the Senate": Stewart and Weingast, "Stacking the Senate," 270

p. 308 "extraordinary stable" pattern of sectional alignments, etc.: Bensel, *Sectionalism*, 6, 5, 6

p. 309 "Perhaps a more scientific method would be to ignore state lines": Turner to W. H. Page, 1896, quoted in Jacobs, *Historical World*, 94

p. 310 "the individual State is still a unit": Davis, "United States," 712

p. 310 "the 'whys' and 'hows' of location": Rowley, *J. Russell Smith*, 76

p. 312 "the need for a thorough study of the physiographic basis of our history": Turner, "Problems in American History," 1892, in *Frontier and Section*, 30–31

p. 312 history as "a comparative and genetic study": Turner, "Problems in American History," 1892, 29

p. 312 "One might ascertain how business houses . . . divided up the 'territory'": Turner to W. H. Page, 1896, in Jacobs, *Historical World*, 95

p. 312 "there is and always has been a sectional geography in America": Turner, "Significance of the Section," in *Frontier and Section*, 131

p. 312 "men of ability": Lodge, "Distribution of Ability," 693

p. 312 *each age writes the history of the past anew*: Turner, "Significance of History," 1891, 17

p. 312 time for "a connected and unified account of the progress of civilization": Turner, "Problems in American History," 1892, in *Frontier and Section*, 29

p. 312 "the existence of an area of free land, its continuous recession": Turner, "Significance of the Frontier," in *Frontier and Section*, 37, 38

p. 312 "the true point of view . . . is the Great West": Turner, "Significance of the Frontier," in *Frontier and Section,* 38

p. 312 "a form of society, rather than an area": Turner, "Problem of the West," 1896, in *Frontier and Section,* 63

p. 313 "That coarseness and strength combined with acuteness and inquisitiveness": Turner, "Significance of the Frontier," in *Frontier and Section,* 61

p. 313 "and now, four centuries from the discovery of America": Turner, "Significance of the Frontier," in *Frontier and Section,* 62

p. 313 "Darwinian metaphors of evolution and organism" had "placed the American West at center stage": Cronon, "Revisiting the Vanished Frontier," 165

p. 314 "Societies are constituted of . . . networks of power": Mann, *Sources of Social Power,* 1

p. 315 "as American society became . . . more integrated": Bodnar, *Bonds of Affection,* 13

p. 315 "Christianity . . . understood to be . . . the national religion": Bryce, *American Commonwealth,* vol. 2, 770

p. 315 "a full-scale, three-dimensional realization of the kind of city": Lowry, *Building a National Image,* 74

p. 316 "from the circumference to the center": *Missouri Democrat,* 10–21–69

p. 316 "there was a restless admiration for Eastern America": Webb, *American Diary,* 110

p. 317 "emulation is not absorption": Jahr, *Urban Establishment,* 729, 728

p. 317 in San Francisco "none of that extreme sensitiveness": Webb, *American Diary,* 141
"What the railroad and telegraph did for the economies": Hall, *Organization of American Culture,* 3

p. 317 "beginning in the 1880s prominent citizens": Jahr, *Urban Establishment,* 728

p. 317 "the role of the college as custodian of culture": Handlin and Handlin, *American College,* 49

p. 318 "the southernmost university of wide resort": Davis, "United States," 731

p. 318 Morrill Act, "such branches of learning": Hofstadter and Smith, *American Higher Education,* vol. 2, 568

p. 318 Washington University, "with Harvard firmly in mind": Adler, *Yankee Merchants,* 105

p. 319 "By a Capital I mean a city which is": Bryce, *American Commonwealth,* vol. 2, 855

p. 319 "societies are much *messier* than our theories": Mann, *Sources of Social Power,* 4

p. 319 "the concentrated essence of Americanism": Teaford, *Cities of the Heartland,* 48

p. 320 "a time of extraordinary civic confidence": Wills, "Sons and Daughters," 56

p. 320 "the sanctity of the agricultural way of life": David D. Anderson, quoted in Cayton and Onuf, *Midwest and Nation,* 121

p. 320 "at the beginning of the twentieth century a great many people": Cayton and Onuf, *Midwest and Nation,* 122

p. 320 Turner on "Center of the Republic": "Problems of the West," in *Frontier and Section,* 76

p. 320 "a cluster of mountains, with their bright peaks": from *Scribner's,* 1899, quoted in Domash, "Imagining New York," 240

p. 320 "the most visited place in the country": Neil Harris, in Taylor, *Inventing Times Square,* 69

p. 320 "Mid-Manhattan became a sort of permanent World's Fair": David Hammack, in Taylor, *Inventing Times Square,* 43

p. 321 "insoluble clots" of "aliens": Ross, "Middle West" (83): 611

p. 321 "by its geographical position, escapes the temptation": Ross, "Middle West" (84): 148

p. 322 "fished out communities": Ross, "Middle West" (83): 613

p. 322 "a cauldron of class conflict": Teaford, *Cities of the Heartland,* 71

p. 323 "from the Atlantic seaboard to the Mississippi": Wilson, *History,* vol. 5, 199–200

p. 323 "provided the scholarly and theoretical basis for the growing celebration": Cayton and Onuf, *Midwest and Nation,* 123

PART FOUR

p. 328 "our individuality—our destiny as a people—will be forever sunk": Weale and Baglole, *Island and Confederation*, 115

p. 328 "from a federation of equal provinces into a veritable empire": Martin, *Foundations*, 409

p. 328 métis "bought like the buffalo": quoted in Martin, *Foundations*, 418

p. 329 Manitoba "embodied the old rivalry": Morton, *Manitoba*, 142

p. 329 Grant, "We must do, in one or two years": *Ocean to Ocean*, 6

p. 330 Macdonald, "little more than a 'geographical expression'": quoted in Berton, *National Dream*, 163

p. 330 "the last link between Europe and Asia": Montreal newspaper, 1869, quoted in Silver, *French-Canadian Idea*, 72

p. 330 "an impetus that will make it a great and powerful country": Sir Charles Tupper, 1880, quoted in Berton, *National Dream*, 229

p. 330 on Vancouver "destined to be a great city": Hull et al., *Vancouver's Past*, 31

p. 332 lands retained "for the purposes of the Dominion": Martin, *Foundations*, 397

p. 332 "making Manitoba a New Quebec": Halliburton letter to Macdonald, 1870, quoted in Owram, *Promise of Eden*, 99

p. 333 "a declaration of war . . . against the French race": Silver, *French-Canadian Idea*, 186

p. 333 "perfect equality of the two races": Montreal newspaper, 1890, quoted in Silver, *French-Canadian Idea*, 187

p. 333 "Manitoba has been to us . . . what Kansas was": quoted in Owram, *Promise of Eden*, 99–100

p. 333 "during the 1870s and 1880s the West was Canadianized": Francis and Palmer, *Prairie West*, 135

p. 334 on Churchill Harbour: quoted in Owram, *Promise of Eden*, 185

p. 336 "the hopper was too big for the spout": Van Horne, quoted in Lower, *Canada*, 142

p. 338 *"We are the Northmen"*: Russell, *Nationalism*, 5, 6

p. 341 "just and generous treatment": Hunt, *Alaska*, 99

p. 341 "a territory . . . capable of supporting a population larger" than Scandinavia: Seattle brief, *Location of Reserve Districts*, S. Doc. 485, 63d Cong., 2d sess., 1914, 337

p. 341 a population "destined to be as numerous as that of the United States": Laurier, Prime Minister, 1911, quoted in Bowles et al., *Canada and the U.S.*, 179

p. 341 "no balance of power in North America": Creighton, "Canada in the English-Speaking World," 120

p. 341 "there remain differences of environment": Shortt and Doughty, *Canada and Its Provinces*, vol. 1, viii

p. 342 "expedient . . . that there should be community of language": Silver, *French-Canadian Idea*, 186

p. 342 "Canada is not Canada for all Canadians": Bourassa, quoted in Careless and Brown, *Canadians*, 162

p. 342 Bourassa on duality: Silver, *French-Canadian Idea*, 193

p. 342 no "ideological Canadianism": Smith, *Canada-American Nation*, 151

p. 343 "Whoever wishes to know what Canada is": Smith, *Canada and Canadian Question*, 1–2

p. 343 that alternative lay "near the centre of Canadian politics": Smith, *Canada-American Nation*, 70

p. 344 Moffett on communications, Greater Canada, and cities: *Americanization*, 61, 14, 67

p. 345 Canada "united by no bond of geography": Smith, *Canada and Canadian Question*, 300

p. 345 "a transcontinental Canadian nation . . . natural and perhaps inevitable": Zeller, *Inventing Canada*, 9

p. 346 "look the Americans in the face": Careless and Brown, *Canadians*, 71

p. 346 "building up a nation without separation": Laurier, 1911, quoted in Bowles et al., *Canada and the U.S.*, 180

p. 346 "This land is ours, we have made it": Bowles et al., *Canada and the U.S.*, 176

p. 346 "once the United States have engulfed . . . North America": Silver, *French-Canadian Idea*, 188

p. 347 "sustained pressure of ninety-three millions to eight millions": Bowles, *Canada and the U.S.*, 176–77

p. 347 "Canadians feared and envied the United States": Brown and Cook, *Canada, 1896–1921*, 6

p. 347 "Border nations are natural enemies": Davids, *American Penetration*, 168

p. 347 Bayard's comment: Davids, *American Penetration*, 165

p. 347 "opened the floodgates of American capital": Pletcher, *Rail, Mines, and Progress*, 24–25

p. 349 "the vast system of railroads is operated generally, . . . by American citizens": Senator Carter, Montana, *Cong. Record*, 54th Cong., 2d sess., February 17, 1897, 1924–25

p. 351 on "Plan de San Diego": Sandos, *Rebellion in the Borderlands*, 79

p. 353 "ironically, as these groups moved back and forth across the boundary": Chávez, *Lost Land*, 78

p. 355 U.S. consul, "*De Facto*, Cuba is already inside": Pérez, *Cuba and United States*, 61

p. 355 "Cubans could not help but stand in awe" and "in habits, tastes, preferences Cubans . . . partook freely": Pérez, *Cuba and United States*, 70, 69

p. 355 "their experiences guaranteed that North American influences": Pérez, *Cuba and United States*, 69

p. 355 Martí, urging compatriots to "block with our blood" annexation: Pérez, *Cuba and United States*, 79

p. 355 President on intervention: McKinley message to Congress, April 11, 1898, in Fitzgibbon, *Cuba and United States*, 267–68

p. 355 "the Cuban war of liberation became the 'Spanish-American War' ": Pérez, *Cuba and United States*, 97

p. 357 Cuban government "not representative of the Cuban people": Major General Leonard Wood, quoted in Pérez, *Cuba and United States*, 108

p. 357 Teller Amendment; "United States hereby disclaims": in Fitzgibbon, *Cuba and United States*, 269

p. 357 Platt Amendment provisions: Fitzgibbon, *Cuba and United States*, 272–73

p. 357 "limited sovereignty or no sovereignty": Pérez, *Cuba and United States*, 112

p. 357 "independence with restrictions was better than continued occupation": Hernández, *Cuba and United States*, 96

p. 357 "Cuba lay in ruins": Hernández, *Cuba and United States*, 49

p. 357 on Leonard Wood; American historian: Fitzgibbon, *Cuba and United States*, 28; Hispanic-American historian: Hernández, *Cuba and United States*, 94

p. 358 American visitor on Cuba and statehood: Forbes Lindsay, 1911, quoted in Pérez, *Cuba and United States*, 51

p. 358 Cuban census takers "displayed an indifference": Fitzgibbon, *Cuba and United States*, 251

p. 358 Americans "arrived as carpetbaggers and gamblers": Pérez, *Cuba and United States*, 123

p. 358 on Isle of Pines: "Adjustment of Title to Isle of Pines": S. Doc. No. 205, 59th Cong., 1st sess., February 1, 1906, 244, 252, and *Cong. Record*, 56th Cong., 2d sess., February 27, 1901, vol. 34, 3149

p. 359 great sugar *centrals* each "a huge feudal territory": quoted in Healy, *Drive to Hegemony*, 205–6

p. 359 "the vastly augmented power of [American] production": Pérez, *Cuba under Platt*, 110

p. 359 U.S. policy "shifted away from armed intervention": Pérez, *Cuba under Platt*, 117

p. 359 Secretary of State (Knox) to minister on American interest: Pérez, *Cuba under Platt*, 122

p. 359 Gómez on "those rich northerners": Hernández, *Cuba and United States*, 87

p. 359 Pérez reflection, "North American resolve to control": *Cuba and United States*, xvi

p. 360 "uncomfortable feeling that imperialism . . . was a betrayal": Leibowitz, *Defining Status*, 20

p. 360 "differing from us in religion, customs, laws": Leibowitz, *Defining Status*, 22

p. 360 on "incorporated" and "unincorporated" territories: Leibowitz, *Defining Status*, 23

p. 360 dissent on "occult" concept of territories: Justice Harlan, quoted in Leibowitz, *Defining Status*, 25

p. 361 "a peaceful invasion" of American schoolteachers, and even changing the name to "Porto Rico": Diana Christopulos in López, *Puerto Ricans*, 130; *National Geographic Magazine* 10 (1899), 112

p. 361 Mahan on "Puerto Rico, considered militarily": *Lessons of the War with Spain*, 29

p. 361 "There is no harbor . . . better fitted than St. Thomas": Vice Admiral Porter, quoted in Leibowitz, *Defining Status*, 244

p. 361 Roosevelt Corollary, "in flagrant cases of such wrongdoing": Bailey, *Diplomatic History*, 558

p. 364 United States in Canal Zone might exercise "all the rights, power and authority": McCullough, *Path between the Seas*, 393

p. 364 "a mandate from civilization" to create an "interoceanic canal": quoted in Bailey, *Diplomatic History*, 544

p. 365 "the annexation of Hawaii would make a canal a necessity": Senator Morgan, Alabama, 1897, quoted in Healy, *Drive to Hegemony*, 80

p. 366 "Hawaii has reached the parting of the ways" and "The Hawaiian pear is now fully ripe": quoted in Pratt, *Expansionists*, 68, 113

p. 366 Hawaii a "necessary outwork," "without sea power no nation has been truly great," "we must abandon the doctrine," "now that the continent is subdued": quoted in Pratt, *Expansionists*, 206, 205, 152, 224

p. 367 Carl Schurz on "manifest destiny": *Harper's* 87 (October 1983): 743

p. 367 Fuchs on Hawaii as "a curious amalgam": *Hawaii Pono*, 37

p. 367 Japanese "attitudes toward family, property, and authority" and "Hawaii of the Hawaiians": Fuchs, *Hawaii Pono*, 36–37

p. 368 "a veritable paradise on earth": Fuchs, *Hawaii Pono*, 153

p. 369 "this island empire is the last land left": Senator Beveridge, quoted in Brands, *Bound to Empire*, 32

p. 369 Manila "the greatest commercial and strategic point": Senator Lodge, quoted in Osborne, *"Empire Can Wait,"* 130

p. 369 "The United States will occupy and hold the city": Offner, *Unwanted War*, 237

p. 369 McKinley on the Filipinos: Bailey, *Diplomatic History*, 520

p. 371 "had spent most of his career terrorizing Apaches": Stuart Creighton Miller, quoted in Linn, *"Long Twilight,"* 159

p. 372 "Spanish element is less than often presumed": Spencer, *Oriental Asia*, 52

p. 372 on Rizal, and "a modernizing convulsion": Stanley, *Nation in the Making*, 47, 267

p. 372 "English is the lingua franca of the Far East": Brands, *Bound to Empire*, 71

p. 373 "American imperialism . . . was progressivism writ large": Brands, *Bound to Empire*, 61

p. 373 "United States refused to be labeled a colonial power" and "emissaries of good will": Karnow, *In Our Image*, 197, 196

p. 373 "cosmopolitan upper class" . . . quickly "demonstrated their mastery": Karnow, *In Our Image*, 174

p. 373 Democrats in 1912, "We condemn the experiment": Brands, *Bound to Empire*, 104

p. 375 "a continuous line of great telegraph poles": Austin, "Problems of the Pacific," 313–15

p. 375 "Commerce follows the cables": Osborne, *"Empire Can Wait,"* 130

p. 375 Mahan on "a renewed China": *Problem of Asia*, 66

p. 375 Dewey and "the best obtainable port in China": Iriye, *Pacific Estrangement*, 55

p. 377 "final movement" . . . "across the great ocean": Austin, "Commercial Prize," 423

p. 377 Coolidge on Pacific Ocean: *United States as a World Power*, 324

p. 377 Gannett on the Philippines: "Philippine Islands," 112

p. 377 Semple on United States in Asiatic affairs: *American History*, 433

p. 377 United States "ill prepared . . . for coping with a totally different phenomenon," an Asian power equally "self-conscious about civilization and race": Iriye, *Pacific Estrangement,* 16, 49

p. 377 "It would be to our great advantage if our countrymen moved outside the limits": Iriye, *Pacific Estrangement,* 39

p. 377 Hawaii as "our branch house": Iriye, *Pacific Estrangement,* 48

p. 377 "if we continue to send emigrants" to the Philippines: 1898 newspaper, quoted in Iriye, *Pacific Estrangement,* 56

p. 379 Japanese on Oahu as "vexatious" question: Linn, "Long Twilight," 156; see also Iriye, *Pacific Estrangement,* 218

p. 379 T. Roosevelt on better to "give up the Philippine Islands": Iriye, *Across the Pacific,* 107

p. 380 President Hayes on "The policy of this country": Message to Congress, March 8, 1880, quoted in Coolidge, *United States as a World Power,* 273

p. 381 "the United States Government built the Canal in order to join the two coasts" and implications thereof: Wheeler, "Meaning of the Canal," 163

p. 381 "ports . . . now find themselves drawn within the circle of New York trade": Wheeler, "Meaning of the Canal," 162

p. 381 Pacific ports "quickened into new life": Abbot, *Panama and the Canal,* 382

p. 381 Canal as symbol of American character: Lane, "City of Realized Dreams," 27; Abbot, *Panama and the Canal,* 412; *Ladies Home Journal,* quoted in Richard, *Panama Canal,* 232

p. 384 "largest public work ever attempted": McCullough, *Path between the Seas,* 446

p. 384 proposal on Blacks "met with strenuous opposition": McCullough, *Path Between the Seas,* 473

p. 385 Canal Zone "a Government owned reservation": Epstein, *Statesman's Year-Book 1931,* 1163

p. 386 San Francisco "the most modern city": Phelan, "California's Invitation," 161

p. 386 Panama-Pacific Exposition to celebrate "the first cutting of . . . the long, broad dyke of the Americas": Wheeler, "Meaning of the Canal," 164, slightly rearranged

p. 386 "the most Titanic war in world-history": "San Francisco Fair," 533, quoting Portland *Oregonian*

p. 386 "Beyond its significance as a great scientific achievement": Macdonald, "California Expositions," 491

p. 389 Semple on "the most important geographic fact" and her conclusion: *American History,* 1, 435

p. 389 Bryce on "dying down of sudden imperialistic impulse": *American Commonwealth,* vol. 2, 585

p. 389 "the youthful American republic had triumphed where old world had failed": Richard, *Panama Canal,* 250

p. 389 Cornish's report: "Panama Canal in 1908," 175

p. 389 "To everyone's surprise the [Suez] Canal only reinforced Britain's domination" and Britain's "ability to make ships pay a profit": Headrick, *Tentacles of Progress,* 27

p. 390 Hugill on British "lead in building first global information infrastructure": "Global Communications" ms, unpaged

p. 391 "*the simultaneous appearance of three new world powers*": Bemis, *United States as a World Power,* 4

p. 391 Senator Lodge on map of "British naval stations": *Cong. Record,* 53d Cong., 3d sess., March 2, 1895, 3082–83

p. 391 "exaggerated sense of right to expand," "unlimited growth," "total immunity": Liska, *Career of Empire,* 115

p. 391 Lippmann on "unearned security": *U.S. Foreign Policy,* 49

p. 391 Mackinder quotations: "Geographical Pivot," 434, 422

p. 394 Mahan on U.S. relations with Europe: *Problem of Asia,* 17

p. 394 "Neither the people of the U.S. nor persons in governance knew what the war was about": Bemis: *United States as a World Power,* 121

p. 394 "Powerful and persuasive minds" . . . "focused on need to transform": Williams, *Empire as a Way of Life,* 101–2

Bibliography

The following list of works used in the preparation of *Transcontinental America* is changed in pattern from that of previous volumes, where they were grouped according to the four major parts of the text. Here the list is subdivided according to the twenty chapters of the book so as to offer a rather quicker and clearer link between text and source in most cases. There were, of course, a number of works pertinent to more than one chapter; a few of the most general of these are noted at the outset, but none of these or others have been listed more than once.

As in previous volumes an array of other materials too numerous, well known, or inaccessible to warrant separate listing was also important. These include many standard federal government documents, especially census reports, annual reports of departments, and the sequential volumes of sessions and debates in Congress (specific quotations from these are identified in the Sources of Quotations). A large number of maps and atlases, some contemporary with these topics and some of more recent publication, some accumulated over many years of professional work, others copied from various collections to serve this project, were always ready at hand and consulted countless times in the writing of every chapter. My own collection of the state guidebooks produced by the Federal Writers' Project of the Works Progress Administration in the late 1930s and early 1940s, a series too numerous and standardized in kind to warrant individual citation, was another source of ready reference on innumerable local details.

GENERAL

Allen, James Paul, and Eugene James Turner. *We the People: An Atlas of America's Ethnic Diversity.* New York: Macmillan, 1988.

Boorstin, Daniel J. *The Americans: The Democratic Experience.* New York: Random House, 1973.

Bryce, James. *The American Commonwealth.* 2 vols. New York: Macmillan, 1888, 1891, 1910, 1915.

Conzen, Michael P., ed. *The Making of the American Landscape.* Boston: Unwin Hyman, 1990.

Davidson, Marshall B. *Life in America.* 2 vols. Boston: Houghton Mifflin, 1951.

Elazar, Daniel J. *The American Mosaic: The Impact of Space, Time, and Culture on American Politics.* Boulder, Colo.: Westview Press, 1994.

Furnas, J. C. *The Americans: A Social History, 1587–1914.* Vol. 2. New York: Capricorn Books, 1969.

Garraty, John A. *The American Nation: A History of the United States.* New York: Harper & Row, 1966.

Garrett, Wilbur E., ed. *Historical Atlas of the United States.* Washington, D.C.: National Geographic Society, 1988.

Henretta, James A., W. Elliot Brownlee, David Brody, and Susan Ware. *America's History.* Chicago: Dorsey Press, 1987.

Historical Statistics of the United States, 1789–1945. Washington, D.C.: Bureau of the Census, Department of Commerce, 1949.

King's Handbook of the United States. Buffalo: Moses King, 1891.

Martis, Kenneth C. *The Historical Atlas of Political Parties in the United States Congress, 1789–1989.* New York: Macmillan, 1989.

Mitchell, Robert D., and Paul A. Groves, eds. *North America: The Historical Geography of a Changing Continent.* Totowa, N.J.: Rowman & Littlefield, 1987.

Paullin, Charles O., and John K. Wright. *Atlas of the Historical Geography of the United States.* Washington, D.C.: Carnegie Institution, 1932.

Thistlethwaite, Frank. *The Great Experiment: An Introduction to the History of the American People.* Cambridge: Cambridge Univ. Press, 1955.

PART ONE

1. Forging the Iron Bond

Boorstin, Daniel J. *The Americans: The National Experience.* New York: Random House, 1965.

Bowles, Samuel. *The Pacific Railroad-Open. How to Go: What to See. Guide for Travel to and through Western America.* Boston: Fields, Osgood, & Co., 1869.

Brown, Dee. *Hear That Lonesome Whistle Blow: Railroads in the West.* New York: Holt, Rinehart and Winston, 1977.

Cronise, Titus Fey. *The Natural Wealth of California.* San Francisco: H. H. Bancroft, 1868.

DeBow, J. D. B. "Intercommunication between the Atlantic and Pacific Coasts." *DeBow's Commercial Review* 17 o.s., 1, no. 1, n.s. (July 1849): 1–37.

Drury, George H. *The Historical Guide to North American Railroads.* Milwaukee: Kalmbach Publishing, 1985.

Dubin, Arthur D. *Some Classic Trains.* Milwaukee: Kalmbach, 1964.

Evans, Cerinda W. *Collis Potter Huntington.* Vol. 1. Newport News, Va.: Mariner's Museum, 1954.

Farnham, Wallace D. "Shadows from the Gilded Age: Pacific Railwaymen and the Race to Promontory—or Ogden?" In *The Golden Spike,* ed. David E. Miller, 1–22. Salt Lake City: Univ. of Utah Press, 1973.

Galloway, John Debo. *The First Transcontinental Railroad: The Central Pacific and the Union Pacific.* New York: Simmons-Boardman, 1950.

Goetzmann, William H. *Army Exploration in the American West, 1803–1863.* New Haven: Yale Univ. Press, 1959.

Haney, Lewis H. *A Congressional History of Railways in the United States.* Vol. 2, *The Railway in Congress: 1850–1887.* Madison, Wis.: Democrat Printing Co., State Printer, 1910.

Jackson, W. Turrentine. *Wagon Roads West: A Study of Federal Road Surveys and Construction in the Trans-Mississippi West, 1846–1869.* New Haven: Yale Univ. Press, 1964.

Keir, Malcolm. *The March of Commerce.* New Haven: Yale Univ. Press, 1927.

Klein, Maury. *Union Pacific: Birth of a Railroad, 1862–1893.* Garden City, N.Y.: Doubleday, 1987.

Loughborough, J. *The Pacific Telegraph and Railway.* St. Louis: Charles & Hammond, 1849.

Martin, Albro. *Railroads Triumphant: The Growth, Rejection, and Rebirth of a Vital American Force.* New York: Oxford Univ. Press, 1992.

Petro, Sir S. Morton. *The Resources and Prospects of America.* London and New York: Alexander Strahan, 1866.

Poor, Henry V. *Manual of the Railroads of the United States.* New York: H. V. & H. W. Poor, 1870.

Potter, David M. *The Impending Crisis, 1848–1861.* New York: Harper & Row, 1976.

Ratzel, Friedrich. *Sketches of Urban and Cultural Life in North America.* [1876] Trans. and ed. Stewart A. Stehlin. New Brunswick, N.J.: Rutgers Univ. Press, 1988.

Russel, Robert R. *Improvement of Communication with the Pacific Coast as an Issue in American Politics, 1783–1864.* Cedar Rapids, Iowa: Torch Press, 1948.

The Statutes at Large, Treaties, and Proclamations of the United States of America from December 5, 1859 to March 3, 1863. Vol. 12. Ed. George P. Sanger. Boston: Little, Brown, 1863.

Taylor, George Rogers, and Irene D. Neu. *The American Railroad Network, 1861–1890.* Cambridge: Harvard Univ. Press, 1956.

Travelers' Official Railway Guide of the United States and Canada. June 1868. Reprint. Ann Arbor: University Microfilms, 1968.

Vance, James E., Jr. *Capturing the Horizon: The Historical Geography of Transportation since the Transportation Revolution of the Sixteenth Century.* New York: Harper & Row, 1986.

Wender, Herbert. "Southern Commercial Conventions, 1837–1859." *Johns Hopkins University Studies in Historical and Political Science* 48 (1930): 423–658.

Wyckoff, William. "Mapping the 'New' El Dorado: Pikes Peak Promotional Cartography, 1859–1861." *Imago Mundi* 40 (1988): 32–45.

PART TWO

1. Delineating the New West

Fisher, Richard Swainson. *A New and Complete Statistical Gazetteer of the United States of America.* New York: J. H. Colton, 1853.

Goetzmann, William H. *Exploration and Empire: The Explorer and the Scientist in the Winning of the American West.* New York: Alfred A. Knopf, 1967.

Hyde, Anne Farrar. *An American Vision: Far Western Landscape and National Culture, 1820–1920.* New York: New York Univ. Press, 1990.

Jackson, John Brinckerhoff. *American Space: The Centennial Years, 1865–1876.* New York: W. W. Norton, 1972.

Reps, John W. *Cities of the American West: A History of Frontier Urban Planning.* Princeton: Princeton Univ. Press, 1979.

Walker, Francis A., comp. *Statistical Atlas of the United States, Based on the Results of the Ninth Census 1870.* [Washington, D.C.]: United States Census Office, 1874.

2. California

Alonzo Delano's California. Ed. Irving McKee. Sacramento: Sacramento Book Club, 1952.

Boline, Frederick C. "The Portuguese in California." *California Historical Society Quarterly* 35 (September 1956): 233–52.

Bowman, Lynn. *Los Angeles: Epic of a City.* Berkeley: Howell-North Books, 1974.

Bunkse, Edmunds V. "The Humboldt Bay Region: A Study in Pioneer Transportation." M.A. thesis, Department of Geography, Univ. of California, Berkeley, 1966.

Burcham, Levi Turner. "Historical Geography of the Range Livestock Industry of California." Ph.D. dissertation, Department of Geography, Univ. of California, Berkeley, 1956.

Cleland, Robert Glass. *The Cattle on a Thousand Hills: Southern California, 1850–1880.* San Marino, Calif.: Huntington Library, 1951.

Colton, Walter. *Three Years in California.* Stanford: Stanford Univ. Press, 1949.

Cook, Sherburne F. *The Conflict between the California Indian and White Civilization.* Berkeley: Univ. of California Press, 1976.

———. *The Population of the California Indians, 1769–1970.* Berkeley: Univ. of California Press, 1976.

Daniels, Roger, and Harry H. L. Kitano. *American Racism: Exploration of the Nature of Prejudice.* Englewood Cliffs, N.J.: Prentice-Hall, 1970.

Davis, William Newell. "California East of the Sierra: A Study in Economic Sectionalism." Ph.D. dissertation, Department of History, Univ. of California, Berkeley, 1942.

DeWitt, Howard A. *California Civilization: An Interpretation.* Dubuque, Iowa: Kendall/Hunt, 1979.

Dunn, H. D. "California—Her Agricultural Resources." In *Report of the Commissioner of Agriculture for the Year 1866,* 581–610. Wash-

ington, D.C.: Government Printing Office, 1867.

Durrenberger, Robert W. *Patterns on the Land: Geographical, Historical and Political Maps of California.* Woodland Hills, Calif.: Aegus, 1965.

Eder, Herbert Michael. "The Geographical Uniqueness of California's North Coast Counties: Humboldt and Del Norte." Ph.D. dissertation, Department of Geography, Univ. of California, Berkeley, 1963.

Ellison, William Henry. *A Self-Governing Dominion: California, 1849–1860.* Berkeley: Univ. of California Press, 1950.

Frémont, John Charles. "Geographical Memoir upon Upper California, in Illustration of His Map of Oregon and California." In *The Expeditions of John Charles Frémont.* Vol. 3, *Travels from 1848 to 1854,* ed. Mary Lee Spence, 495–570. Urbana: Univ. of Illinois Press, 1984.

Garner, William Robert. *Letters from California, 1846–1847.* Ed. Donald Munro Craig. Berkeley: Univ. of California Press, 1970.

Griswold, Richard del Castillo. *The Los Angeles Barrio, 1850–1890: A Social History.* Berkeley: Univ. of California Press, 1979.

Gudde, Erwin G. *California Gold Camps.* Ed. Elizabeth K. Gudde. Berkeley: Univ. of California Press, 1975.

Guest, Anna Lee. "The Historical Development of Southern Oregon, 1825–1852." M.A. thesis, Department of History, Univ. of California, Berkeley, 1929.

Heizer, Robert F., and Alan J. Almquist. *The Other Californians: Prejudice and Discrimination under Spain, Mexico, and the United States to 1920.* Berkeley: Univ. of California Press, 1971.

Higgins, F. Hal. "John M. Horner and the Development of the Combined Harvester." *Agricultural History* 32 (January 1958): 14–24.

Hilgard, E. W. "The Agriculture and Soils of California." In *Annual Report of the Commissioner of Agriculture for the Year 1878*, 476–507. Washington, D.C.: Government Printing Office, 1879.

[Hill, Laurance L.]. *La Reina: Los Angeles in Three Centuries*. 4th ed. Los Angeles: Security-First National Bank, 1931.

Hornbeck, David. "Mexican-American Land Tenure Conflict in California." *Journal of Geography* 74 (April 1976): 209–21.

———. "Land Tenure and Rancho Expansion in Alta California, 1784–1846." *Journal of Historical Geography* 4 (October 1978): 371–90.

———. "The California Indian before European Contact." *Journal of Cultural Geography* 2 (Spring–Summer 1982): 23–39.

———. *California Patterns: A Geographical and Historical Atlas*. Mountainview, Calif.: Mayfield, 1983.

Hunt, Rockwell D. "History of the California State Division Controversy." *Publication of the Historical Society of Southern California* 13 (1924): 37–53.

Jarvis, Chester Edward. "The Capitals of California, 1849–1854." M.A. thesis, Department of History, Univ. of California, Berkeley, 1942.

Kemble, John Haskell. *San Francisco Bay: A Pictorial Maritime History*. New York: Bonanza Books, 1957.

Kroeber, A. L. "The Nature of Land-Holding Groups in Aboriginal California." In *Aboriginal California: Three Studies in Culture History*, ed. Robert F. Heizer, 81–120. Berkeley: Univ. of California Archaeological Research Facility, 1963.

Lamb, Edith Jane. "The Formation of the State of Nevada, 1840–1864." M.A. thesis, Department of History, Univ. of California, Berkeley, 1917.

Lantis, David W., Rodney Steiner, and Arthur E. Karinen. *California: Land of Contrast*. Belmont, Calif.: Wadsworth, 1963.

Los Angeles: A Guide to the City and Its Environs. American Guide Series. New York: Hastings House, 1941.

Lotchin, Roger W. *San Francisco, 1846–1856: From Hamlet to City*. New York: Oxford Univ. Press, 1974.

[McEntire, Davis]. *The Population of California*.

San Francisco: Commonwealth Club of California, 1946.

McKain, Walter C., Jr., and Sara Miles. "Santa Barbara County between Two Social Orders." *California Historical Society Quarterly* 25 (December 1946): 311–18.

MacKinnon, Richard M. "The Sonoran Miners: A Case of Historical Accident in the California Gold Rush." *California Geographer* 9 (1970): 21–28.

McWilliams, Carey. *Southern California Country: An Island in the Land*. New York: Duell, Sloan & Pearce, 1946.

———. *California: The Great Exception*. New York: A. A. Wyn, 1949.

Mann, Ralph. *After the Gold Rush: Society in Grass Valley and Nevada City, California, 1849–1870*. Stanford: Stanford Univ. Press, 1982.

Monaghan, Jay. *Chile, Peru, and the California Gold Rush of 1849*. Berkeley: Univ. of California Press, 1973.

Morefield, Richard Henry. "The Mexican Adaptation in American California: 1846–1875." M.A. Thesis, Department of History, Univ. of California, Berkeley, 1956.

Nelson, Howard J. "The Spread of an Artificial Landscape over Southern California." *Annals of the Association of American Geographers* 49, pt. 2 (September 1959): 80–99.

Odell, Kerry A. "The Integration of Regional and Interregional Capital Markets: Evidence from the Pacific Coast, 1883–1913." *Journal of Economic History* 49 (June 1989): 297–310.

Pacific Railroad Guide. Vol. 2. San Francisco: Wilson & Lawrence, January 1870.

Palmer, Hans Christian. "Italian Immigration and the Development of California Agriculture." Ph.D. dissertation, Department of Economics, University of California, Berkeley, 1965.

Parsons, James J. "The Uniqueness of California." *American Quarterly* 7 (Spring 1955): 45–55.

Paul, Rodman W. *California Gold: The Beginnings of Mining in the Far West*. Lincoln: Univ. of Nebraska Press, 1947.

Pitt, Leonard. *The Decline of the Californios: A Social History of the Spanish-Speaking Californians, 1846–1890*. Berkeley: Univ. of California Press, 1966.

Railroad Gazetteer. No. 26. San Francisco: H. S. Crocker, October 1871.

Raup, H. F. "San Bernardino, California: Settlement and Growth of a Pass-Site City." *University of California Publications in Geography* 8, no. 1 (1940): 1–64.

————. "The Italian-Swiss in California." *California Historical Society Quarterly* 30 (December 1951): 305–14.

————. "Transformation of Southern California to a Cultivated Land." *Annals of the Association of American Geographers* 49, pt. 2 (September 1959): 58–78.

Report of the Commissioner of Agriculture for the Year 1873. Washington, D.C.: Government Printing Office, 1874.

Riegel, Martin P. *California's Maritime Heritage.* San Clemente, Calif.: Riegel, 1987.

Robinson, W. W. *Land in California.* Berkeley: Univ. of California Press, 1948.

Roske, Ralph J. "The World Impact of the California Gold Rush, 1849–1857." *Arizona and the West* 5 (Autumn 1963): 187–232.

————. *Everyman's Eden: A History of California.* New York: Macmillan, 1968.

San Francisco: The Bay and Its Cities. 2d ed. American Guide Series. New York: Hastings House, 1947.

Scott, Mel. *The San Francisco Bay Area: A Metropolis in Perspective.* Berkeley: Univ. of California Press, 1959.

Smith, Michael L. *Pacific Visions: California Scientists and the Environment, 1850–1915.* New Haven: Yale Univ. Press, 1987.

Smith, Wallace. *Garden of the Sun: A History of the San Joaquin Valley, 1772–1939.* Los Angeles: Lymanhouse, 1939.

Spaulding, Imogene. "The Attitude of California to the Civil War." *Publications of the Historical Society of Southern California* 9 (1912–14): 104–31.

Starr, Kevin. *Americans and the California Dream, 1850–1915.* New York: Oxford Univ. Press, 1973.

Thomas, Benjamin E. "The California-Nevada Boundary." *Annals of the Association of American Geographers* 42 (March 1952): 51–68.

Vance, James E., Jr. *Geography and Urban Evolution in the San Francisco Bay Area.* Berkeley: Institute of Governmental Studies, Univ. of California, 1964.

Wickson, E. J. *Rural California.* New York: Macmillan, 1923.

Wright, Doris Marion. "The Making of Cosmopolitan California—An Analysis of Immigration, 1848–1870." *California Historical Society Quarterly* 19 (December 1940): 323–43; 20 (March 1941): 65–79.

Zelinsky, Edward Galland, and Nancy Olmsted. "Upriver Boats—When Red Bluff Was the Head of Navigation." *California History* 64 (Spring 1985): 86–117.

3. Southern California

Arreola, Daniel D., and James R. Curtis. *The Mexican Border Cities: Landscape Anatomy and Place Personality.* Tucson: Univ. of Arizona Press, 1993.

Banham, Reyner. *Los Angeles: The Architecture of Four Ecologies.* New York: Harper & Row, 1971.

Baur, John E. *The Health Seekers of Southern California, 1870–1900.* San Marino, Calif.: Huntington Library, 1959.

Beach, Frank L. "The Transformation of California, 1900–1920: The Effects of the Westward Movement on California's Growth and Development in the Progressive Period." Ph.D. dissertation, Department of History, Univ. of California, Berkeley, 1963.

Bemis, George. "Sectionalism and Representation in the California State Legislature, 1911–1931." Ph.D. dissertation, Department of Political Science, Univ. of California, Berkeley, 1935.

Brown, Robert Gregory. "The California Bungalow in Los Angeles: A Study in Origins and Classification." M.A. thesis, Department of Geography, Univ. of California, Los Angeles, 1964.

Carpenter, Bruce. "Rancho Encino: Its Historical Geography." M.A. thesis, Department of Geography, Univ. of California, Los Angeles, 1948.

Chamberlin, Eugene Keith. "Mexican Colonization versus American Interests in Lower California." *Pacific Historical Review* 20 (February 1951): 43–55.

Cooper, Frederic Taber. *Rider's California: A Guide-book for Travelers.* New York: Macmillan, 1925.

Dumke, Glenn S. *The Boom of the Eighties in Southern California.* San Marino, Calif.: Huntington Library, 1944.

Gentilcore, R. Louis. "Ontario, California and the Agricultural Boom of the 1880s." *Agricultural History* 34 (April 1960): 77–87.

Gerhard, Peter. "The Socialist Invasion of Baja California, 1911." *Pacific Historical Review* 15 (September 1940): 295–304.

Hutchinson, W. H. *California: Two Centuries of Man, Land, and Growth in the Golden State.* Palo Alto, Calif.: American West, 1969.

Kirker, Harold. *California's Architectural Frontier: Style and Tradition in the Nineteenth Century.* San Marino, Calif.: Huntington Library, 1960.

Lyman, Edward W. "Outmaneuvering the Octopus: Atchison, Topeka and Santa Fe." *California History* 67 (June 1988): 94–107.

Marshall, James. *Santa Fe: The Railroad That Built an Empire.* New York: Random House, 1945.

Meinig, Donald W. "The Growth of Agricultural Regions in the Far West: 1850–1910." *Journal of Geography* 54 (May 1955): 221–32.

Nadeau, Remi. *City-Makers: The Story of Southern California's First Boom, 1868–76.* Los Angeles: Trans-Anglo Books, 1965.

Nelson, Howard J. *The Los Angeles Metropolis.* Dubuque, Iowa: Kendall/Hunt, 1983.

Nordhoff, Charles. *California: For Health, Pleasure, and Residence.* 1874. New York: Harper & Brothers, 1882.

Pomeroy, Earl. *The Pacific Slope: A History of California, Oregon, Washington, Idaho, Utah, and Nevada.* New York: Alfred A. Knopf, 1965.

Roberts, James Arthur. "Stockton's Manufacturing: The Development, Effects, and Future of Manufacturing in Stockton, California." Ph.D. dissertation, Department of Geography, Univ. of California, Los Angeles, 1963.

Starrs, Paul F. "The Navel of California and Other Oranges: Images of California and the Orange Crate." *California Geographer* 28 (1988): 1–41.

Wheat: An Illustrated Description of California's Leading Industry. San Francisco: Commercial, 1887.

Winther, Oscar Osburn. "The Rise of Metropolitan Los Angeles, 1870–1900." *Huntington Library Quarterly* 10 (August 1940): 391–405.

4. Oregon and the Pacific Northwest

Applegate, Jesse. "Report from Umpqua Valley, Oregon, December 28, 1851." In *Report of the Commissioner of Patents for the Year 1851.* Part 2, Agriculture, 468–74. 32d Cong., 1st sess., 1852. H. Ex. Doc. 102.

Boag, Peter G. *Environment and Experience: Settlement Culture in Nineteenth-Century Oregon.* Berkeley: Univ. of California Press, 1992.

Bowen, William A. *The Willamette Valley: Migration and Settlement on the Oregon Frontier.* Seattle: Univ. of Washington Press, 1978.

Carstensen, Vern. "The Fisherman's Frontier on the Pacific Coast: The Rise of the Salmon-Canning Industry." In *The Frontier Challenge: Responses to the Trans-Mississippi West,* ed. John C. Clark, 57–79. Lawrence: Univ. Press of Kansas, 1971.

Clark, Norman H. *Mill Town: A Social History of Everett, Washington, . . .* Seattle: Univ. of Washington Press, 1970.

Coman, Edwin T., Jr. *Time, Tide and Timber: A Century of Pope & Talbot.* New York: Greenwood Press, 1968.

Cox, Thomas R. *Mills and Markets: A History of the Pacific Coast Lumber Industry to 1900.* Seattle: Univ. of Washington Press, 1974.

Dicken, Samuel N., and Emily F. Dicken. *The Making of Oregon: A Study in Historical Geography.* Portland: Oregon Historical Society, 1979.

Dole, Philip. "Farmhouse and Barn in Early Lane County." *Lane County Historian* 10 (August 1965): 22–44.

Edwards, G. Thomas, and Carlos A. Schwantes, eds. *Experiences in a Promised Land: Essays in Pacific Northwest History.* Seattle: Univ. of Washington Press, 1986.

Fahey, John. *The Inland Empire: Unfolding Years, 1879–1929.* Seattle: Univ. of Washington Press, 1986.

Gates, Charles M. *Messages of the Governors of the Territory of Washington to the Legislative Assembly, 1854–1889.* Seattle: Univ. of Washington Press, 1940.

Johansen, Dorothy O., and Charles M. Gates. *Empire of the Columbia: A History of the Pacific Northwest.* 2d ed. New York: Harper & Row, 1967.

Johnson, David Alan. *Founding the Far West: California, Oregon, and Nevada, 1840–1890.* Berkeley: Univ. of California Press, 1992.

Kensel, W. Hudson. "Inland Empire Mining and the Growth of Spokane, 1883–1905." *Pacific Northwest Quarterly* 60 (April 1969): 84–97.

Kingston, C. S. "The Walla Walla Separation Movement." *Washington Historical Quarterly* 24 (April 1933): 91–109.

Kirk, Ruth, and Carmela Alexander. *Exploring Washington's Past: A Road Guide to History.* Seattle: Univ. of Washington Press, 1990.

MacColl, E. Kimbark. *Merchants, Money and Power: The Portland Establishment, 1843–1913.* [Portland]: Georgian Press, 1988.

MacDonald, Norbert. *Distant Neighbors: A Comparative History of Seattle and Vancouver.* Lincoln: Univ. of Nebraska Press, 1987.

Martin, Albro. *James J. Hill and the Opening of the Northwest.* New York: Oxford Univ. Press, 1976.

Matthews, Henry C. *Kirtland Cutter: Architecture in the Land of Promise.* Seattle: Univ. of Washington Press, 1998.

Meinig, D. W. *The Great Columbia Plain: A Historical Geography, 1805–1910.* Seattle: Univ. of Washington Press, 1968.

Mills, Randall V. *Stern-Wheelers Up Columbia: A Century of Steamboating in the Oregon Country.* Palo Alto, Calif.: Pacific Books, 1947.

Morgan, Murray. *Puget's Sound: A Narrative of Early Tacoma and the Southern Sound.* Seattle: Univ. of Washington Press, 1979.

Nesbit, Robert C. *"He Built Seattle": A Biography of Judge Thomas Burke.* Seattle: Univ. of Washington Press, 1961.

The Oregonian's Handbook of the Pacific Northwest. Portland: Oregonian, 1894.

Pollard, Lancaster. "The Pacific Northwest." In *Regionalism in America,* ed. Merrill Jensen, 187–212. Madison: Univ. of Wisconsin Press, 1952.

"Report of Committee on New State, submitted to the Spokane Chamber of Commerce." Spokane, [c. 1909].

Reps, John W. *Panoramas of Promise: Pacific Northwest Cities and Towns on Nineteenth-Century Lithographs.* Pullman: Washington State Univ. Press, 1984.

Sale, Roger. *Seattle Past to Present.* Seattle: Univ. of Washington Press, 1976.

Schwantes, Carlos A. *The Pacific Northwest: An Interpretive History.* Lincoln: Univ. of Nebraska Press, 1989.

Stratton, David H., ed. *Spokane and the Inland Empire: An Interior Pacific Northwest Anthology.* Pullman: Washington State Univ. Press, 1991.

White, Richard. *Land Use, Environment, and Social Change: The Shaping of Island County, Washington.* Seattle: Univ. of Washington Press, 1980.

Winther, Oscar Osburn. *The Old Oregon Country: A History of Frontier Trade, Transportation, and Travel.* Bloomington: Indiana Univ. Publications, Social Science Series, no. 7, 1950.

5. Zion, Deseret, and Utah

Alexander, Thomas G. *Mormonism in Transition: A History of the Latter-Day Saints, 1890–1930.* Urbana: Univ. of Illinois Press, 1986.

Alexander, Thomas G., and James B. Allen. *Mormons and Gentiles: A History of Salt Lake City.* Boulder, Colo.: Pruett, 1984.

Anderson, Nels. *Desert Saints: The Mormon Frontier in Utah.* Chicago: Univ. of Chicago Press, 1942.

Arrington, Leonard J. *Great Basin Kingdom: An Economic History of the Latter-Day Saints.* Cambridge: Harvard Univ. Press, 1958.

———. *Brigham Young: American Moses.* New York: Alfred A. Knopf, 1985.

Arrington, Leonard, and Davis Bitton. *The Mormon Experience: A History of the Latter-Day Saints.* New York: Alfred A. Knopf, 1979.

Beal, M. D. *A History of Southeastern Idaho.* Caldwell, Idaho: Caxton Printers, 1942.

Bennion, Lowell C. "Mormon Country a Century Ago: A Geographer's View." In *The Mormon People, Their Character and Traditions*, ed. Thomas G. Alexander, 1–26. Provo: Brigham Young Univ. Press, 1980.

Boyce, Ronald R. "An Historical Geography of Greater Salt Lake City." M.A. thesis, Department of Geography, Univ. of Utah, 1957.

Campbell, Eugene E. *Establishing Zion: The Mormon Church in the American West.* Salt Lake City: Signature Books, 1988.

Flanders, Robert Bruce. *Nauvoo: Kingdom on the Mississippi.* Urbana: Univ. of Illinois Press, 1965.

Hansen, Klaus J. *Quest for Empire: The Political Kingdom of God and the Council of Fifty in Mormon History.* [East Lansing]: Michigan State Univ. Press, 1967.

Hill, Marvin S., and James B. Allen, eds. *Mormonism and American Culture.* New York: Harper & Row, 1972.

Hunter, Milton R. *Brigham Young the Colonizer.* Independence, Mo.: Zion's Printing and Publishing, 1945.

Irving, Gordon. "Encouraging the Saints: Brigham Young's Annual Tours of the Mormon Settlements." *Utah Historical Quarterly* 45 (Summer 1977): 233–51.

Ivins, S. S. "The Deseret Alphabet." *Utah Humanities Review* 1 (July 1947): 223–39.

Jackson, Richard H. "The Mormon Village: Genesis and Antecedents of the City of Zion Plan." *Brigham Young Univ. Studies* 17 (Winter 1977): 223–40.

———. "Religion and Landscape in the Mormon Cultural Region." In *Dimensions of Human Geography*, ed. Karl W. Butzer, 100–127. Chicago: Univ. of Chicago, Department of Geography Research Paper 186, 1978.

———. "The Mormon Experience: The Plains as Sinai, the Great Salt Lake as the Dead Sea, and the Great Basin as Desert-cum-Promised Land." *Journal of Historical Geography* 18 (January 1992): 41–58.

———, ed. *The Mormon Role in the Settlement of the West.* Provo: Brigham Young Univ. Press, 1978.

Lamar, Howard Roberts. *The Far Southwest, 1846–1912: A Territorial History.* New York: W. W. Norton, 1970.

Lyman, Edward Leo. *Political Deliverance: The Mormon Quest for Utah Statehood.* Urbana: Univ. of Illinois Press, 1986.

McClintock, J. H. *Mormon Settlement in Arizona.* Phoenix: Manufacturing Stationers, 1921.

Meinig, D. W. "The Mormon Culture Region: Strategies and Patterns in the Geography of the American West, 1847–1964." *Annals of the Association of American Geographers* 55 (June 1965): 191–220.

Mortensen, A. R. "Main Street: Salt Lake City." *Utah Historical Quarterly* 27 (July 1959): 274–83.

Mulder, William. *Homeward to Zion: The Mormon Migration from Scandinavia.* Minneapolis: Univ. of Minnesota Press, 1957.

———. "The Mormons in American History." *Bulletin of the University of Utah* 48 (January 14, 1957).

———. "Mormon Angles of Historical Vision: Some Maverick Reflections." *Journal of Mormon History* 3 (1976): 13–22.

Mulder, William, and A. Russell Mortensen, eds. *Among the Mormons: Historic Accounts by Contemporary Observers.* New York: Alfred A. Knopf, 1958.

Peterson, Charles S. "A Mormon Village: One Man's West." *Journal of Mormon History* 3 (1976): 3–12.

———. *Utah: A Bicentennial History.* New York: W. W. Norton, 1977.

Peterson, Gary B., and Lowell C. Bennion. *Sanpete Scenes: A Guide to Utah's Heart.* Eureka, Utah: Basin Plateau Press, 1987.

Pollock, N. C., and Swanzie Agnew. *An Historical Geography of South Africa.* London: Longmans, Green, 1963.

Roberts, Richard C. "Railroad Depots in Ogden: Microcosm of a Community." *Utah Historical Quarterly* 53 (Winter 1985): 74–99.

Robinson, Phil. *Sinners and Saints: A Tour Across the States, and Round Them; with Three Months among the Mormons.* Boston: Roberts Brothers, 1883.

Russell, Osborne. *Osborne Russell's Journal of a Trapper.* Portland: Oregon Historical Society, 1955.

Sauder, Robert A. "State v. Society: Public Land Law and Mormon Settlement in the Sevier

Valley, Utah." *Agricultural History* 70 (Winter 1996): 57–89.

Shepherd, Gordon, and Gary Shepherd. *A Kingdom Transformed: Themes in the Development of Mormonism.* Salt Lake City: Univ. of Utah Press, 1984.

Shipps, Jan. *Mormonism: The Story of a New Religious Tradition.* Urbana: Univ. of Illinois Press, 1985.

Soffer, Arnon. "The Settlement Process of the Mormons in Utah and the Jews in Israel." *Comparative Social Research* 9 (1986): 197–229.

Stansbury, Howard. *Exploration and Survey of the Valley of the Great Salt Lake of Utah.* 32d Cong., special sess., March 1851. S. Ex. Doc. 3.

Taylor, P. A. M. *Expectations Westward: The Mormons and the Emigration of Their British Converts in the Nineteenth Century.* Edinburgh and London: Oliver & Boyd, 1965.

Wahlquist, Wayne L. *Atlas of Utah.* Provo: Brigham Young Univ. Press, 1981.

White, Jean Bickmore. "Prelude to Statehood: Coming Together in the 1890s." *Utah Historical Quarterly* 62 (Fall 1994): 300–315.

Wright, John B. *Rocky Mountain Divide: Selling and Saving the West.* Austin: Univ. of Texas Press, 1993.

Wright, Paul A. "The Growth and Distribution of the Mormon and Non-Mormon Populations in Salt Lake City." M.A. thesis, Department of Geography, Univ. of Chicago, 1970.

6. *New Mexico: Hispano, Indian, Anglo*

Athearn, Robert G. *William Tecumseh Sherman and the Settlement of the West.* Norman: Univ. of Oklahoma Press, 1956.

Barrows, William. *The United States of Yesterday and of To-morrow.* Boston: Roberts Brothers, 1888.

Beck, Warren. *New Mexico: A History of Four Centuries.* Norman: Univ. of Oklahoma Press, 1962.

Beck, Warren A., and Ynez D. Haase. *Historical Atlas of New Mexico.* Norman: Univ. of Oklahoma Press, 1969.

Briggs, Charles L., and John R. Van Ness. *Land, Water, and Culture: New Perspectives on Hispanic Land Grants.* Albuquerque: Univ. of New Mexico Press, 1978.

Carlson, Alvar W. *The Spanish-American Homeland: Four Centuries in New Mexico's Río Arriba.* Baltimore: Johns Hopkins Univ. Press, 1990.

Chavez, Thomas E. *An Illustrated History of New Mexico.* Niwot: Univ. Press of Colorado, 1992.

Davis, W. W. H. *El Gringo; or, New Mexico and Her People.* New York: Harper & Brothers, 1857.

Goodman, James M. *The Navajo Atlas.* Norman: Univ. of Oklahoma Press, 1982.

Hall, Thomas D. *Social Change in the Southwest, 1350–1880.* Lawrence: Univ. Press of Kansas, 1989.

Jett, Stephen C., ed. "The Destruction of Navajo Orchards in 1864: Captain John Thompson's Report." *Arizona and the West* 16 (Winter 1974): 365–78.

Lang, Herbert H. "The New Mexico Bureau of Immigration, 1880–1912." *New Mexico Historical Review* 51 (July 1976): 193–214.

Larson, Robert W. *New Mexico's Quest for Statehood, 1846–1912.* Albuquerque: Univ. of New Mexico Press, 1968.

Leonard, Glen Milton. "Western Boundary-Making: Texas and the Mexican Cession, 1844–1850." Ph.D. dissertation, Department of History, Univ. of Utah, 1970.

McCall, Colonel George Archibald. *New Mexico in 1850: A Military View.* Ed. and intro. Robert W. Frazer. Norman: Univ. of Oklahoma Press, 1968.

Meinig, D. W. *Southwest: Three Peoples in Geographical Change, 1600–1970.* New York: Oxford Univ. Press, 1971.

Miller, Darlis A. "Cross-Cultural Marriages in the Southwest: The New Mexico Experience, 1846–1900." *New Mexico Historical Review* 57 (October 1982): 335–59.

Noggle, Burl. "Anglo Observers of the Southwest Borderland, 1825–1890: The Rise of a Concept." *Arizona and the West* 1 (1959): 105–31.

Nostrand, Richard L. "Mexican Americans circa 1850." *Annals of the Association of American*

Geographers 65 (September 1975): 378–90.

———. *The Hispano Homeland.* Norman: Univ. of Oklahoma Press, 1992.

Parish, William J. "The German Jew and the Commercial Revolution in Territorial New Mexico, 1850–1900." *New Mexico Quarterly* 29 (Autumn 1959): 307–32.

Rosenbaum, Robert J. *Mexicano Resistance in the Southwest: "The Sacred Right of Self-Preservation."* Austin: Univ. of Texas Press, 1981.

Simmons, Marc. *Albuquerque: A Narrative History.* Albuquerque: Univ. of New Mexico Press, 1982.

Spicer, Edward H. *Cycles of Conquest: The Impact of Spain, Mexico, and the United States on the Indians of the Southwest, 1533–1960.* Tucson: Univ. of Arizona Press, 1962.

Sumner, Lieut. Col. E. V. "Reports from the Ninth Military Department, New Mexico." Santa Fe, May 27, 1852. H. Ex. Doc. 1, Part 2, 23–26.

Sunseri, Alvin R. *Seeds of Discord: New Mexico in the Aftermath of the American Conquest, 1846–1861.* Chicago: Nelson-Hall, 1979.

Tobias, Henry J., and Charles E. Woodhouse. "New York Investment Bankers and New Mexico Merchants: Group Formation and Elite Status among German Jewish Businessmen." *New Mexico Historical Review* 65 (January 1990): 21–47.

Williams, Jerry L., and Paul E. McAllister, eds. *New Mexico in Maps.* [Albuquerque]: Technology Application Center, Univ. of New Mexico, 1979.

7. The Colorado Complex

Abbott, Carl. *Colorado: A History of the Centennial State.* Boulder: Colorado Associated Univ. Press, 1976.

Athearn, Robert G. *Rebel of the Rockies: The Denver and Rio Grande Western Railroad.* New Haven: Yale Univ. Press, 1962.

———. *The Coloradans.* Albuquerque: Univ. of New Mexico Press, 1976.

Baedeker, Karl. *The United States, with Excursions to Mexico, Cuba, Porto Rico, and Alaska: Handbook for Travellers.* Leipzig: Karl Baedeker, 1909.

Barth, Gunther. *Instant Cities: Urbanization and the Rise of San Francisco and Denver.* New York: Oxford Univ. Press, 1975.

Buckman, Geo. Rex. *Colorado Springs, Colorado and Its Famous Scenic Environs.* 2d ed. Colorado Springs: Geo. Rex Buchman, 1893.

Colorado and the American Renaissance, 1876–1917. Denver: Denver Art Museum, 1980.

Dorsett, Phyllis Flanders. *The New Eldorado: The Story of Colorado's Gold and Silver Rushes.* New York: Macmillan, 1970.

Fossett, Frank. *Colorado: Its Gold and Silver Mines, Farms and Stock Ranges, and Health and Pleasure Resorts.* New York: C. G. Crawford, 1880.

Hafen, Leroy, ed. *Colorado and Its People: A Narrative and Topical History of the Centennial State.* 4 vols. New York: Lewis, 1948.

Helphand, Kenneth I., and Ellen Manchester, photo ed. *Colorado: Visions of an American Landscape.* Niwot: Roberts Rinehart, 1991.

Ingersoll, Ernest. *Crest of the Continent.* Chicago: R. R. Donnelley & Sons, 1889.

Karnes, Thomas L. *William Gilpin: Western Nationalist.* Austin: Univ. of Texas Press, 1970.

Kedro, M. James. "Czechs and Slovaks in Colorado, 1860–1920." *Colorado Magazine* 54 (Spring 1977): 92–125.

Kelsey, Harry E., Jr. *Frontier Capitalist: The Life of John Evans.* [Denver]: State Historical Society of Colorado and Pruett, 1969.

Leonard, Stephen J. "The Irish, English, and Germans in Denver, 1860–90." *Colorado Magazine* 54 (Spring 1977): 126–54.

Leonard, Stephen J., and Thomas J. Noel. *Denver: Mining Camp to Metropolis.* Niwot: Univ. Press of Colorado, 1990.

Mehls, Steven F. "An Area the Size of Pennsylvania: David H. Moffat and the Opening of Northwest Colorado." *Midwest Review* 7 (Spring 1985): 15–30.

Ormes, Robert M. *Railroads and the Rockies: A Record of Lines in and near Colorado.* Denver: Sage Books, 1963.

Pomeroy, Earl. *In Search of the Golden West: The Tourist in Western America.* New York: Alfred A. Knopf, 1957.

Rock, Kenneth W. "*Unsere Leute:* The Germans

from Russia in Colorado." *Colorado Magazine* 54 (Spring 1977): 154–83.

Smythe, William E. *The Conquest of Arid America.* New York: Harper & Brothers, 1900.

Thode, Jackson C. *George L. Beam and the Denver and Rio Grande.* 2 vols. Denver: Sundance Publications, 1989.

Ubbelohde, Carl, ed. *A Colorado Reader.* Boulder, Colo.: Pruett, 1962.

Wilson, Owen Meredith. "A History of the Denver and Rio Grande Project, 1870–1901." Ph.D. dissertation, Department of History, Univ. of California, Berkeley, 1942.

Worster, Donald. *Rivers of Empire: Water, Aridity, and the Growth of the American West.* New York: Pantheon Books, 1985.

Wyckoff, William. "Incorporation as a Factor in Formation of an Urban System." *Geographical Review* 77 (July 1987): 281–92.

———. "Revising the Meyer Model: Denver and the National Urban System, 1859–1879." *Urban Geography* 9 (January–March 1988): 1–18.

———. "Central Place Theory and the Location of Services in Colorado in 1899." *Social Science Journal* 26, no. 4 (1989): 383–98.

8. The Rest of the West

Alwin, John A. *Montana Portrait.* Helena: American & World Geographic, 1993.

Andrist, Ralph K. *The Long Death: The Last Days of the Plains Indian.* New York: Macmillan, 1964.

Borchert, John R. *America's Northern Heartland: An Economic and Historical Geography of the Upper Midwest.* Minneapolis: Univ. of Minnesota Press, 1987.

Bowden, Martyn J. "Desert Wheat Belt, Plains Corn Belt: Environmental Cognition and Behavior of Settlers in the Plains Margin, 1850–99." In *Images of the Plains: The Role of Human Nature in Settlement,* ed. Brian W. Blouet and Merlin P. Lawson, 189–201. Lincoln: Univ. of Nebraska Press, 1975.

Bowman, Isaiah. *The Pioneer Fringe.* New York: American Geographical Society, 1931.

Briggs, Harold E. *Frontiers of the Northwest: A History of the Upper Missouri Valley.* New York: D. Appleton-Century, 1940.

Brown, Robert Harold. *Wyoming: A Geography.* Boulder, Colo.: Westview Press, 1980.

Cleland, Robert Glass. *A History of Phelps Dodge, 1834–1950.* New York: Alfred A. Knopf, 1952.

Davis, Leslie B., and Michael Wilson, eds. "Bison Procurement and Utilization: A Symposium." *Plains Anthropologist* 23 (November 1978): v–361.

Fielder, Mildred. *Railroads of the Black Hills.* New York: Bonanza Books, 1964.

Flores, Dan. "Bison Ecology and Bison Diplomacy: The Southern Plains from 1800 to 1850." *Journal of American History* 78 (September 1991): 465–85.

Garcia, Mario T. *Desert Immigrants: The Mexicans of El Paso, 1880–1920.* New Haven: Yale Univ. Press, 1981.

Greever, William S. *The Bonanza West: The Story of Western Mining Rushes, 1848–1900.* Norman: Univ. of Oklahoma Press, 1963.

Hamilton, Leonidas. *Border States of Mexico: Sonora, Sinaloa, Chihuahua and Durango.* San Francisco: Bacon, 1881.

Hudson, John C. *Plains Country Towns.* Minneapolis: Univ. of Minnesota Press, 1985.

Jordan, Terry G. *North American Cattle-Ranching Frontiers: Origins, Diffusion, and Differentiation.* Albuquerque: Univ. of New Mexico Press, 1993.

Kollmorgen, Walter M. "The Woodsman's Assault on the Domain of the Cattleman." *Annals of the Association of American Geographers* 59 (June 1969): 215–39.

Lamar, Howard Roberts. *Dakota Territory, 1861–1889: A Study of Frontier Politics.* New Haven: Yale Univ. Press, 1956.

Larson, T. A. *History of Wyoming.* Lincoln: Univ. of Nebraska Press, 1965.

Lewis, G. M. "Regional Ideas and Reality in the Cis-Rocky Mountain West." *Transactions and Papers, Institute of British Geographers,* Publication No. 38 (1966): 135–50.

Lillard, Richard G. *Desert Challenge: An Interpretation of Nevada.* New York: Alfred A. Knopf, 1949.

Malin, James C. *The Grassland of North America:*

Prolegomena to Its History. Lawrence: James C. Malin, 1947.

———. "The Agricultural Regionalism of the Trans-Mississippi West as Delineated by Cyrus Thomas." *Agricultural History* 21 (October 1947): 208–17.

———. *History and Ecology: Studies of the Grassland.* Ed. Robert P. Swierenga. Lincoln: Univ. of Nebraska Press, 1984.

Malone, Michael P., and Richard B. Roeder. *Montana: A History of Two Centuries.* Seattle: Univ. of Washington Press, 1976.

Martinez, Oscar J. *Border Boom Town: Ciudad Juárez since 1848.* Austin: Univ. of Texas Press, 1978.

Meinig, D. W. *Imperial Texas: An Interpretive Essay in Cultural Geography.* Austin: Univ. of Texas Press, 1969.

Mood, Fulmer. "The Origin, Evolution, and Application of the Sectional Concept, 1750–1900." In *Regionalism in America,* ed. Merrill Jensen, 5–98. Madison: Univ. of Wisconsin Press, 1952.

Nelson, Paula M. *After the West Was Won: Homesteaders and Town-Builders in Western South Dakota, 1900–1917.* Iowa City: Univ. of Iowa Press, 1986.

Officer, James. "Historical Factors in Interethnic Relations in the Community of Tucson." *Arizoniana* 1 (Fall 1960): 12–16.

Osgood, Ernest Staples. *The Day of the Cattleman.* Chicago: Univ. of Chicago Press, 1929.

Paul, Rodman Wilson. *Mining Frontiers of the Far West, 1848–1880.* New York: Holt, Rinehart and Winston, 1963.

———. *The Far West and the Great Plains in Transition, 1859–1900.* New York: Harper & Row, 1988.

Pletcher, David M. *Rails, Mines, and Progress: Seven American Promoters in Mexico, 1867–1911.* Port Washington, N.J.: Kennikat Press, 1972.

Prucha, Francis Paul, ed. *Documents of United States Indian Policy.* Lincoln: Univ. of Nebraska Press, 1975.

Roark, Michael Owen. "Oklahoma Territory: Frontier Development, Migration, and Culture Areas." Ph.D. dissertation, Department of Geography, Syracuse University, 1979.

Ruíz, Ramón Eduardo. *The People of Sonora and Yankee Capitalists.* Tucson: Univ. of Arizona Press, 1988.

Salas, Miguel Tinker. "Sonora: The Making of a Border Society, 1880–1910." *Journal of the Southwest* 34 (Winter 1992): 429–56.

Schell, Herbert S. *History of South Dakota.* Lincoln: Univ. of Nebraska Press, 1968.

Schwantes, Carlos A., ed. *Bisbee: Urban Outpost on the Frontier.* Tucson: Univ. of Arizona Press, 1992.

Shortridge, James R. "The Post Office Frontier in Kansas." *Journal of the West* 13 (July 1974): 83–97.

———. *The Middle West: Its Meaning in American Culture.* Lawrence: Univ. Press of Kansas, 1989.

Smits, David D. "The Frontier Army and the Destruction of the Buffalo: 1865–1883." *Western Historical Quarterly* 25 (Autumn 1994): 313–38.

Voss, Stuart F. *On the Periphery of Nineteenth-Century Mexico: Sonora and Sinaloa, 1810–1877.* Tucson: Univ. of Arizona Press, 1982.

Wasserman, Mark. *Capitalists, Caciques, and Revolution: The Native Elite and Foreign Enterprise in Chihuahua, Mexico, 1854–1911.* Chapel Hill: Univ. of North Carolina Press, 1984.

Wells, Merle W. "Territorial Government in the Inland Empire: The Movement to Create Columbia Territory, 1864–69." *Pacific Northwest Quarterly* 44 (April 1953): 80–87.

———. "Politics in the Panhandle: Opposition to the Admission of Washington and North Idaho, 1886–1888." *Pacific Northwest Quarterly* 46 (July 1955): 79–89.

Wessel, Thomas R., ed. *Agriculture in the Great Plains, 1876–1936.* Washington, D.C.: Agricultural History Society, 1977.

West, Robert C. *Sonora: Its Geographical Personality.* Austin: Univ. of Texas Press, 1993.

Wishart, David J. "The Changing Position of the Frontier of Settlement on the Eastern Margins of the Central and Northern Great Plains, 1854–1890." *Professional Geographer* 21 (May 1969): 153–57.

9. Indians and Empire

Albers, Patricia, and Jeanne Kay. "Sharing the Land: A Study in American Indian Territoriality." In *A Cultural Geography of North American Indians*, ed. Thomas E. Ross and Tyrel G. Moore. Boulder, Colo.: Westview Press, 1987.

Berkhofer, Robert F., Jr. *The White Man's Indian: Images of the American Indian from Columbus to the Present*. New York: Vintage Books, 1979.

Dippie, Brian W. *The Vanishing American: White Attitudes and U.S. Indian Policy*. Middletown, Conn.: Wesleyan Univ. Press, 1982.

Hewes, Leslie. *Occupying the Cherokee Country of Oklahoma*. Lincoln: Univ. of Nebraska Studies, n.s., no. 57, 1978.

Hoxie, Frederick E. *A Final Promise: The Campaign to Assimilate the Indians, 1880–1920*. Lincoln: Univ. of Nebraska Press, 1984.

Jenness, Theodora R. "The Indian Territory." *Atlantic Monthly* 43 (April 1879): 444–52.

King, Henry. "The Indian Country." *Century Magazine* 30 (August 1885): 599–606.

Kvasnicka, Robert M., and Herman J. Viola, eds. *The Commissioners of Indian Affairs, 1824–1977*. Lincoln: Univ. of Nebraska Press, 1979.

McReynolds, Edwin C. *Oklahoma: A History of the Sooner State*. Norman: Univ. of Oklahoma Press, 1954.

Maxwell, Amos. "The Sequoyah Convention." *Chronicles of Oklahoma* 28 (Summer 1950): 161–92; (Autumn 1950): 299–340.

Morris, John W., and Edwin C. McReynolds. *Historical Atlas of Oklahoma*. Norman: Univ. of Oklahoma Press, 1965.

Report of the Commissioner of Indian Affairs. [Cato Sells.] Vol. 2, *Reports of the Department of the Interior . . . June 30, 1913*. Washington, D.C.: Government Printing Office, 1914.

Royce, Charles C. *Indian Land Cessions in the United States*. Washington, D.C.: Government Printing Office, 1900. Arno Press Reprint Edition, 1971.

Stuart, Paul. *The Indian Office: Growth and Development of an American Institution, 1865–1900*. Ann Arbor: UMI Research Press, 1978.

White, Richard. *The Roots of Dependency: Subsistence, Environment, and Social Change among the Choctaws, Pawnees, and Navajos*. Lincoln: Univ. of Nebraska Press, 1983.

Wooster, Robert. *The Military and United States Indian Policy, 1865–1903*. New Haven: Yale Univ. Press, 1988.

10. American Wests-American Domain

Bartlett, Richard A. *Great Surveys of the American West*. Norman: Univ. of Oklahoma Press, 1962.

Berkhofer, Robert F., Jr. "The North American Frontier as Process and Context." In *The Frontier in History: North America and Southern Africa Compared*, ed. Howard Lamar and Leonard Thompson, 43–75. New Haven: Yale Univ. Press, 1981.

Meinig, D. W. "American Wests: Preface to a Geographical Interpretation." *Annals of the Association of American Geographers* 62 (June 1972): 159–84.

Stegner, Wallace. *Beyond the Hundredth Meridian: John Wesley Powell and the Second Opening of the West*. Boston: Houghton Mifflin, 1962.

White, Richard. *"It's Your Misfortune and None of My Own": A History of the American West*. Norman: Univ. of Oklahoma Press, 1991.

PART THREE

1. A Re-United States

Aiken, Charles S. "The Evolution of Cotton Ginning in the Southeastern United States." *Geographical Review* 63 (April 1973): 196–224.

———. "New Settlement Patterns of Rural Blacks in the American South." *Geographical Review* 75 (October 1985): 383–404.

Alexander, Thomas B. "The Dimensions of

Continuity across the Civil War." In *The Old South in the Crucible of War*, ed. Harry P. Owens and James J. Cooke. Jackson: Univ. Press of Mississippi, 1983.

Anderson, Hugh George. *Lutheranism in the Southeastern States, 1860–1886: A Social History*. The Hague: Mouton, 1969.

Andrews, Sidney. *The South since the War as Shown by Fourteen Weeks of Travel and Observation in Georgia and the Carolinas*. [1866] Boston: Houghton Mifflin, 1971.

Asante, Molefi K., and Mark T. Mattson. *Historical and Cultural Atlas of African Americans*. New York: Macmillan, 1992.

Ayers, Edward L. *The Promise of the New South: Life after Reconstruction*. New York: Oxford Univ. Press, 1992.

Bailey, Kenneth K. "The Post-Civil War Racial Separatism in Southern Protestantism: Another Look." *Church History* 46 (December 1977): 453–73.

[Barrow, David]. "A Georgia Plantation." *Scribner's Monthly* 21 (April 1881): 830–36.

Benzel, Richard Franklin. *Yankee Leviathan: The Origins of Central State Authority in America, 1859–1877*. Cambridge: Cambridge Univ. Press, 1990.

Berthoff, Rowland T. "Southern Attitudes toward Immigration, 1865–1914." *Journal of Southern History* 17 (August 1951): 328–60.

Billington, Monroe L., ed. *The South: A Central Theme?* New York: Holt, Rinehart and Winston, 1969.

Bond, Bradley G. *Political Culture in the Nineteenth-Century South: Mississippi, 1830–1900*. Baton Rouge: Louisiana State Univ. Press, 1995.

Bonner, James C. "Legislative Apportionment and County Unit Voting in Georgia since 1777." *Georgia Historical Quarterly* 47 (December 1963): 351–74.

Brandfon, Robert L. *Cotton Kingdom of the New South: A History of the Yazoo Delta from Reconstruction to the Twentieth Century*. Cambridge: Harvard Univ. Press, 1967.

Bruce, Christopher. "The Black Population, 1860." *Historical Geography* 21 (1992): 10–11.

Buck, Paul H. *The Road to Reunion, 1865–1900*. Boston: Little, Brown, 1937.

Burton, Orville Vernon. "The Rise and Fall of Afro-American Town Life: Town and Country in Reconstructed Edgefield, South Carolina." In *Toward a New South? Studies in Post-Civil War Southern Communities*, ed. Orville Vernon Burton and Robert C. McMath, Jr., 152–92. Westport, Conn.: Greenwood Press, 1982.

Campbell, John G. *The Southern Highlander and His Homeland*. New York: Russell Sage Foundation, 1921.

Campbell, Sir George. *White and Black: The Outcome of a Visit to the United States*. New York: R. Worthington, 1879.

Carlton, David L. *Mill and Town in South Carolina, 1880–1920*. Baton Rouge: Louisiana State Univ. Press, 1982.

———. "The Revolution from Above: The National Market and the Beginnings of Industrialization in North Carolina." *Journal of American History* 77 (September 1990): 445–75.

———. "How American Is the American South?" In *The South as an American Problem*, ed. Larry J. Griffin and Don H. Doyle, 33–56. Athens: Univ. of Georgia Press, 1995.

Cash, W. J. *The Mind of the South*. New York: Alfred A. Knopf, 1941.

Coulter, E. Merton. *The South during Reconstruction, 1865–1877*. Baton Rouge: Louisiana State Univ. Press, 1947.

Current, Richard N. *Northernizing the South*. Athens: Univ. of Georgia Press, 1983.

Currie, James T. *Enclave: Vicksburg and Her Plantations, 1863–1870*. Jackson: Univ. Press of Mississippi, 1980.

Curry, Leonard P. *Rail Routes South: Louisville's Fight for the Southern Market, 1865–1872*. Lexington: Univ. of Kentucky Press, 1969.

Davis, George A., and O. Fred Donaldson. *Blacks in the United States: A Geographic Perspective*. Boston: Houghton Mifflin, 1975.

Degler, Carl N. *Place over Time: The Continuity of Southern Distinctiveness*. Baton Rouge: Louisiana State Univ. Press, 1977.

DuBois, W. E. Burghardt. *The Souls of Black Folk: Essays and Sketches*. Chicago: A. C. McClurg, 1903.

Estaville, Lawrence E., Jr. "The Louisiana French in 1900." *Journal of Historical Geography* 14 (October 1988): 342–59.

Fields, Barbara J. "Ideology and Race in American History." In *Region, Race, and Reconstruc-*

tion: *Essays in Honor of C. Vann Woodward*, ed. J. Morgan Kousser and James M. McPherson, 143–77. New York: Oxford Univ. Press, 1982.

Foner, Eric. *Reconstruction: America's Unfinished Revolution, 1863–1877*. New York: Harper & Row, 1988.

———. "Writing about Reconstruction: A Personal Reflection." In *Looking South: Chapters in the Story of an American Region*, ed. Winifred B. Moore and Joseph F. Tripp, 3–13. New York: Greenwood Press, 1989.

Franklin, John Hope. *Reconstruction after the Civil War*. Chicago: Univ. of Chicago Press, 1961.

Gatewood, Willard B. *Aristocrats of Color: The Black Elite, 1880–1920*. Bloomington: Univ. of Indiana Press, 1990.

Gillette, William. *Retreat from Reconstruction, 1869–1879*. Baton Rouge: Louisiana State Univ. Press, 1979.

Goldfield, David R. "The Urban South: A Regional Framework." *American Historical Review* 86 (December 1981): 1009–34.

Graves, Lawrence L., ed. *A History of Lubbock*. Lubbock: West Texas Museum Association, 1962.

Groves, Paul A., and Edward K. Muller. "The Evolution of Black Residential Areas in Late Nineteenth-Century Cities." *Journal of Historical Geography* 1 (April 1975): 169–91.

Hamilton, Kenneth Marvin. *Black Towns and Profit: Promotion and Development in the Trans-Appalachian West, 1877–1915*. Urbana: Univ. of Illinois Press, 1991.

Harris, J. William. "Plantations and Power: Emancipation on the David Barrow Plantations." In *Toward a New South? Studies in Post-Civil War Southern Communities*, ed. Orville Vernon Burton and Robert C. McMath, Jr., 246–64. Westport, Conn.: Greenwood Press, 1982.

Hart, Albert Bushnell. *The Southern South*. New York: D. Appleton, 1912.

Hilgard, Eugene W. *Report on Cotton Production in the United States*. 2 vols. Washington, D.C.: Government Printing Office, 1884.

Jordan, Terry. "The German Settlement of Texas after 1865." *Southwestern Historical Quarterly* 73 (October 1969): 193–212.

———. "The Texas Appalachia." *Annals of the*

Association of American Geographers 60 (September 1970): 409–27.

Kellogg, John. "Negro Urban Clusters in the Postbellum South." *Geographical Review* 67 (October 1977): 310–21.

King, Edward. *The Great South: A Record of Journeys . . .* Hartford, Conn.: American, 1875.

Kollmorgen, Walter M. "A Reconnaissance of Some Cultural-Agricultural Islands in the South." *Economic Geography* 17 (October 1941): 409–30.

Kopf, Jennifer. "Neighborhood Hygiene and 'Renewal' in the U.S. South: The Purification of Pralltown during the Civil War Reconstruction and 1960s Urban Renewal Eras." *Historical Geography* 25 (1997): 148–64.

Kremer, Gary, and Lynn Morrow. "Pennytown: A Freedmen's Hamlet, 1871–1945." *Missouri Folklore Society Journal* 11–12 (1989–90): 77–92.

Lee, Willie Rose. *Rehearsal for Reconstruction: The Port Royal Experiment*. New York: Oxford Univ. Press, 1964.

Lieberman, Robert C. "The Freedmen's Bureau and the Politics of Institutional Structure." *Social Science History* 18 (Fall 1994): 405–37.

Litwack, Leon F. *Been in the Storm So Long: The Aftermath of Slavery*. New York: Alfred A. Knopf, 1979.

McCorkle, James L., Jr. "Moving Perishables to Market: Southern Railroads and the Nineteenth-Century Origins of Southern Truck Farming." *Agricultural History* 66 (Winter 1992): 42–62.

McFeely, William S. *Yankee Stepfather: General O. O. Howard and the Freedmen*. New Haven: Yale Univ. Press, 1968.

McMillen, Neil R. *Dark Journey: Black Mississippians in the Age of Jim Crow*. Urbana: Univ. of Illinois Press, 1989.

McPherson, James M. *The Struggle for Equality: Abolitionists and the Negro in the Civil War and Reconstruction*. Princeton: Princeton Univ. Press, 1964.

Meier, August. *Negro Thought in America, 1880–1915: Racial Ideologies in the Age of Booker T. Washington*. Ann Arbor: Univ. of Michigan Press, 1963.

Meyer, David R. "Industry in Southern Cities in the Nineteenth Century." *Geoscience and Man* 25 (1988): 129–37.

Morland, John Kenneth. *Millways of Kent*. Chapel Hill: Univ. of North Carolina Press, 1958.

Morrill, Richard L., and O. Fred Donaldson. "Geographical Perspectives on the History of Black America." *Economic Geography* 48 (January 1972): 1–23.

Morrow, Ralph E. *Northern Methodism and Reconstruction*. East Lansing: Michigan State Univ. Press, 1956.

Murphy, Edgar Gardner. *Problems of the Present South: A Discussion of Certain of the Educational, Industrial and Political Issues in the Southern States*. New York: Longmans, Green, 1910.

Newby, I. A. *Plain Folk in the New South: Social Change and Cultural Persistence*. Baton Rouge: Louisiana State Univ. Press, 1989.

Newton, Milton B., Jr. "The Darlings Creek Peasant Settlements of St. Helena Parish, Louisiana." *Southern Anthropological Society Proceedings* 4 (1971): 38–48.

———. *Atlas of Louisiana: A Guide for Students*. Baton Rouge: School of Geoscience, Louisiana State Univ., 1972.

———. "Settlement Patterns as Artifacts of Social Structure." In *The Human Mirror: Material and Spatial Images of Man*, ed. Miles Richardson, 339–61. Baton Rouge: Louisiana State Univ. Press, 1974.

———. "Louisiana Geography: A Syllabus." 3d ed. Baton Rouge: School of Geoscience, Louisiana State Univ., 1976.

Nordhoff, Charles. *The Cotton States in the Spring and Summer of 1875*. New York: D. Appleton & Company, 1876.

Official Guide of the Railway and Steam Navigation Lines in the United States, Canada and Mexico. New York: National Railway, September 1897.

Oubre, Claude F. *Forty Acres and a Mule: The Freedmen's Bureau and Black Land Ownership*. Baton Rouge: Louisiana State Univ. Press, 1978.

Painter, Nell Irvin. *Exodusters: Black Migration to Kansas after Reconstruction*. New York: Alfred A. Knopf, 1977.

Panzer, Mary. *In My Studio: Rudolf Eickemeyer, Jr. and the Art of the Camera, 1885–1930*. Yonkers, N.Y.: Hudson River Museum, 1986.

Parkins, A. E. *The South: Its Economic-Geographic Development*. New York: John Wiley, 1938.

Powell, Lawrence N. *New Masters: Northern Planters during the Civil War and Reconstruction*. New Haven: Yale Univ. Press, 1980.

Power, Richard Lyle. *Planting Corn Belt Culture: The Impress of the Upland Southerner and Yankee in the Old Northwest*. Indianapolis: Indiana Historical Society, 1953.

Pruett, Katherine M., and John D. Fair. "Promoting a New South: Immigration, Racism, and 'Alabama on Wheels.'" *Agricultural History* 66 (Winter 1992): 19–41.

Prunty, Merle, Jr. "The Renaissance of the Southern Plantation." *Geographical Review* 45 (October 1955): 459–91.

Rabinowitz, Howard N. *Race Relations in the Urban South, 1865–1890*. New York: Oxford Univ. Press, 1978.

———. *Race, Ethnicity, and Urbanization: Selected Essays*. Columbia: Univ. of Missouri Press, 1994.

Radford, John P. "Race, Residence, and Ideology: Charleston, South Carolina in the Mid-Nineteenth Century." *Journal of Historical Geography* 2 (October 1976): 329–46.

Ransom, Roger L., and Richard Sutch. *One Kind of Freedom: The Economic Consequences of Emancipation*. Cambridge: Cambridge Univ. Press, 1977.

Reed, John Shelton. *The Enduring South: Subcultural Persistence in Mass Society*. Lexington, Mass.: D. C. Heath, 1972.

Reid, Whitelaw. *After the War: A Southern Tour. May 1, 1865, to May 1, 1866*. Cincinnati: Moore, Wilstach & Baldwin, 1866.

Reidy, Joseph P. *From Slavery to Agrarian Capitalism in the Cotton Plantation South: Central Georgia, 1800–1880*. Chapel Hill: Univ. of North Carolina Press, 1992.

Richardson, Joe M. *Christian Reconstruction: The American Missionary Association and Southern Blacks, 1861–1890*. Athens: Univ. of Georgia Press, 1986.

Roark, James L. "From Lords to Landlords." *Wilson Quarterly* 2 (Spring 1978): 124–34.

Russell, James Michael. *Atlanta, 1847–1890: City Building in the Old South and the New*. Baton Rouge: Louisiana State Univ. Press, 1988.

Schweninger, Loren. "Prosperous Blacks in the South, 1790–1880." *American Historical Review* 95 (February 1990): 31–55.

Sefton, James E. *The United States Army and Reconstruction, 1865–1877.* Baton Rouge: Louisiana State Univ. Press, 1967.

Smith, Peter C., and Karl B. Raitz. "Negro Hamlets and Agricultural Estates in Kentucky's Inner Bluegrass." *Geographical Review* 64 (April 1974): 217–34.

Somers, Robert. *The Southern States since the War, 1870–1.* London: Macmillan, 1871.

Stampp, Kenneth M. *The Era of Reconstruction, 1865–1877.* New York: Alfred A. Knopf, 1969.

Stover, John F. *The Railroads of the South, 1865–1900: A Study in Finance and Control.* Chapel Hill: Univ. of North Carolina Press, 1955.

Tullos, Allen. *Habits of Industry: White Culture and the Transformation of the Carolina Piedmont.* Chapel Hill: Univ. of North Carolina Press, 1989.

U.S. Bureau of the Census. *Negroes in the United States.* Bulletin 8. Washington, D.C.: Government Printing Office, 1904.

Vance, Rupert B. *Human Geography of the South: A Study of Regional Resources and Human Adequacy.* 1932. New York: Russell and Russell, 1968.

Waddell, Eric. "French Louisiana: An Outpost of L'Amérique Française, or Another Country and Another Culture?" *Projet Louisiane Working Paper,* no. 4, Département de Géographie, Université Laval, Quebec, 1979.

Warren, Kenneth. *The American Steel Industry, 1850–1970: A Geographical Interpretation.* Oxford: Oxford Univ. Press, 1973.

Wayne, Michael. *The Reshaping of Plantation Society: The Natchez District, 1860–1880.* Baton Rouge: Louisiana State Univ. Press, 1983.

Weiher, Kenneth. "The Cotton Industry and Southern Urbanization, 1880–1930." *Explorations in Economic History* 14 (April 1977): 120–40.

Wharton, Vernon L. "Reconstruction." In *Writing Southern History,* ed. Arthur S. Link and Rembert W. Patrick. Baton Rouge: Louisiana State Univ. Press, 1965.

Wiener, Jonathan M. "Planter Persistence and Social Change: Alabama, 1850–1870." *Journal of Interdisciplinary History* 7 (Autumn 1976): 235–60.

Williams, Michael. *Americans and Their Forests: A Historical Geography.* New York: Cambridge Univ. Press, 1989.

Williamson, Joel. *The Crucible of Race: Black-White Relations in the American South since Emancipation.* New York: Oxford Univ. Press, 1984.

Wilson, Charles Reagan. *Baptized in Blood: The Religion of the Lost Cause, 1865–1920.* Athens: Univ. of Georgia Press, 1980.

Woodward, C. Vann. *Origins of the New South.* Baton Rouge: Louisiana State Univ. Press, 1951.

———. "Gone with the Wind." *New York Review of Books,* July 17, 1986, 3–6.

2. New Economic Regions

Bennett, Sari, and Carville Earle. *The Geography of American Labor and Industrialization, 1865–1908: An Atlas.* Catonsville, Md.: Department of Geography, Univ. of Maryland Baltimore County, 1980.

Bolles, Albert S. *Industrial History of the United States, from the Earliest Settlements to the Present Time: Being a Complete Survey of American Industries.* Norwich, Conn.: Henry Bill, 1879.

Broehl, Wayne G., Jr. *Cargill: Trading the World's Grain.* Hanover: Univ. Press of New England, 1992.

Chandler, Alfred D., Jr. *The Visible Hand: The Managerial Revolution in American Business.* Cambridge: Harvard Univ. Press, 1977.

———. *Scale and Scope: The Dynamics of Industrial Capitalism.* Cambridge: Harvard Univ. Press, 1990.

Clark, Victor S. *History of Manufactures in the United States.* Vol. 2, 1860–1893; Vol. 3, 1893–1928. New York: McGraw-Hill, 1929.

Clemen, Rudolf Alexander. *The American Livestock and Meat Industry.* New York: Ronald Press, 1923.

Conzen, Michael P., Glenn M. Richard, and Carl A. Zimring, eds. *The Industrial Revolution in the Upper Illinois Valley.* Chicago: Committee on Geographical Studies, Univ. of Chicago, 1993.

Cronon, William. *Nature's Metropolis: Chicago and the Great West.* New York: W. W. Norton, 1991.

Danhof, Clarence H. *Change in Agriculture: The Northern United States, 1820–1870.* Cambridge: Harvard Univ. Press, 1969.

Edwards, Everett E. "American Agriculture—The First 300 Years." *Farmers in a Changing World: The Yearbook of Agriculture,* 171–276. U.S. Department of Agriculture. Washington, D.C.: Government Printing Office, 1940.

Faulkner, Harold Underwood. *American Economic History.* New York: Harper & Brothers, 1943.

Fite, Emerson David. *Social and Industrial Conditions in the North during the Civil War.* New York: Macmillan, 1910.

Glazier, Captain Willard. *Down the Great River.* Philadelphia: Hubbard Brothers, 1889.

Glover, John George, and William Bouck Cornell, eds. *The Development of American Industries: Their Economic Significance.* New York: Prentice-Hall, 1932.

Hatcher, Harlan, and Erich A. Walter. *A Pictorial History of the Great Lakes.* New York: Crown, 1963.

Hogan, William T. *Economic History of the Iron and Steel Industry in the United States.* Vol. 1. Lexington, Mass.: D. C. Heath, 1971.

Hudson, John C. *Making the Corn Belt: A Geographical History of Middle-Western Agriculture.* Bloomington: Indiana Univ. Press, 1994.

Keir, Malcolm. *The Epic of Industry.* New Haven: Yale Univ. Press, 1926.

Kirkland, Edward C. *Industry Comes of Age: Business, Labor, and Public Policy, 1860–1897.* New York: Holt, Rinehart and Winston, 1961.

Lamoreaux, Naomi R. *The Great Merger Movement in American Business, 1895–1904.* Cambridge: Cambridge Univ. Press, 1985.

Licht, Walter. *Industrializing America: The Nineteenth Century.* Baltimore: Johns Hopkins Univ. Press, 1995.

Meyer, David R. "Emergence of the American Manufacturing Belt: An Interpretation." *Journal of Historical Geography* 9 (April 1983): 145–74.

———. "Midwestern Industrialization and the American Manufacturing Belt in the Nineteenth Century." *Journal of Economic History* 49 (December 1989): 921–37.

Mumford, Lewis. *Technics and Civilization.* New York: Harcourt, Brace, 1934.

Perloff, Harvey S., Edgar S. Dunn, Jr., Eric E. Lampard, and Richard F. Muth. *Regions, Resources and Economic Growth.* Baltimore: Johns Hopkins Univ. Press, 1960.

Pudup, Mary Beth. "From Farm to Factory: Structuring and Location of the U.S. Farm Machinery Industry." *Economic Geography* 63 (July 1987): 203–22.

Rothwell, Richard P., ed. *The Mineral Industry: Its Statistics, Technology and Trade in the United States and Other Countries from the Earliest Times to the End of 1892.* New York: Scientific, 1893.

Shannon, Fred A. *The Farmer's Last Frontier: Agriculture, 1860–1897.* New York: Holt, Rinehart and Winston, 1945.

Smith, J. Russell, and M. Ogden Phillips. *North America: Its People and the Resources, Development and Prospects of the Continent as the Home of Man.* New York: Harcourt, Brace, 1942.

Temin, Peter. *Iron and Steel in Nineteenth-Century America: An Economic Inquiry.* Cambridge: MIT Press, 1964.

Trading and Shipping on the Great Lakes. [1899] Toronto: Coles, 1980.

Walsh, Margaret. "The Spatial Evolution of the Mid-Western Pork Industry, 1835–75." *Journal of Historical Geography* 4 (January 1978): 1–22.

Warntz, William. "An Historical Consideration of the Terms, 'Corn' and 'Corn Belt' in the United States." *Agricultural History* 31 (January 1957): 40–45.

Weaver, John C. *American Barley Production: A Study in Agricultural Geography.* Minneapolis: Burgess, 1950.

Williamson, Harold F., and Arnold R. Daum. *The American Petroleum Industry: The Age of Illumination, 1859–1899.* Evanston, Ill.: Northwestern Univ. Press, 1959.

Winder, Gordon M. "Before the Corporation and Mass Production: The Licensing Regime in the Manufacture of North American Harvesting Machinery, 1830–1910." *Annals of the Association of American Geographers* 85 (September 1995): 521–52.

3. Railroads: The Contest for Territory

Anderson, George L. "Banks, Mails, and Rails, 1880–1915." In *The Frontier Challenge: Responses to the Trans-Mississippi West*, ed. John C. Clark, 275–307. Lawrence: Univ. of Kansas Press, 1971.

Baker, George Pierce. *The Formation of the New England Railroad Systems*. New York: Greenwood Press, 1968.

Clarke, Thomas Curtis, et al. *The American Railway: Its Construction, Development, Management and Appliances*. [1889] Secaucus, N.J.: Castle, 1988.

Conzen, Michael P. "A Transport Interpretation of the Growth of Urban Regions: An American Example." *Journal of Historical Geography* 1 (October 1975): 361–82.

The Day of Two Noons. 9th ed. Washington, D.C.: Association of American Railroads, 1959.

Grodinsky, Julius. *Transcontinental Railway Strategy, 1869–1893: A Study of Businessmen*. Philadelphia: Univ. of Pennsylvania Press, 1962.

Interstate Commerce Commission. *Annual Reports*. Washington, D.C.: Government Printing Office, 1887–1910.

———. *Thirteenth Annual Report on the Statistics of Railways in the United States for the Year Ending June 30, 1900*. Washington, D.C.: Government Printing Office, 1901.

Joubert, William H. *Southern Freight Rates in Transition*. Gainesville: Univ. of Florida Press, 1949.

Klein, Maury. *Unfinished Business: The Railroad in American Life*. Hanover: Univ. Press of New England, 1994.

McLeod, Richard. "The Development of Superior, Wisconsin, as a Western Transportation Center." *Journal of the West* 8 (July 1974): 17–27.

Martin, Albro. *Enterprise Denied: Origins of the Decline of American Railroads, 1897–1917*. New York: Columbia Univ. Press, 1971.

Meinig, D. W. "A Comparative Historical Geography of Two Railnets: Columbia Basin and South Australia." *Annals of the Association of American Geographers* 52 (December 1962): 394–413.

Nimmo, Joseph, Jr. *First Annual Report of the Internal Commerce of the United States*. 44th Cong., 2d sess., 1877. H. Ex. Doc. 46, Part 2.

O'Connell, John. *Railroad Album*. Chicago: Popular Mechanics Press, 1954.

Official Guide of the Railways and Steam Navigation Lines of the United States, Porto Rico, Canada, Mexico and Cuba. New York: National Railway Publication, May 1915.

O'Malley, Michael. *Keeping Watch: A History of American Time*. New York: Viking Penguin, 1990.

Pred, Allan R. *The Spatial Dynamics of U.S. Urban-Industrial Growth, 1800–1914: Interpretive and Theoretical Essays*. Cambridge: MIT Press, 1966.

Quastler, I. E. "A Descriptive Model of Railroad Network Growth in the American Midwest, 1865–1915." *Journal of Geography* 77 (March 1978): 87–93.

Ringwalt, J. L. *Development of Transportation Systems in the United States*. Philadelphia: Railway World Office, 1888.

Schonberger, Howard B. *Transportation to the Seaboard: The "Communications Revolution" and American Foreign Policy, 1860–1900*. Westport, Conn.: Greenwood Press, 1971.

Smart, Douglas. "Spokane's Battle for Freight Rates." *Pacific Northwest Quarterly* 45 (January 1954): 19–27.

Stilgoe, John R. *Metropolitan Corridor: Railroads and the American Scene*. New Haven: Yale Univ. Press, 1983.

U.S. Congress. Senate. *Report of the Select Committee on Transportation-Routes to the Seaboard*. 43d Cong., 1st sess., 1874. S. Report 307, Part 1.

Vance, James E., Jr. *The North American Railroad: Its Origin, Evolution, and Geography*. Baltimore: Johns Hopkins Univ. Press, 1995.

Wilgus, William J. *The Railway Interrelations of the United States and Canada*. New Haven: Yale Univ. Press, 1937.

4. Populations and Peoples

Ahlstrom, Sydney E. *A Religious History of the American People*. New Haven: Yale Univ. Press, 1972.

Arends, Shirley Fischer. *The Central Dakota Germans: Their History, Language, and Culture*. Washington, D.C.: Georgetown Univ. Press, 1989.

Balch, Emily Greene. *Our Slavic Fellow Citizens*. New York: Charities Publication Committee, 1910.

Baltensperger, Bradley H. *Nebraska: A Geography*. Boulder, Colo.: Westview Press, 1985.

Bennett, John W., and Seena B. Kohl. *Settling the Canadian-American West, 1890–1915*. Lincoln: Univ. of Nebraska Press, 1995.

Bennion, Lowell Colton. "German Migration and Colonization: Inventory and Prologue to Geographic Study." M.A. thesis, Department of Geography, Syracuse Univ., 1963.

Bodnar, John. *Immigration and Industrialization: Ethnicity in an American Mill Town, 1870–1940*. Pittsburgh: Univ. of Pittsburgh Press, 1977.

Busch, Briton Cooper. "Cape Verdeans in the American Whaling and Sealing Industry, 1850–1900." *American Neptune* 45 (Spring 1985): 104–116.

Commons, John R. *Races and Immigrants in America*. New York: Macmillan, 1908.

Conzen, Kathleen Neils, David A. Gerber, Ewa Morawska, George E. Pozzetta, and Rudolph J. Vecoli. "The Invention of Ethnicity: A Perspective from the U.S.A." *Journal of American Ethnic History* 12 (Fall 1992): 3–41.

Conzen, Michael. "The German-Speaking Ethnic Archipelago in America." In *Ethnic Persistence and Change in Europe and America*, ed. Klaus Frantz and Robert A. Sauder, 67–92. Innsbruck, Austria: Univ. of Innsbruck, 1966.

Coolidge, Mary Roberts. *Chinese Immigration*. New York: Henry Holt, 1909.

Daniels, Roger. *Coming to America: A History of Immigration and Ethnicity in American Life*. New York: HarperCollins, 1990.

Davie, Maurice R. *World Immigration, with Special Reference to the United States*. New York: Macmillan, 1949.

Dinnerstein, Leonard, and David M. Reimers. *Ethnic Americas*. 2d ed. New York: Harper & Row, 1982.

Dockendorff, Thomas P. "Upper Mississippi Valley Landscape: A Legacy of German Catholic Settlement in Central Minnesota." *Pioneer America Society Transactions* 8 (1985): 85–90.

Dolan, Jay P. *The Immigrant Church: New York's Irish and German Catholics, 1815–1865*. Baltimore: Johns Hopkins Univ. Press, 1975.

Elazar, Daniel J. *Cities of the Prairie: The Metropolitan Frontier and American Politics*. New York: Basic Books, 1970.

Erickson, Charlotte. *American Industry and the European Immigrant, 1860–1885*. Cambridge: Harvard Univ. Press, 1957.

Gaustad, Edwin Scott. *Historical Atlas of Religion in America*. New York: Harper & Row, 1962.

Glaab, Charles N., and A. Theodore Brown. *A History of Urban America*. New York: Macmillan, 1967.

Golab, Caroline. *Immigrant Destinations*. Philadelphia: Temple Univ. Press, 1977.

Gordon, Milton M. *Assimilation in American Life: The Role of Race, Religion, and National Origins*. New York: Oxford Univ. Press, 1964.

Greeley, Andrew M. *The American Catholic: A Social Portrait*. New York: Basic Books, 1977.

Handlin, Oscar. *Race and Nationality in American Life*. Garden City, N.Y.: Anchor Books, 1957.

Hansen, Marcus Lee. *The Mingling of the Canadian and American Peoples*. New Haven: Yale Univ. Press, 1940.

Hauk, Mary Ursula. "Changing Patterns of Catholic Population in Eastern United States (1790–1950)." Ph.D. dissertation, Graduate School of Geography, Clark University, 1959.

Hennesey, James. *American Catholics: A History of the Roman Catholic Community in the United States*. New York: Oxford Univ. Press, 1981.

Herberg, Will. *Protestant-Catholic-Jew: An Essay in American Religious Sociology*. Garden City, N.Y.: Anchor Books, 1960.

Higham, John. *Send These to Me: Jews and Other Immigrants in Urban America*. New York: Atheneum, 1975.

Hudson, John C. "Migration to an American Frontier." *Annals of the Association of American Geographers* 66 (June 1976): 242–65.

———. "North American Origins of Middlewestern Frontier Populations." *Annals of the Association of American Geographers* 78 (September 1988): 395–413.

Jakle, John A., and James O. Wheeler. "The Changing Residential Structure of the Dutch Population in Kalamazoo." *Annals of the Association of American Geographers* 59 (September 1969): 441–60.

Jenks, Jeremiah W., and W. Jett Lauk. *The Immigration Problem: A Study of American Immigration Conditions and Needs.* New York: Funk & Wagnalls, 1913.

Johnson, Hildegard Binder. "The Location of German Immigrants in the Middle West." *Annals of the Association of American Geographers* 41 (March 1951): 1–41.

Jones, Maldwyn Allen. *American Immigration.* Chicago: Univ. of Chicago Press, 1960.

King's Illustrated Portfolio of Our Country. Philadelphia: W. C. King, 1906.

LaGumina, Salvatore J., and Frank J. Cavaioli. *The Ethnic Dimension in American Society.* Boston: Holbrook Press, 1974.

Liptak, Dolores. *Immigrants and Their Church.* New York: Macmillan, 1989.

McKee, Jesse O., ed. *Ethnicity in Contemporary America: A Geographical Appraisal.* Dubuque: Kendall/Hunt, 1985.

McQuillan, D. Aidan. *Prevailing over Time: Ethnic Adjustment on the Kansas Prairies, 1875–1925.* Lincoln: Univ. of Nebraska Press, 1990.

Markus, Neil A. "Areal Patterns of Religious Denominationalism in Minnesota, 1950." M.A. thesis, Department of Geography, Univ. of Minnesota, n.d.

Meyer, Judith M. "The Historical Geography of the Lutheran Church-Missouri Synod, 1847–1967: A Case Study in Religious Geography." M.A. thesis, Department of Geography, Southern Illinois Univ., 1967.

Montejano, David. *Anglos and Mexicans in the Making of Texas, 1836–1986.* Austin: Univ. of Texas Press, 1987.

Niebuhr, H. Richard. *The Social Sources of Denominationalism.* Cleveland: World, 1957.

Noble, Allen G. *To Build in a New Land: Ethnic Landscapes in North America.* Baltimore: Johns Hopkins Univ. Press, 1992.

Ostergren, Robert C. *A Community Transplanted: The Trans-Atlantic Experience of a Swedish Immigrant Settlement in the Upper Middle West, 1835–1915.* Madison: Univ. of Wisconsin Press, 1988.

Paterson, Donald H. "Comments on the Underenumeration of the U.S. Census, 1850–1880." *Social Science History* 15 (Winter 1991): 509–15.

Raitz, Karl B. "Ethnic Maps of North America." *Geographical Review* 68 (July 1978): 335–50.

———. "Themes in the Cultural Geography of European Ethnic Groups in the United States." *Geographical Review* 69 (January 1979): 79–94.

Riis, Jacob. *How the Other Half Lives: Studies among the Tenements of New York.* New York: Charles Scribner's Sons, 1907.

Ripley, William Z. *The Races of Europe: A Sociological Study.* New York: D. Appleton Century, 1899.

Sherman, William C. *Prairie Mosaic: An Ethnic Atlas of Rural North Dakota.* Fargo: North Dakota Institute for Regional Studies, 1983.

Shortridge, James R. *Peopling the Plains: Who Settled Where in Frontier Kansas.* Lawrence: Univ. Press of Kansas, 1995.

Speek, Peter A. *A Stake in the Land.* New York: Harper & Brothers, 1921.

"Statistical Review of Immigration, 1820–1910" and "Distribution of Immigrants, 1850–1900." *Reports of the Immigration Commission,* Vol. 3. 61st Cong., 3d sess., December 5, 1910. S. Doc. 756.

Stolarik, M. Mark, ed. *Forgotten Doors: The Other Ports of Entry to the United States.* Philadelphia: Balch Institute Press, 1988.

Taylor, Philip. *The Distant Magnet: European Emigration to the U.S.A.* New York: Harper & Row, 1971.

Thernstrom, Stephen B., ed. *Harvard Encyclopedia of American Ethnic Groups.* Cambridge: Harvard Univ. Press, 1980.

U.S. Department of Commerce and Labor. Bureau of Statistics. *Emigration to the United States.* Special Consular Reports, Vol. 30. 58th Cong., 2d sess., 1904. H. Doc. 732.

Vogeler, Ingolf. *Wisconsin: A Geography.* Boulder, Colo.: Westview Press, 1986.

Ward, David. *Cities and Immigrants: A Geography of Change in Nineteenth Century America.* New York: Oxford Univ. Press, 1971.

———. *Poverty, Ethnicity, and the American City, 1840–1925.* Cambridge: Cambridge Univ. Press, 1989.

Warne, Frank Julian. *The Immigrant Invasion.* New York: Dodd, Mead, 1913.

Wattenberg, Ben J. "Introduction and User's Guide." In *The Statistical History of the United States: From Colonial Times to the Present,* comp. Francis A. Walker. New York: Basic Books, 1976.

Widdis, Randy William. "With Scarcely a Ripple: English Canadians in Northern New York State at the Beginning of the Twentieth Century." *Journal of Historical Geography* 13 (1987): 169–92.

Wyman, Mark. *Round-Trip to America.: The Immigrants Return to Europe, 1880–1930.* Ithaca: Cornell Univ. Press, 1993.

5. Systems and Symbols

Abbott, Carl. "Dimensions of Regional Change in Washington, D.C." *American Historical Review* 95 (December 1990): 1367–93.

Abler, Ronald. "The Telephone and the Evolution of the American Metropolitan System." In *The Social Impact of the Telephone,* ed. Ithiel de Sola Pool, 318–41. Cambridge: MIT Press, 1977.

Adler, Jeffrey S. *Yankee Merchants and the Making of the Urban West: The Rise and Fall of Antebellum St. Louis.* Cambridge: Cambridge Univ. Press, 1991.

Bender, Thomas. "New York as a Center of 'Difference.'" *Dissent* 34 (Fall 1987): 429–35.

Bennett, Arnold. *Your United States: Impressions of a First Visit.* New York: Harper & Brothers, 1912.

Bensel, Richard Franklin. *Sectionalism and American Political Development, 1880–1980.* Madison: Univ. of Wisconsin Press, 1984.

Benson, Lee. *Turner and Beard: American Historical Writing Reconsidered.* New York: Free Press, 1960.

Bodnar, John, ed. *Bonds of Affection: Americans Define Their Patriotism.* Princeton: Princeton Univ. Press, 1996.

Borchert, John R. "American Metropolitan Evolution." *Geographical Review* 57 (July 1967): 301–32.

———. "Major Control Points in American Economic Geography." *Annals of the Association of American Geographers* 68 (June 1978): 214–32.

Brigham, Albert P. *Geographic Influences in American History.* Boston: Ginn, 1903.

Bright, Charles C. "The State in the United States during the Nineteenth Century." In *Statemaking and Social Movements: Essays in History and Theory,* ed. Charles Bright and Susan Harding, 121–57. Ann Arbor: Univ. of Michigan Press, 1984.

Brunn, Stanley D. *Geography and Politics in America.* New York: Harper & Row, 1974.

Cayton, Andrew R. L., and Peter S. Onuf. *The Midwest and the Nation: Rethinking the History of an American Region.* Bloomington: Indiana Univ. Press, 1990.

Cochran, Edwin A. *The Cathedral of Commerce.* [New York]: Broadway Park Place, 1917.

Conzen, Michael P. "The Maturing Urban System in the United States, 1840–1910." *Annals of the Association of American Geographers* 67 (March 1977): 88–108.

———. "The Moral Tenets of American Urban Form." In *Human Geography in North America,* ed. Klaus Frantz, 275–87. *Innsbrucker Geographische Studien* 26 (Innsbruck, 1996).

———, ed. *Chicago Mapmakers: Essays on the Rise of the City's Map Trade.* Chicago: Chicago Historical Society, 1984.

Cronon, William. "Revisiting the Vanishing Frontier: The Legacy of Frederick Jackson Turner." *Western Historical Quarterly* 18 (April 1987): 157–76.

Davis, Lance E. "The Investment Market, 1870–1914: The Evolution of a National Market." *Journal of Economic History* 25 (September 1965): 355–93.

Davis, William Morris. "The United States of America." In *The International Geography,* ed. Hugh Robert Mill, 710–73. New York: D. Appleton, 1915.

Dodge, Richard Elwood. *Dodge's Advanced Geography.* Chicago: Rand McNally, 1907.

Domosh, Mona. "Imagining New York's First Skyscrapers, 1875–1910." *Journal of Historical Geography* 13 (July 1987): 233–48.

———. *Invented Cities: The Creation of Landscape in Nineteenth-Century New York and Boston.* New Haven: Yale Univ. Press, 1996.

Duis, Perry. *Chicago: Creating New Traditions.* Chicago: Chicago Historical Society, 1976.

Elazar, Daniel J. *American Federalism: A View from the States.* New York: Thomas Crowell, 1966.

Gannett, Henry. *The Building of a Nation: The Growth, Present Condition and Resources of the United States with a Forecast of the Future.* New York: Henry T. Thomas, 1895.

Glazier, Willard. *Peculiarities of American Cities.* Philadelphia: Hubbard Brothers, 1886.

Greenfeld, Liah. *Nationalism: Five Roads to Modernity.* Cambridge: Harvard Univ. Press, 1992.

Hall, Peter Dobkin. *The Organization of American Culture, 1700–1900: Private Institutions, Elites, and the Origins of American Nationality.* New York: New York Univ. Press, 1982.

Handlin, Oscar, and Mary F. Handlin. *The American College and American Culture: Socialization as a Function of Higher Education.* New York: McGraw-Hill, 1970.

Harris, Neil, ed. *The Land of Contrasts, 1880–1901.* New York: George Braziller, 1970.

Hart, Albert Bushnell, and Herbert Ronald Ferleger, eds. *Theodore Roosevelt Encyclopedia.* New York: Roosevelt Memorial Association, 1941.

Heise, Kenan. *The Chicagoization of America, 1893–1917.* Evanston, Ill.: Chicago Historical Bookworks, 1990.

Hilton, George W., and John F. Due. *The Electric Interurban Railways in America.* Stanford: Stanford Univ. Press, 1960.

Hofstadter, Richard, and Wilson Smith, eds. *American Higher Education: A Documentary History.* Vol. 2. Chicago: Univ. of Chicago Press, 1961.

Jacobs, Wilbur R. *The Historical World of Frederick Jackson Turner, with Selections from His Correspondence.* New Haven: Yale Univ. Press, 1968.

Jaher, Frederic Cople. *The Urban Establishment: Upper Strata in Boston, New York, Charleston, Chicago, and Los Angeles.* Urbana: Univ. of Illinois Press, 1982.

James, Preston E. *All Possible Worlds: A History of Geographical Ideas.* New York: Odyssey Press, 1972.

Kammen, Michael. *Mystic Chords of Memory: The Transformation of Tradition in American Culture.* New York: Vintage Books, 1993.

Landau, Sarah Bradford, and Carl W. Condit. *Rise of the New York Skyscraper, 1865–1913.* New Haven: Yale Univ. Press, 1996.

Langdale, John V. "The Growth of Long-Distance Telephony in the Bell System: 1875–1907." *Journal of Historical Geography* 4 (April 1978): 145–59.

Livingstone, David N. *The Geographical Tradition: Episodes in the History of a Contested Enterprise.* Oxford: Blackwell, 1992.

Lodge, Henry Cabot. "The Distribution of Ability in the United States." *Century Magazine* 42 (September 1891): 687–914.

Lowry, Bates. *Building a National Image: Architectural Drawings for the American Democracy, 1789–1912.* Washington, D.C.: National Building Museum, 1985.

Mann, Michael. *The Sources of Social Power.* Vol. 1, *A History of Power from the Beginning to A.D. 1760.* Cambridge: Cambridge Univ. Press, 1986.

Meinig, D. W. "Symbolic Landscapes." In *The Interpretation of Ordinary Landscapes: Geographical Essays,* ed. D. W. Meinig, 164–92. New York: Oxford Univ. Press, 1979.

Murray, John J., ed. *The Heritage of the Middle West.* Norman: Univ. of Oklahoma Press, 1958.

Parmele, Mary Platt. *The Evolution of an Empire: A Brief Historical Sketch of the United States.* New York: William Beverley Harison, 1896.

Pierson, George W. *The Education of American Leaders: Comparative Contributions of U.S. Colleges and Universities.* New York: Frederick A. Praeger, 1969.

Pomeroy, Earl S. *The Territories and the United States, 1861–1890.* Seattle: Univ. of Washington Press, 1969.

Porter, Glenn, and Harold C. Livesay. *Merchants and Manufacturers: Studies in the Changing Structure of Nineteenth-Century Marketing.* Baltimore: Johns Hopkins Univ. Press, 1971.

Read-Miller, Cynthia, ed. *Main Street, U.S.A. in Early Photographs: 113 Detroit Publishing Co. Views*. New York: Dover, 1988.

Reavis, L. U. *A Change of National Empire; or, Arguments in Favor of the Removal of the National Capital from Washington City to the Mississippi Valley*. St. Louis: J. F. Torrey, 1869.

———. *The National Capital Is Movable*. St. Louis: Missouri Democrat Book and Job, 1871.

Richey, Russell E., and Donald G. Jones, eds. *American Civil Religion*. New York: Harper & Row, 1974.

Ross, Edward Alsworth. "The Middle West: Being Studies of Its People in Comparison with Those of the East." *Century Magazine* 83 (February, March, April 1912): 609–15, 686–92, 874–80; 84 (May 1912): 142–48.

Rowley, Virginia M. *J. Russell Smith: Geographer, Educator, and Conservationist*. Philadelphia: Univ. of Pennsylvania Press, 1964.

Schneirov, Matthew. *The Dream of a New Social Order: Popular Magazines in America, 1893–1914*. New York: Columbia Univ. Press, 1994.

Semple, Ellen Churchill. *American History and Its Geographic Conditions*. Boston: Houghton Mifflin, 1903.

Shils, Edward. "Center and Periphery: An Idea and Its Career, 1935–1987." In *Center: Ideas and Institutions*, ed. Liah Greenfeld and Michael Martin, 250–82. Chicago: Univ. of Chicago Press, 1988.

Smith, Timothy L. "Uncommon Schools: Christian Colleges and Social Idealism in Midwestern America, 1820–1950." In *The History of Education in the Middle West: Lectures, 1976–1977*. Indianapolis: Indiana Historical Society, 1978.

Stewart, Paul W. *Market Data Handbook of United States*. Domestic Commerce Series, No. 30. United States Department of Commerce. Washington, D.C.: Government Printing Office, 1929.

Stewart, Charles, III, and Barry R. Weingast. "Stacking the Senate, Changing the Nation: Republican Rotten Boroughs, Statehood Politics, and American Political Development. *Studies in American Political Development* 6 (Fall 1992): 223–71.

Taylor, William R. *Inventing Times Square: Commerce and Culture at the Crossroads of the World*. New York: Russell Sage Foundation, 1991.

Teaford, Jon C. *Cities of the Heartland: The Rise and Fall of the Industrial Midwest*. Bloomington: Indiana Univ. Press, 1993.

Tunnard, Christopher, and Henry Hope Read. *American Skyline: The Growth and Form of Our Cities and Towns*. New York: Mentor Books, 1956.

Turner, Frederick Jackson. *The United States, 1830–1850: The Nation and Its Sections*. New York: Henry Holt, 1935.

———. *Frontier and Section: Selected Essays of Frederick Jackson Turner*. Ed. and intro. Ray Allen Billington. Englewood Cliffs, N.J.: Prentice-Hall, 1961.

———. *Rise of the New West, 1819–1829*. [1906] New York: Collier Books, 1962.

Ubbelohde, Carl. "History and the Midwest as a Region." *Wisconsin Magazine of History* 78 (Autumn 1994): 35–47.

U.S. Congress. Senate. *Location of Reserve Districts in the United States*. 63d Cong., 2d sess., May 28, 1914. S. Doc. 485.

Watson, J. Wreford, and Timothy O'Riordan. *The American Environment: Perceptions and Policies*. London: John Wiley, 1976.

Webb, Beatrice. *Beatrice Webb's American Diary, 1898*. Ed. David A. Shannon. Madison: Univ. of Wisconsin Press, 1963.

Whitney, Gordon G. *From Coastal Wilderness to Fruited Plain: A History of Environmental Change in Temperate North America, 1500 to the Present*. New York: Cambridge Univ. Press, 1994.

Wiebe, Robert H. *The Search for Order, 1877–1920*. New York: Hill and Wang, 1967.

Wills, Gary. "Sons and Daughters of Chicago." *New York Review of Books*, June 4, 1994, 52–59.

Wilson, Woodrow. *A History of the American People*. Vol. 5. New York: Harper & Brothers, 1902.

———. "The Ideals of America." *Atlantic Monthly* 90 (December 1902): 721–34.

Woodward, C. Vann, ed. *The Comparative Approach to American History*. New York: Basic Books, 1968.

PART FOUR
1. Canada and Continentalism

Alaska's Great Interior. Vol. 7, No. 1. Anchorage: Alaska Geographic Society, 1980.

Allen, James P. "Migration Fields of French Canadian Immigrants to Southern Maine." *Geographical Review* 62 (July 1972): 366–83.

Anchorage and the Cook Inlet Basin. Vol. 10, No. 2. Anchorage: Alaska Geographic Society, 1983.

Berger, Carl. *The Sense of Power: Studies in the Ideas of Canadian Imperialism, 1867–1914.* Toronto: Univ. of Toronto Press, 1970.

Berton, Pierre. *The National Dream: The Last Spike.* Toronto: McClelland and Stewart, 1974.

Bowles, Richard P., James L. Hanley, Bruce W. Hodgins, George A. Rawlyk. *Canada and the U.S.: Continental Partners or Wary Neighbours?* Scarborough: Prentice-Hall of Canada, 1973.

Brown, Robert Craig. *Canada's National Policy, 1883–1900: A Study in Canadian-American Relations.* Princeton: Princeton Univ. Press, 1964.

———. "The Nationalism of the National Policy." In *Readings in Canadian History: Post-Confederation,* ed. R. Douglas Francis and Donald B. Smith, 22–28. Toronto: Holt, Rinehart and Winston, 1982.

Brown, Robert Craig, and Ramsey Cook. *Canada, 1896–1921: A Nation Transformed.* Toronto: McClelland and Stewart, 1974.

Careless, J. M. S. *Canada: A Story of Challenge.* Toronto: Macmillan, 1970.

Careless, J. M. S., and R. Craig Brown, eds. *The Canadians, 1867–1967.* Toronto: Macmillan, 1968.

Cornell, Paul G., Jean Hamelin, Fernand Ouellet, and Marcel Trudel. *Canada: Unity in Diversity.* Toronto: Holt, Rinehart and Winston, 1967.

Creighton, D. G. "Canada in the English-Speaking World." *Canadian Historical Review* 26 (June 1945): 119–27.

Easterbrook, W. T., and Hugh G. J. Aitken. *Canadian Economic History.* Toronto: Macmillan, 1956.

Francis, R. Douglas, and Howard Palmer. *The Prairie West: Historical Readings.* Edmonton: Pica Pica Press, 1985.

Gentilcore, Louis, ed. *Ontario: Studies in Canadian Geography.* Toronto: Univ. of Toronto Press, 1972.

———, ed. *Historical Atlas of Canada.* Vol. 2, *The Land Transformed, 1800–1891.* Toronto: Univ. of Toronto Press, 1993.

Glazebrook, G. P. de T. *A History of Transportation in Canada.* Vol. 2, *National Economy 1867–1936.* Toronto: McClelland and Stewart, 1964.

Goheen, Peter G. "Currents of Change in Toronto, 1850–1900." In *Readings in Canadian History: Post-Confederation,* ed. R. Douglas Francis and Donald B. Smith, 217–47. Toronto: Holt, Rinehart and Winston, 1982.

Grant, George M. *Ocean to Ocean: Sanford Fleming's Expedition through Canada in 1872.* Rev. ed. Toronto: Radisson Society of Canada, 1925.

Homes for Millions in Western Canada's Vast Agricultural Domain. Issued by direction of Hon. Clifford Sifton, Minister of the Interior. Ottawa, Canada, [c. 1904].

Hull, Raymond, Gordon Soules, and Christine Soules. *Vancouver's Past.* Seattle: Univ. of Washington Press, 1974.

Hunt, William R. *Alaska: A Bicentennial History.* New York: W. W. Norton, 1976.

Johnson, George. *Canada: Its History, Productions and Natural Resources.* Ottawa: Department of Agriculture of Canada, 1904.

Kerr, D. G. G., and R. I. K. Davidson. *An Illustrated History of Canada.* Toronto: Thomas Nelson & Sons, 1966.

Kerr, Donald, and Deryck W. Holdsworth, eds. *Historical Atlas of Canada.* Vol. 3, *Addressing the Twentieth Century, 1891–1961.* Toronto: Univ. of Toronto Press, 1990.

Koroscil, Paul M. "The Historical Development of Whitehorse: 1898–1945." *American Review of Canadian Studies* 18 (Autumn 1988): 271–94.

Levitt, Joseph. *A Vision beyond Reach: A Century of Images of Canadian Destiny.* Ottawa: Deneau, n.d.

Lower, J. A. *Canada: An Outline History*. Toronto: Ryerson Press, 1966.

McCann, L. D., ed. *Heartland and Hinterland: A Geography of Canada*. 2d ed. Scarborough: Prentice-Hall, 1987.

MacDonald, Norbert. "Seattle, Vancouver, and the Klondike." *Canadian Historical Review* 49 (September 1968): 234–46.

MacGibbon, D. A. *The Canadian Grain Trade*. Toronto: Macmillan, 1932.

McIlwraith, Thomas E. "Transport in the Borderlands, 1763–1920." In *Borderlands: Essays in Canadian-American Relations*. Borderlands Project. Toronto: ECW Press, 1991.

Mackintosh, W. A. *Prairie Settlement: The Geographical Setting*. Toronto: Macmillan, 1934.

McQuillan, D. Aidan. "Creation of Indian Reserves on the Canadian Prairies, 1870–1885." *Geographical Review* 70 (October 1980): 379–96.

Martin, Chester. *Foundations of Canadian Nationhood*. Toronto: Univ. of Toronto Press, 1955.

Mika, Nick, and Helma Mika. *Railways of Canada: A Pictorial History*. Toronto: McGraw-Hill Ryerson, 1972.

Moffett, Samuel E. *The Americanization of Canada*. Intro. Allan Smith. Toronto: Univ. of Toronto Press, 1972.

Morchain, Janet. *Sharing a Continent: An Introduction to Canadian-American Relations*. Toronto: McGraw-Hill Ryerson, 1973.

Morton, W. L. *Manitoba: A History*. Toronto: Univ. of Toronto Press, 1957.

———. *The Canadian Identity*. Madison: Univ. of Wisconsin Press, 1961.

———. *Contexts of Canada's Past: Selected Essays*. Ed. and intro. A. B. McKillop. Toronto: Macmillan, 1980.

Nicholson, Norman L. *The Boundaries of the Canadian Confederation*. Toronto: Macmillan, 1979.

Owram, Doug. *Promise of Eden: The Canadian Expansionist Movement and the Idea of the West, 1856–1900*. Toronto: Univ. of Toronto Press, 1980.

Robinson, J. Lewis, and Walter G. Hardwick. *British Columbia: One Hundred Years of Geographical Change*. Vancouver: Talonbooks, 1973.

Russell, Peter, ed. *Nationalism in Canada*. Toronto: McGraw-Hill Ryerson, 1966.

Sage, Walter N. "British Columbia Becomes Canadian (1871–1901)." In *Readings in Canadian History: Post-Confederation*, ed. R. Douglas Francis and Donald B. Smith, 10–20. Toronto: Holt, Rinehart and Winston, 1982.

Shortt, Adam, and Arthur G. Doughty, eds. *Canada and Its Provinces: A History of the Canadian People and Their Institutions by One Hundred Associates*. 22 vols., plus index. Toronto: Publishers Association of Canada, 1914–17.

Silver, A. I. *The French-Canadian Idea of Confederation, 1864–1900*. Toronto: Univ. of Toronto Press, 1982.

Smith, Allan. *Canada—An American Nation? Essays on Continentalism, Identity, and the Canadian Frame of Mind*. Montreal and Kingston: McGill-Queen's Univ. Press, 1994.

Smith, Goldwin. *Canada and the Canadian Question*. Toronto: Macmillan, 1891.

Stone, Kirk H. "Populating Alaska: The United States Phase." *Geographical Review* 42 (October 1952): 384–404.

Tansill, Charles Callan. *Canadian-American Relations, 1875–1911*. Gloucester, Mass.: Peter Smith, 1964.

Underhill, Frank H. *The Image of Confederation*. Toronto: Canadian Broadcasting, 1964.

Weale, David, and Harry Baglole. *The Island and Confederation: The End of an Era*. [Charlottetown]: Williams & Crue, 1973.

Wynn, Graeme, ed. *People Places Patterns Processes: Geographical Perspective on the Canadian Past*. Toronto: Copp Clark Pitman, 1990.

Zeller, Suzanne. *Inventing Canada: Early Victorian Science and the Idea of a Transcontinental Nation*. Toronto: Univ. of Toronto Press, 1987.

2. Mexico and an American Mediterranean

Arreola, Daniel D. "The Mexican American Cultural Capital." *Geographical Review* 77 (January 1987): 17–34.

———. "Mexico Origins of South Texas Mexican Americans, 1930." *Journal of Historical Geography* 19 (January 1993): 48–63.

Bailey, Thomas A. *A Diplomatic History of the American People.* 3d ed. New York: F. S. Crofts, 1947.

Brameld, Theodore. *The Remaking of a Culture: Life and Education in Puerto Rico.* New York: Harper & Brothers, 1959.

Cerutti, Mario. "The Formation and Consolidation of a Regional Bourgeoisie in Northeastern Mexico." In *Region, State and Capitalism in Mexico: Nineteenth and Twentieth Centuries,* ed. Wil Pansters and Arij Ouweneel, 47–58. Amsterdam: Centrum voor Studie en Documentatie van Latijns Amerika, 1989.

Chávez, John R. *The Lost Land: The Chicano Image of the Southwest.* Albuquerque: Univ. of New Mexico Press, 1984.

Cline, Howard F. *The United States and Mexico.* Cambridge: Harvard Univ. Press, 1961.

Conkling, Alfred R. *Appleton's Guide to Mexico.* New York: D. Appleton, 1893.

Davids, Jules. *American Political and Economic Penetration of Mexico, 1877–1920.* New York: Arno Press, 1976.

De León, Arnoldo. *The Tejano Community, 1836–1900.* Albuquerque: Univ. of New Mexico Press, 1982.

Fitzgibbon, Russell H. *Cuba and the United States, 1900–1935.* Menasha, Wis.: George Banta, 1935.

Hall, Linda D., and Don M. Coerver. *Revolution on the Border: The United States and Mexico, 1910–1920.* Albuquerque: Univ. of New Mexico Press, 1988.

Hanson, Earl Parker. *Puerto Rico: Ally for Progress.* Princeton: D. Van Nostrand, 1962.

Healy, David. *Drive to Hegemony: The United States in the Caribbean, 1898–1917.* Madison: Univ. of Wisconsin Press, 1988.

Hernández, José M. *Cuba and the United States: Intervention and Militarism, 1868–1933.* Austin: Univ. of Texas Press, 1993.

Hill, Robert T. *Cuba and Porto Rico with the Other Islands of the West Indies.* New York: Century, 1898.

Knight, Alan. *U.S.-Mexican Relations, 1910–1940.* San Diego: Center for U.S.-Mexican Studies, Univ. of California–San Diego, 1987.

Langley, Lester D. *The United States in the Carib-bean, 1900–1970.* Athens: Univ. of Georgia Press, 1980.

Leibowitz, Arnold H. *Defining Status: A Comprehensive Analysis of United States Territorial Relations.* Dordrecht, The Netherlands: Martinus Nijhoff, 1989.

López, Adalberto, ed. *The Puerto Ricans: Their History, Culture, and Society.* Cambridge, Mass.: Schenkman, 1980.

Mahan, Alfred T. *Lessons of the War with Spain and Other Articles.* Boston: Little, Brown, 1899.

———. *Mahan on Naval Warfare: Selections from the Writings of Rear Admiral Alfred T. Mahan.* Ed. Allan Westcott. Boston: Little, Brown, 1942.

Martinez, Oscar J. *Border People: Life and Society in the U.S.-Mexico Borderlands.* Tucson: Univ. of Arizona Press, 1994.

May, Ernest R. *Imperial Democracy: The Emergence of America as a World Power.* New York: Harcourt, Brace & World, 1961.

Mexico: A General Sketch. Washington, D.C.: Pan American Union, 1911.

Meyer, Michael C., and William L. Sherman. *The Course of Mexican History.* New York: Oxford Univ. Press, 1979.

Offner, John L. *The Unwanted War: The Diplomacy of the United States and Spain over Cuba, 1895–1898.* Chapel Hill: Univ. of North Carolina Press, 1992.

Paz, Octavio. *The Labyrinth of Solitude: Life and Thought in Mexico.* New York: Grove Press, 1961.

Pérez, Louis A., Jr. *Cuba under the Platt Amendment, 1902–1934.* Pittsburgh: Univ. of Pittsburgh Press, 1986.

———. *Cuba and the United States: Ties of Singular Intimacy.* Athens: Univ. of Georgia Press, 1990.

Pratt, Julius W. *Expansionists of 1898: The Acquisition of Hawaii and the Spanish Islands.* Baltimore: Johns Hopkins Univ. Press, 1936.

Puerto Rico: A Guide to the Island of Boriquén. American Guide Series, Works Progress Administration. New York: University Society, 1940.

Raat, W. Dirk. *Mexico and the United States: Ambivalent Vistas.* Athens: Univ. of Georgia Press, 1992.

Report on the Census of Cuba, 1899. Cuban

Census Office, U.S. War Department. Washington, D.C.: Government Printing Office, 1900.

Sandos, James A. *Rebellion in the Borderlands: Anarchism and the Plan of San Diego, 1904–1923.* Norman: Univ. of Oklahoma Press, 1992.

Saragoza, Alex M. *The Monterrey Elite and the Mexican State, 1880–1940.* Austin: Univ. of Texas Press, 1988.

Sprout, Harold, and Margaret Sprout. *The Rise of American Naval Power, 1776–1918.* Princeton: Princeton Univ. Press, 1944.

Taylor, Nathaniel Alston. *The Coming Empire or Two Thousand Miles in Texas on Horseback.* [1877] Houston: N. T. Carlisle, 1936.

3. Hawaii and an American Pacific

Austin, O. P. "Problems of the Pacific—The Commerce of the Great Ocean." *National Geographic Magazine* 13 (August 1902): 303–18.

———. "Commercial Prize of the Orient." *National Geographic Magazine* 16 (September 1905): 399–423.

Brands, H. W. *Bound to Empire: The United States and the Philippines.* New York: Oxford Univ. Press, 1992.

Coolidge, Archibald Cary. *The United States as a World Power.* New York: Macmillan, 1908.

Doeppers, Daniel F. "The Development of Philippine Cities before 1900." *Journal of Asian Studies* 31 (August 1972): 769–92.

———. "The Evolution of the Geography of Religious Adherence in the Philippines before 1898." *Journal of Historical Geography* 2 (April 1976): 95–110.

Farrell, Don A. *The Pictorial History of Guam: The Americanization, 1898–1918.* 2d ed. Tamuning, Guam: Micronesian Productions, 1986.

Fuchs, Lawrence H. *Hawaii Pono: A Social History.* New York: Harcourt Brace Jovanovich, 1961.

Gagelonia, Pedro A. *Philippine History.* Navotas: Navotas Press, 1974.

Gannett, Henry. "The Philippine Islands and Their People." *National Geographic Magazine* 15 (March 1904): 91–112.

Iriye, Akira. *Across the Pacific: An Inner History of American-East Asian Relations.* New York: Harcourt, Brace & World, 1967.

———. *Pacific Estrangement: Japanese and American Expansion, 1897–1911.* Cambridge: Harvard Univ. Press, 1972.

Karnow, Stanley. *In Our Image: America's Empire in the Philippines.* London: Century, 1990.

Karolle, Bruce G. *Atlas of Micronesia.* 2d ed. Honolulu: Bess Press, 1993.

Linn, Brian McAllister. "The Long Twilight of the Frontier Army." *Western Historical Quarterly* 27 (Summer 1996): 141–67.

Mahan, A. T. *The Problem of Asia and Its Effect upon International Policies.* Boston: Little, Brown, 1900.

Mullins, Joseph G. *Hawaiian Journey.* Honolulu: Mutual, 1978.

Nordyke, Eleanor C. *The Peopling of Hawaii.* Honolulu: Univ. Press of Hawaii, 1977.

Osborne, Thomas J. *"Empire Can Wait": American Opposition to Hawaiian Expansion, 1893–1898.* Kent, Ohio: Kent State Univ. Press, 1981.

Reed, Robert R. "Landscape as Witness: Origin and Spread of the Philippine *Iglesia ni Christo.*" Unpublished paper, International Congress of Historical Geographers, Jerusalem, 1989.

Reports of the Philippine Commission, the Civil Governor and the Heads of the Executive Departments (1900–1903). Bureau of Insular Affairs, War Department. Washington, D.C.: Government Printing Office, 1904.

Schurz, Carl. "'Manifest Destiny.'" *Harper's New Monthly Magazine* 87 (October 1893): 737–46.

Spencer, Joseph E. *Oriental Asia: Themes toward a Geography.* Englewood Cliffs, N.J.: Prentice-Hall, 1973.

Stanley, Peter W. *A Nation in the Making: The Philippines and the United States, 1899–1921.* Cambridge: Harvard Univ. Press, 1974.

Wernstedt, Frederick L., and J. E. Spencer. *The Philippine Island World: A Physical, Cultural, and Regional Geography.* Berkeley: Univ. of California Press, 1967.

Yearbook of the Philippine Islands, 1920. Cámara de Comercio de las Islas Filipinas. Manila: Bureau of Printing, 1920.

4. Panama and Transcontinental Completion

Abbot, Willis J. *Panama and the Canal in Picture and Prose.* New York: Syndicate Publishing, 1913.

Bemis, Samuel Flagg. *The United States as a World Power: A Diplomatic History, 1900–1955.* New York: Henry Holt, 1955.

Cornish, Vaughan. "The Panama Canal in 1908." *Geographical Journal* 33 (February 1909): 153–80.

Epstein, M., ed. *The Statesman's Year-Book.* London: Macmillan, 1931.

Frenkel, Stephen. "Geography, Empire, and Environmental Determinism." *Geographical Review* 82 (April 1992): 143–53.

Goethals, George W. *Government of the Canal Zone.* Princeton: Princeton Univ. Press, 1915.

Headrick, Daniel R. *The Tentacles of Progress: Technology Transfer in the Age of Imperialism, 1850–1940.* New York: Oxford Univ. Press, 1988.

Healy, David. *U.S. Expansionism: The Imperialist Urge in the 1890s.* Madison: Univ. of Wisconsin Press, 1970.

Howse, Derek. *Greenwich Time and the Discovery of Longitude.* Oxford: Oxford Univ. Press, 1980.

Hugill, Peter J. *Global Communications since 1844: Geopolitics and Technology.* Baltimore: Johns Hopkins Univ. Press, in press.

Johnson, Emory R. *The Panama Canal and Commerce.* New York: D. Appleton, 1916.

Kern, Stephen. *The Culture of Time and Space, 1880–1918.* Cambridge, Mass.: Harvard Univ. Press, 1983.

Lane, Franklin K. "A City of Realized Dreams." *National Geographic Magazine* 27 (February 1915): 169–71.

Laut, Agnes C. "Preparations on the Pacific for Panama." *American Review of Reviews* 44 (1911): 705–13.

Lippmann, Walter. *U.S. Foreign Policy: Shield of the Republic.* Boston: Little, Brown, 1943.

Liska, George. *Career of Empire: America and Imperial Expansion over Land and Sea.* Baltimore: Johns Hopkins Univ. Press, 1978.

McCullough, David. *The Path between the Seas: The Creation of the Panama Canal, 1870–1914.* New York: Simon and Schuster, 1977.

Macdonald, William. "The California Expositions." *Nation* 101 (October 21, 1915): 490–92.

McGee, W. J. "National Growth and National Character." *National Geographic Magazine* 10 (June 1899): 185–206.

Mackinder, H. J. "The Geographical Pivot of History." *Geographical Journal* 23 (April 1904): 421–44.

Major, John. *Prize Possession: The United States and the Panama Canal, 1903–1979.* Cambridge: Cambridge Univ. Press, 1993.

New Imperial Atlas of the World. Chicago: Rand McNally, 1900.

Phelan, James D. "California's Invitation to the Country." *American Review of Reviews* 51 (1915): 160–61.

Pratt, Julius W. *Challenge and Rejection: The United States and World Leadership, 1900–1921.* New York: Macmillan, 1967.

Richard, Alfred Charles, Jr. *The Panama Canal in American National Consciousness.* New York: Garland Publishing, 1990.

Richardson, Bonham C. *The Caribbean in the Wider World, 1492–1992.* Cambridge: Cambridge Univ. Press, 1992.

Rosenberg, Emily S. *Spreading the American Dream: American Economic and Cultural Expansionism, 1890–1945.* New York: Hill and Wang, 1982.

"The San Francisco Fair." *Literary Digest* 50 (March 13, 1915): 533–35.

Stead, W. T. *The Americanisation of the World; or, The Trend of the Twentieth Century.* London: The "Review of Reviews," 1902.

Wheeler, Benjamin Ide. "The Meaning of the Canal." *American Review of Reviews* 51 (1915): 161–64.

Williams, William Appleman. *Empire as a Way of Life.* New York: Oxford Univ. Press, 1982.

INDEX

443